ULTIMATE
X
MEN

W9-AEC-468

ULTIMATE X-MEN

ULTIMATE COLLECTION

"The Tomorrow People"
Ultimate X-Men #1-6

Writer
Mark Millar

Pencils
Adam Kubert & Andy Kubert

Inks
Art Thibert with Danny Miki

Colors
**Richard Isanove
with Brian Haberlin**

Letters
**Richard Starkings
& Comicraft's Wes Abbott**

"Burial Service"
Ultimate X-Men #1/2

Writer
Geoff Johns

Pencils
Aaron Lopresti

Inks
Danny Miki

Colors
Hi-Fi Design

Letters
Comicraft

Assistant Editor, Original Series
Pete Franco

Editor, Original Series
Mark Powers

"Return to Weapon X"
Ultimate X-Men #7-12

Writer
Mark Millar

Pencils
**Adam Kubert
with Tom Raney & Tom Derenick**

Inks
**Art Thibert with Scott Hanna,
Joe Kubert, Danny Miki & Lary Stucker**

Colors
**Transparency Digital
with Richard Isanove & Dave Stewart**

Letters
**Richard Starkings
& Comicraft's Wes 'n' Saida!**

Collection Cover
Leinil Francis Yu

Collection Editor
Jennifer Grünwald

Assistant Editor
Michael Short

Senior Editor, Special Projects
Jeff Youngquist

Vice President of Sales
David Gabriel

Production
Jerry Kalinowski

Book Designer
Jhonson Eteng

Creative Director
Tom Marvelli

Editor in Chief
Joe Quesada

Publisher
Dan Buckley

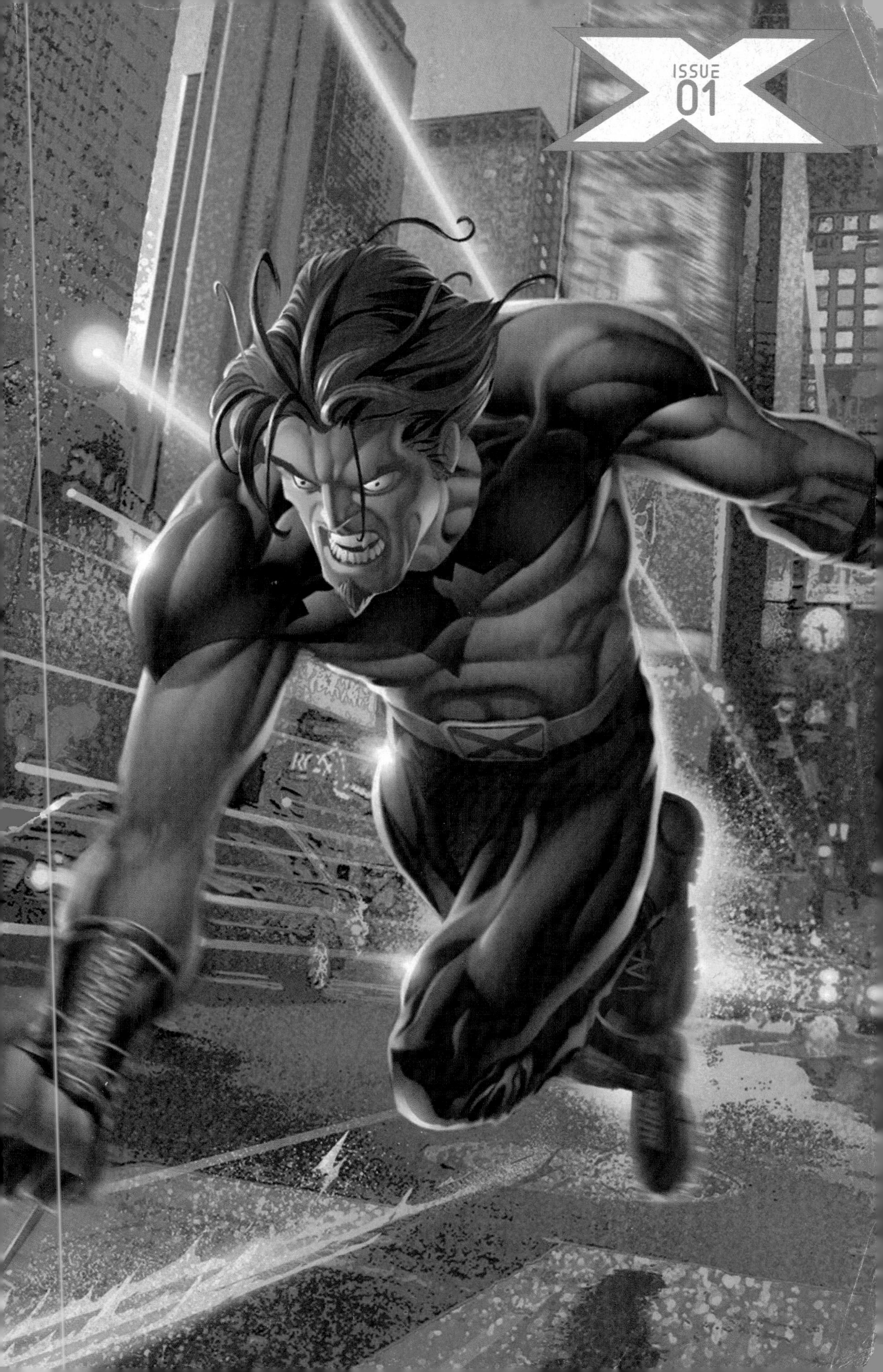
ISSUE
01

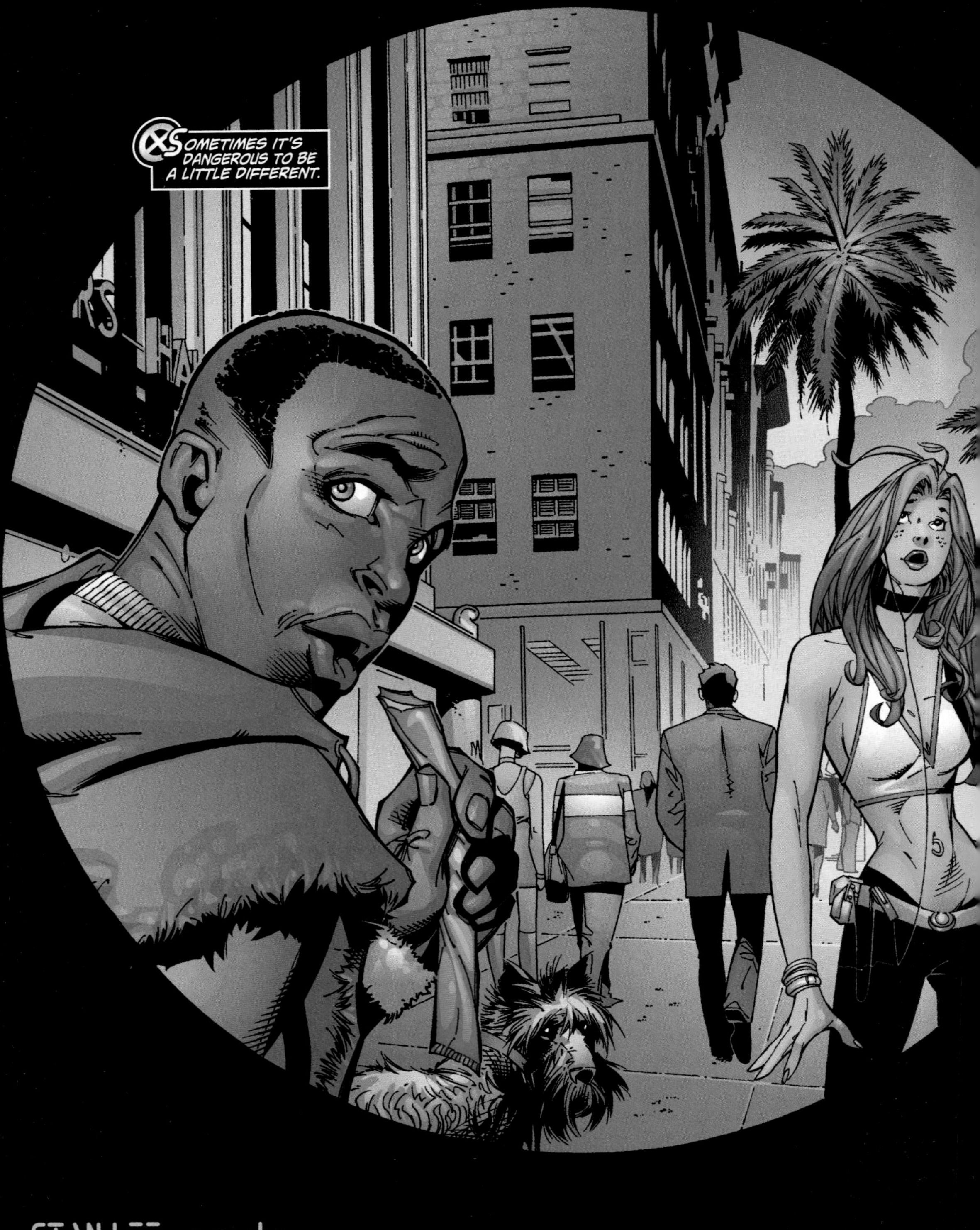
SOMETIMES IT'S DANGEROUS TO BE A LITTLE DIFFERENT.

STAN LEE presents:

The TOMORROW PEOPLE

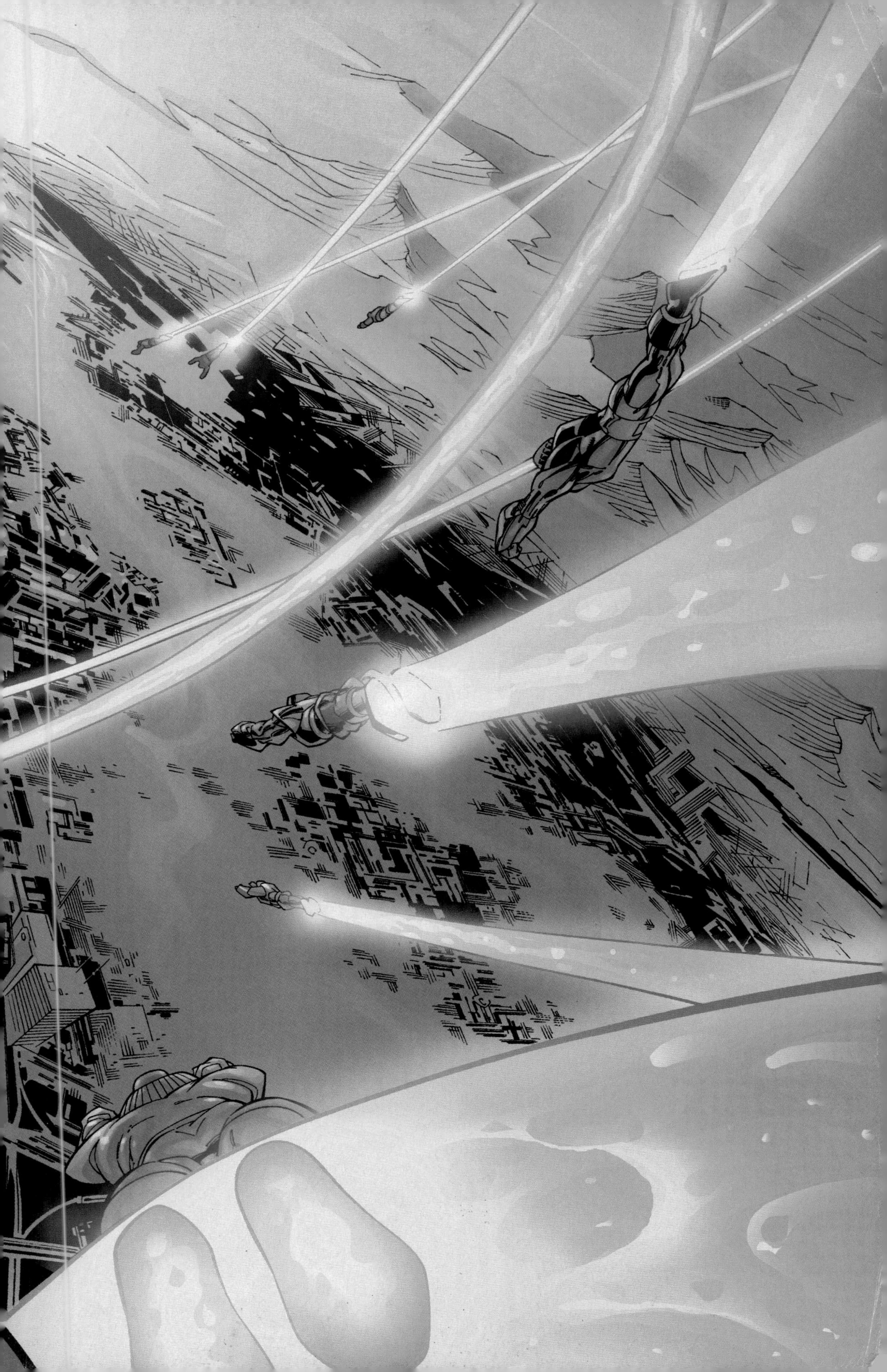

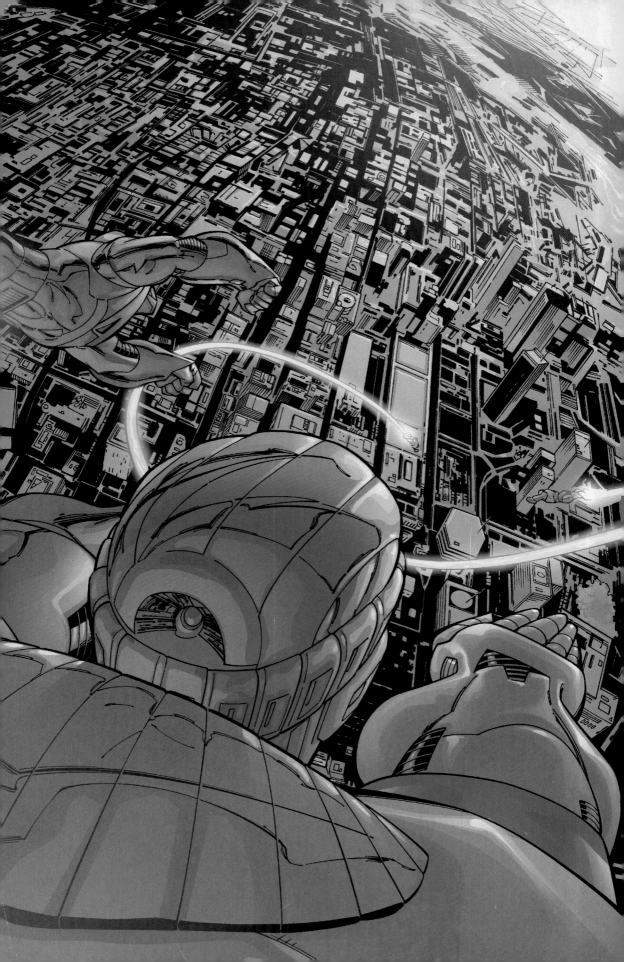

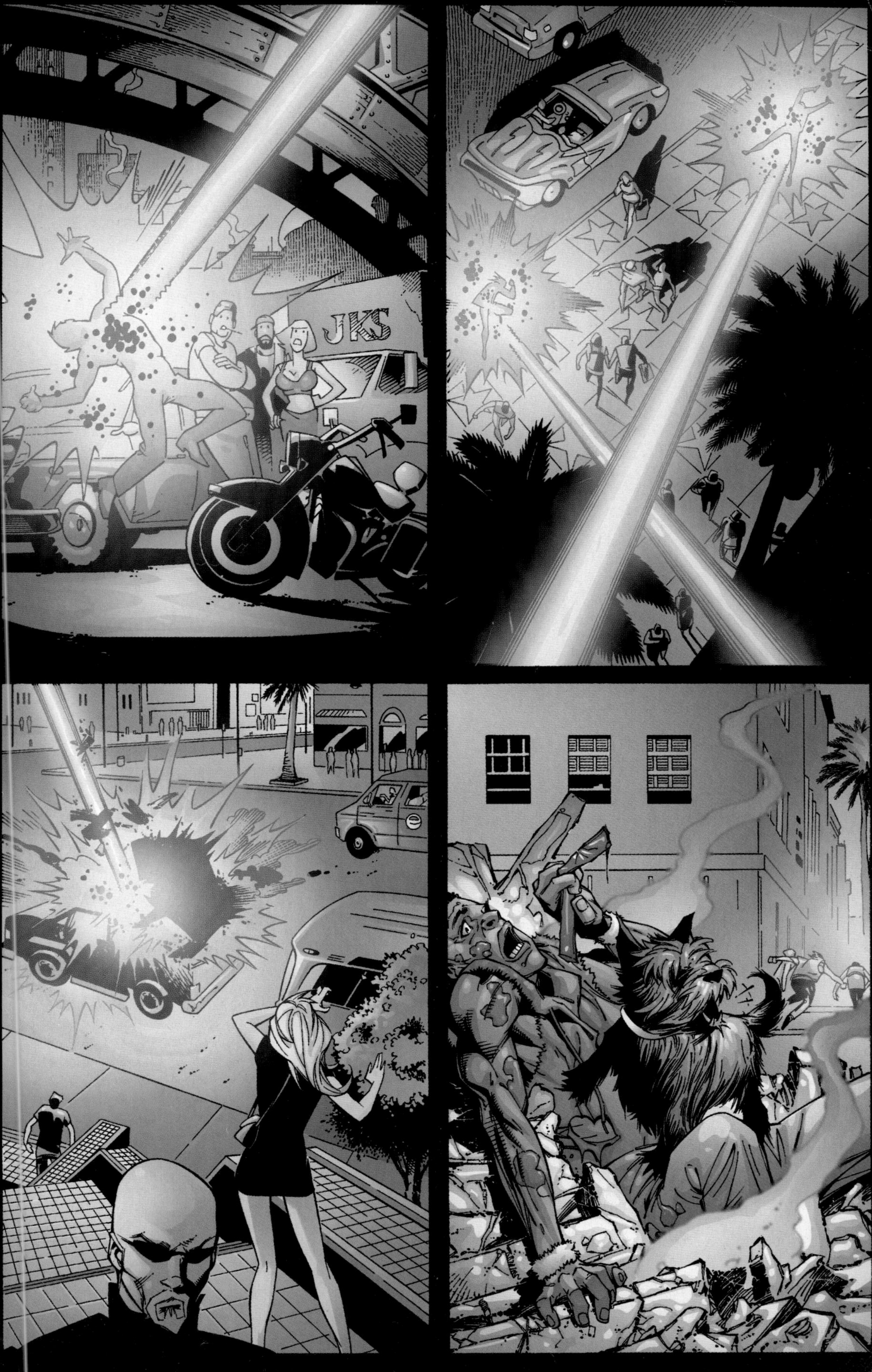
JKS

ГНВУ–7–8888–ФТѰ95
ННГНЕХФГΞР999–9875

Mutant Gene CONFIRMED
Proceed with TERMINATION

ΚѰϭ.Κ
λ 19С99–
0897В–ВВΝε
ΙϴϴϹϴΙϴϴΙΙΙΙΙϴΙϴΙϴΙϴϴϴΙϴΙ
М ГНКΦВ–98/Т435

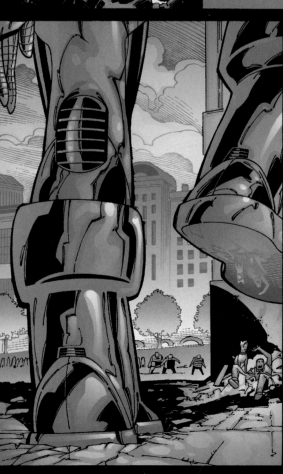

CRUNCH

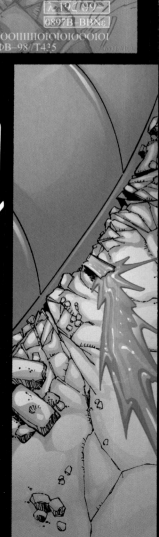

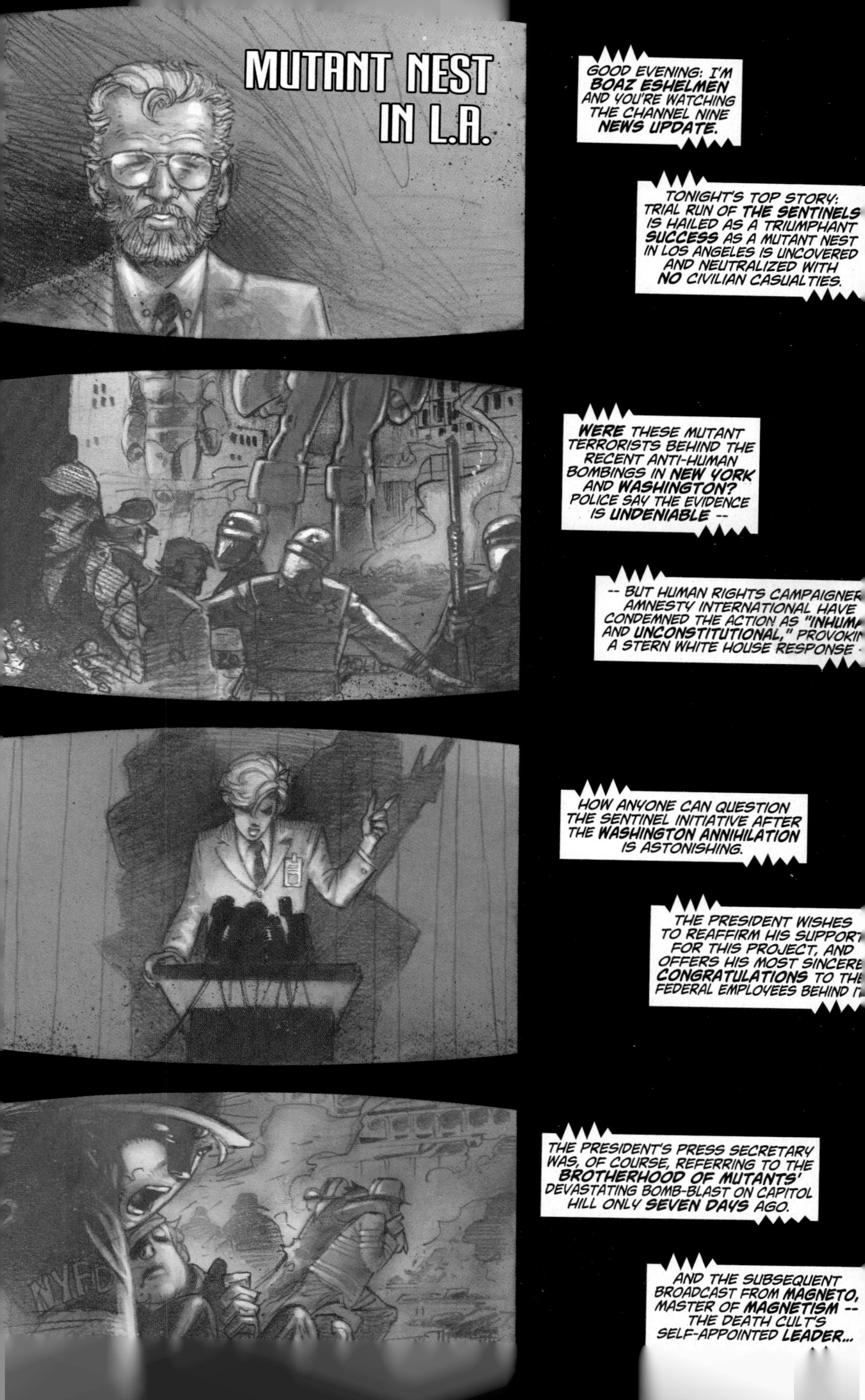

MUTANT NEST IN L.A.
GOOD EVENING: I'M BOAZ ESHELMEN AND YOU'RE WATCHING THE CHANNEL NINE NEWS UPDATE.
TONIGHT'S TOP STORY: TRIAL RUN OF THE SENTINELS IS HAILED AS A TRIUMPHANT SUCCESS AS A MUTANT NEST IN LOS ANGELES IS UNCOVERED AND NEUTRALIZED WITH NO CIVILIAN CASUALTIES.
WERE THESE MUTANT TERRORISTS BEHIND THE RECENT ANTI-HUMAN BOMBINGS IN NEW YORK AND WASHINGTON? POLICE SAY THE EVIDENCE IS UNDENIABLE --
-- BUT HUMAN RIGHTS CAMPAIGNER AMNESTY INTERNATIONAL HAVE CONDEMNED THE ACTION AS "INHUMA AND UNCONSTITUTIONAL," PROVOKIN A STERN WHITE HOUSE RESPONSE
HOW ANYONE CAN QUESTION THE SENTINEL INITIATIVE AFTER THE WASHINGTON ANNIHILATION IS ASTONISHING.
THE PRESIDENT WISHES TO REAFFIRM HIS SUPPOR FOR THIS PROJECT, AND OFFERS HIS MOST SINCERE CONGRATULATIONS TO TH FEDERAL EMPLOYEES BEHIND I
THE PRESIDENT'S PRESS SECRETARY WAS, OF COURSE, REFERRING TO THE BROTHERHOOD OF MUTANTS' DEVASTATING BOMB-BLAST ON CAPITOL HILL ONLY SEVEN DAYS AGO.
NYPD
AND THE SUBSEQUENT BROADCAST FROM MAGNETO, MASTER OF MAGNETISM -- THE DEATH CULT'S SELF-APPOINTED LEADER...

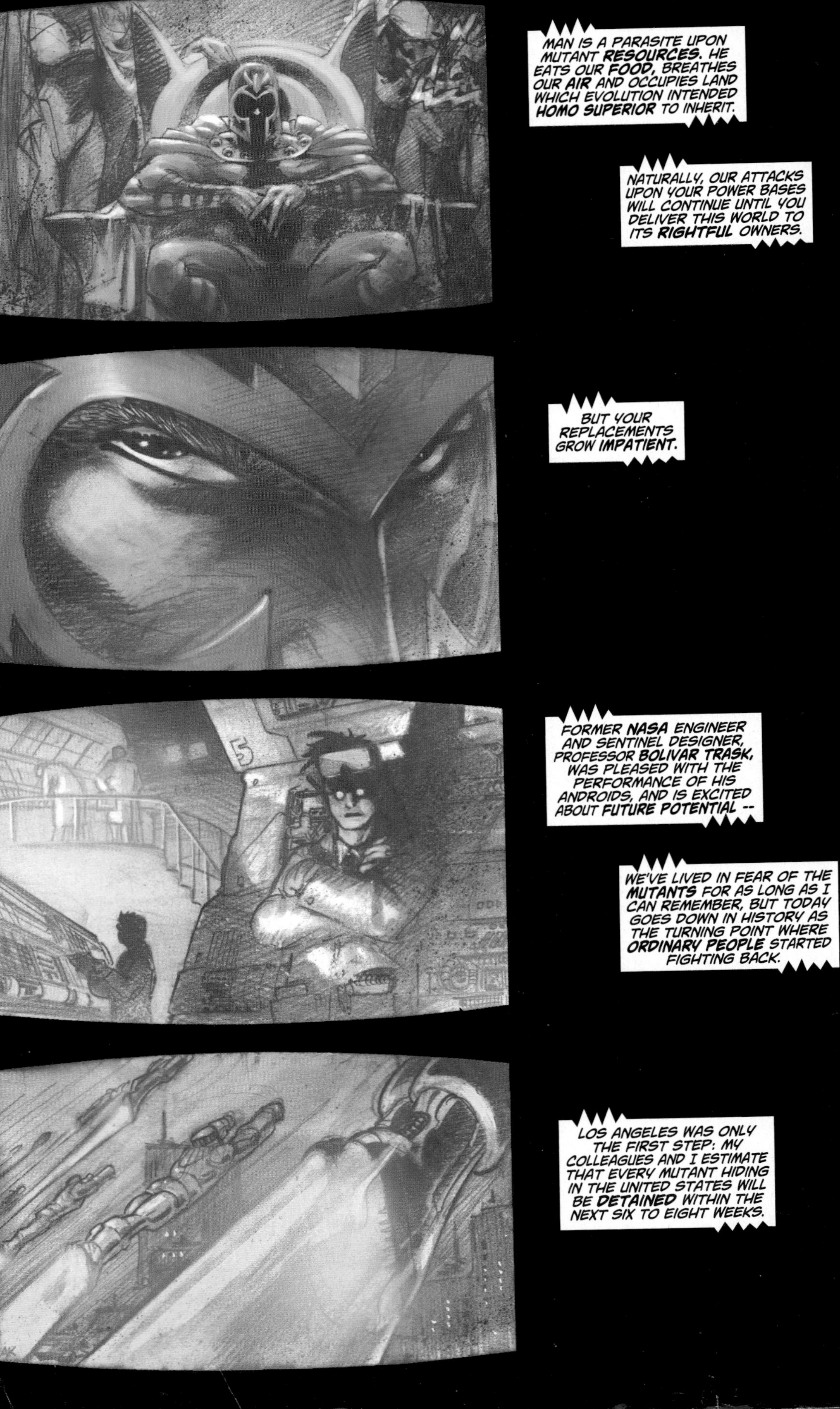
MAN IS A PARASITE UPON MUTANT RESOURCES. HE EATS OUR FOOD, BREATHES OUR AIR AND OCCUPIES LAND WHICH EVOLUTION INTENDED HOMO SUPERIOR TO INHERIT.
NATURALLY, OUR ATTACKS UPON YOUR POWER BASES WILL CONTINUE UNTIL YOU DELIVER THIS WORLD TO ITS RIGHTFUL OWNERS.
BUT YOUR REPLACEMENTS GROW IMPATIENT.
FORMER NASA ENGINEER AND SENTINEL DESIGNER, PROFESSOR BOLIVAR TRASK, WAS PLEASED WITH THE PERFORMANCE OF HIS ANDROIDS, AND IS EXCITED ABOUT FUTURE POTENTIAL --
WE'VE LIVED IN FEAR OF THE MUTANTS FOR AS LONG AS I CAN REMEMBER, BUT TODAY GOES DOWN IN HISTORY AS THE TURNING POINT WHERE ORDINARY PEOPLE STARTED FIGHTING BACK.
LOS ANGELES WAS ONLY THE FIRST STEP: MY COLLEAGUES AND I ESTIMATE THAT EVERY MUTANT HIDING IN THE UNITED STATES WILL BE DETAINED WITHIN THE NEXT SIX TO EIGHT WEEKS.

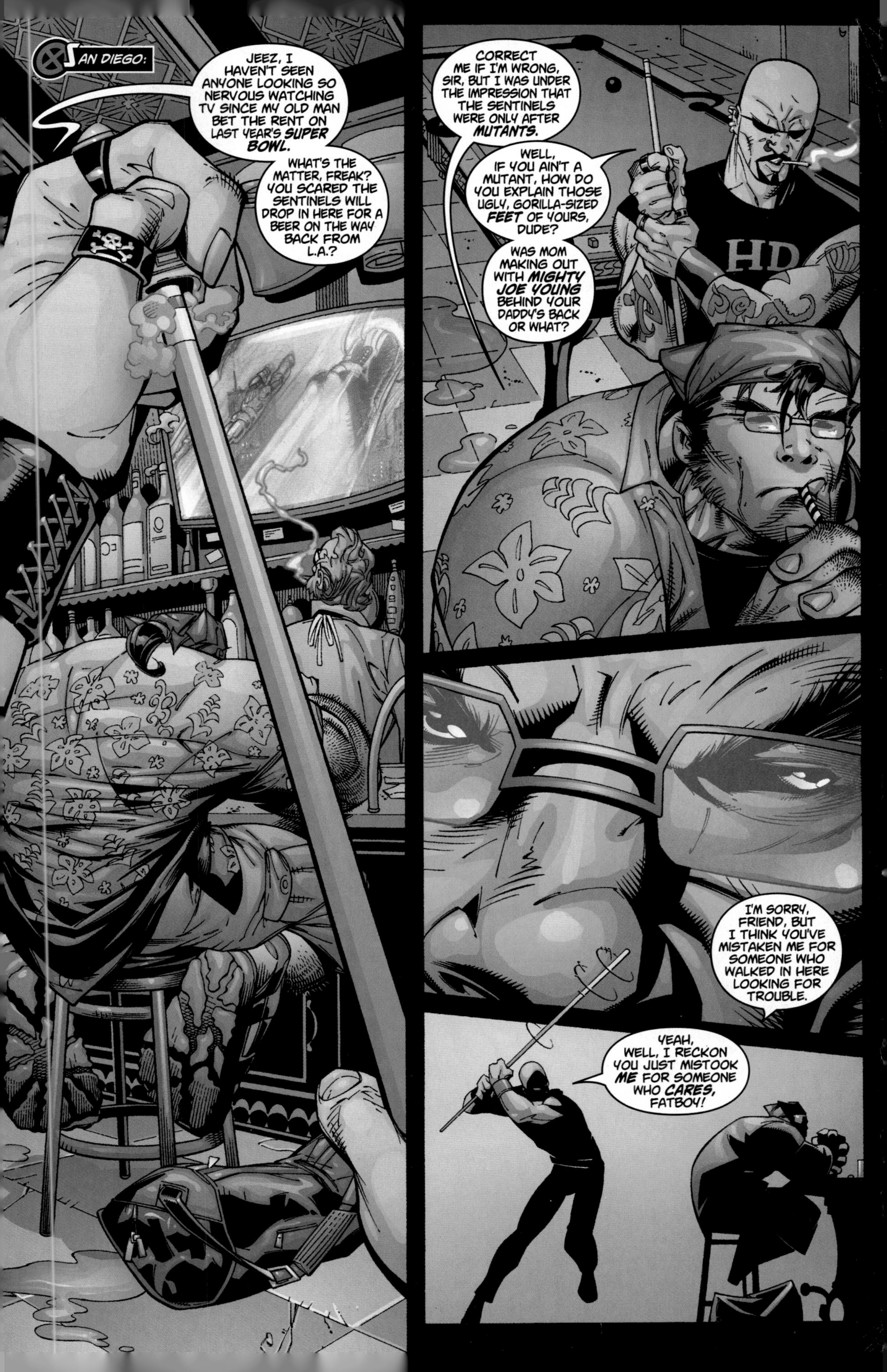
SAN DIEGO:
JEEZ, I HAVEN'T SEEN ANYONE LOOKING SO NERVOUS WATCHING TV SINCE MY OLD MAN BET THE RENT ON LAST YEAR'S SUPER BOWL.
WHAT'S THE MATTER, FREAK? YOU SCARED THE SENTINELS WILL DROP IN HERE FOR A BEER ON THE WAY BACK FROM L.A.?
CORRECT ME IF I'M WRONG, SIR, BUT I WAS UNDER THE IMPRESSION THAT THE SENTINELS WERE ONLY AFTER MUTANTS.
WELL, IF YOU AIN'T A MUTANT, HOW DO YOU EXPLAIN THOSE UGLY, GORILLA-SIZED FEET OF YOURS, DUDE?
WAS MOM MAKING OUT WITH MIGHTY JOE YOUNG BEHIND YOUR DADDY'S BACK OR WHAT?
HD
I'M SORRY, FRIEND, BUT I THINK YOU'VE MISTAKEN ME FOR SOMEONE WHO WALKED IN HERE LOOKING FOR TROUBLE.
YEAH, WELL, I RECKON YOU JUST MISTOOK ME FOR SOMEONE WHO CARES, FATBOY!

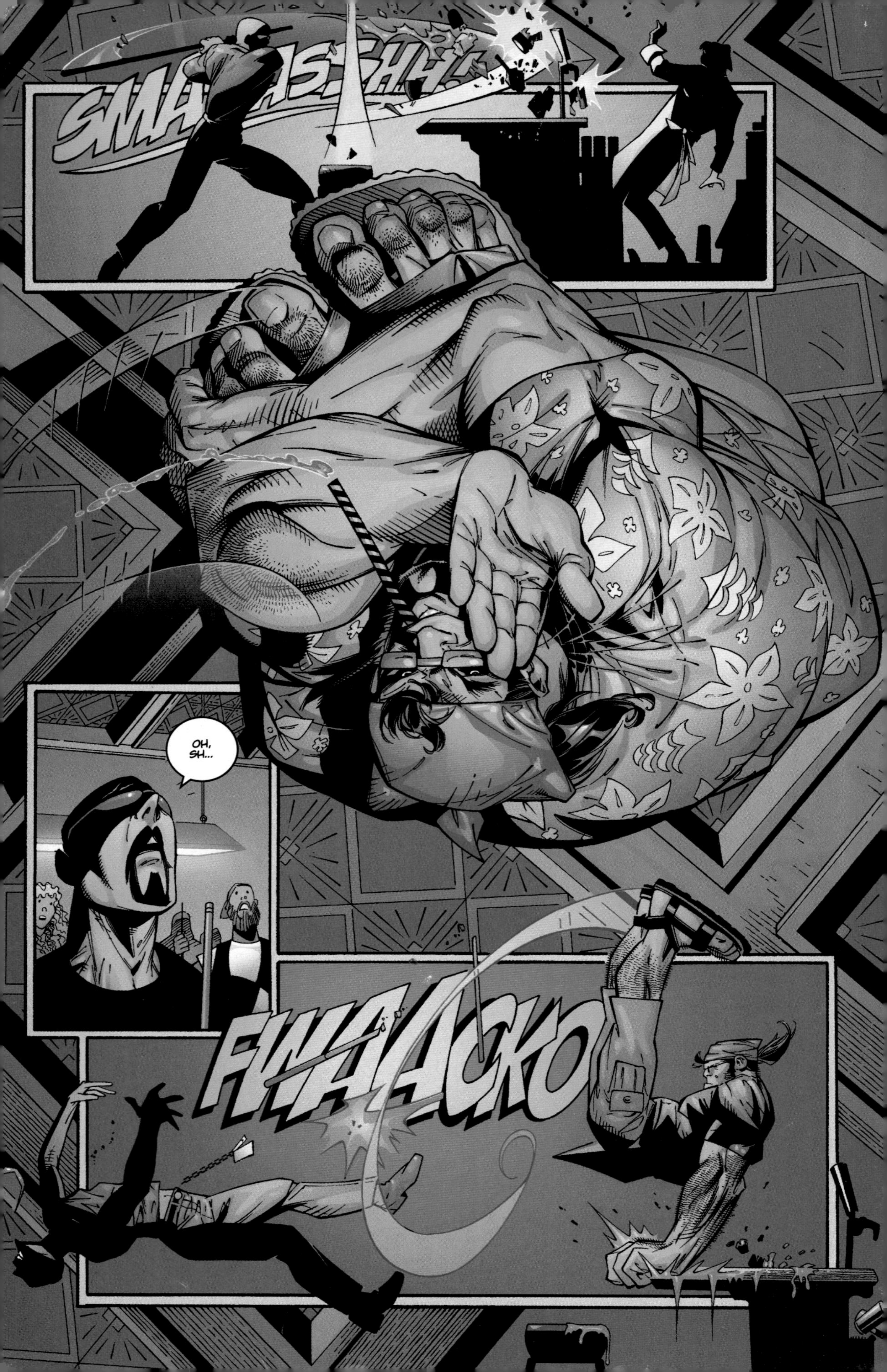
SMASSHH!
OH, SH...
FWHACKO

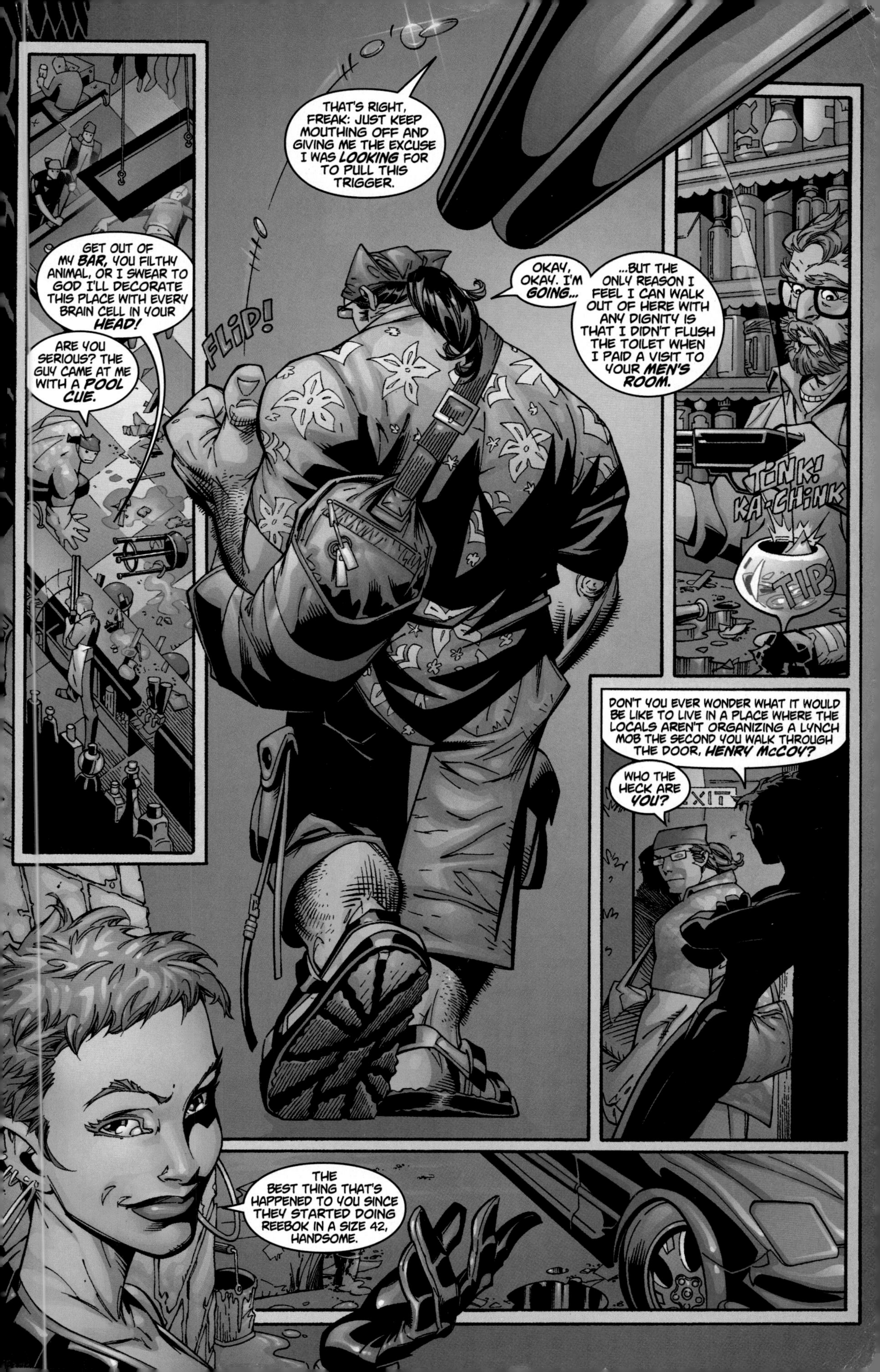
GET OUT OF MY BAR, YOU FILTHY ANIMAL, OR I SWEAR TO GOD I'LL DECORATE THIS PLACE WITH EVERY BRAIN CELL IN YOUR HEAD!
ARE YOU SERIOUS? THE GUY CAME AT ME WITH A POOL CUE.
THAT'S RIGHT, FREAK: JUST KEEP MOUTHING OFF AND GIVING ME THE EXCUSE I WAS LOOKING FOR TO PULL THIS TRIGGER.
FLIP!
OKAY, OKAY. I'M GOING...
...BUT THE ONLY REASON I FEEL I CAN WALK OUT OF HERE WITH ANY DIGNITY IS THAT I DIDN'T FLUSH THE TOILET WHEN I PAID A VISIT TO YOUR MEN'S ROOM.
TINK! KA-CHINK
TIPS
DON'T YOU EVER WONDER WHAT IT WOULD BE LIKE TO LIVE IN A PLACE WHERE THE LOCALS AREN'T ORGANIZING A LYNCH MOB THE SECOND YOU WALK THROUGH THE DOOR, HENRY McCOY?
WHO THE HECK ARE YOU?
EXIT
THE BEST THING THAT'S HAPPENED TO YOU SINCE THEY STARTED DOING REEBOK IN A SIZE 42, HANDSOME.

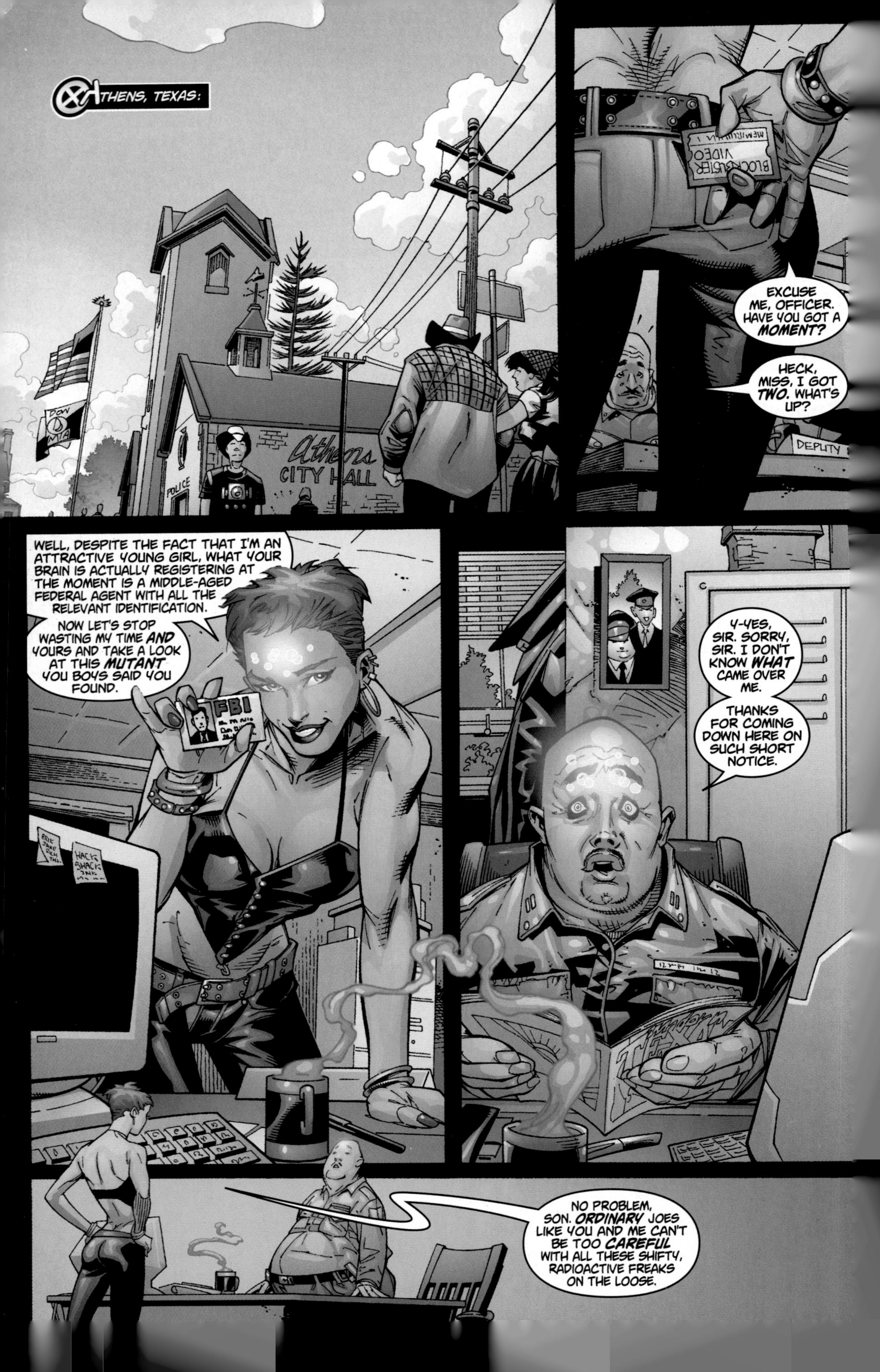
ATHENS, TEXAS:
BLOCKBUSTER VIDEO MEMBERSHIP
ATHENS CITY HALL
POLICE
POW MIA
EXCUSE ME, OFFICER. HAVE YOU GOT A MOMENT?
HECK, MISS, I GOT TWO. WHAT'S UP?
DEPUTY
WELL, DESPITE THE FACT THAT I'M AN ATTRACTIVE YOUNG GIRL, WHAT YOUR BRAIN IS ACTUALLY REGISTERING AT THE MOMENT IS A MIDDLE-AGED FEDERAL AGENT WITH ALL THE RELEVANT IDENTIFICATION.
NOW LET'S STOP WASTING MY TIME AND YOURS AND TAKE A LOOK AT THIS MUTANT YOU BOYS SAID YOU FOUND.
FBI
Y-YES, SIR. SORRY, SIR. I DON'T KNOW WHAT CAME OVER ME.
THANKS FOR COMING DOWN HERE ON SUCH SHORT NOTICE.
HACK SHACK
NO PROBLEM, SON. ORDINARY JOES LIKE YOU AND ME CAN'T BE TOO CAREFUL WITH ALL THESE SHIFTY, RADIOACTIVE FREAKS ON THE LOOSE.

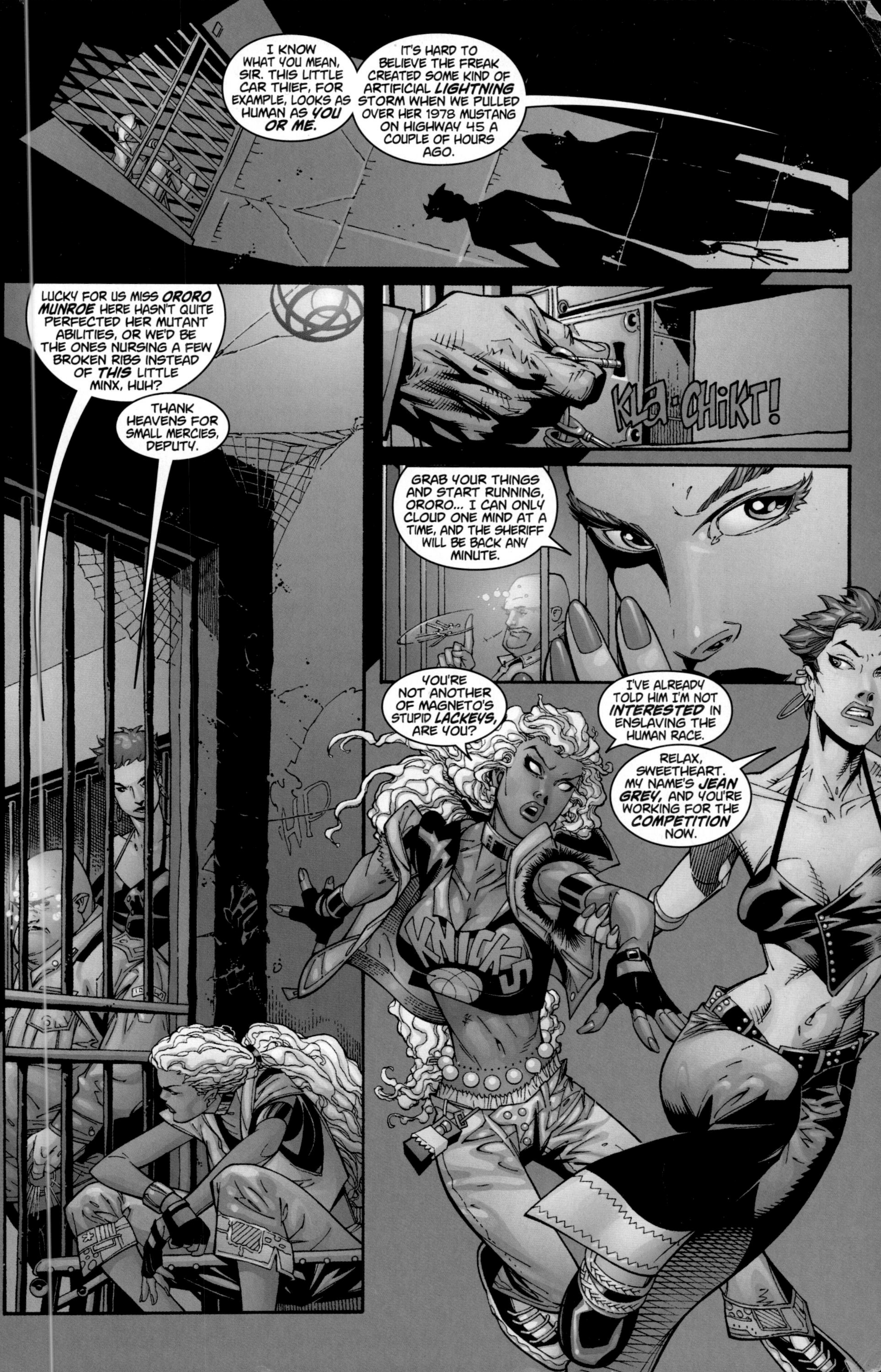
I KNOW WHAT YOU MEAN, SIR. THIS LITTLE CAR THIEF, FOR EXAMPLE, LOOKS AS HUMAN AS YOU OR ME.
IT'S HARD TO BELIEVE THE FREAK CREATED SOME KIND OF ARTIFICIAL LIGHTNING STORM WHEN WE PULLED OVER HER 1978 MUSTANG ON HIGHWAY 45 A COUPLE OF HOURS AGO.
LUCKY FOR US MISS ORORO MUNROE HERE HASN'T QUITE PERFECTED HER MUTANT ABILITIES, OR WE'D BE THE ONES NURSING A FEW BROKEN RIBS INSTEAD OF THIS LITTLE MINX, HUH?
THANK HEAVENS FOR SMALL MERCIES, DEPUTY.
KLA-CHIKT!
GRAB YOUR THINGS AND START RUNNING, ORORO... I CAN ONLY CLOUD ONE MIND AT A TIME, AND THE SHERIFF WILL BE BACK ANY MINUTE.
YOU'RE NOT ANOTHER OF MAGNETO'S STUPID LACKEYS, ARE YOU?
I'VE ALREADY TOLD HIM I'M NOT INTERESTED IN ENSLAVING THE HUMAN RACE.
RELAX, SWEETHEART. MY NAME'S JEAN GREY, AND YOU'RE WORKING FOR THE COMPETITION NOW.

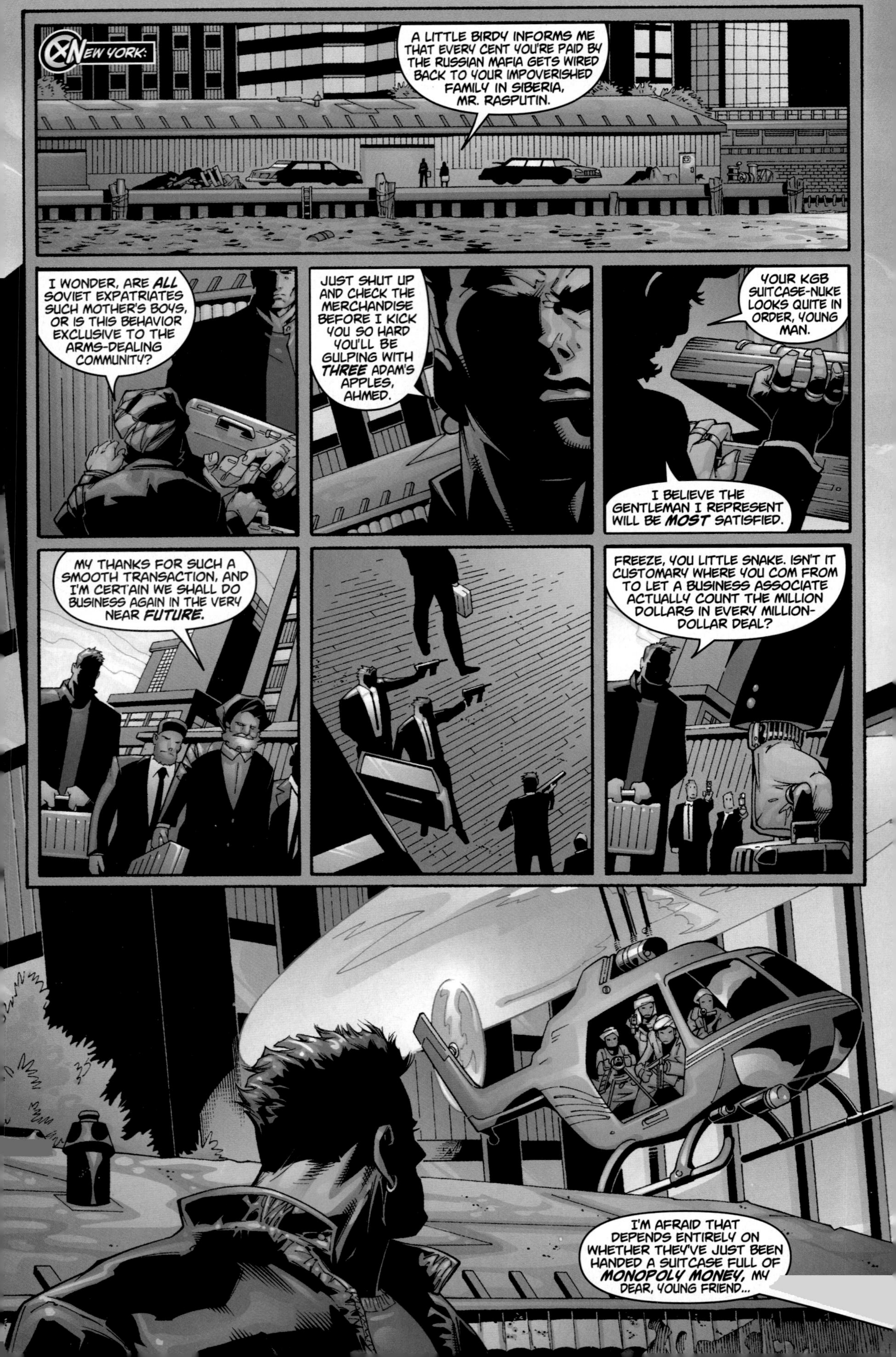
NEW YORK:
A LITTLE BIRDY INFORMS ME THAT EVERY CENT YOU'RE PAID BY THE RUSSIAN MAFIA GETS WIRED BACK TO YOUR IMPOVERISHED FAMILY IN SIBERIA, MR. RASPUTIN.
I WONDER, ARE ALL SOVIET EXPATRIATES SUCH MOTHER'S BOYS, OR IS THIS BEHAVIOR EXCLUSIVE TO THE ARMS-DEALING COMMUNITY?
JUST SHUT UP AND CHECK THE MERCHANDISE BEFORE I KICK YOU SO HARD YOU'LL BE GULPING WITH THREE ADAM'S APPLES, AHMED.
YOUR KGB SUITCASE-NUKE LOOKS QUITE IN ORDER, YOUNG MAN.
I BELIEVE THE GENTLEMAN I REPRESENT WILL BE MOST SATISFIED.
MY THANKS FOR SUCH A SMOOTH TRANSACTION, AND I'M CERTAIN WE SHALL DO BUSINESS AGAIN IN THE VERY NEAR FUTURE.
FREEZE, YOU LITTLE SNAKE. ISN'T IT CUSTOMARY WHERE YOU COM FROM TO LET A BUSINESS ASSOCIATE ACTUALLY COUNT THE MILLION DOLLARS IN EVERY MILLION-DOLLAR DEAL?
I'M AFRAID THAT DEPENDS ENTIRELY ON WHETHER THEY'VE JUST BEEN HANDED A SUITCASE FULL OF MONOPOLY MONEY, MY DEAR, YOUNG FRIEND...

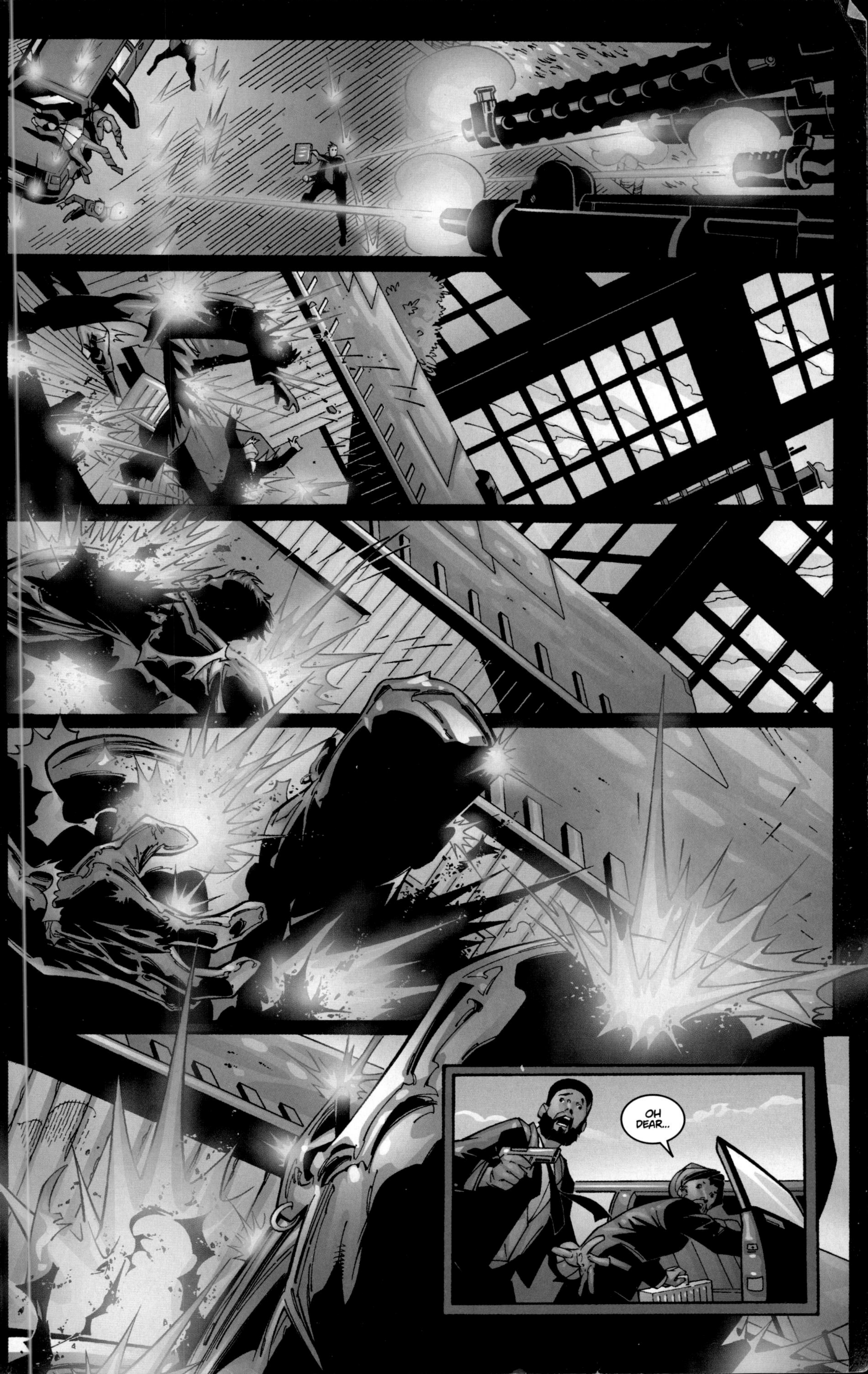
OH DEAR...

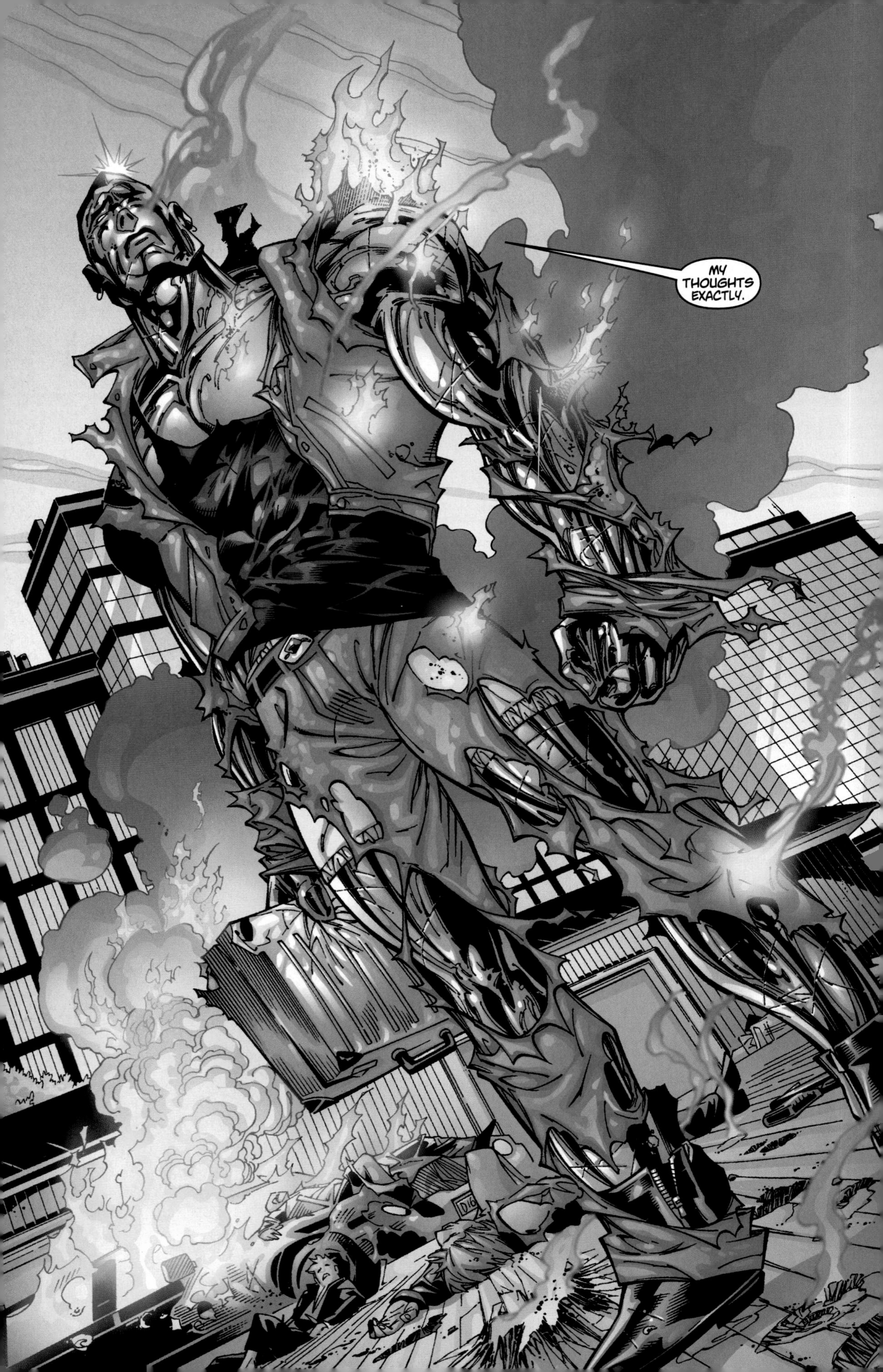
MY THOUGHTS EXACTLY.

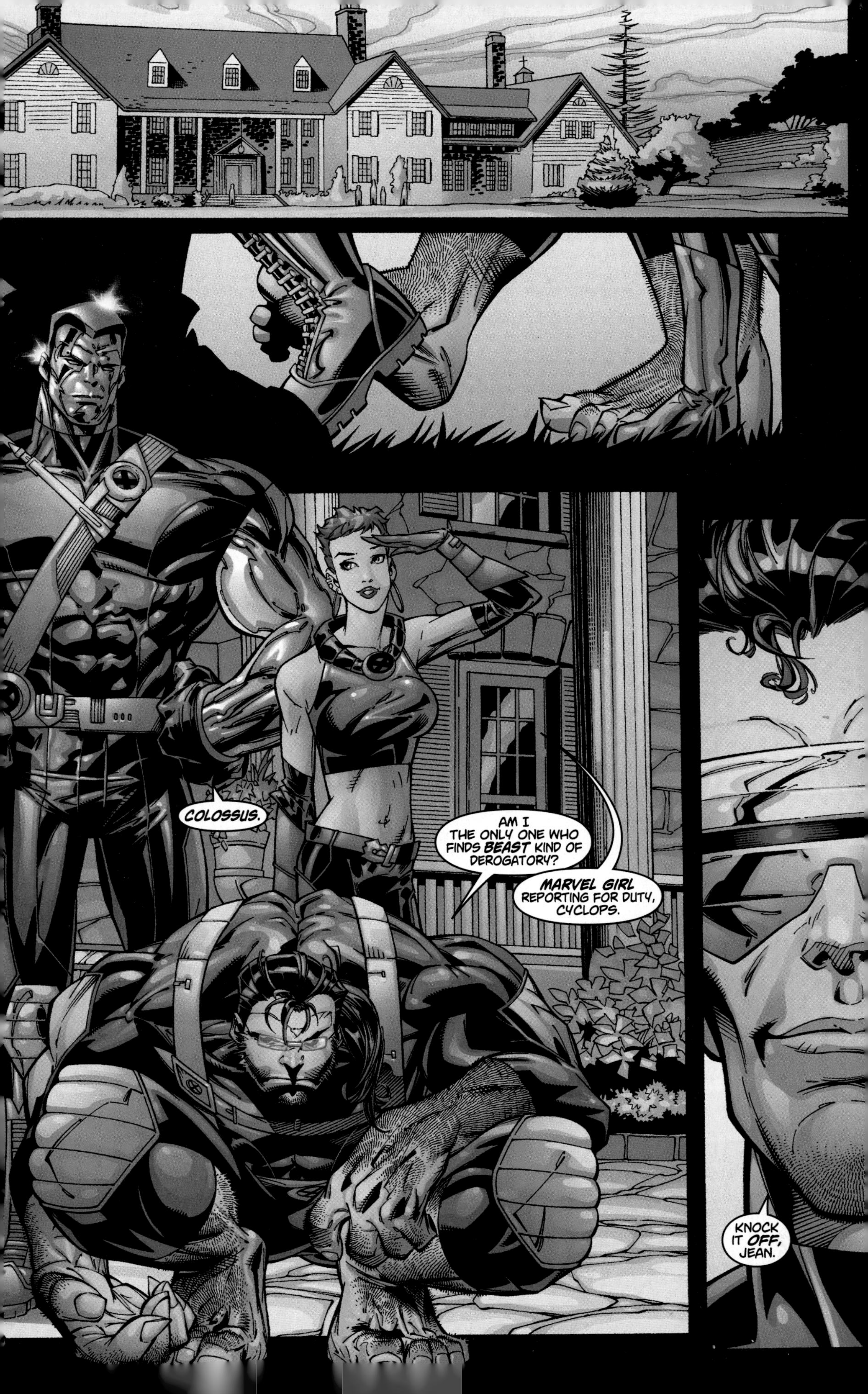
COLOSSUS.
AM I THE ONLY ONE WHO FINDS BEAST KIND OF DEROGATORY?
MARVEL GIRL REPORTING FOR DUTY, CYCLOPS.
KNOCK IT OFF, JEAN.

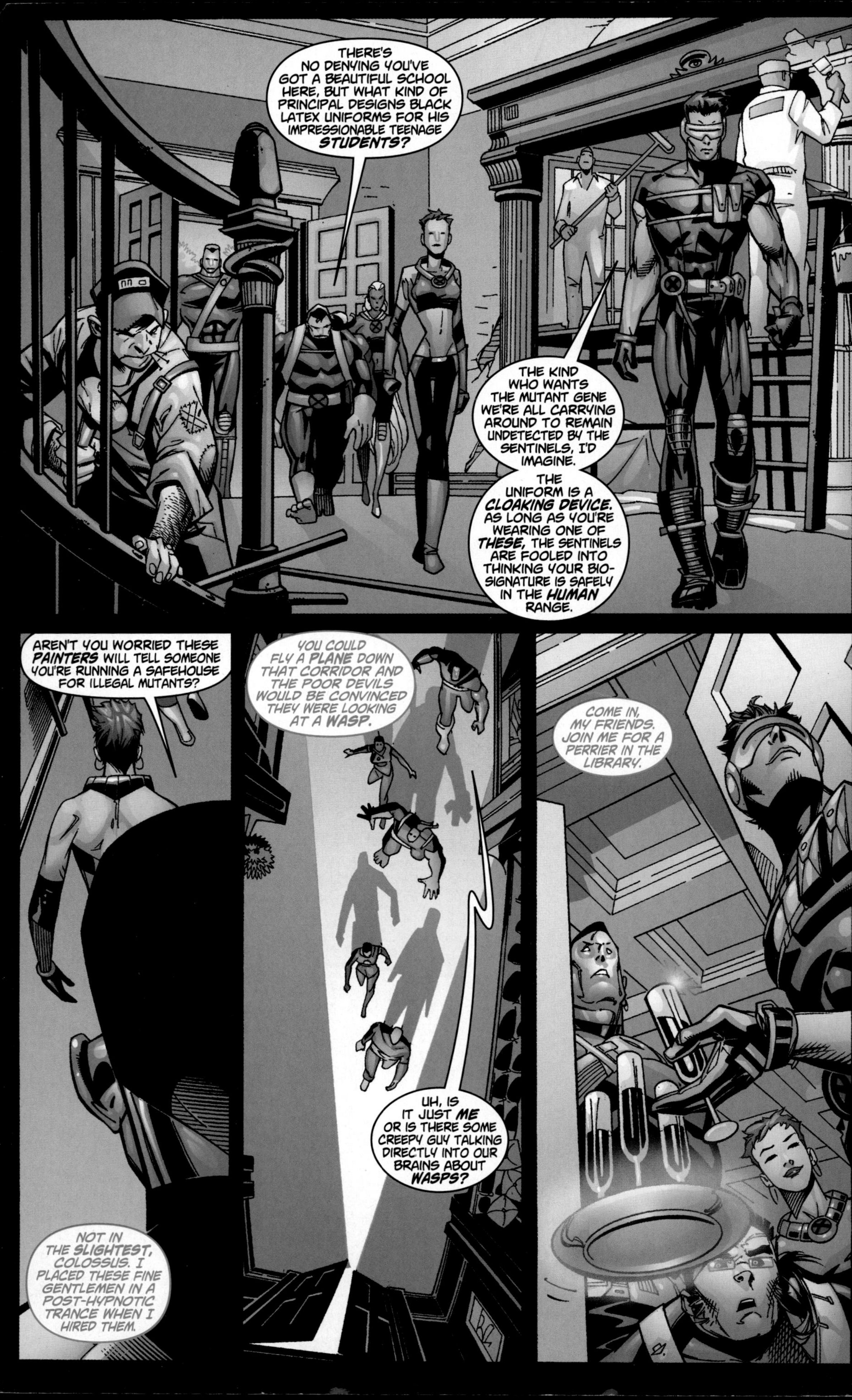
THERE'S NO DENYING YOU'VE GOT A BEAUTIFUL SCHOOL HERE, BUT WHAT KIND OF PRINCIPAL DESIGNS BLACK LATEX UNIFORMS FOR HIS IMPRESSIONABLE TEENAGE STUDENTS?
THE KIND WHO WANTS THE MUTANT GENE WE'RE ALL CARRYING AROUND TO REMAIN UNDETECTED BY THE SENTINELS, I'D IMAGINE.
THE UNIFORM IS A CLOAKING DEVICE. AS LONG AS YOU'RE WEARING ONE OF THESE, THE SENTINELS ARE FOOLED INTO THINKING YOUR BIO-SIGNATURE IS SAFELY IN THE HUMAN RANGE.
AREN'T YOU WORRIED THESE PAINTERS WILL TELL SOMEONE YOU'RE RUNNING A SAFEHOUSE FOR ILLEGAL MUTANTS?
NOT IN THE SLIGHTEST, COLOSSUS. I PLACED THESE FINE GENTLEMEN IN A POST-HYPNOTIC TRANCE WHEN I HIRED THEM.
YOU COULD FLY A PLANE DOWN THAT CORRIDOR AND THE POOR DEVILS WOULD BE CONVINCED THEY WERE LOOKING AT A WASP.
UH, IS IT JUST ME OR IS THERE SOME CREEPY GUY TALKING DIRECTLY INTO OUR BRAINS ABOUT WASPS?
COME IN, MY FRIENDS. JOIN ME FOR A PERRIER IN THE LIBRARY.

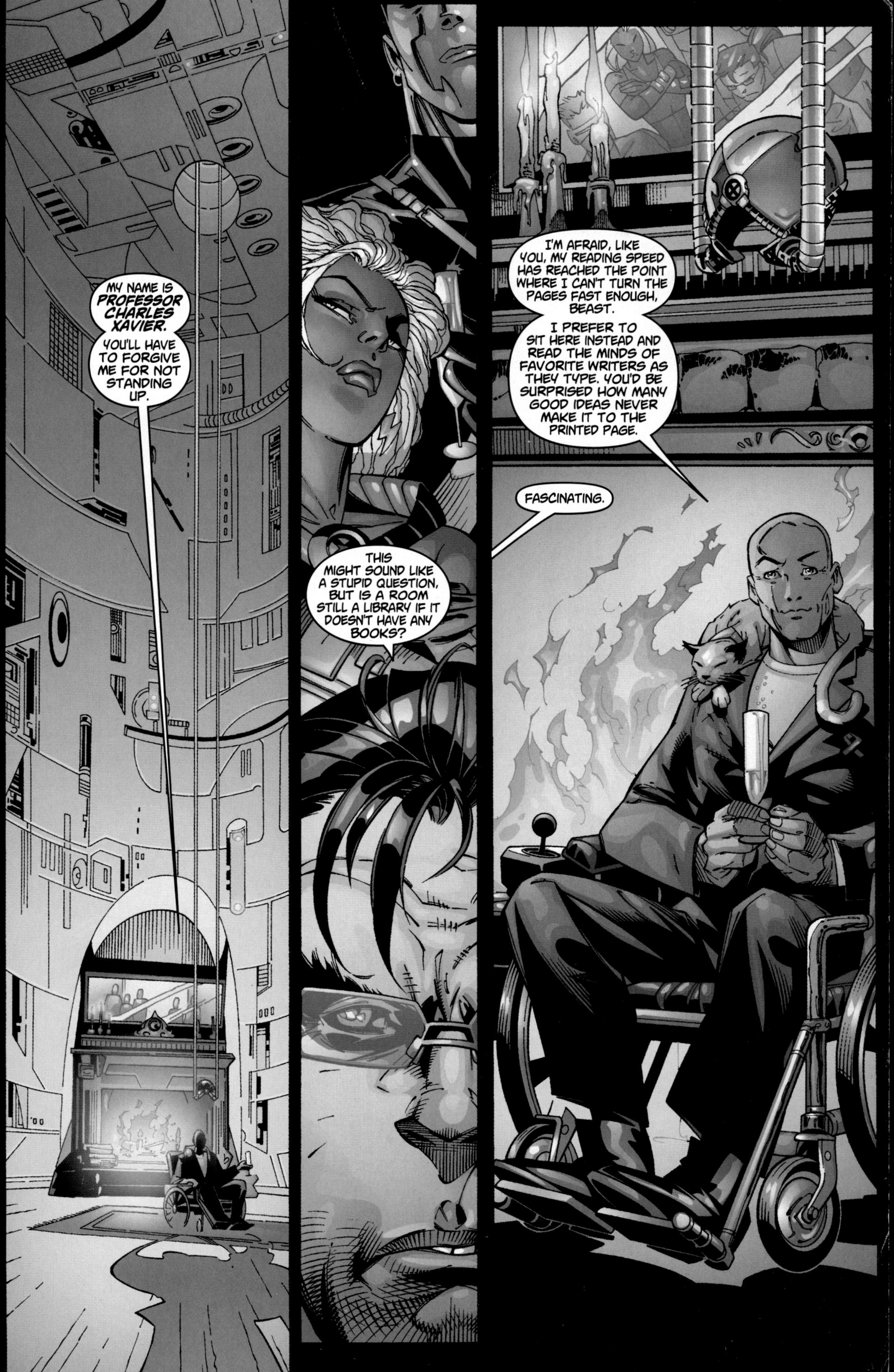
MY NAME IS **PROFESSOR CHARLES XAVIER.**
YOU'LL HAVE TO FORGIVE ME FOR NOT STANDING UP.
THIS MIGHT SOUND LIKE A STUPID QUESTION, BUT IS A ROOM STILL A LIBRARY IF IT DOESN'T HAVE ANY BOOKS?
I'M AFRAID, LIKE YOU, MY READING SPEED HAS REACHED THE POINT WHERE I CAN'T TURN THE PAGES FAST ENOUGH, BEAST.
I PREFER TO SIT HERE INSTEAD AND READ THE MINDS OF FAVORITE WRITERS AS THEY TYPE. YOU'D BE SURPRISED HOW MANY GOOD IDEAS NEVER MAKE IT TO THE PRINTED PAGE.
FASCINATING.

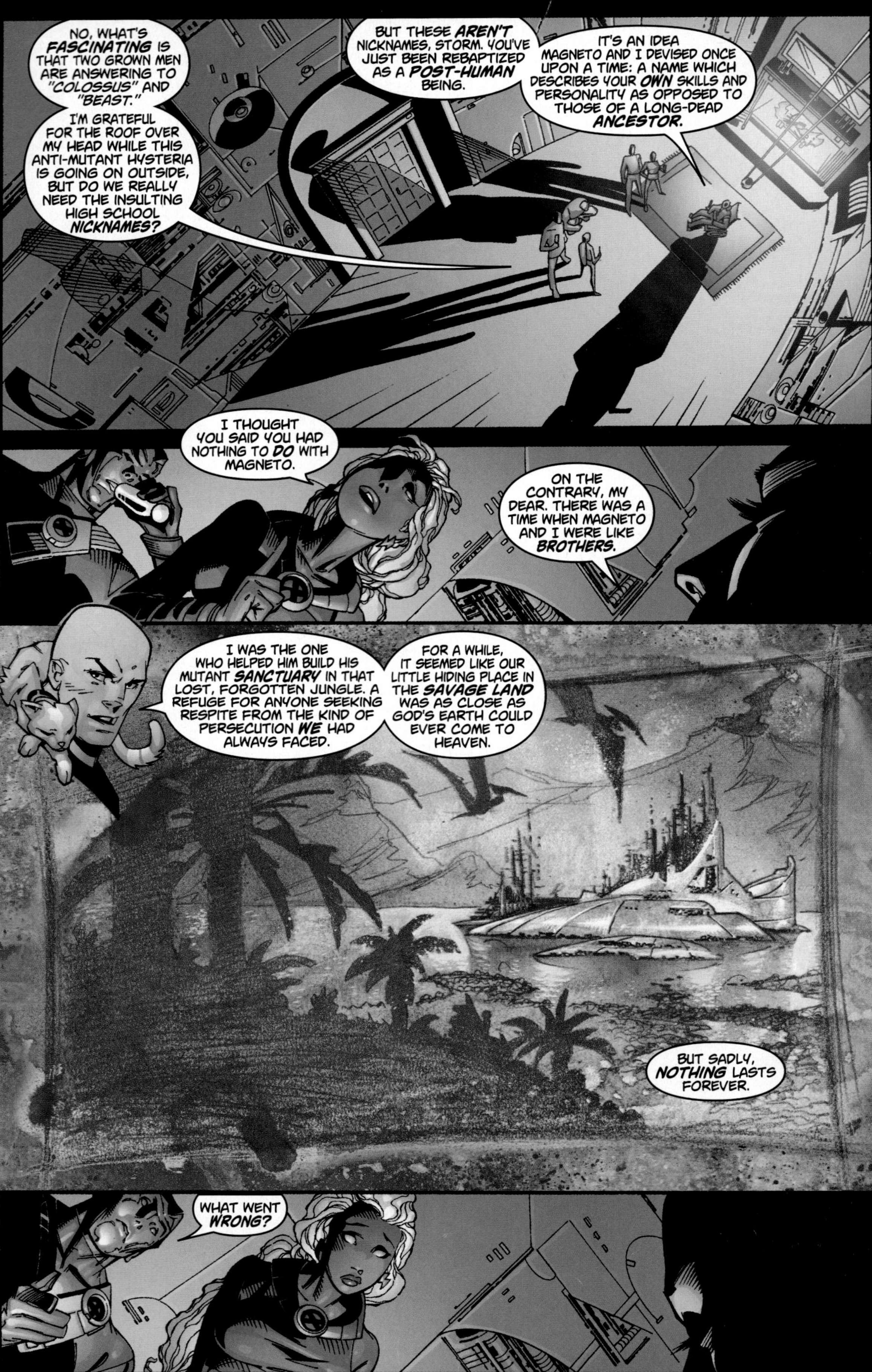

NO, WHAT'S FASCINATING IS THAT TWO GROWN MEN ARE ANSWERING TO "COLOSSUS" AND "BEAST."
I'M GRATEFUL FOR THE ROOF OVER MY HEAD WHILE THIS ANTI-MUTANT HYSTERIA IS GOING ON OUTSIDE, BUT DO WE REALLY NEED THE INSULTING HIGH SCHOOL NICKNAMES?
BUT THESE AREN'T NICKNAMES, STORM. YOU'VE JUST BEEN REBAPTIZED AS A POST-HUMAN BEING.
IT'S AN IDEA MAGNETO AND I DEVISED ONCE UPON A TIME: A NAME WHICH DESCRIBES YOUR OWN SKILLS AND PERSONALITY AS OPPOSED TO THOSE OF A LONG-DEAD ANCESTOR.
I THOUGHT YOU SAID YOU HAD NOTHING TO DO WITH MAGNETO.
ON THE CONTRARY, MY DEAR. THERE WAS A TIME WHEN MAGNETO AND I WERE LIKE BROTHERS.
I WAS THE ONE WHO HELPED HIM BUILD HIS MUTANT SANCTUARY IN THAT LOST, FORGOTTEN JUNGLE. A REFUGE FOR ANYONE SEEKING RESPITE FROM THE KIND OF PERSECUTION WE HAD ALWAYS FACED.
FOR A WHILE, IT SEEMED LIKE OUR LITTLE HIDING PLACE IN THE SAVAGE LAND WAS AS CLOSE AS GOD'S EARTH COULD EVER COME TO HEAVEN.
BUT SADLY, NOTHING LASTS FOREVER.
WHAT WENT WRONG?

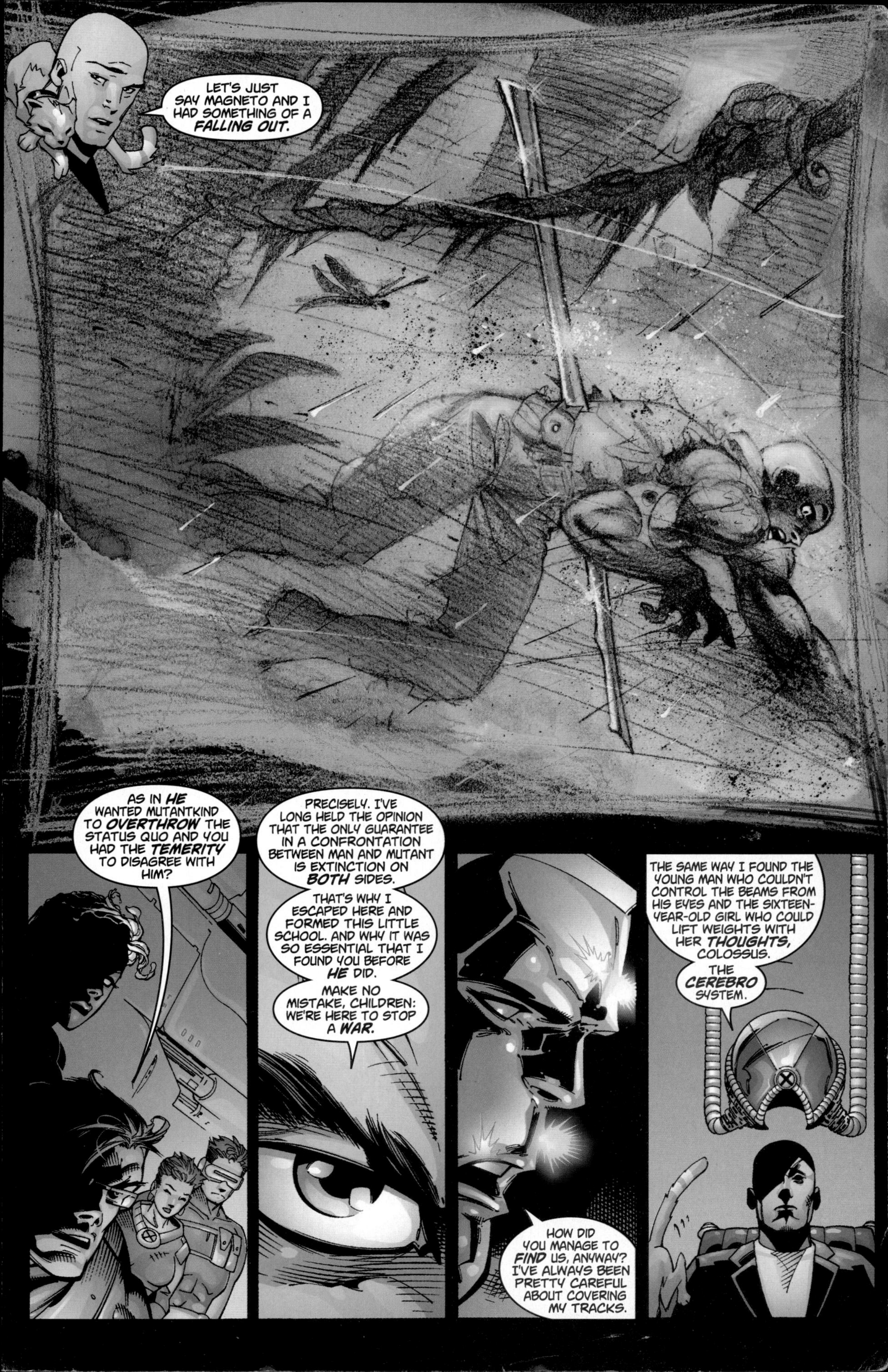
LET'S JUST SAY MAGNETO AND I HAD SOMETHING OF A FALLING OUT.
AS IN HE WANTED MUTANTKIND TO OVERTHROW THE STATUS QUO AND YOU HAD THE TEMERITY TO DISAGREE WITH HIM?
PRECISELY. I'VE LONG HELD THE OPINION THAT THE ONLY GUARANTEE IN A CONFRONTATION BETWEEN MAN AND MUTANT IS EXTINCTION ON BOTH SIDES.
THAT'S WHY I ESCAPED HERE AND FORMED THIS LITTLE SCHOOL. AND WHY IT WAS SO ESSENTIAL THAT I FOUND YOU BEFORE HE DID.
MAKE NO MISTAKE, CHILDREN: WE'RE HERE TO STOP A WAR.
HOW DID YOU MANAGE TO FIND US, ANYWAY? I'VE ALWAYS BEEN PRETTY CAREFUL ABOUT COVERING MY TRACKS.
THE SAME WAY I FOUND THE YOUNG MAN WHO COULDN'T CONTROL THE BEAMS FROM HIS EYES AND THE SIXTEEN-YEAR-OLD GIRL WHO COULD LIFT WEIGHTS WITH HER THOUGHTS, COLOSSUS.
THE CEREBRO SYSTEM.

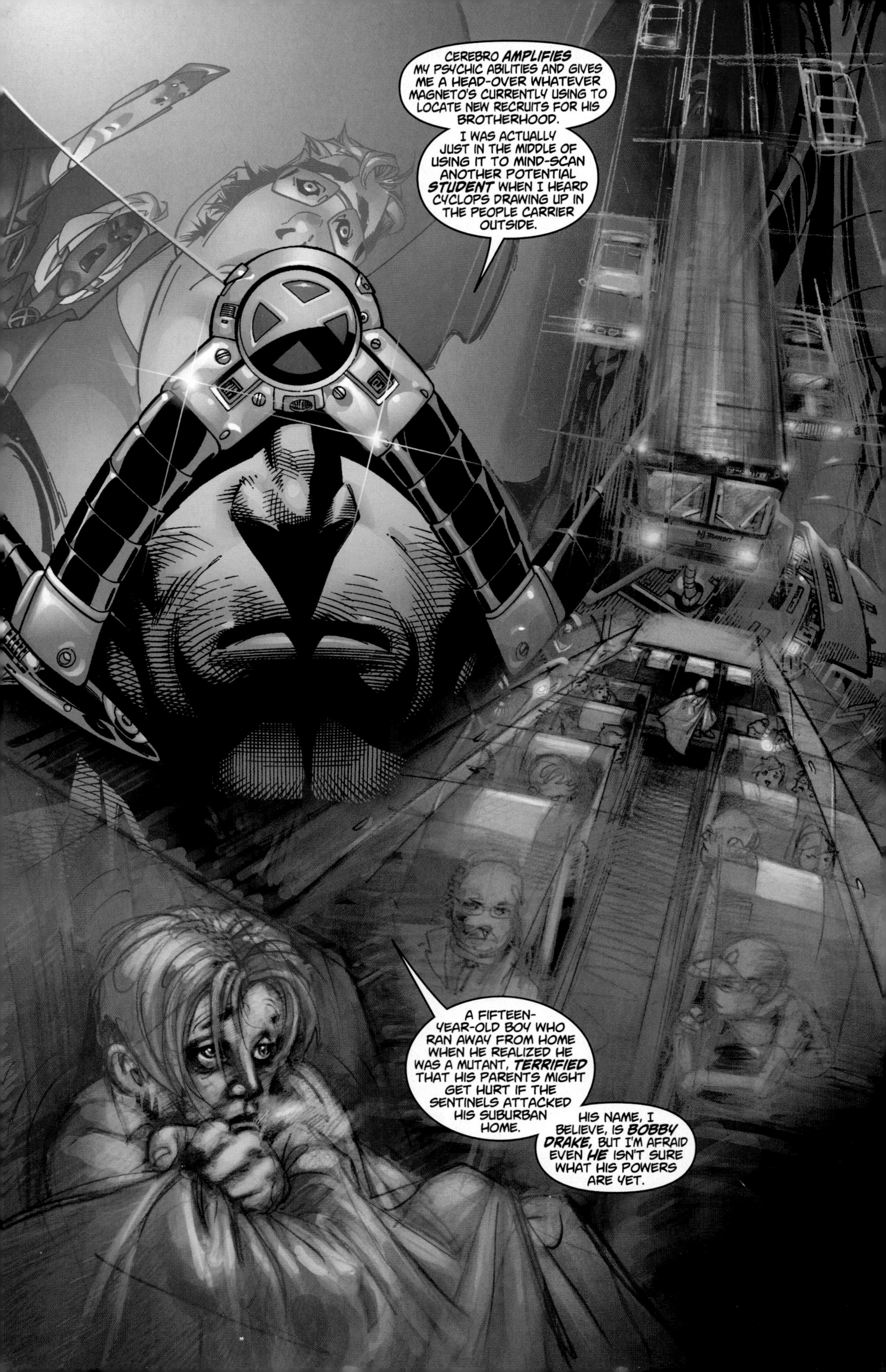
CEREBRO AMPLIFIES MY PSYCHIC ABILITIES AND GIVES ME A HEAD-OVER WHATEVER MAGNETO'S CURRENTLY USING TO LOCATE NEW RECRUITS FOR HIS BROTHERHOOD.
I WAS ACTUALLY JUST IN THE MIDDLE OF USING IT TO MIND-SCAN ANOTHER POTENTIAL STUDENT WHEN I HEARD CYCLOPS DRAWING UP IN THE PEOPLE CARRIER OUTSIDE.
A FIFTEEN-YEAR-OLD BOY WHO RAN AWAY FROM HOME WHEN HE REALIZED HE WAS A MUTANT, TERRIFIED THAT HIS PARENTS MIGHT GET HURT IF THE SENTINELS ATTACKED HIS SUBURBAN HOME.
HIS NAME, I BELIEVE, IS BOBBY DRAKE, BUT I'M AFRAID EVEN HE ISN'T SURE WHAT HIS POWERS ARE YET.

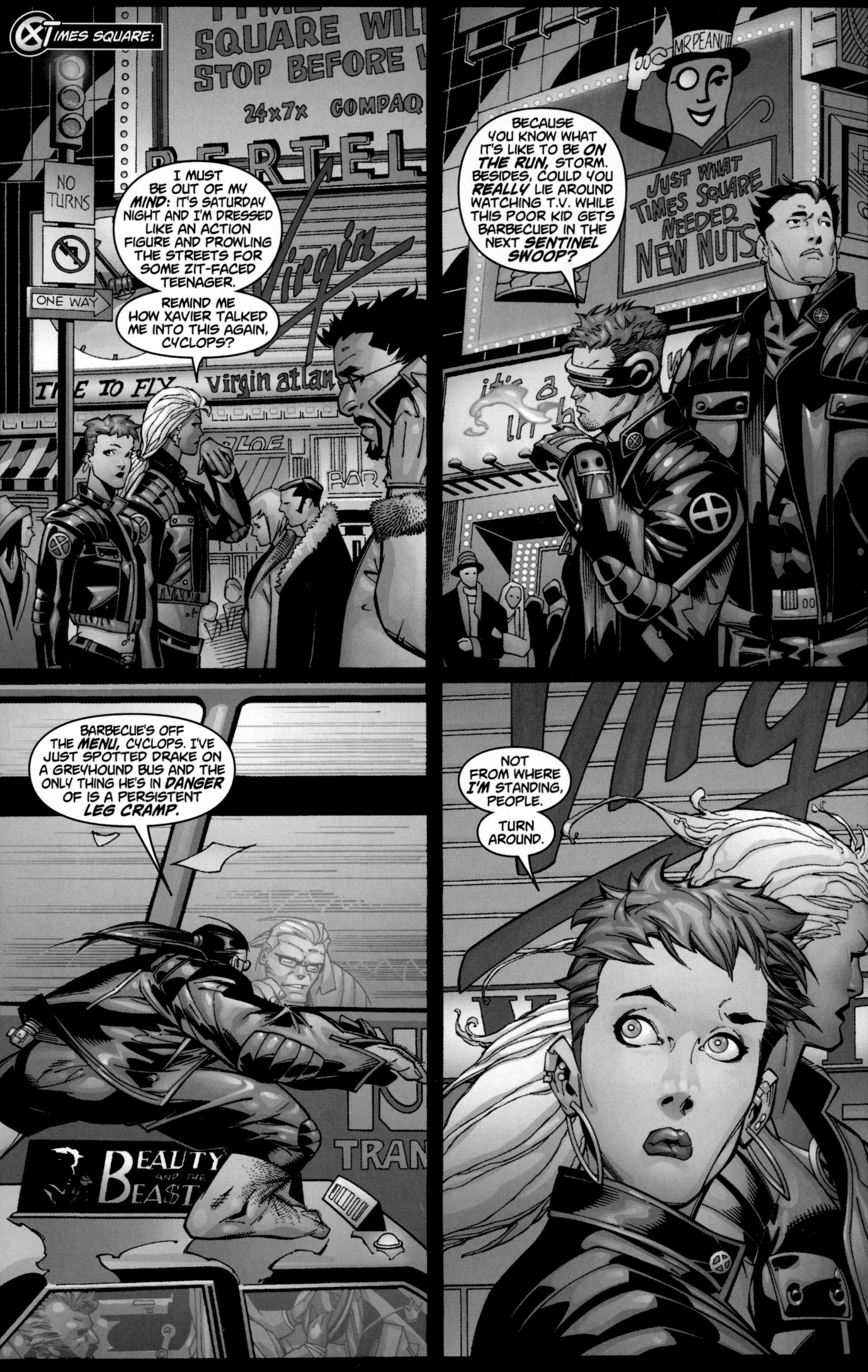
TIMES SQUARE:
I MUST BE OUT OF MY MIND: IT'S SATURDAY NIGHT AND I'M DRESSED LIKE AN ACTION FIGURE AND PROWLING THE STREETS FOR SOME ZIT-FACED TEENAGER.
REMIND ME HOW XAVIER TALKED ME INTO THIS AGAIN, CYCLOPS?
BECAUSE YOU KNOW WHAT IT'S LIKE TO BE ON THE RUN, STORM. BESIDES, COULD YOU REALLY LIE AROUND WATCHING T.V. WHILE THIS POOR KID GETS BARBECUED IN THE NEXT SENTINEL SWOOP?
JUST WHAT TIMES SQUARE NEEDED. NEW NUTS
BARBECUE'S OFF THE MENU, CYCLOPS. I'VE JUST SPOTTED DRAKE ON A GREYHOUND BUS AND THE ONLY THING HE'S IN DANGER OF IS A PERSISTENT LEG CRAMP.
NOT FROM WHERE I'M STANDING, PEOPLE.
TURN AROUND.

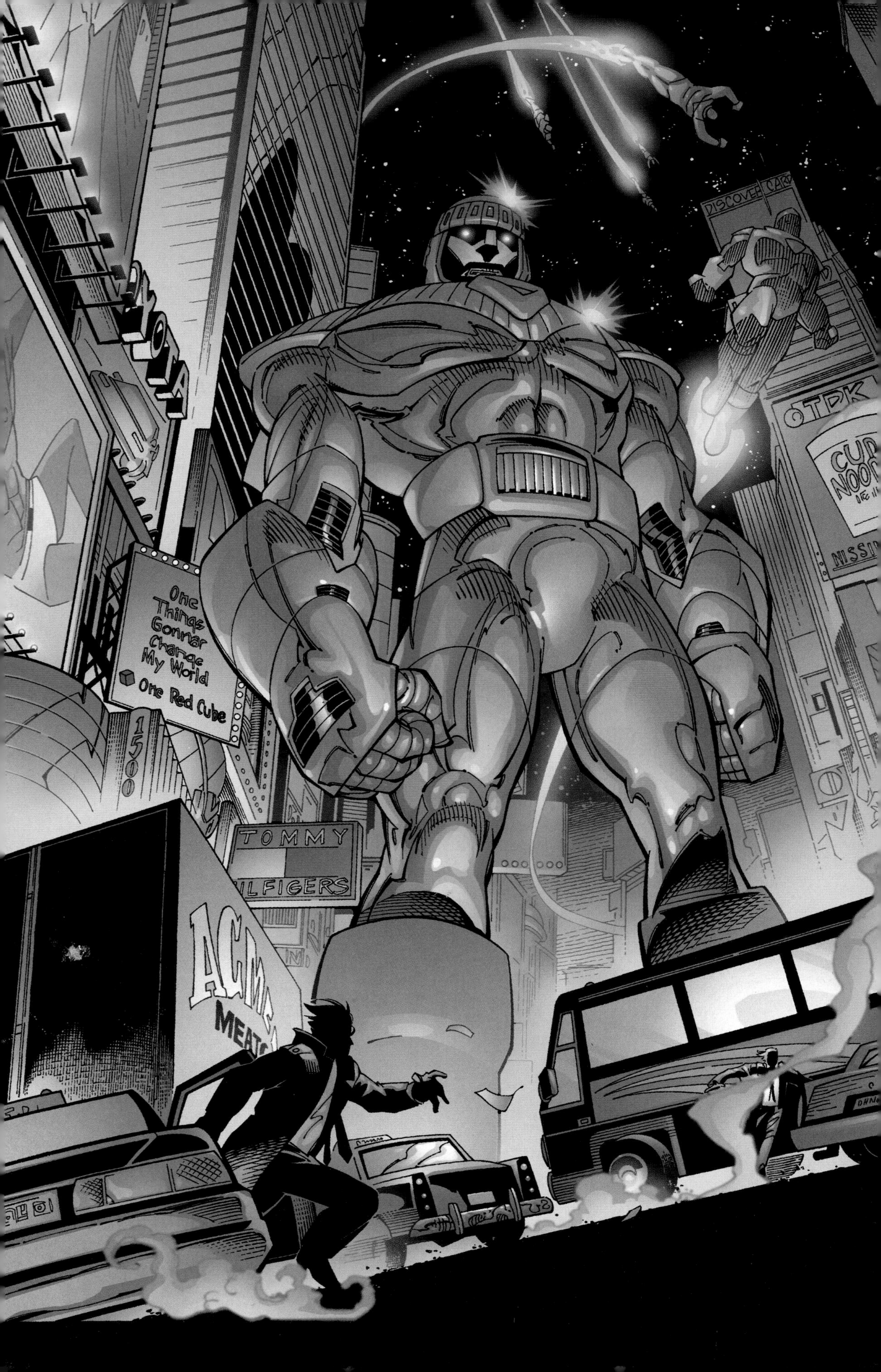

One Things Gonnar Change My World
One Red Cube
1500
TOMMY
ILFIGERS
ACME
MEAT
DISCOVER CARD
TDK
CUP NOOD
NISSI

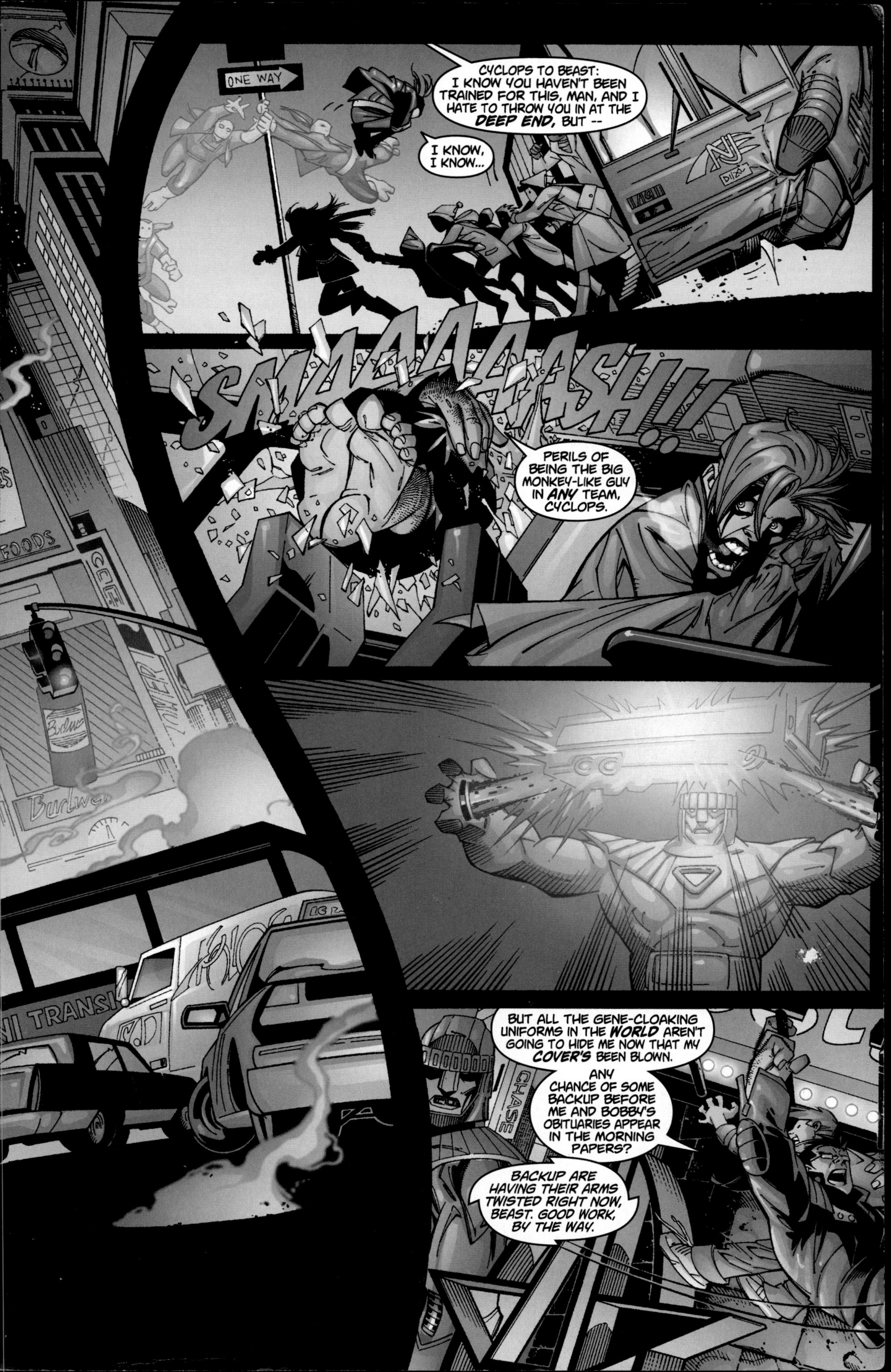

ONE WAY
CYCLOPS TO BEAST: I KNOW YOU HAVEN'T BEEN TRAINED FOR THIS, MAN, AND I HATE TO THROW YOU IN AT THE DEEP END, BUT --
I KNOW, I KNOW...
SMAAAAASH!!
PERILS OF BEING THE BIG MONKEY-LIKE GUY IN ANY TEAM, CYCLOPS.
FOODS
TRANSI
CHASE
BUT ALL THE GENE-CLOAKING UNIFORMS IN THE WORLD AREN'T GOING TO HIDE ME NOW THAT MY COVER'S BEEN BLOWN.
ANY CHANCE OF SOME BACKUP BEFORE ME AND BOBBY'S OBITUARIES APPEAR IN THE MORNING PAPERS?
BACKUP ARE HAVING THEIR ARMS TWISTED RIGHT NOW, BEAST. GOOD WORK, BY THE WAY.

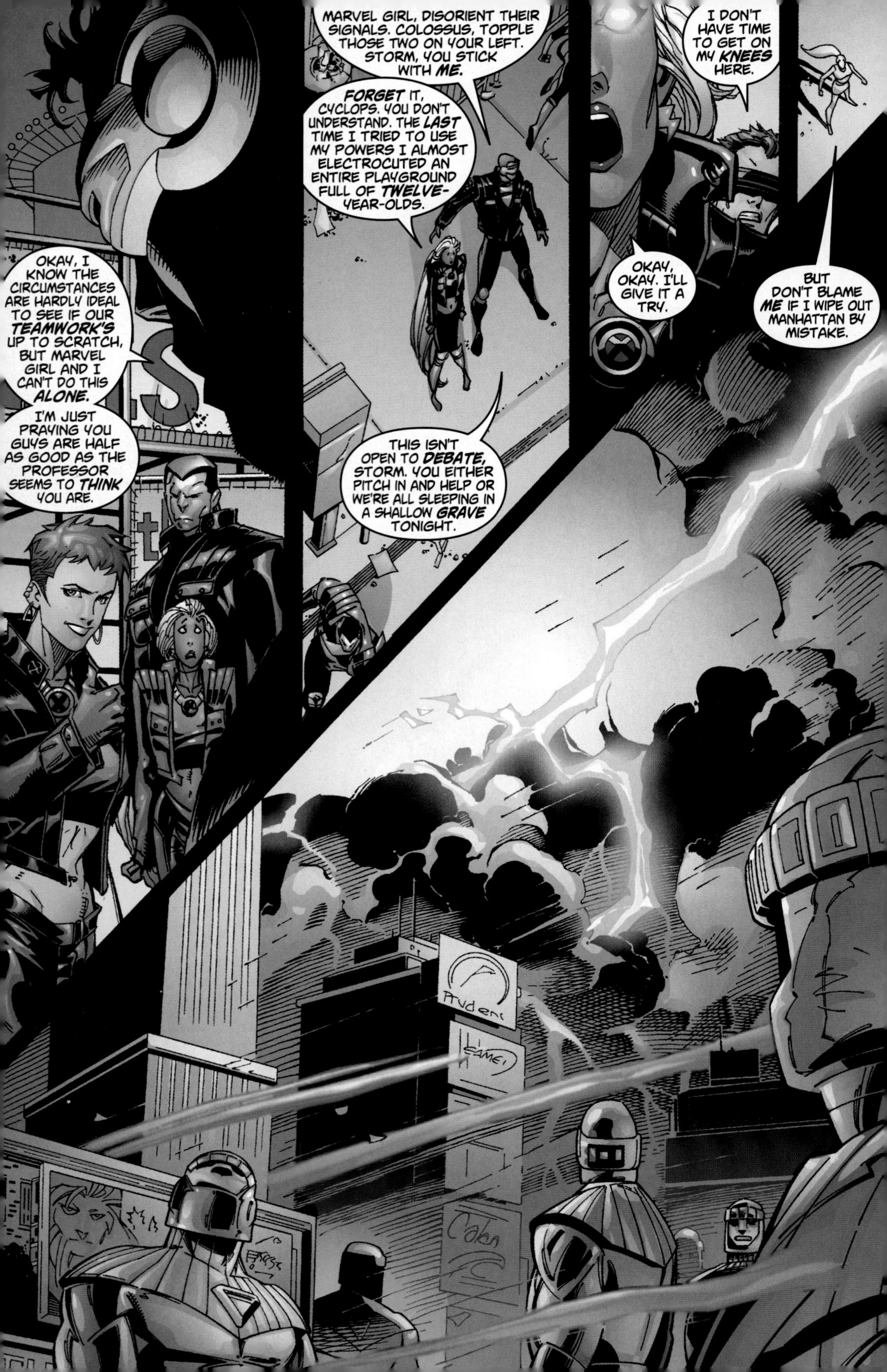

OKAY, I KNOW THE CIRCUMSTANCES ARE HARDLY IDEAL TO SEE IF OUR TEAMWORK'S UP TO SCRATCH, BUT MARVEL GIRL AND I CAN'T DO THIS ALONE.
I'M JUST PRAYING YOU GUYS ARE HALF AS GOOD AS THE PROFESSOR SEEMS TO THINK YOU ARE.
MARVEL GIRL, DISORIENT THEIR SIGNALS. COLOSSUS, TOPPLE THOSE TWO ON YOUR LEFT. STORM, YOU STICK WITH ME.
FORGET IT, CYCLOPS. YOU DON'T UNDERSTAND. THE LAST TIME I TRIED TO USE MY POWERS I ALMOST ELECTROCUTED AN ENTIRE PLAYGROUND FULL OF TWELVE-YEAR-OLDS.
THIS ISN'T OPEN TO DEBATE, STORM. YOU EITHER PITCH IN AND HELP OR WE'RE ALL SLEEPING IN A SHALLOW GRAVE TONIGHT.
I DON'T HAVE TIME TO GET ON MY KNEES HERE.
OKAY, OKAY. I'LL GIVE IT A TRY.
BUT DON'T BLAME ME IF I WIPE OUT MANHATTAN BY MISTAKE.

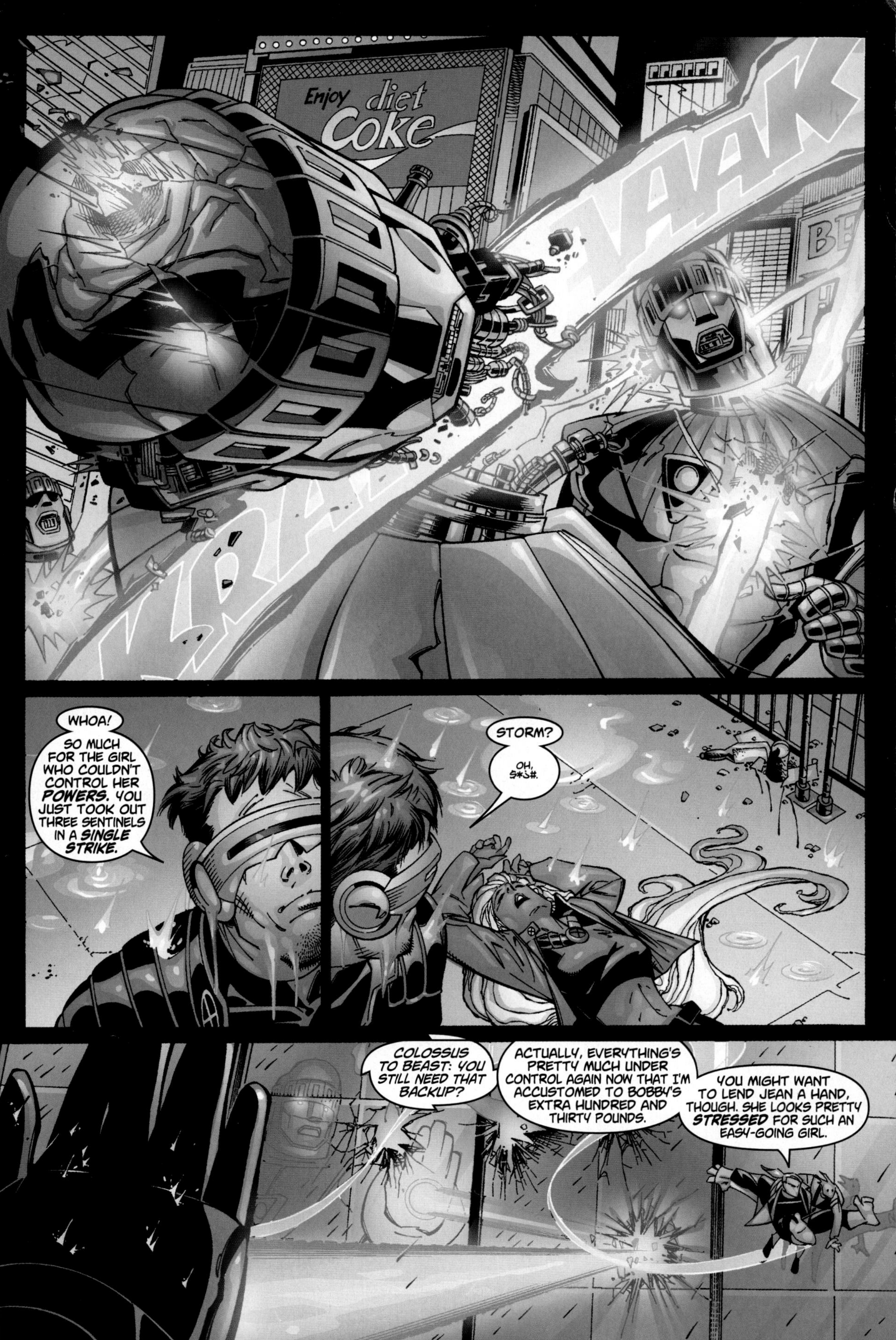

Enjoy diet Coke
KRAAAK
WHOA!
SO MUCH FOR THE GIRL WHO COULDN'T CONTROL HER POWERS. YOU JUST TOOK OUT THREE SENTINELS IN A SINGLE STRIKE.
STORM?
OH, S*J#.
COLOSSUS TO BEAST: YOU STILL NEED THAT BACKUP?
ACTUALLY, EVERYTHING'S PRETTY MUCH UNDER CONTROL AGAIN NOW THAT I'M ACCUSTOMED TO BOBBY'S EXTRA HUNDRED AND THIRTY POUNDS.
YOU MIGHT WANT TO LEND JEAN A HAND, THOUGH. SHE LOOKS PRETTY STRESSED FOR SUCH AN EASY-GOING GIRL.

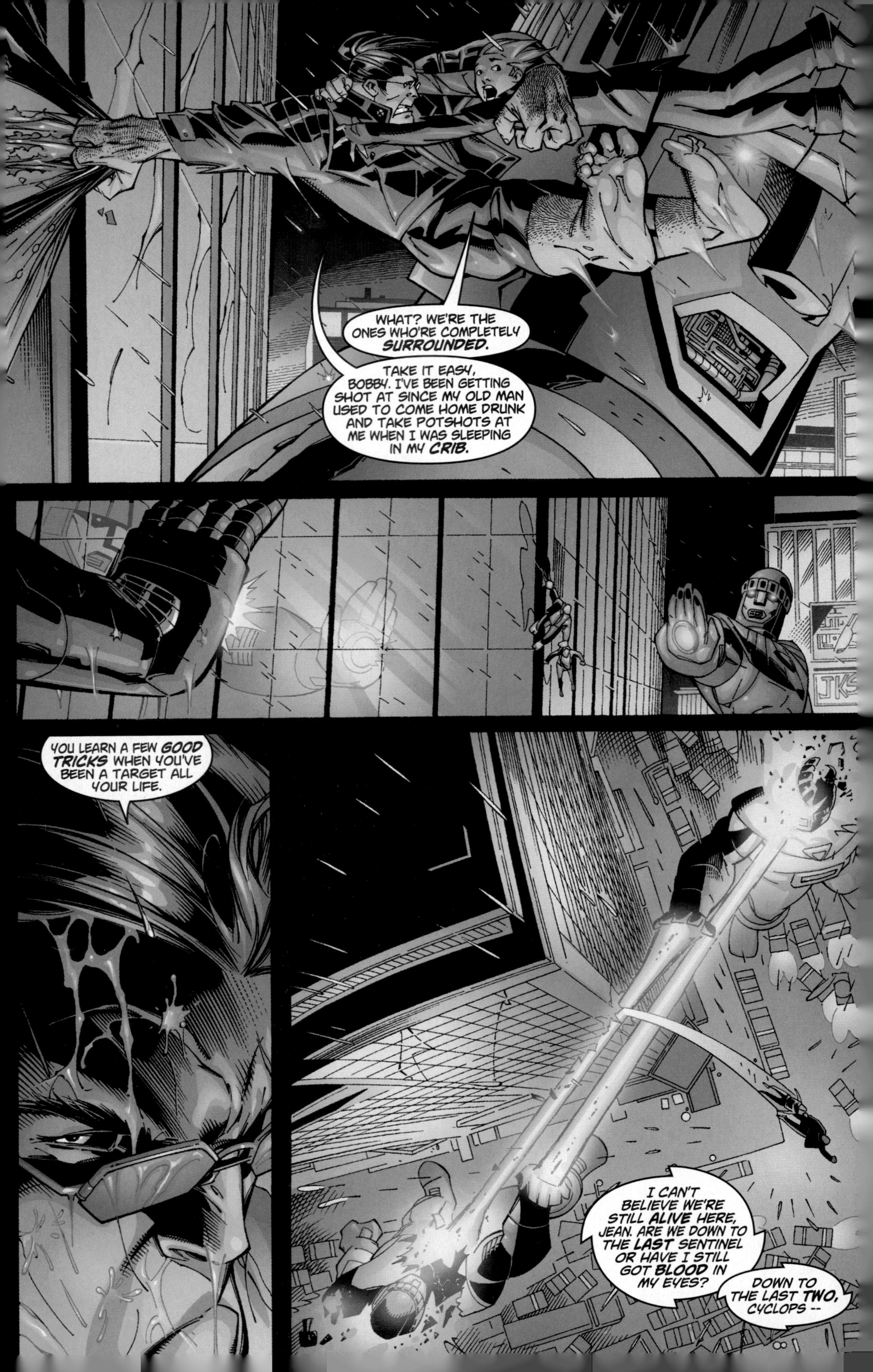
WHAT? WE'RE THE ONES WHO'RE COMPLETELY SURROUNDED.
TAKE IT EASY, BOBBY. I'VE BEEN GETTING SHOT AT SINCE MY OLD MAN USED TO COME HOME DRUNK AND TAKE POTSHOTS AT ME WHEN I WAS SLEEPING IN MY CRIB.
YOU LEARN A FEW GOOD TRICKS WHEN YOU'VE BEEN A TARGET ALL YOUR LIFE.
I CAN'T BELIEVE WE'RE STILL ALIVE HERE, JEAN. ARE WE DOWN TO THE LAST SENTINEL OR HAVE I STILL GOT BLOOD IN MY EYES?
DOWN TO THE LAST TWO, CYCLOPS --

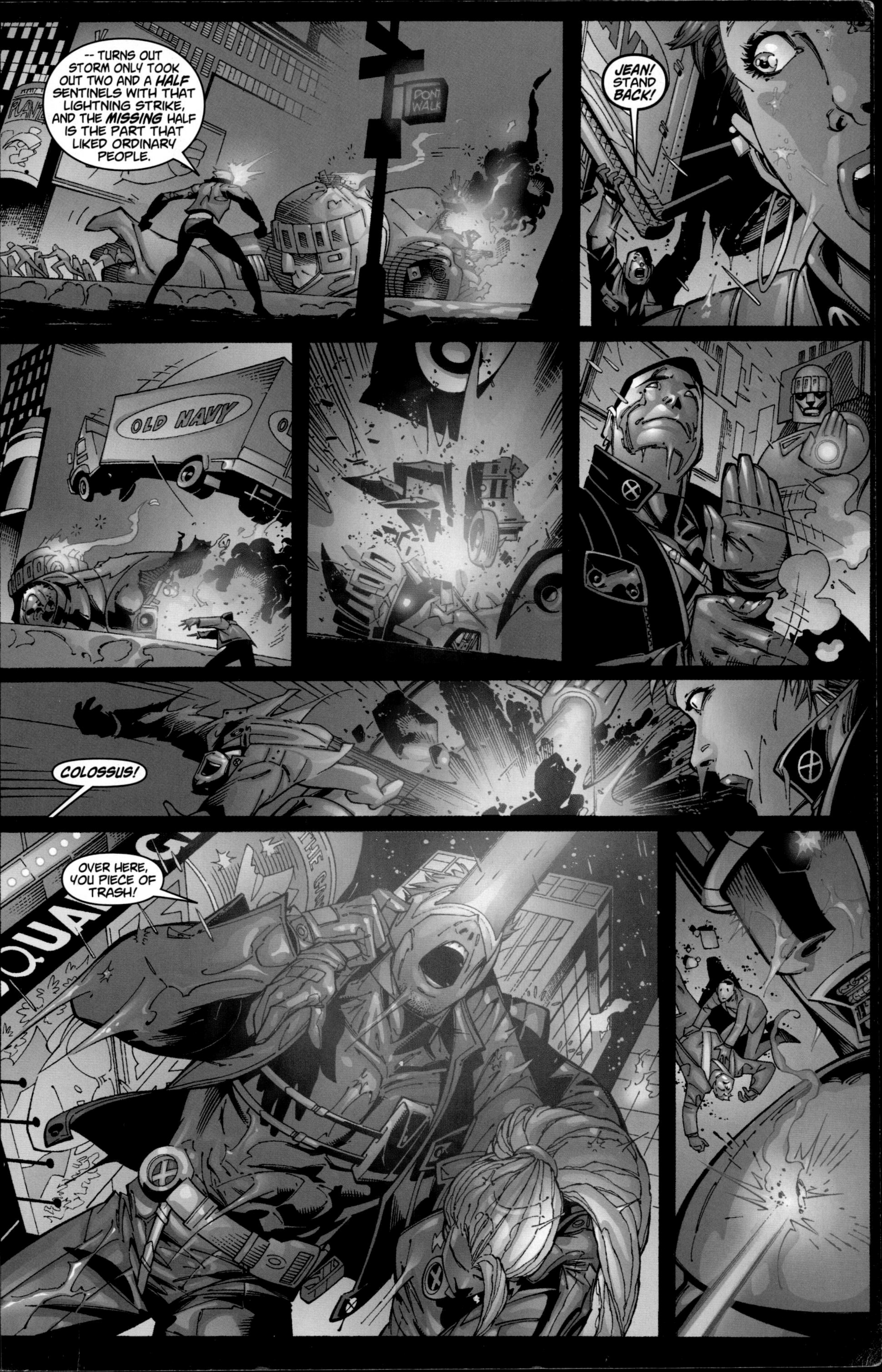
-- TURNS OUT STORM ONLY TOOK OUT TWO AND A HALF SENTINELS WITH THAT LIGHTNING STRIKE, AND THE MISSING HALF IS THE PART THAT LIKED ORDINARY PEOPLE.
DON'T WALK
JEAN! STAND BACK!
OLD NAVY
COLOSSUS!
OVER HERE, YOU PIECE OF TRASH!

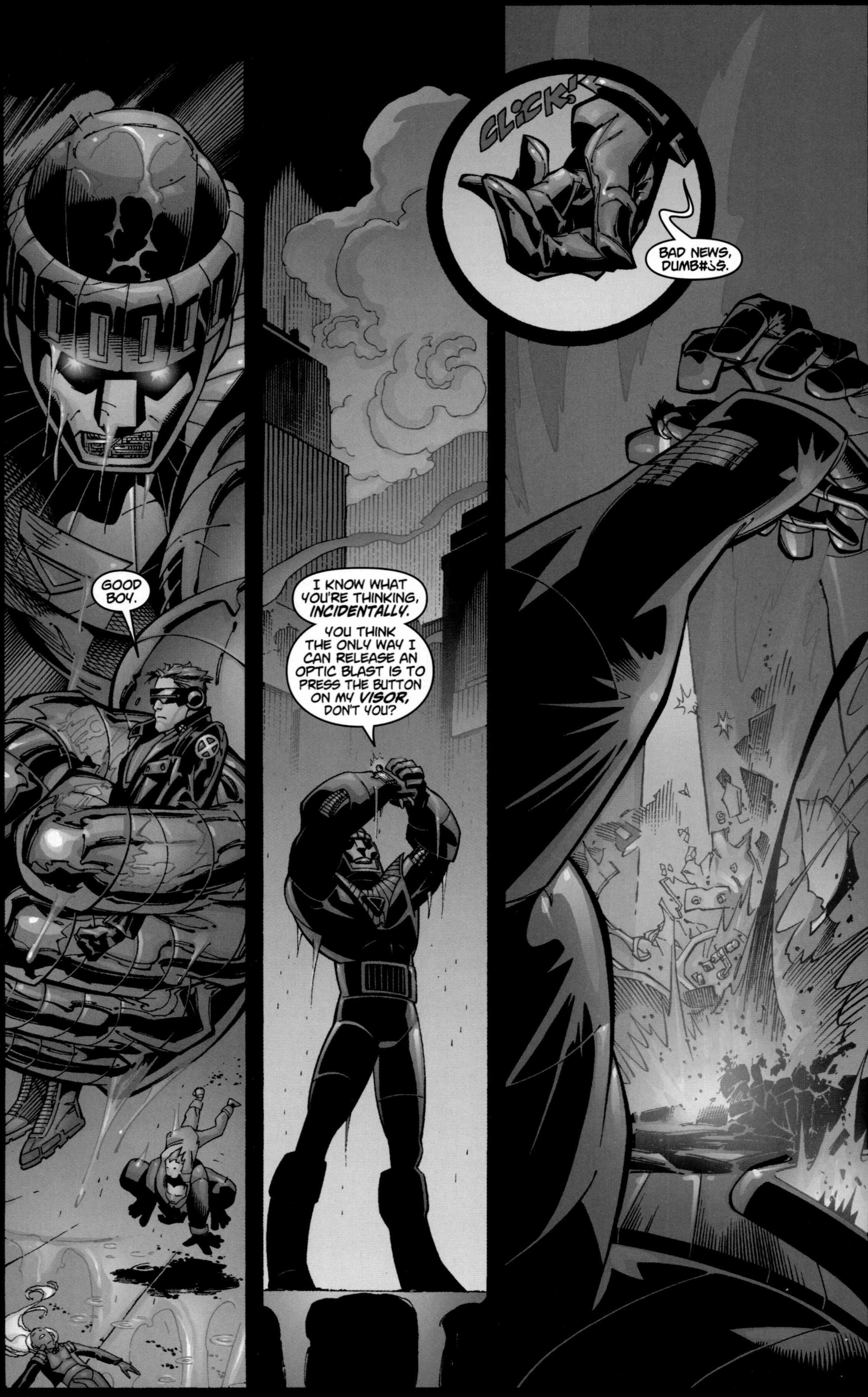
GOOD BOY.
I KNOW WHAT YOU'RE THINKING, INCIDENTALLY.
YOU THINK THE ONLY WAY I CAN RELEASE AN OPTIC BLAST IS TO PRESS THE BUTTON ON MY VISOR, DON'T YOU?
CLICK!
BAD NEWS, DUMB#$S.

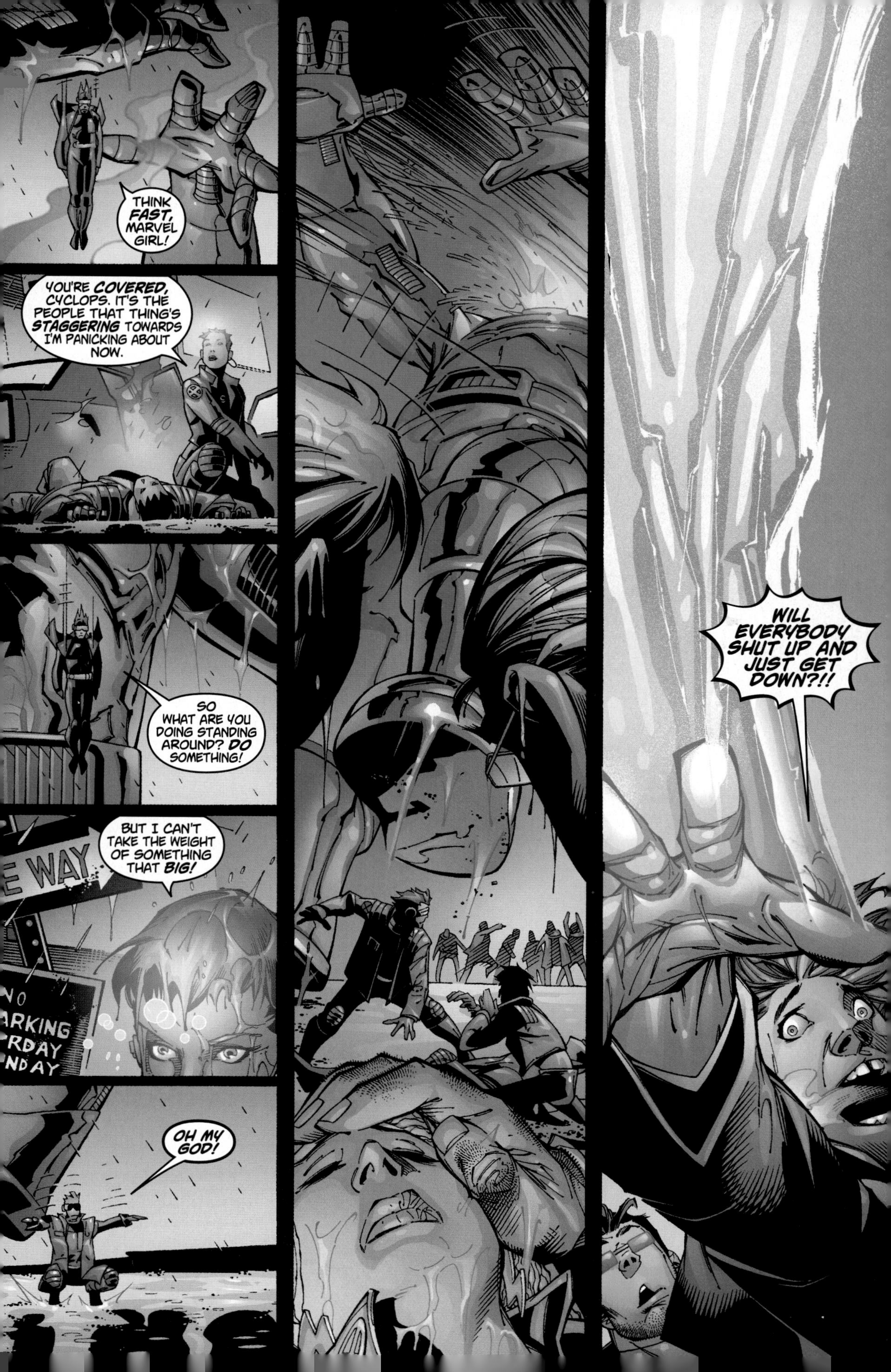
THINK FAST, MARVEL GIRL!
YOU'RE COVERED, CYCLOPS. IT'S THE PEOPLE THAT THING'S STAGGERING TOWARDS I'M PANICKING ABOUT NOW.
SO WHAT ARE YOU DOING STANDING AROUND? DO SOMETHING!
BUT I CAN'T TAKE THE WEIGHT OF SOMETHING THAT BIG!
E WAY
NO
ARKING
RDAY
NDAY
OH MY GOD!
WILL EVERYBODY SHUT UP AND JUST GET DOWN?!!

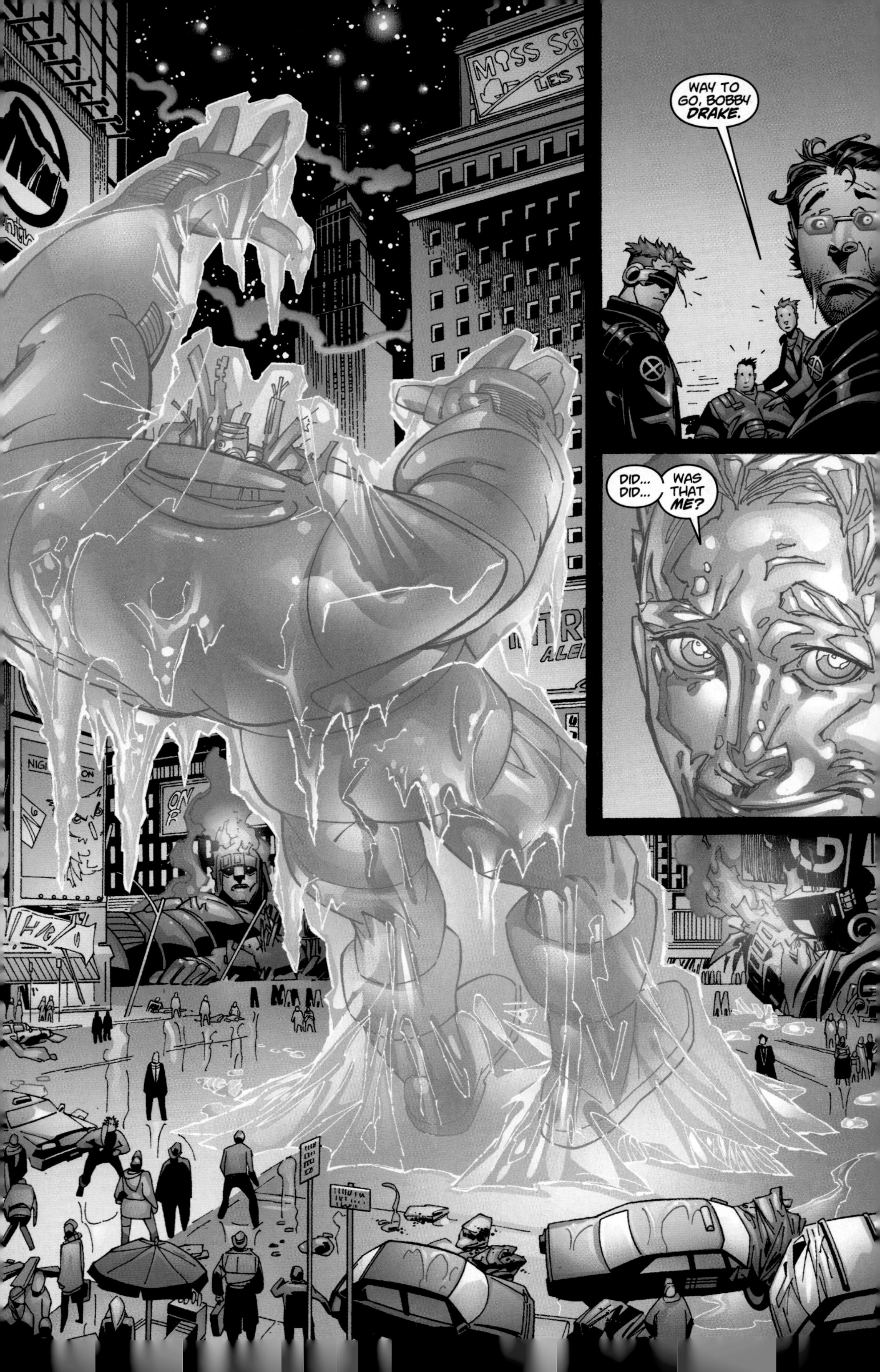
WAY TO GO, BOBBY DRAKE.
DID... DID...
WAS THAT ME?

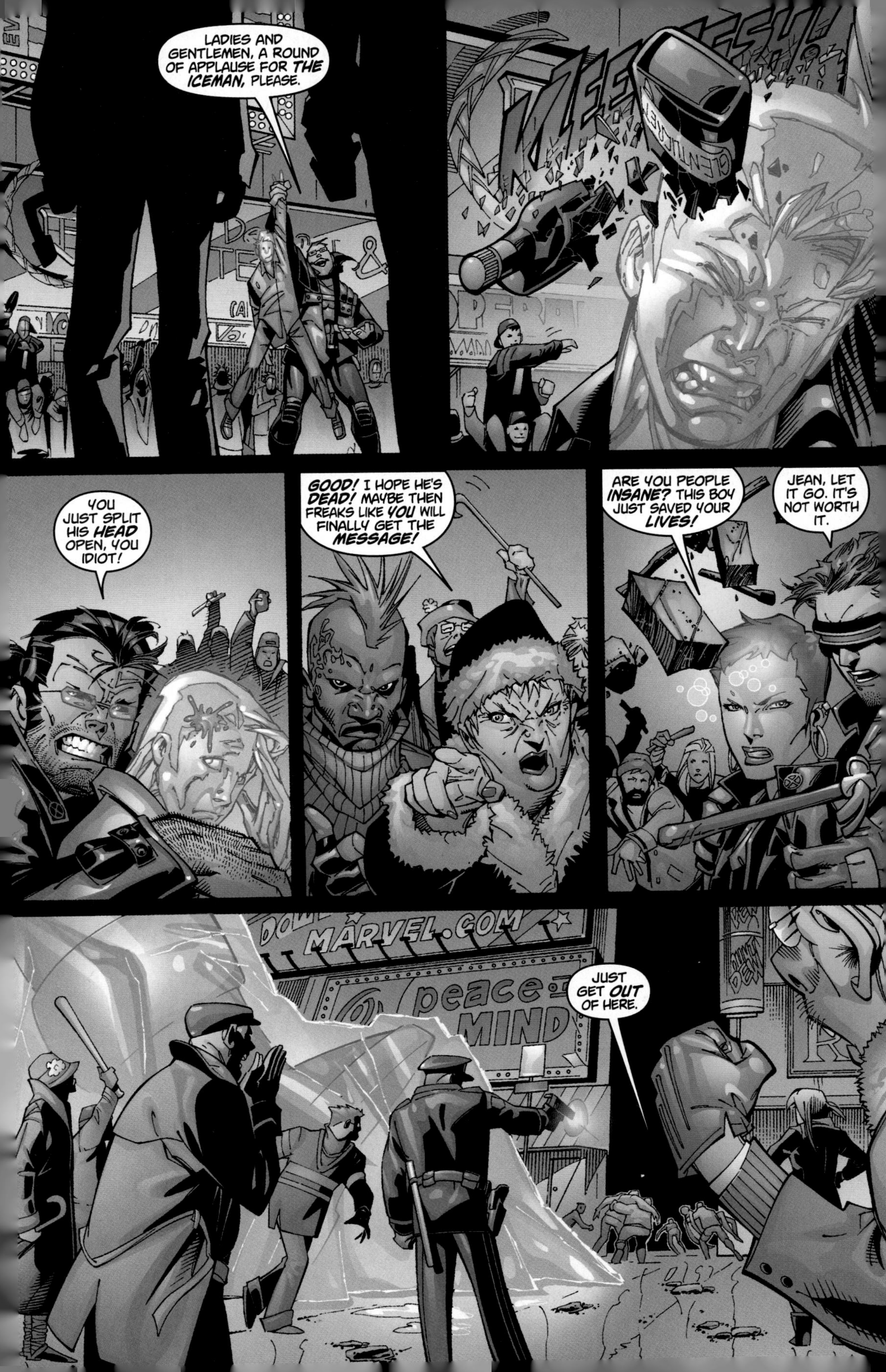

LADIES AND GENTLEMEN, A ROUND OF APPLAUSE FOR THE ICEMAN, PLEASE.
YOU JUST SPLIT HIS HEAD OPEN, YOU IDIOT!
GOOD! I HOPE HE'S DEAD! MAYBE THEN FREAKS LIKE YOU WILL FINALLY GET THE MESSAGE!
ARE YOU PEOPLE INSANE? THIS BOY JUST SAVED YOUR LIVES!
JEAN, LET IT GO. IT'S NOT WORTH IT.
JUST GET OUT OF HERE.

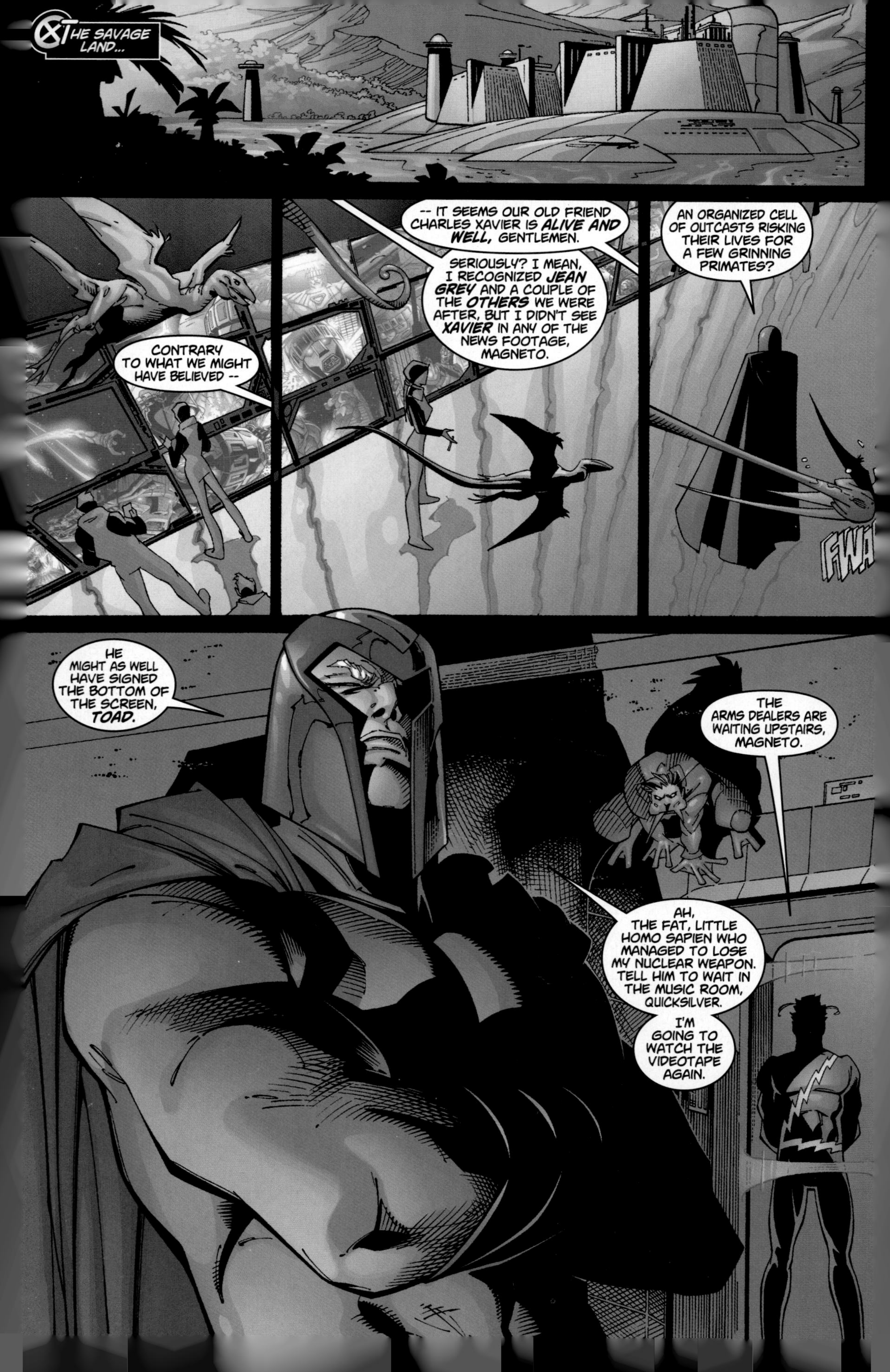
THE SAVAGE LAND...
CONTRARY TO WHAT WE MIGHT HAVE BELIEVED --
-- IT SEEMS OUR OLD FRIEND CHARLES XAVIER IS ALIVE AND WELL, GENTLEMEN.
SERIOUSLY? I MEAN, I RECOGNIZED JEAN GREY AND A COUPLE OF THE OTHERS WE WERE AFTER, BUT I DIDN'T SEE XAVIER IN ANY OF THE NEWS FOOTAGE, MAGNETO.
AN ORGANIZED CELL OF OUTCASTS RISKING THEIR LIVES FOR A FEW GRINNING PRIMATES?
FWA
HE MIGHT AS WELL HAVE SIGNED THE BOTTOM OF THE SCREEN, TOAD.
THE ARMS DEALERS ARE WAITING UPSTAIRS, MAGNETO.
AH, THE FAT, LITTLE HOMO SAPIEN WHO MANAGED TO LOSE MY NUCLEAR WEAPON. TELL HIM TO WAIT IN THE MUSIC ROOM, QUICKSILVER.
I'M GOING TO WATCH THE VIDEOTAPE AGAIN.

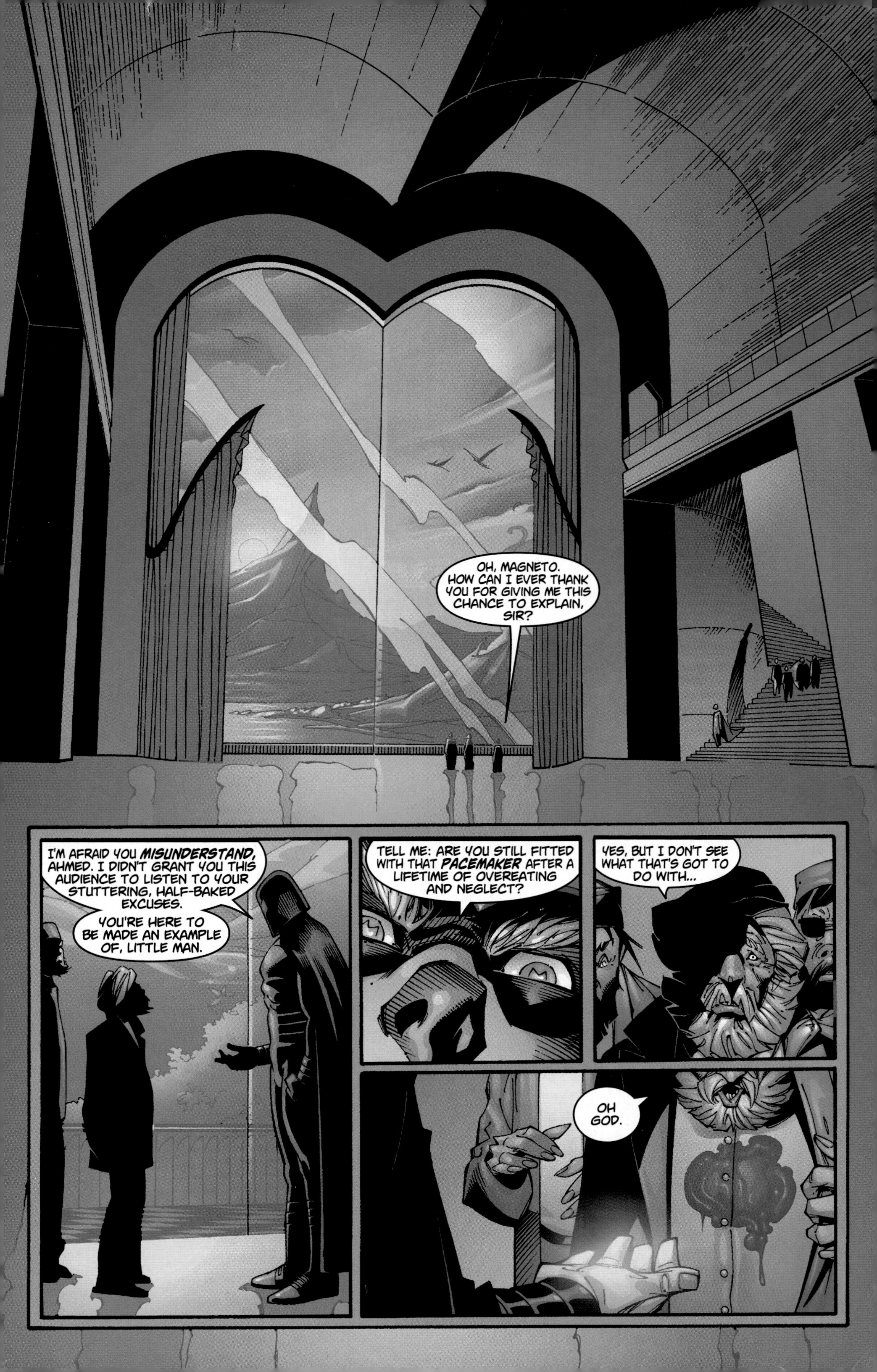
OH, MAGNETO. HOW CAN I EVER THANK YOU FOR GIVING ME THIS CHANCE TO EXPLAIN, SIR?
I'M AFRAID YOU MISUNDERSTAND, AHMED. I DIDN'T GRANT YOU THIS AUDIENCE TO LISTEN TO YOUR STUTTERING, HALF-BAKED EXCUSES.
YOU'RE HERE TO BE MADE AN EXAMPLE OF, LITTLE MAN.
TELL ME: ARE YOU STILL FITTED WITH THAT PACEMAKER AFTER A LIFETIME OF OVEREATING AND NEGLECT?
YES, BUT I DON'T SEE WHAT THAT'S GOT TO DO WITH...
OH GOD.

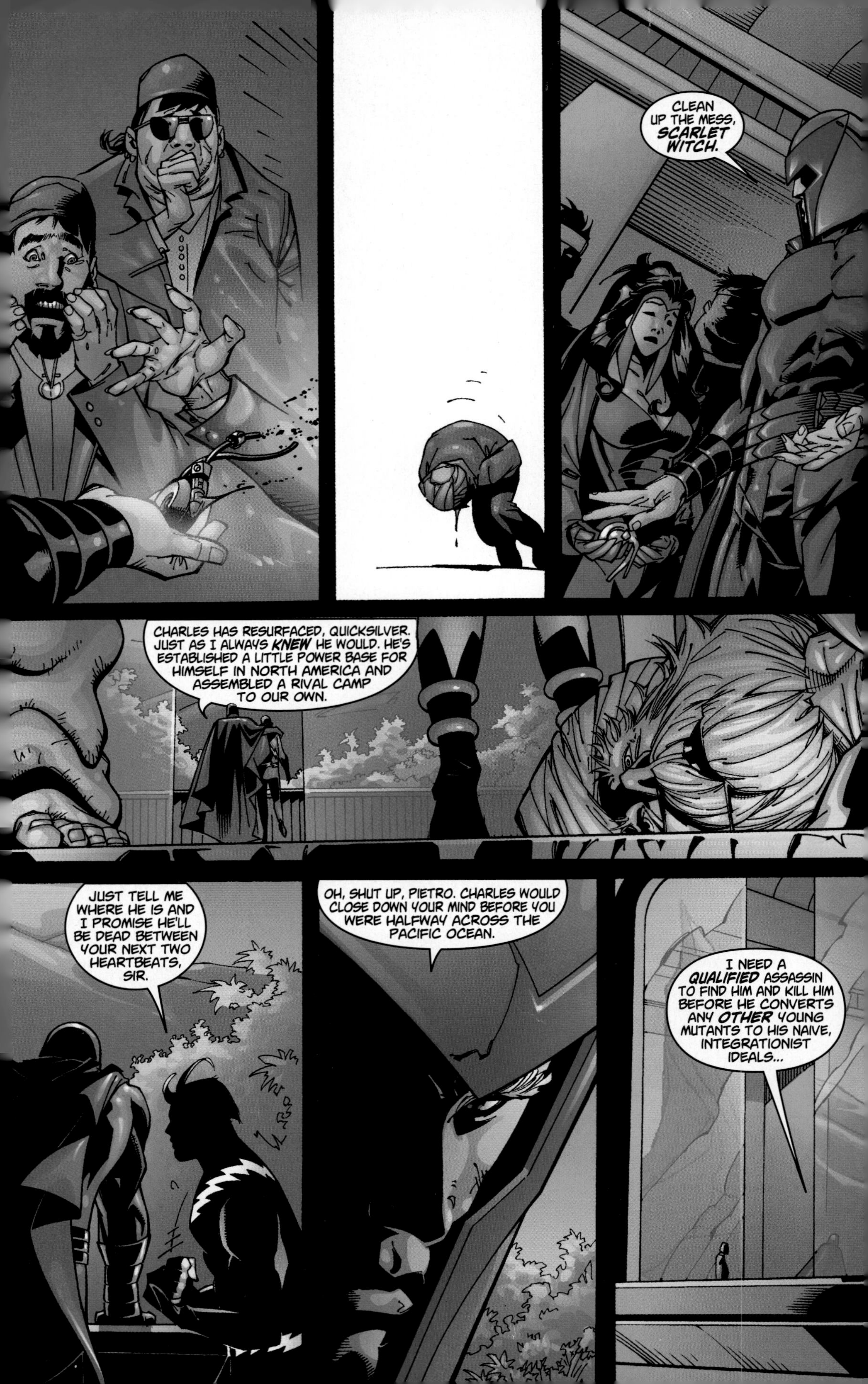
CLEAN UP THE MESS, SCARLET WITCH.
CHARLES HAS RESURFACED, QUICKSILVER. JUST AS I ALWAYS KNEW HE WOULD. HE'S ESTABLISHED A LITTLE POWER BASE FOR HIMSELF IN NORTH AMERICA AND ASSEMBLED A RIVAL CAMP TO OUR OWN.
JUST TELL ME WHERE HE IS AND I PROMISE HE'LL BE DEAD BETWEEN YOUR NEXT TWO HEARTBEATS, SIR.
OH, SHUT UP, PIETRO. CHARLES WOULD CLOSE DOWN YOUR MIND BEFORE YOU WERE HALFWAY ACROSS THE PACIFIC OCEAN.
I NEED A QUALIFIED ASSASSIN TO FIND HIM AND KILL HIM BEFORE HE CONVERTS ANY OTHER YOUNG MUTANTS TO HIS NAIVE, INTEGRATIONIST IDEALS...

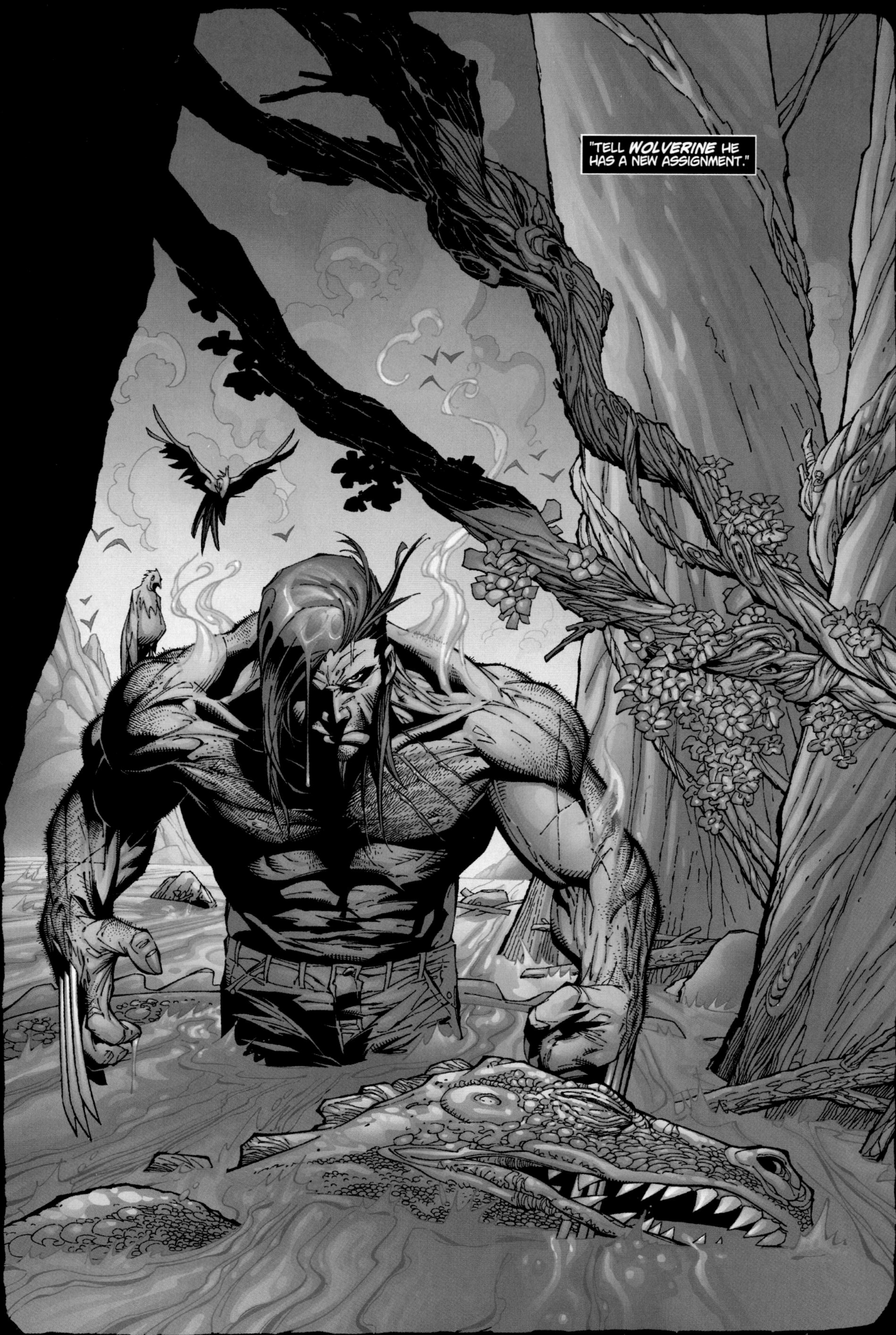
"TELL WOLVERINE HE HAS A NEW ASSIGNMENT."

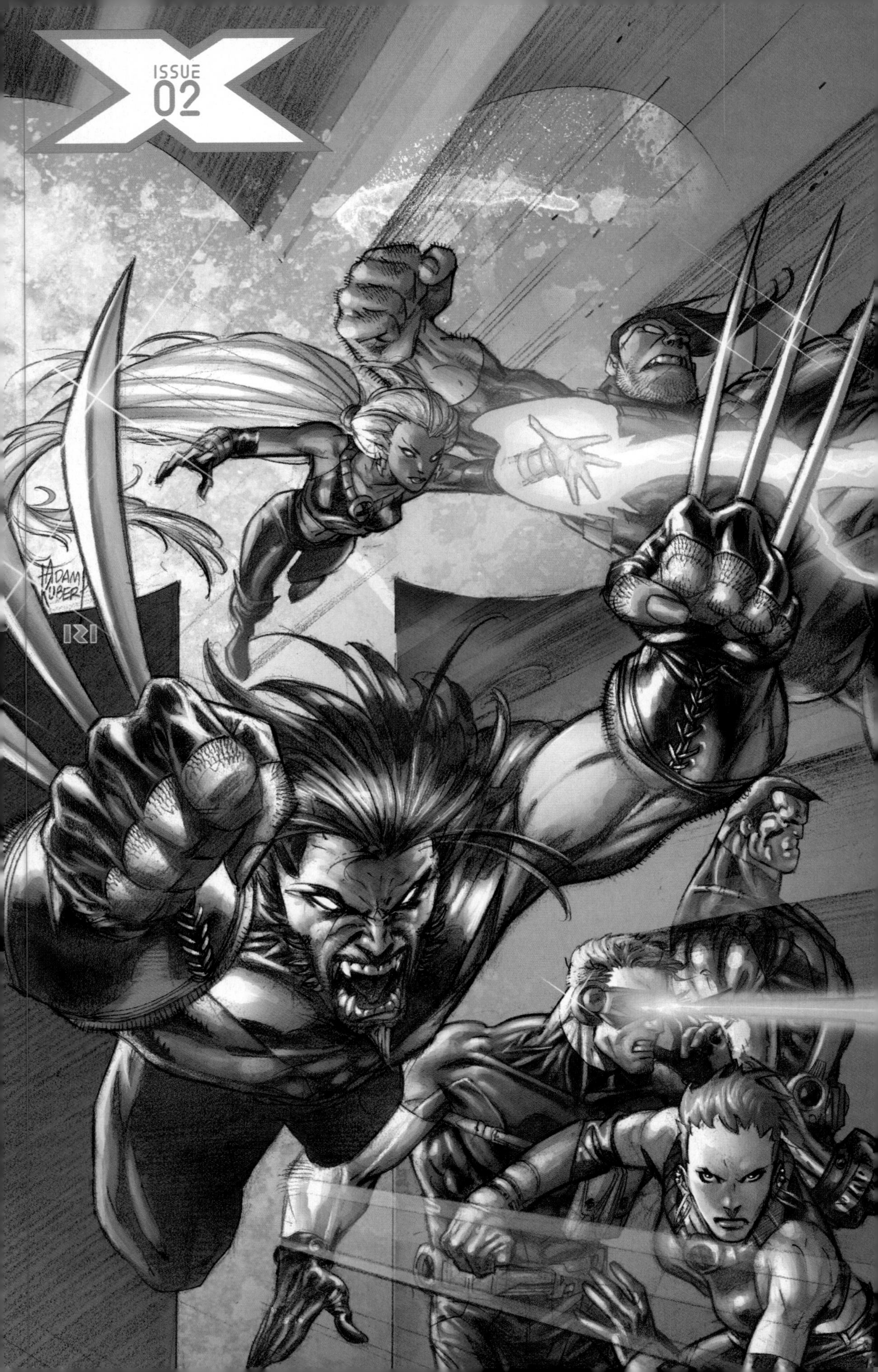
X
ISSUE
02
ADAM KUBERT

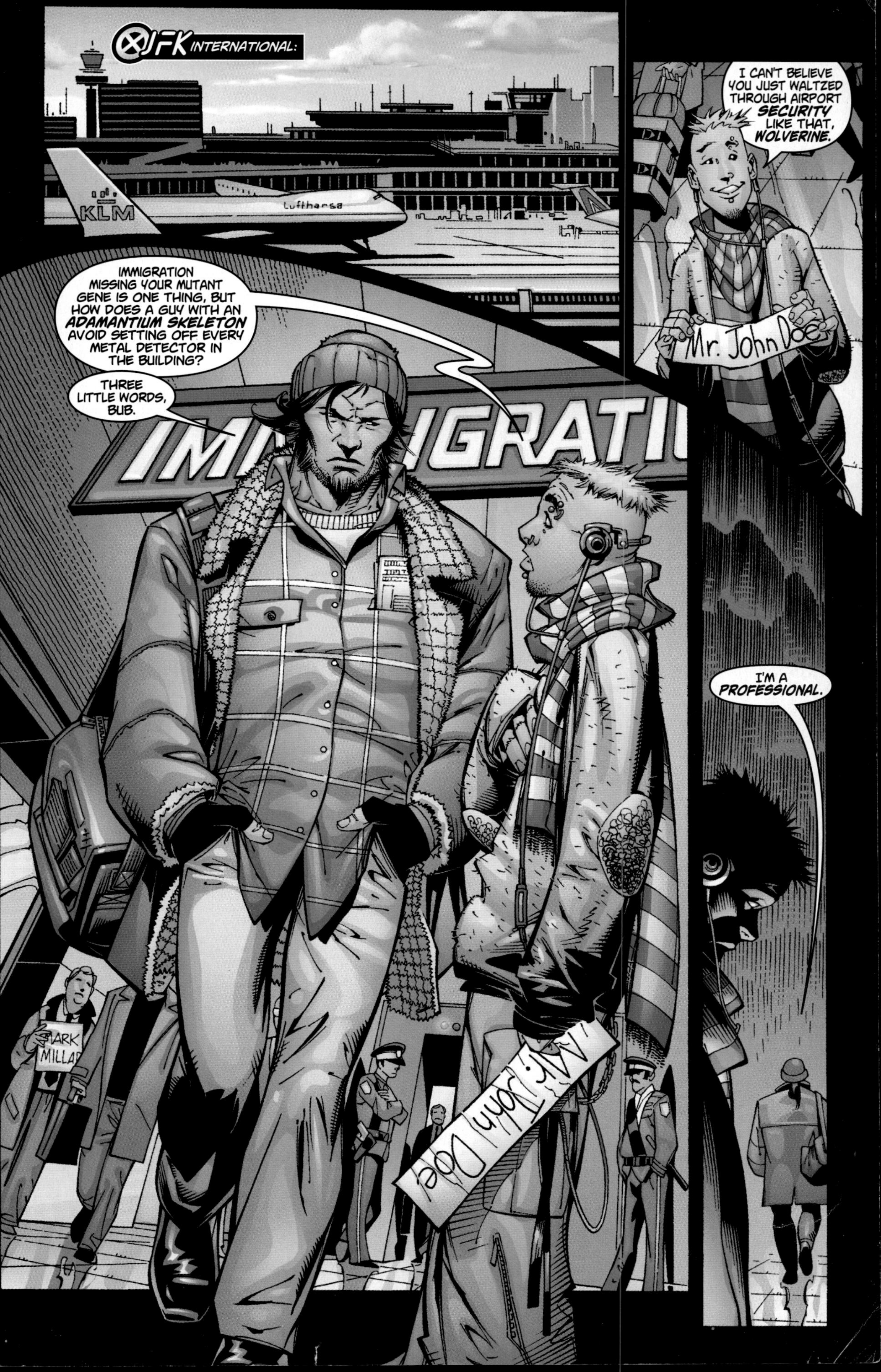
JFK INTERNATIONAL:
KLM
Lufthansa
I CAN'T BELIEVE YOU JUST WALTZED THROUGH AIRPORT SECURITY LIKE THAT, WOLVERINE.
Mr. John Doe
IMMIGRATION MISSING YOUR MUTANT GENE IS ONE THING, BUT HOW DOES A GUY WITH AN ADAMANTIUM SKELETON AVOID SETTING OFF EVERY METAL DETECTOR IN THE BUILDING?
THREE LITTLE WORDS, BUB.
I'M A PROFESSIONAL.
IMMIGRATI
MARK MILLAR
Mr. John Doe

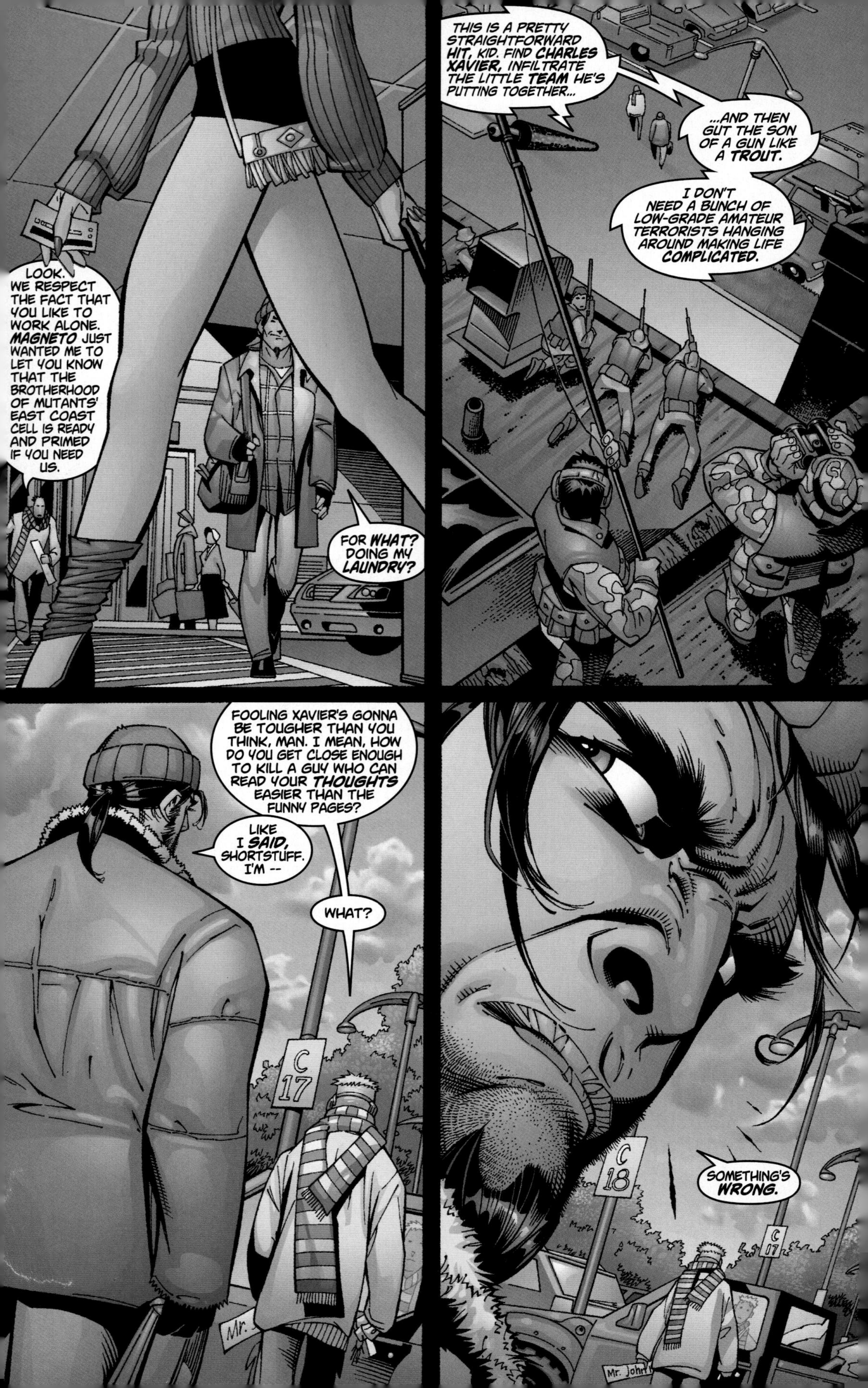
LOOK. WE RESPECT THE FACT THAT YOU LIKE TO WORK ALONE. MAGNETO JUST WANTED ME TO LET YOU KNOW THAT THE BROTHERHOOD OF MUTANTS' EAST COAST CELL IS READY AND PRIMED IF YOU NEED US.
FOR WHAT? DOING MY LAUNDRY?
THIS IS A PRETTY STRAIGHTFORWARD HIT, KID. FIND CHARLES XAVIER, INFILTRATE THE LITTLE TEAM HE'S PUTTING TOGETHER...
...AND THEN GUT THE SON OF A GUN LIKE A TROUT.
I DON'T NEED A BUNCH OF LOW-GRADE AMATEUR TERRORISTS HANGING AROUND MAKING LIFE COMPLICATED.
FOOLING XAVIER'S GONNA BE TOUGHER THAN YOU THINK, MAN. I MEAN, HOW DO YOU GET CLOSE ENOUGH TO KILL A GUY WHO CAN READ YOUR THOUGHTS EASIER THAN THE FUNNY PAGES?
LIKE I SAID, SHORTSTUFF. I'M --
WHAT?
C 17
SOMETHING'S WRONG.
C 18
C 17

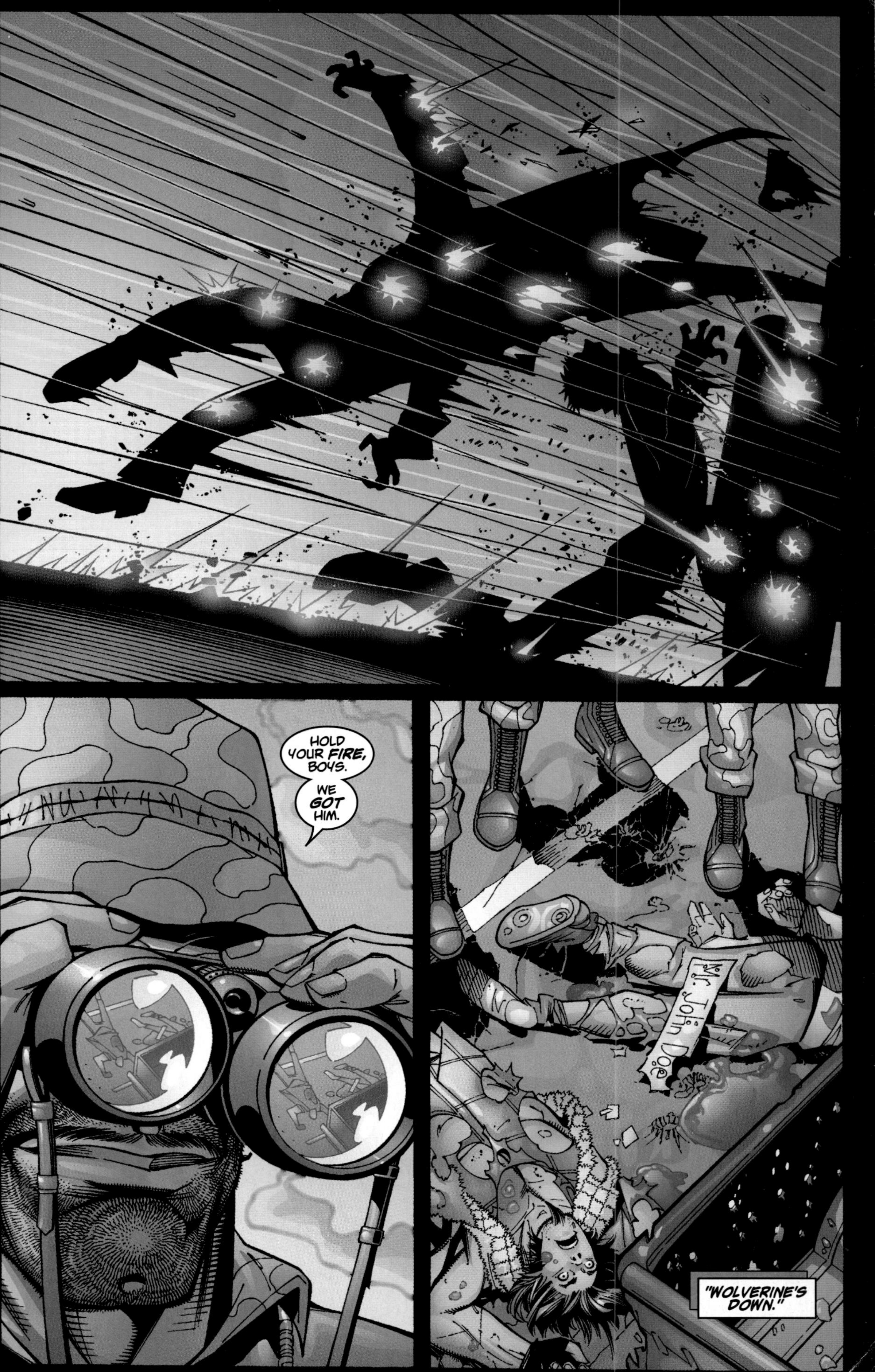
HOLD YOUR FIRE, BOYS.
WE GOT HIM.
Mr. John Doe
"WOLVERINE'S DOWN."

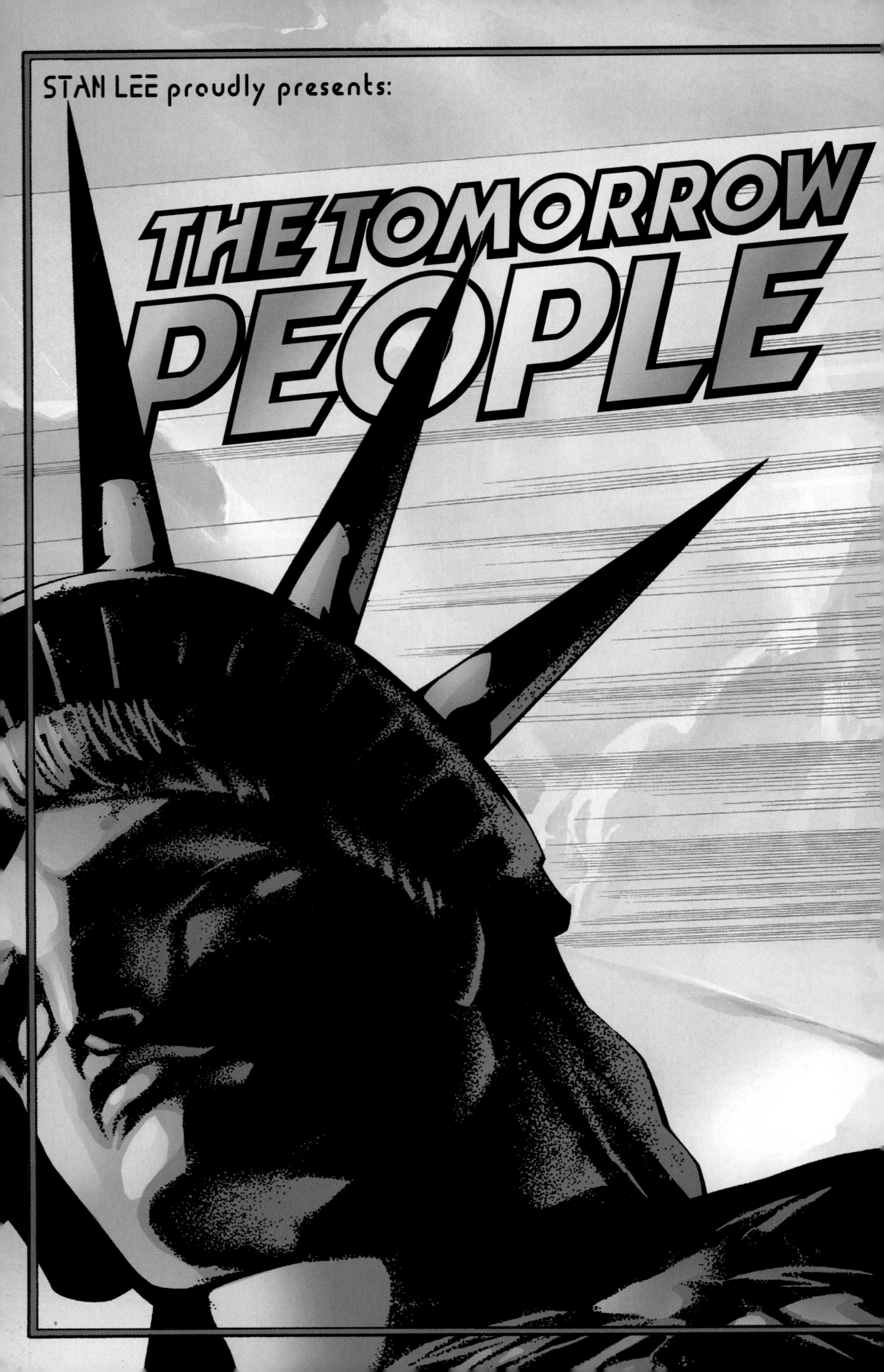
STAN LEE proudly presents:
THE TOMORROW PEOPLE

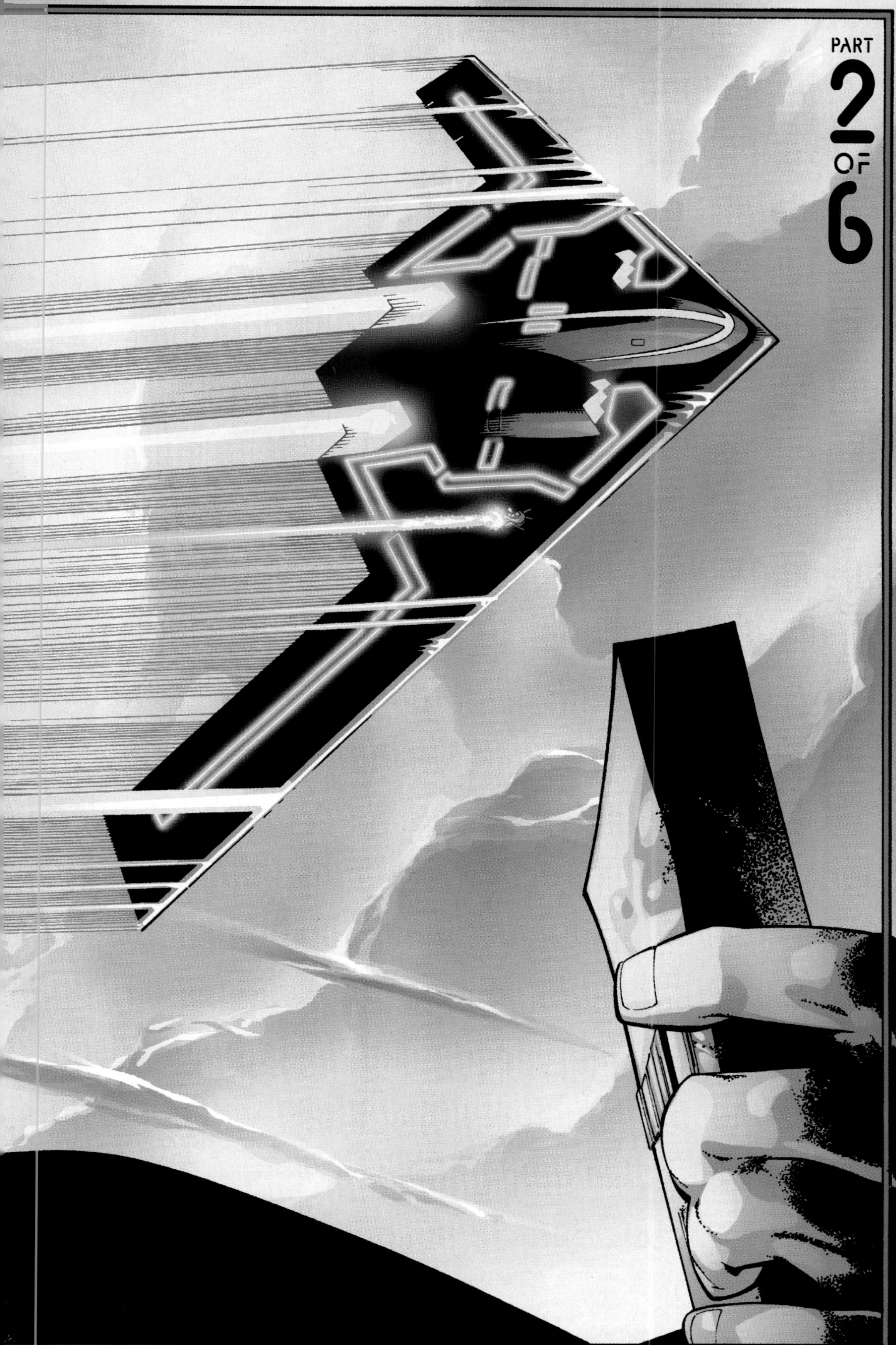
PART
2
OF
6

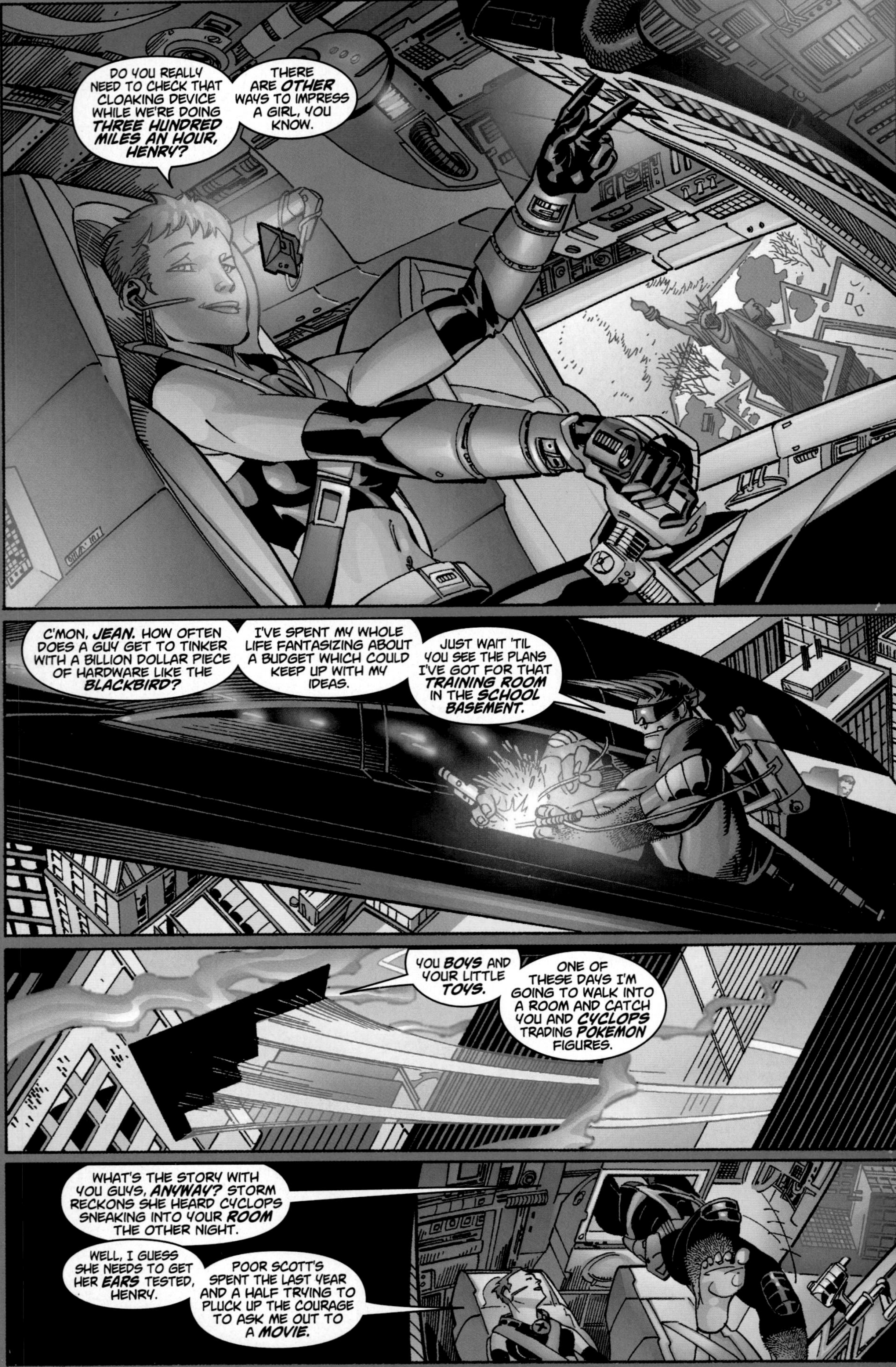
DO YOU REALLY NEED TO CHECK THAT CLOAKING DEVICE WHILE WE'RE DOING THREE HUNDRED MILES AN HOUR, HENRY?
THERE ARE OTHER WAYS TO IMPRESS A GIRL, YOU KNOW.
C'MON, JEAN. HOW OFTEN DOES A GUY GET TO TINKER WITH A BILLION DOLLAR PIECE OF HARDWARE LIKE THE BLACKBIRD?
I'VE SPENT MY WHOLE LIFE FANTASIZING ABOUT A BUDGET WHICH COULD KEEP UP WITH MY IDEAS.
JUST WAIT 'TIL YOU SEE THE PLANS I'VE GOT FOR THAT TRAINING ROOM IN THE SCHOOL BASEMENT.
YOU BOYS AND YOUR LITTLE TOYS.
ONE OF THESE DAYS I'M GOING TO WALK INTO A ROOM AND CATCH YOU AND CYCLOPS TRADING POKEMON FIGURES.
WHAT'S THE STORY WITH YOU GUYS, ANYWAY? STORM RECKONS SHE HEARD CYCLOPS SNEAKING INTO YOUR ROOM THE OTHER NIGHT.
WELL, I GUESS SHE NEEDS TO GET HER EARS TESTED, HENRY.
POOR SCOTT'S SPENT THE LAST YEAR AND A HALF TRYING TO PLUCK UP THE COURAGE TO ASK ME OUT TO A MOVIE.

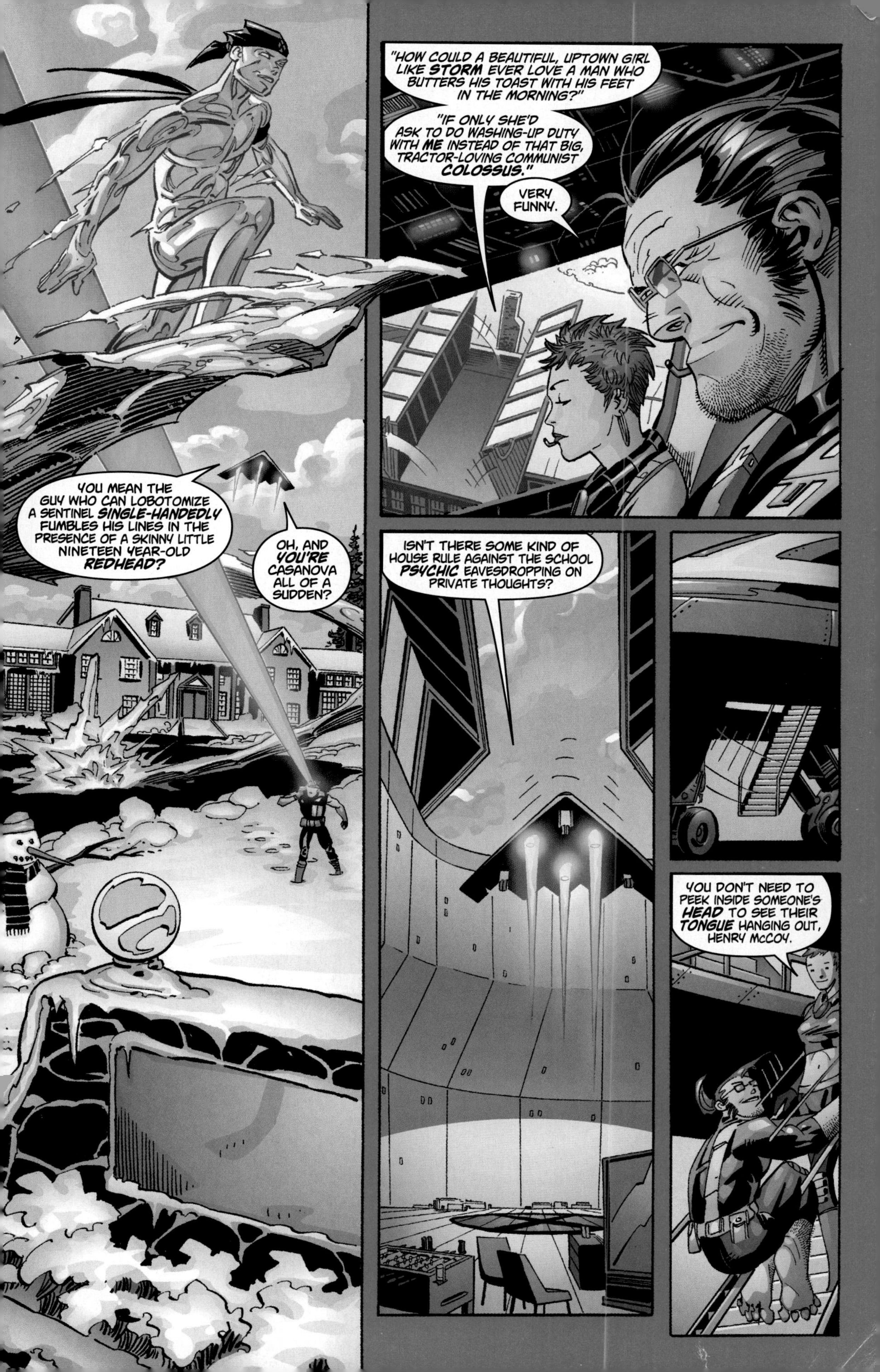
YOU MEAN THE GUY WHO CAN LOBOTOMIZE A SENTINEL SINGLE-HANDEDLY FUMBLES HIS LINES IN THE PRESENCE OF A SKINNY LITTLE NINETEEN YEAR-OLD REDHEAD?
OH, AND YOU'RE CASANOVA ALL OF A SUDDEN?
"HOW COULD A BEAUTIFUL, UPTOWN GIRL LIKE STORM EVER LOVE A MAN WHO BUTTERS HIS TOAST WITH HIS FEET IN THE MORNING?"
"IF ONLY SHE'D ASK TO DO WASHING-UP DUTY WITH ME INSTEAD OF THAT BIG, TRACTOR-LOVING COMMUNIST COLOSSUS."
VERY FUNNY.
ISN'T THERE SOME KIND OF HOUSE RULE AGAINST THE SCHOOL PSYCHIC EAVESDROPPING ON PRIVATE THOUGHTS?
YOU DON'T NEED TO PEEK INSIDE SOMEONE'S HEAD TO SEE THEIR TONGUE HANGING OUT, HENRY McCOY.

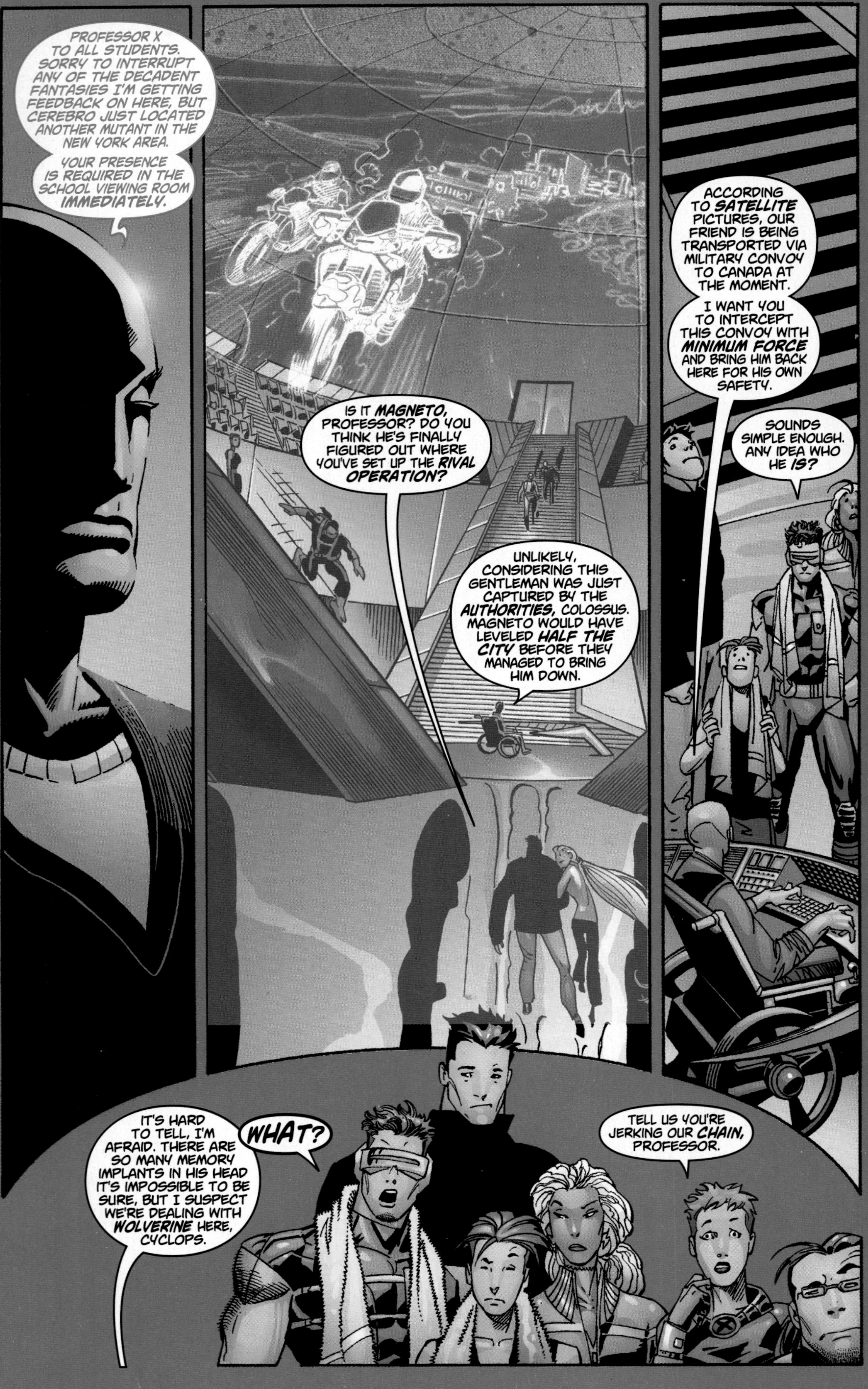
PROFESSOR X TO ALL STUDENTS. SORRY TO INTERRUPT ANY OF THE DECADENT FANTASIES I'M GETTING FEEDBACK ON HERE, BUT CEREBRO JUST LOCATED ANOTHER MUTANT IN THE NEW YORK AREA.
YOUR PRESENCE IS REQUIRED IN THE SCHOOL VIEWING ROOM IMMEDIATELY.
IS IT MAGNETO, PROFESSOR? DO YOU THINK HE'S FINALLY FIGURED OUT WHERE YOU'VE SET UP THE RIVAL OPERATION?
UNLIKELY, CONSIDERING THIS GENTLEMAN WAS JUST CAPTURED BY THE AUTHORITIES, COLOSSUS. MAGNETO WOULD HAVE LEVELED HALF THE CITY BEFORE THEY MANAGED TO BRING HIM DOWN.
ACCORDING TO SATELLITE PICTURES, OUR FRIEND IS BEING TRANSPORTED VIA MILITARY CONVOY TO CANADA AT THE MOMENT.
I WANT YOU TO INTERCEPT THIS CONVOY WITH MINIMUM FORCE AND BRING HIM BACK HERE FOR HIS OWN SAFETY.
SOUNDS SIMPLE ENOUGH. ANY IDEA WHO HE IS?
IT'S HARD TO TELL, I'M AFRAID. THERE ARE SO MANY MEMORY IMPLANTS IN HIS HEAD IT'S IMPOSSIBLE TO BE SURE, BUT I SUSPECT WE'RE DEALING WITH WOLVERINE HERE, CYCLOPS.
WHAT?
TELL US YOU'RE JERKING OUR CHAIN, PROFESSOR.

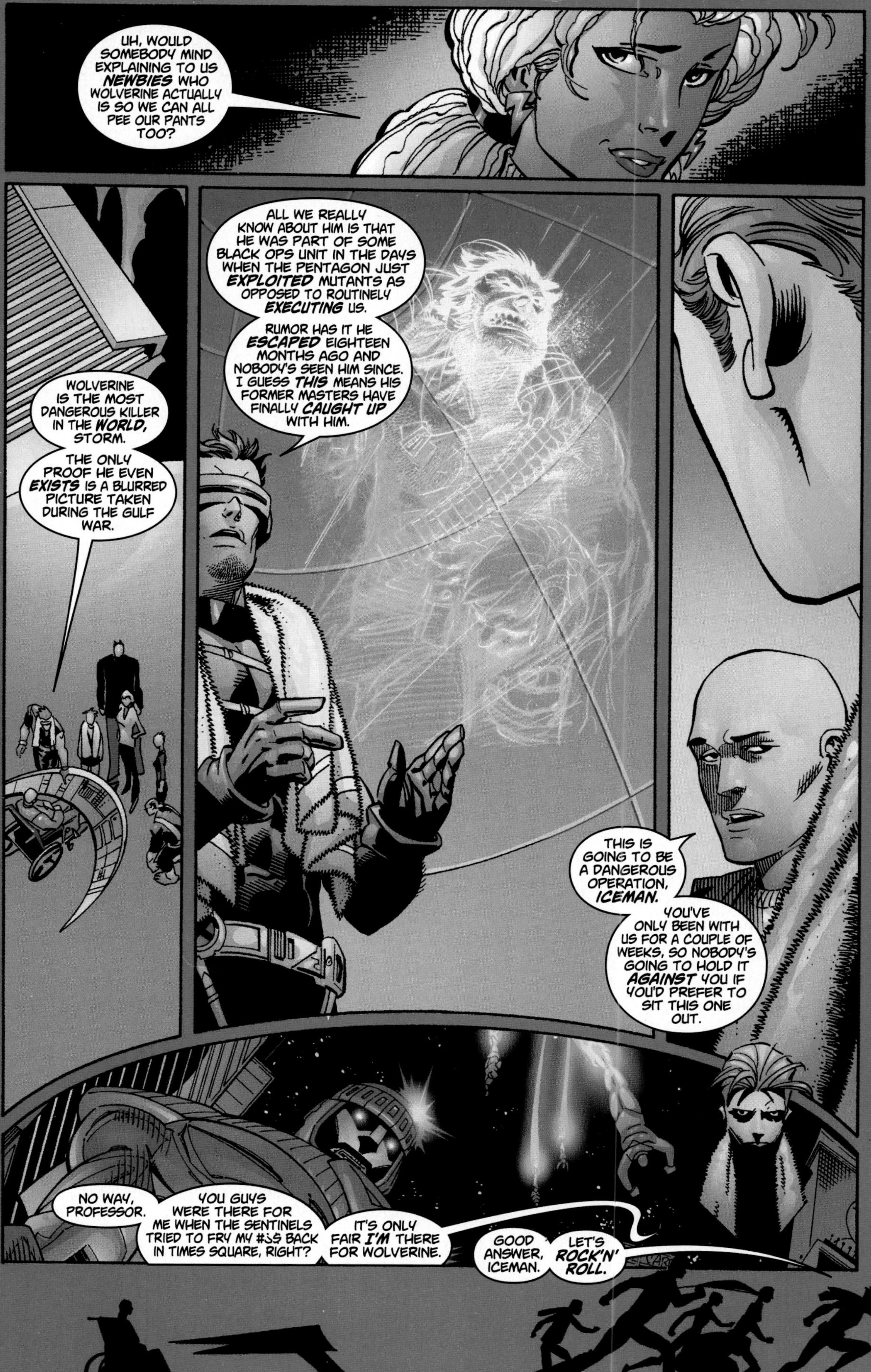

UH, WOULD SOMEBODY MIND EXPLAINING TO US NEWBIES WHO WOLVERINE ACTUALLY IS SO WE CAN ALL PEE OUR PANTS TOO?
WOLVERINE IS THE MOST DANGEROUS KILLER IN THE WORLD, STORM.
THE ONLY PROOF HE EVEN EXISTS IS A BLURRED PICTURE TAKEN DURING THE GULF WAR.
ALL WE REALLY KNOW ABOUT HIM IS THAT HE WAS PART OF SOME BLACK OPS UNIT IN THE DAYS WHEN THE PENTAGON JUST EXPLOITED MUTANTS AS OPPOSED TO ROUTINELY EXECUTING US.
RUMOR HAS IT HE ESCAPED EIGHTEEN MONTHS AGO AND NOBODY'S SEEN HIM SINCE. I GUESS THIS MEANS HIS FORMER MASTERS HAVE FINALLY CAUGHT UP WITH HIM.
THIS IS GOING TO BE A DANGEROUS OPERATION, ICEMAN.
YOU'VE ONLY BEEN WITH US FOR A COUPLE OF WEEKS, SO NOBODY'S GOING TO HOLD IT AGAINST YOU IF YOU'D PREFER TO SIT THIS ONE OUT.
NO WAY, PROFESSOR.
YOU GUYS WERE THERE FOR ME WHEN THE SENTINELS TRIED TO FRY MY #$$ BACK IN TIMES SQUARE, RIGHT?
IT'S ONLY FAIR I'M THERE FOR WOLVERINE.
GOOD ANSWER, ICEMAN.
LET'S ROCK'N' ROLL.

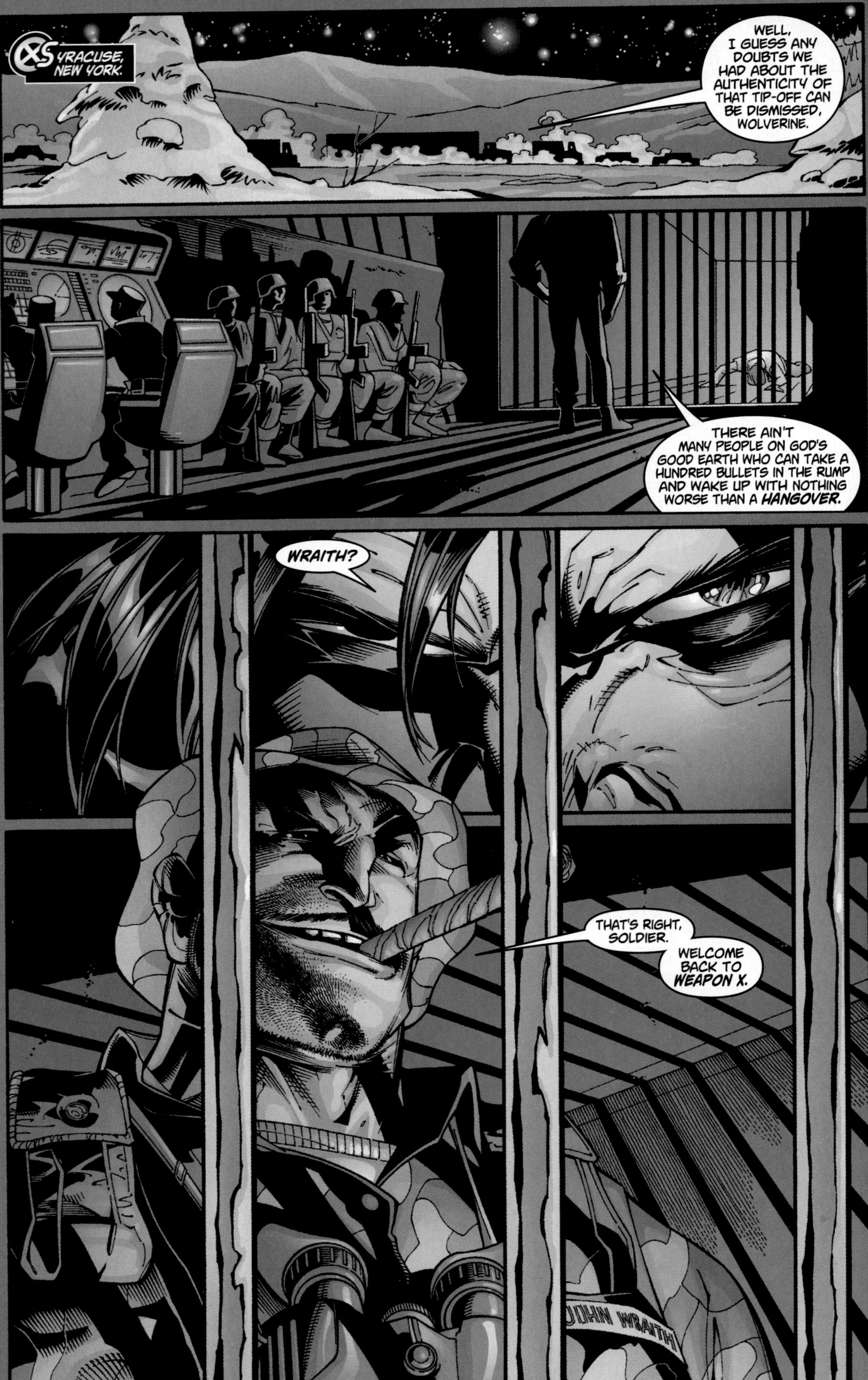
SYRACUSE, NEW YORK.
WELL, I GUESS ANY DOUBTS WE HAD ABOUT THE AUTHENTICITY OF THAT TIP-OFF CAN BE DISMISSED, WOLVERINE.
THERE AIN'T MANY PEOPLE ON GOD'S GOOD EARTH WHO CAN TAKE A HUNDRED BULLETS IN THE RUMP AND WAKE UP WITH NOTHING WORSE THAN A HANGOVER.
WRAITH?
THAT'S RIGHT, SOLDIER.
WELCOME BACK TO WEAPON X.
JOHN WRAITH

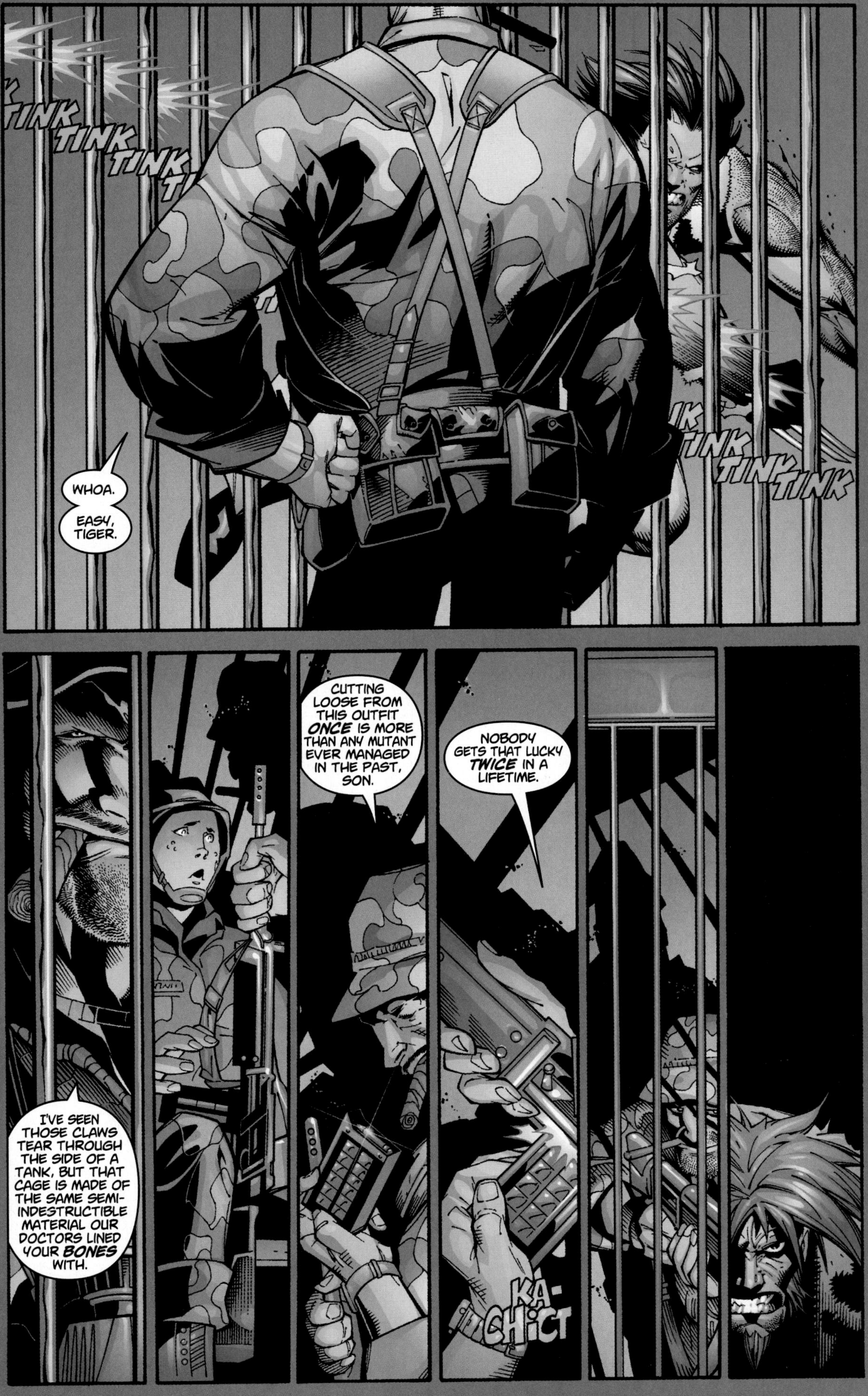
TINK TINK TINK
WHOA.
EASY, TIGER.
TINK TINK TINK
I'VE SEEN THOSE CLAWS TEAR THROUGH THE SIDE OF A TANK, BUT THAT CAGE IS MADE OF THE SAME SEMI-INDESTRUCTIBLE MATERIAL OUR DOCTORS LINED YOUR BONES WITH.
CUTTING LOOSE FROM THIS OUTFIT ONCE IS MORE THAN ANY MUTANT EVER MANAGED IN THE PAST, SON.
NOBODY GETS THAT LUCKY TWICE IN A LIFETIME.
KA-CHICT

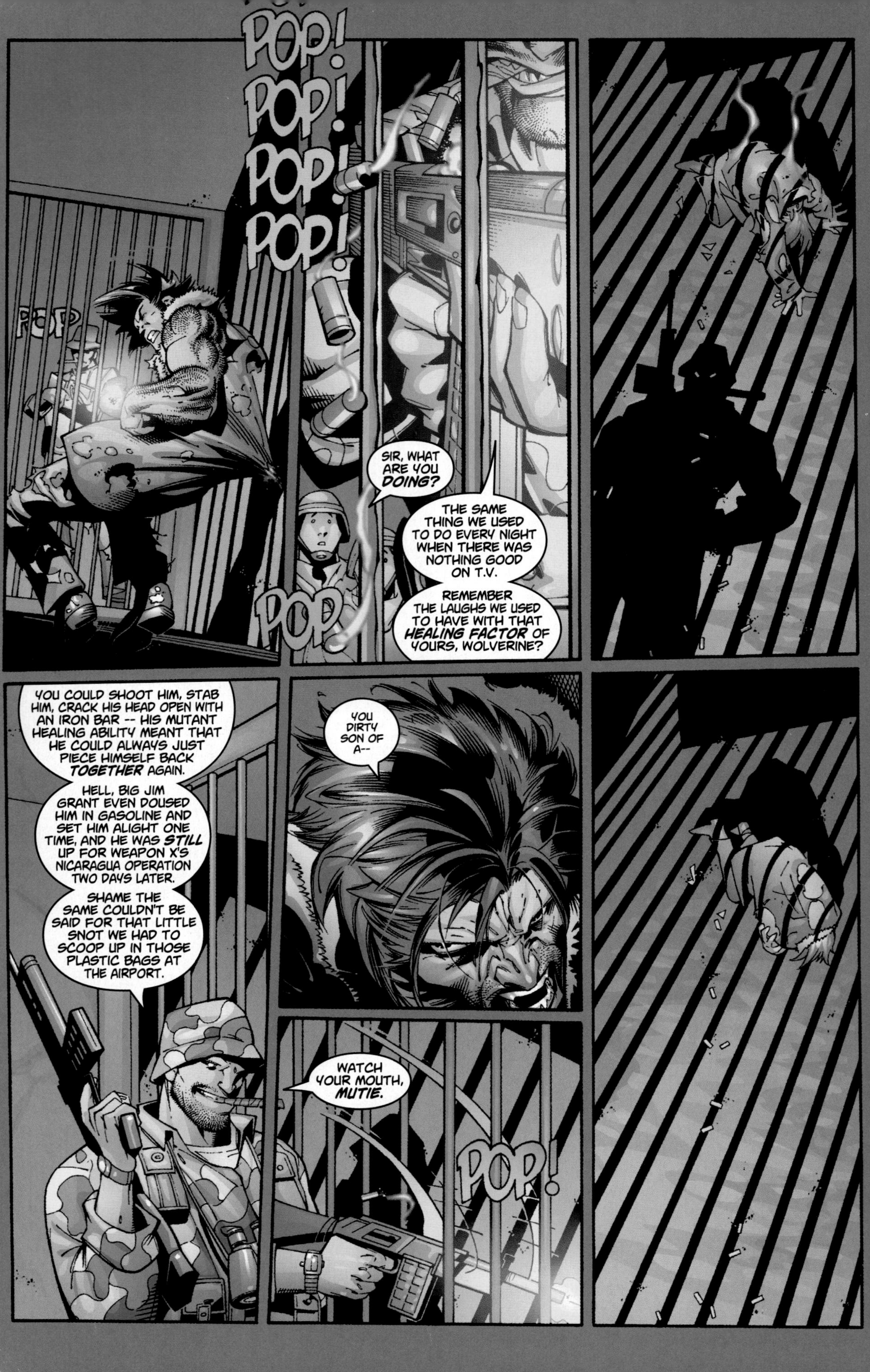
POP! POP! POP! POP!
POP
SIR, WHAT ARE YOU DOING?
THE SAME THING WE USED TO DO EVERY NIGHT WHEN THERE WAS NOTHING GOOD ON T.V.
REMEMBER THE LAUGHS WE USED TO HAVE WITH THAT HEALING FACTOR OF YOURS, WOLVERINE?
POP
YOU COULD SHOOT HIM, STAB HIM, CRACK HIS HEAD OPEN WITH AN IRON BAR -- HIS MUTANT HEALING ABILITY MEANT THAT HE COULD ALWAYS JUST PIECE HIMSELF BACK TOGETHER AGAIN.
HELL, BIG JIM GRANT EVEN DOUSED HIM IN GASOLINE AND SET HIM ALIGHT ONE TIME, AND HE WAS STILL UP FOR WEAPON X'S NICARAGUA OPERATION TWO DAYS LATER.
SHAME THE SAME COULDN'T BE SAID FOR THAT LITTLE SNOT WE HAD TO SCOOP UP IN THOSE PLASTIC BAGS AT THE AIRPORT.
YOU DIRTY SON OF A--
WATCH YOUR MOUTH, MUTIE.
POP!

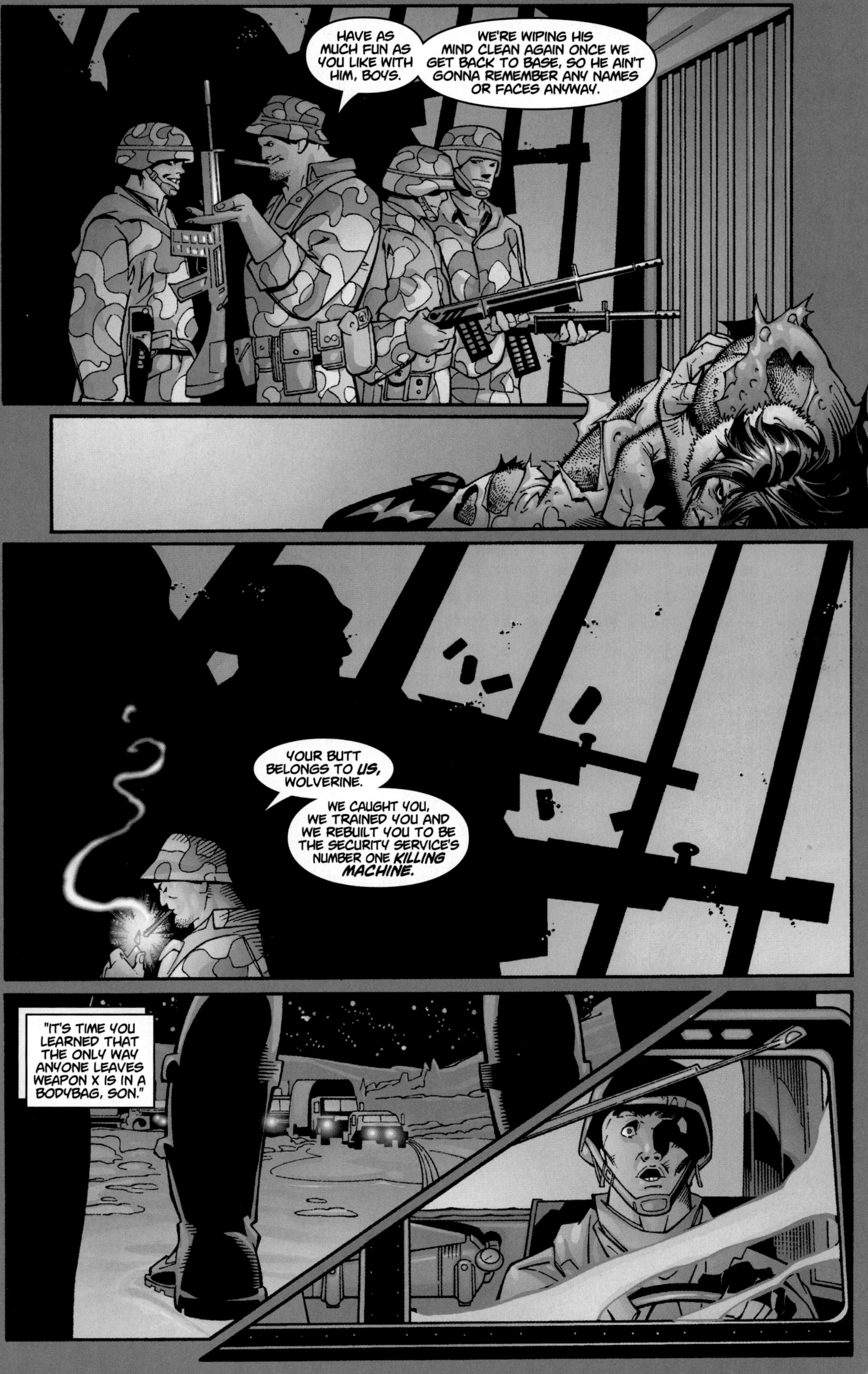
HAVE AS MUCH FUN AS YOU LIKE WITH HIM, BOYS.
WE'RE WIPING HIS MIND CLEAN AGAIN ONCE WE GET BACK TO BASE, SO HE AIN'T GONNA REMEMBER ANY NAMES OR FACES ANYWAY.
YOUR BUTT BELONGS TO US, WOLVERINE.
WE CAUGHT YOU, WE TRAINED YOU AND WE REBUILT YOU TO BE THE SECURITY SERVICE'S NUMBER ONE KILLING MACHINE.
"IT'S TIME YOU LEARNED THAT THE ONLY WAY ANYONE LEAVES WEAPON X IS IN A BODYBAG, SON."

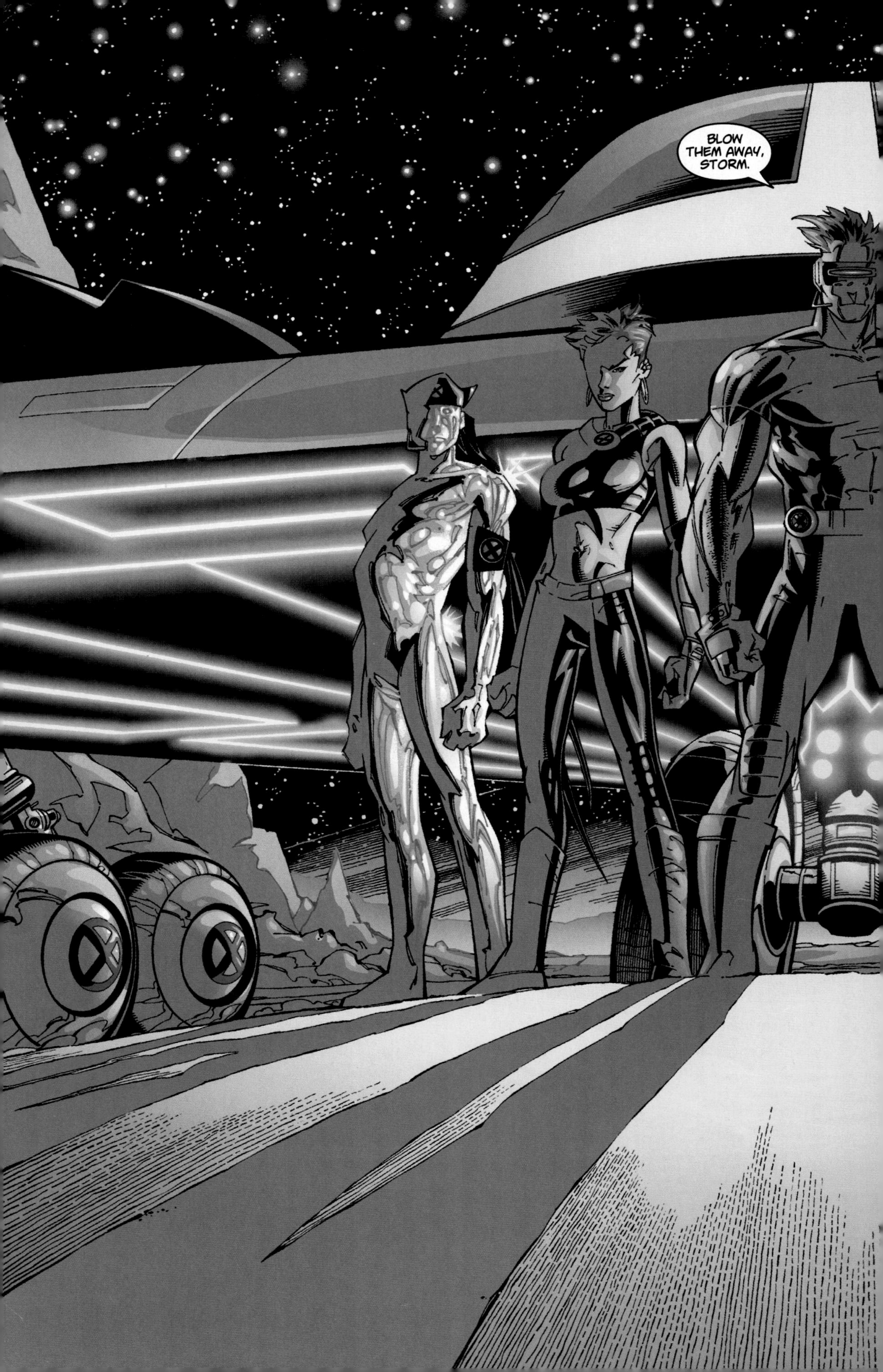
BLOW THEM AWAY, STORM.

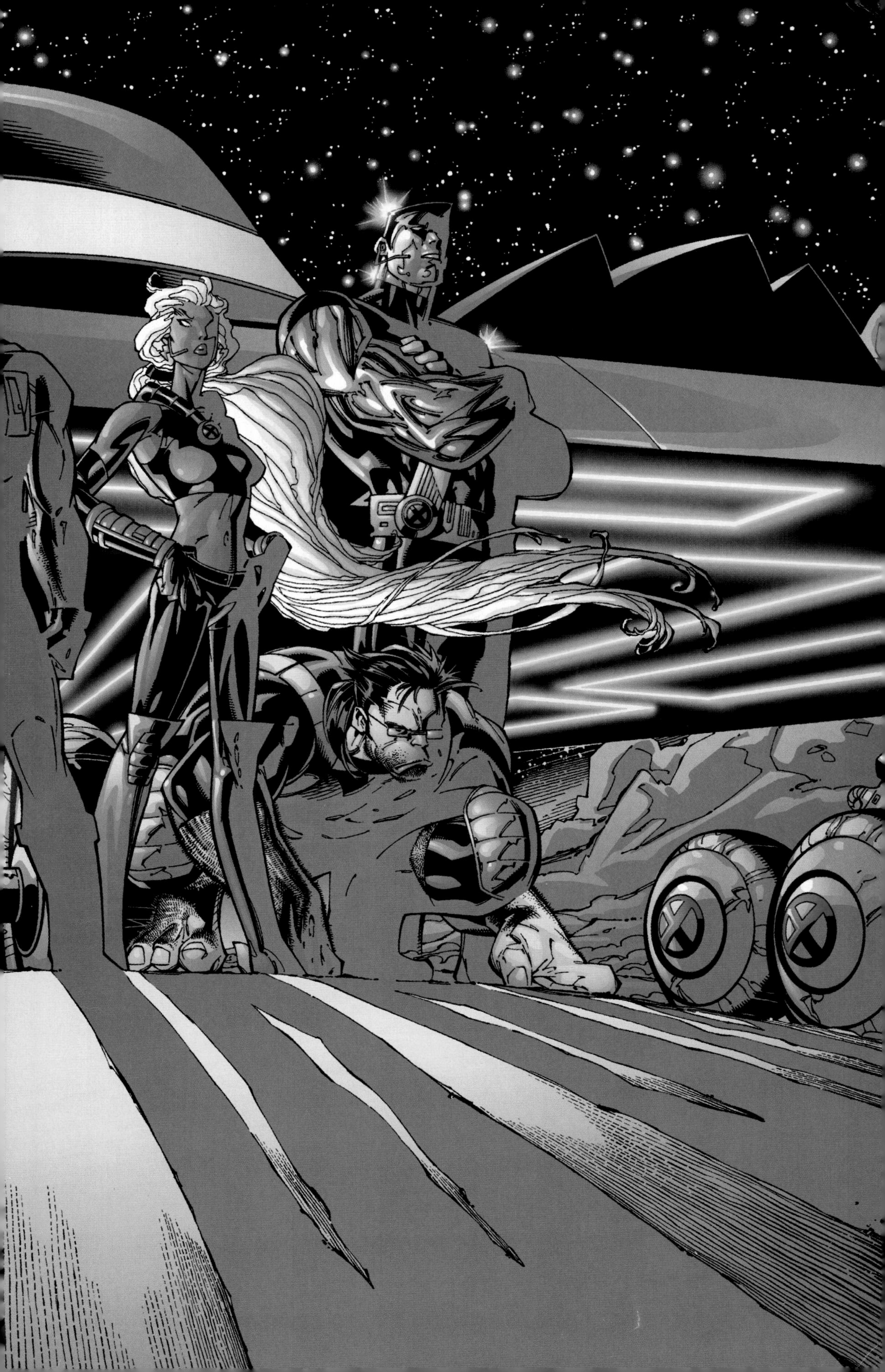

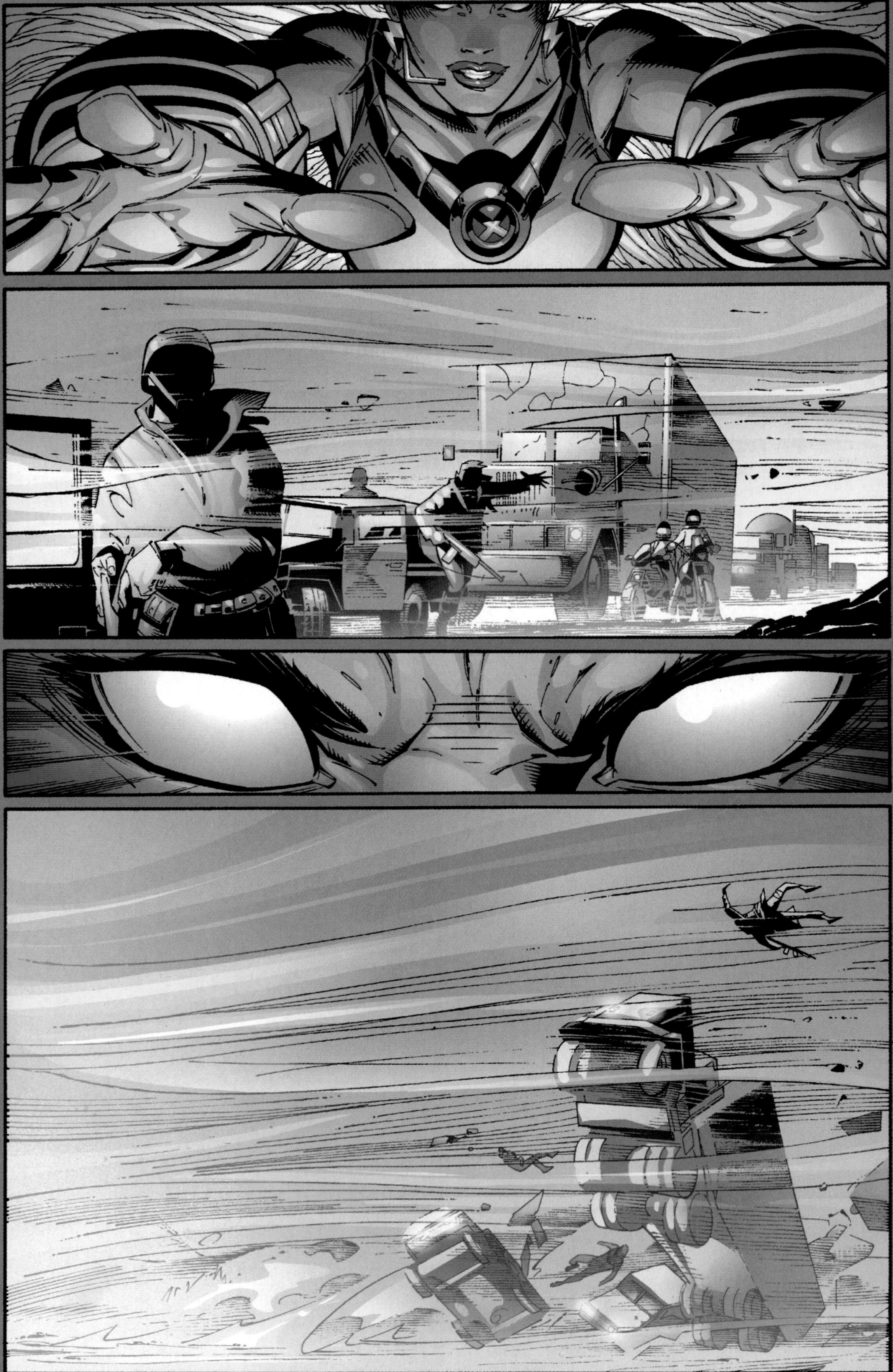

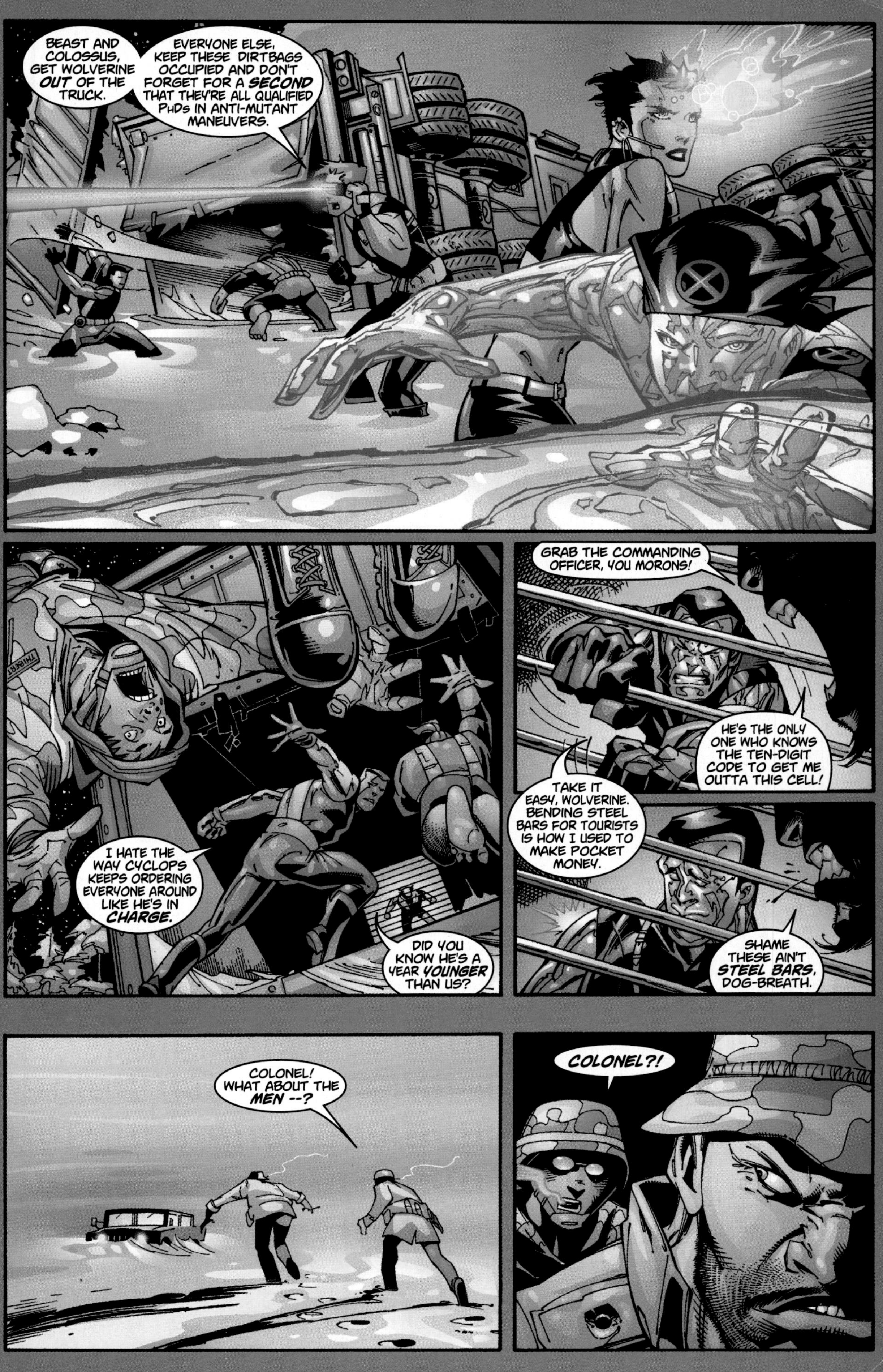
BEAST AND COLOSSUS, GET WOLVERINE OUT OF THE TRUCK.
EVERYONE ELSE, KEEP THESE DIRTBAGS OCCUPIED AND DON'T FORGET FOR A SECOND THAT THEY'RE ALL QUALIFIED PHDs IN ANTI-MUTANT MANEUVERS.
I HATE THE WAY CYCLOPS KEEPS ORDERING EVERYONE AROUND LIKE HE'S IN CHARGE.
DID YOU KNOW HE'S A YEAR YOUNGER THAN US?
GRAB THE COMMANDING OFFICER, YOU MORONS!
HE'S THE ONLY ONE WHO KNOWS THE TEN-DIGIT CODE TO GET ME OUTTA THIS CELL!
TAKE IT EASY, WOLVERINE. BENDING STEEL BARS FOR TOURISTS IS HOW I USED TO MAKE POCKET MONEY.
SHAME THESE AIN'T STEEL BARS, DOG-BREATH.
COLONEL! WHAT ABOUT THE MEN --?
COLONEL?!

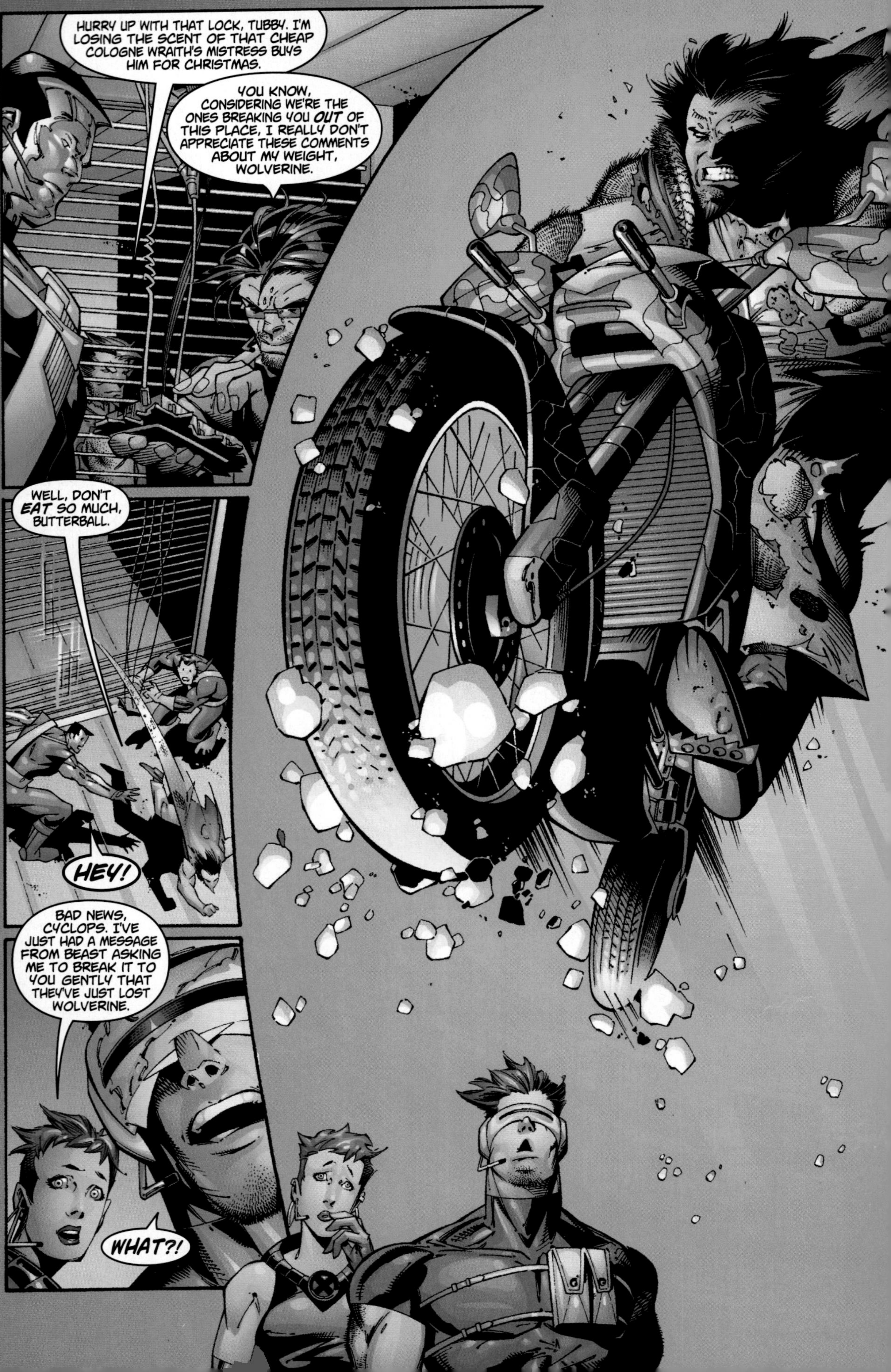
HURRY UP WITH THAT LOCK, TUBBY. I'M LOSING THE SCENT OF THAT CHEAP COLOGNE WRAITH'S MISTRESS BUYS HIM FOR CHRISTMAS.
YOU KNOW, CONSIDERING WE'RE THE ONES BREAKING YOU *OUT* OF THIS PLACE, I REALLY DON'T APPRECIATE THESE COMMENTS ABOUT MY WEIGHT, WOLVERINE.
WELL, DON'T *EAT* SO MUCH, BUTTERBALL.
HEY!
BAD NEWS, CYCLOPS. I'VE JUST HAD A MESSAGE FROM BEAST ASKING ME TO BREAK IT TO YOU GENTLY THAT THEY'VE JUST LOST WOLVERINE.
WHAT?!

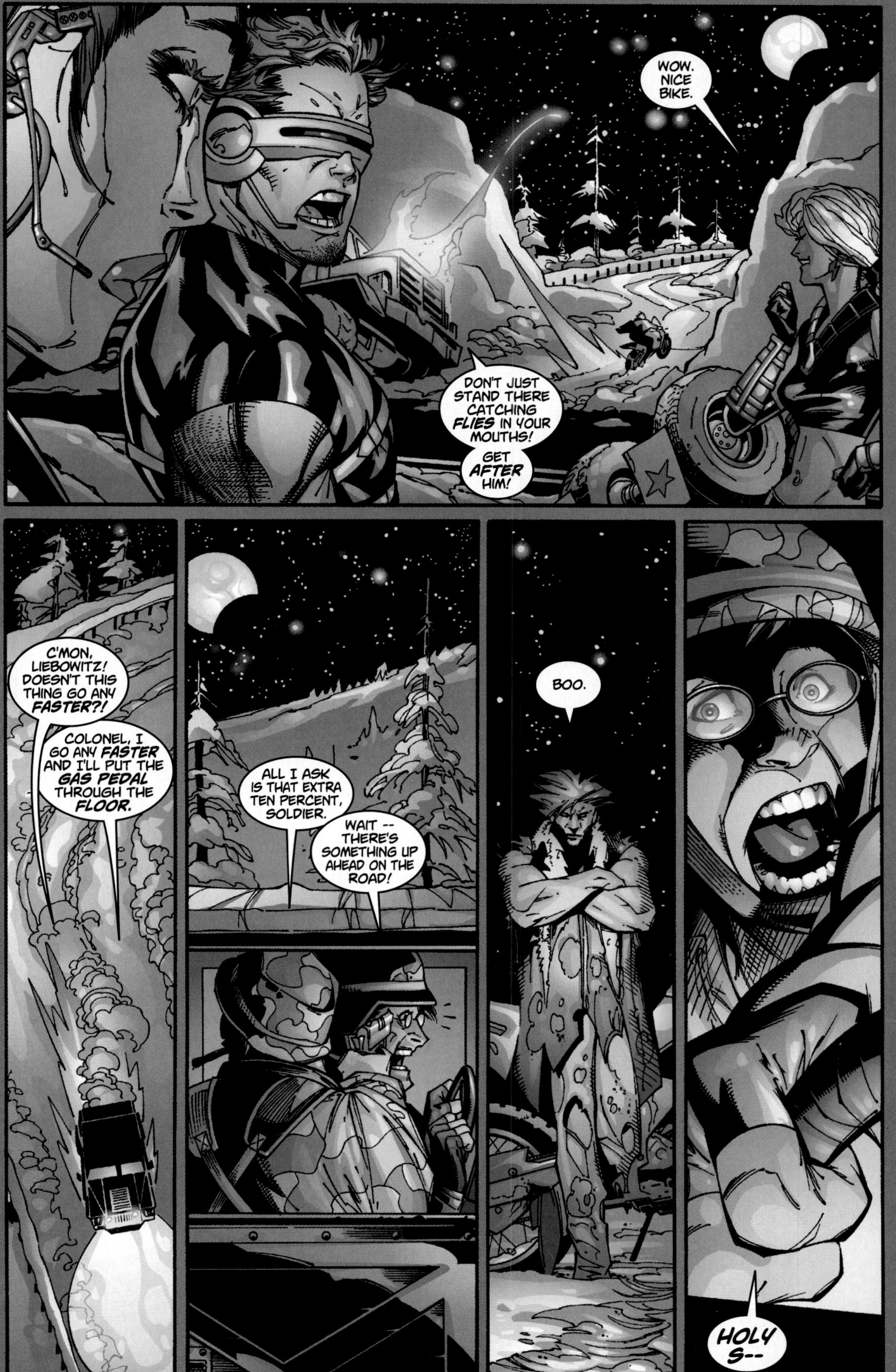
WOW. NICE BIKE.
DON'T JUST STAND THERE CATCHING FLIES IN YOUR MOUTHS!
GET AFTER HIM!
C'MON, LIEBOWITZ! DOESN'T THIS THING GO ANY FASTER?!
COLONEL, I GO ANY FASTER AND I'LL PUT THE GAS PEDAL THROUGH THE FLOOR.
ALL I ASK IS THAT EXTRA TEN PERCENT, SOLDIER.
WAIT -- THERE'S SOMETHING UP AHEAD ON THE ROAD!
BOO.
HOLY S--

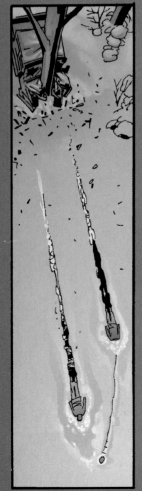

LIEBOWITZ?! HOLY MOTHER OF GOD --! YOU JUST BROKE HIS FREAKIN' NECK!

LUCKY LIEBOWITZ.

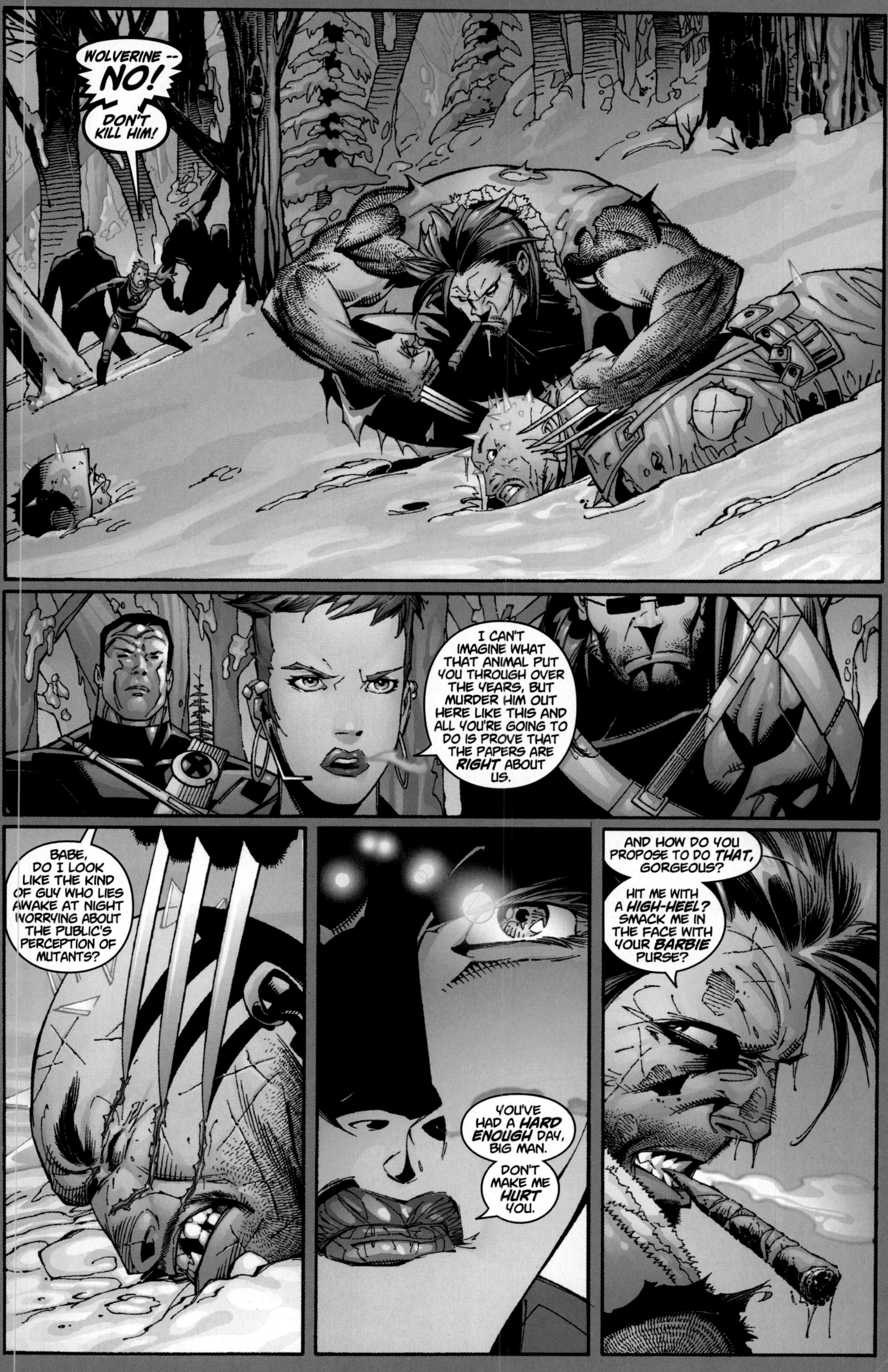
WOLVERINE -- NO!
DON'T KILL HIM!
I CAN'T IMAGINE WHAT THAT ANIMAL PUT YOU THROUGH OVER THE YEARS, BUT MURDER HIM OUT HERE LIKE THIS AND ALL YOU'RE GOING TO DO IS PROVE THAT THE PAPERS ARE RIGHT ABOUT US.
BABE, DO I LOOK LIKE THE KIND OF GUY WHO LIES AWAKE AT NIGHT WORRYING ABOUT THE PUBLIC'S PERCEPTION OF MUTANTS?
YOU'VE HAD A HARD ENOUGH DAY, BIG MAN.
DON'T MAKE ME HURT YOU.
AND HOW DO YOU PROPOSE TO DO THAT, GORGEOUS?
HIT ME WITH A HIGH-HEEL? SMACK ME IN THE FACE WITH YOUR BARBIE PURSE?

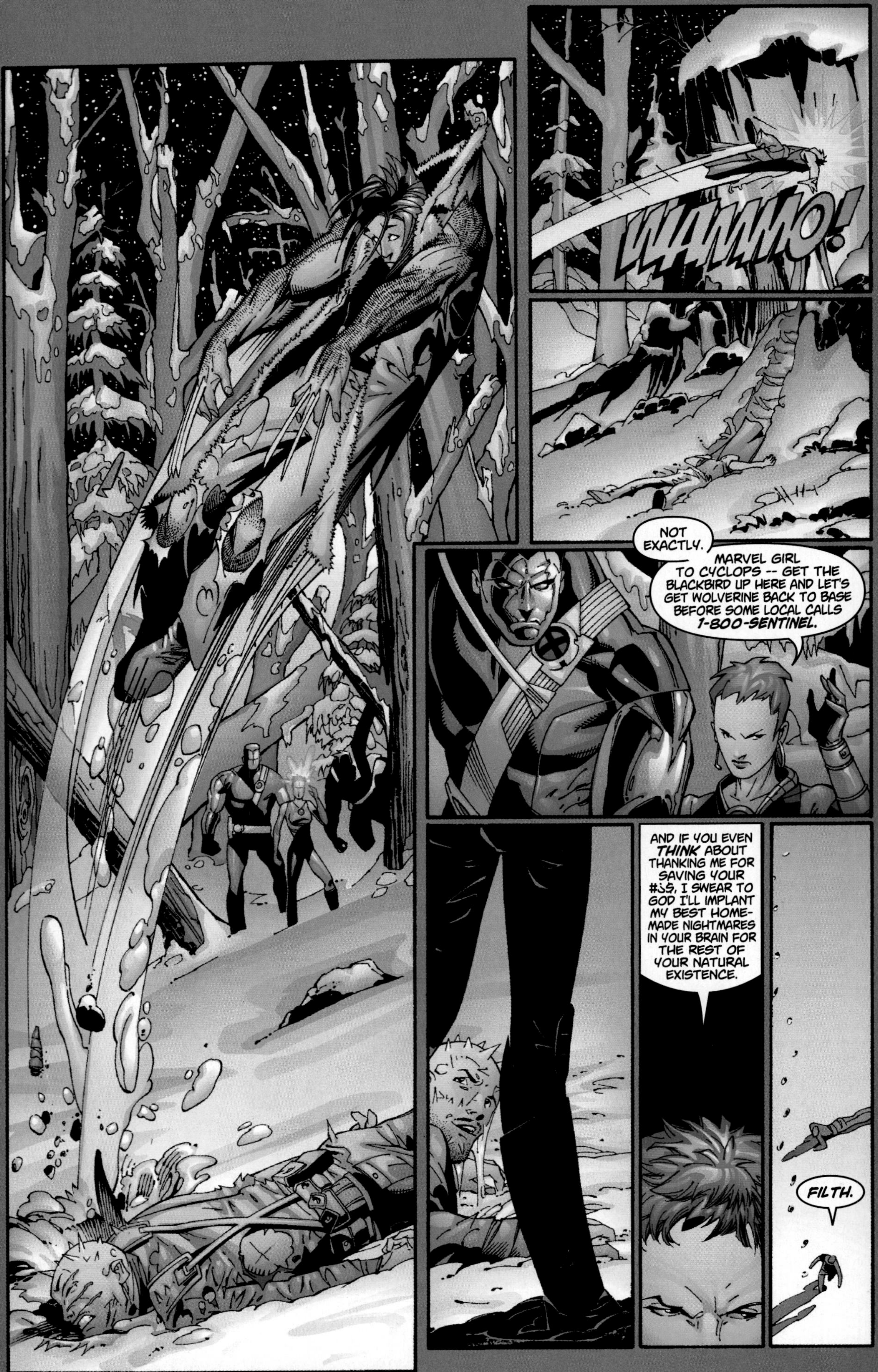
WHAMMO!
NOT EXACTLY.
MARVEL GIRL TO CYCLOPS -- GET THE BLACKBIRD UP HERE AND LET'S GET WOLVERINE BACK TO BASE BEFORE SOME LOCAL CALLS 1-800-SENTINEL.
AND IF YOU EVEN THINK ABOUT THANKING ME FOR SAVING YOUR #$S, I SWEAR TO GOD I'LL IMPLANT MY BEST HOME-MADE NIGHTMARES IN YOUR BRAIN FOR THE REST OF YOUR NATURAL EXISTENCE.
FILTH.

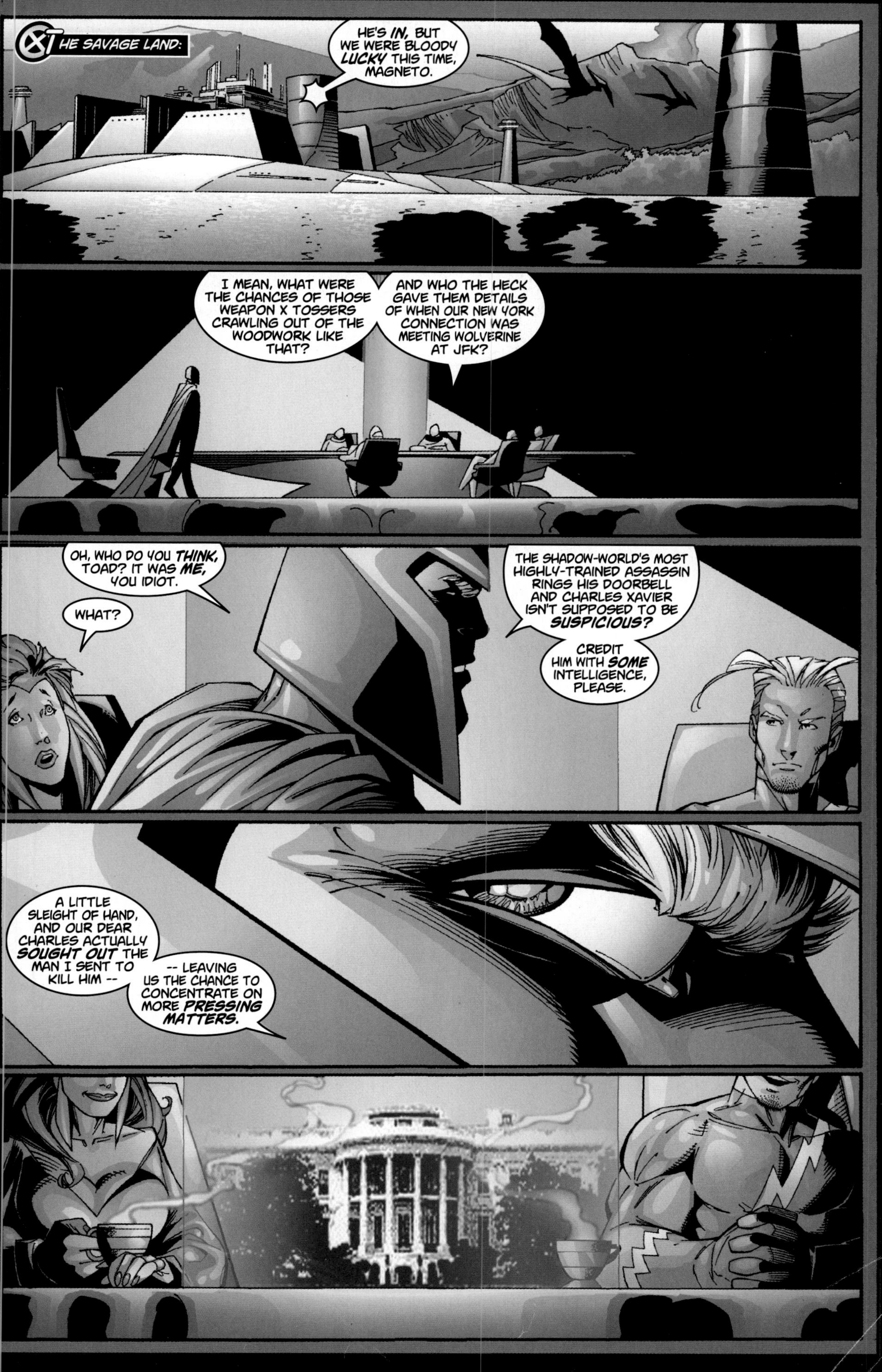
THE SAVAGE LAND:
HE'S IN, BUT WE WERE BLOODY LUCKY THIS TIME, MAGNETO.
I MEAN, WHAT WERE THE CHANCES OF THOSE WEAPON X TOSSERS CRAWLING OUT OF THE WOODWORK LIKE THAT?
AND WHO THE HECK GAVE THEM DETAILS OF WHEN OUR NEW YORK CONNECTION WAS MEETING WOLVERINE AT JFK?
OH, WHO DO YOU THINK, TOAD? IT WAS ME, YOU IDIOT.
WHAT?
THE SHADOW-WORLD'S MOST HIGHLY-TRAINED ASSASSIN RINGS HIS DOORBELL AND CHARLES XAVIER ISN'T SUPPOSED TO BE SUSPICIOUS?
CREDIT HIM WITH SOME INTELLIGENCE, PLEASE.
A LITTLE SLEIGHT OF HAND, AND OUR DEAR CHARLES ACTUALLY SOUGHT OUT THE MAN I SENT TO KILL HIM --
-- LEAVING US THE CHANCE TO CONCENTRATE ON MORE PRESSING MATTERS.

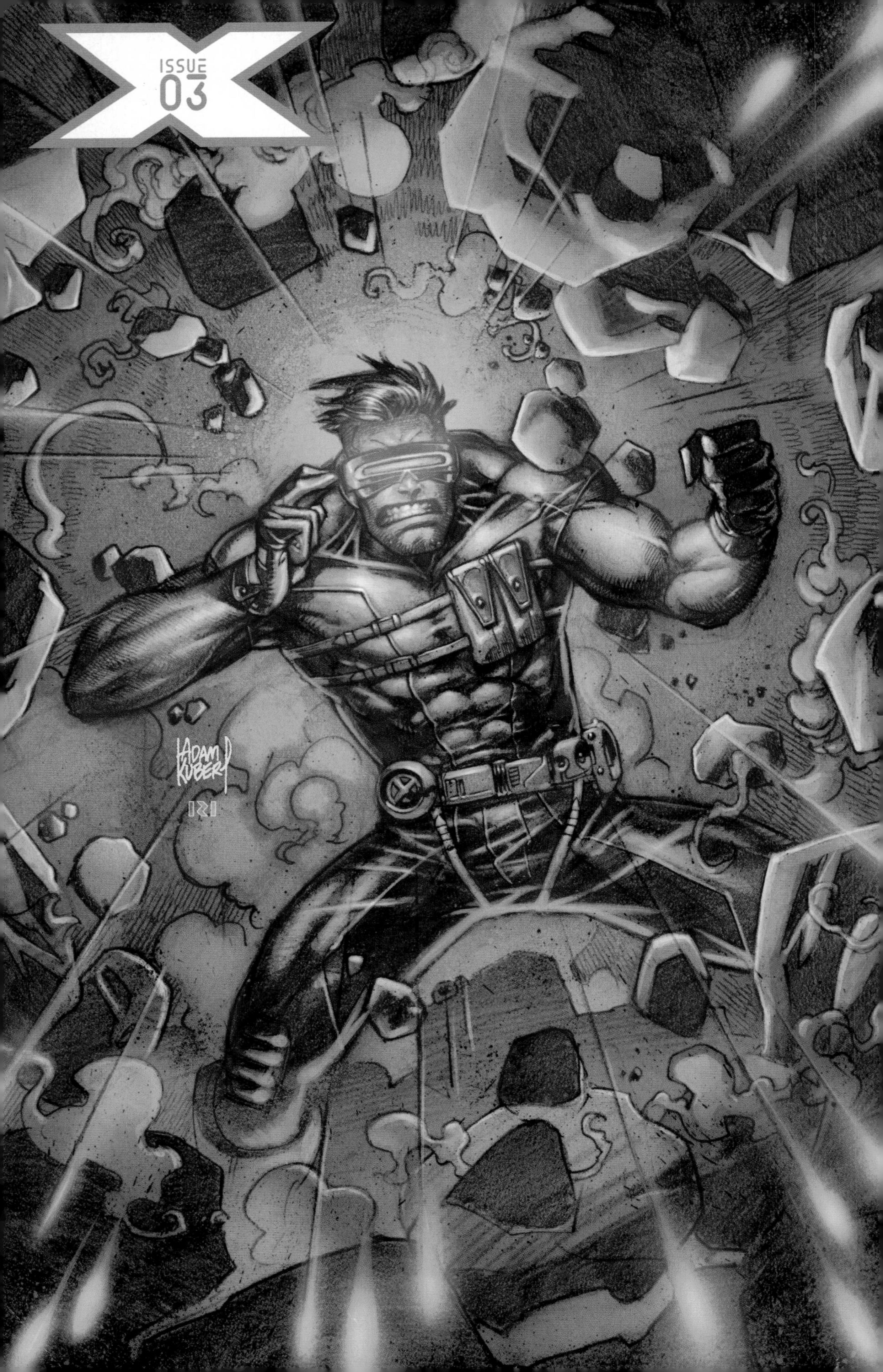
ISSUE
03
ADAM KUBERT

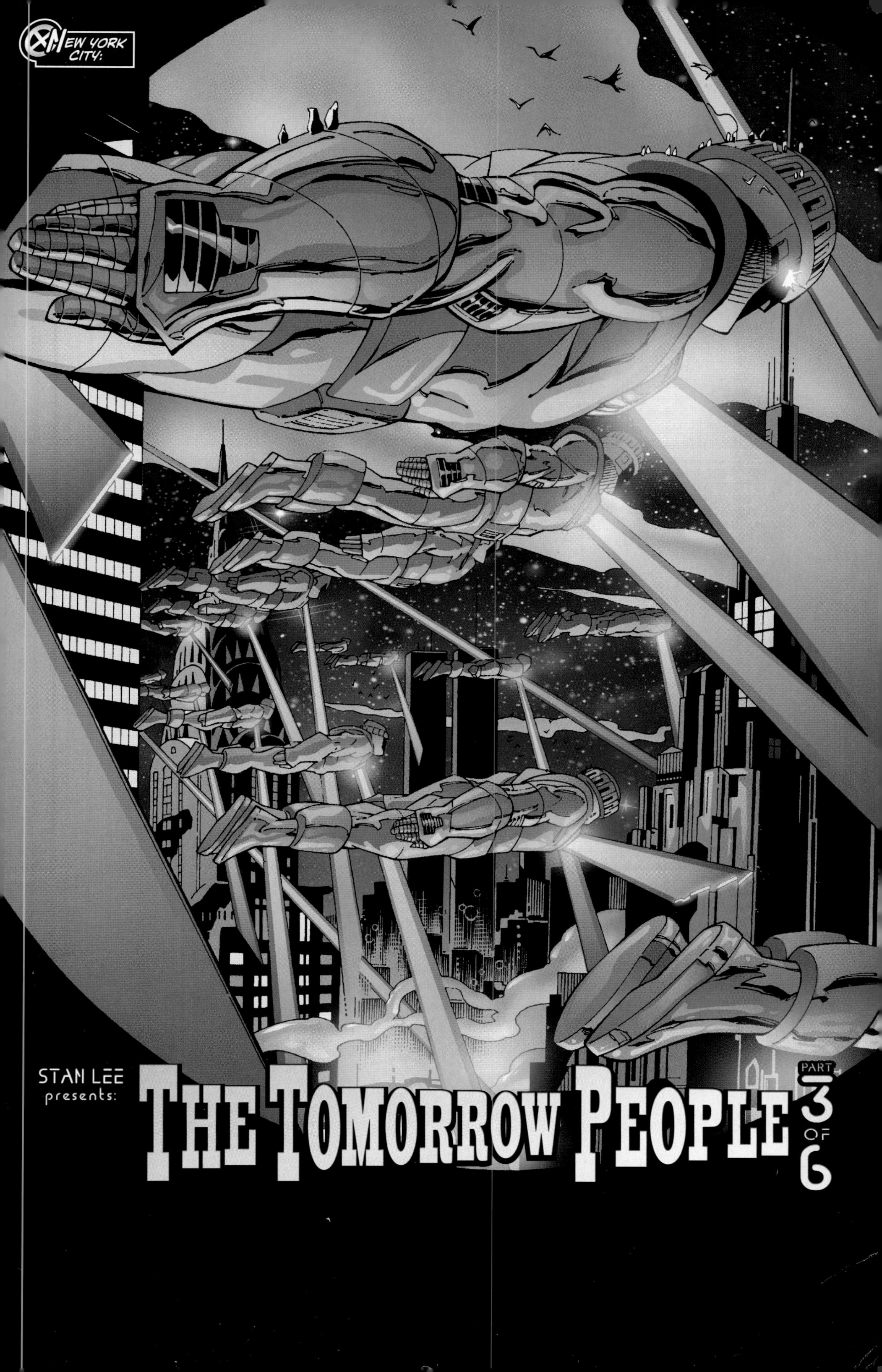
NEW YORK CITY:
STAN LEE presents:
THE TOMORROW PEOPLE
PART 3 OF 6

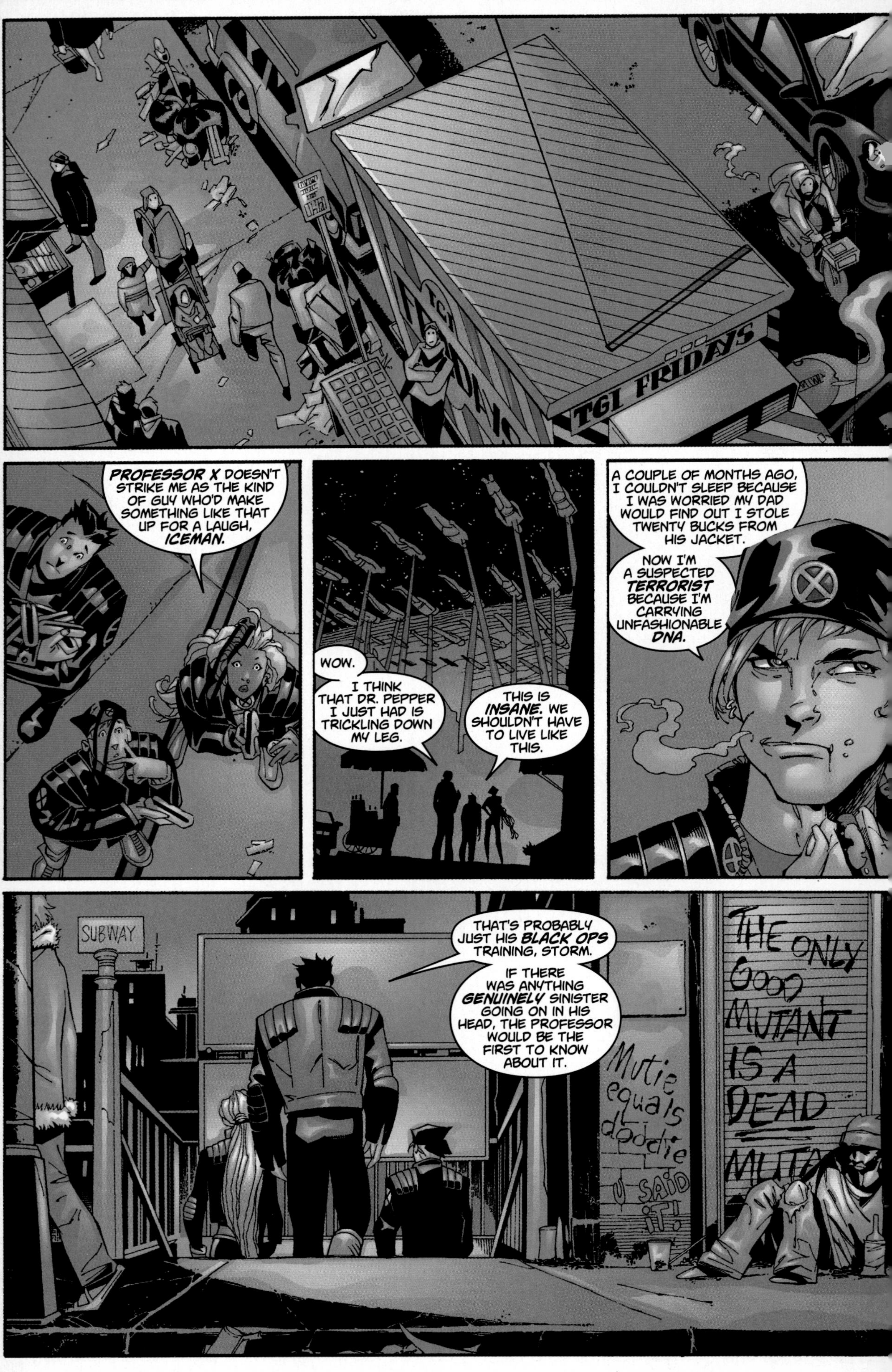

TGI FRIDAYS
PROFESSOR X DOESN'T STRIKE ME AS THE KIND OF GUY WHO'D MAKE SOMETHING LIKE THAT UP FOR A LAUGH, ICEMAN.
WOW.
I THINK THAT DR. PEPPER I JUST HAD IS TRICKLING DOWN MY LEG.
THIS IS INSANE. WE SHOULDN'T HAVE TO LIVE LIKE THIS.
A COUPLE OF MONTHS AGO, I COULDN'T SLEEP BECAUSE I WAS WORRIED MY DAD WOULD FIND OUT I STOLE TWENTY BUCKS FROM HIS JACKET.
NOW I'M A SUSPECTED TERRORIST BECAUSE I'M CARRYING UNFASHIONABLE DNA.
SUBWAY
THAT'S PROBABLY JUST HIS BLACK OPS TRAINING, STORM.
IF THERE WAS ANYTHING GENUINELY SINISTER GOING ON IN HIS HEAD, THE PROFESSOR WOULD BE THE FIRST TO KNOW ABOUT IT.
Mutie equals doodie
U SAID IT!
THE ONLY GOOD MUTANT IS A DEAD

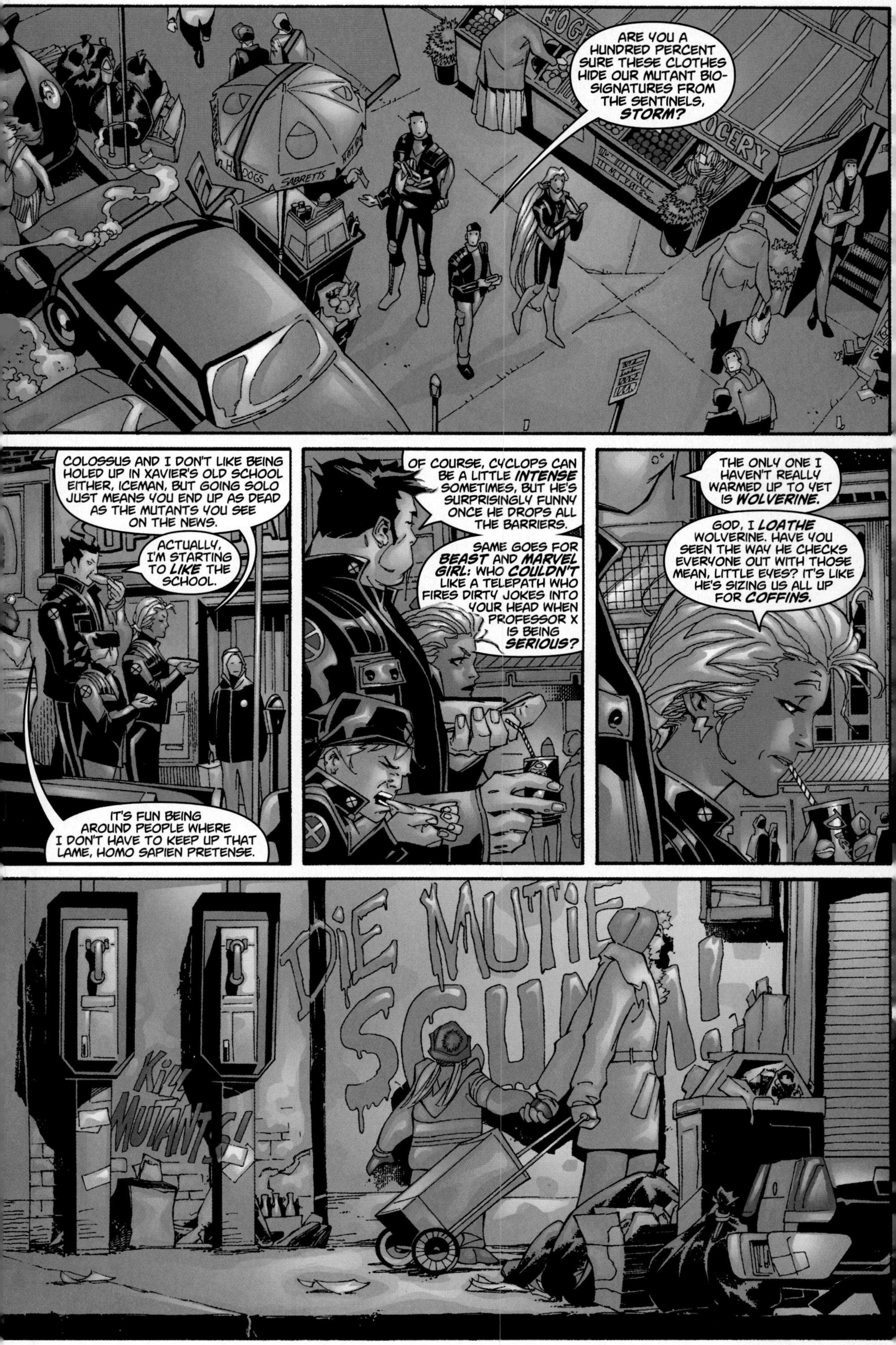
ARE YOU A HUNDRED PERCENT SURE THESE CLOTHES HIDE OUR MUTANT BIO-SIGNATURES FROM THE SENTINELS, STORM?
COLOSSUS AND I DON'T LIKE BEING HOLED UP IN XAVIER'S OLD SCHOOL EITHER, ICEMAN, BUT GOING SOLO JUST MEANS YOU END UP AS DEAD AS THE MUTANTS YOU SEE ON THE NEWS.
ACTUALLY, I'M STARTING TO LIKE THE SCHOOL.
IT'S FUN BEING AROUND PEOPLE WHERE I DON'T HAVE TO KEEP UP THAT LAME, HOMO SAPIEN PRETENSE.
OF COURSE, CYCLOPS CAN BE A LITTLE INTENSE SOMETIMES, BUT HE'S SURPRISINGLY FUNNY ONCE HE DROPS ALL THE BARRIERS.
SAME GOES FOR BEAST AND MARVEL GIRL: WHO COULDN'T LIKE A TELEPATH WHO FIRES DIRTY JOKES INTO YOUR HEAD WHEN PROFESSOR X IS BEING SERIOUS?
THE ONLY ONE I HAVEN'T REALLY WARMED UP TO YET IS WOLVERINE.
GOD, I LOATHE WOLVERINE. HAVE YOU SEEN THE WAY HE CHECKS EVERYONE OUT WITH THOSE MEAN, LITTLE EYES? IT'S LIKE HE'S SIZING US ALL UP FOR COFFINS.
DIE MUTIE SCUM!
KILL MUTANTS!

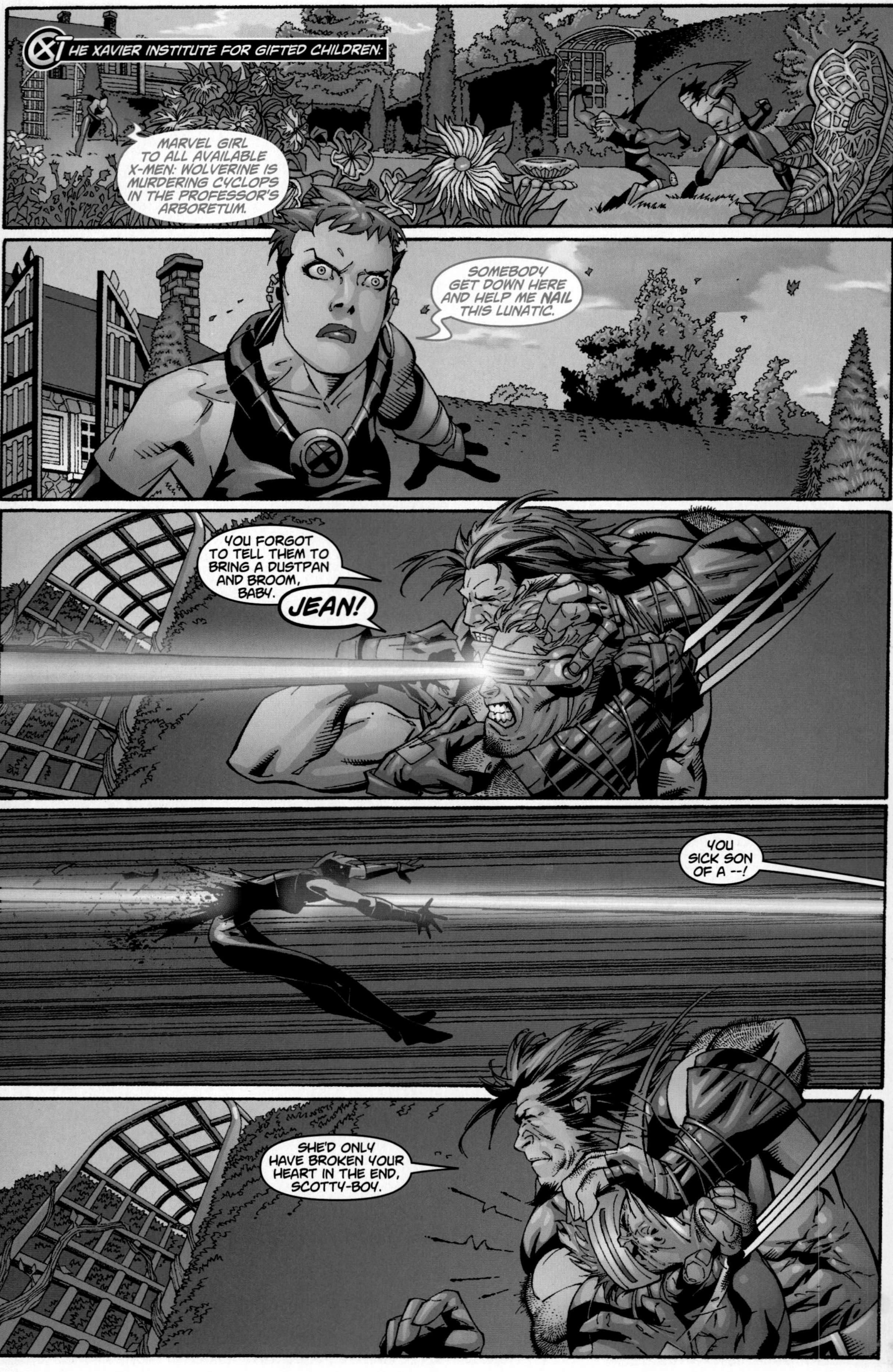
THE XAVIER INSTITUTE FOR GIFTED CHILDREN:
MARVEL GIRL TO ALL AVAILABLE X-MEN: WOLVERINE IS MURDERING CYCLOPS IN THE PROFESSOR'S ARBORETUM.
SOMEBODY GET DOWN HERE AND HELP ME NAIL THIS LUNATIC.
YOU FORGOT TO TELL THEM TO BRING A DUSTPAN AND BROOM, BABY.
JEAN!
YOU SICK SON OF A --!
SHE'D ONLY HAVE BROKEN YOUR HEART IN THE END, SCOTTY-BOY.

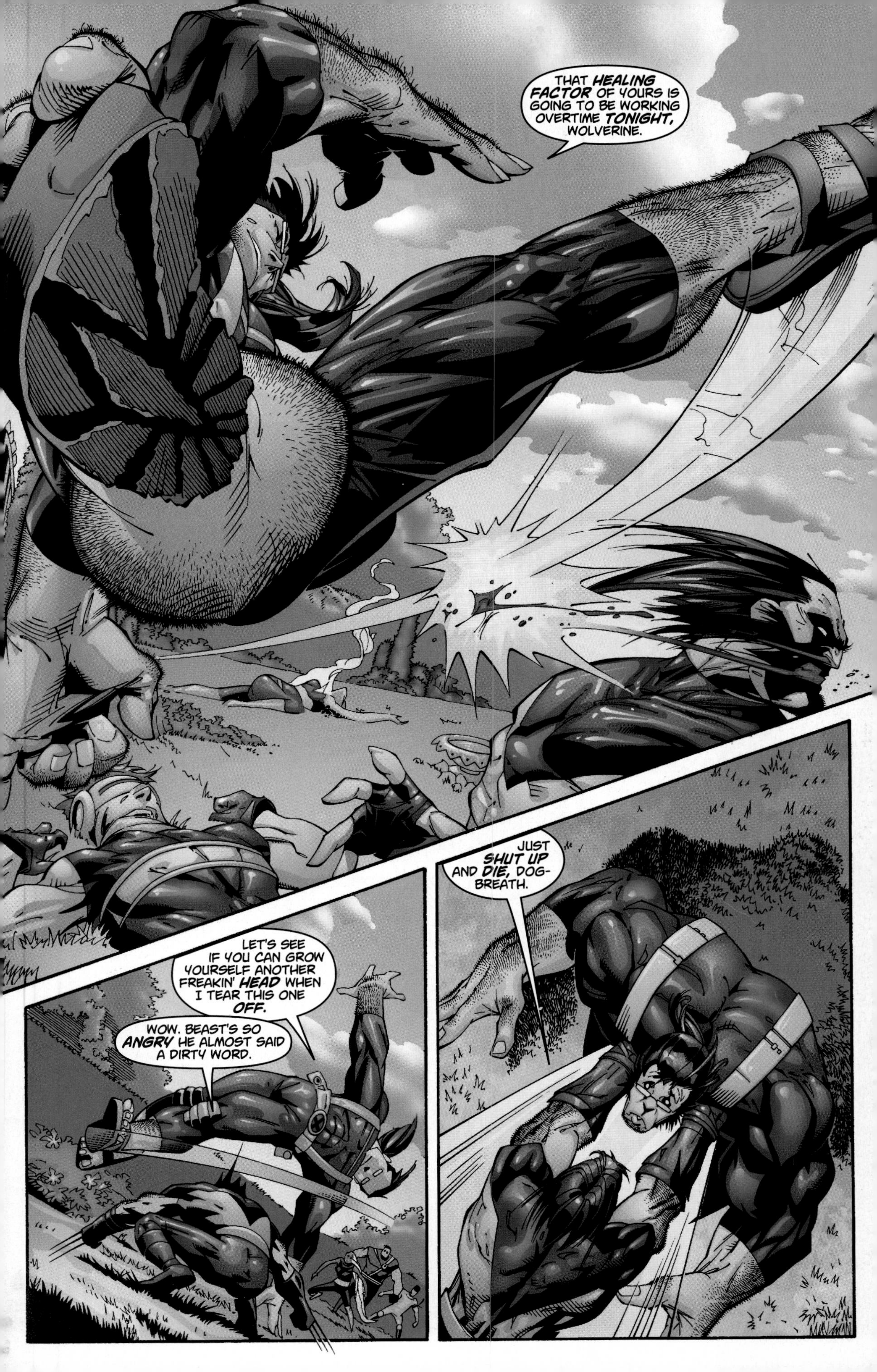
THAT HEALING FACTOR OF YOURS IS GOING TO BE WORKING OVERTIME TONIGHT, WOLVERINE.
LET'S SEE IF YOU CAN GROW YOURSELF ANOTHER FREAKIN' HEAD WHEN I TEAR THIS ONE OFF.
WOW. BEAST'S SO ANGRY HE ALMOST SAID A DIRTY WORD.
JUST SHUT UP AND DIE, DOG-BREATH.

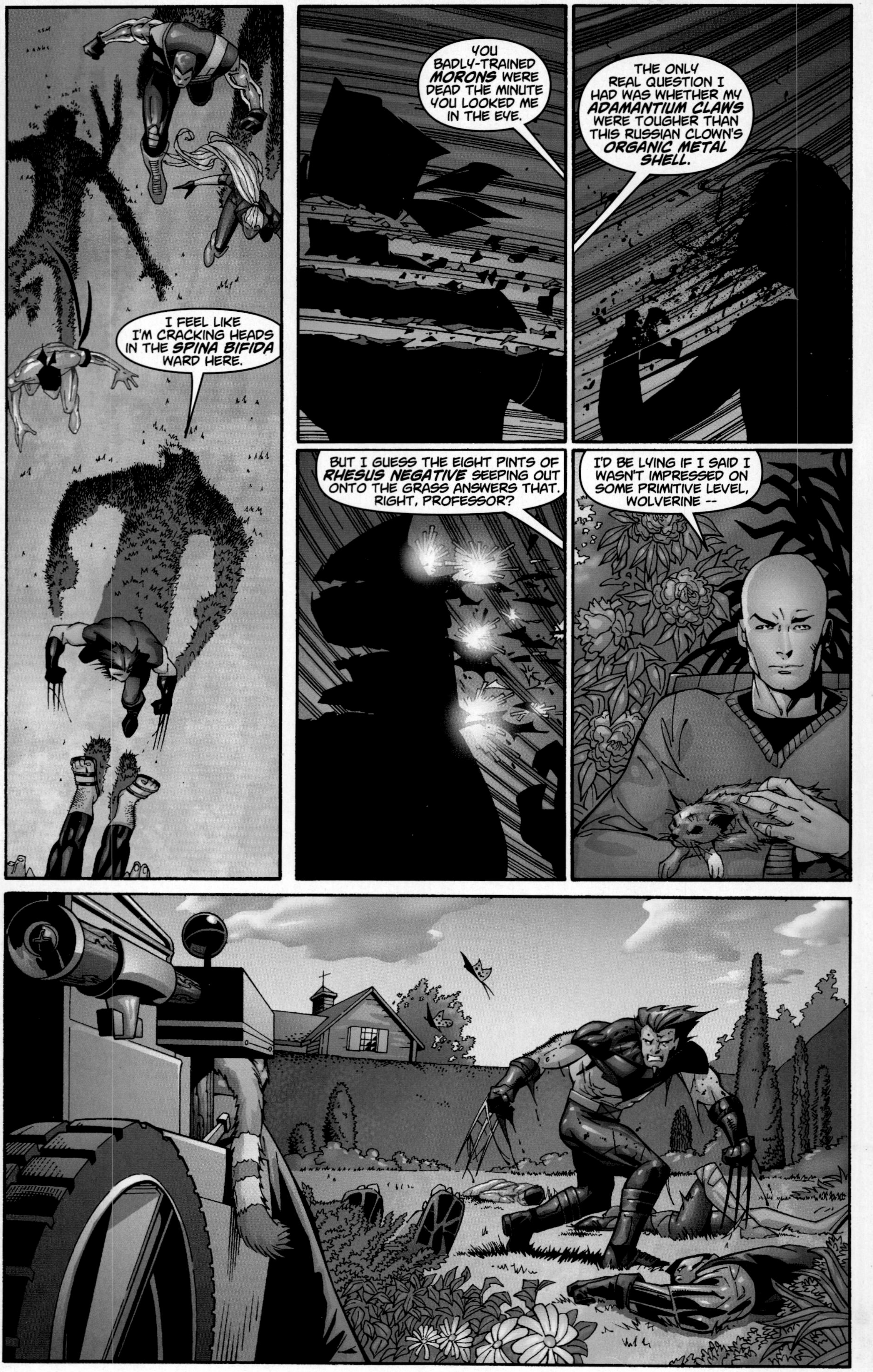
I FEEL LIKE I'M CRACKING HEADS IN THE SPINA BIFIDA WARD HERE.
YOU BADLY-TRAINED MORONS WERE DEAD THE MINUTE YOU LOOKED ME IN THE EYE.
THE ONLY REAL QUESTION I HAD WAS WHETHER MY ADAMANTIUM CLAWS WERE TOUGHER THAN THIS RUSSIAN CLOWN'S ORGANIC METAL SHELL.
BUT I GUESS THE EIGHT PINTS OF RHESUS NEGATIVE SEEPING OUT ONTO THE GRASS ANSWERS THAT. RIGHT, PROFESSOR?
I'D BE LYING IF I SAID I WASN'T IMPRESSED ON SOME PRIMITIVE LEVEL, WOLVERINE --

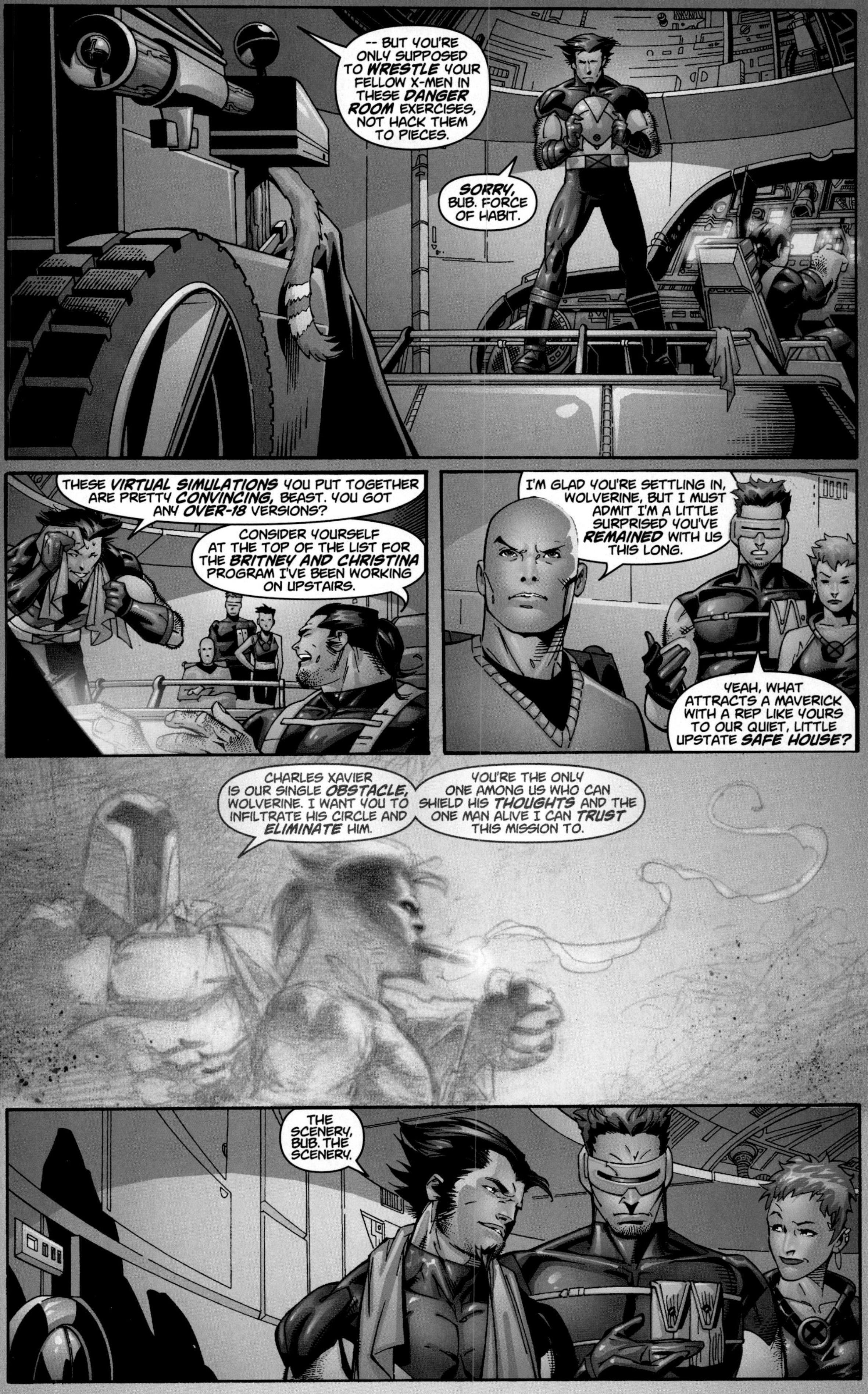
-- BUT YOU'RE ONLY SUPPOSED TO WRESTLE YOUR FELLOW X-MEN IN THESE DANGER ROOM EXERCISES, NOT HACK THEM TO PIECES.
SORRY, BUB. FORCE OF HABIT.
THESE VIRTUAL SIMULATIONS YOU PUT TOGETHER ARE PRETTY CONVINCING, BEAST. YOU GOT ANY OVER-18 VERSIONS?
CONSIDER YOURSELF AT THE TOP OF THE LIST FOR THE BRITNEY AND CHRISTINA PROGRAM I'VE BEEN WORKING ON UPSTAIRS.
I'M GLAD YOU'RE SETTLING IN, WOLVERINE, BUT I MUST ADMIT I'M A LITTLE SURPRISED YOU'VE REMAINED WITH US THIS LONG.
YEAH, WHAT ATTRACTS A MAVERICK WITH A REP LIKE YOURS TO OUR QUIET, LITTLE UPSTATE SAFE HOUSE?
CHARLES XAVIER IS OUR SINGLE OBSTACLE, WOLVERINE. I WANT YOU TO INFILTRATE HIS CIRCLE AND ELIMINATE HIM.
YOU'RE THE ONLY ONE AMONG US WHO CAN SHIELD HIS THOUGHTS AND THE ONE MAN ALIVE I CAN TRUST THIS MISSION TO.
THE SCENERY, BUB. THE SCENERY.

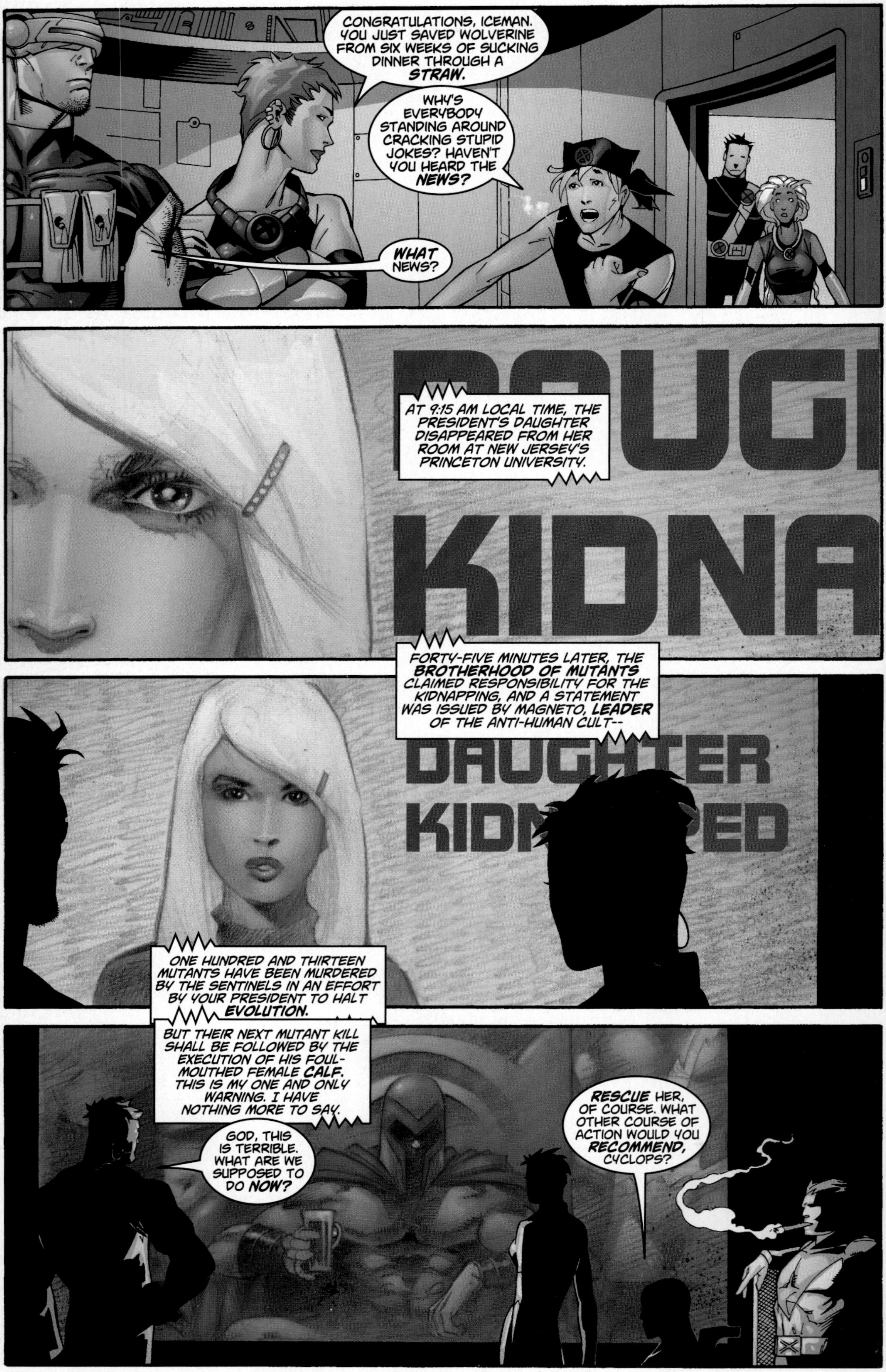
CONGRATULATIONS, ICEMAN. YOU JUST SAVED WOLVERINE FROM SIX WEEKS OF SUCKING DINNER THROUGH A **STRAW.**
WHY'S EVERYBODY STANDING AROUND CRACKING STUPID JOKES? HAVEN'T YOU HEARD THE **NEWS?**
WHAT NEWS?
AT 9:15 AM LOCAL TIME, THE PRESIDENT'S DAUGHTER DISAPPEARED FROM HER ROOM AT NEW JERSEY'S PRINCETON UNIVERSITY.
KIDNA
FORTY-FIVE MINUTES LATER, THE **BROTHERHOOD OF MUTANTS** CLAIMED RESPONSIBILITY FOR THE KIDNAPPING, AND A STATEMENT WAS ISSUED BY MAGNETO, **LEADER** OF THE ANTI-HUMAN CULT--
DAUGHTER
ONE HUNDRED AND THIRTEEN MUTANTS HAVE BEEN MURDERED BY THE SENTINELS IN AN EFFORT BY YOUR PRESIDENT TO HALT **EVOLUTION.**
BUT THEIR NEXT MUTANT KILL SHALL BE FOLLOWED BY THE EXECUTION OF HIS FOUL-MOUTHED FEMALE **CALF.** THIS IS MY ONE AND ONLY WARNING. I HAVE NOTHING MORE TO SAY.
GOD, THIS IS TERRIBLE. WHAT ARE WE SUPPOSED TO DO **NOW?**
RESCUE HER, OF COURSE. WHAT OTHER COURSE OF ACTION WOULD YOU **RECOMMEND,** CYCLOPS?

BUT RESCUING THE *FIRST DAUGHTER* OR WHATEVER THEY *CALL* HER, MEANS THE SENTINELS ARE GOING TO BE OUT THERE *FOREVER*, PROFESSOR.

I DON'T LIKE MAGNETO ANY MORE THAN *YOU* DO, BUT AT LEAST HE'S STOPPED THE GOVERNMENT FROM KILLING *MUTANTS*.

THE ONLY *LASTING* SOLUTION TO THE TENSION BETWEEN MANKIND AND THE MUTANT POPULATION IS A *PEACEFUL* ONE, STORM.

TURN YOUR BACK ON THIS GIRL NOW AND YOU MIGHT AS WELL SIGN UP WITH *MAGNETO*.

CYCLOPS?

I HATE TO SAY IT, BUT HE'S RIGHT.

WE *ALL* WANT TO SEE THE SENTINELS TAKEN OUT OF THE PICTURE, BUT WE CAN'T LET THE BROTHERHOOD USE THIS GIRL AS A *BARGAINING CHIP*.

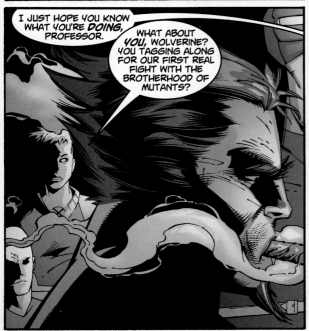

I JUST HOPE YOU KNOW WHAT YOU'RE *DOING*, PROFESSOR.

WHAT ABOUT *YOU*, WOLVERINE? YOU TAGGING ALONG FOR OUR FIRST REAL FIGHT WITH THE BROTHERHOOD OF MUTANTS?

WELL, I KINDA HAD MY HEART SET ON PLAYIN' *BACKGAMMON* WITH THE *PROFESSOR* HERE, BUT WHY THE HECK NOT?

SOUNDS LIKE IT COULD BE A *LAUGH*.

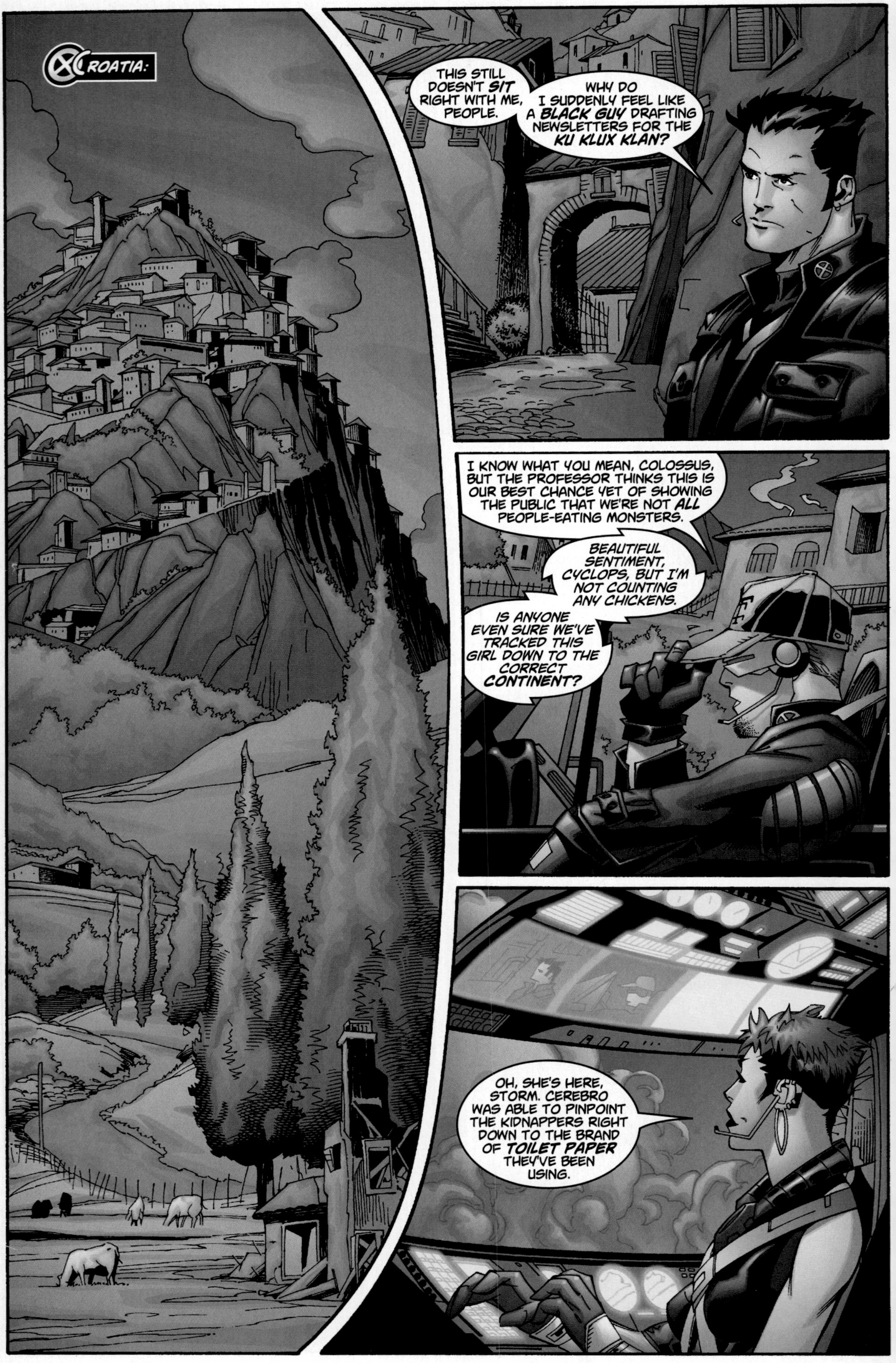
CROATIA:
THIS STILL DOESN'T SIT RIGHT WITH ME, PEOPLE.
WHY DO I SUDDENLY FEEL LIKE A BLACK GUY DRAFTING NEWSLETTERS FOR THE KU KLUX KLAN?
I KNOW WHAT YOU MEAN, COLOSSUS, BUT THE PROFESSOR THINKS THIS IS OUR BEST CHANCE YET OF SHOWING THE PUBLIC THAT WE'RE NOT ALL PEOPLE-EATING MONSTERS.
BEAUTIFUL SENTIMENT, CYCLOPS, BUT I'M NOT COUNTING ANY CHICKENS.
IS ANYONE EVEN SURE WE'VE TRACKED THIS GIRL DOWN TO THE CORRECT CONTINENT?
OH, SHE'S HERE, STORM. CEREBRO WAS ABLE TO PINPOINT THE KIDNAPPERS RIGHT DOWN TO THE BRAND OF TOILET PAPER THEY'VE BEEN USING.

THEIR JET BACK TO THE SAVAGE LAND WON'T BE HERE FOR ANOTHER EIGHTEEN MINUTES, BUT I WANT EVERYBODY OUT OF THIS CREEPY, LITTLE COUNTRY WITH FIVE GIANT-SIZED MINUTES TO *SPARE.*

DOWN BELOW:

WHAT HAPPENED TO MY SODDING CIGARETTES? THERE WERE *FIFTEEN* IN THE PACK BEFORE I WENT FOR A SLASH.

I CAN SMOKE FIFTEEN BEFORE THE *MATCH* GOES OUT, *TOAD.* THIRTY IF I'M REALLY *TRYING.*

REALLY? WHAT A WONDERFUL *MUTANT ABILITY,* QUICKSILVER.

THANK GOD WE'VE GOT *EACH OTHER* FOR INTELLIGENT CONVERSATION, SCARLET WITCH.

ACTUALLY, THE ONLY INTELLIGENT CONVERSATION I GET AROUND HERE...

...IS WHEN I TALK TO *MYSELF,* MASTERMIND.

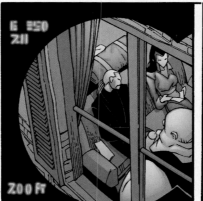

READY WHEN *YOU* ARE, COLOSSUS.

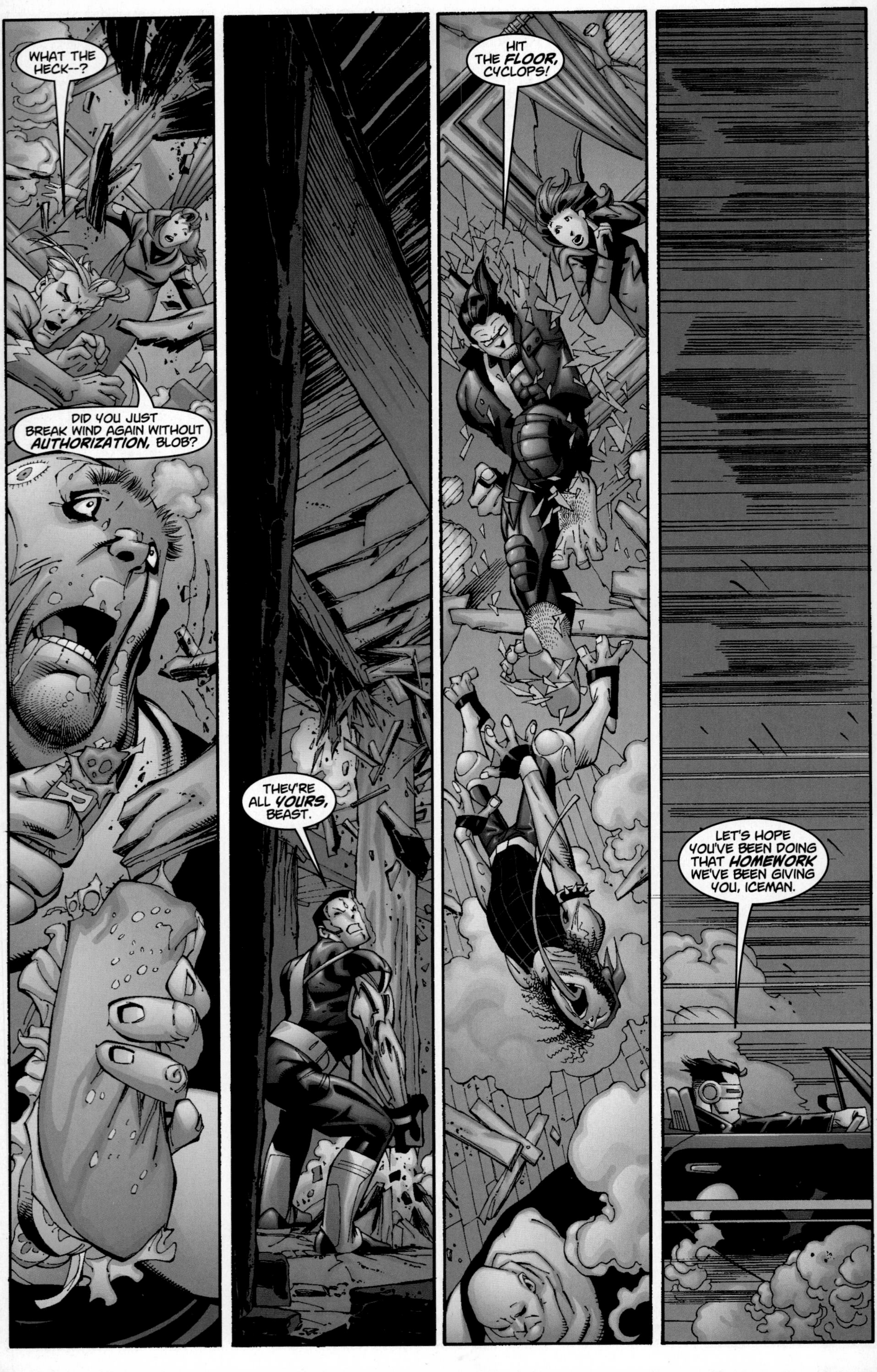
WHAT THE HECK--?
DID YOU JUST BREAK WIND AGAIN WITHOUT AUTHORIZATION, BLOB?
THEY'RE ALL YOURS, BEAST.
HIT THE FLOOR, CYCLOPS!
LET'S HOPE YOU'VE BEEN DOING THAT HOMEWORK WE'VE BEEN GIVING YOU, ICEMAN.

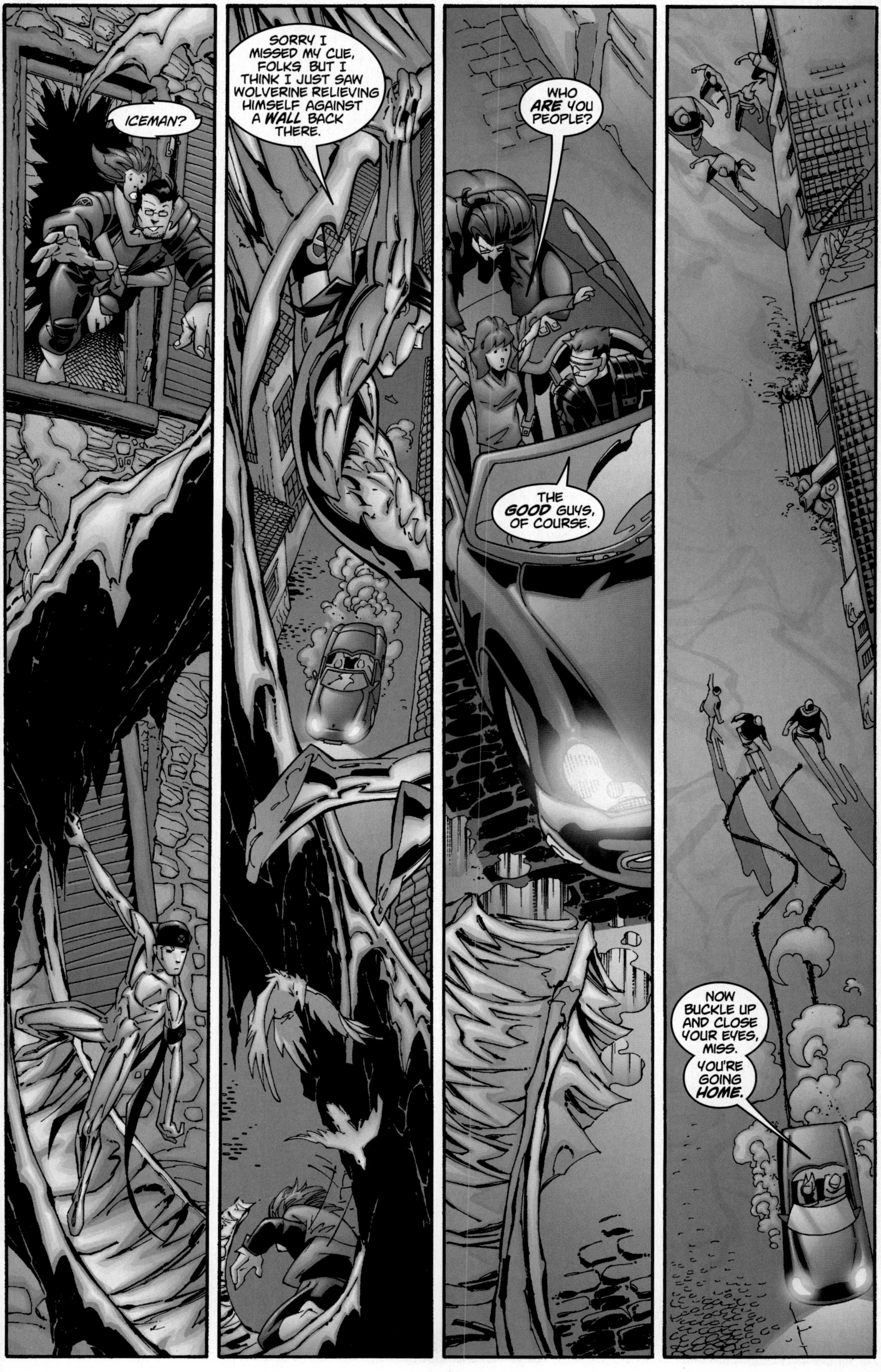
ICEMAN?
SORRY I MISSED MY CUE, FOLKS BUT I THINK I JUST SAW WOLVERINE RELIEVING HIMSELF AGAINST A WALL BACK THERE.
WHO ARE YOU PEOPLE?
THE GOOD GUYS, OF COURSE.
NOW BUCKLE UP AND CLOSE YOUR EYES, MISS.
YOU'RE GOING HOME.

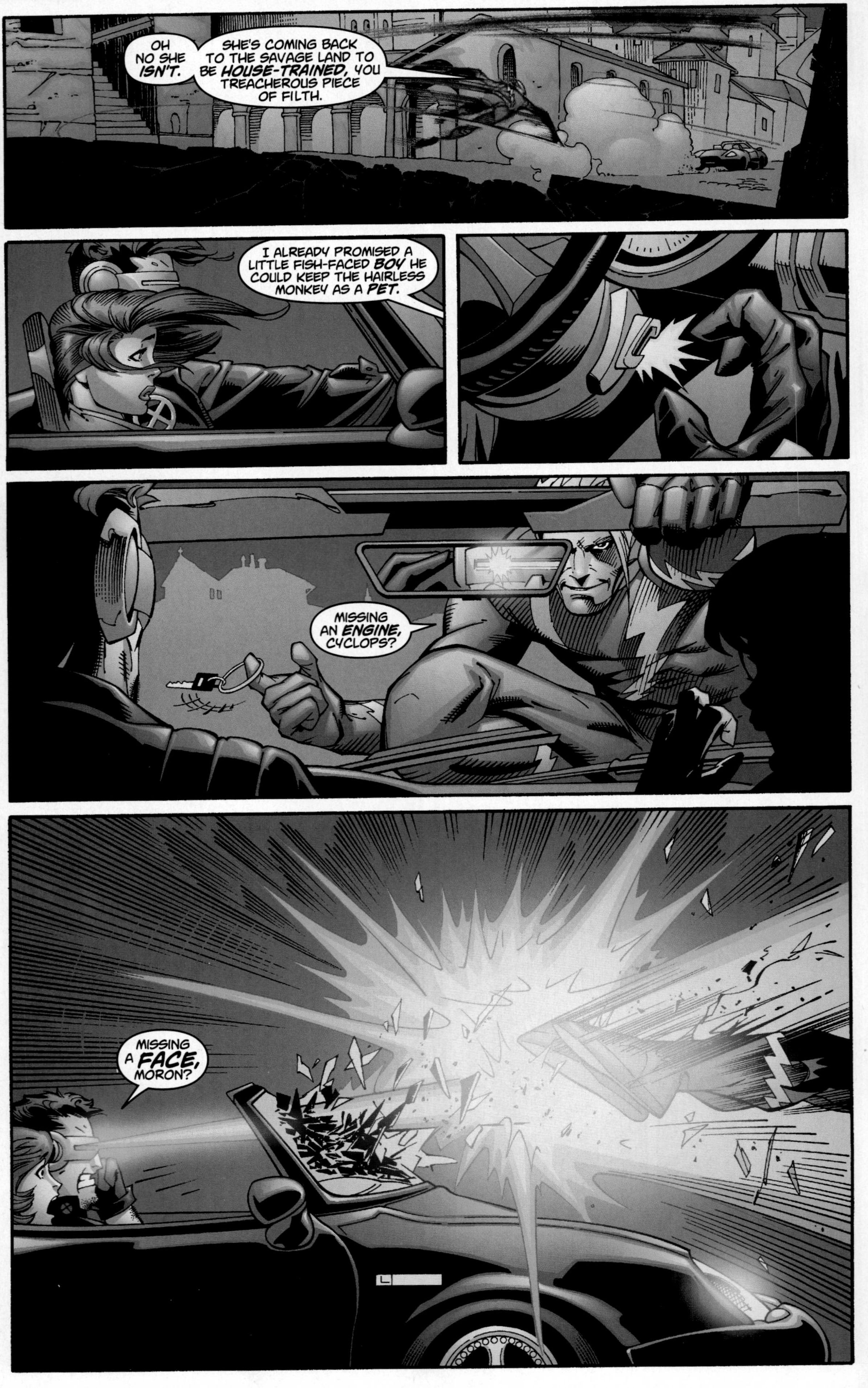
OH NO SHE ISN'T.
SHE'S COMING BACK TO THE SAVAGE LAND TO BE HOUSE-TRAINED, YOU TREACHEROUS PIECE OF FILTH.
I ALREADY PROMISED A LITTLE FISH-FACED BOY HE COULD KEEP THE HAIRLESS MONKEY AS A PET.
MISSING AN ENGINE, CYCLOPS?
MISSING A FACE, MORON?

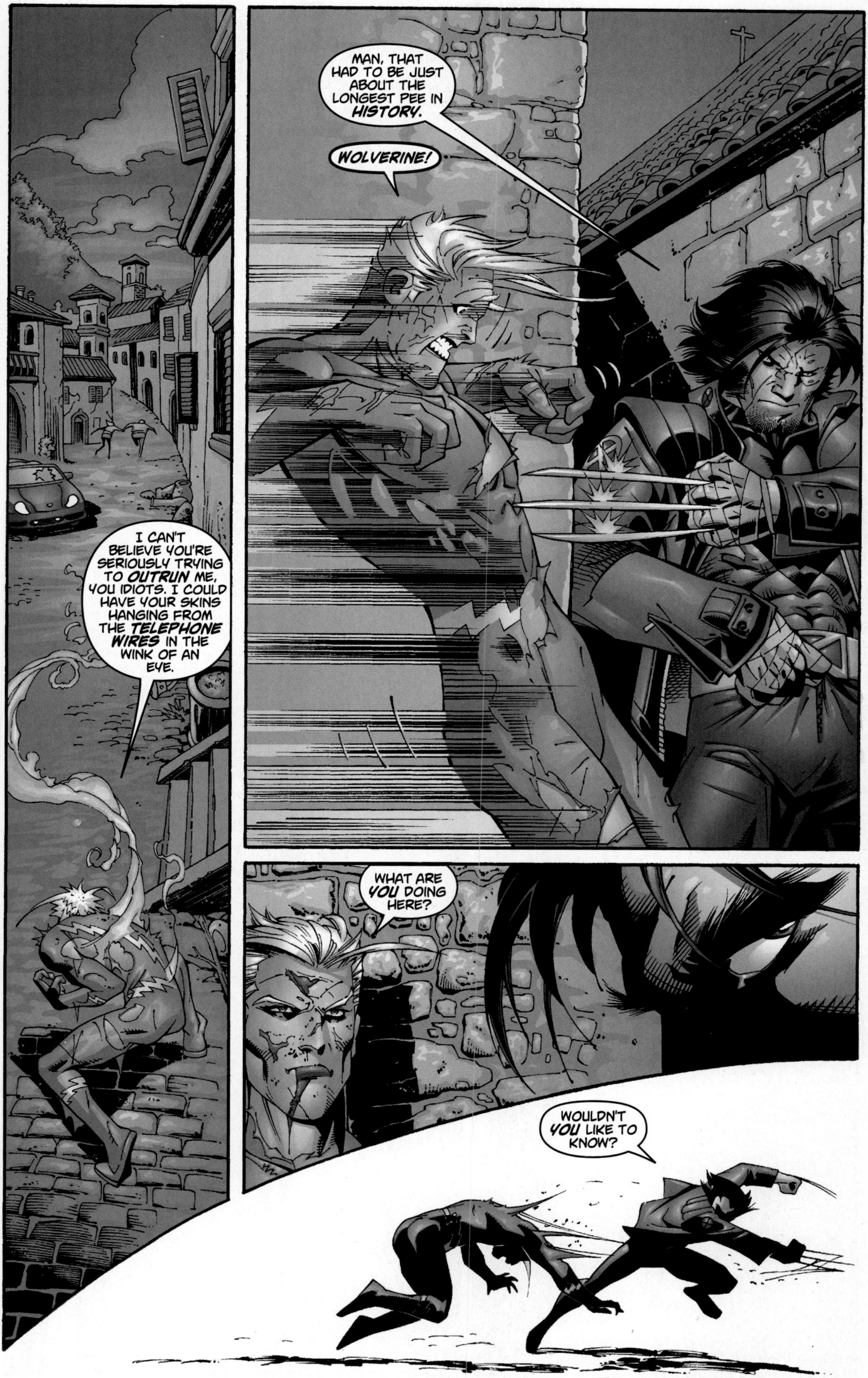
I CAN'T BELIEVE YOU'RE SERIOUSLY TRYING TO OUTRUN ME, YOU IDIOTS. I COULD HAVE YOUR SKINS HANGING FROM THE TELEPHONE WIRES IN THE WINK OF AN EYE.
MAN, THAT HAD TO BE JUST ABOUT THE LONGEST PEE IN HISTORY.
WOLVERINE!
WHAT ARE YOU DOING HERE?
WOULDN'T YOU LIKE TO KNOW?

YOU KNOW, WHOEVER SAID THAT TIGHT, LITTLE T-SHIRT DOESN'T MAKE YOU LOOK LIKE THE TEAM PANSY WAS LYING, CYCLOPS.
WAM
YOU'RE NEXT, BY THE WAY, YOU STUPID-LOOKING AMERICAN COW.
WHAT?
BEAST TO ALL POINTS: COLOSSUS AND I JUST DISABLED MASTERMIND AND THE BLOB --
WAM
-- BUT MORE OF THEM ARE CRAWLING OUT OF THE WOODWORK EVERY SECOND. ANYONE FIT TO LEND A HAND?
SORRY, BEAST. PROBLEMS OF OUR OWN RIGHT NOW.
OH, BLOODY--

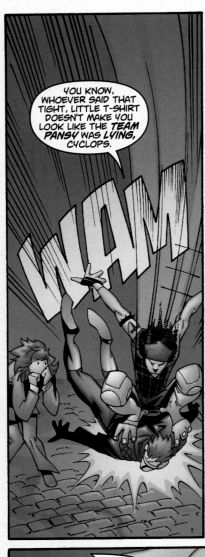

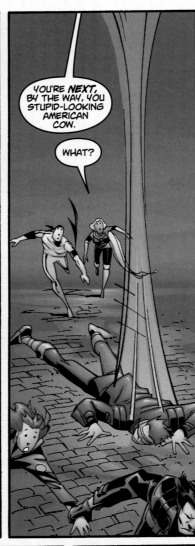

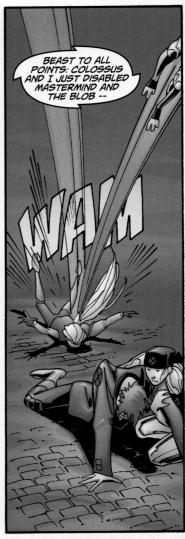

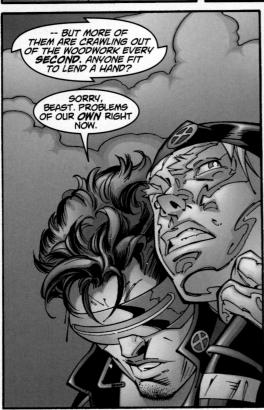

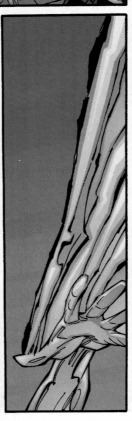

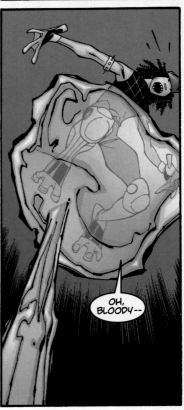

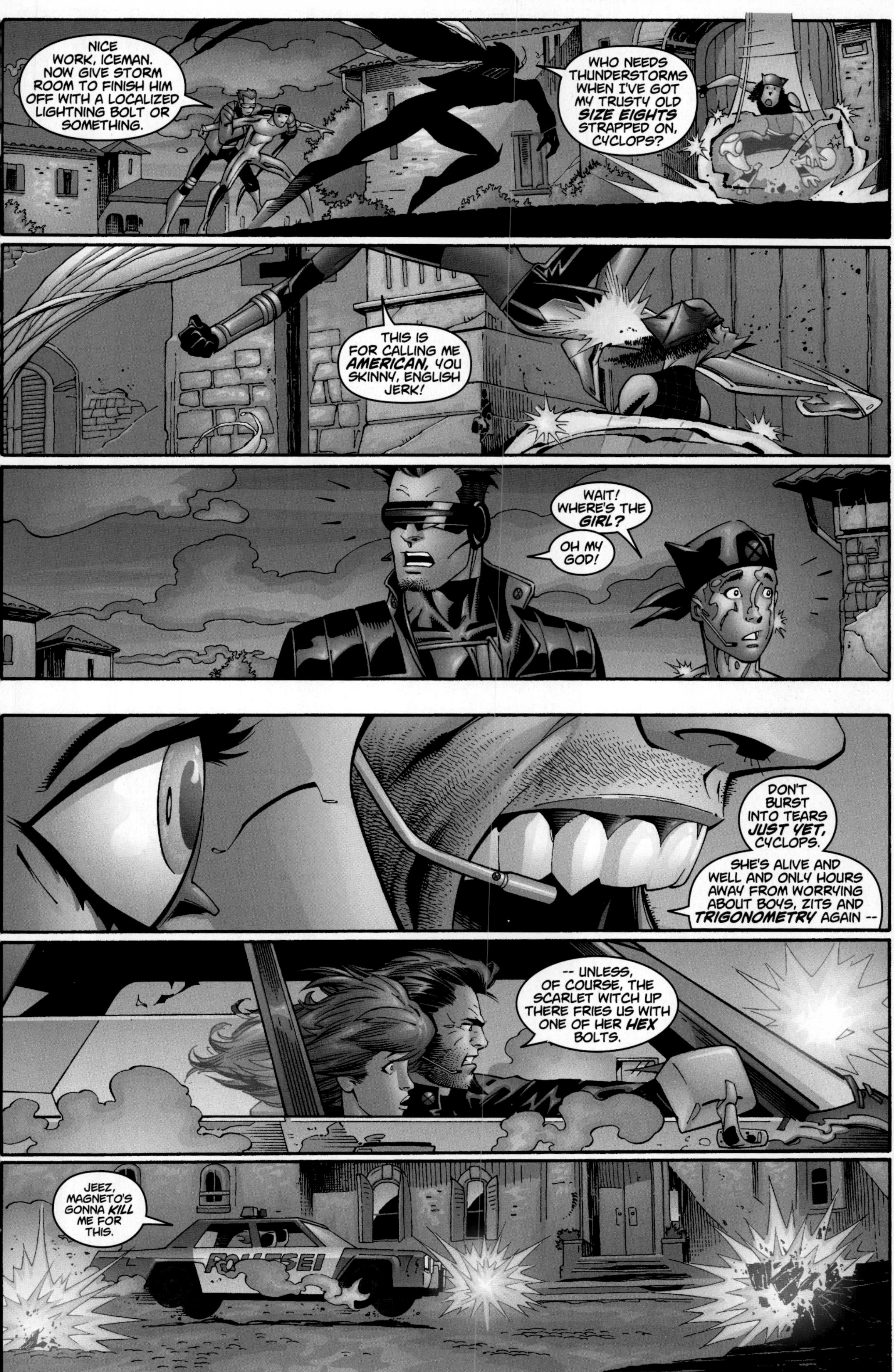
NICE WORK, ICEMAN. NOW GIVE STORM ROOM TO FINISH HIM OFF WITH A LOCALIZED LIGHTNING BOLT OR SOMETHING.
WHO NEEDS THUNDERSTORMS WHEN I'VE GOT MY TRUSTY OLD SIZE EIGHTS STRAPPED ON, CYCLOPS?
THIS IS FOR CALLING ME AMERICAN, YOU SKINNY, ENGLISH JERK!
WAIT! WHERE'S THE GIRL?
OH MY GOD!
DON'T BURST INTO TEARS JUST YET, CYCLOPS.
SHE'S ALIVE AND WELL AND ONLY HOURS AWAY FROM WORRYING ABOUT BOYS, ZITS AND TRIGONOMETRY AGAIN --
-- UNLESS, OF COURSE, THE SCARLET WITCH UP THERE FRIES US WITH ONE OF HER HEX BOLTS.
JEEZ, MAGNETO'S GONNA KILL ME FOR THIS.

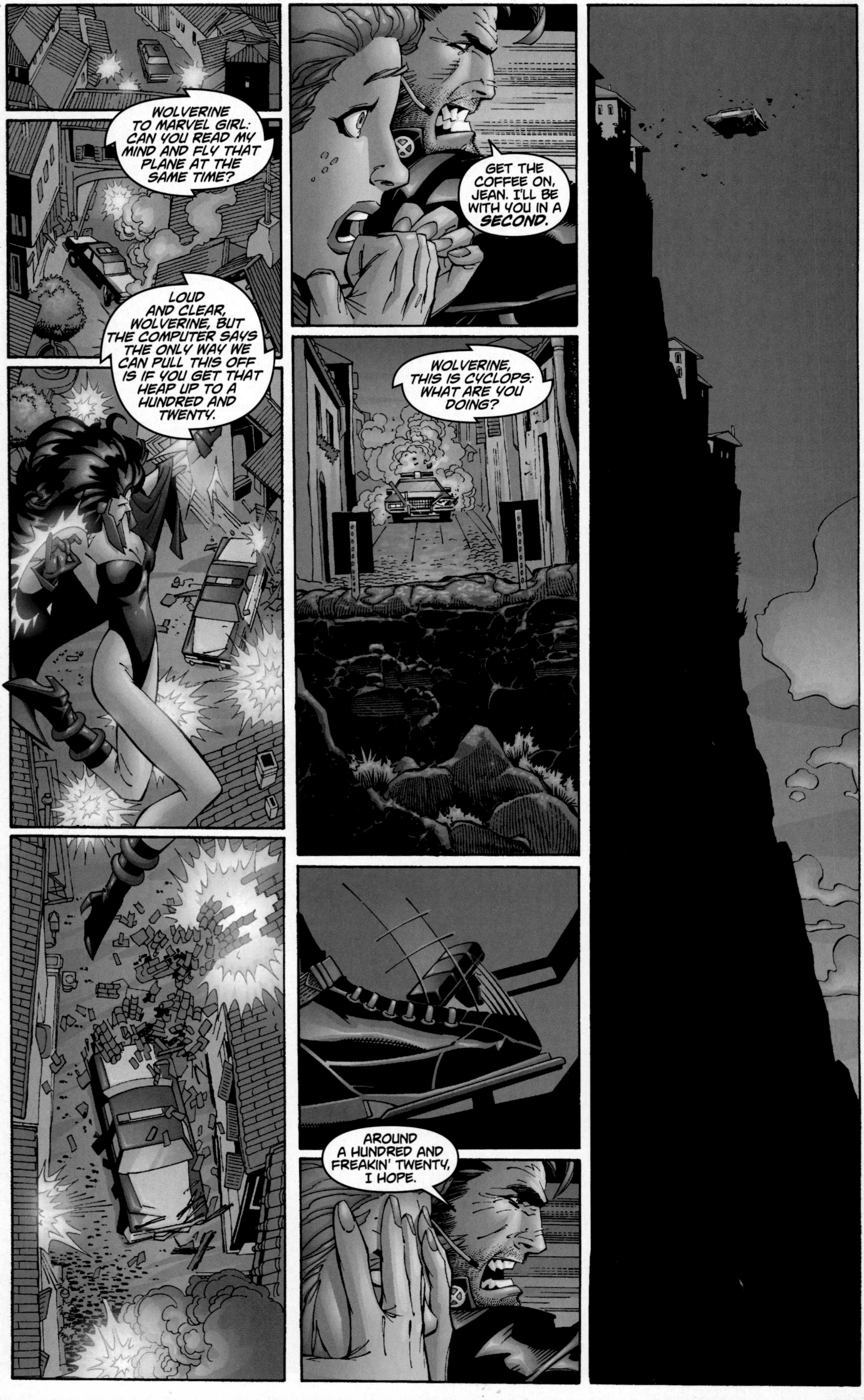
WOLVERINE TO MARVEL GIRL: CAN YOU READ MY MIND AND FLY THAT PLANE AT THE SAME TIME?
LOUD AND CLEAR, WOLVERINE, BUT THE COMPUTER SAYS THE ONLY WAY WE CAN PULL THIS OFF IS IF YOU GET THAT HEAP UP TO A HUNDRED AND TWENTY.
GET THE COFFEE ON, JEAN. I'LL BE WITH YOU IN A SECOND.
WOLVERINE, THIS IS CYCLOPS: WHAT ARE YOU DOING?
AROUND A HUNDRED AND FREAKIN' TWENTY, I HOPE.

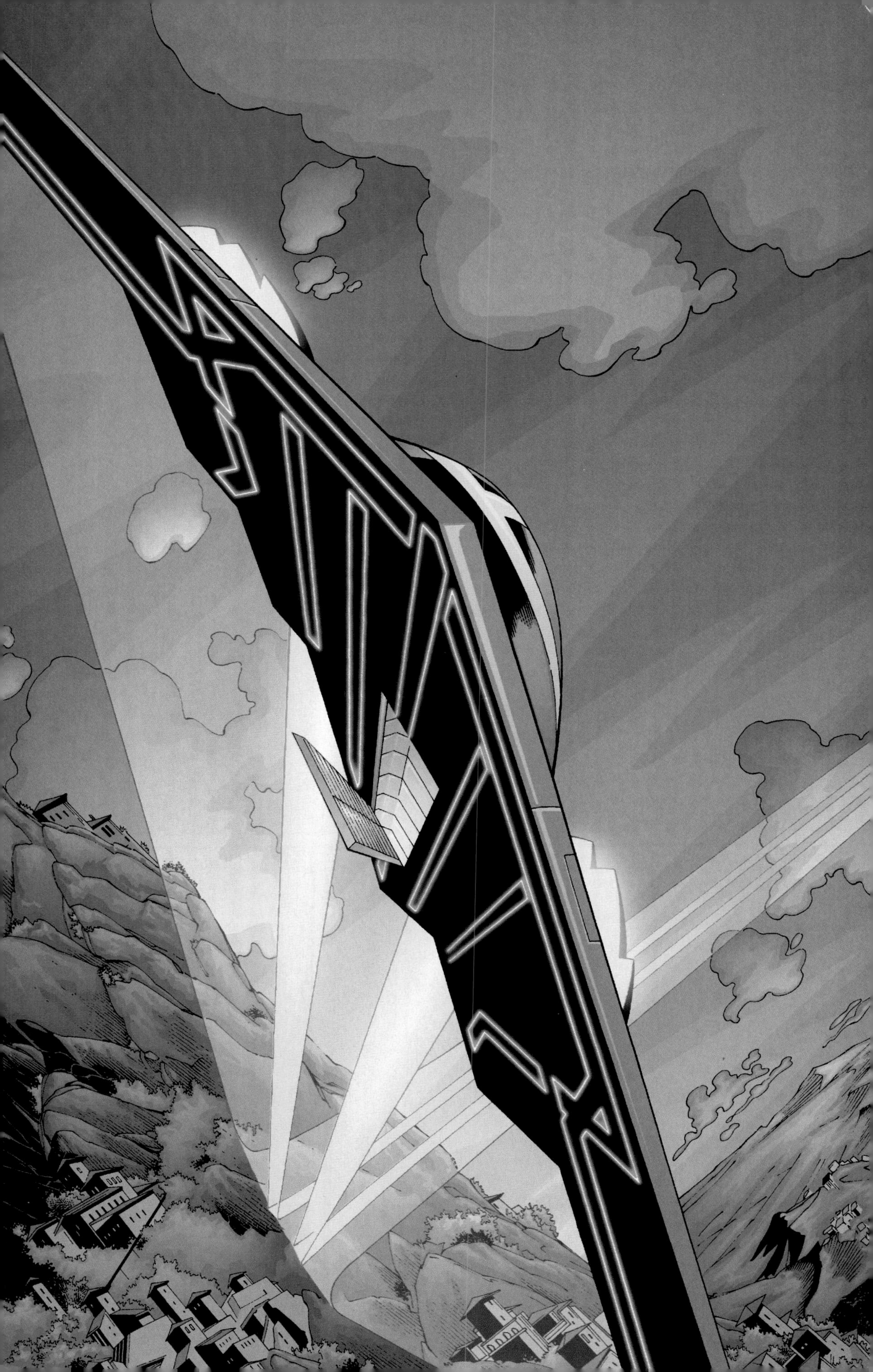

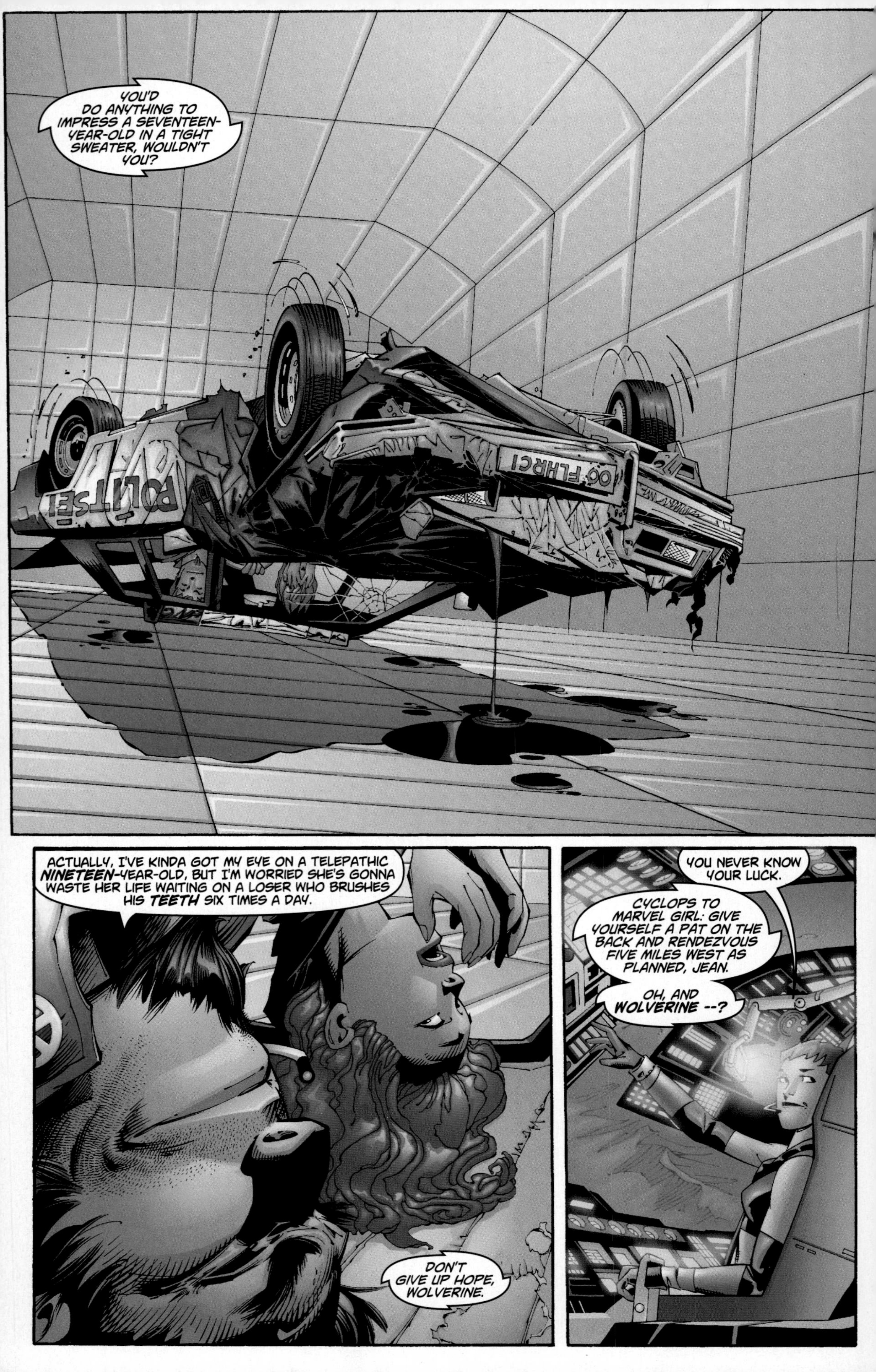
YOU'D DO ANYTHING TO IMPRESS A SEVENTEEN-YEAR-OLD IN A TIGHT SWEATER, WOULDN'T YOU?
ACTUALLY, I'VE KINDA GOT MY EYE ON A TELEPATHIC NINETEEN-YEAR-OLD, BUT I'M WORRIED SHE'S GONNA WASTE HER LIFE WAITING ON A LOSER WHO BRUSHES HIS TEETH SIX TIMES A DAY.
DON'T GIVE UP HOPE, WOLVERINE.
YOU NEVER KNOW YOUR LUCK.
CYCLOPS TO MARVEL GIRL: GIVE YOURSELF A PAT ON THE BACK AND RENDEZVOUS FIVE MILES WEST AS PLANNED, JEAN.
OH, AND WOLVERINE --?

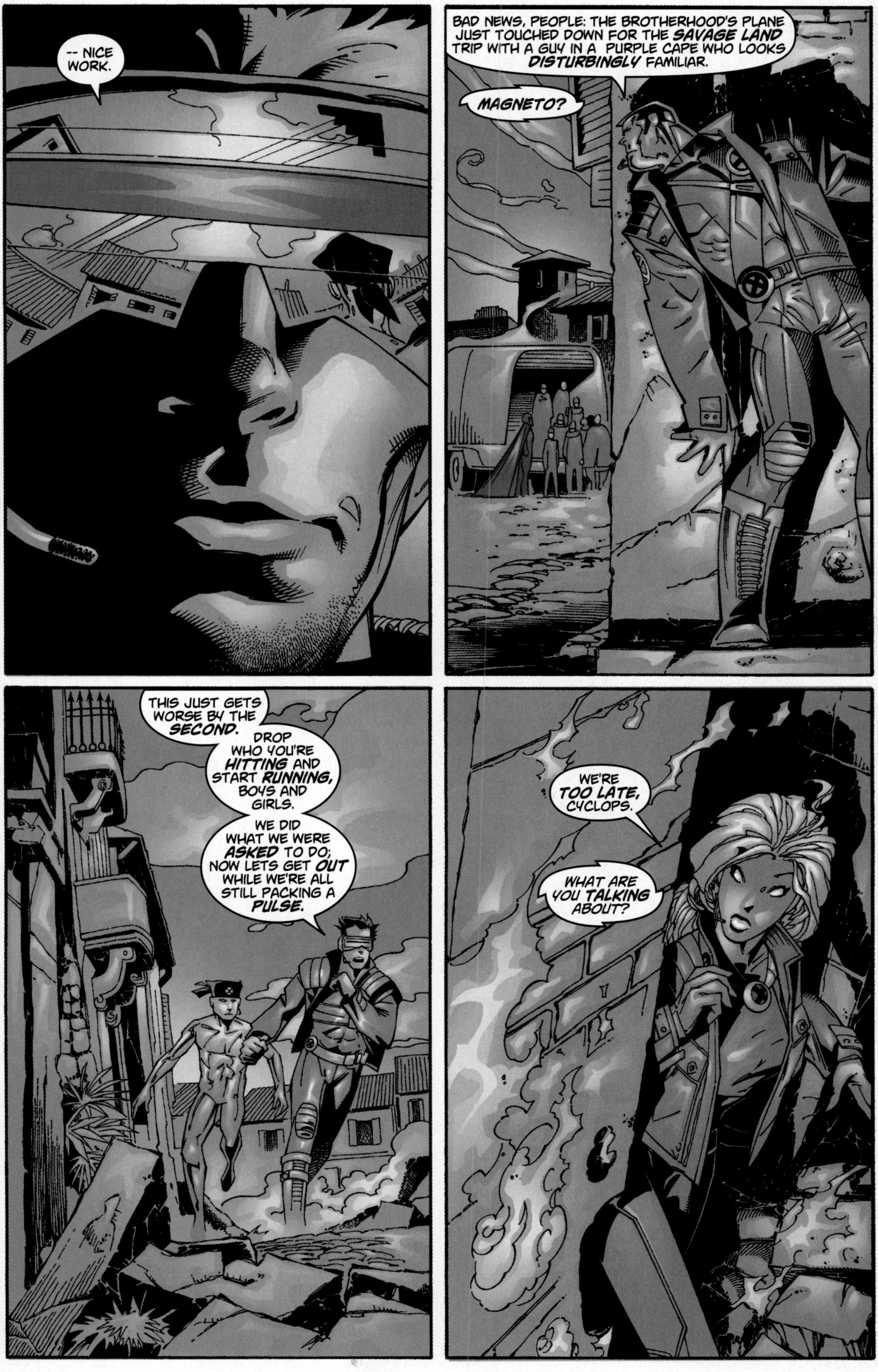
-- NICE WORK.
BAD NEWS, PEOPLE: THE BROTHERHOOD'S PLANE JUST TOUCHED DOWN FOR THE SAVAGE LAND TRIP WITH A GUY IN A PURPLE CAPE WHO LOOKS DISTURBINGLY FAMILIAR.
MAGNETO?
THIS JUST GETS WORSE BY THE SECOND.
DROP WHO YOU'RE HITTING AND START RUNNING, BOYS AND GIRLS.
WE DID WHAT WE WERE ASKED TO DO; NOW LETS GET OUT WHILE WE'RE ALL STILL PACKING A PULSE.
WE'RE TOO LATE, CYCLOPS.
WHAT ARE YOU TALKING ABOUT?

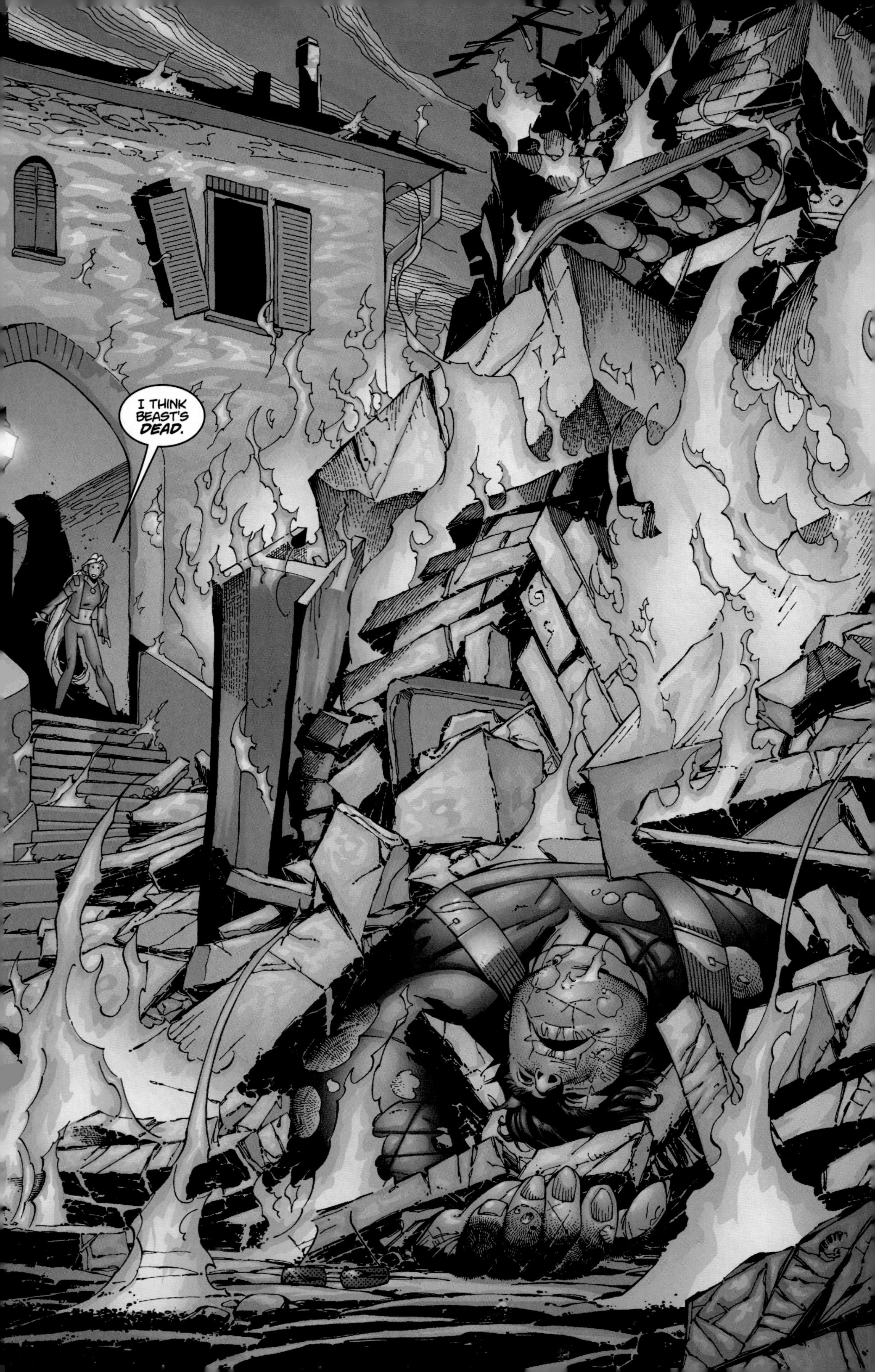
I THINK BEAST'S *DEAD*.

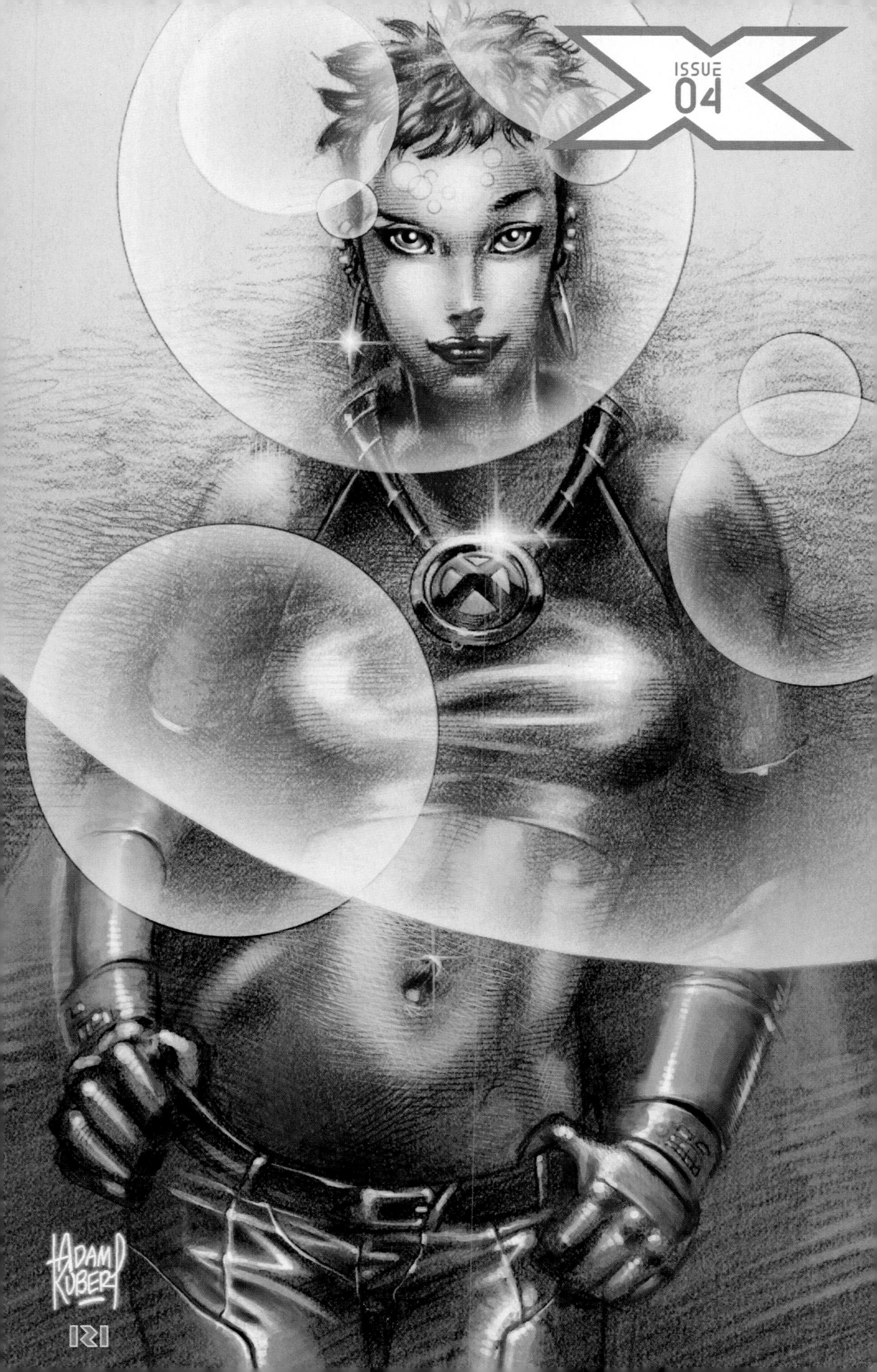

X
ISSUE
04
ADAM KUBERT

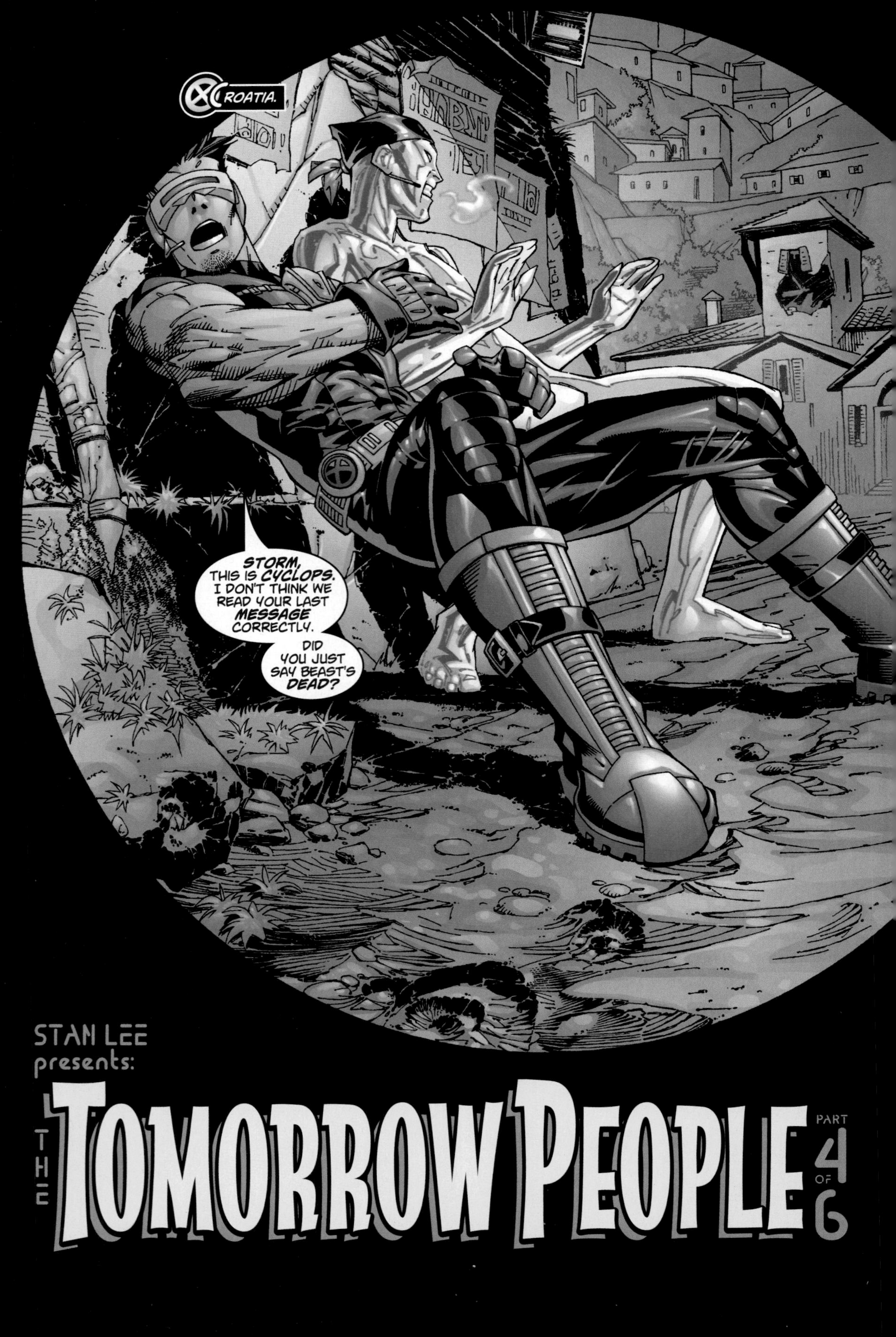
CROATIA.
STORM, THIS IS CYCLOPS. I DON'T THINK WE READ YOUR LAST MESSAGE CORRECTLY.
DID YOU JUST SAY BEAST'S DEAD?
STAN LEE presents:
THE TOMORROW PEOPLE
PART 4 OF 6

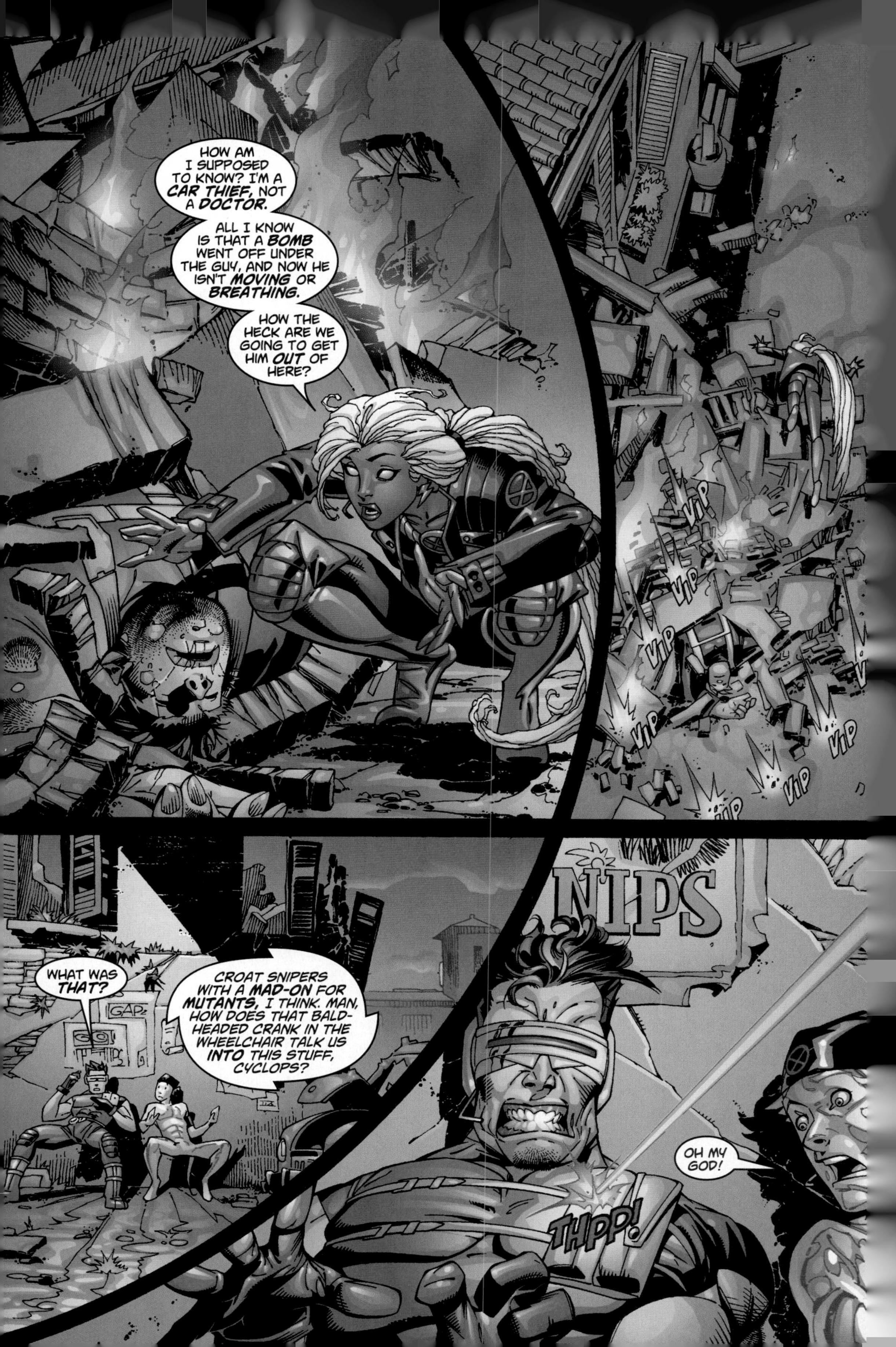

HOW AM I SUPPOSED TO KNOW? I'M A CAR THIEF, NOT A DOCTOR.
ALL I KNOW IS THAT A BOMB WENT OFF UNDER THE GUY, AND NOW HE ISN'T MOVING OR BREATHING.
HOW THE HECK ARE WE GOING TO GET HIM OUT OF HERE?
VIP
VIP
VIP
VIP
VIP
VIP
VIP
WHAT WAS THAT?
CROAT SNIPERS WITH A MAD-ON FOR MUTANTS, I THINK. MAN, HOW DOES THAT BALD-HEADED CRANK IN THE WHEELCHAIR TALK US INTO THIS STUFF, CYCLOPS?
NIPS
THPP!
OH MY GOD!

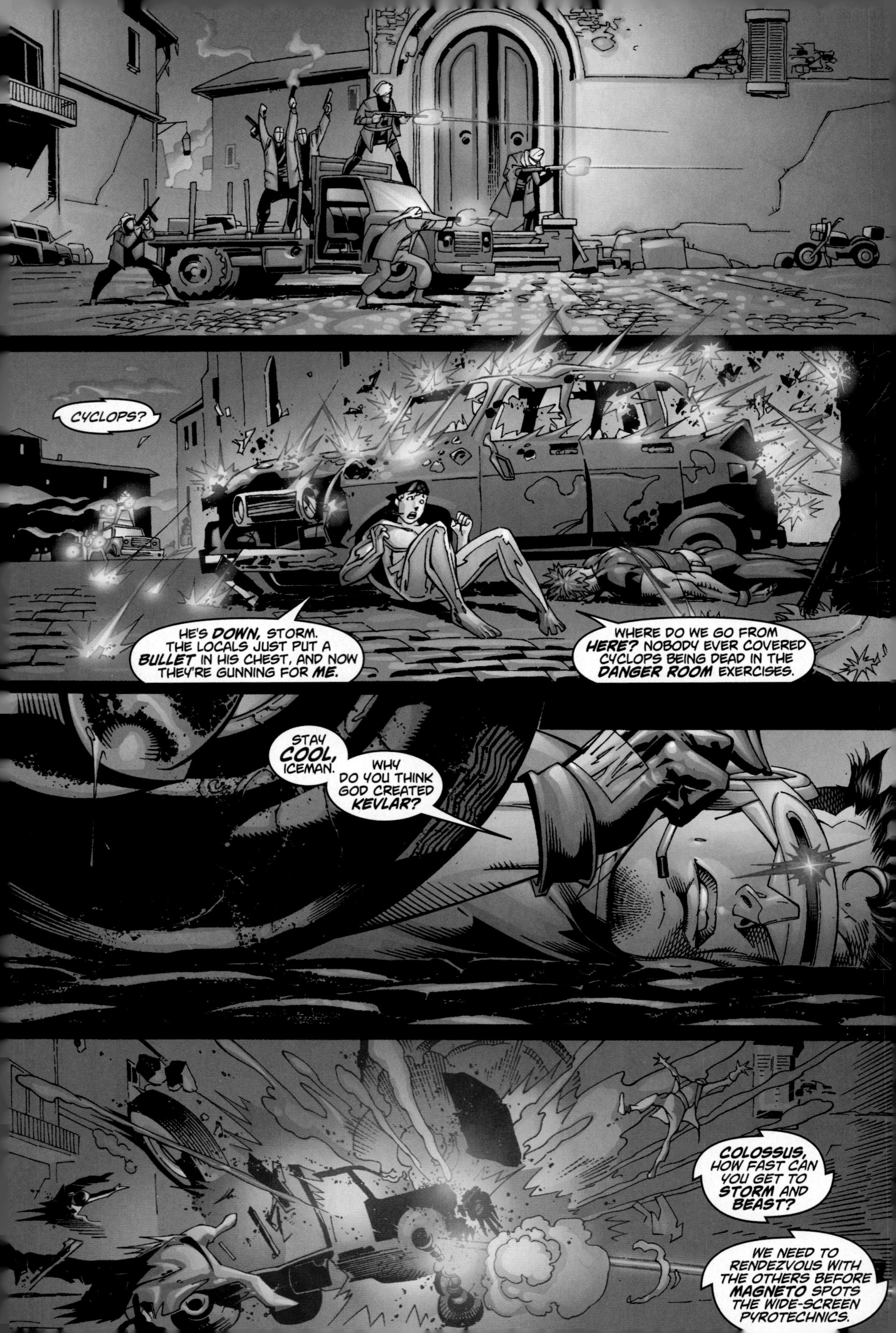
CYCLOPS?
HE'S DOWN, STORM. THE LOCALS JUST PUT A BULLET IN HIS CHEST, AND NOW THEY'RE GUNNING FOR ME.
WHERE DO WE GO FROM HERE? NOBODY EVER COVERED CYCLOPS BEING DEAD IN THE DANGER ROOM EXERCISES.
STAY COOL, ICEMAN.
WHY DO YOU THINK GOD CREATED KEVLAR?
COLOSSUS, HOW FAST CAN YOU GET TO STORM AND BEAST?
WE NEED TO RENDEZVOUS WITH THE OTHERS BEFORE MAGNETO SPOTS THE WIDE-SCREEN PYROTECHNICS.

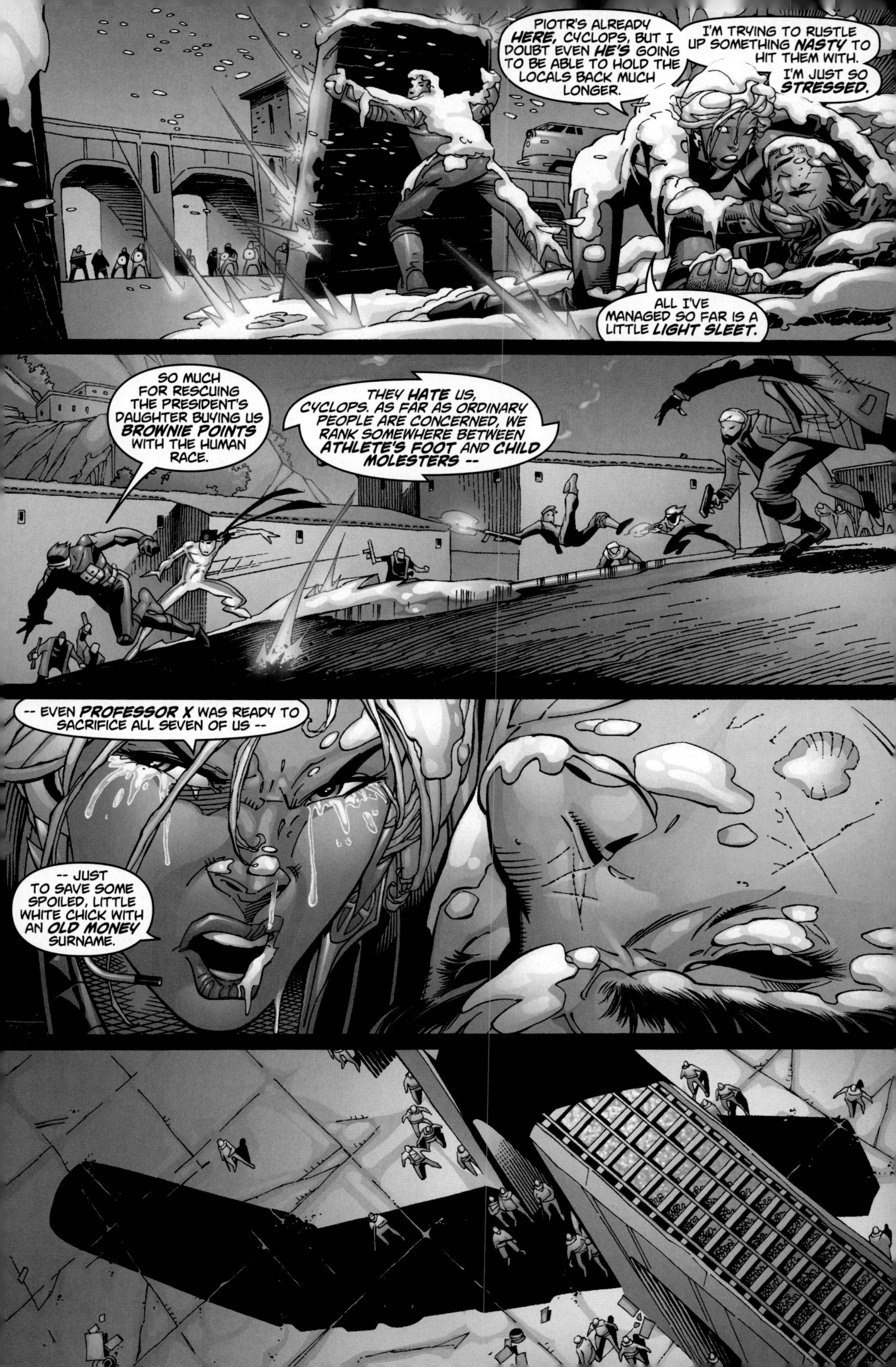
PIOTR'S ALREADY HERE, CYCLOPS, BUT I DOUBT EVEN HE'S GOING TO BE ABLE TO HOLD THE LOCALS BACK MUCH LONGER.
I'M TRYING TO RUSTLE UP SOMETHING NASTY TO HIT THEM WITH.
I'M JUST SO STRESSED.
ALL I'VE MANAGED SO FAR IS A LITTLE LIGHT SLEET.
SO MUCH FOR RESCUING THE PRESIDENT'S DAUGHTER BUYING US BROWNIE POINTS WITH THE HUMAN RACE.
THEY HATE US, CYCLOPS. AS FAR AS ORDINARY PEOPLE ARE CONCERNED, WE RANK SOMEWHERE BETWEEN ATHLETE'S FOOT AND CHILD MOLESTERS --
-- EVEN PROFESSOR X WAS READY TO SACRIFICE ALL SEVEN OF US --
-- JUST TO SAVE SOME SPOILED, LITTLE WHITE CHICK WITH AN OLD MONEY SURNAME.

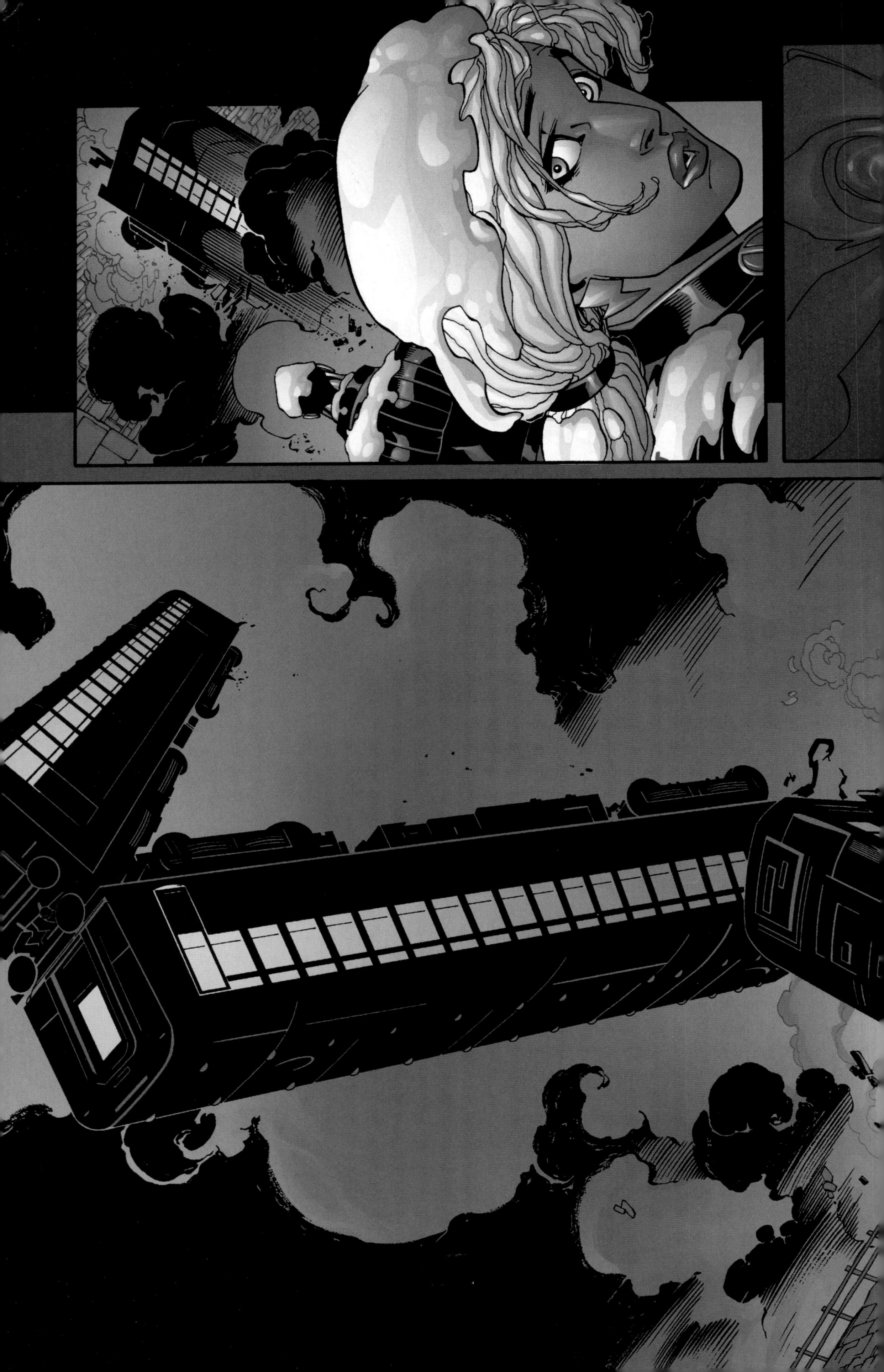

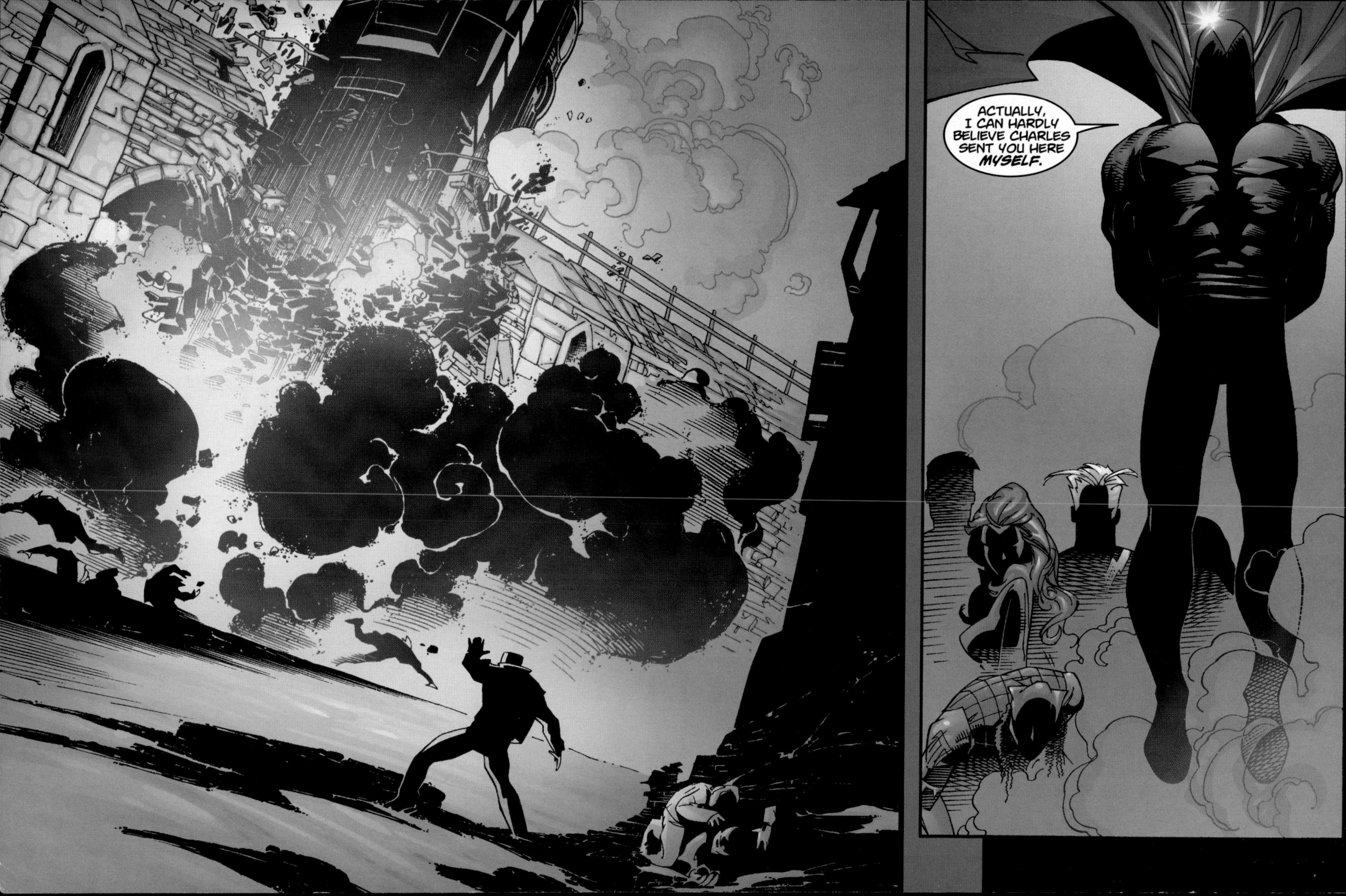
ACTUALLY, I CAN HARDLY BELIEVE CHARLES SENT YOU HERE MYSELF.

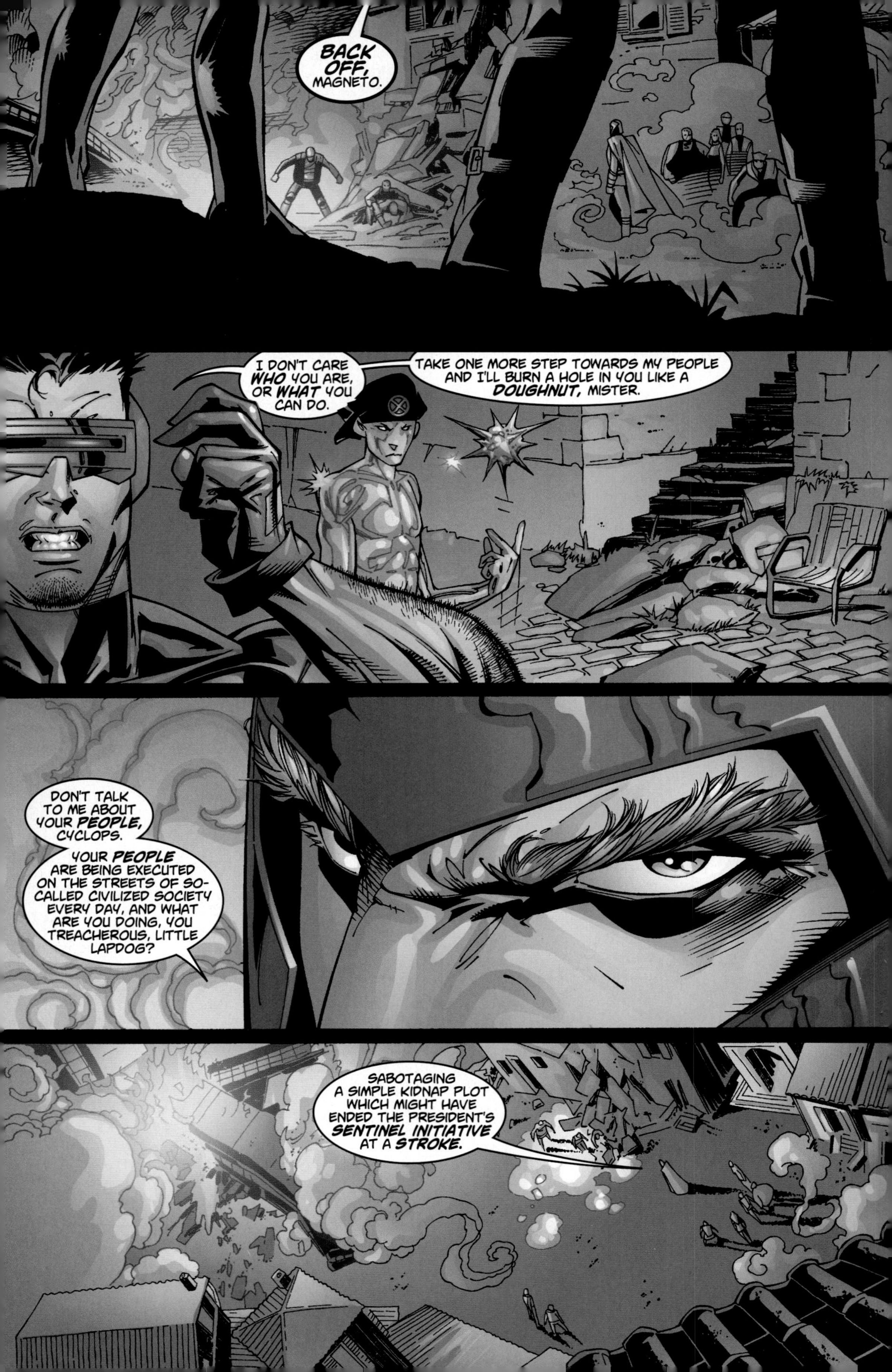
BACK OFF, MAGNETO.
I DON'T CARE WHO YOU ARE, OR WHAT YOU CAN DO.
TAKE ONE MORE STEP TOWARDS MY PEOPLE AND I'LL BURN A HOLE IN YOU LIKE A DOUGHNUT, MISTER.
DON'T TALK TO ME ABOUT YOUR PEOPLE, CYCLOPS.
YOUR PEOPLE ARE BEING EXECUTED ON THE STREETS OF SO-CALLED CIVILIZED SOCIETY EVERY DAY, AND WHAT ARE YOU DOING, YOU TREACHEROUS, LITTLE LAPDOG?
SABOTAGING A SIMPLE KIDNAP PLOT WHICH MIGHT HAVE ENDED THE PRESIDENT'S SENTINEL INITIATIVE AT A STROKE.

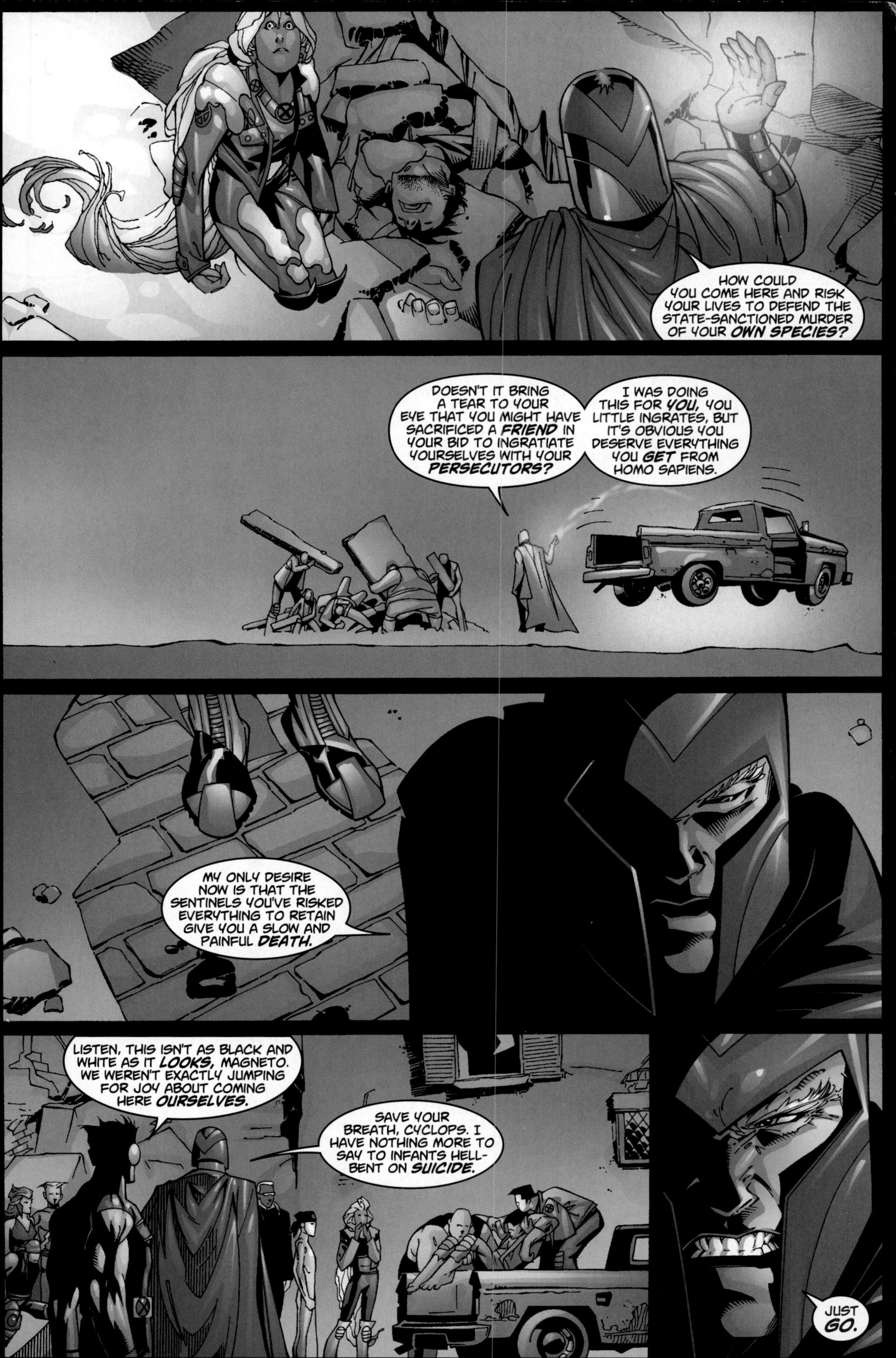
HOW COULD YOU COME HERE AND RISK YOUR LIVES TO DEFEND THE STATE-SANCTIONED MURDER OF YOUR OWN SPECIES?
DOESN'T IT BRING A TEAR TO YOUR EYE THAT YOU MIGHT HAVE SACRIFICED A FRIEND IN YOUR BID TO INGRATIATE YOURSELVES WITH YOUR PERSECUTORS?
I WAS DOING THIS FOR YOU, YOU LITTLE INGRATES, BUT IT'S OBVIOUS YOU DESERVE EVERYTHING YOU GET FROM HOMO SAPIENS.
MY ONLY DESIRE NOW IS THAT THE SENTINELS YOU'VE RISKED EVERYTHING TO RETAIN GIVE YOU A SLOW AND PAINFUL DEATH.
LISTEN, THIS ISN'T AS BLACK AND WHITE AS IT LOOKS, MAGNETO. WE WEREN'T EXACTLY JUMPING FOR JOY ABOUT COMING HERE OURSELVES.
SAVE YOUR BREATH, CYCLOPS. I HAVE NOTHING MORE TO SAY TO INFANTS HELL-BENT ON SUICIDE.
JUST GO.

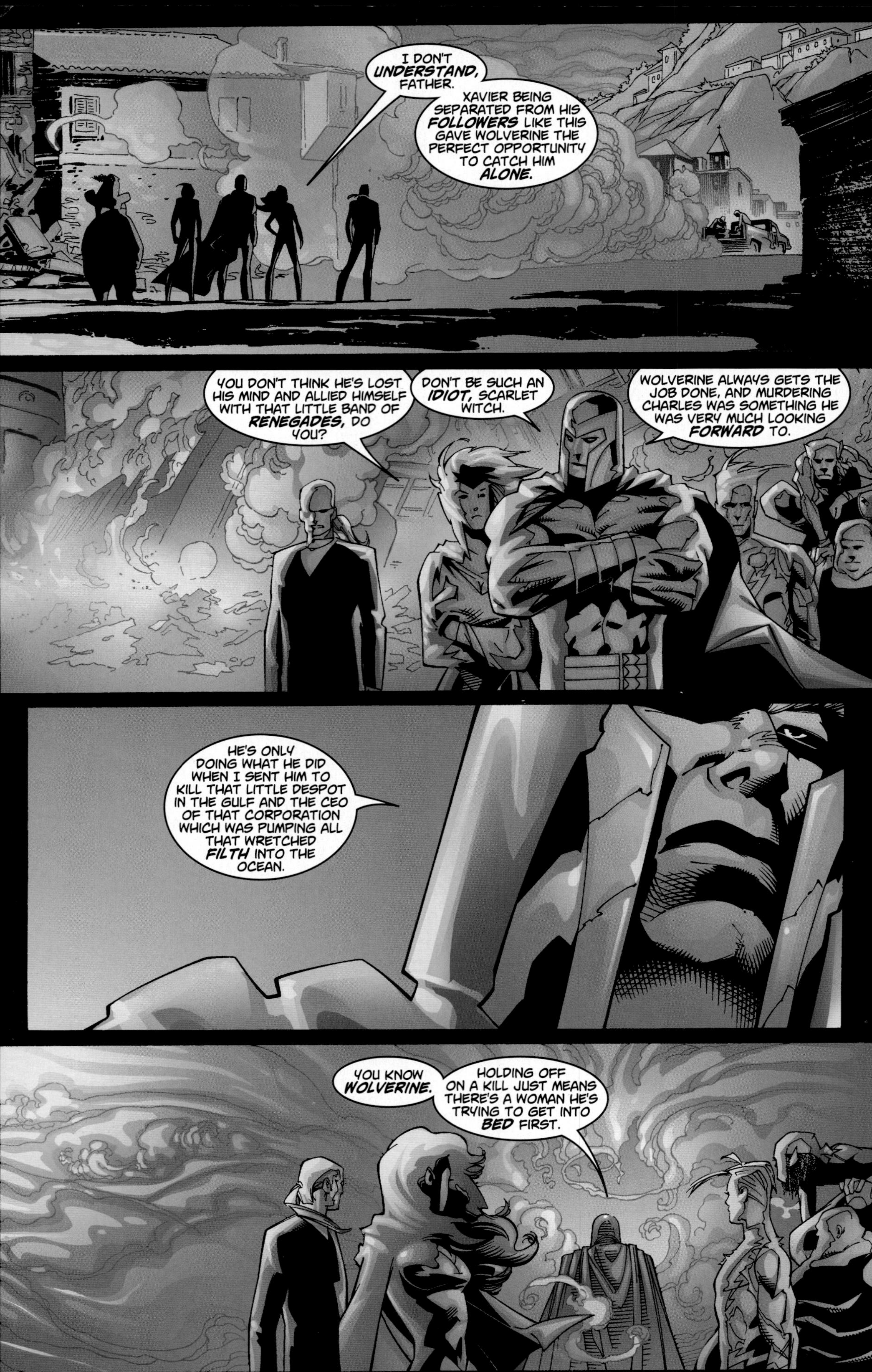
I DON'T UNDERSTAND, FATHER.
XAVIER BEING SEPARATED FROM HIS FOLLOWERS LIKE THIS GAVE WOLVERINE THE PERFECT OPPORTUNITY TO CATCH HIM ALONE.
YOU DON'T THINK HE'S LOST HIS MIND AND ALLIED HIMSELF WITH THAT LITTLE BAND OF RENEGADES, DO YOU?
DON'T BE SUCH AN IDIOT, SCARLET WITCH.
WOLVERINE ALWAYS GETS THE JOB DONE, AND MURDERING CHARLES WAS SOMETHING HE WAS VERY MUCH LOOKING FORWARD TO.
HE'S ONLY DOING WHAT HE DID WHEN I SENT HIM TO KILL THAT LITTLE DESPOT IN THE GULF AND THE CEO OF THAT CORPORATION WHICH WAS PUMPING ALL THAT WRETCHED FILTH INTO THE OCEAN.
YOU KNOW WOLVERINE.
HOLDING OFF ON A KILL JUST MEANS THERE'S A WOMAN HE'S TRYING TO GET INTO BED FIRST.

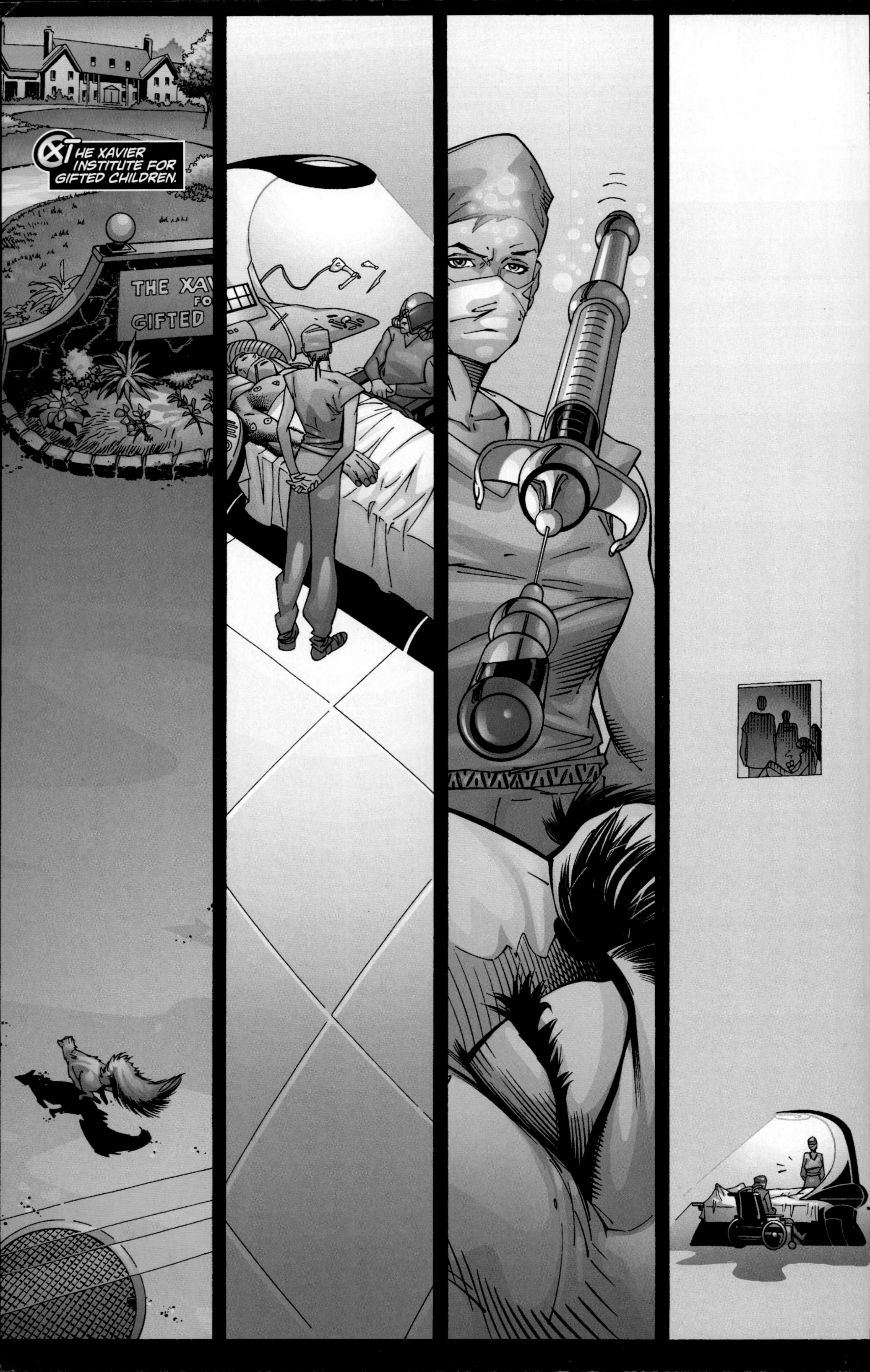
THE XAVIER INSTITUTE FOR GIFTED CHILDREN.
THE XAV
FO
GIFTED

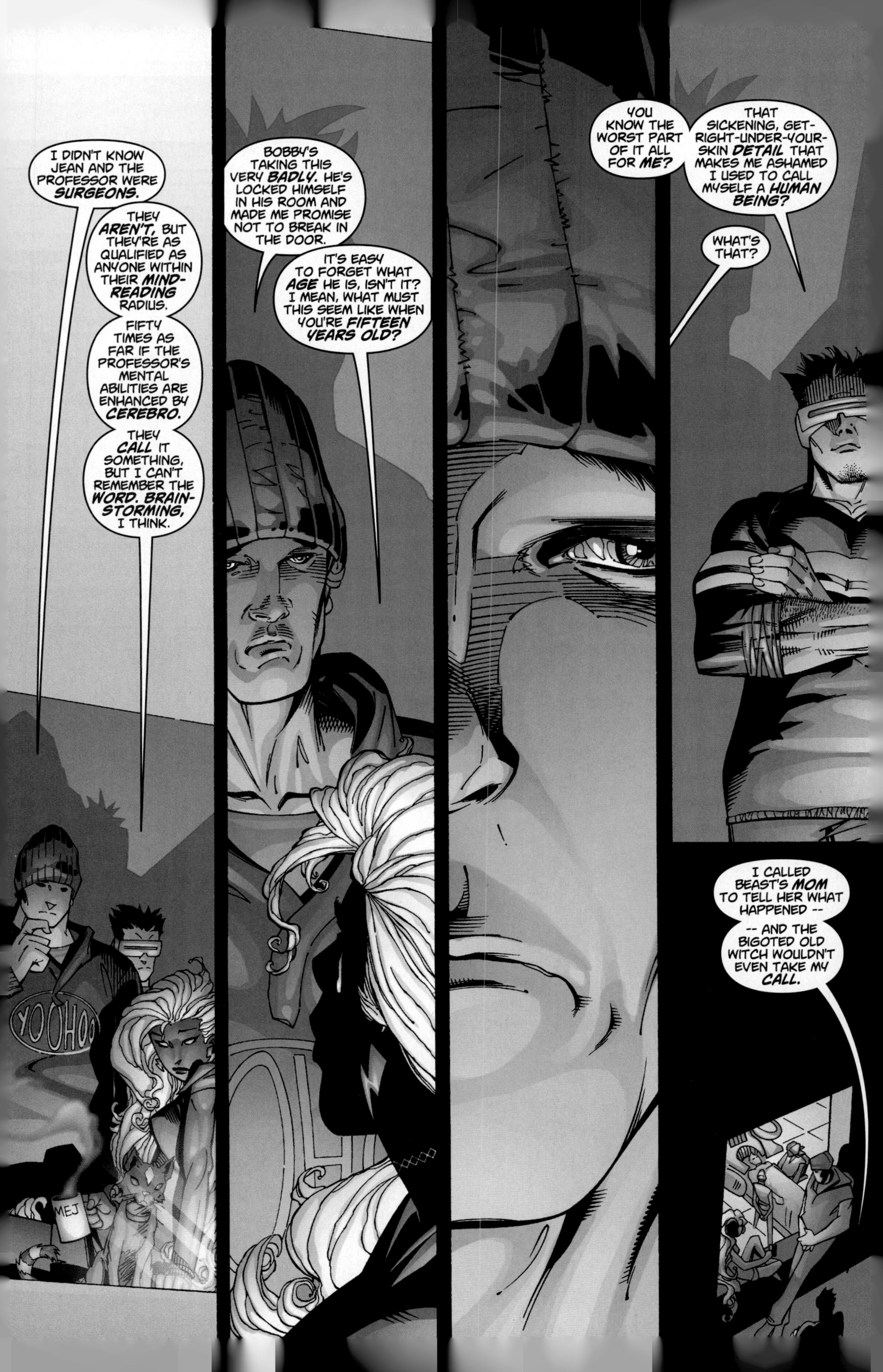
I DIDN'T KNOW JEAN AND THE PROFESSOR WERE SURGEONS.
THEY AREN'T, BUT THEY'RE AS QUALIFIED AS ANYONE WITHIN THEIR MIND-READING RADIUS.
FIFTY TIMES AS FAR IF THE PROFESSOR'S MENTAL ABILITIES ARE ENHANCED BY CEREBRO.
THEY CALL IT SOMETHING, BUT I CAN'T REMEMBER THE WORD. BRAIN-STORMING, I THINK.
YOOHOO
MEJ
BOBBY'S TAKING THIS VERY BADLY. HE'S LOCKED HIMSELF IN HIS ROOM AND MADE ME PROMISE NOT TO BREAK IN THE DOOR.
IT'S EASY TO FORGET WHAT AGE HE IS, ISN'T IT? I MEAN, WHAT MUST THIS SEEM LIKE WHEN YOU'RE FIFTEEN YEARS OLD?
YOU KNOW THE WORST PART OF IT ALL FOR ME?
WHAT'S THAT?
THAT SICKENING, GET-RIGHT-UNDER-YOUR-SKIN DETAIL THAT MAKES ME ASHAMED I USED TO CALL MYSELF A HUMAN BEING?
I CALLED BEAST'S MOM TO TELL HER WHAT HAPPENED --
-- AND THE BIGOTED OLD WITCH WOULDN'T EVEN TAKE MY CALL.

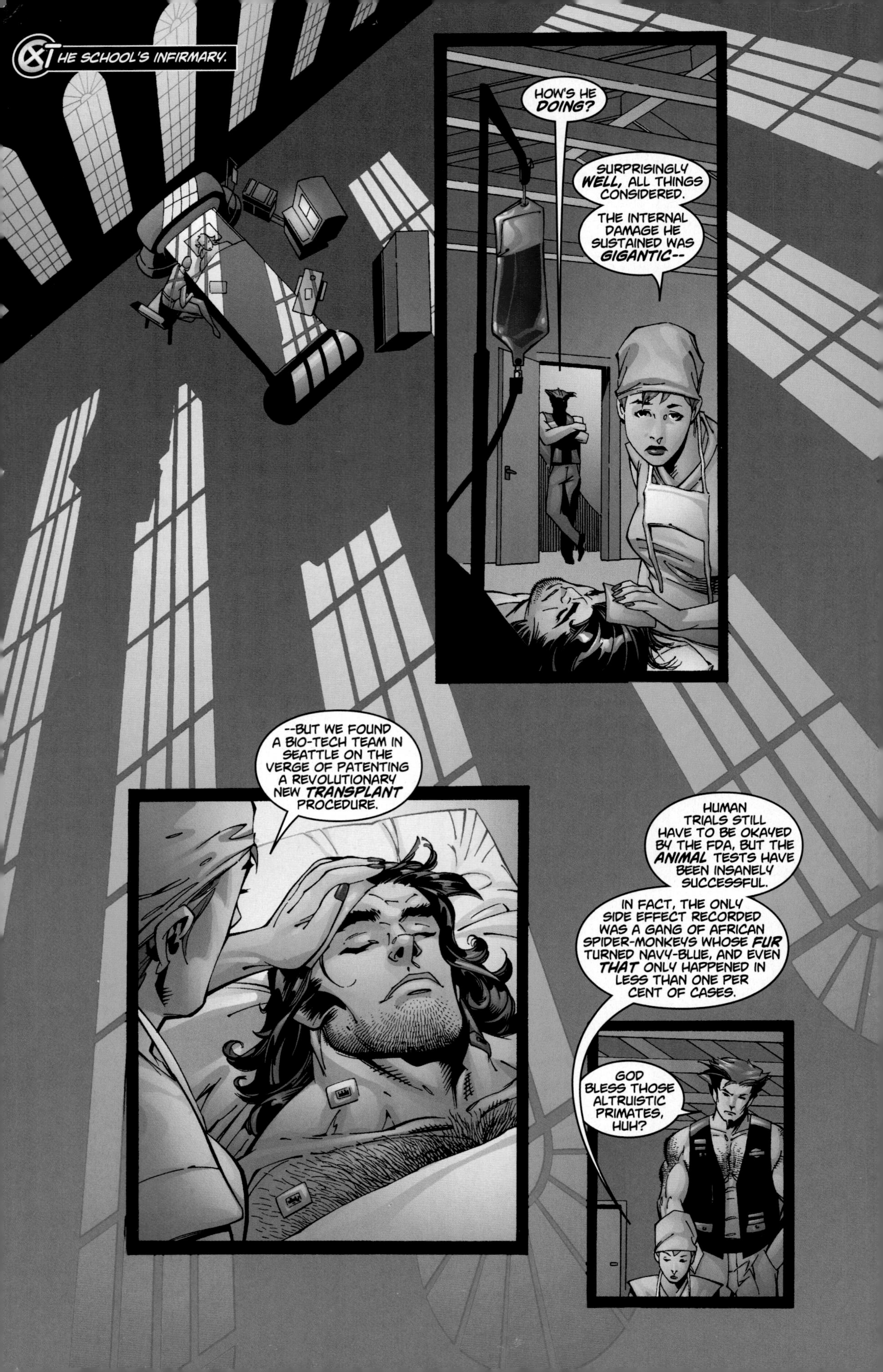
THE SCHOOL'S INFIRMARY.
HOW'S HE DOING?
SURPRISINGLY WELL, ALL THINGS CONSIDERED.
THE INTERNAL DAMAGE HE SUSTAINED WAS GIGANTIC--
--BUT WE FOUND A BIO-TECH TEAM IN SEATTLE ON THE VERGE OF PATENTING A REVOLUTIONARY NEW TRANSPLANT PROCEDURE.
HUMAN TRIALS STILL HAVE TO BE OKAYED BY THE FDA, BUT THE ANIMAL TESTS HAVE BEEN INSANELY SUCCESSFUL.
IN FACT, THE ONLY SIDE EFFECT RECORDED WAS A GANG OF AFRICAN SPIDER-MONKEYS WHOSE FUR TURNED NAVY-BLUE, AND EVEN THAT ONLY HAPPENED IN LESS THAN ONE PER CENT OF CASES.
GOD BLESS THOSE ALTRUISTIC PRIMATES, HUH?

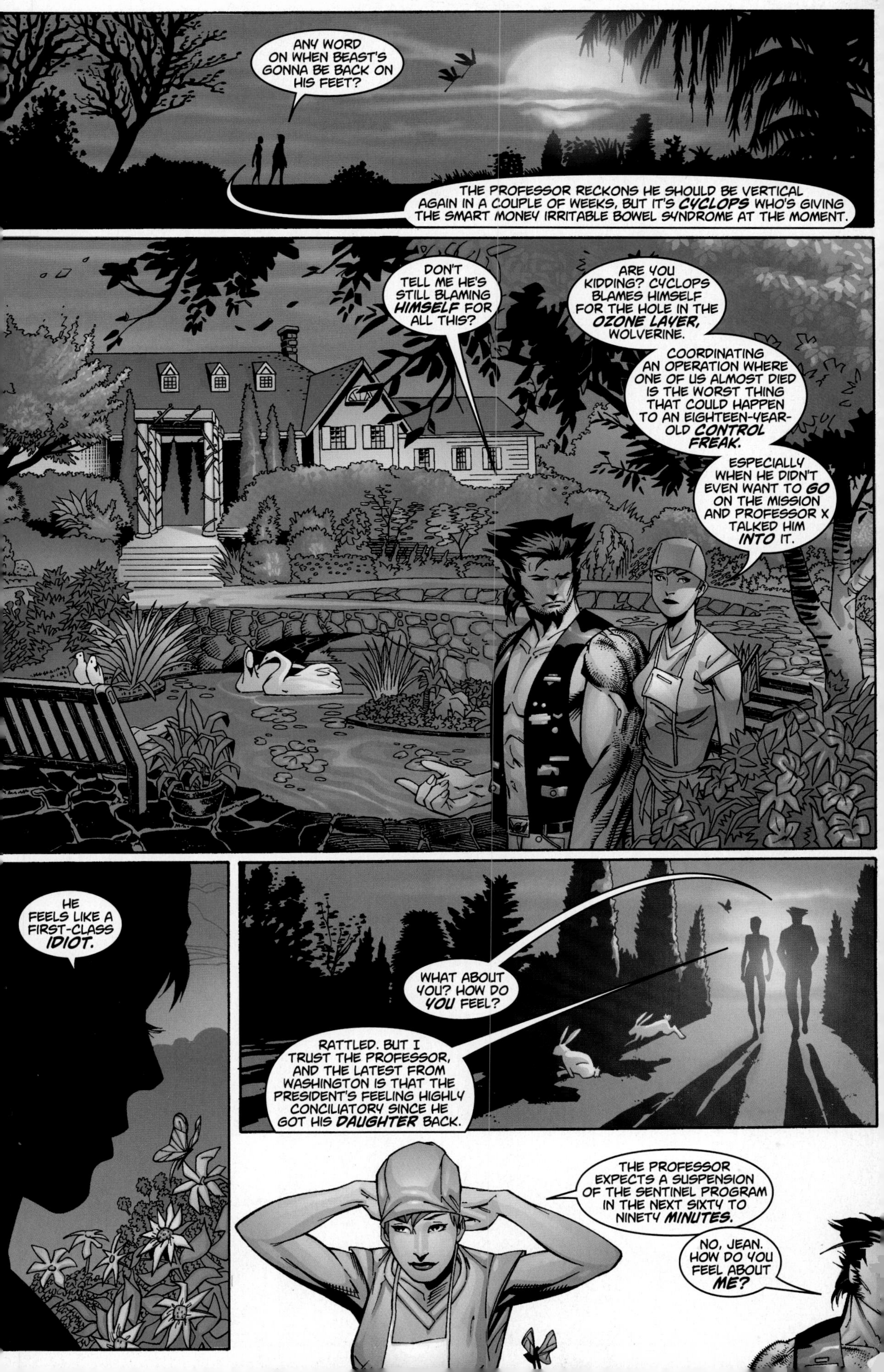
ANY WORD ON WHEN BEAST'S GONNA BE BACK ON HIS FEET?
THE PROFESSOR RECKONS HE SHOULD BE VERTICAL AGAIN IN A COUPLE OF WEEKS, BUT IT'S CYCLOPS WHO'S GIVING THE SMART MONEY IRRITABLE BOWEL SYNDROME AT THE MOMENT.
DON'T TELL ME HE'S STILL BLAMING HIMSELF FOR ALL THIS?
ARE YOU KIDDING? CYCLOPS BLAMES HIMSELF FOR THE HOLE IN THE OZONE LAYER, WOLVERINE.
COORDINATING AN OPERATION WHERE ONE OF US ALMOST DIED IS THE WORST THING THAT COULD HAPPEN TO AN EIGHTEEN-YEAR-OLD CONTROL FREAK.
ESPECIALLY WHEN HE DIDN'T EVEN WANT TO GO ON THE MISSION AND PROFESSOR X TALKED HIM INTO IT.
HE FEELS LIKE A FIRST-CLASS IDIOT.
WHAT ABOUT YOU? HOW DO YOU FEEL?
RATTLED. BUT I TRUST THE PROFESSOR, AND THE LATEST FROM WASHINGTON IS THAT THE PRESIDENT'S FEELING HIGHLY CONCILIATORY SINCE HE GOT HIS DAUGHTER BACK.
THE PROFESSOR EXPECTS A SUSPENSION OF THE SENTINEL PROGRAM IN THE NEXT SIXTY TO NINETY MINUTES.
NO, JEAN. HOW DO YOU FEEL ABOUT ME?

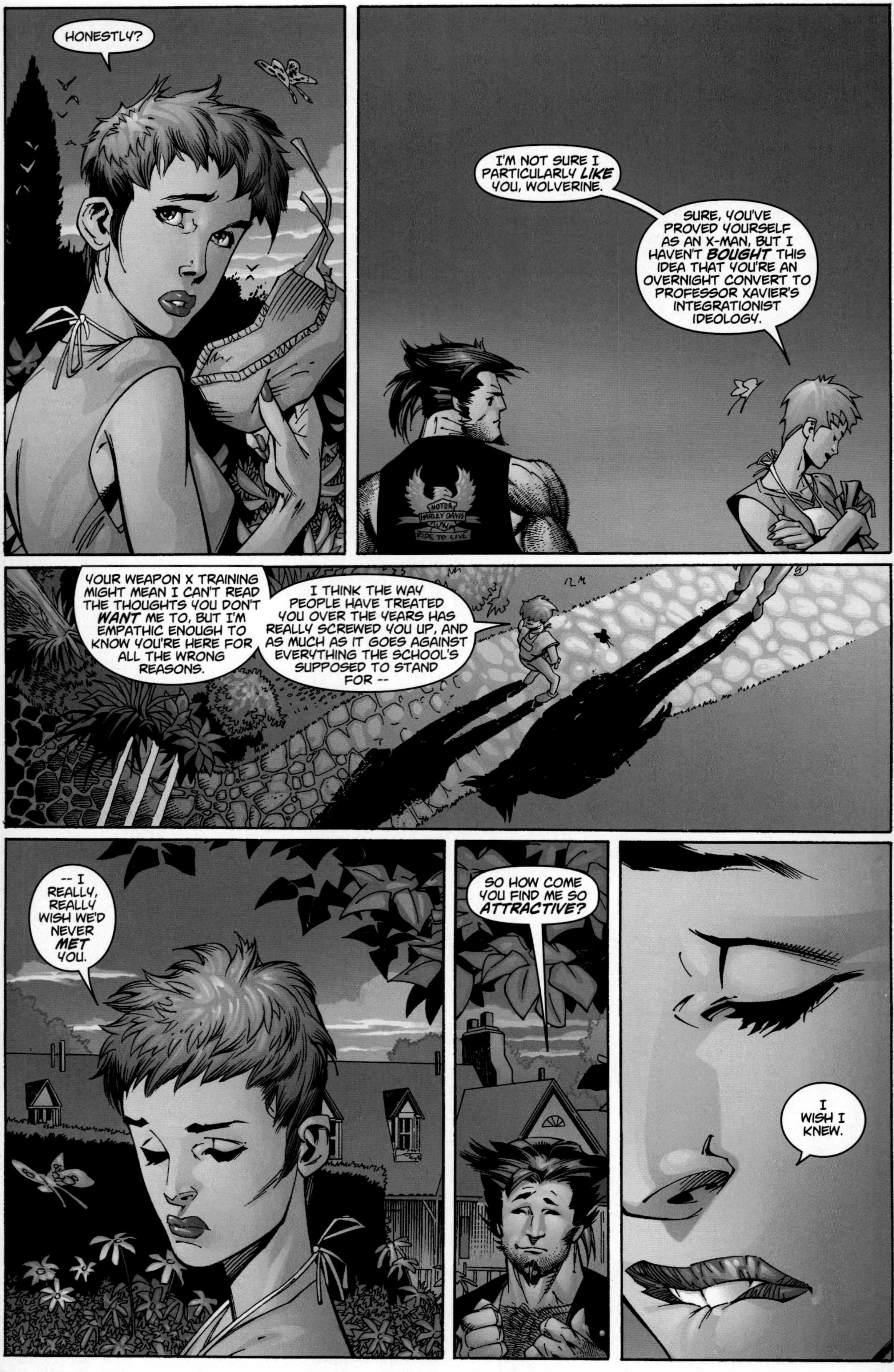
HONESTLY?
I'M NOT SURE I PARTICULARLY LIKE YOU, WOLVERINE.
SURE, YOU'VE PROVED YOURSELF AS AN X-MAN, BUT I HAVEN'T BOUGHT THIS IDEA THAT YOU'RE AN OVERNIGHT CONVERT TO PROFESSOR XAVIER'S INTEGRATIONIST IDEOLOGY.
HARLEY DAVIS
RIDE TO LIVE
YOUR WEAPON X TRAINING MIGHT MEAN I CAN'T READ THE THOUGHTS YOU DON'T WANT ME TO, BUT I'M EMPATHIC ENOUGH TO KNOW YOU'RE HERE FOR ALL THE WRONG REASONS.
I THINK THE WAY PEOPLE HAVE TREATED YOU OVER THE YEARS HAS REALLY SCREWED YOU UP, AND AS MUCH AS IT GOES AGAINST EVERYTHING THE SCHOOL'S SUPPOSED TO STAND FOR --
-- I REALLY, REALLY WISH WE'D NEVER MET YOU.
SO HOW COME YOU FIND ME SO ATTRACTIVE?
I WISH I KNEW.

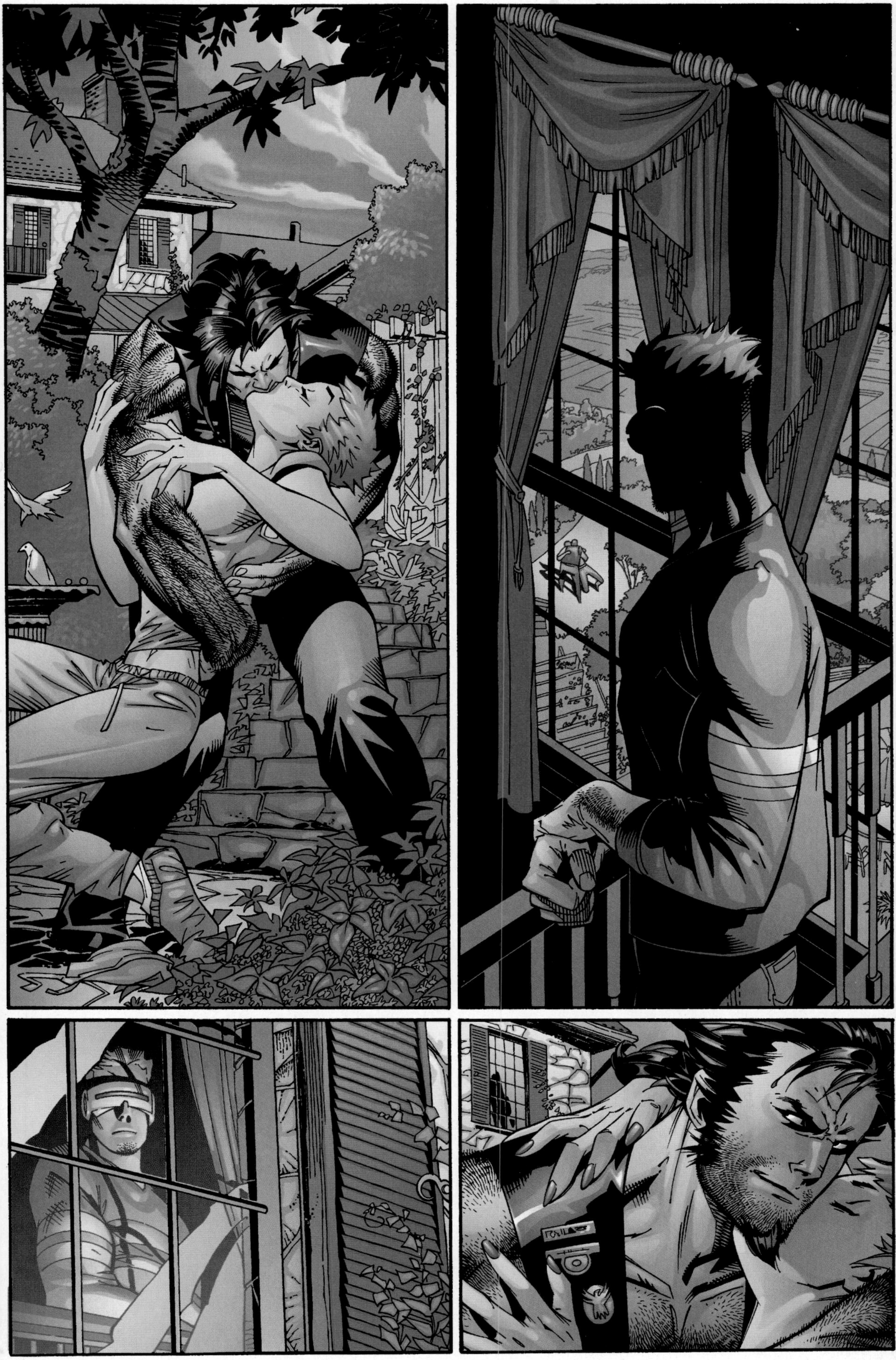

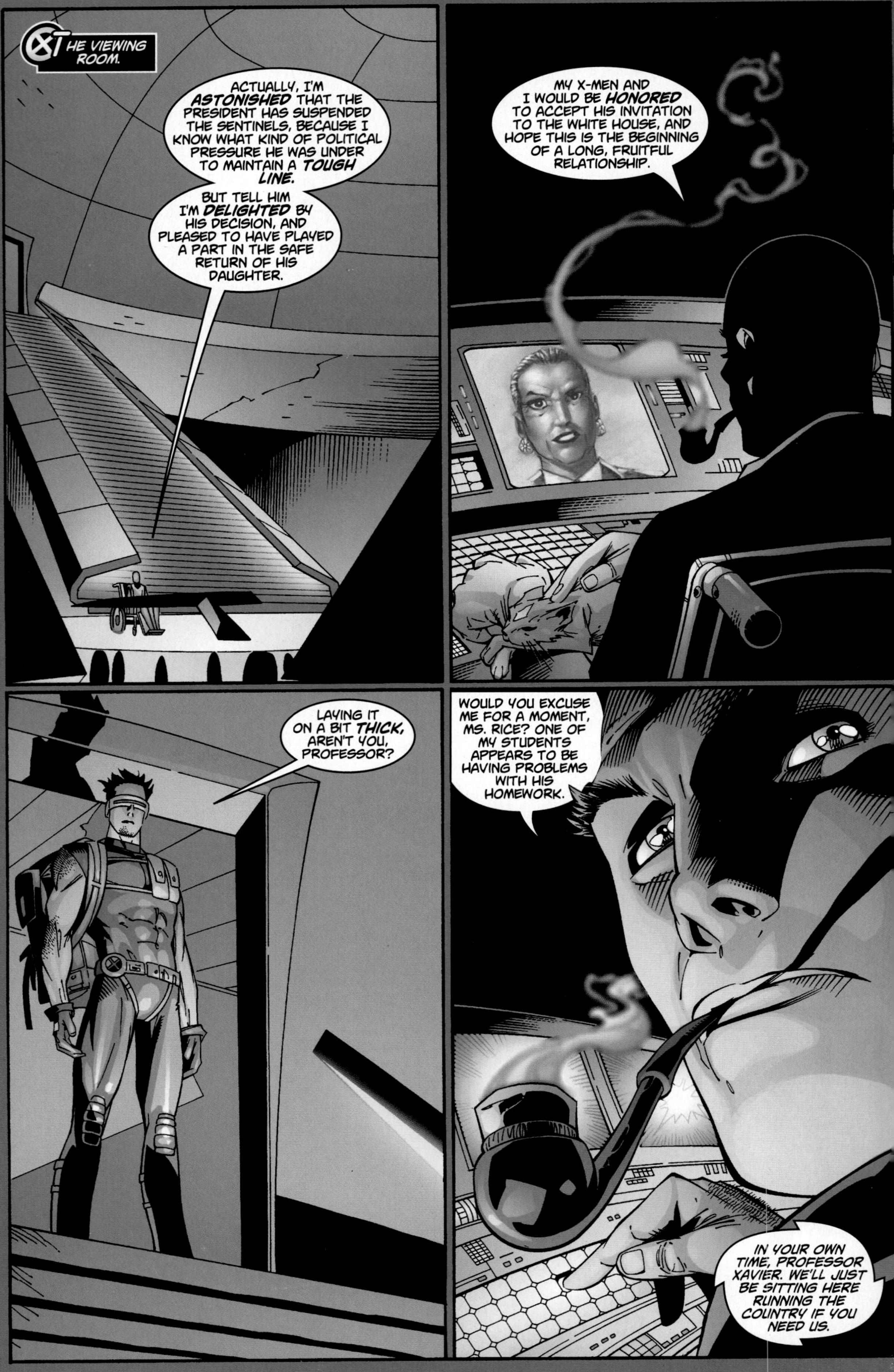
THE VIEWING ROOM.
ACTUALLY, I'M ASTONISHED THAT THE PRESIDENT HAS SUSPENDED THE SENTINELS, BECAUSE I KNOW WHAT KIND OF POLITICAL PRESSURE HE WAS UNDER TO MAINTAIN A TOUGH LINE.
BUT TELL HIM I'M DELIGHTED BY HIS DECISION, AND PLEASED TO HAVE PLAYED A PART IN THE SAFE RETURN OF HIS DAUGHTER.
MY X-MEN AND I WOULD BE HONORED TO ACCEPT HIS INVITATION TO THE WHITE HOUSE, AND HOPE THIS IS THE BEGINNING OF A LONG, FRUITFUL RELATIONSHIP.
LAYING IT ON A BIT THICK, AREN'T YOU, PROFESSOR?
WOULD YOU EXCUSE ME FOR A MOMENT, MS. RICE? ONE OF MY STUDENTS APPEARS TO BE HAVING PROBLEMS WITH HIS HOMEWORK.
IN YOUR OWN TIME, PROFESSOR XAVIER. WE'LL JUST BE SITTING HERE RUNNING THE COUNTRY IF YOU NEED US.

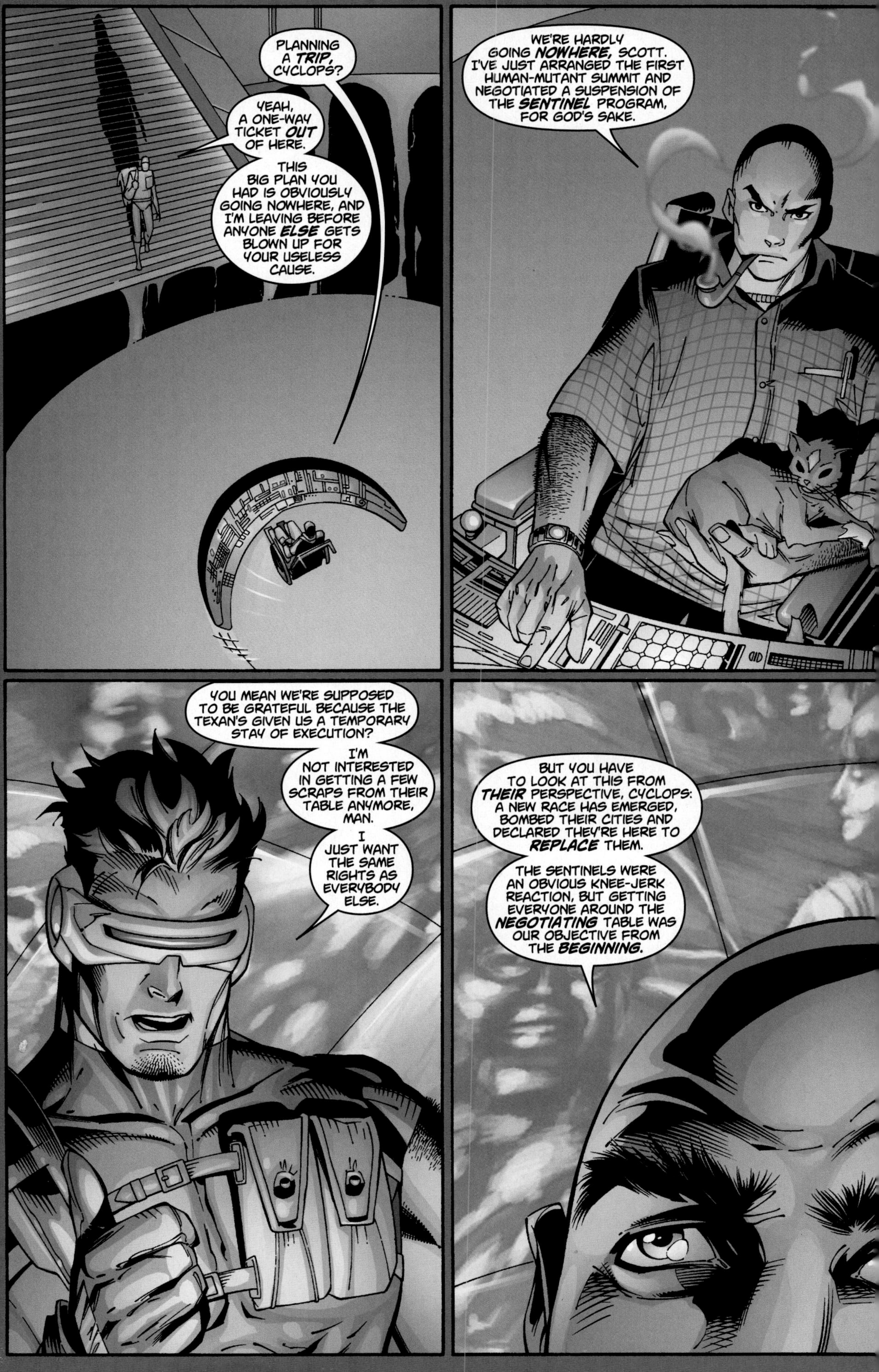
PLANNING A *TRIP,* CYCLOPS?
YEAH, A ONE-WAY TICKET *OUT* OF HERE.
THIS BIG PLAN YOU HAD IS OBVIOUSLY GOING NOWHERE, AND I'M LEAVING BEFORE ANYONE *ELSE* GETS BLOWN UP FOR YOUR USELESS CAUSE.
WE'RE HARDLY GOING *NOWHERE,* SCOTT. I'VE JUST ARRANGED THE FIRST HUMAN-MUTANT SUMMIT AND NEGOTIATED A SUSPENSION OF THE *SENTINEL* PROGRAM, FOR GOD'S SAKE.
YOU MEAN WE'RE SUPPOSED TO BE GRATEFUL BECAUSE THE TEXAN'S GIVEN US A TEMPORARY STAY OF EXECUTION?
I'M NOT INTERESTED IN GETTING A FEW SCRAPS FROM THEIR TABLE ANYMORE, MAN.
I JUST WANT THE SAME RIGHTS AS EVERYBODY ELSE.
BUT YOU HAVE TO LOOK AT THIS FROM *THEIR* PERSPECTIVE, CYCLOPS: A NEW RACE HAS EMERGED, BOMBED THEIR CITIES AND DECLARED THEY'RE HERE TO *REPLACE* THEM.
THE SENTINELS WERE AN OBVIOUS KNEE-JERK REACTION, BUT GETTING EVERYONE AROUND THE *NEGOTIATING* TABLE WAS OUR OBJECTIVE FROM THE *BEGINNING.*

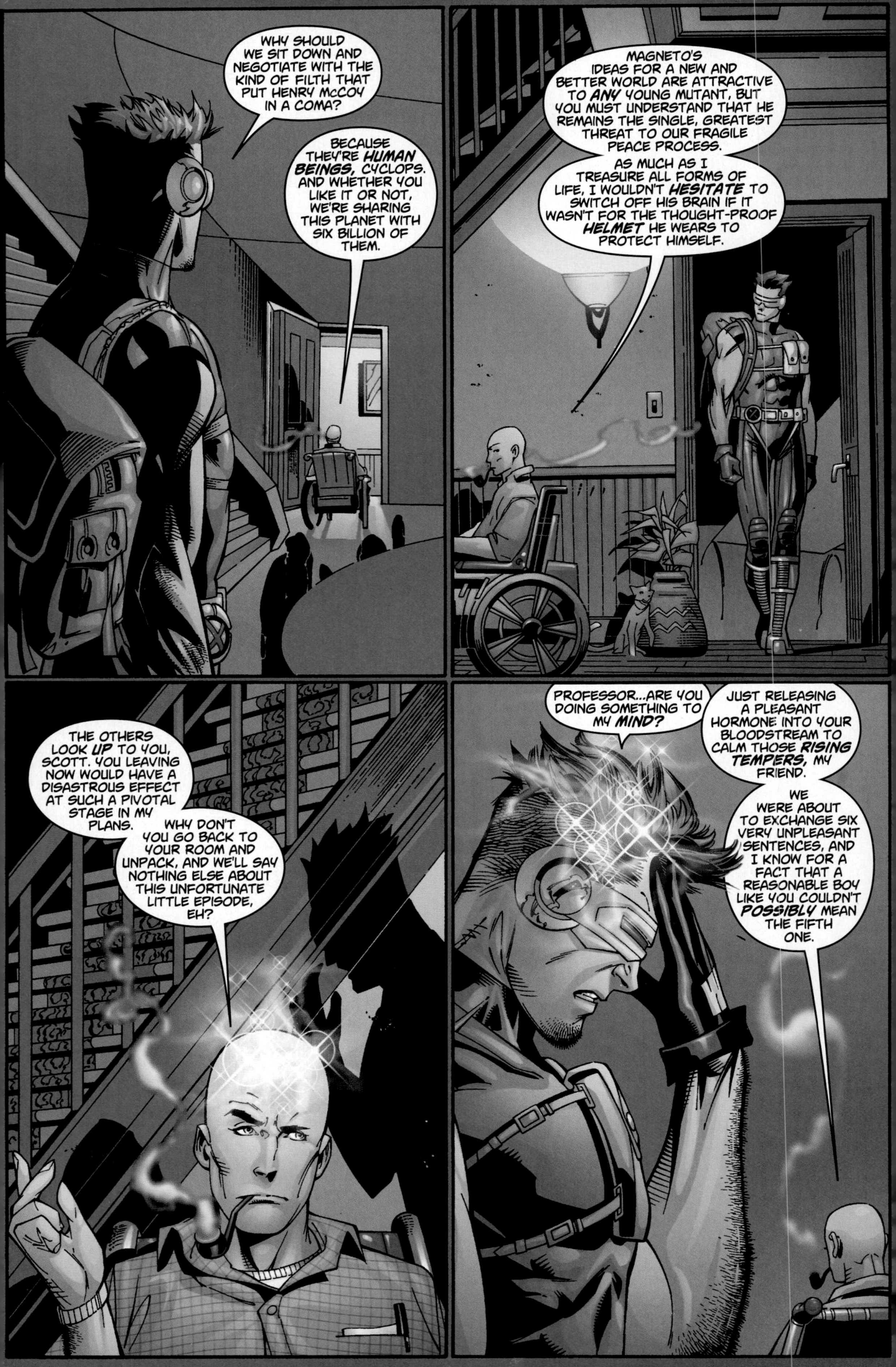
WHY SHOULD WE SIT DOWN AND NEGOTIATE WITH THE KIND OF FILTH THAT PUT HENRY McCOY IN A COMA?
BECAUSE THEY'RE HUMAN BEINGS, CYCLOPS. AND WHETHER YOU LIKE IT OR NOT, WE'RE SHARING THIS PLANET WITH SIX BILLION OF THEM.
MAGNETO'S IDEAS FOR A NEW AND BETTER WORLD ARE ATTRACTIVE TO ANY YOUNG MUTANT, BUT YOU MUST UNDERSTAND THAT HE REMAINS THE SINGLE, GREATEST THREAT TO OUR FRAGILE PEACE PROCESS.
AS MUCH AS I TREASURE ALL FORMS OF LIFE, I WOULDN'T HESITATE TO SWITCH OFF HIS BRAIN IF IT WASN'T FOR THE THOUGHT-PROOF HELMET HE WEARS TO PROTECT HIMSELF.
THE OTHERS LOOK UP TO YOU, SCOTT. YOU LEAVING NOW WOULD HAVE A DISASTROUS EFFECT AT SUCH A PIVOTAL STAGE IN MY PLANS.
WHY DON'T YOU GO BACK TO YOUR ROOM AND UNPACK, AND WE'LL SAY NOTHING ELSE ABOUT THIS UNFORTUNATE LITTLE EPISODE, EH?
PROFESSOR...ARE YOU DOING SOMETHING TO MY MIND?
JUST RELEASING A PLEASANT HORMONE INTO YOUR BLOODSTREAM TO CALM THOSE RISING TEMPERS, MY FRIEND.
WE WERE ABOUT TO EXCHANGE SIX VERY UNPLEASANT SENTENCES, AND I KNOW FOR A FACT THAT A REASONABLE BOY LIKE YOU COULDN'T POSSIBLY MEAN THE FIFTH ONE.

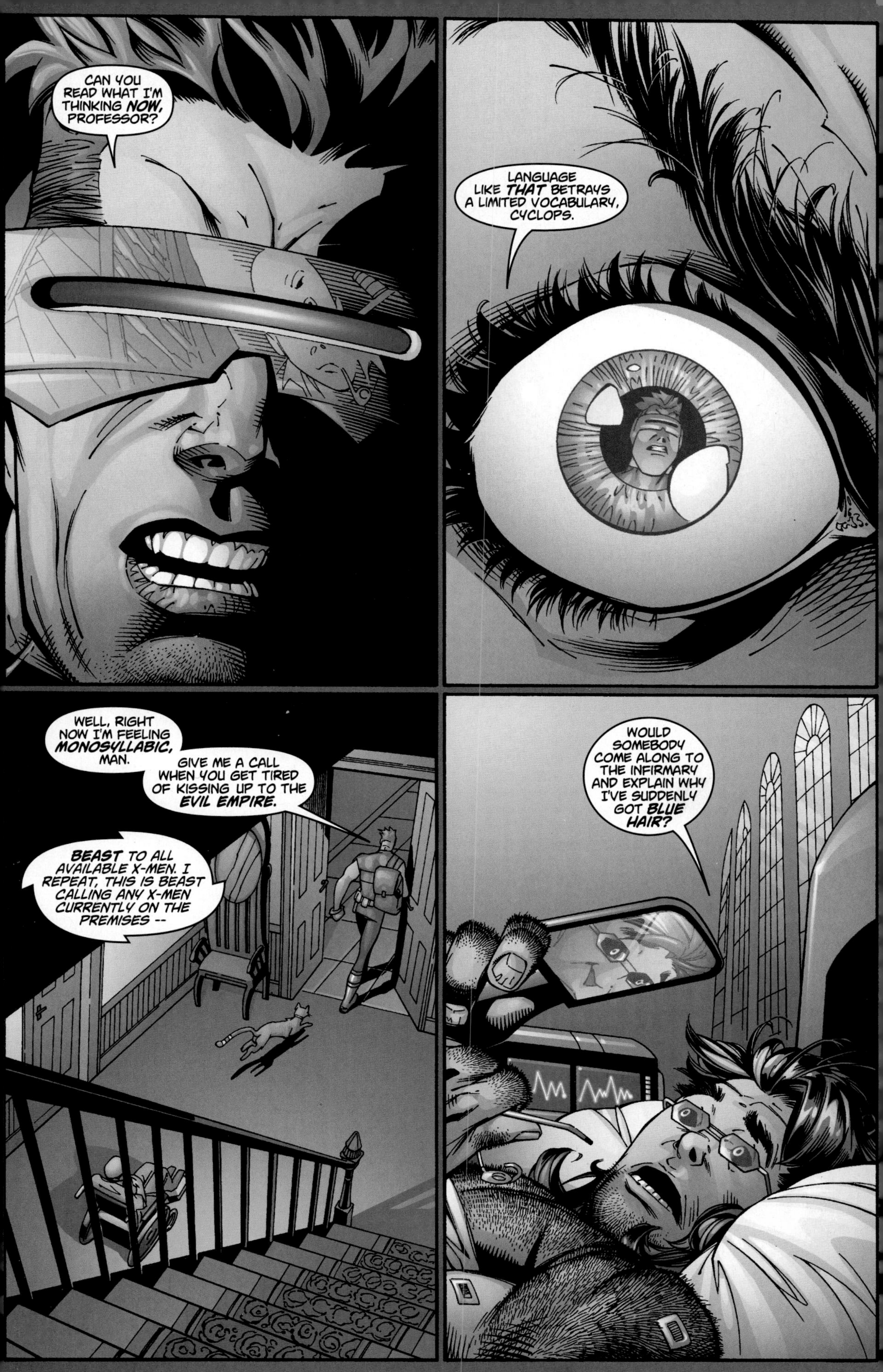
CAN YOU READ WHAT I'M THINKING *NOW*, PROFESSOR?
LANGUAGE LIKE *THAT* BETRAYS A LIMITED VOCABULARY, CYCLOPS.
WELL, RIGHT NOW I'M FEELING *MONOSYLLABIC*, MAN.
GIVE ME A CALL WHEN YOU GET TIRED OF KISSING UP TO THE *EVIL EMPIRE*.
BEAST TO ALL AVAILABLE X-MEN. I REPEAT, THIS IS BEAST CALLING ANY X-MEN CURRENTLY ON THE PREMISES --
WOULD SOMEBODY COME ALONG TO THE INFIRMARY AND EXPLAIN WHY I'VE SUDDENLY GOT *BLUE HAIR*?

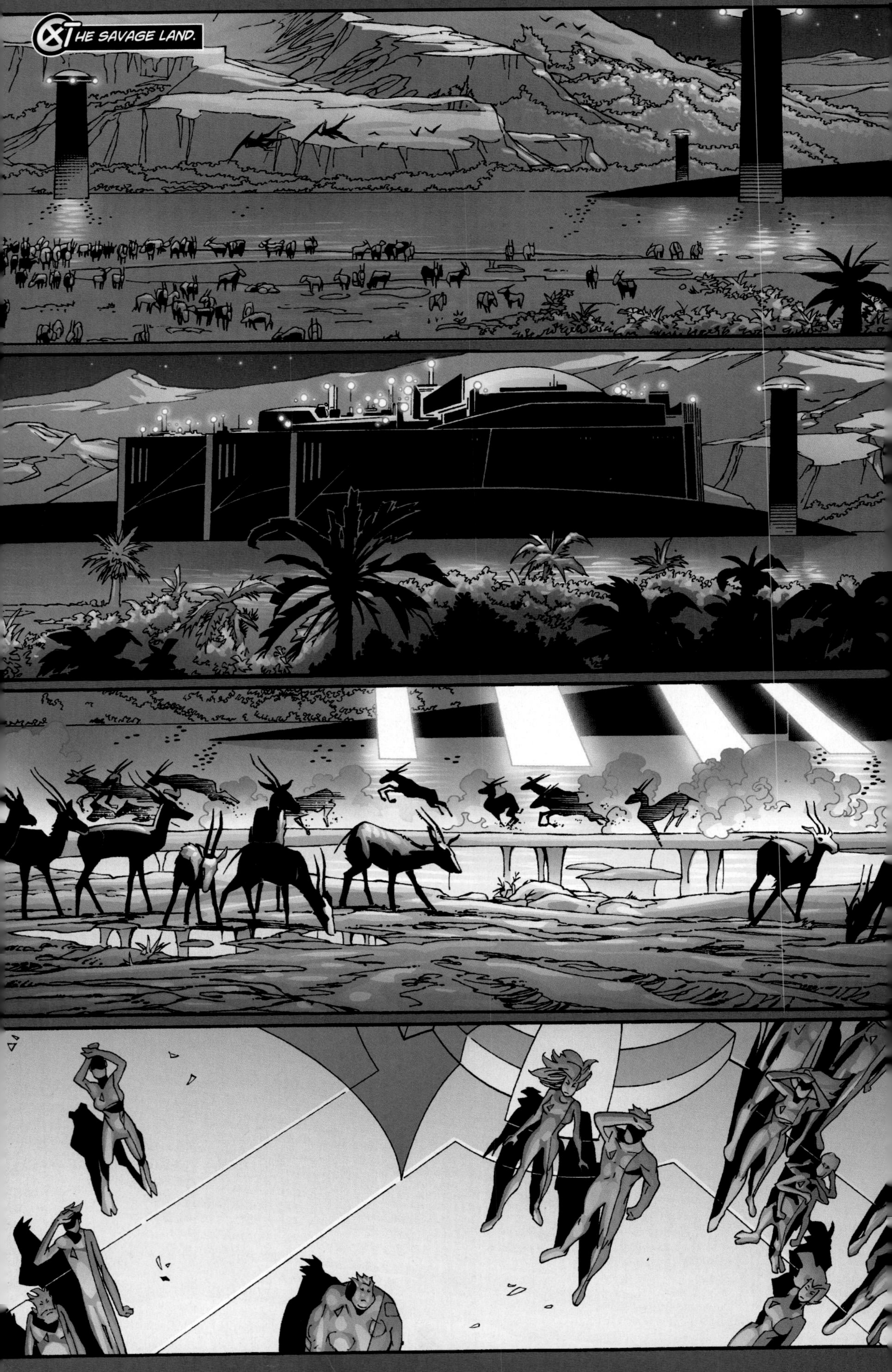
THE SAVAGE LAND.

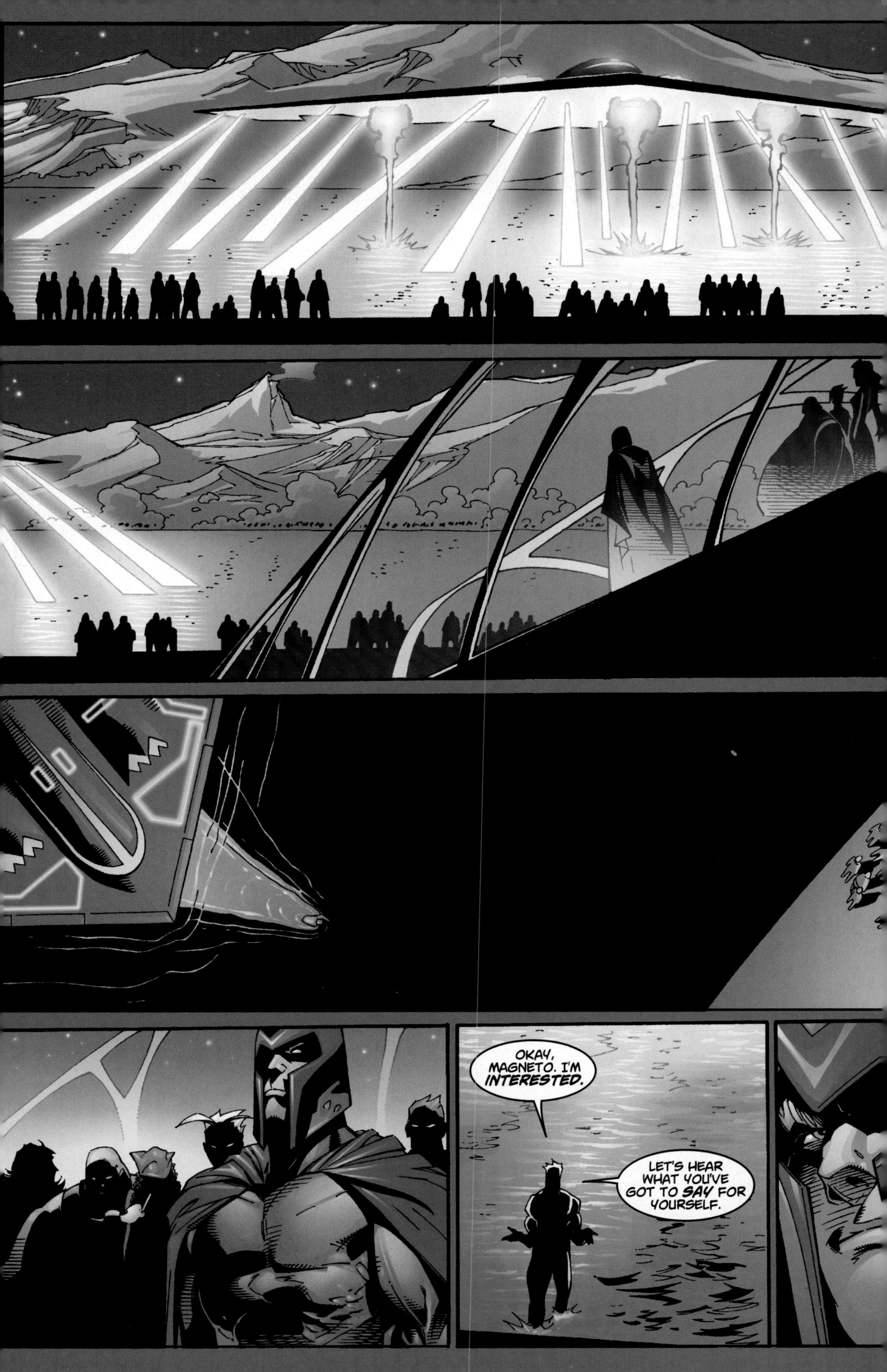
OKAY, MAGNETO. I'M *INTERESTED.*
LET'S HEAR WHAT YOU'VE GOT TO *SAY* FOR YOURSELF.

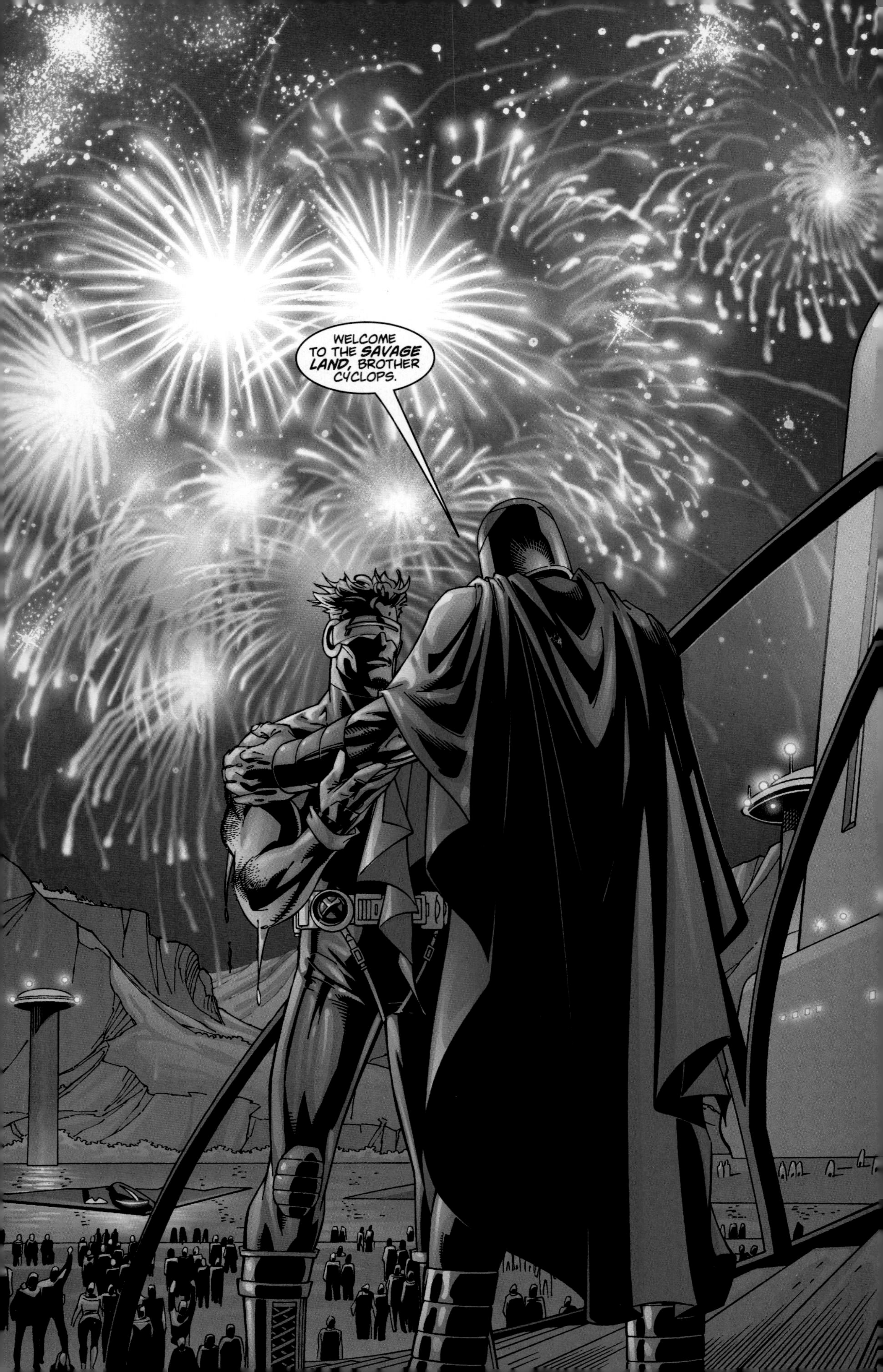
WELCOME TO THE SAVAGE LAND, BROTHER CYCLOPS.

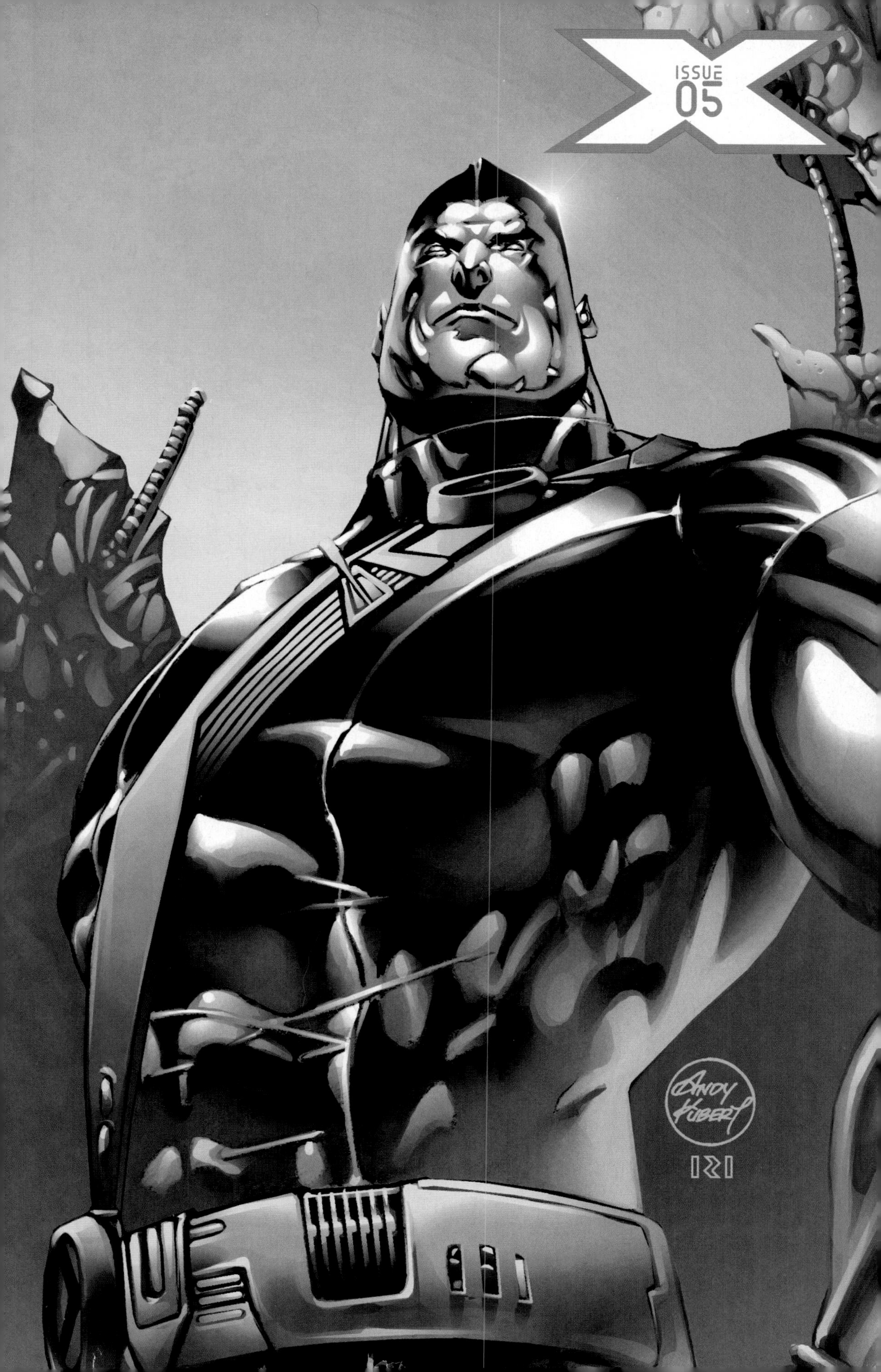
ISSUE
05
ANDY KUBERT

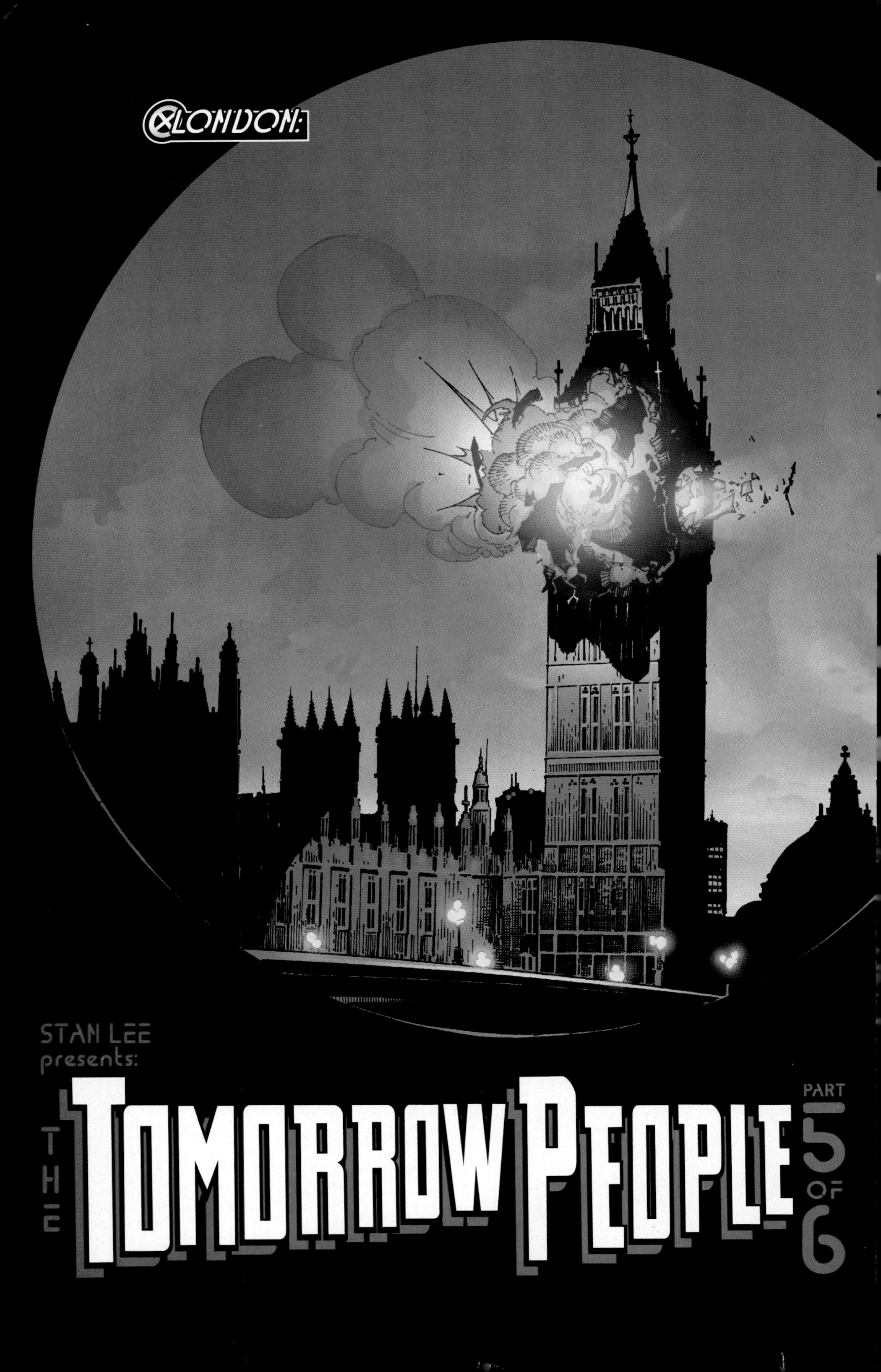
LONDON:
STAN LEE
presents:
THE TOMORROW PEOPLE
PART 5 OF 6

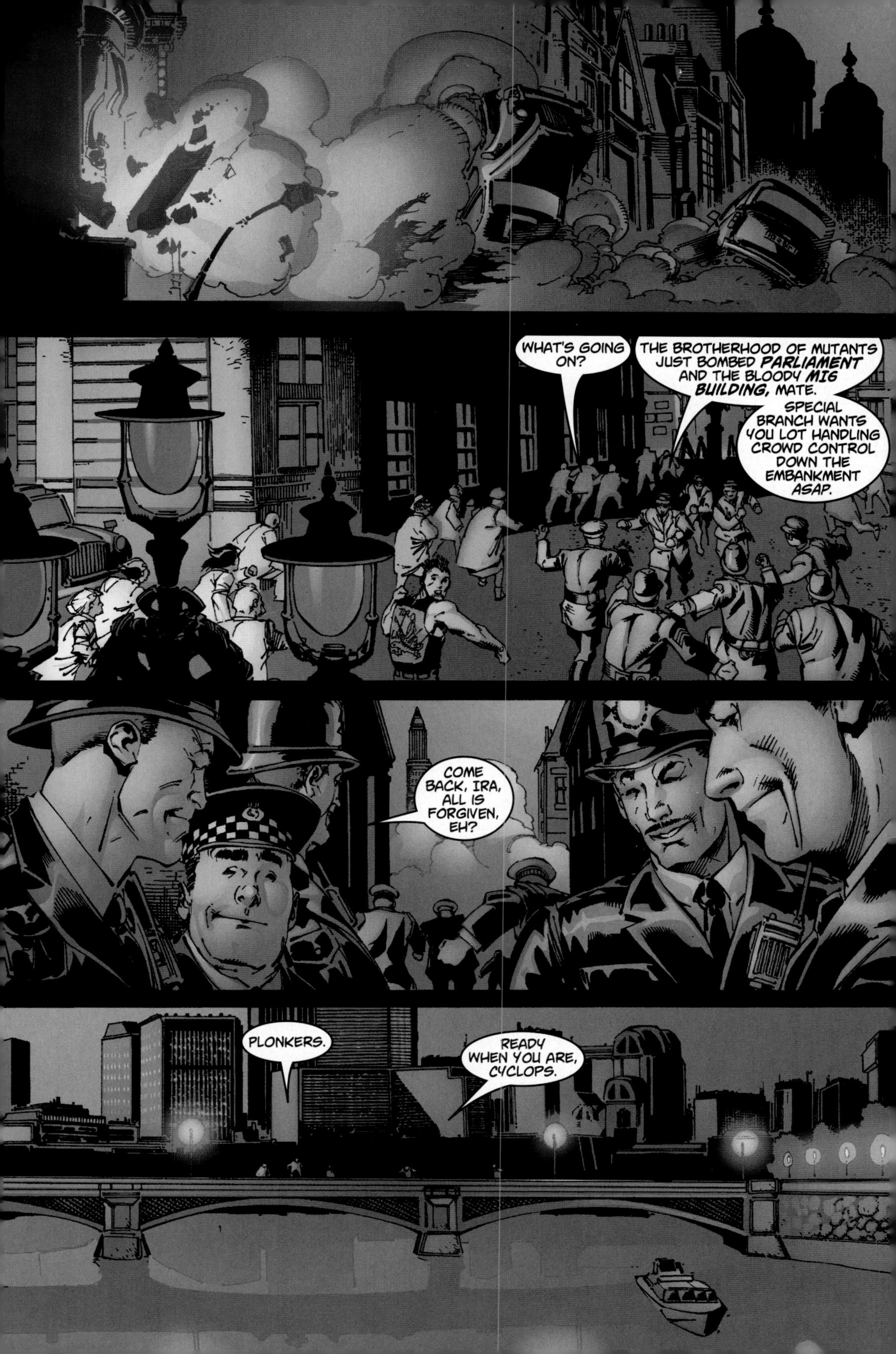
WHAT'S GOING ON?
THE BROTHERHOOD OF MUTANTS JUST BOMBED PARLIAMENT AND THE BLOODY MI6 BUILDING, MATE.
SPECIAL BRANCH WANTS YOU LOT HANDLING CROWD CONTROL DOWN THE EMBANKMENT ASAP.
COME BACK, IRA, ALL IS FORGIVEN, EH?
PLONKERS.
READY WHEN YOU ARE, CYCLOPS.

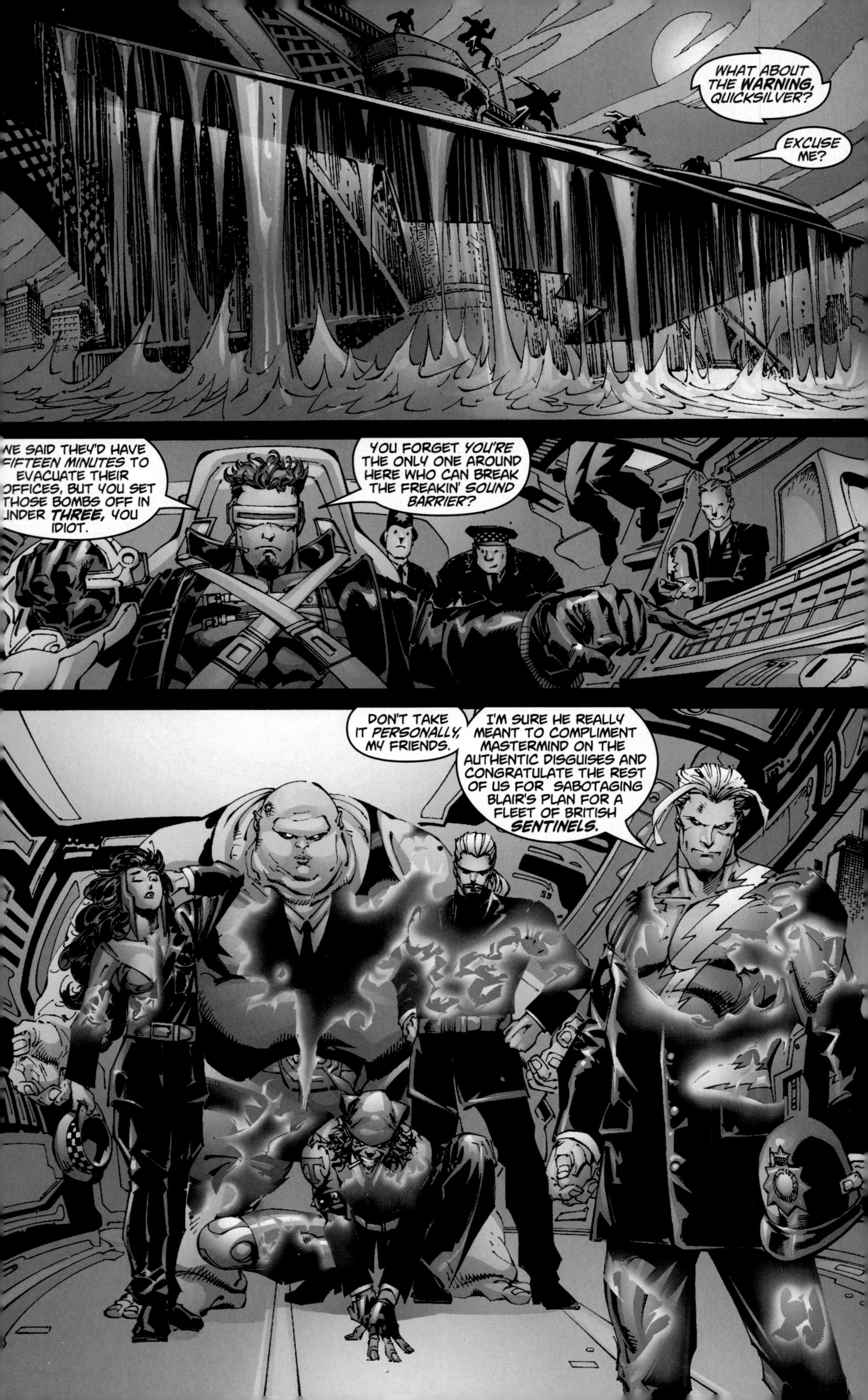
WHAT ABOUT THE WARNING, QUICKSILVER?
EXCUSE ME?
WE SAID THEY'D HAVE FIFTEEN MINUTES TO EVACUATE THEIR OFFICES, BUT YOU SET THOSE BOMBS OFF IN UNDER THREE, YOU IDIOT.
YOU FORGET YOU'RE THE ONLY ONE AROUND HERE WHO CAN BREAK THE FREAKIN' SOUND BARRIER?
DON'T TAKE IT PERSONALLY, MY FRIENDS.
I'M SURE HE REALLY MEANT TO COMPLIMENT MASTERMIND ON THE AUTHENTIC DISGUISES AND CONGRATULATE THE REST OF US FOR SABOTAGING BLAIR'S PLAN FOR A FLEET OF BRITISH SENTINELS.

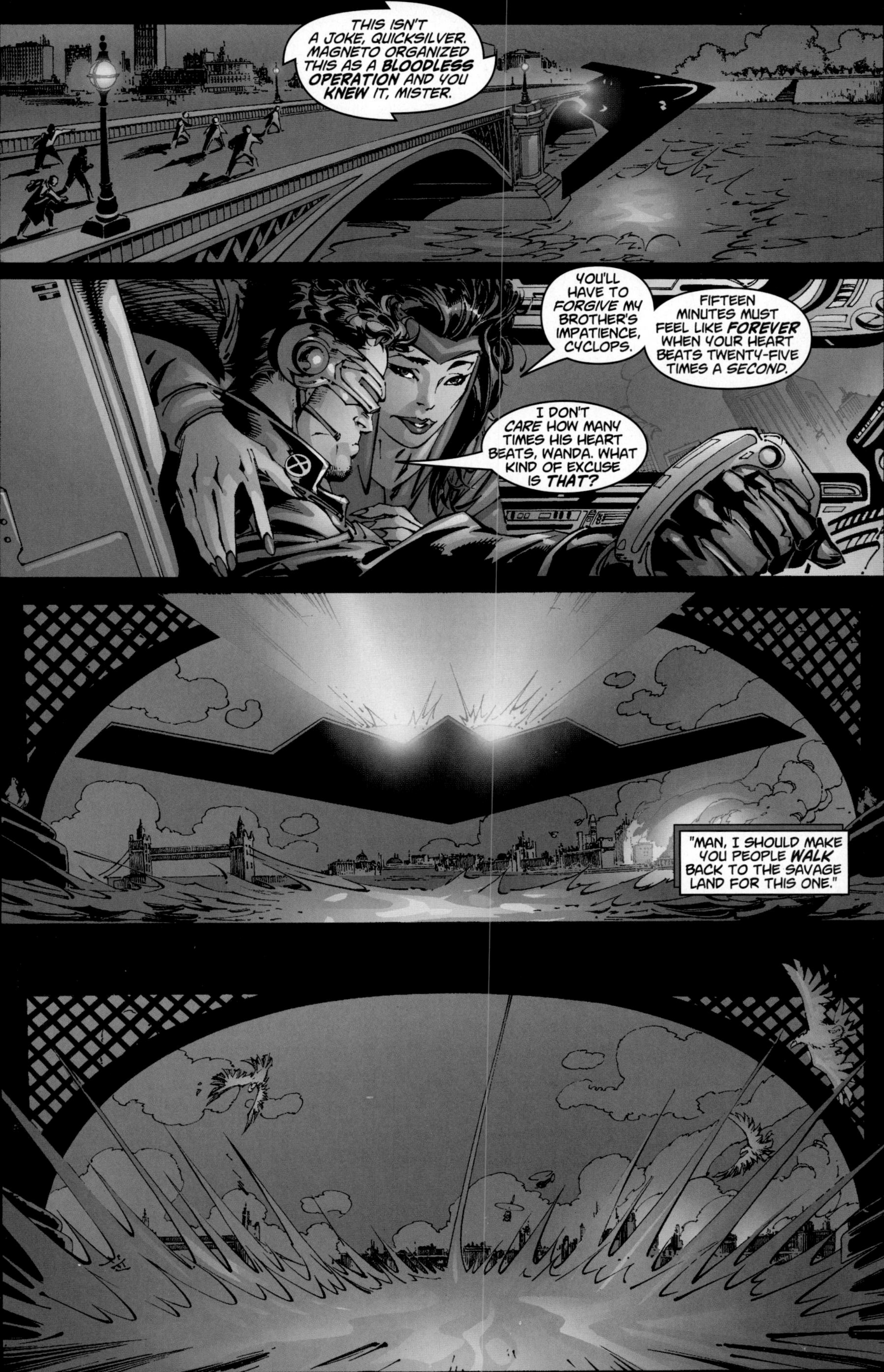

THIS ISN'T A JOKE, QUICKSILVER. MAGNETO ORGANIZED THIS AS A BLOODLESS OPERATION AND YOU KNEW IT, MISTER.
YOU'LL HAVE TO FORGIVE MY BROTHER'S IMPATIENCE, CYCLOPS.
FIFTEEN MINUTES MUST FEEL LIKE FOREVER WHEN YOUR HEART BEATS TWENTY-FIVE TIMES A SECOND.
I DON'T CARE HOW MANY TIMES HIS HEART BEATS, WANDA. WHAT KIND OF EXCUSE IS THAT?
"MAN, I SHOULD MAKE YOU PEOPLE WALK BACK TO THE SAVAGE LAND FOR THIS ONE."

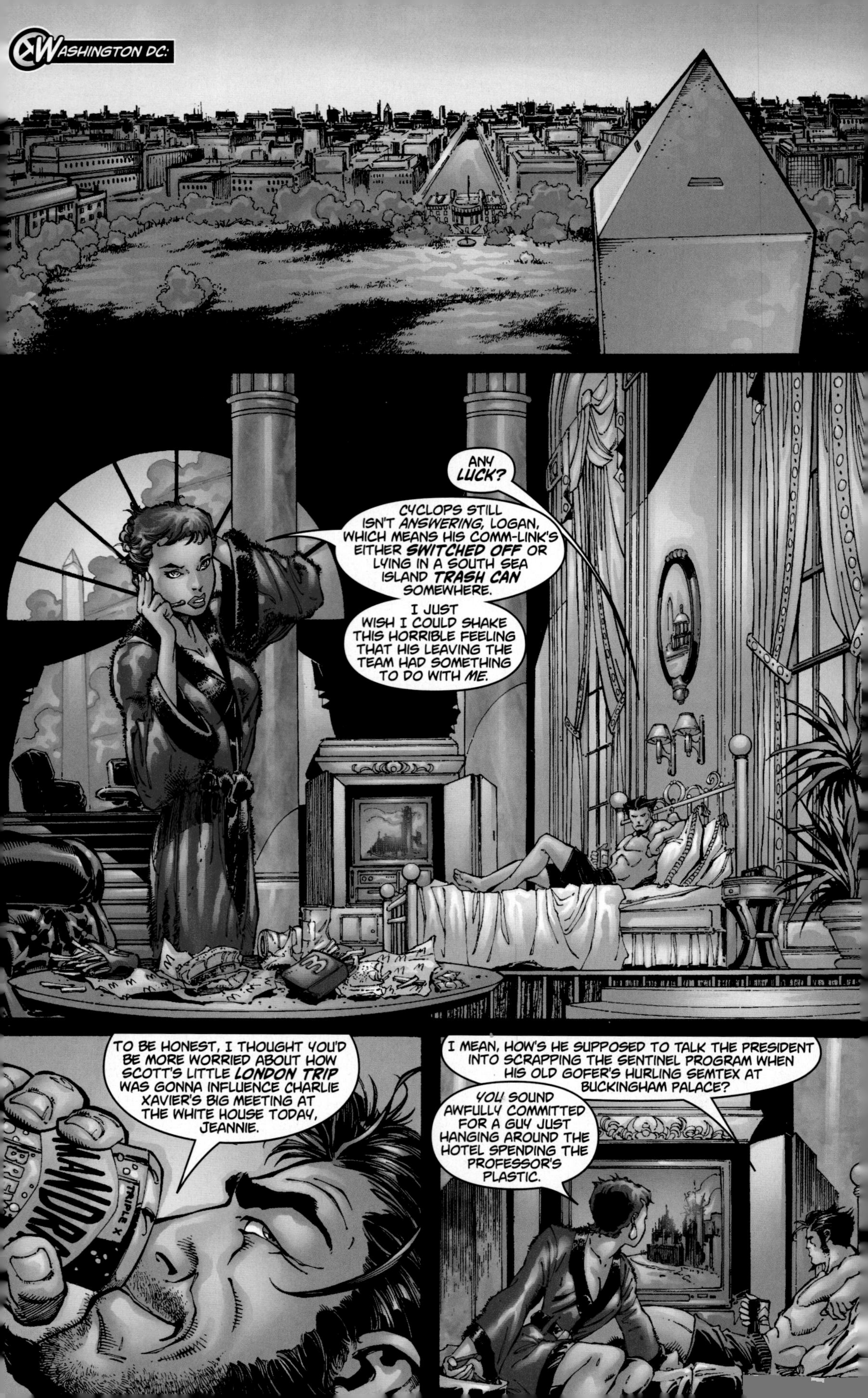
WASHINGTON DC:
ANY LUCK?
CYCLOPS STILL ISN'T ANSWERING, LOGAN, WHICH MEANS HIS COMM-LINK'S EITHER SWITCHED OFF OR LYING IN A SOUTH SEA ISLAND TRASH CAN SOMEWHERE.
I JUST WISH I COULD SHAKE THIS HORRIBLE FEELING THAT HIS LEAVING THE TEAM HAD SOMETHING TO DO WITH ME.
TO BE HONEST, I THOUGHT YOU'D BE MORE WORRIED ABOUT HOW SCOTT'S LITTLE LONDON TRIP WAS GONNA INFLUENCE CHARLIE XAVIER'S BIG MEETING AT THE WHITE HOUSE TODAY, JEANNIE.
MANDRAKE
TRIPLE X
I MEAN, HOW'S HE SUPPOSED TO TALK THE PRESIDENT INTO SCRAPPING THE SENTINEL PROGRAM WHEN HIS OLD GOFER'S HURLING SEMTEX AT BUCKINGHAM PALACE?
YOU SOUND AWFULLY COMMITTED FOR A GUY JUST HANGING AROUND THE HOTEL SPENDING THE PROFESSOR'S PLASTIC.

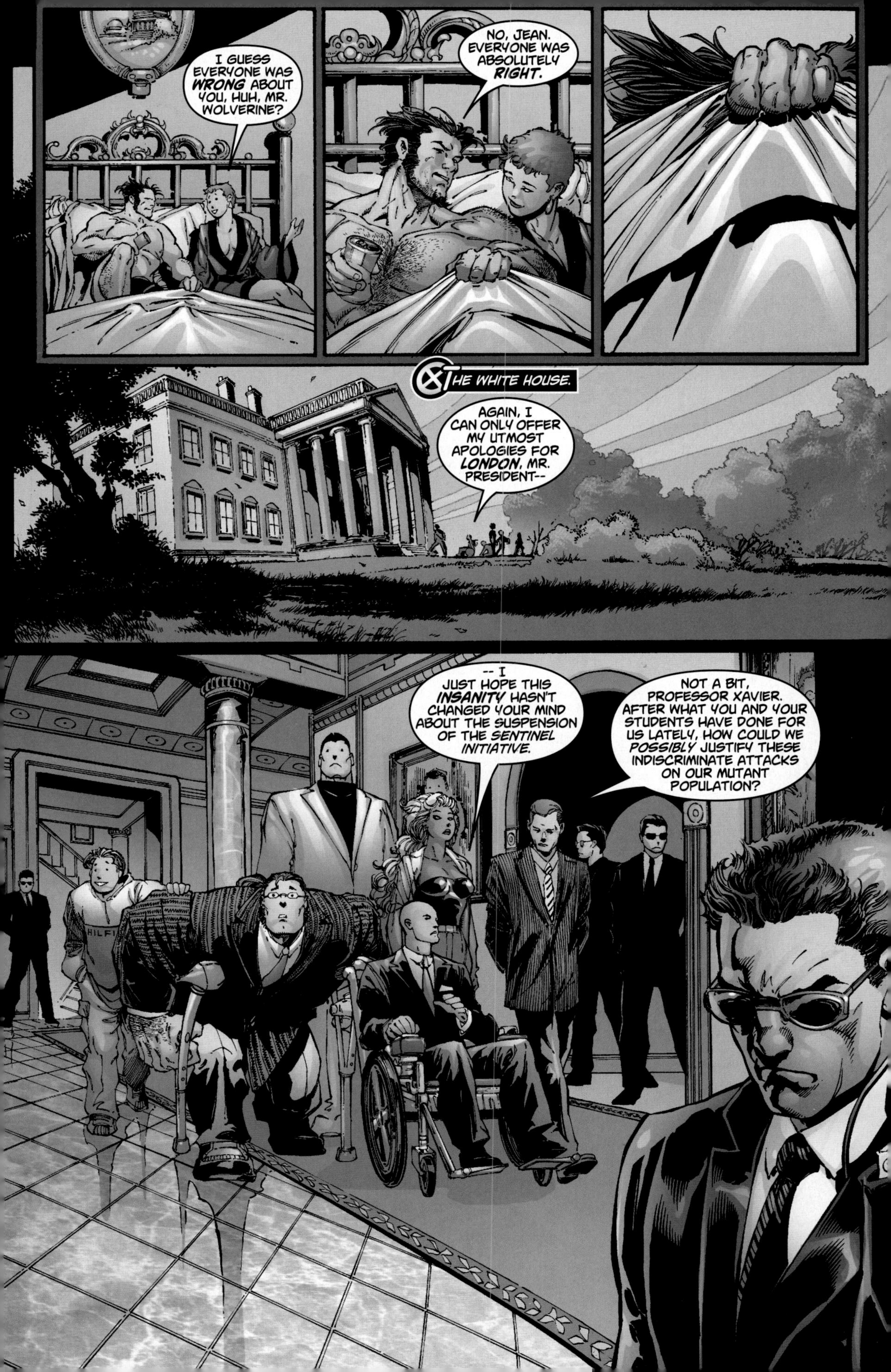
I GUESS EVERYONE WAS WRONG ABOUT YOU, HUH, MR. WOLVERINE?
NO, JEAN. EVERYONE WAS ABSOLUTELY RIGHT.
THE WHITE HOUSE.
AGAIN, I CAN ONLY OFFER MY UTMOST APOLOGIES FOR LONDON, MR. PRESIDENT--
--I JUST HOPE THIS INSANITY HASN'T CHANGED YOUR MIND ABOUT THE SUSPENSION OF THE SENTINEL INITIATIVE.
NOT A BIT, PROFESSOR XAVIER. AFTER WHAT YOU AND YOUR STUDENTS HAVE DONE FOR US LATELY, HOW COULD WE POSSIBLY JUSTIFY THESE INDISCRIMINATE ATTACKS ON OUR MUTANT POPULATION?
HILFI

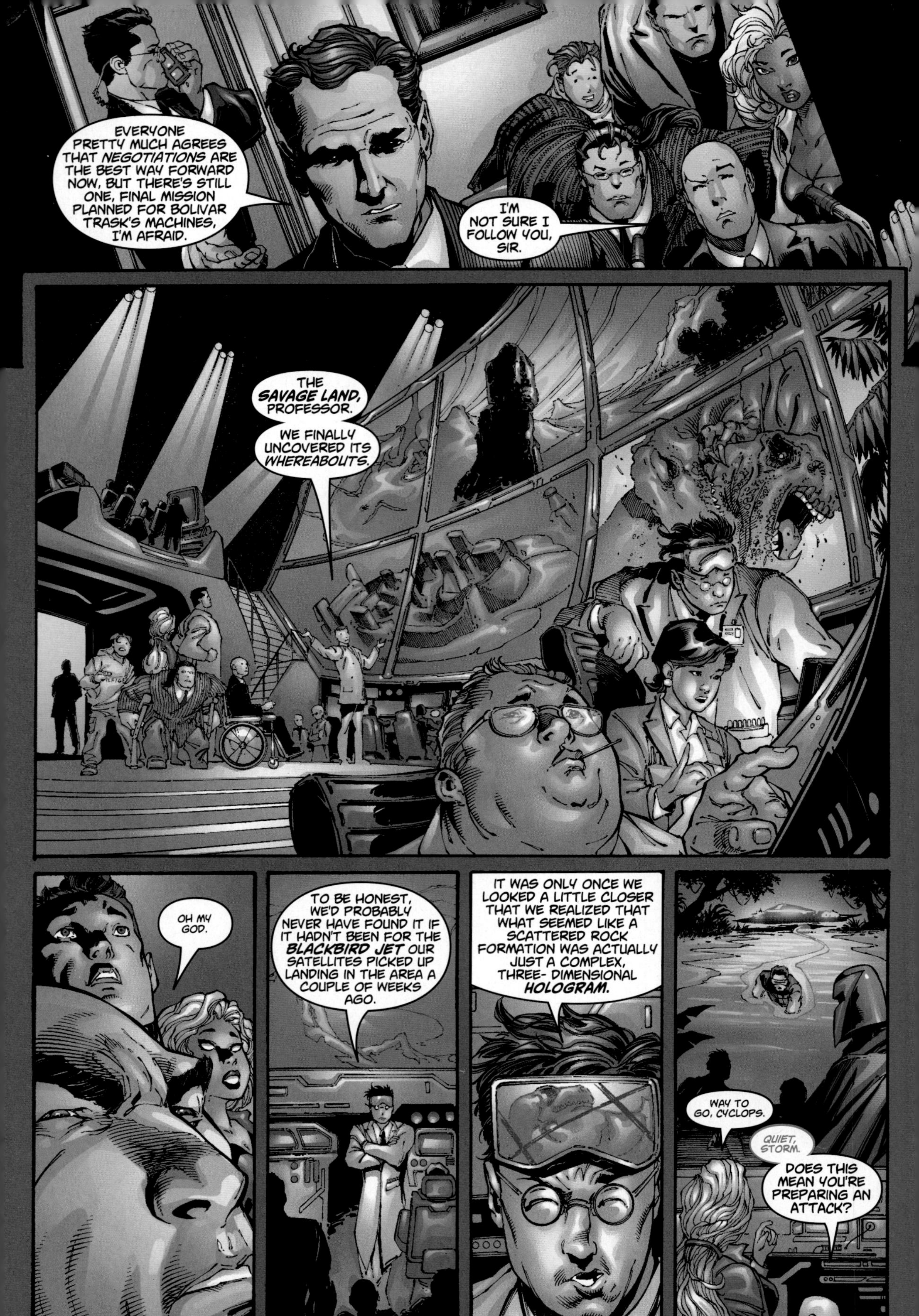

EVERYONE PRETTY MUCH AGREES THAT NEGOTIATIONS ARE THE BEST WAY FORWARD NOW, BUT THERE'S STILL ONE, FINAL MISSION PLANNED FOR BOLIVAR TRASK'S MACHINES, I'M AFRAID.
I'M NOT SURE I FOLLOW YOU, SIR.
THE SAVAGE LAND, PROFESSOR.
WE FINALLY UNCOVERED ITS WHEREABOUTS.
OH MY GOD.
TO BE HONEST, WE'D PROBABLY NEVER HAVE FOUND IT IF IT HADN'T BEEN FOR THE BLACKBIRD JET OUR SATELLITES PICKED UP LANDING IN THE AREA A COUPLE OF WEEKS AGO.
IT WAS ONLY ONCE WE LOOKED A LITTLE CLOSER THAT WE REALIZED THAT WHAT SEEMED LIKE A SCATTERED ROCK FORMATION WAS ACTUALLY JUST A COMPLEX, THREE- DIMENSIONAL HOLOGRAM.
WAY TO GO, CYCLOPS.
QUIET, STORM.
DOES THIS MEAN YOU'RE PREPARING AN ATTACK?

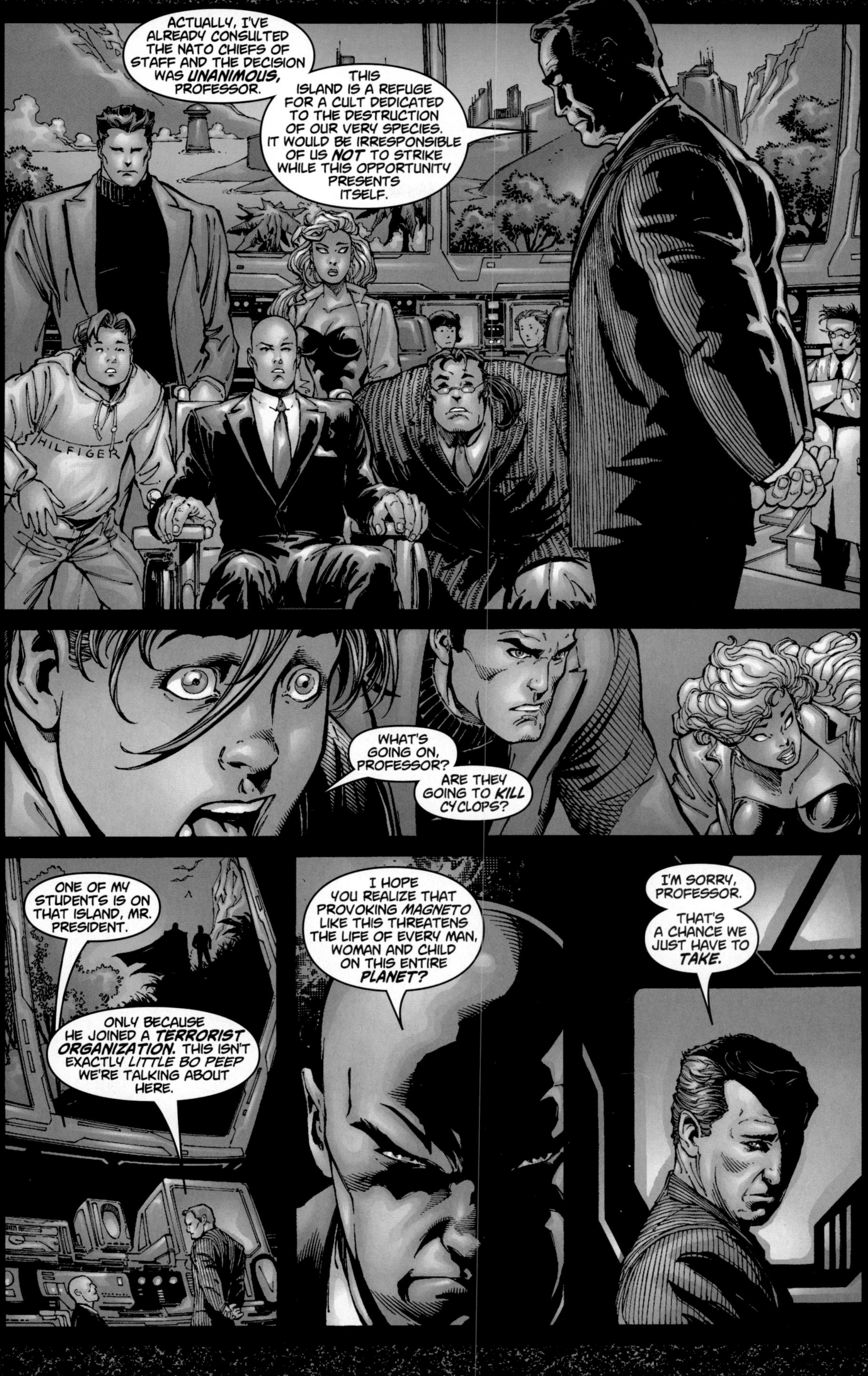
ACTUALLY, I'VE ALREADY CONSULTED THE NATO CHIEFS OF STAFF AND THE DECISION WAS UNANIMOUS, PROFESSOR.
THIS ISLAND IS A REFUGE FOR A CULT DEDICATED TO THE DESTRUCTION OF OUR VERY SPECIES. IT WOULD BE IRRESPONSIBLE OF US NOT TO STRIKE WHILE THIS OPPORTUNITY PRESENTS ITSELF.
HILFIGER
WHAT'S GOING ON, PROFESSOR?
ARE THEY GOING TO KILL CYCLOPS?
ONE OF MY STUDENTS IS ON THAT ISLAND, MR. PRESIDENT.
ONLY BECAUSE HE JOINED A TERRORIST ORGANIZATION. THIS ISN'T EXACTLY LITTLE BO PEEP WE'RE TALKING ABOUT HERE.
I HOPE YOU REALIZE THAT PROVOKING MAGNETO LIKE THIS THREATENS THE LIFE OF EVERY MAN, WOMAN AND CHILD ON THIS ENTIRE PLANET?
I'M SORRY, PROFESSOR.
THAT'S A CHANCE WE JUST HAVE TO TAKE.

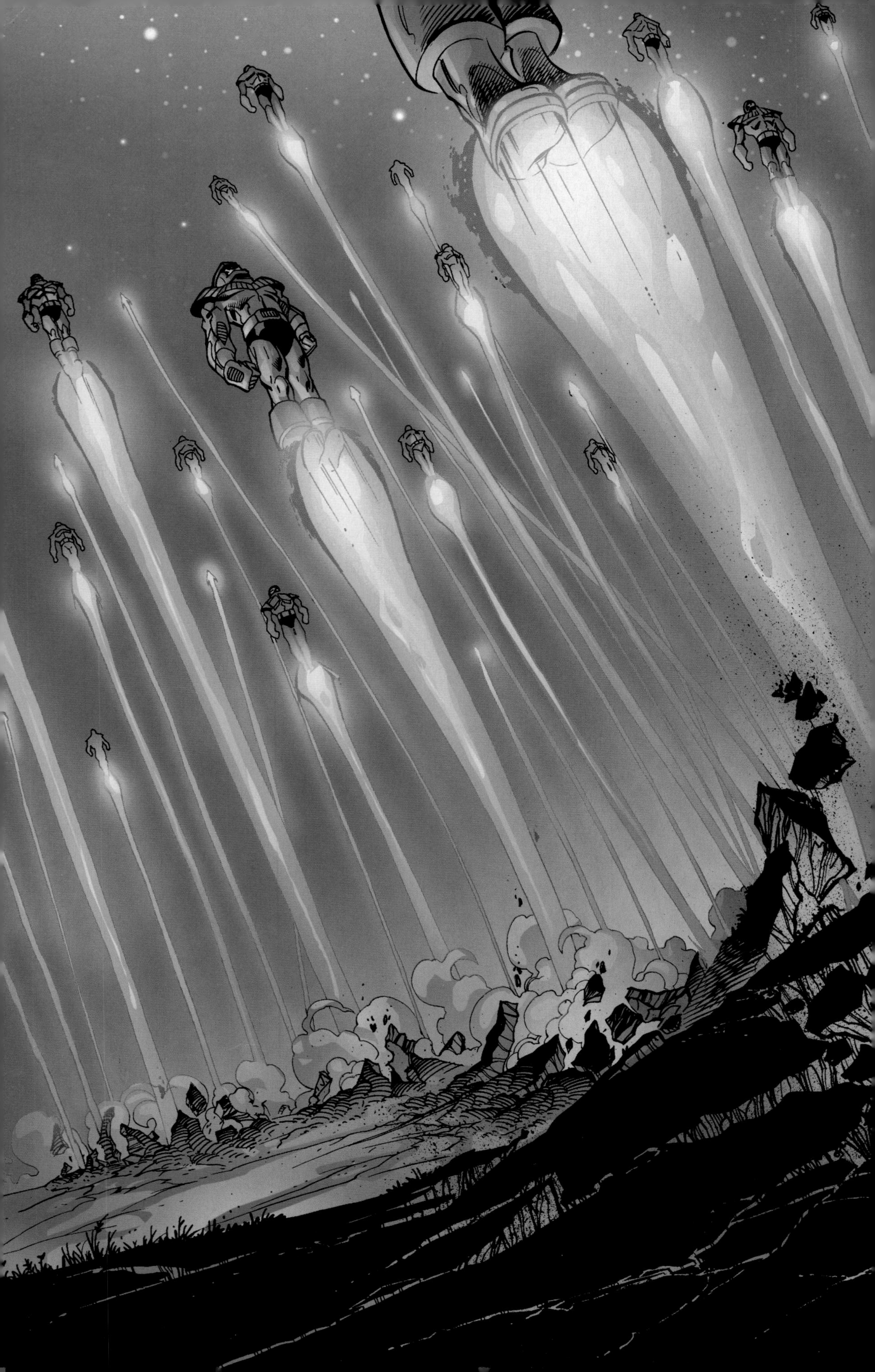

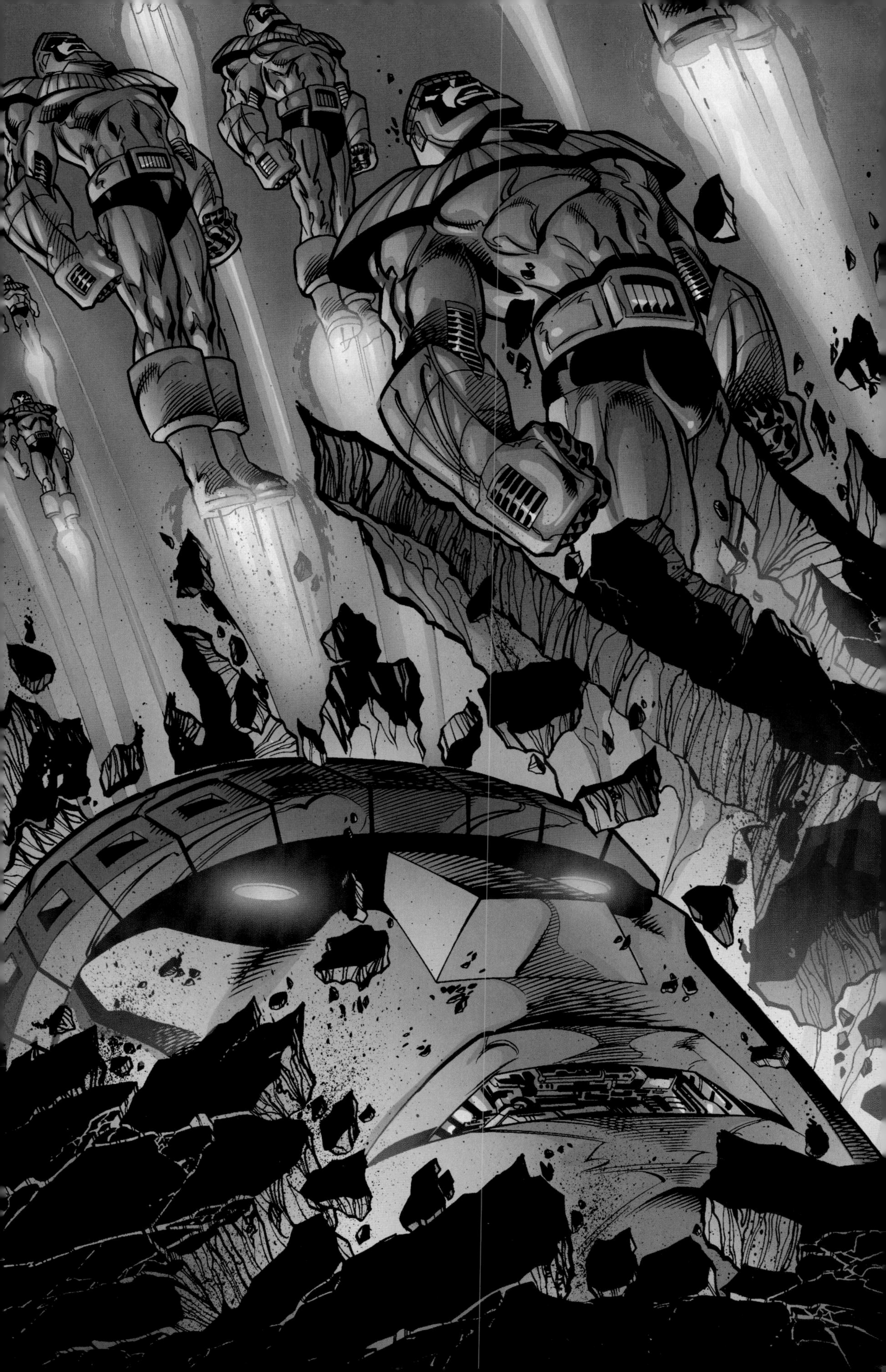

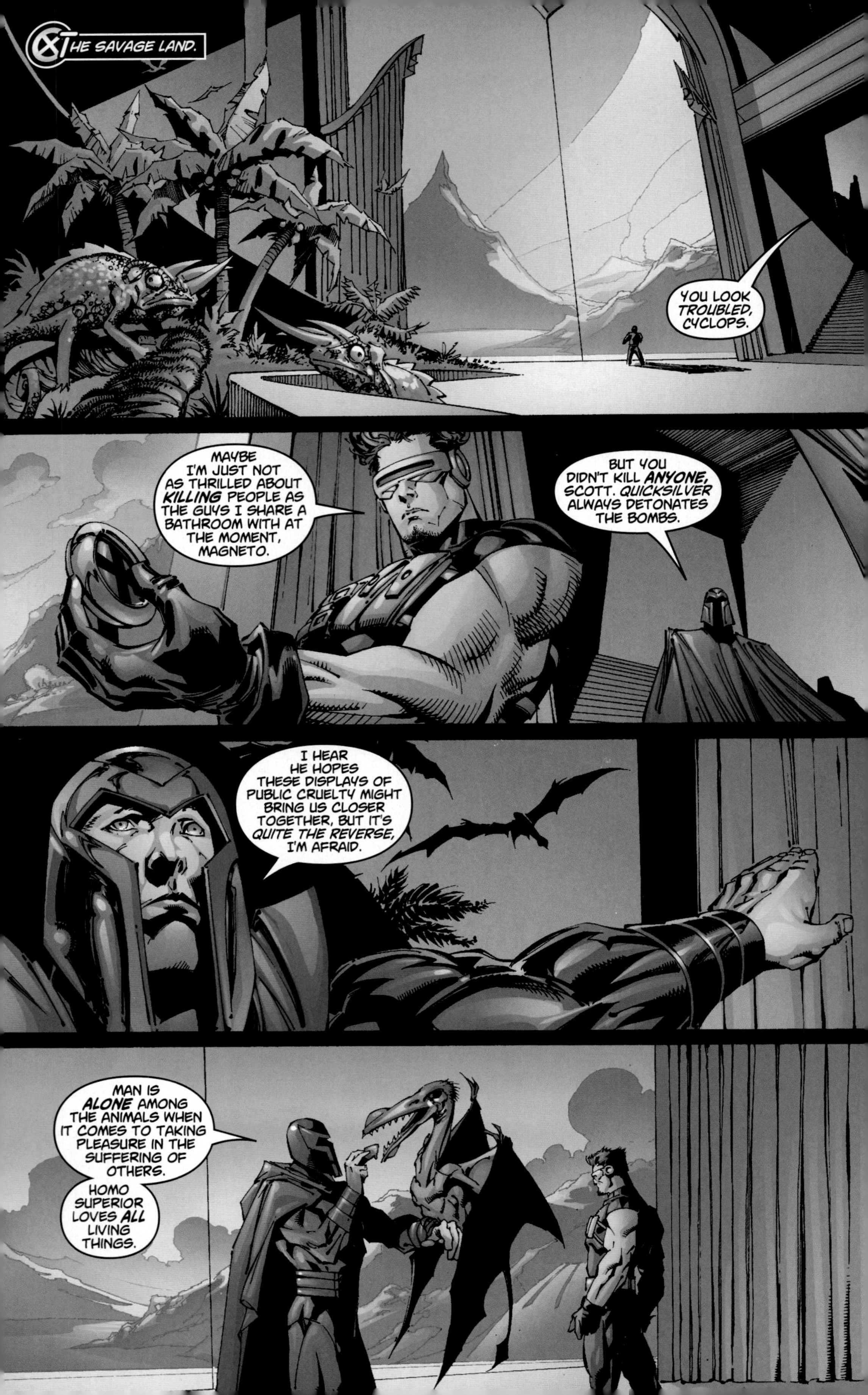
THE SAVAGE LAND.
YOU LOOK TROUBLED, CYCLOPS.
MAYBE I'M JUST NOT AS THRILLED ABOUT KILLING PEOPLE AS THE GUYS I SHARE A BATHROOM WITH AT THE MOMENT, MAGNETO.
BUT YOU DIDN'T KILL ANYONE, SCOTT. QUICKSILVER ALWAYS DETONATES THE BOMBS.
I HEAR HE HOPES THESE DISPLAYS OF PUBLIC CRUELTY MIGHT BRING US CLOSER TOGETHER, BUT IT'S QUITE THE REVERSE, I'M AFRAID.
MAN IS ALONE AMONG THE ANIMALS WHEN IT COMES TO TAKING PLEASURE IN THE SUFFERING OF OTHERS.
HOMO SUPERIOR LOVES ALL LIVING THINGS.

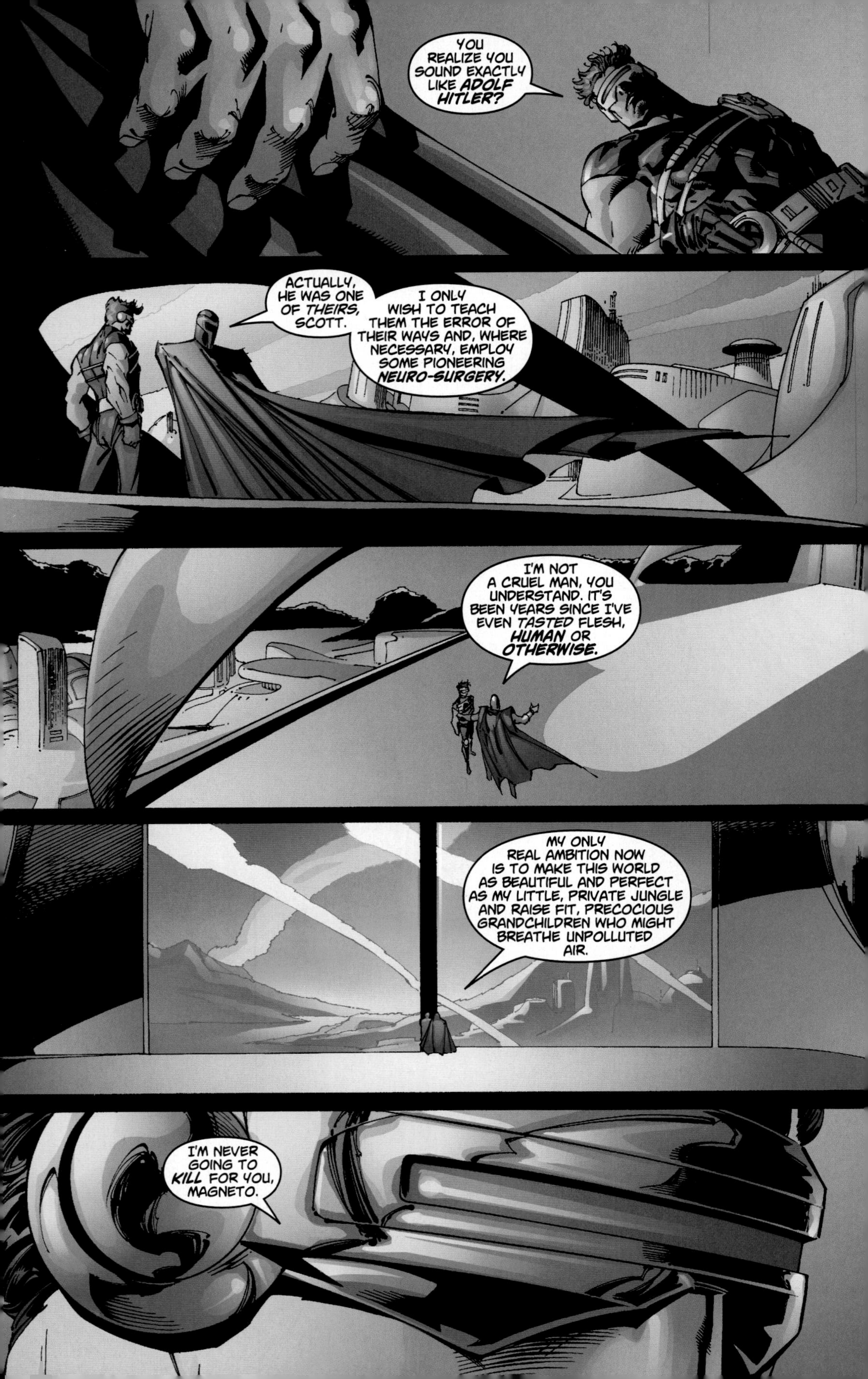
YOU REALIZE YOU SOUND EXACTLY LIKE ADOLF HITLER?
ACTUALLY, HE WAS ONE OF THEIRS, SCOTT.
I ONLY WISH TO TEACH THEM THE ERROR OF THEIR WAYS AND, WHERE NECESSARY, EMPLOY SOME PIONEERING NEURO-SURGERY.
I'M NOT A CRUEL MAN, YOU UNDERSTAND. IT'S BEEN YEARS SINCE I'VE EVEN TASTED FLESH, HUMAN OR OTHERWISE.
MY ONLY REAL AMBITION NOW IS TO MAKE THIS WORLD AS BEAUTIFUL AND PERFECT AS MY LITTLE, PRIVATE JUNGLE AND RAISE FIT, PRECOCIOUS GRANDCHILDREN WHO MIGHT BREATHE UNPOLLUTED AIR.
I'M NEVER GOING TO KILL FOR YOU, MAGNETO.

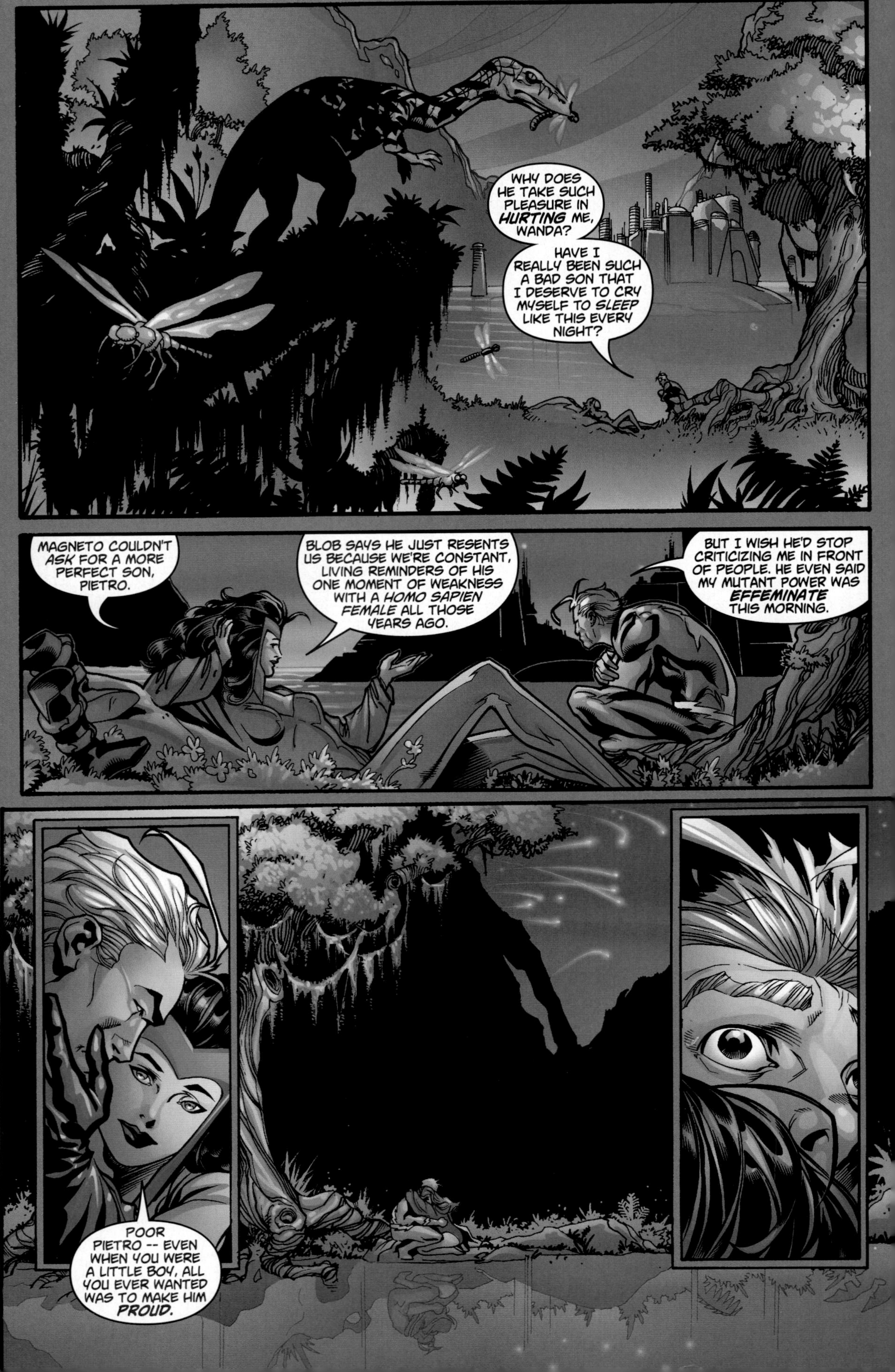
WHY DOES HE TAKE SUCH PLEASURE IN HURTING ME, WANDA?
HAVE I REALLY BEEN SUCH A BAD SON THAT I DESERVE TO CRY MYSELF TO SLEEP LIKE THIS EVERY NIGHT?
MAGNETO COULDN'T ASK FOR A MORE PERFECT SON, PIETRO.
BLOB SAYS HE JUST RESENTS US BECAUSE WE'RE CONSTANT, LIVING REMINDERS OF HIS ONE MOMENT OF WEAKNESS WITH A HOMO SAPIEN FEMALE ALL THOSE YEARS AGO.
BUT I WISH HE'D STOP CRITICIZING ME IN FRONT OF PEOPLE. HE EVEN SAID MY MUTANT POWER WAS EFFEMINATE THIS MORNING.
POOR PIETRO -- EVEN WHEN YOU WERE A LITTLE BOY, ALL YOU EVER WANTED WAS TO MAKE HIM PROUD.

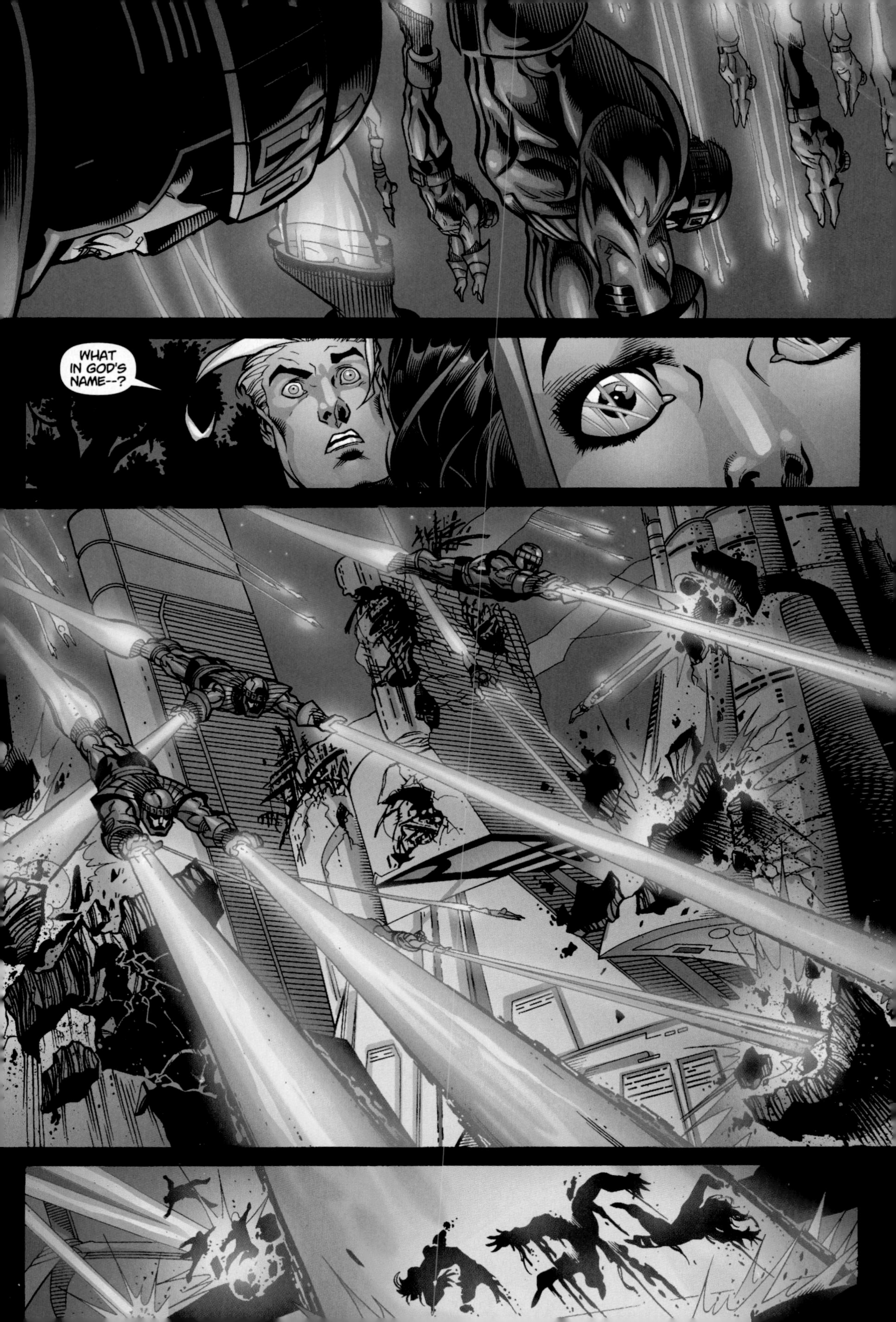
WHAT IN GOD'S NAME--?

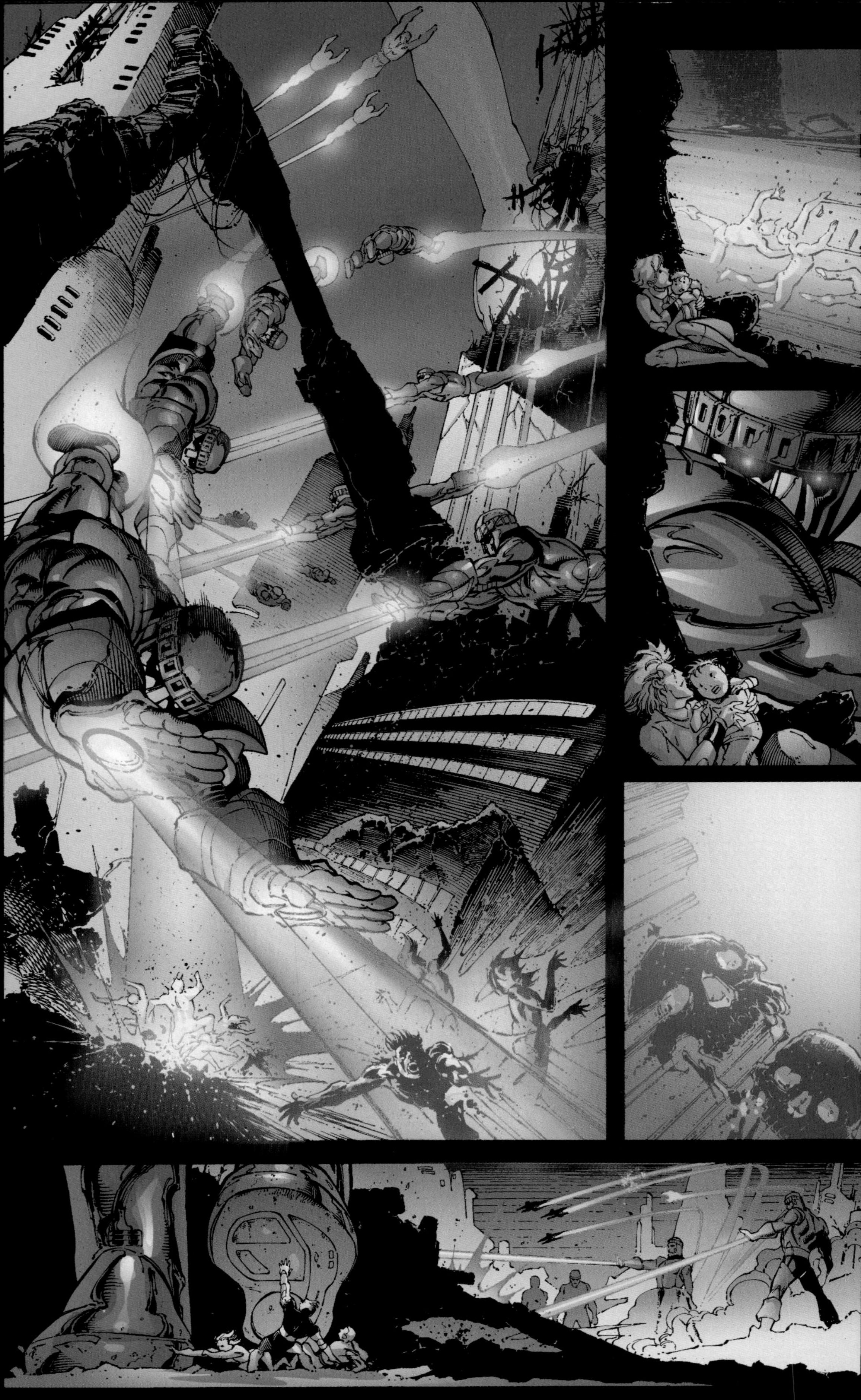

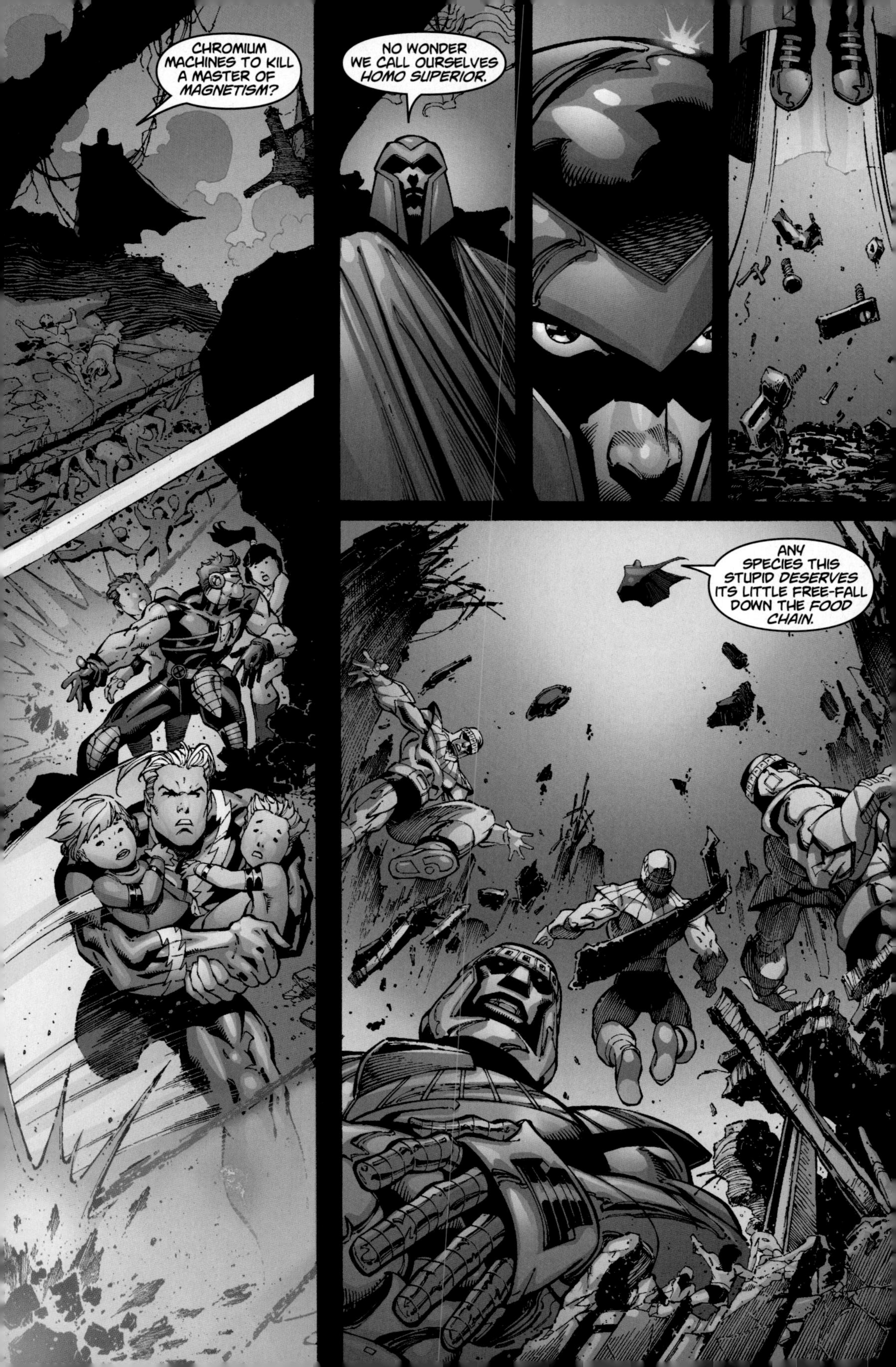
CHROMIUM MACHINES TO KILL A MASTER OF MAGNETISM?
NO WONDER WE CALL OURSELVES HOMO SUPERIOR.
ANY SPECIES THIS STUPID DESERVES ITS LITTLE FREE-FALL DOWN THE FOOD CHAIN.

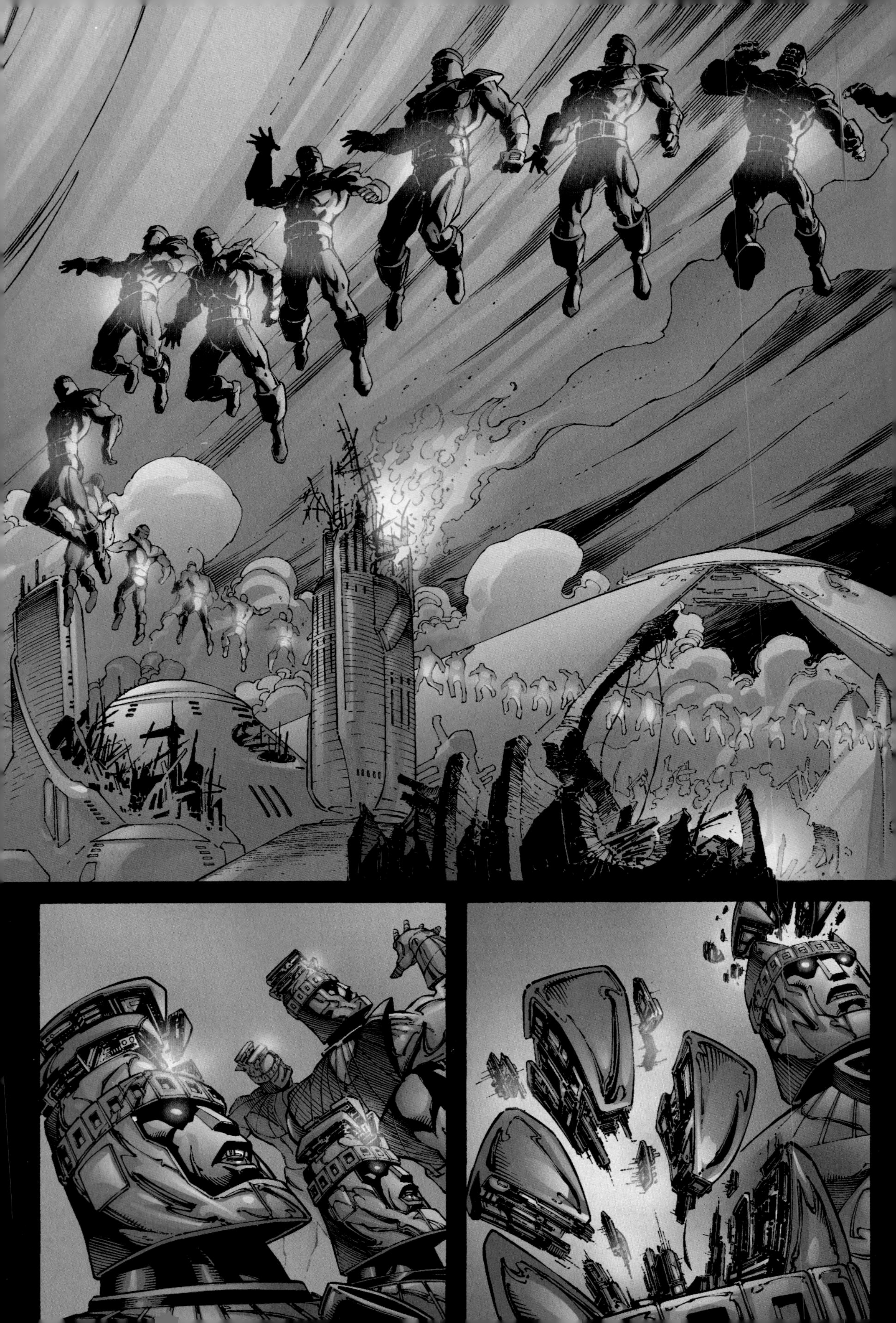

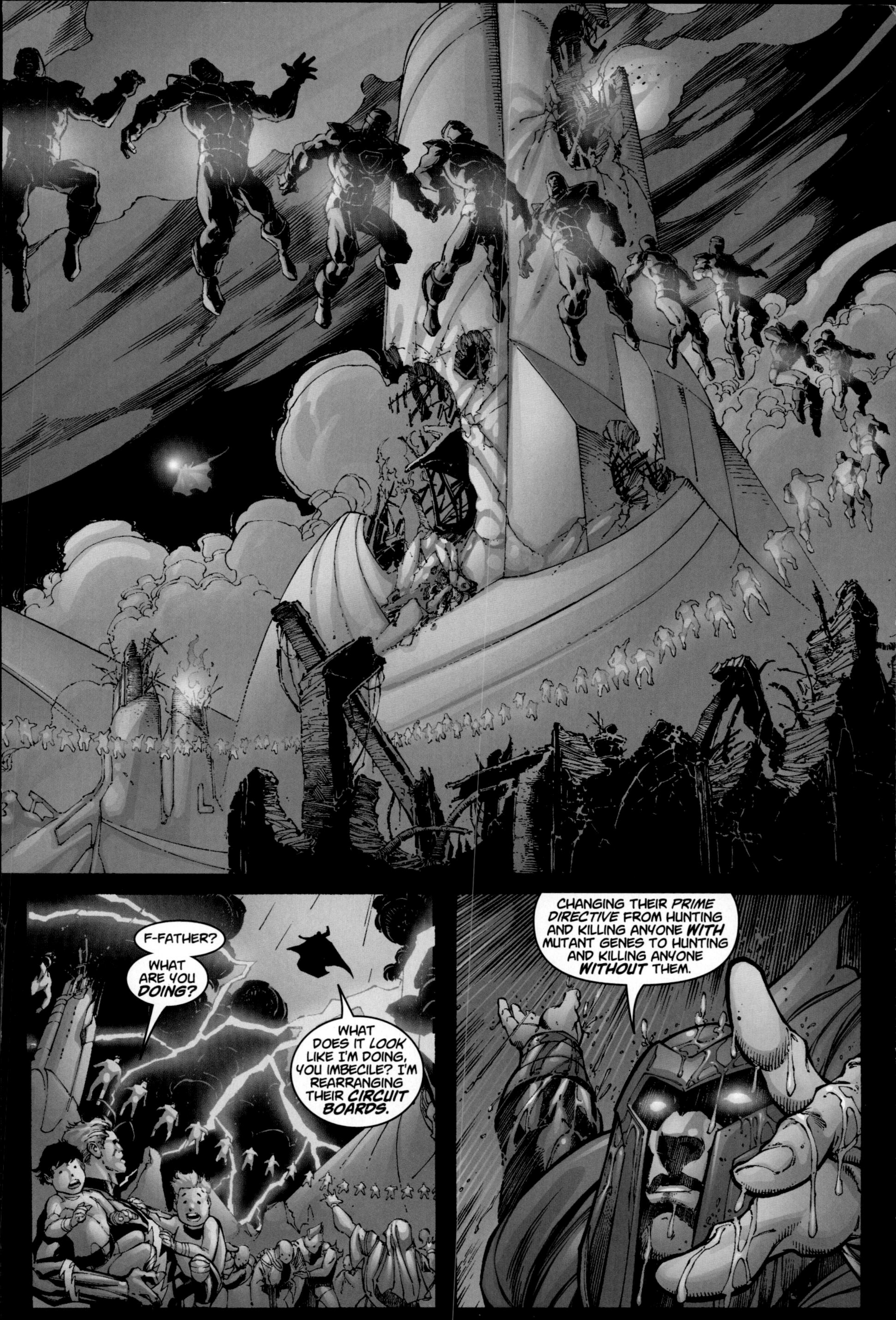
F-FATHER?
WHAT ARE YOU DOING?
WHAT DOES IT LOOK LIKE I'M DOING, YOU IMBECILE? I'M REARRANGING THEIR CIRCUIT BOARDS.
CHANGING THEIR PRIME DIRECTIVE FROM HUNTING AND KILLING ANYONE WITH MUTANT GENES TO HUNTING AND KILLING ANYONE WITHOUT THEM.

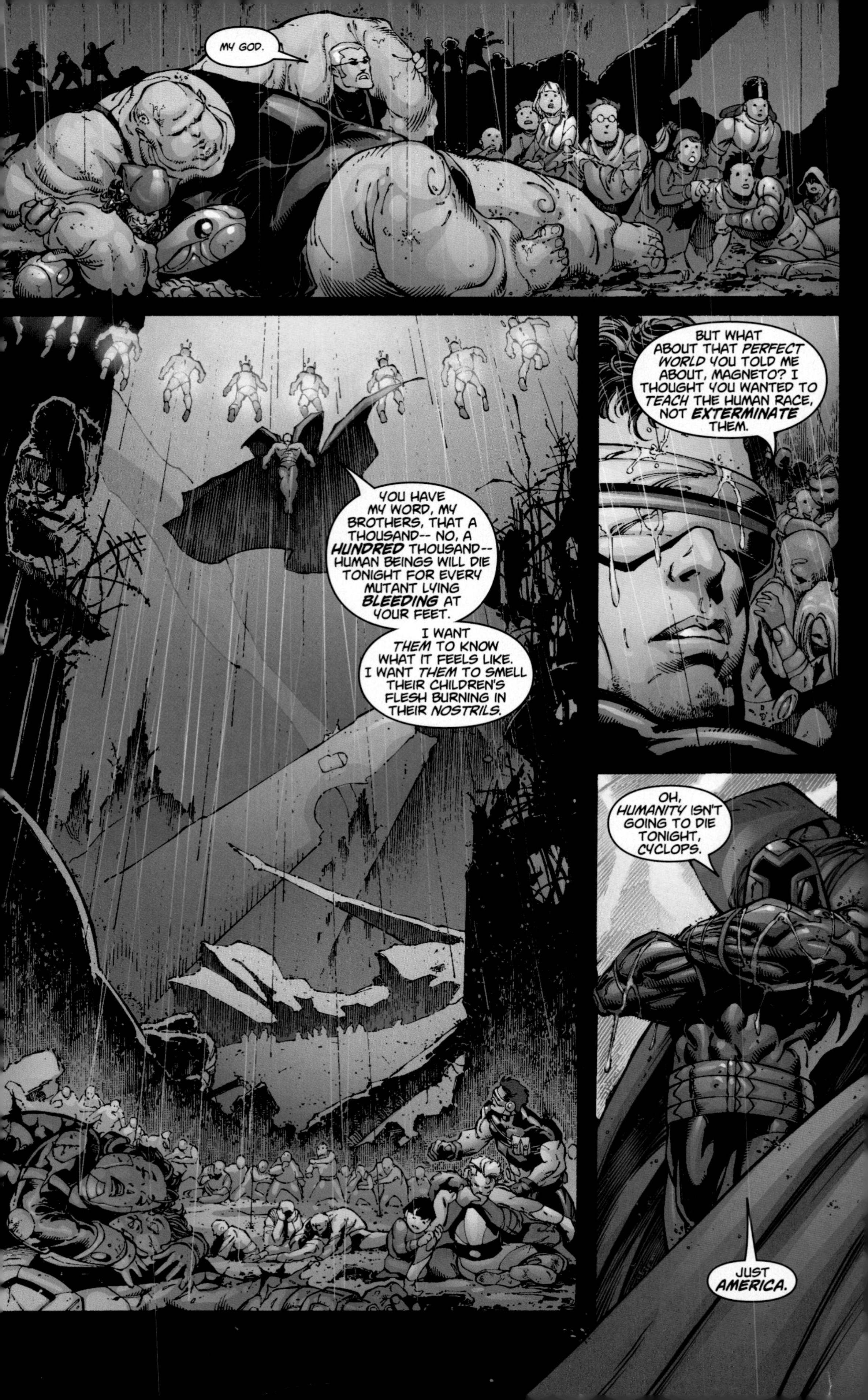
MY GOD.
YOU HAVE MY WORD, MY BROTHERS, THAT A THOUSAND-- NO, A HUNDRED THOUSAND-- HUMAN BEINGS WILL DIE TONIGHT FOR EVERY MUTANT LYING BLEEDING AT YOUR FEET.
I WANT THEM TO KNOW WHAT IT FEELS LIKE. I WANT THEM TO SMELL THEIR CHILDREN'S FLESH BURNING IN THEIR NOSTRILS.
BUT WHAT ABOUT THAT PERFECT WORLD YOU TOLD ME ABOUT, MAGNETO? I THOUGHT YOU WANTED TO TEACH THE HUMAN RACE, NOT EXTERMINATE THEM.
OH, HUMANITY ISN'T GOING TO DIE TONIGHT, CYCLOPS.
JUST AMERICA.

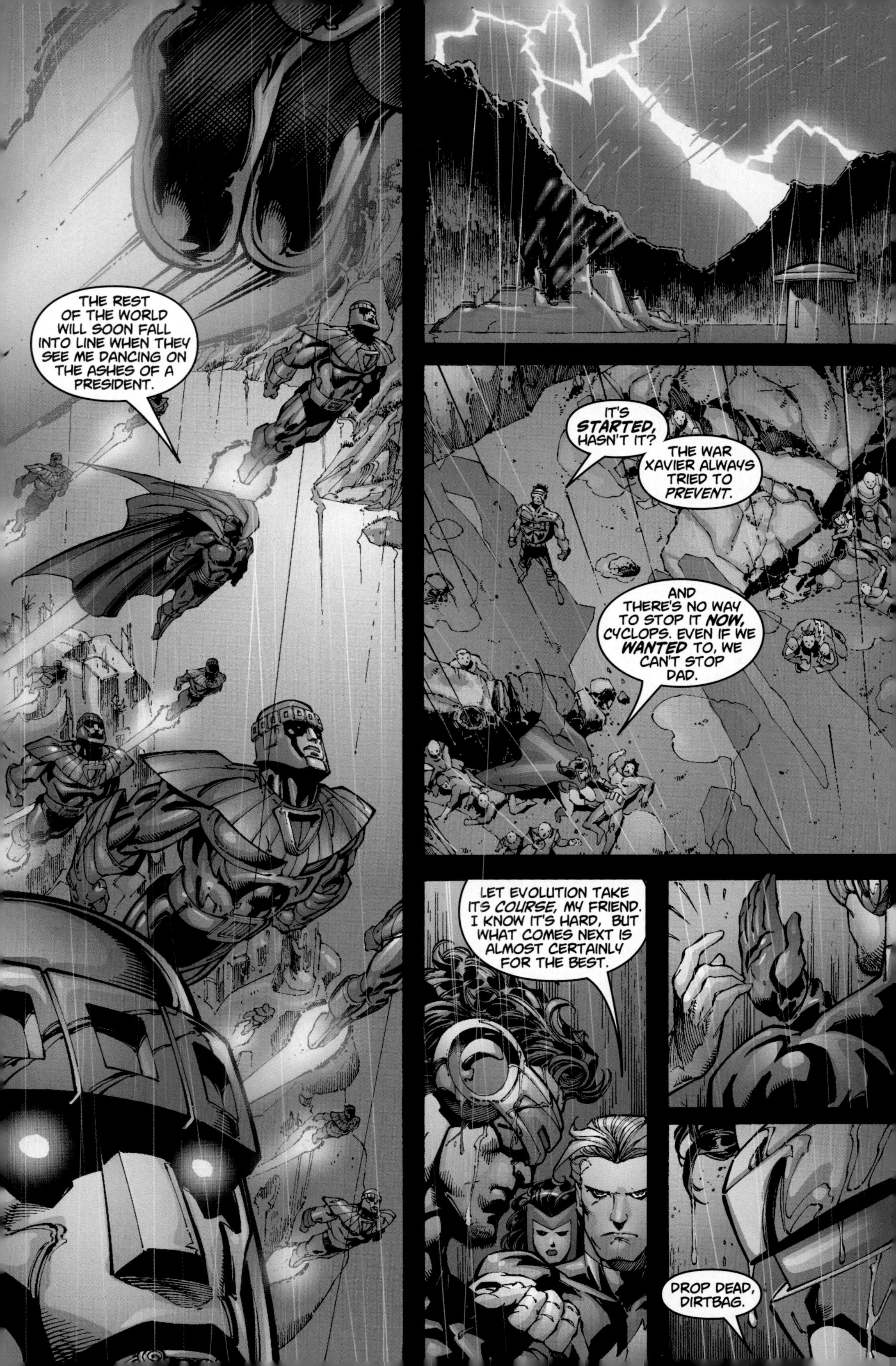
THE REST OF THE WORLD WILL SOON FALL INTO LINE WHEN THEY SEE ME DANCING ON THE ASHES OF A PRESIDENT.
IT'S STARTED, HASN'T IT?
THE WAR XAVIER ALWAYS TRIED TO PREVENT.
AND THERE'S NO WAY TO STOP IT NOW, CYCLOPS. EVEN IF WE WANTED TO, WE CAN'T STOP DAD.
LET EVOLUTION TAKE ITS COURSE, MY FRIEND. I KNOW IT'S HARD, BUT WHAT COMES NEXT IS ALMOST CERTAINLY FOR THE BEST.
DROP DEAD, DIRTBAG.

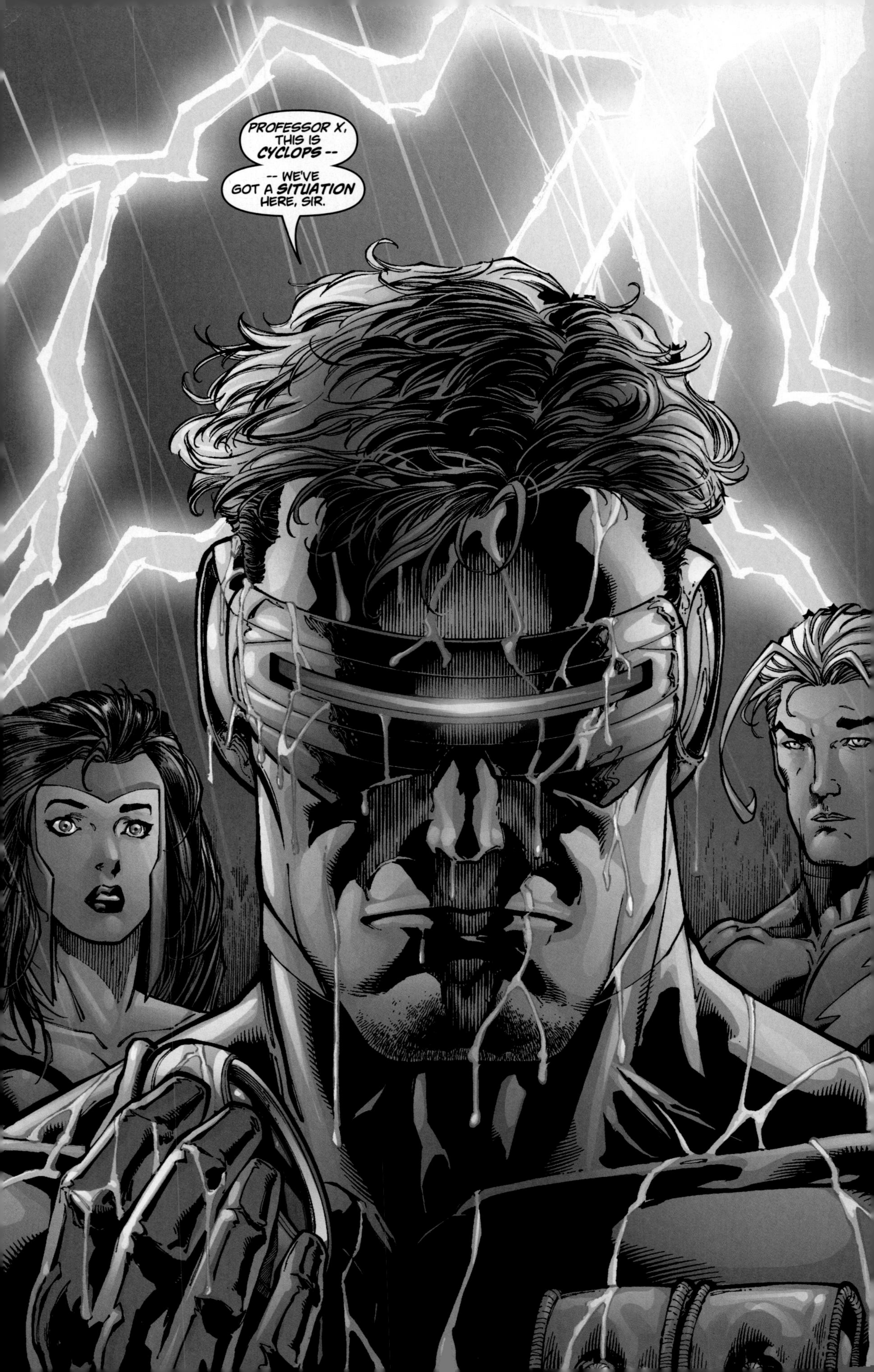
PROFESSOR X, THIS IS CYCLOPS --
-- WE'VE GOT A SITUATION HERE, SIR.

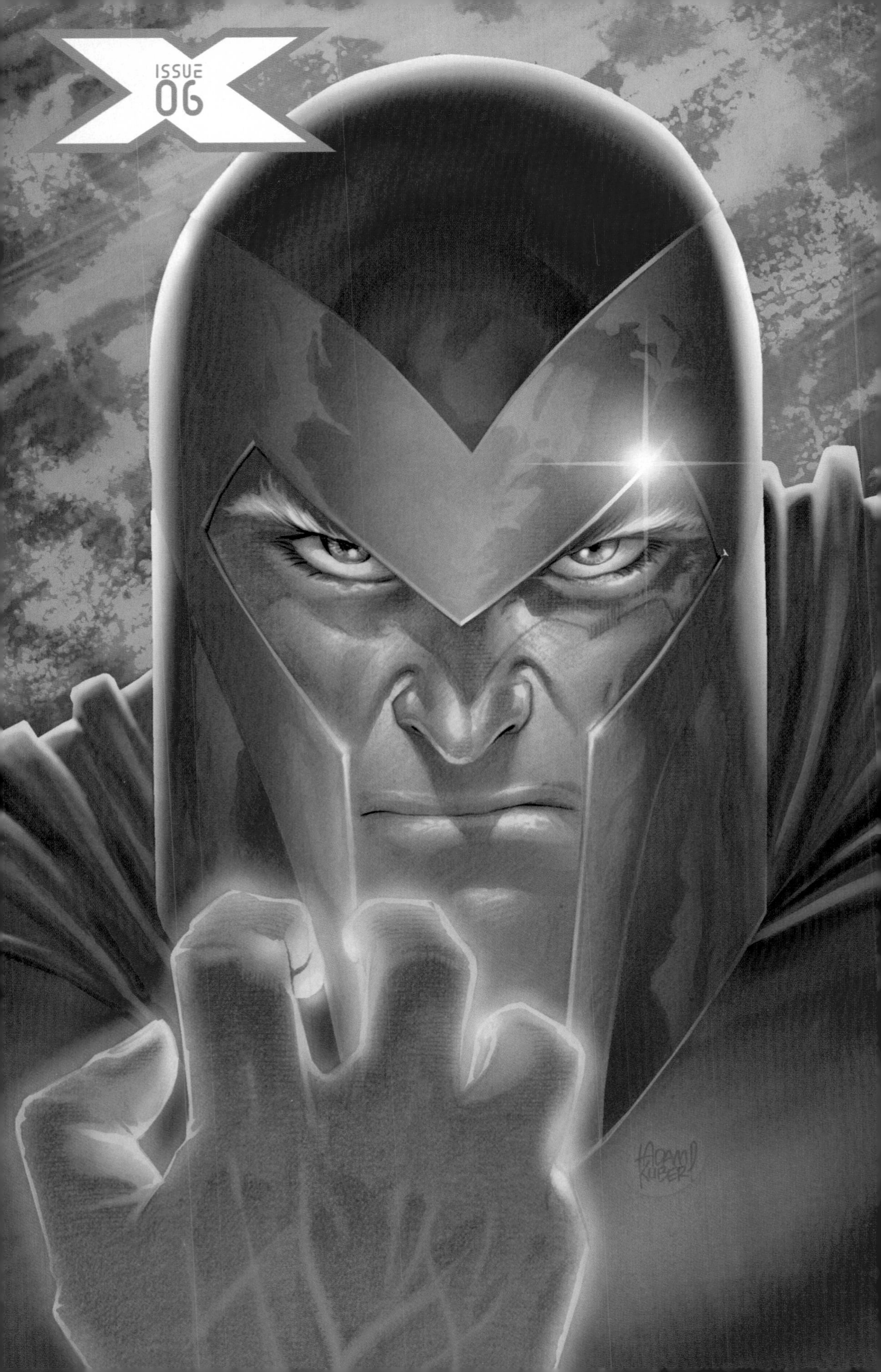
ISSUE
06
ADAM KUBERT

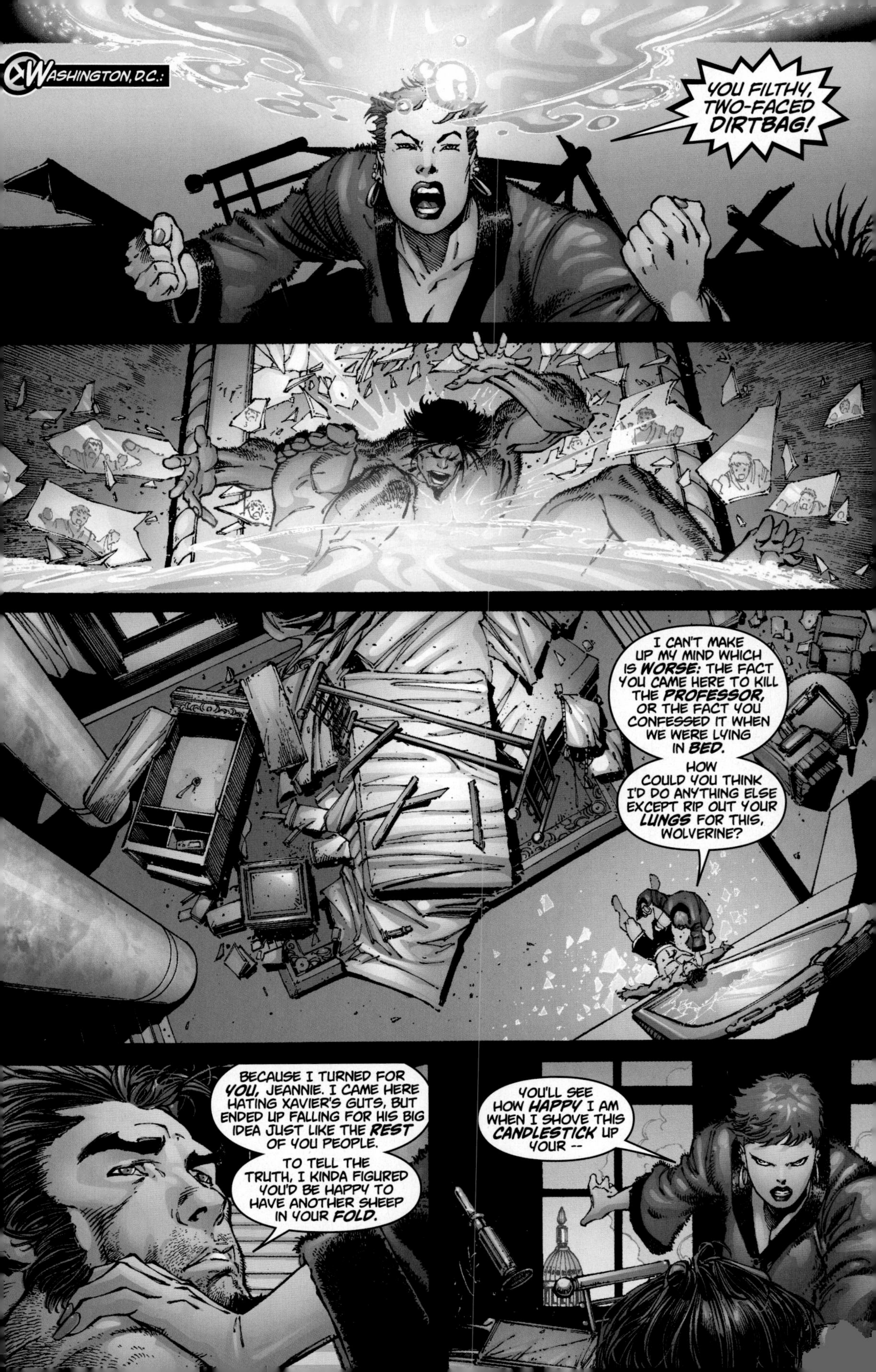
WASHINGTON, D.C.:
YOU FILTHY, TWO-FACED DIRTBAG!
I CAN'T MAKE UP MY MIND WHICH IS WORSE: THE FACT YOU CAME HERE TO KILL THE PROFESSOR, OR THE FACT YOU CONFESSED IT WHEN WE WERE LYING IN BED.
HOW COULD YOU THINK I'D DO ANYTHING ELSE EXCEPT RIP OUT YOUR LUNGS FOR THIS, WOLVERINE?
BECAUSE I TURNED FOR YOU, JEANNIE. I CAME HERE HATING XAVIER'S GUTS, BUT ENDED UP FALLING FOR HIS BIG IDEA JUST LIKE THE REST OF YOU PEOPLE.
TO TELL THE TRUTH, I KINDA FIGURED YOU'D BE HAPPY TO HAVE ANOTHER SHEEP IN YOUR FOLD.
YOU'LL SEE HOW HAPPY I AM WHEN I SHOVE THIS CANDLESTICK UP YOUR --

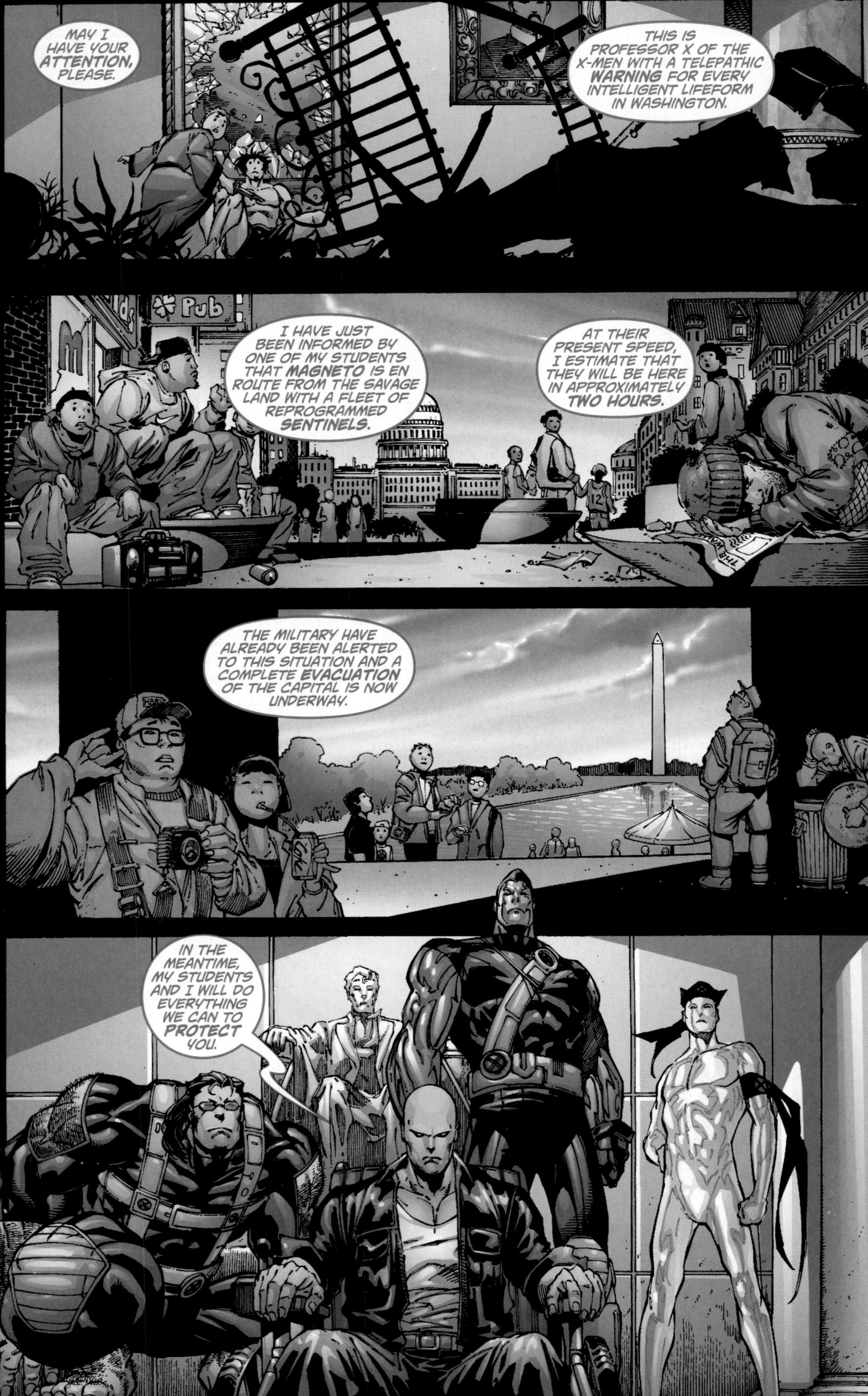
MAY I HAVE YOUR ATTENTION, PLEASE.
THIS IS PROFESSOR X OF THE X-MEN WITH A TELEPATHIC WARNING FOR EVERY INTELLIGENT LIFEFORM IN WASHINGTON.
Pub
I HAVE JUST BEEN INFORMED BY ONE OF MY STUDENTS THAT MAGNETO IS EN ROUTE FROM THE SAVAGE LAND WITH A FLEET OF REPROGRAMMED SENTINELS.
AT THEIR PRESENT SPEED, I ESTIMATE THAT THEY WILL BE HERE IN APPROXIMATELY TWO HOURS.
THE MILITARY HAVE ALREADY BEEN ALERTED TO THIS SITUATION AND A COMPLETE EVACUATION OF THE CAPITAL IS NOW UNDERWAY.
IN THE MEANTIME, MY STUDENTS AND I WILL DO EVERYTHING WE CAN TO PROTECT YOU.

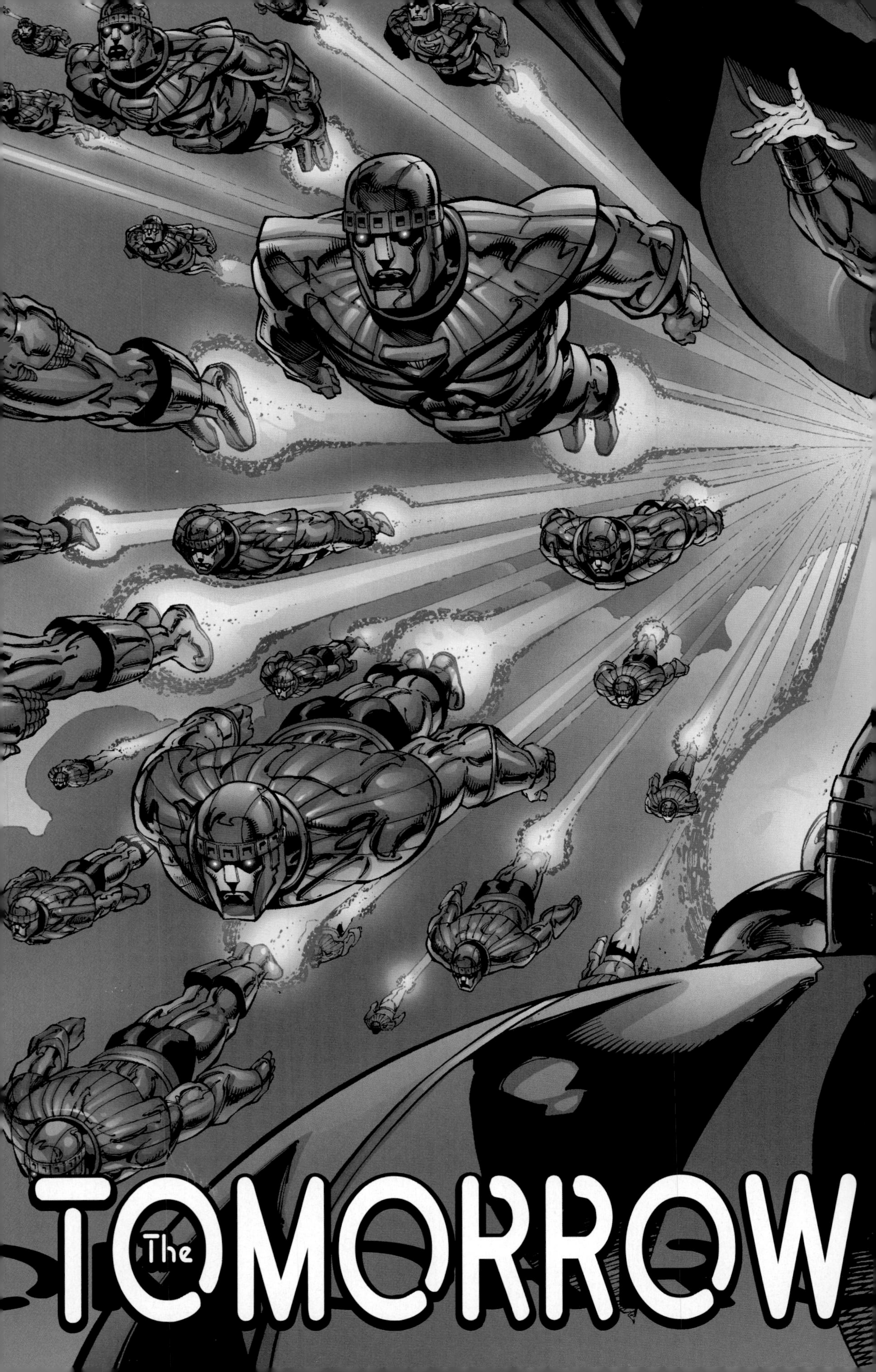
The TOMORROW

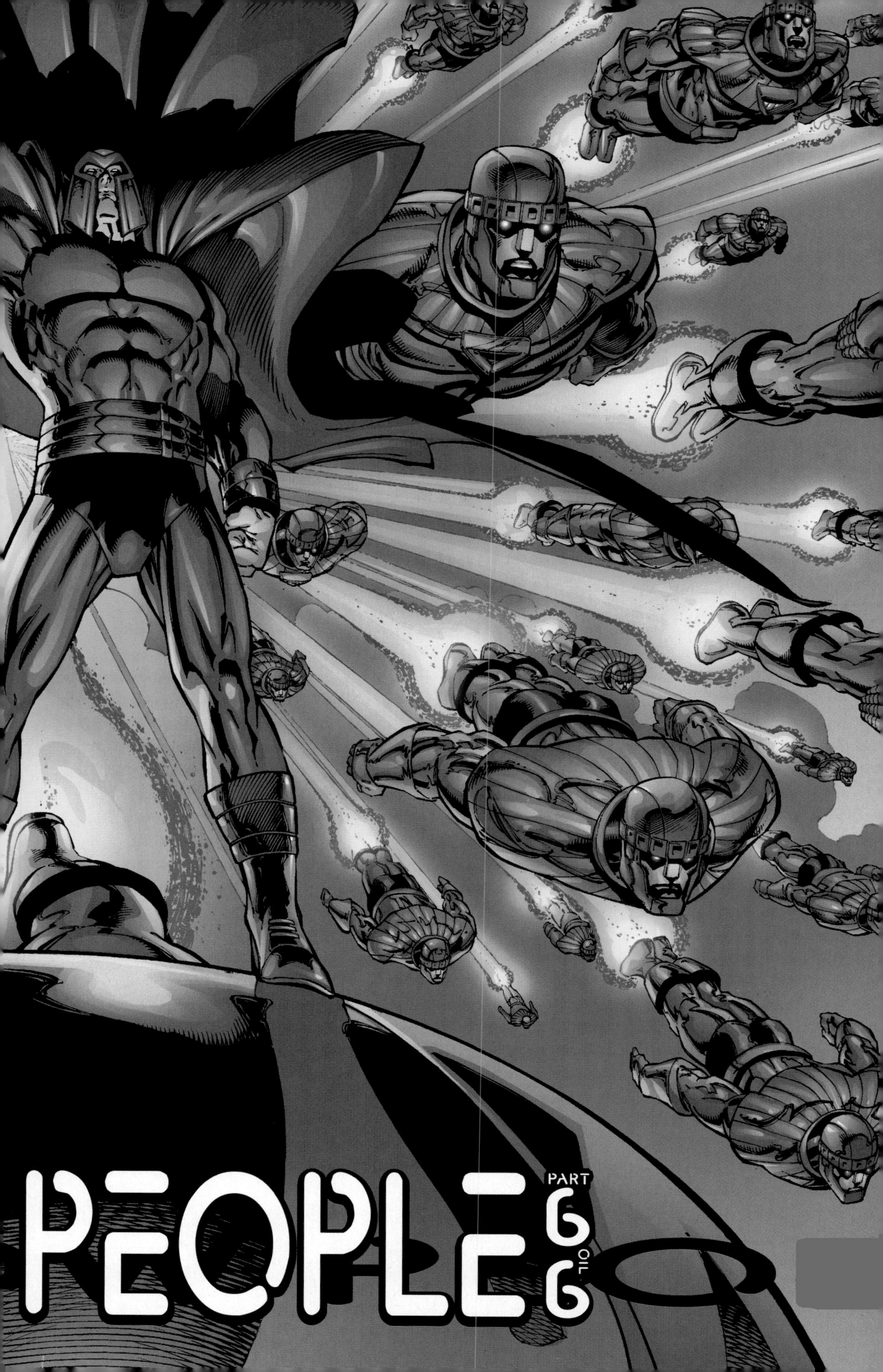
PEOPLE
PART
6
OF
6

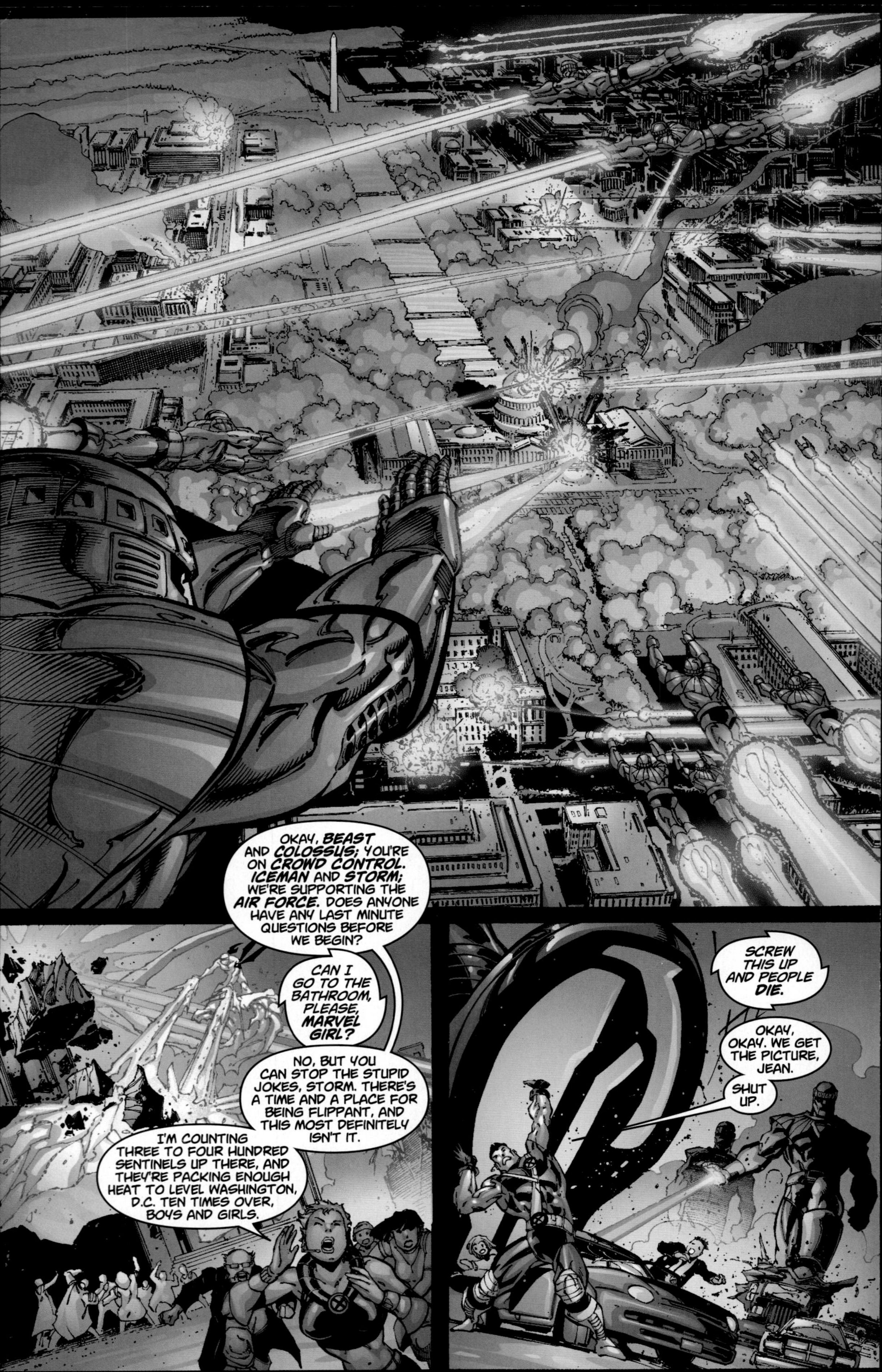
OKAY, BEAST AND COLOSSUS; YOU'RE ON CROWD CONTROL. ICEMAN AND STORM; WE'RE SUPPORTING THE AIR FORCE. DOES ANYONE HAVE ANY LAST MINUTE QUESTIONS BEFORE WE BEGIN?
CAN I GO TO THE BATHROOM, PLEASE, MARVEL GIRL?
NO, BUT YOU CAN STOP THE STUPID JOKES, STORM. THERE'S A TIME AND A PLACE FOR BEING FLIPPANT, AND THIS MOST DEFINITELY ISN'T IT.
I'M COUNTING THREE TO FOUR HUNDRED SENTINELS UP THERE, AND THEY'RE PACKING ENOUGH HEAT TO LEVEL WASHINGTON, D.C. TEN TIMES OVER, BOYS AND GIRLS.
SCREW THIS UP AND PEOPLE DIE.
OKAY, OKAY. WE GET THE PICTURE, JEAN.
SHUT UP.

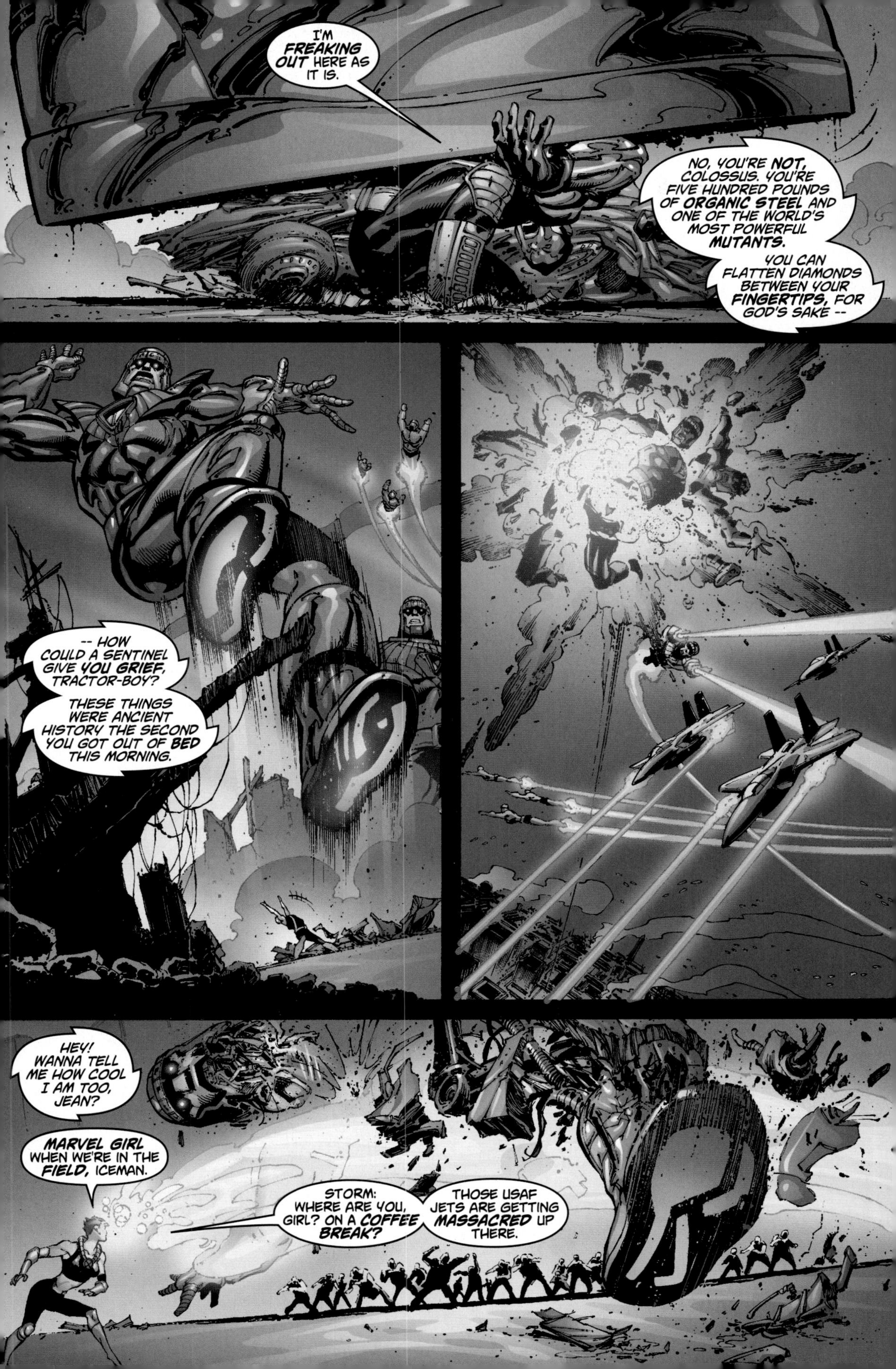
I'M FREAKING OUT HERE AS IT IS.
NO, YOU'RE NOT, COLOSSUS. YOU'RE FIVE HUNDRED POUNDS OF ORGANIC STEEL AND ONE OF THE WORLD'S MOST POWERFUL MUTANTS.
YOU CAN FLATTEN DIAMONDS BETWEEN YOUR FINGERTIPS, FOR GOD'S SAKE --
-- HOW COULD A SENTINEL GIVE YOU GRIEF, TRACTOR-BOY?
THESE THINGS WERE ANCIENT HISTORY THE SECOND YOU GOT OUT OF BED THIS MORNING.
HEY! WANNA TELL ME HOW COOL I AM TOO, JEAN?
MARVEL GIRL WHEN WE'RE IN THE FIELD, ICEMAN.
STORM: WHERE ARE YOU, GIRL? ON A COFFEE BREAK?
THOSE USAF JETS ARE GETTING MASSACRED UP THERE.

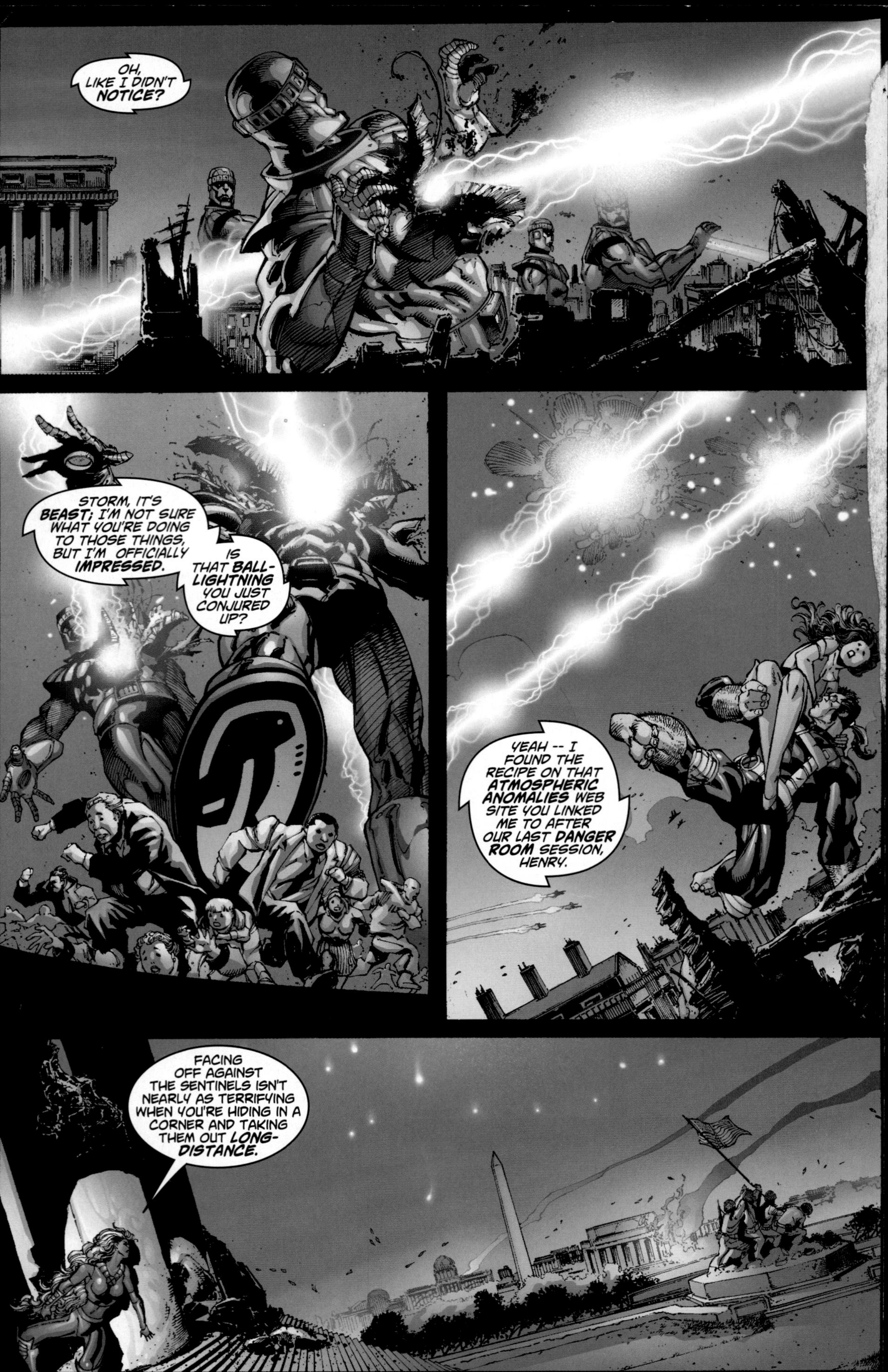

OH, LIKE I DIDN'T NOTICE?
STORM, IT'S BEAST; I'M NOT SURE WHAT YOU'RE DOING TO THOSE THINGS, BUT I'M OFFICIALLY IMPRESSED.
IS THAT BALL-LIGHTNING YOU JUST CONJURED UP?
YEAH -- I FOUND THE RECIPE ON THAT ATMOSPHERIC ANOMALIES WEB SITE YOU LINKED ME TO AFTER OUR LAST DANGER ROOM SESSION, HENRY.
FACING OFF AGAINST THE SENTINELS ISN'T NEARLY AS TERRIFYING WHEN YOU'RE HIDING IN A CORNER AND TAKING THEM OUT LONG-DISTANCE.

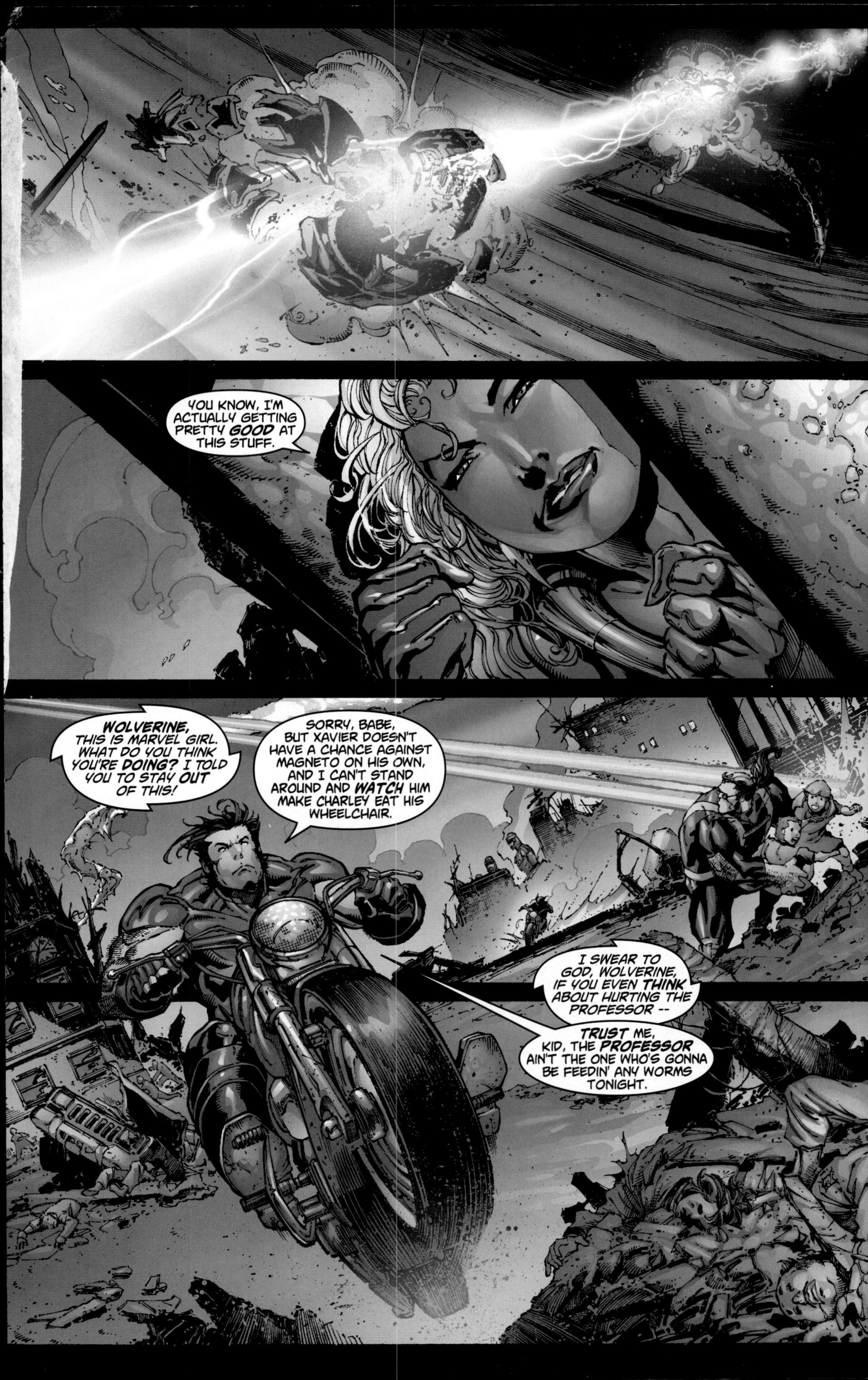
YOU KNOW, I'M ACTUALLY GETTING PRETTY GOOD AT THIS STUFF.
WOLVERINE, THIS IS MARVEL GIRL. WHAT DO YOU THINK YOU'RE DOING? I TOLD YOU TO STAY OUT OF THIS!
SORRY, BABE, BUT XAVIER DOESN'T HAVE A CHANCE AGAINST MAGNETO ON HIS OWN, AND I CAN'T STAND AROUND AND WATCH HIM MAKE CHARLEY EAT HIS WHEELCHAIR.
I SWEAR TO GOD, WOLVERINE, IF YOU EVEN THINK ABOUT HURTING THE PROFESSOR --
TRUST ME, KID, THE PROFESSOR AIN'T THE ONE WHO'S GONNA BE FEEDIN' ANY WORMS TONIGHT.

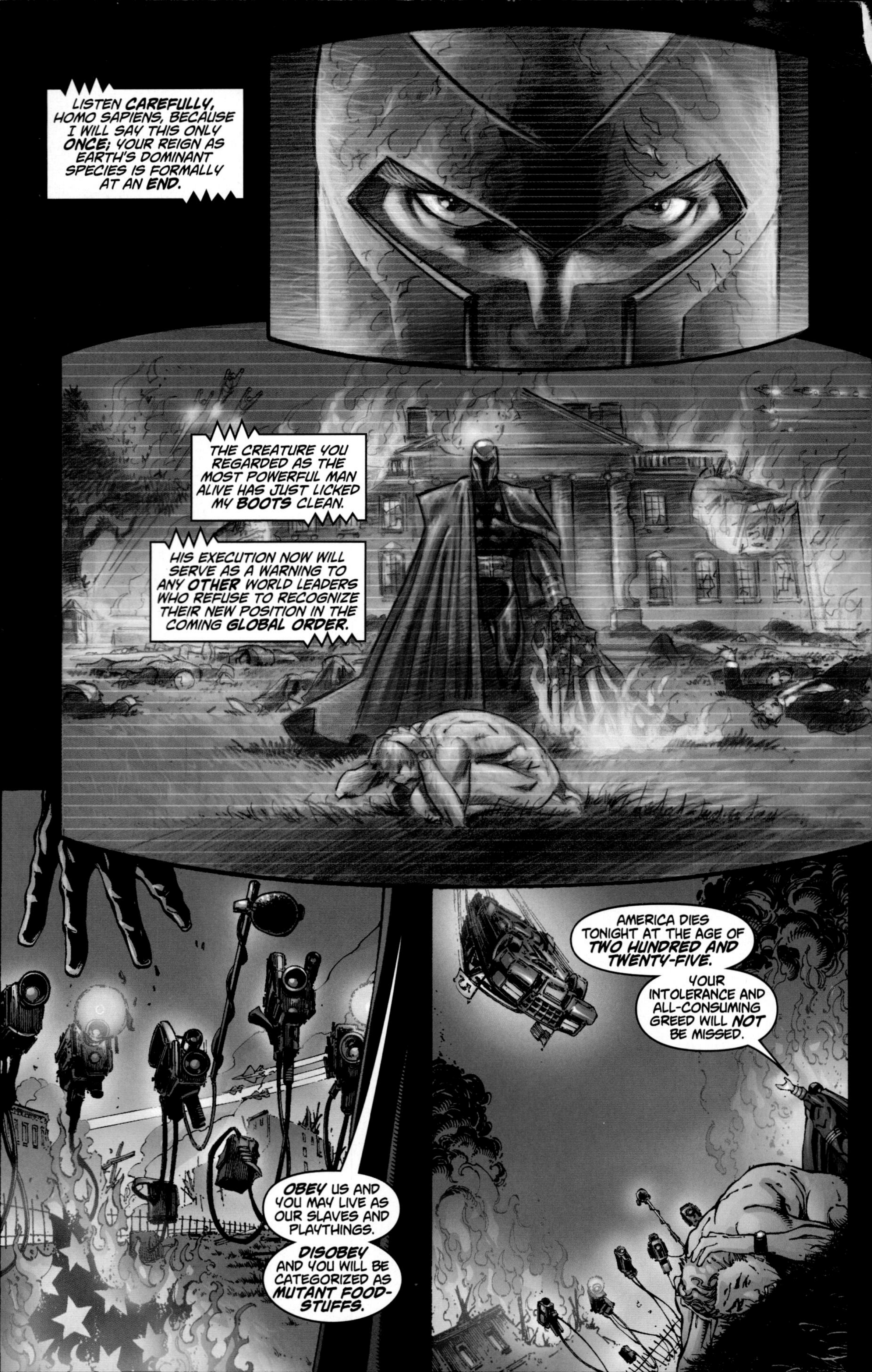
LISTEN **CAREFULLY**, HOMO SAPIENS, BECAUSE I WILL SAY THIS ONLY **ONCE**; YOUR REIGN AS EARTH'S DOMINANT SPECIES IS FORMALLY AT AN **END**.
THE CREATURE YOU REGARDED AS THE MOST POWERFUL MAN ALIVE HAS JUST LICKED MY **BOOTS** CLEAN.
HIS EXECUTION NOW WILL SERVE AS A WARNING TO ANY **OTHER** WORLD LEADERS WHO REFUSE TO RECOGNIZE THEIR NEW POSITION IN THE COMING **GLOBAL ORDER**.
OBEY US AND YOU MAY LIVE AS OUR SLAVES AND PLAYTHINGS.
DISOBEY AND YOU WILL BE CATEGORIZED AS **MUTANT FOOD-STUFFS.**
AMERICA DIES TONIGHT AT THE AGE OF **TWO HUNDRED AND TWENTY-FIVE.**
YOUR INTOLERANCE AND ALL-CONSUMING GREED WILL **NOT** BE MISSED.

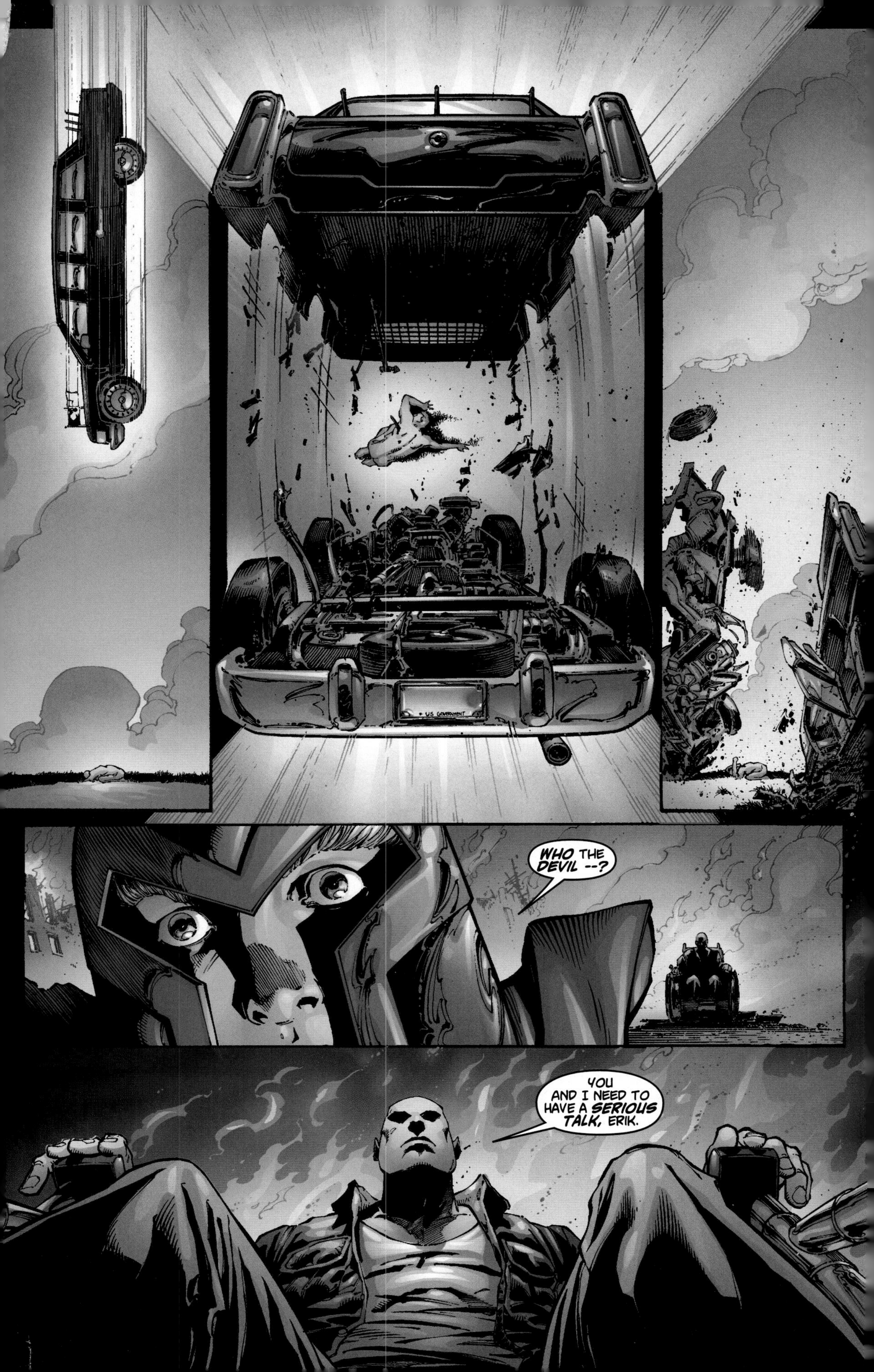
WHO THE DEVIL --?
YOU AND I NEED TO HAVE A SERIOUS TALK, ERIK.

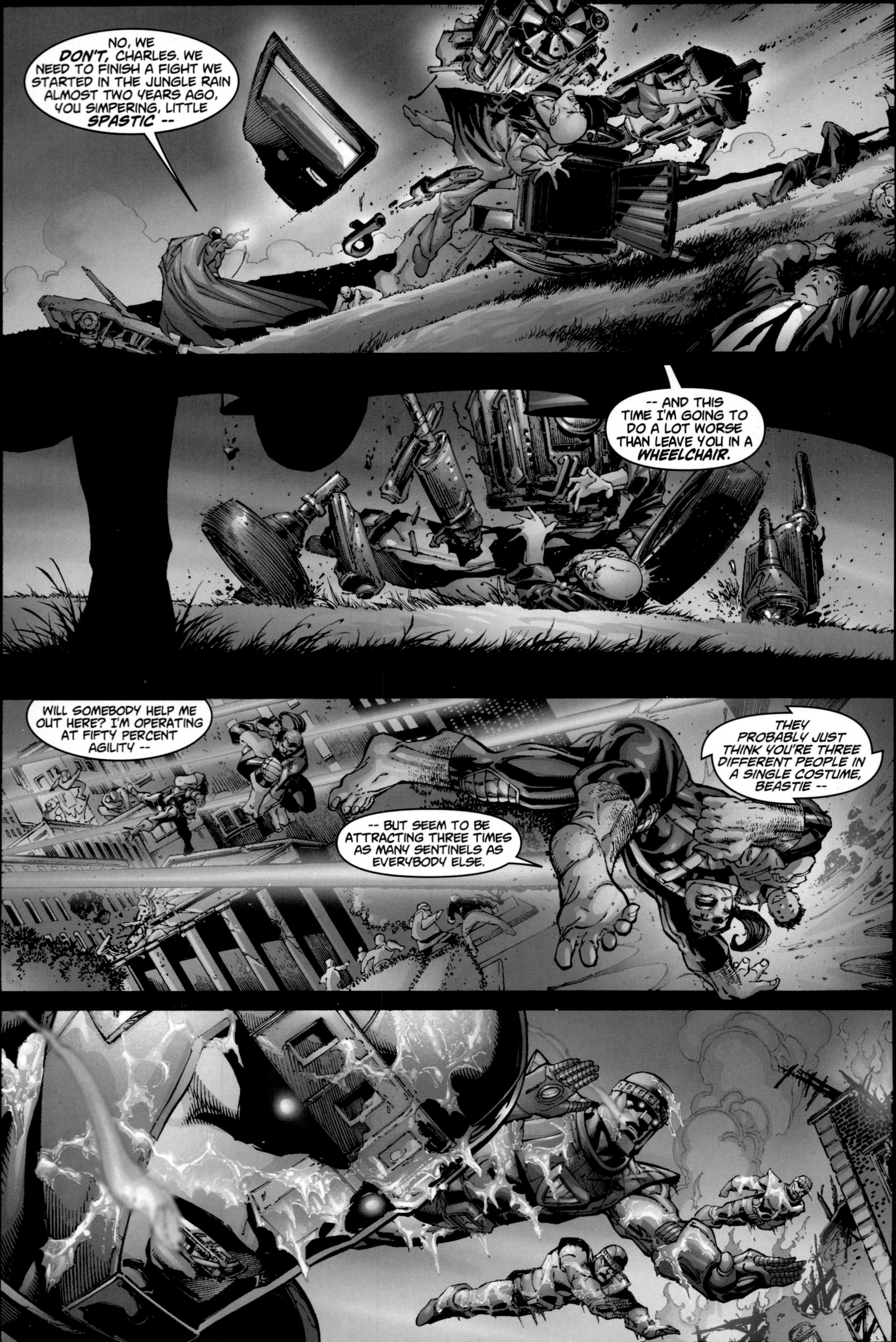
NO, WE DON'T, CHARLES. WE NEED TO FINISH A FIGHT WE STARTED IN THE JUNGLE RAIN ALMOST TWO YEARS AGO, YOU SIMPERING, LITTLE SPASTIC --
-- AND THIS TIME I'M GOING TO DO A LOT WORSE THAN LEAVE YOU IN A WHEELCHAIR.
WILL SOMEBODY HELP ME OUT HERE? I'M OPERATING AT FIFTY PERCENT AGILITY --
-- BUT SEEM TO BE ATTRACTING THREE TIMES AS MANY SENTINELS AS EVERYBODY ELSE.
THEY PROBABLY JUST THINK YOU'RE THREE DIFFERENT PEOPLE IN A SINGLE COSTUME, BEASTIE --

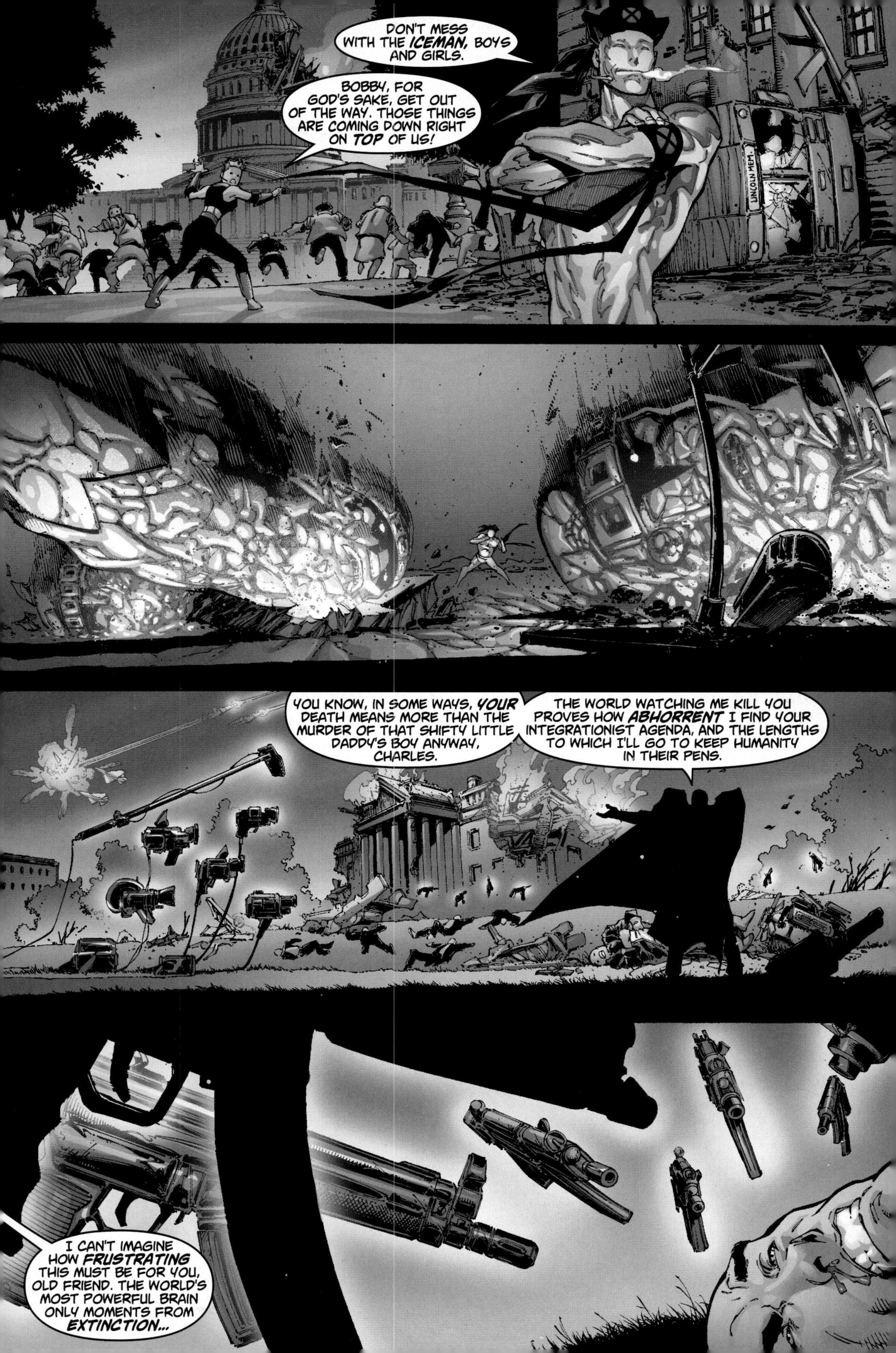

DON'T MESS WITH THE *ICEMAN,* BOYS AND GIRLS.
BOBBY, FOR GOD'S SAKE, GET OUT OF THE WAY. THOSE THINGS ARE COMING DOWN RIGHT ON *TOP* OF US!
LINCOLN MEM.
YOU KNOW, IN SOME WAYS, *YOUR* DEATH MEANS MORE THAN THE MURDER OF THAT SHIFTY LITTLE DADDY'S BOY ANYWAY, CHARLES.
THE WORLD WATCHING ME KILL YOU PROVES HOW *ABHORRENT* I FIND YOUR INTEGRATIONIST AGENDA, AND THE LENGTHS TO WHICH I'LL GO TO KEEP HUMANITY IN THEIR PENS.
I CAN'T IMAGINE HOW *FRUSTRATING* THIS MUST BE FOR YOU, OLD FRIEND. THE WORLD'S MOST POWERFUL BRAIN ONLY MOMENTS FROM *EXTINCTION...*

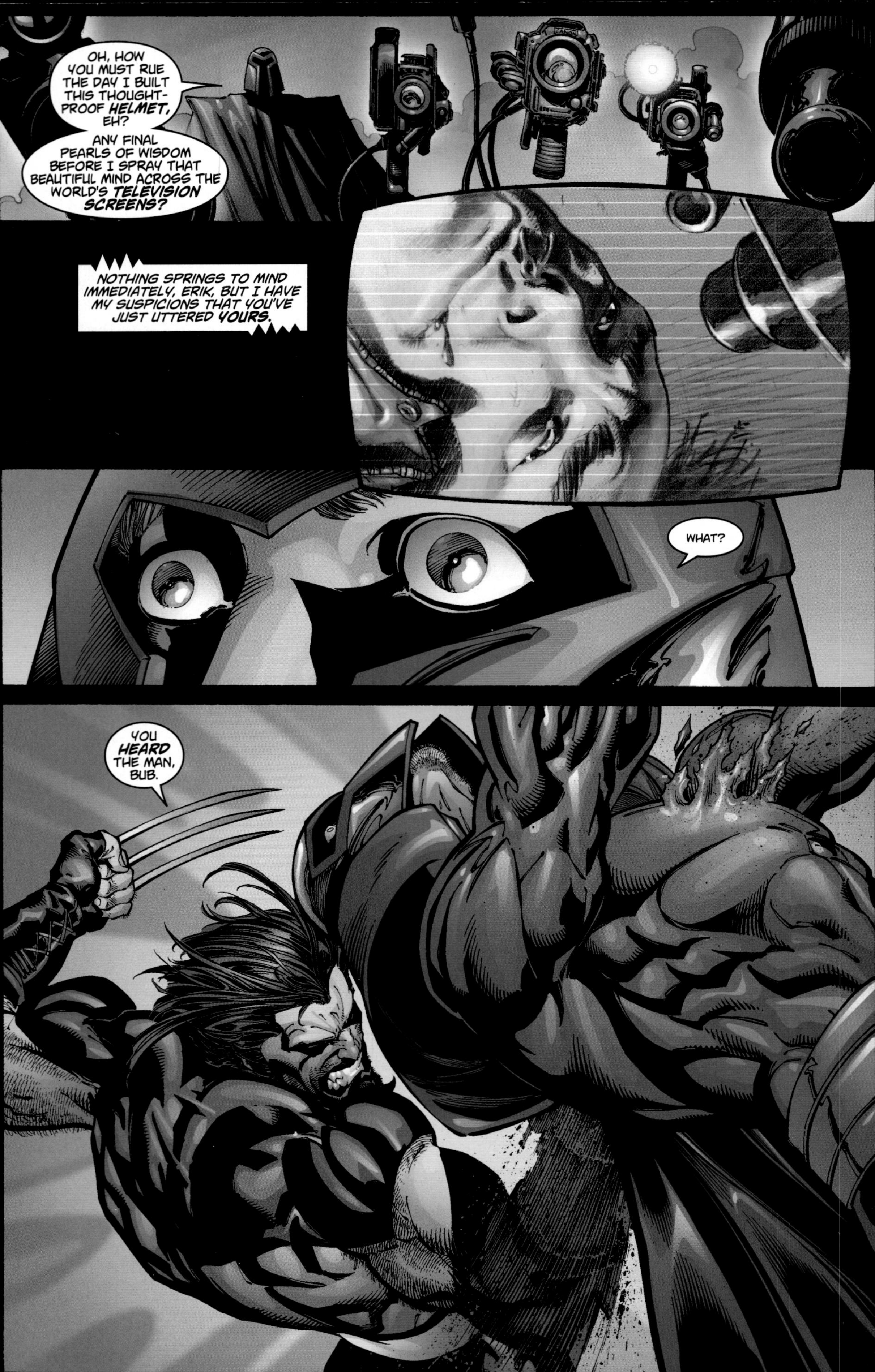
OH, HOW YOU MUST RUE THE DAY I BUILT THIS THOUGHT-PROOF HELMET, EH?
ANY FINAL PEARLS OF WISDOM BEFORE I SPRAY THAT BEAUTIFUL MIND ACROSS THE WORLD'S TELEVISION SCREENS?
NOTHING SPRINGS TO MIND IMMEDIATELY, ERIK, BUT I HAVE MY SUSPICIONS THAT YOU'VE JUST UTTERED YOURS.
WHAT?
YOU HEARD THE MAN, BUB.

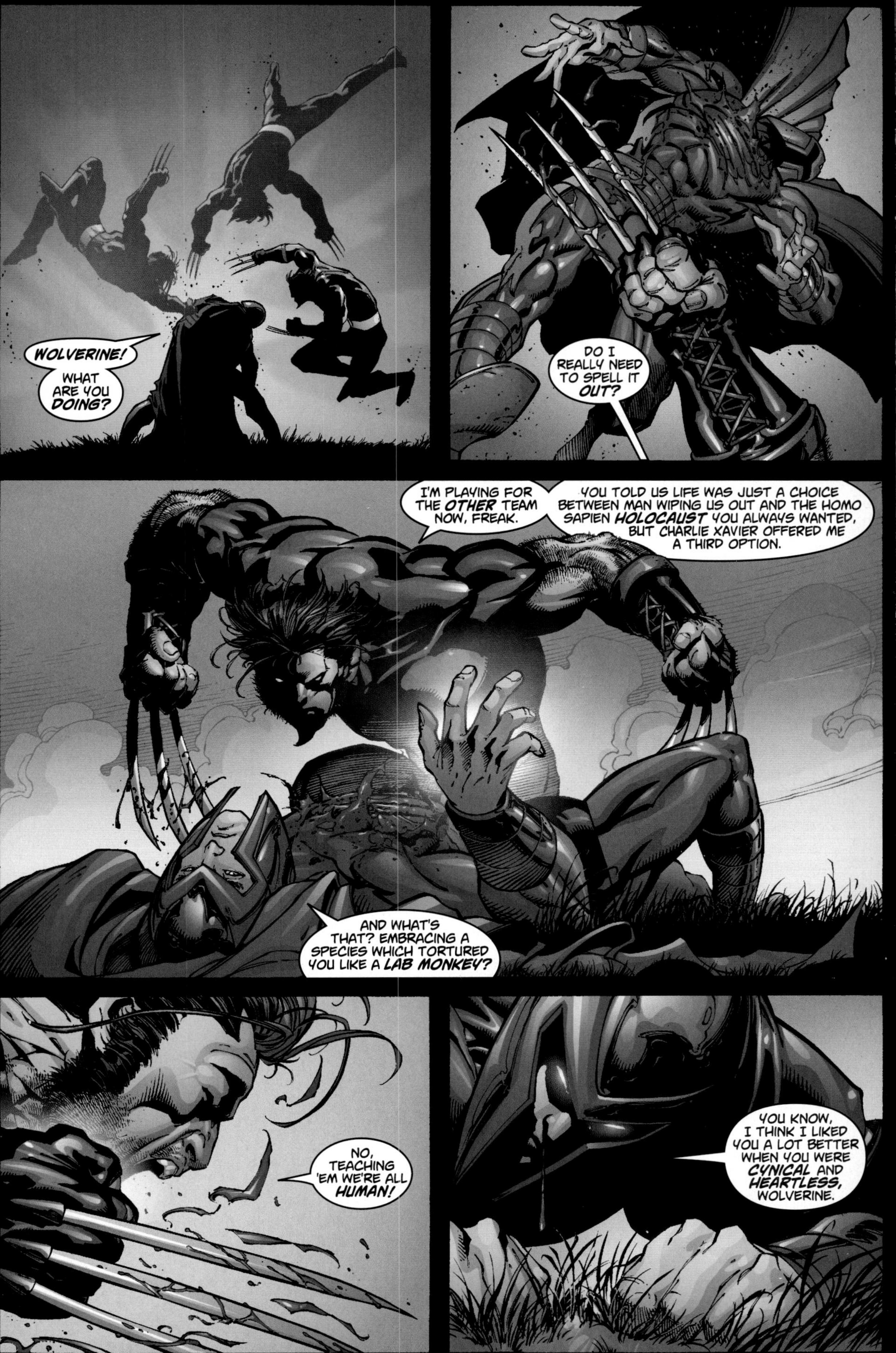

WOLVERINE! WHAT ARE YOU DOING?
DO I REALLY NEED TO SPELL IT OUT?
I'M PLAYING FOR THE OTHER TEAM NOW, FREAK.
YOU TOLD US LIFE WAS JUST A CHOICE BETWEEN MAN WIPING US OUT AND THE HOMO SAPIEN HOLOCAUST YOU ALWAYS WANTED, BUT CHARLIE XAVIER OFFERED ME A THIRD OPTION.
AND WHAT'S THAT? EMBRACING A SPECIES WHICH TORTURED YOU LIKE A LAB MONKEY?
NO, TEACHING 'EM WE'RE ALL HUMAN!
YOU KNOW, I THINK I LIKED YOU A LOT BETTER WHEN YOU WERE CYNICAL AND HEARTLESS, WOLVERINE.

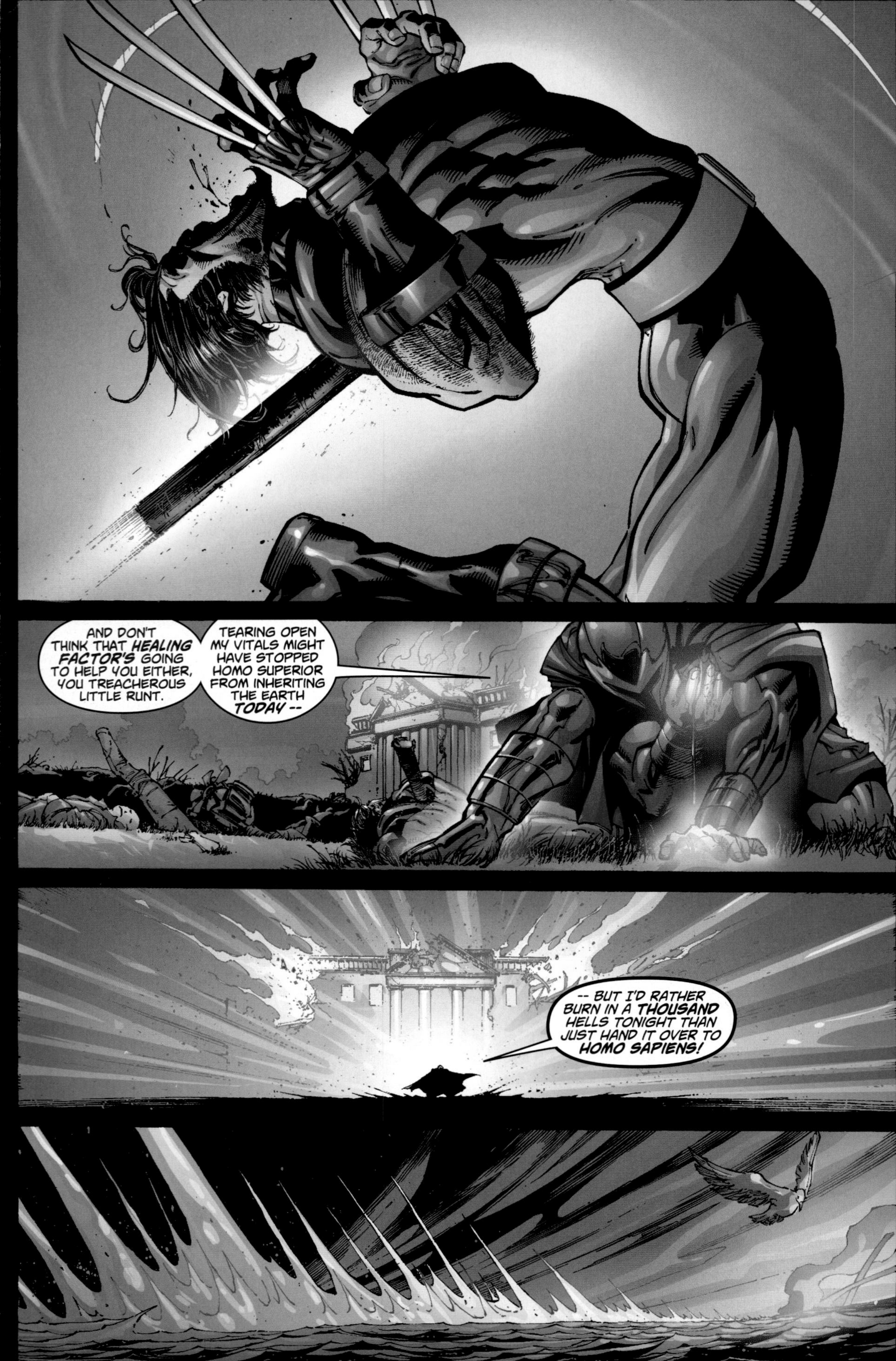

AND DON'T THINK THAT HEALING FACTOR'S GOING TO HELP YOU EITHER, YOU TREACHEROUS LITTLE RUNT.
TEARING OPEN MY VITALS MIGHT HAVE STOPPED HOMO SUPERIOR FROM INHERITING THE EARTH TODAY --
-- BUT I'D RATHER BURN IN A THOUSAND HELLS TONIGHT THAN JUST HAND IT OVER TO HOMO SAPIENS!

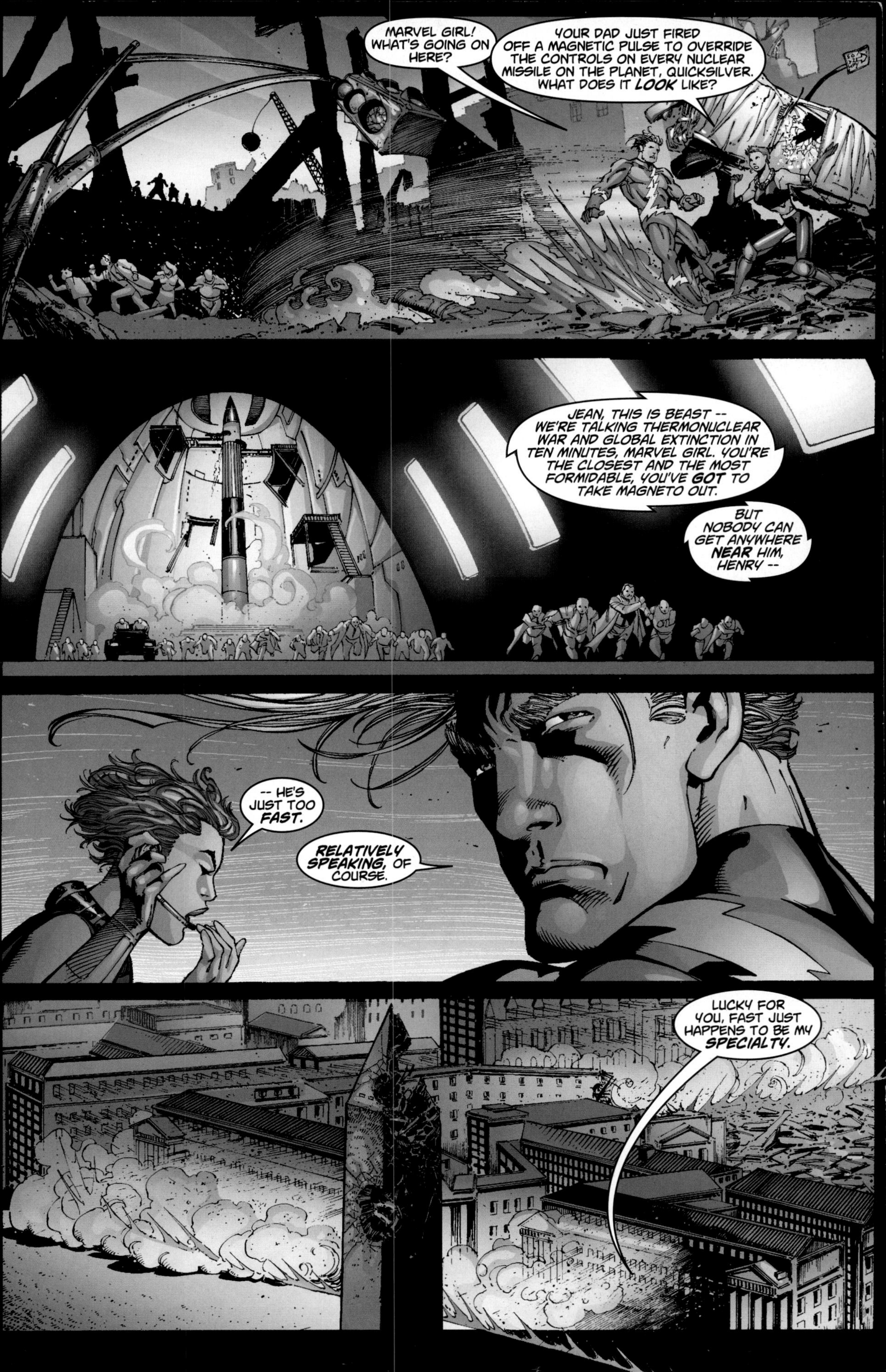
MARVEL GIRL! WHAT'S GOING ON HERE?
YOUR DAD JUST FIRED OFF A MAGNETIC PULSE TO OVERRIDE THE CONTROLS ON EVERY NUCLEAR MISSILE ON THE PLANET, QUICKSILVER. WHAT DOES IT LOOK LIKE?
JEAN, THIS IS BEAST -- WE'RE TALKING THERMONUCLEAR WAR AND GLOBAL EXTINCTION IN TEN MINUTES, MARVEL GIRL. YOU'RE THE CLOSEST AND THE MOST FORMIDABLE, YOU'VE GOT TO TAKE MAGNETO OUT.
BUT NOBODY CAN GET ANYWHERE NEAR HIM, HENRY --
-- HE'S JUST TOO FAST.
RELATIVELY SPEAKING, OF COURSE.
LUCKY FOR YOU, FAST JUST HAPPENS TO BE MY SPECIALTY.

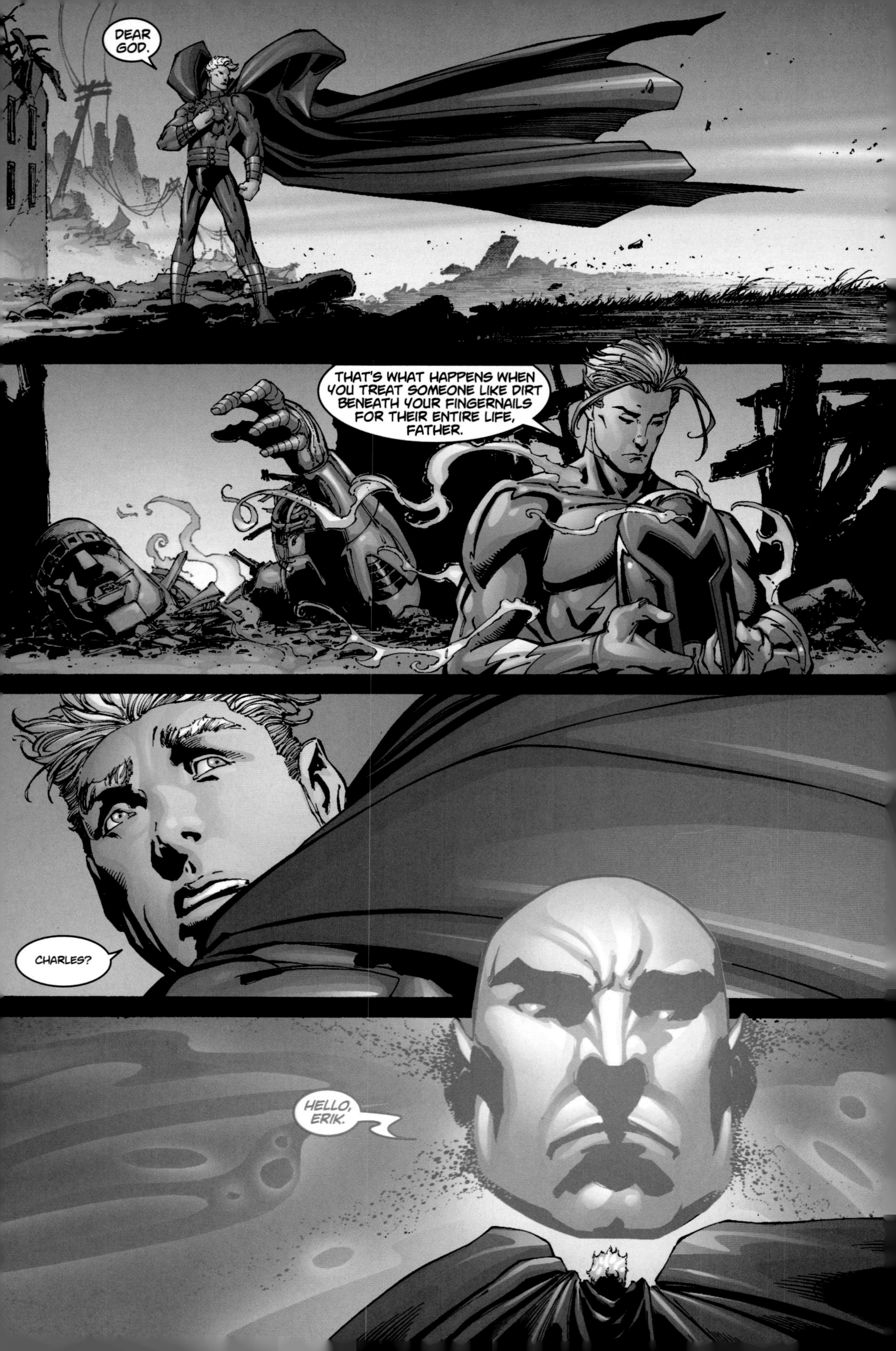
DEAR GOD.
THAT'S WHAT HAPPENS WHEN YOU TREAT SOMEONE LIKE DIRT BENEATH YOUR FINGERNAILS FOR THEIR ENTIRE LIFE, FATHER.
CHARLES?
HELLO, ERIK.

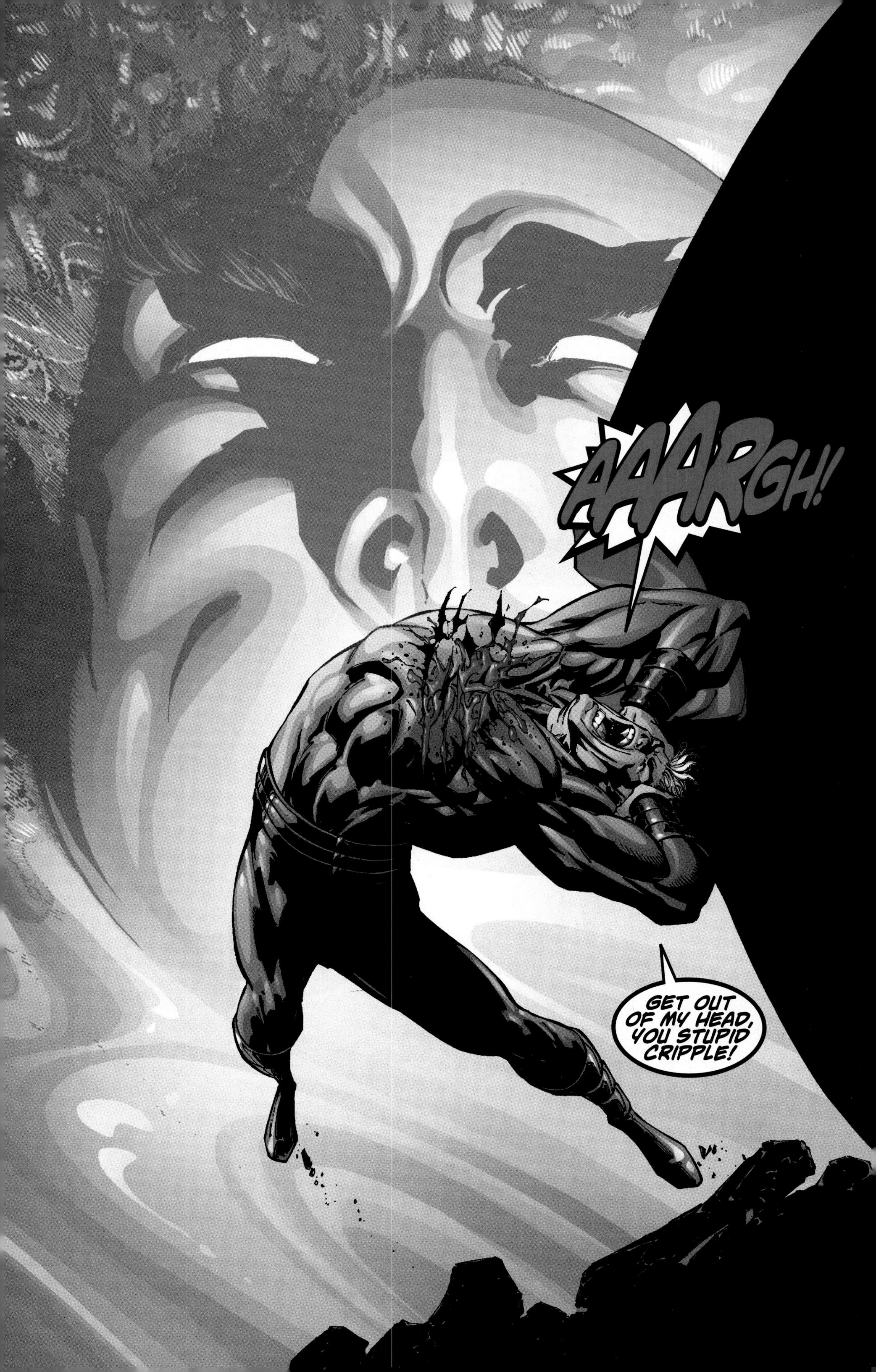
AAARGH!
GET OUT OF MY HEAD, YOU STUPID CRIPPLE!

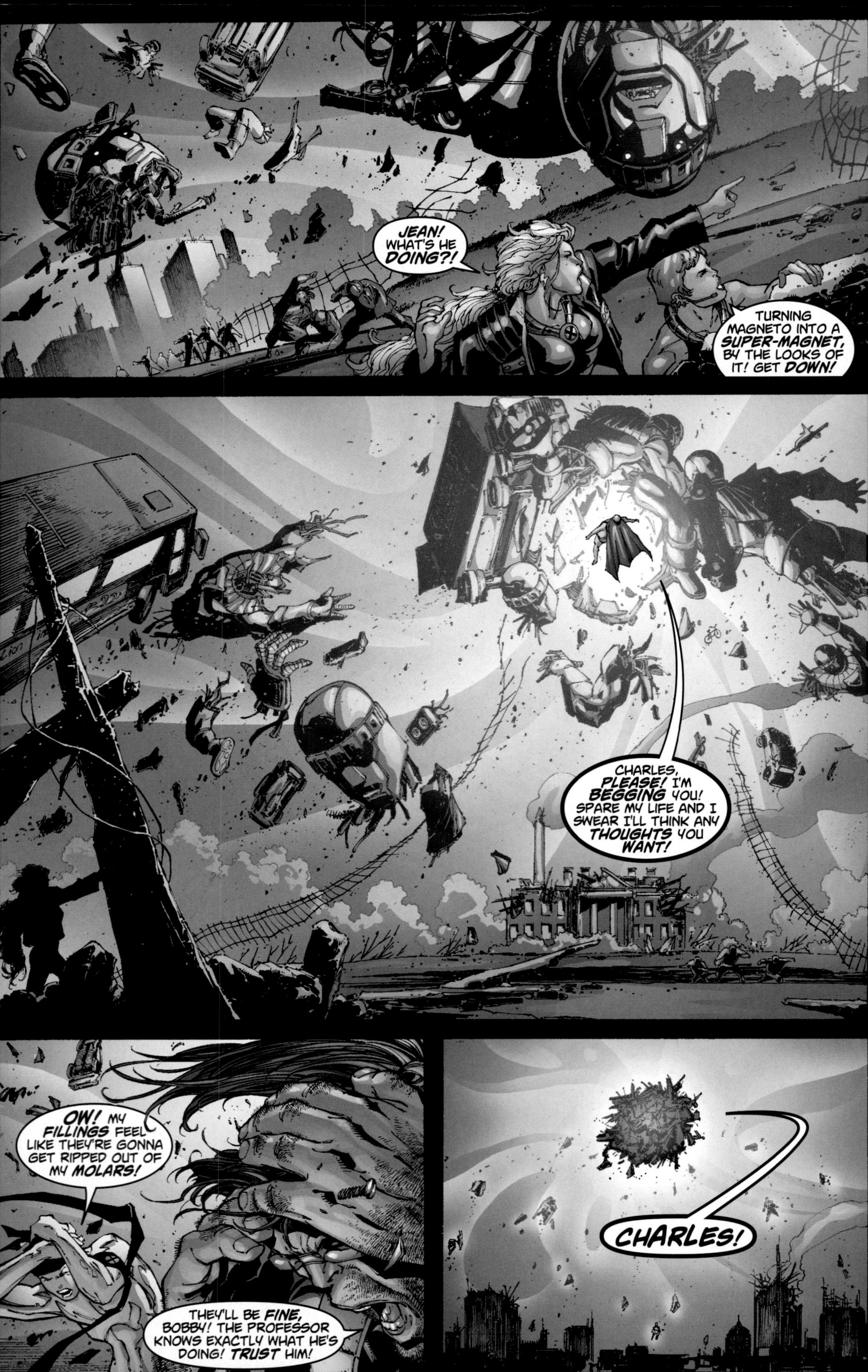
JEAN! WHAT'S HE DOING?!
TURNING MAGNETO INTO A SUPER-MAGNET, BY THE LOOKS OF IT! GET DOWN!
CHARLES, PLEASE! I'M BEGGING YOU! SPARE MY LIFE AND I SWEAR I'LL THINK ANY THOUGHTS YOU WANT!
OW! MY FILLINGS FEEL LIKE THEY'RE GONNA GET RIPPED OUT OF MY MOLARS!
THEY'LL BE FINE, BOBBY! THE PROFESSOR KNOWS EXACTLY WHAT HE'S DOING! TRUST HIM!
CHARLES!

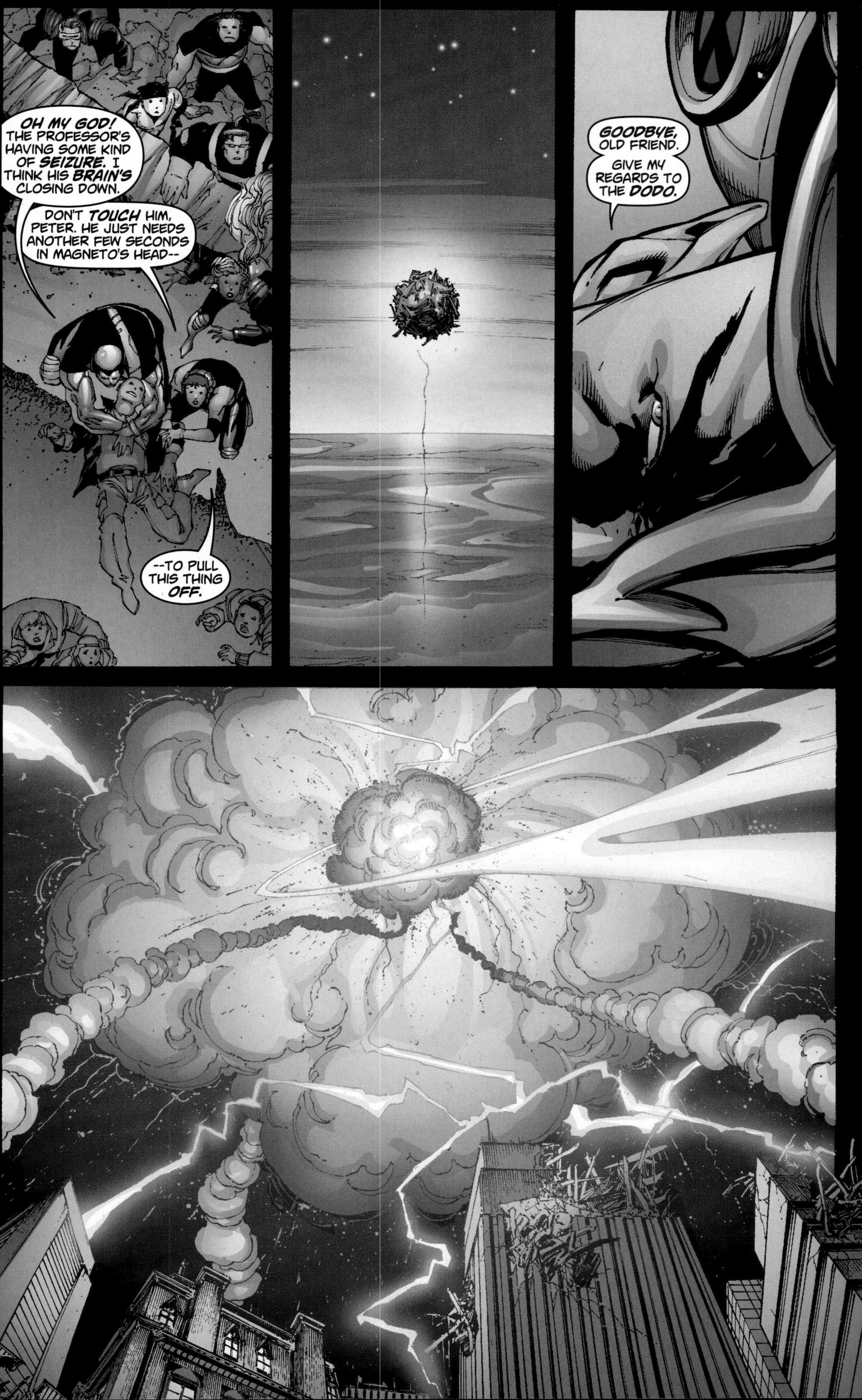
OH MY GOD! THE PROFESSOR'S HAVING SOME KIND OF SEIZURE. I THINK HIS BRAIN'S CLOSING DOWN.
DON'T TOUCH HIM, PETER. HE JUST NEEDS ANOTHER FEW SECONDS IN MAGNETO'S HEAD--
--TO PULL THIS THING OFF.
GOODBYE, OLD FRIEND.
GIVE MY REGARDS TO THE DODO.

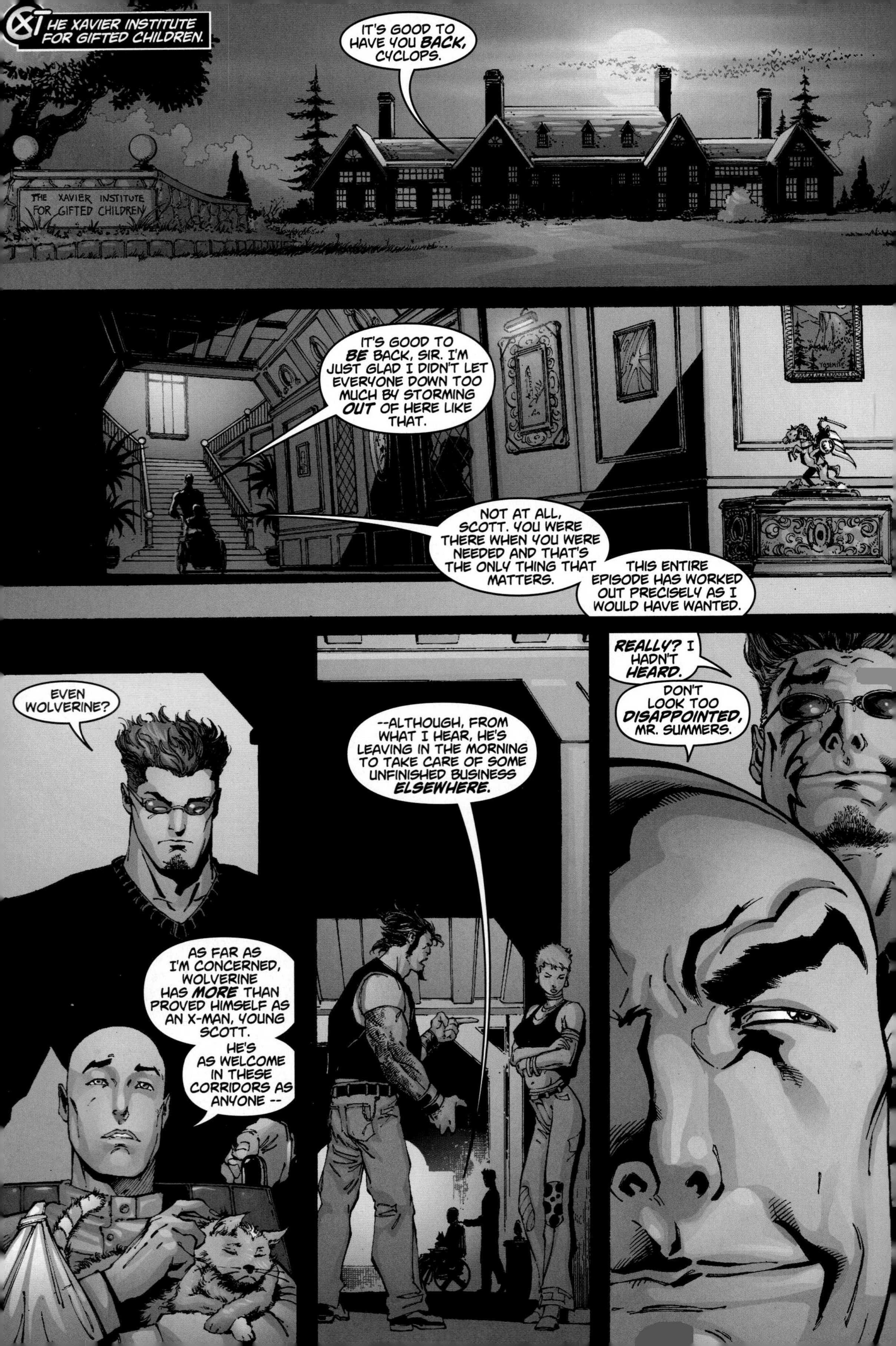
THE XAVIER INSTITUTE FOR GIFTED CHILDREN.
IT'S GOOD TO HAVE YOU BACK, CYCLOPS.
THE XAVIER INSTITUTE FOR GIFTED CHILDREN
IT'S GOOD TO BE BACK, SIR. I'M JUST GLAD I DIDN'T LET EVERYONE DOWN TOO MUCH BY STORMING OUT OF HERE LIKE THAT.
NOT AT ALL, SCOTT. YOU WERE THERE WHEN YOU WERE NEEDED AND THAT'S THE ONLY THING THAT MATTERS.
THIS ENTIRE EPISODE HAS WORKED OUT PRECISELY AS I WOULD HAVE WANTED.
EVEN WOLVERINE?
AS FAR AS I'M CONCERNED, WOLVERINE HAS MORE THAN PROVED HIMSELF AS AN X-MAN, YOUNG SCOTT.
HE'S AS WELCOME IN THESE CORRIDORS AS ANYONE --
--ALTHOUGH, FROM WHAT I HEAR, HE'S LEAVING IN THE MORNING TO TAKE CARE OF SOME UNFINISHED BUSINESS ELSEWHERE.
REALLY? I HADN'T HEARD.
DON'T LOOK TOO DISAPPOINTED, MR. SUMMERS.

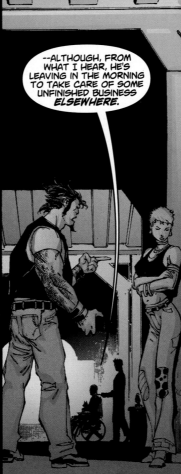

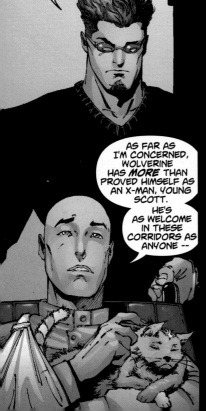

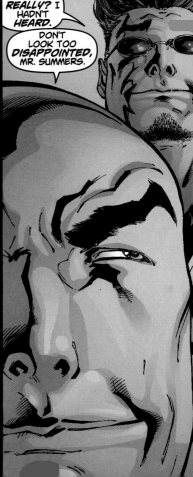

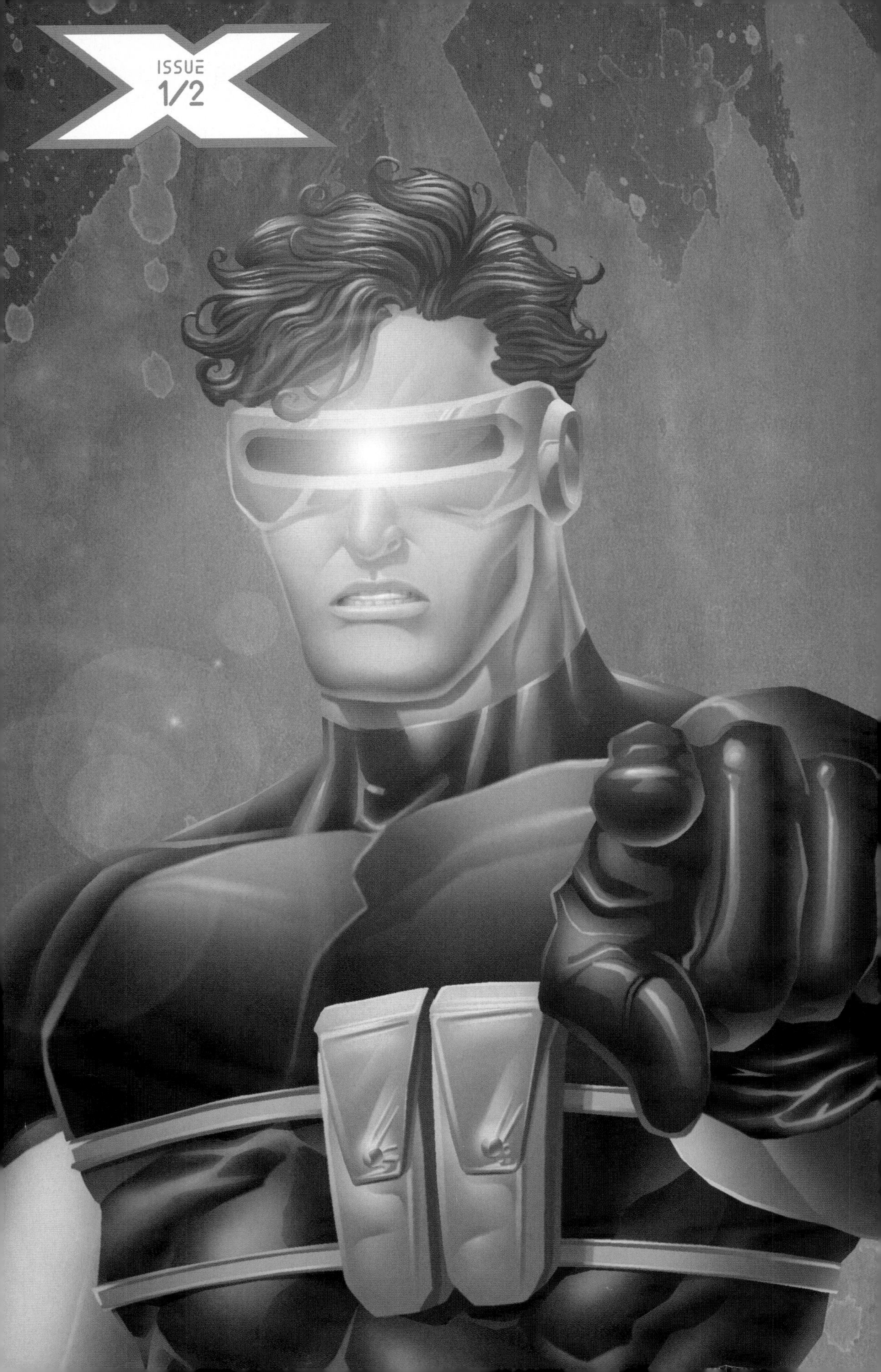
ISSUE
1/2

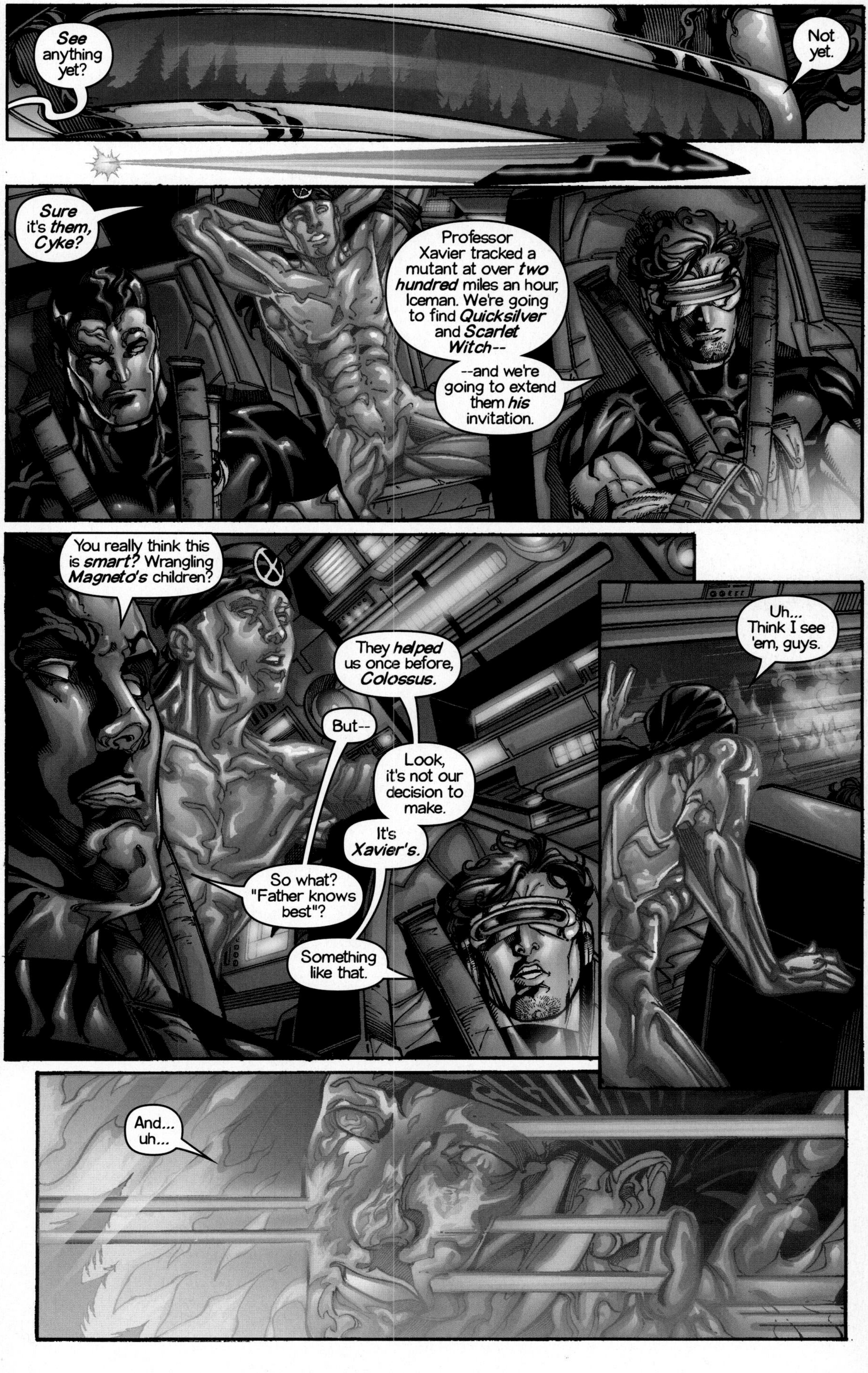
See anything yet?
Not yet.
Sure it's them, Cyke?
Professor Xavier tracked a mutant at over two hundred miles an hour, Iceman. We're going to find Quicksilver and Scarlet Witch--
--and we're going to extend them his invitation.
You really think this is smart? Wrangling Magneto's children?
They helped us once before, Colossus.
But--
Look, it's not our decision to make.
It's Xavier's.
So what? "Father knows best"?
Something like that.
Uh... Think I see 'em, guys.
And... uh...

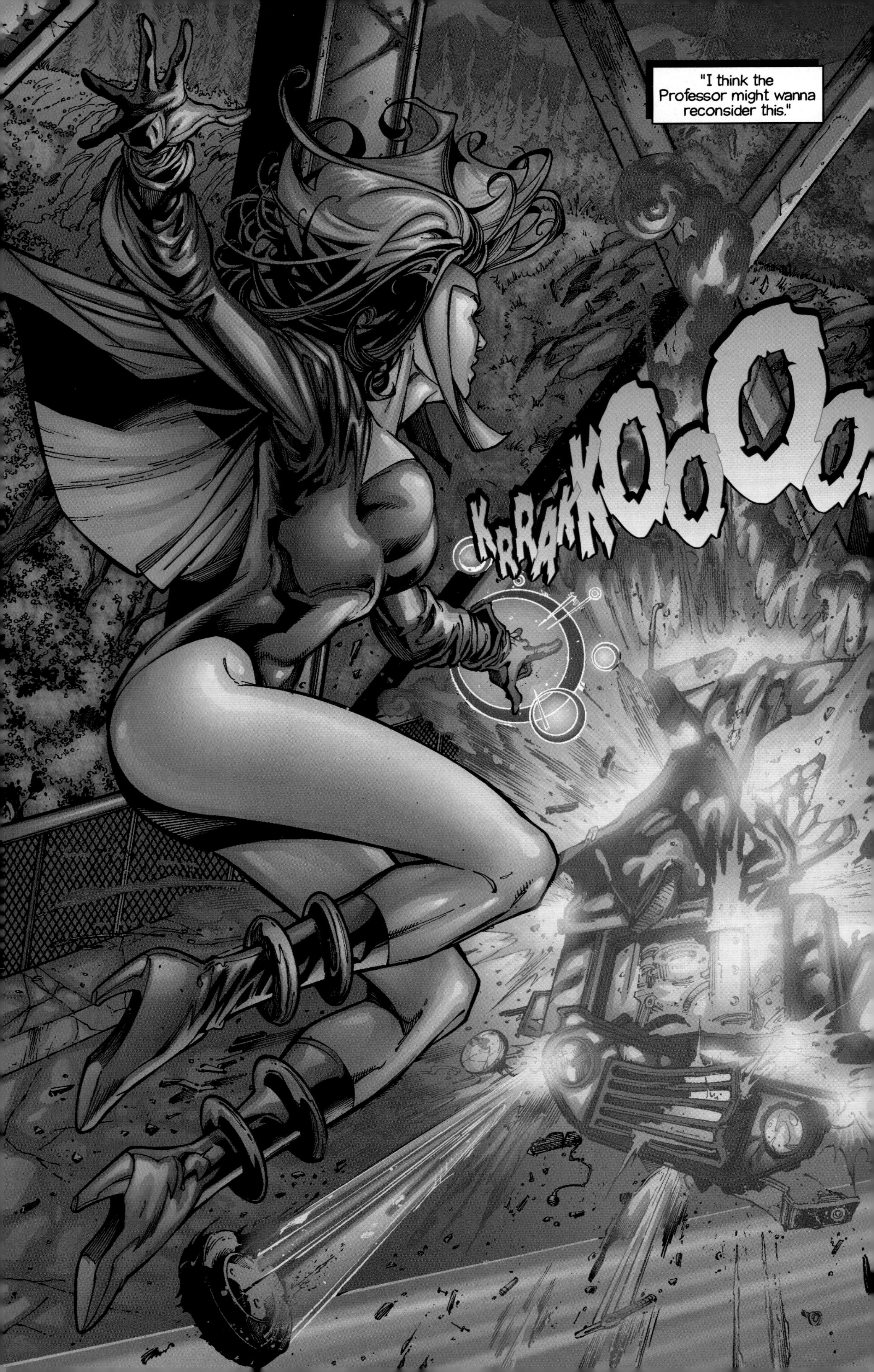
"I think the Professor might wanna reconsider this."
KRRAKKOOOOO

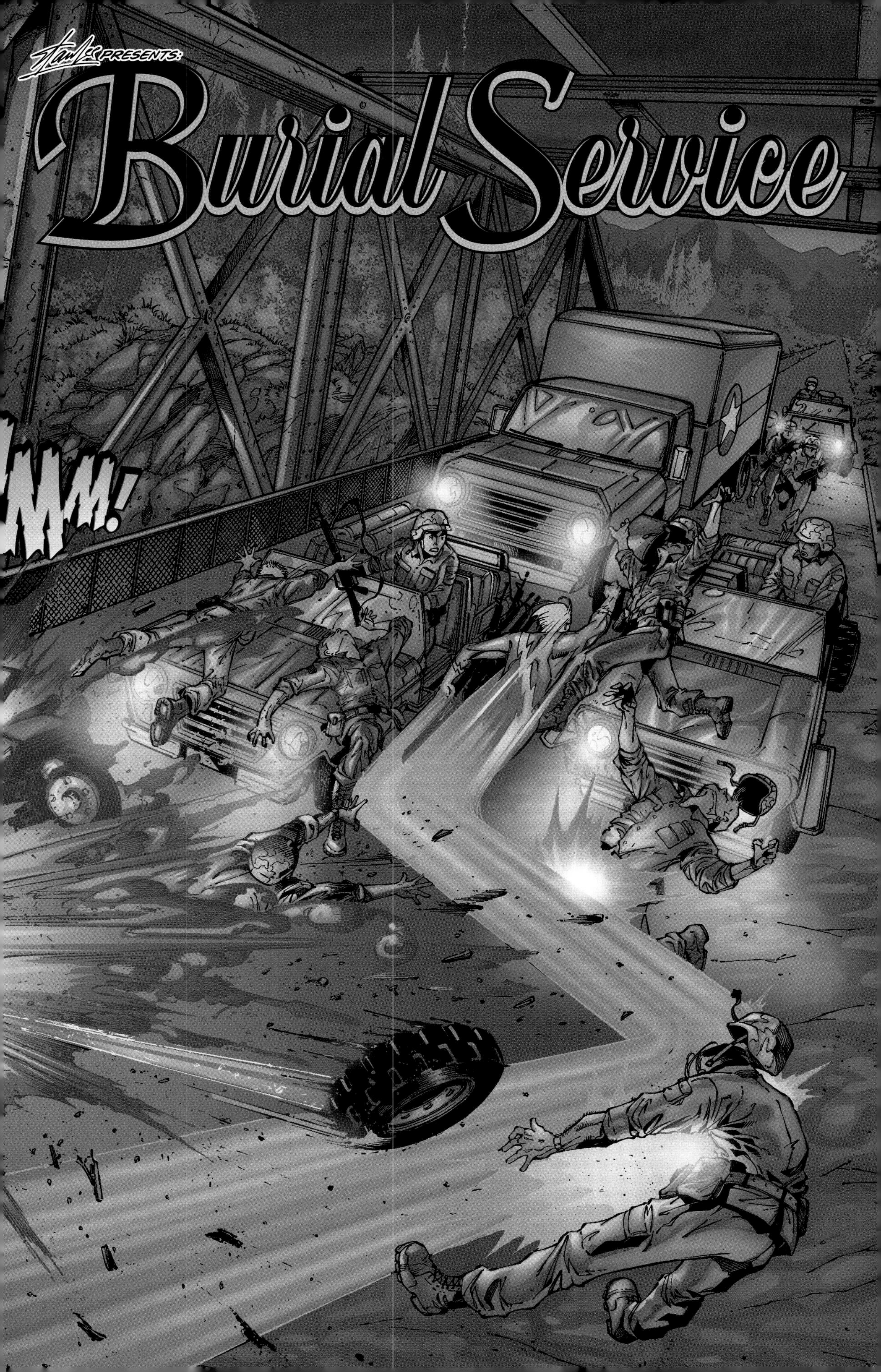
PRESENTS:
Burial Service
MM!

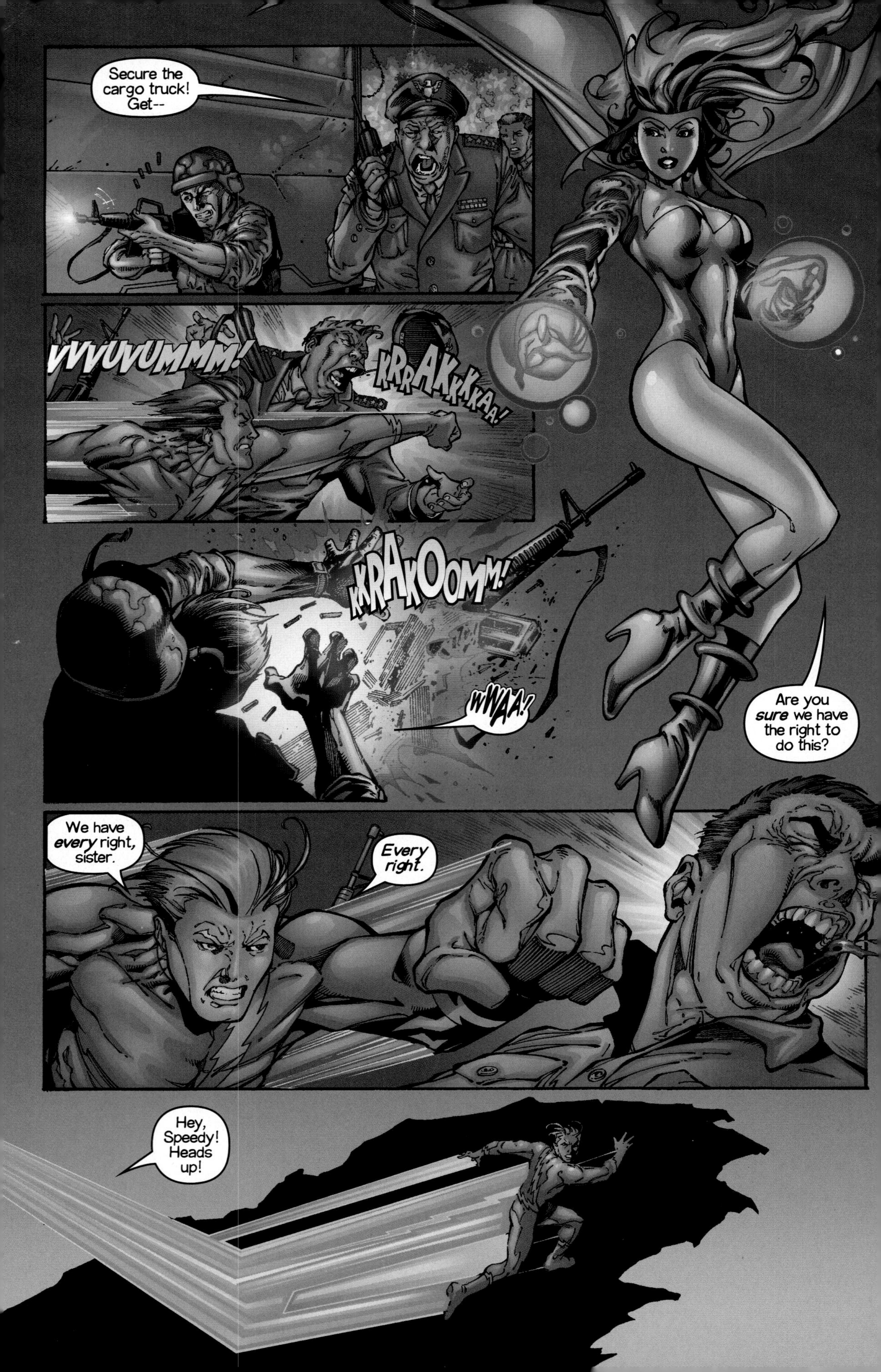
Secure the cargo truck! Get--
VVVUVUMMM!
KRRAKKKKAA!
KKRAKOOMM!
WWAA!
Are you *sure* we have the right to do this?
We have *every* right, sister.
Every right.
Hey, Speedy! Heads up!

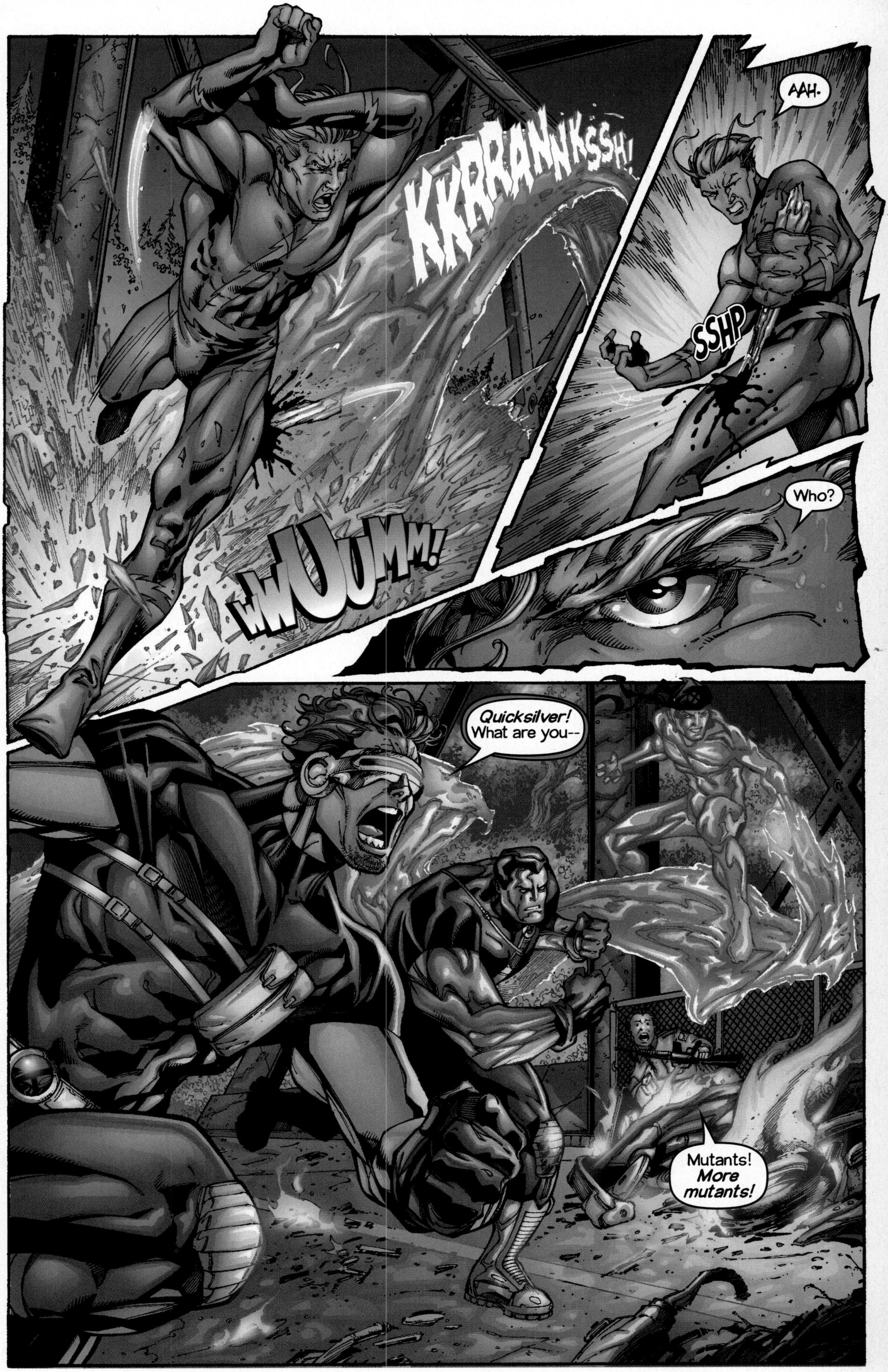
KKRRANNKSSH!
WWUUMM!
AAH.
SSHP
Who?
Quicksilver! What are you--
Mutants! More mutants!

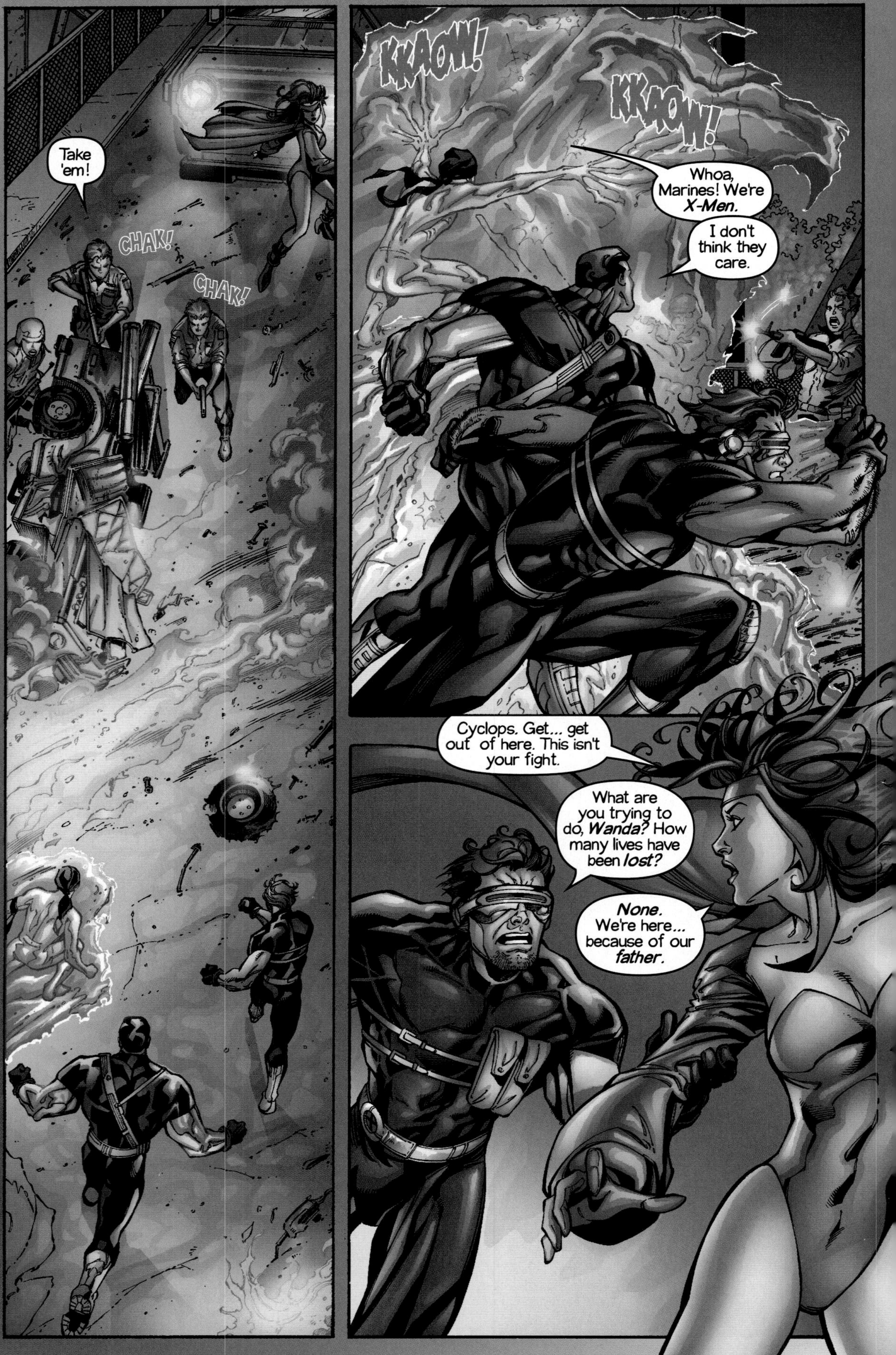
Take 'em!
CHAK!
CHAK!
KKAOW!
KKAOW!
Whoa, Marines! We're *X-Men.*
I don't think they care.
Cyclops. Get... get out of here. This isn't your fight.
What are you trying to do, *Wanda?* How many lives have been *lost?*
None. We're here... because of our *father.*

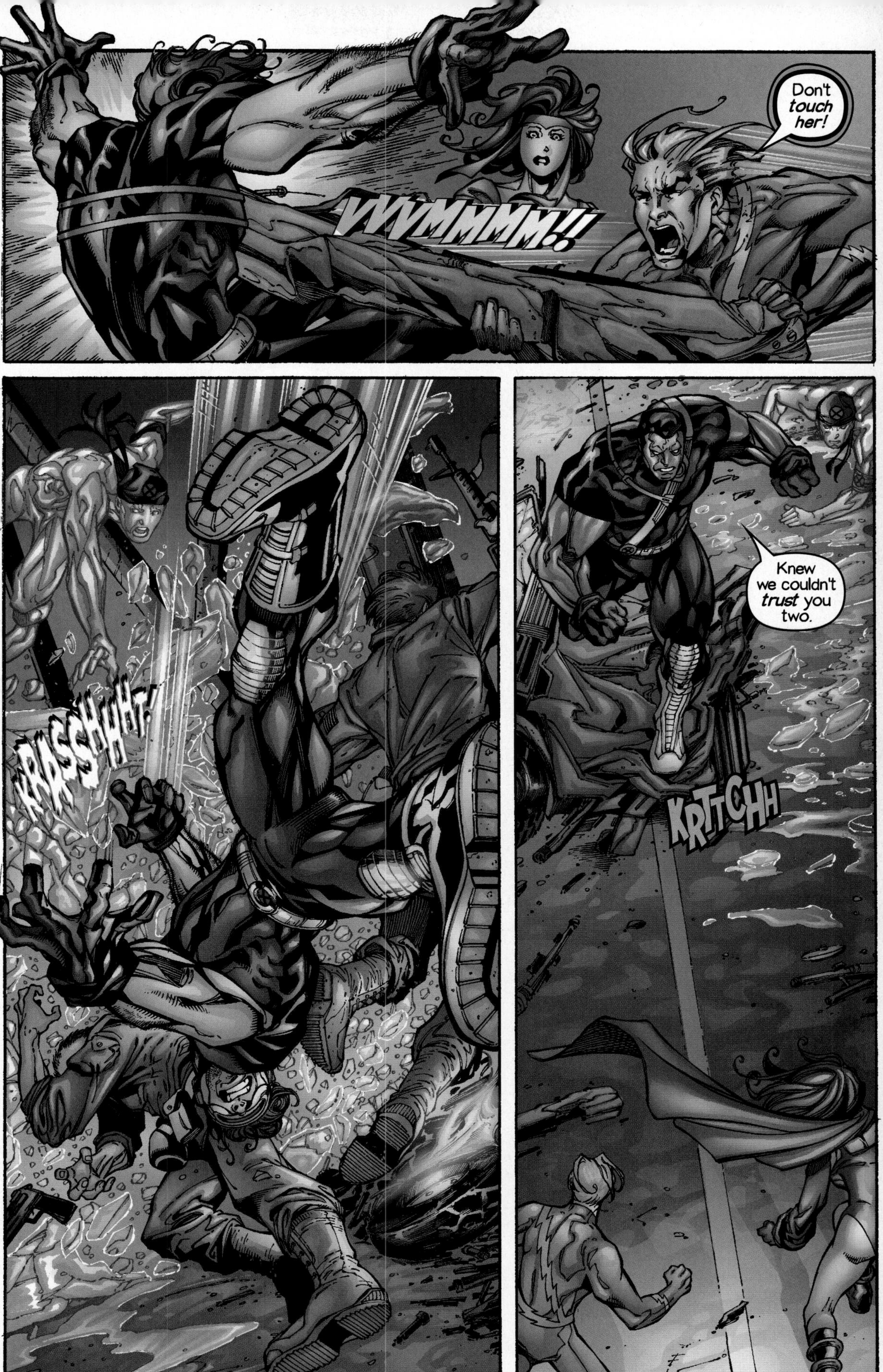
Don't touch her!
VVVMMMM!!
KRASSHHHT!
Knew we couldn't trust you two.
KRTTCHH

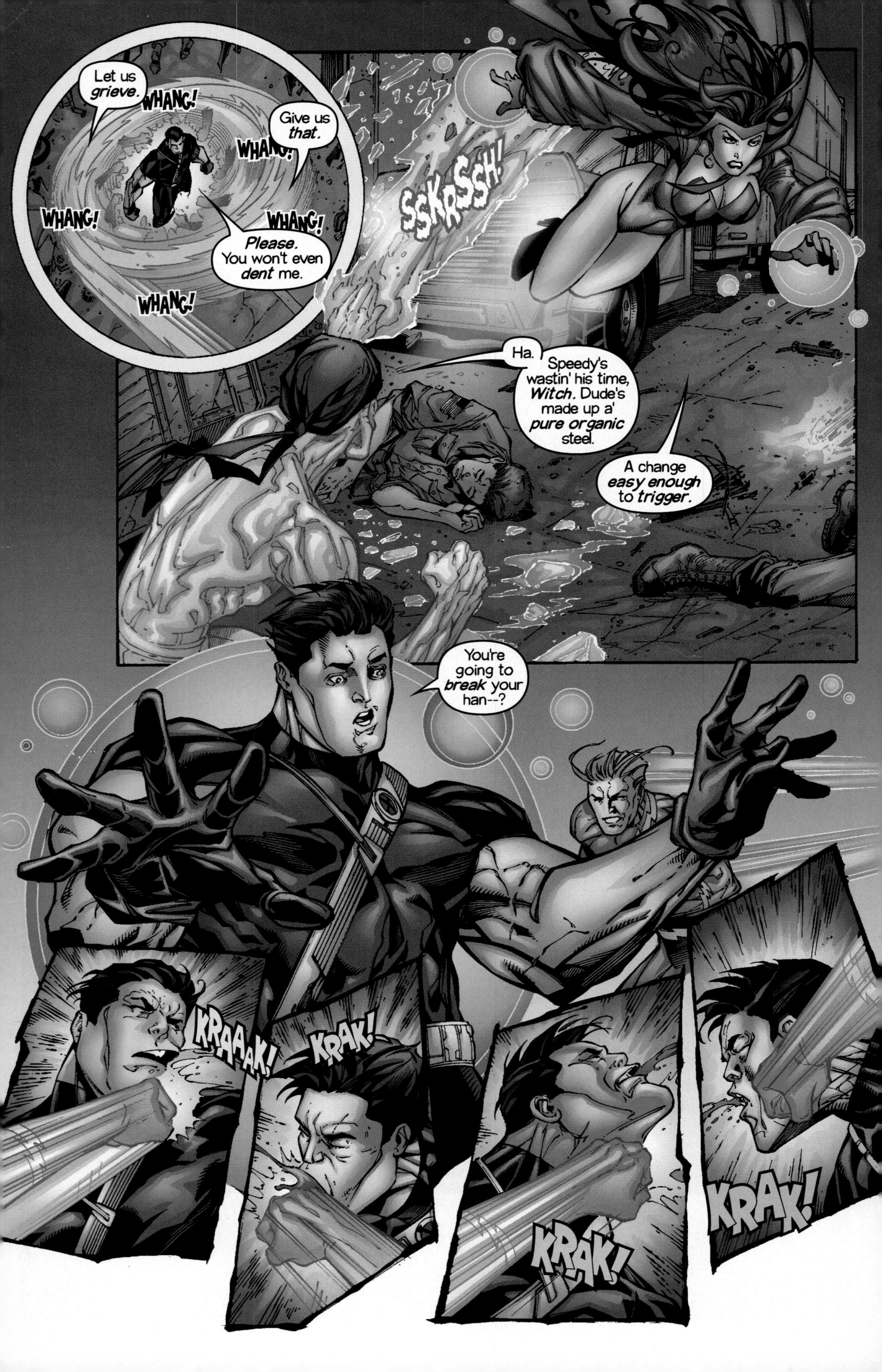
Let us grieve.
WHANG!
Give us that.
WHANG!
WHANG!
WHANG!
Please. You won't even dent me.
WHANG!
SSKRSSH!
Ha.
Speedy's wastin' his time, Witch. Dude's made up a' pure organic steel.
A change easy enough to trigger.
You're going to break your han--?
KRAAAK!
KRAK!
KRAK!
KRAK!

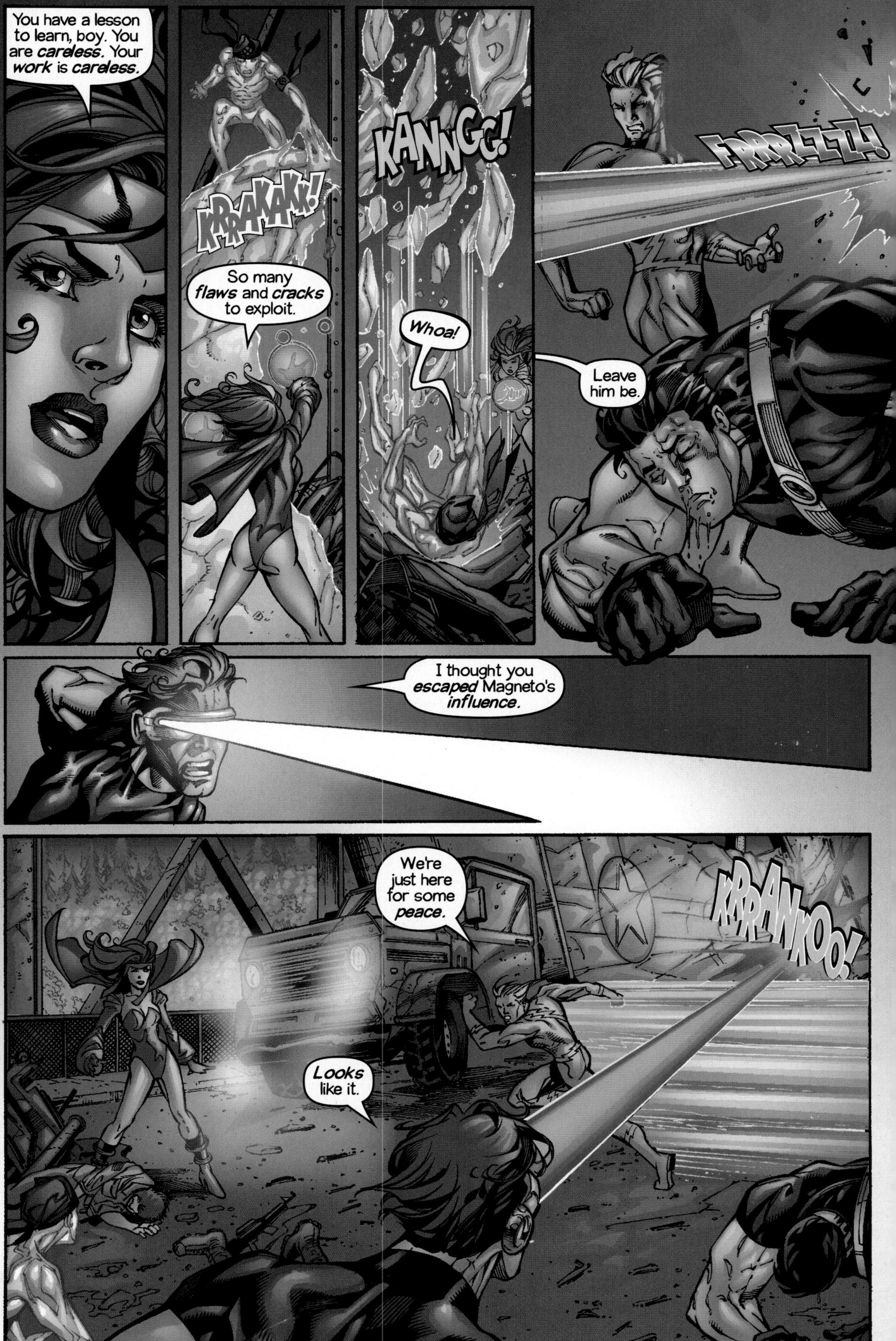
You have a lesson to learn, boy. You are *careless.* Your *work* is *careless.*
KRRAKAKK!
So many *flaws* and *cracks* to exploit.
KANNGG!
Whoa!
FRRRZZZZ!
Leave him be.
I thought you *escaped* Magneto's *influence.*
We're just here for some *peace.*
KRRANKOO!
Looks like it.

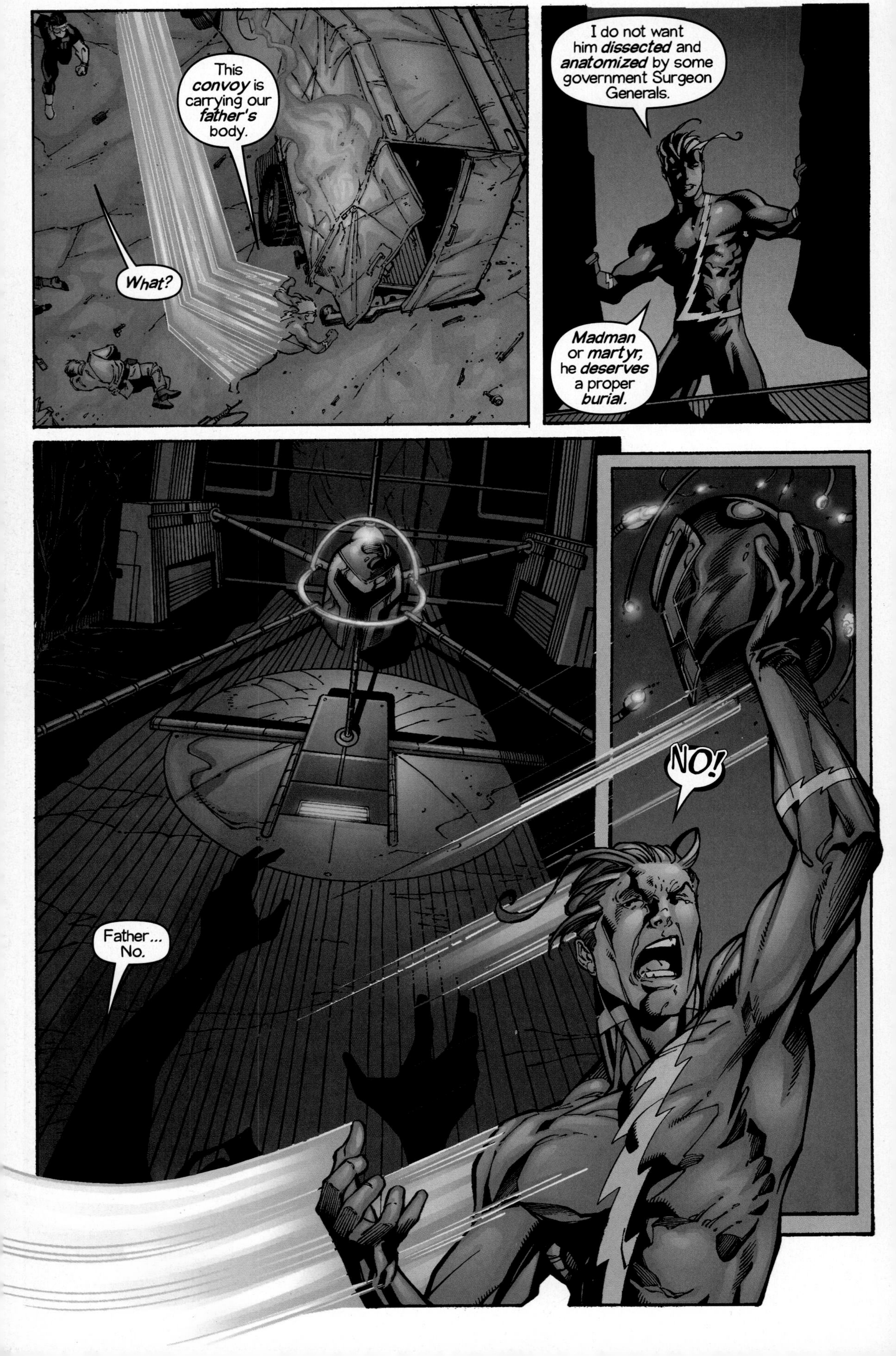
This convoy is carrying our father's body.
What?
I do not want him dissected and anatomized by some government Surgeon Generals.
Madman or martyr, he deserves a proper burial.
NO!
Father... No.

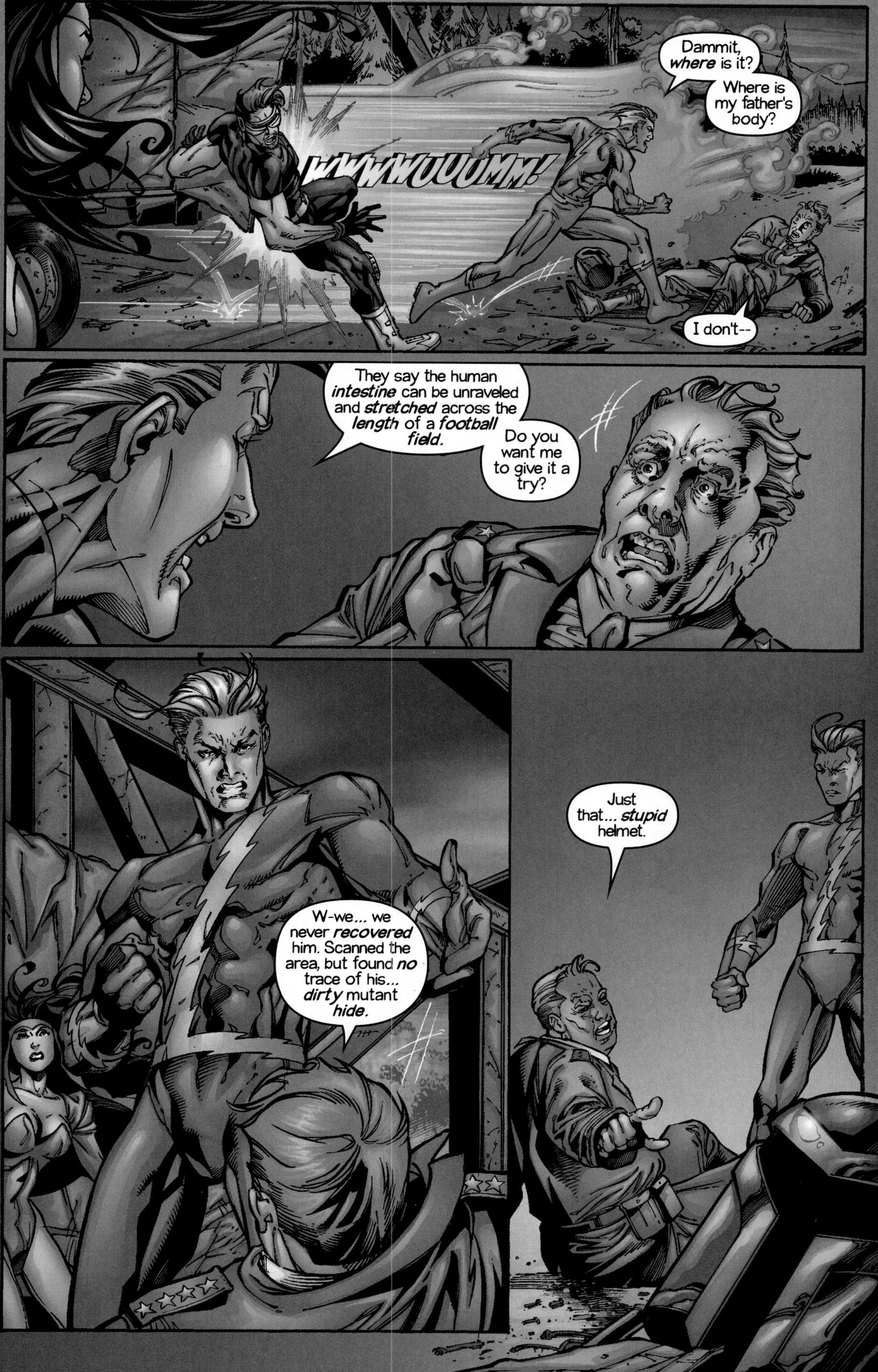

Dammit, *where* is it?
Where is my father's body?
WWWWOUUUMM!
I don't--
They say the human *intestine* can be unraveled and *stretched* across the *length* of a *football field.*
Do you want me to give it a try?
W-we... we never *recovered* him. Scanned the area, but found *no* trace of his... *dirty* mutant *hide.*
Just that... *stupid* helmet.

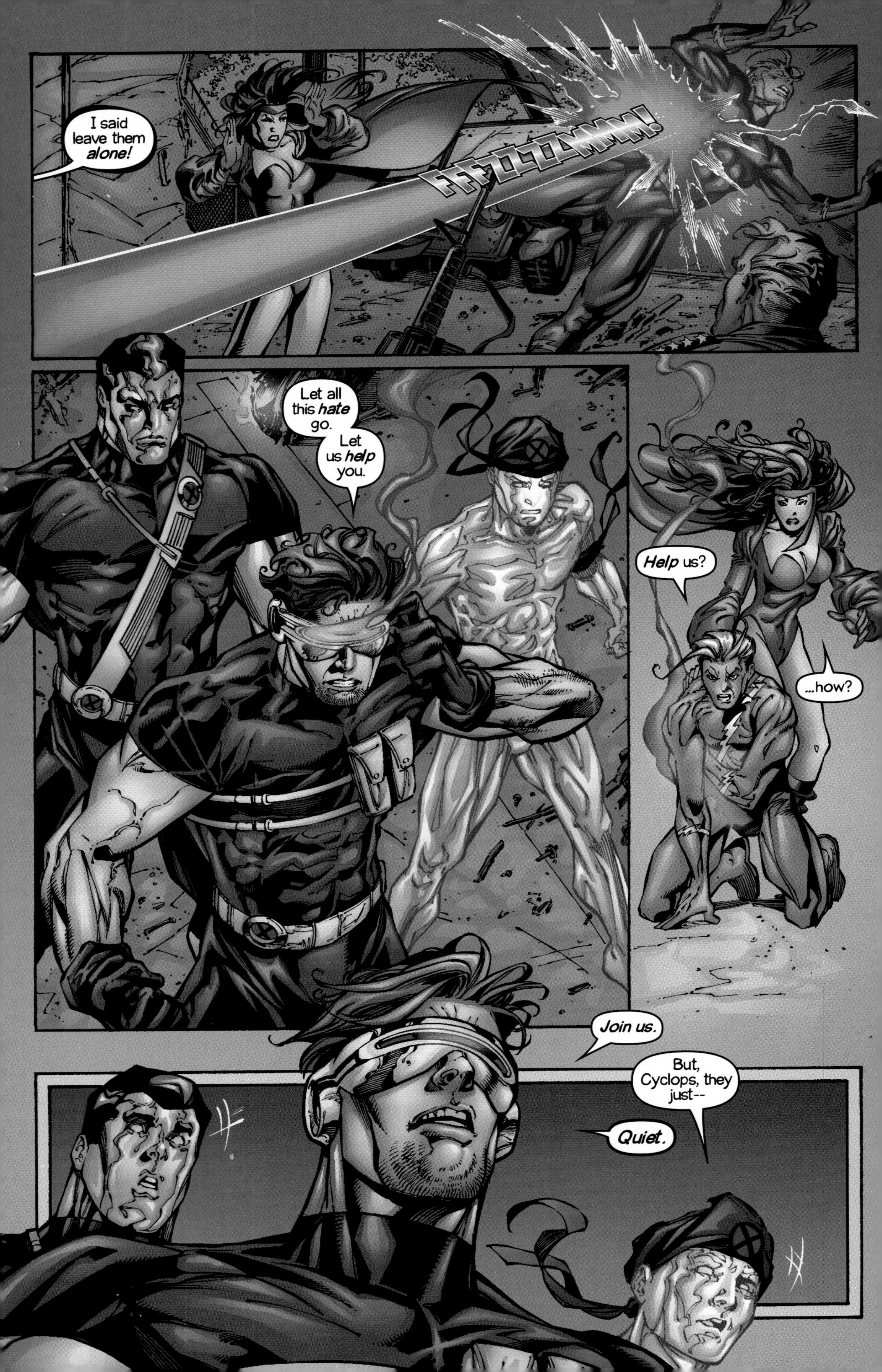
I said leave them *alone!*
FFFZZZZMMM!
Let all this *hate* go.
Let us *help* you.
Help us?
...how?
Join us.
But, Cyclops, they just--
Quiet.

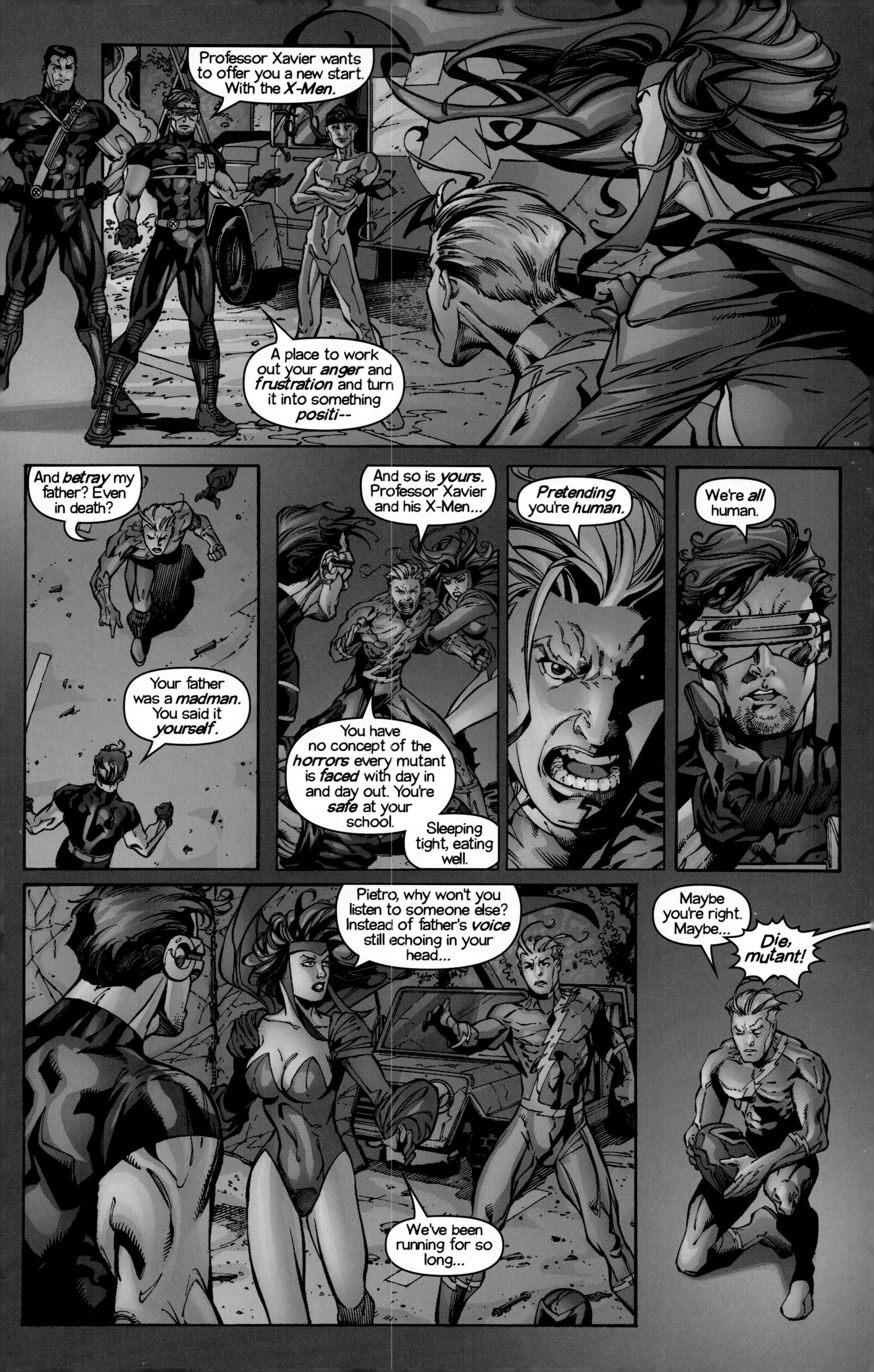
Professor Xavier wants to offer you a new start. With the X-Men.
A place to work out your anger and frustration and turn it into something positi--
And betray my father? Even in death?
Your father was a madman. You said it yourself.
And so is yours. Professor Xavier and his X-Men...
You have no concept of the horrors every mutant is faced with day in and day out. You're safe at your school.
Sleeping tight, eating well.
Pretending you're human.
We're all human.
Pietro, why won't you listen to someone else? Instead of father's voice still echoing in your head...
We've been running for so long...
Maybe you're right. Maybe...
Die, mutant!

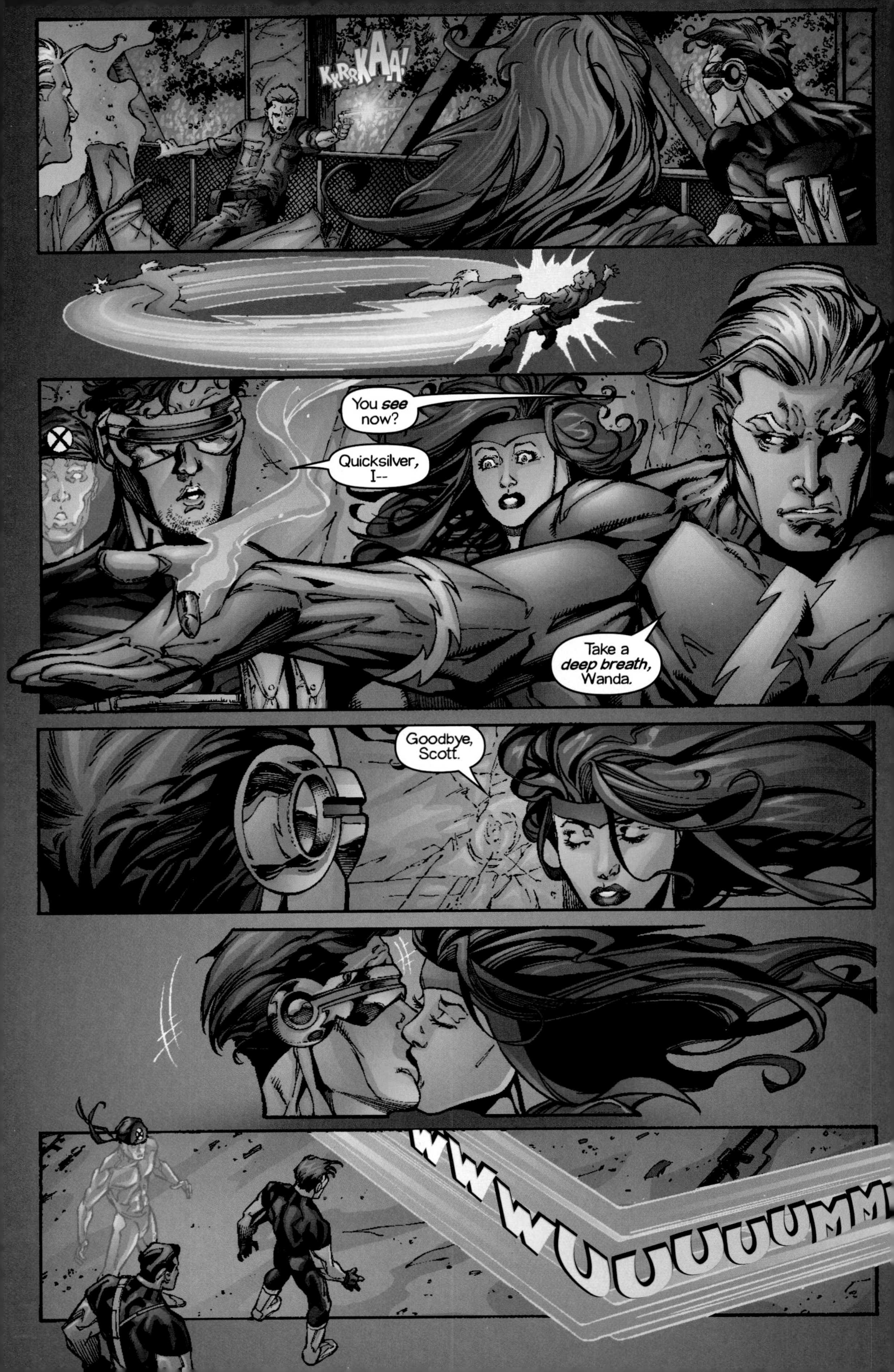
KKRRKAA!
You see now?
Quicksilver, I--
Take a deep breath, Wanda.
Goodbye, Scott.
WWWUUUUUMM

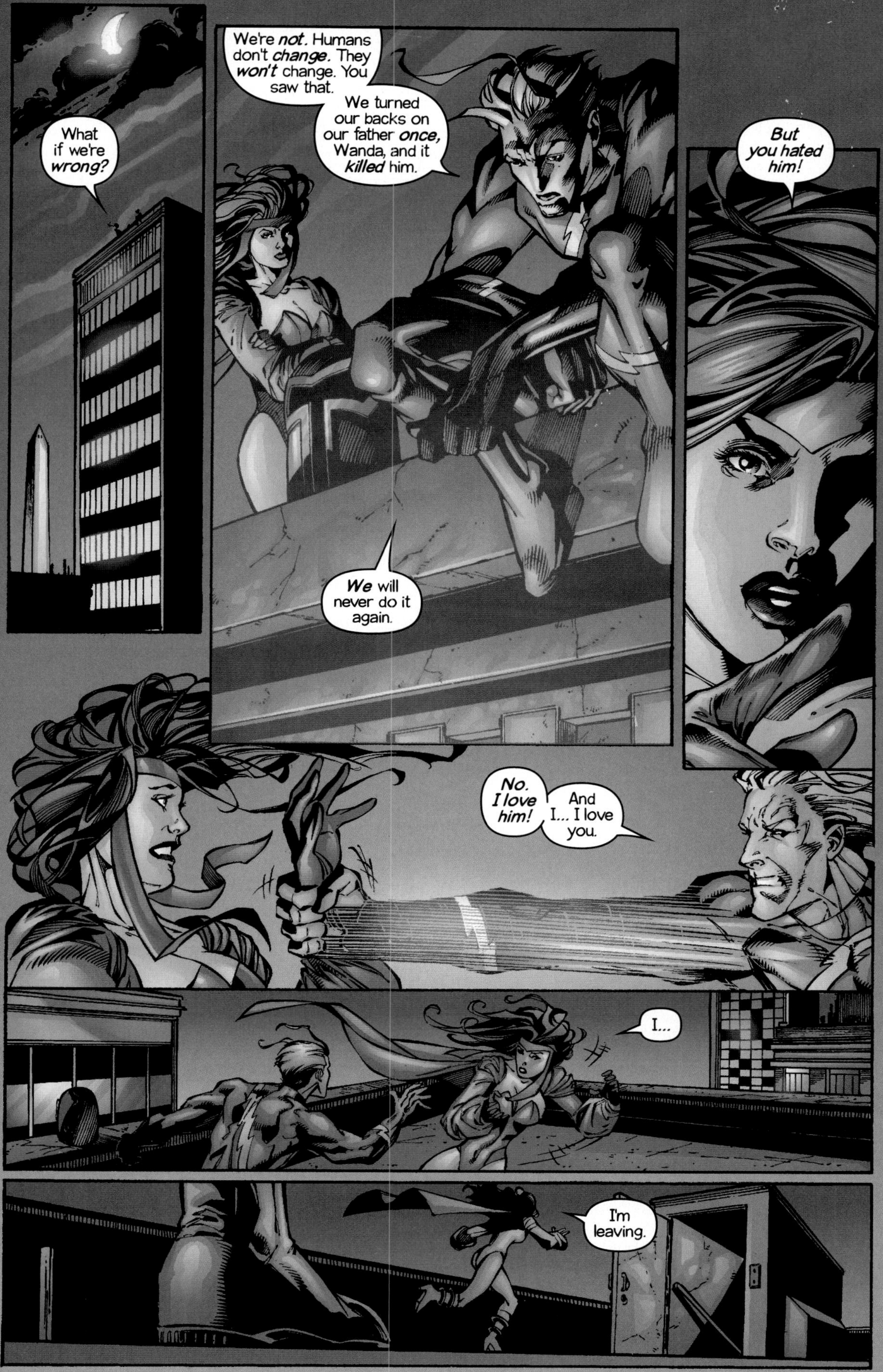
What if we're *wrong?*
We're ***not.*** Humans don't ***change.*** They ***won't*** change. You saw that.
We turned our backs on our father ***once,*** Wanda, and it ***killed*** him.
We will never do it again.
But you hated him!
No. I love him!
And I... I love you.
I...
I'm leaving.

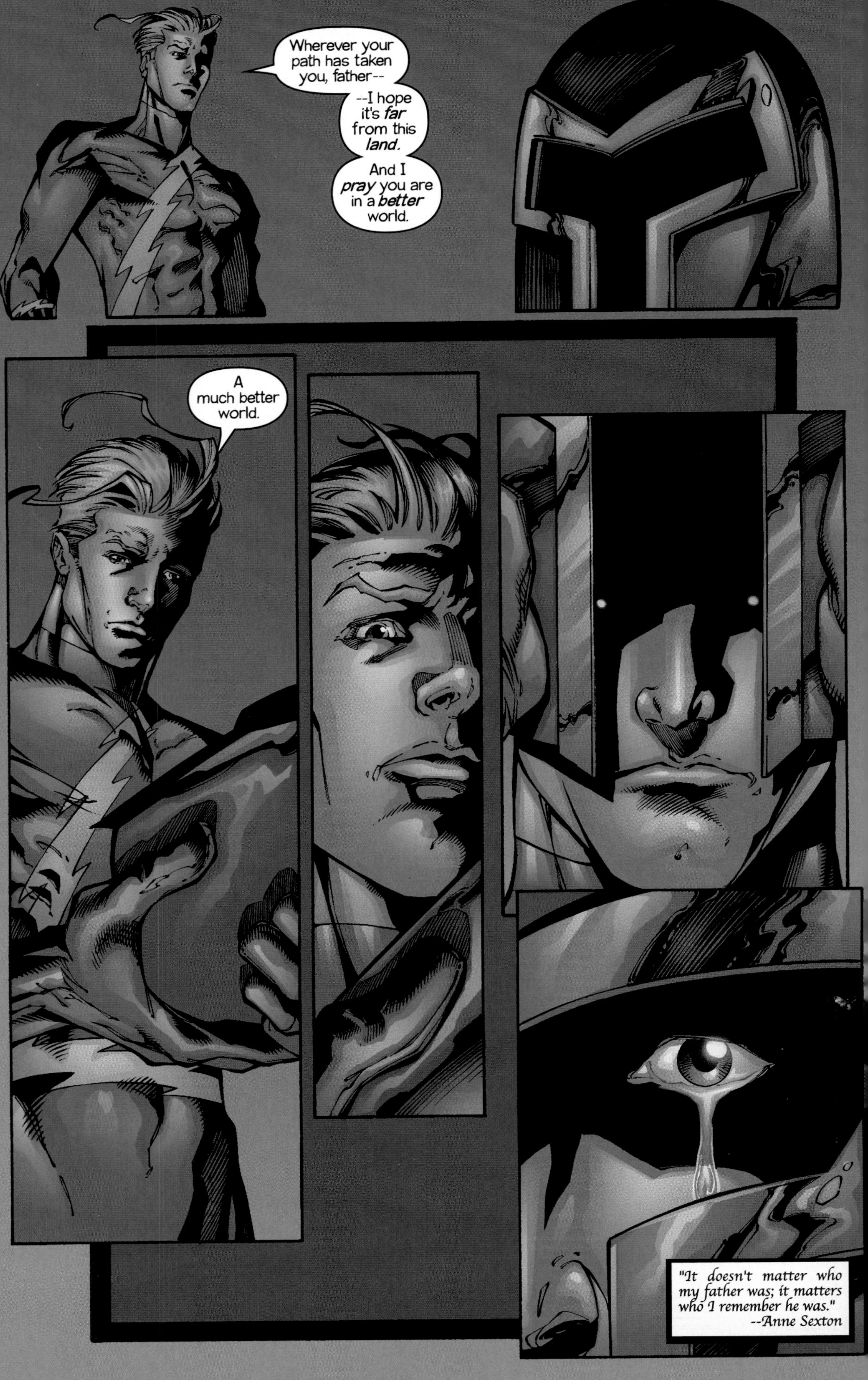
Wherever your path has taken you, father--
--I hope it's *far* from this *land.*
And I *pray* you are in a *better* world.
A much better world.
"It doesn't matter who my father was; it matters who I remember he was."
--Anne Sexton

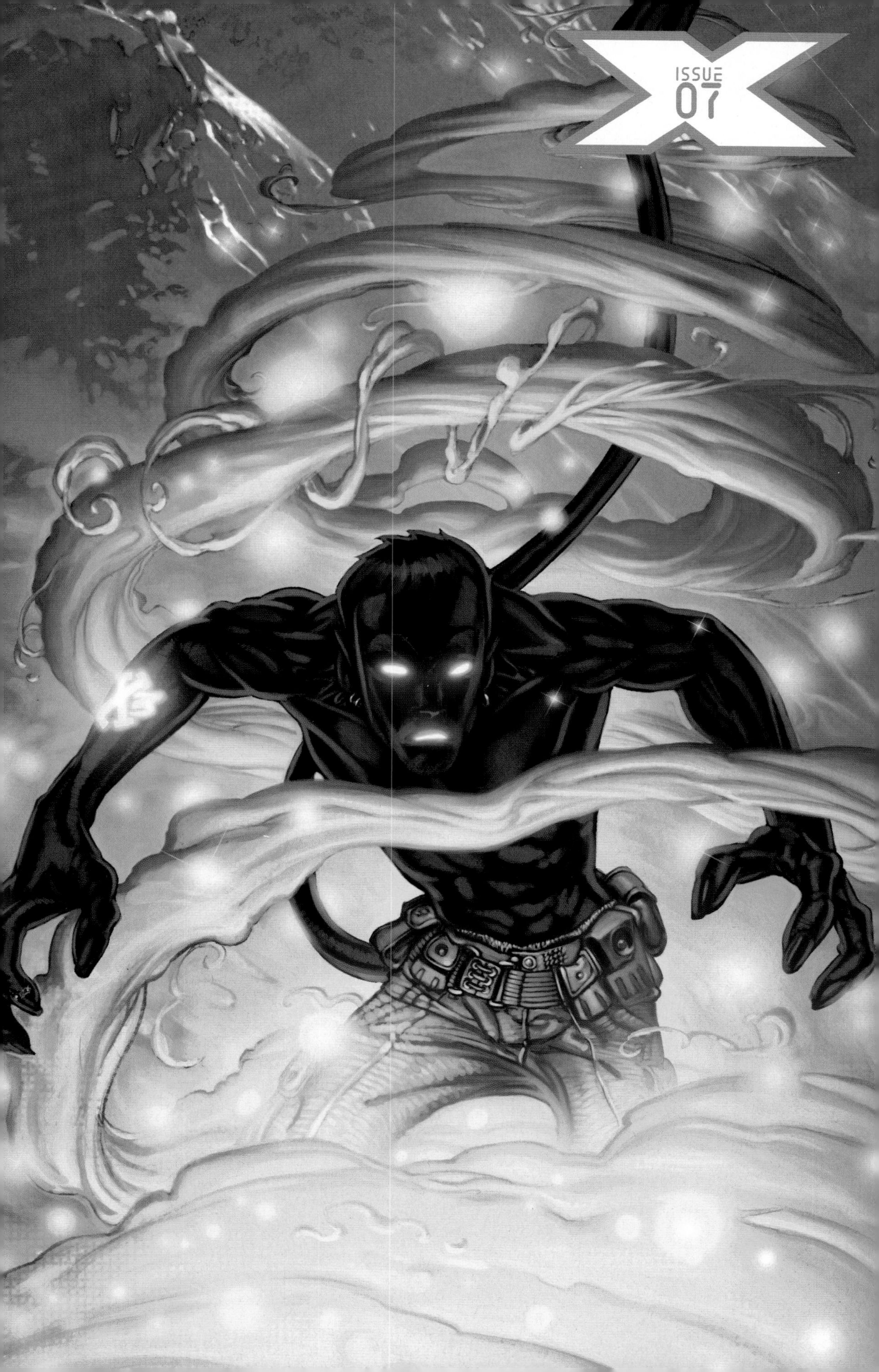
ISSUE
07

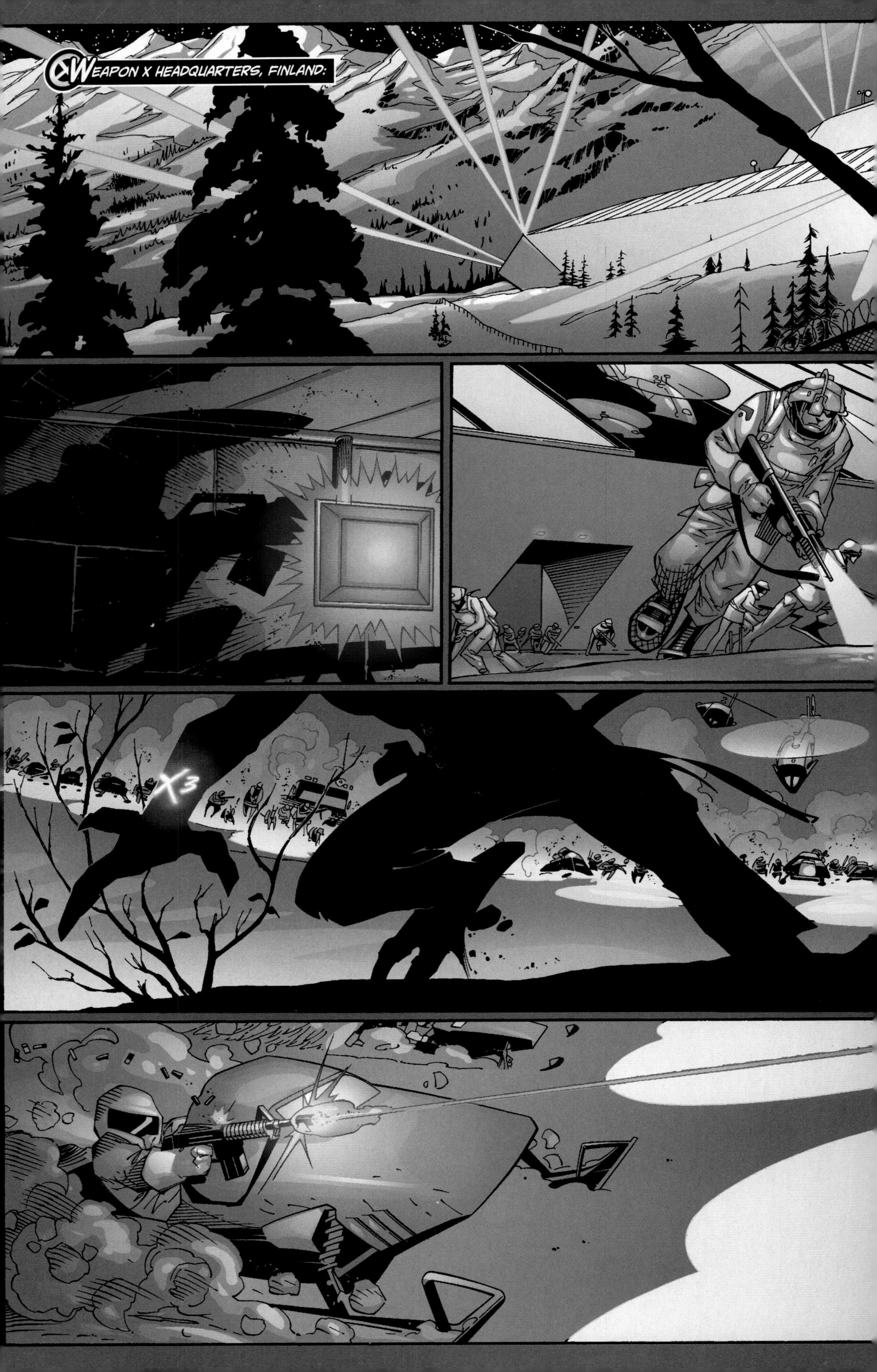
WEAPON X HEADQUARTERS, FINLAND:
X3

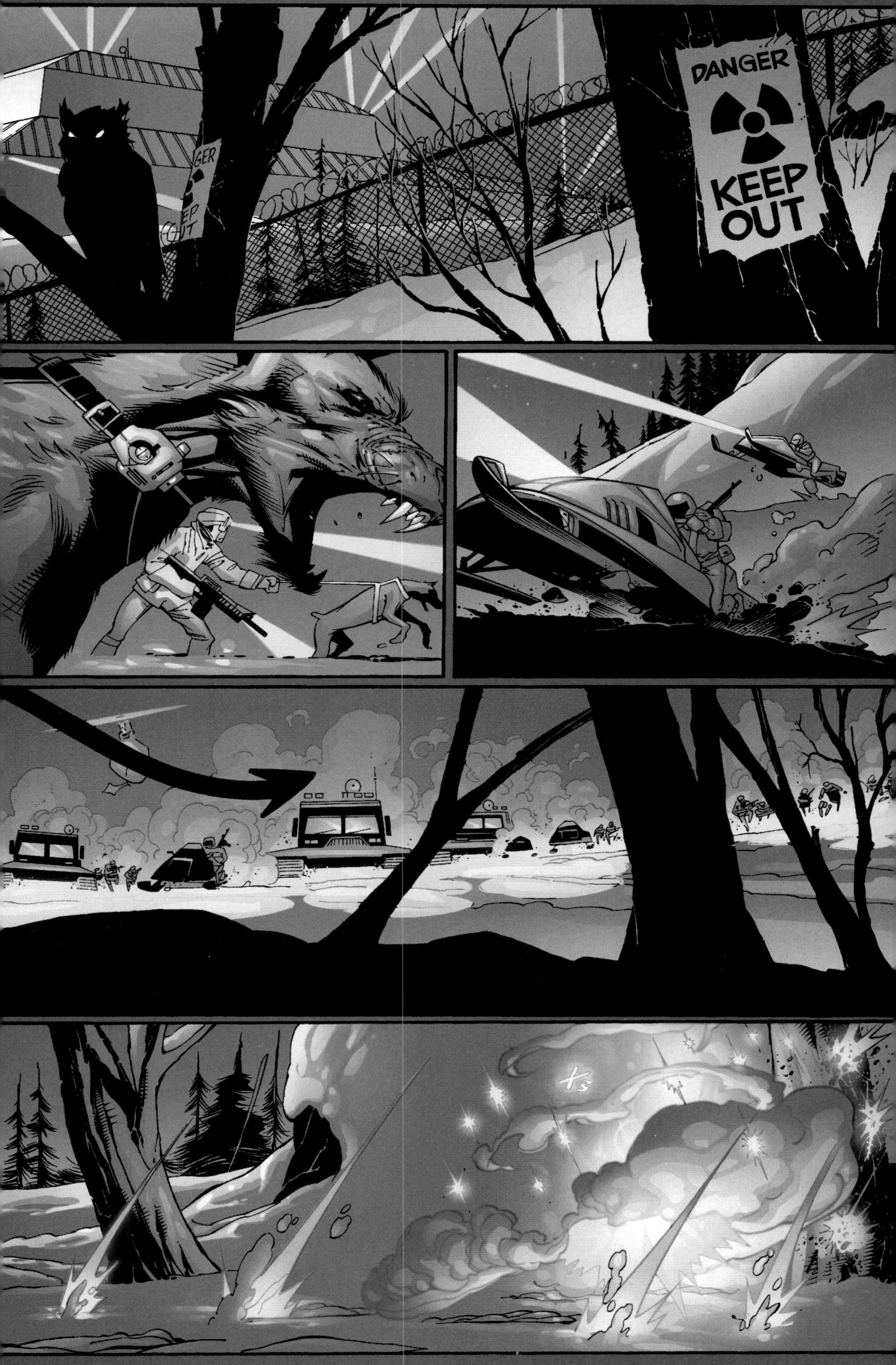
DANGER
KEEP OUT

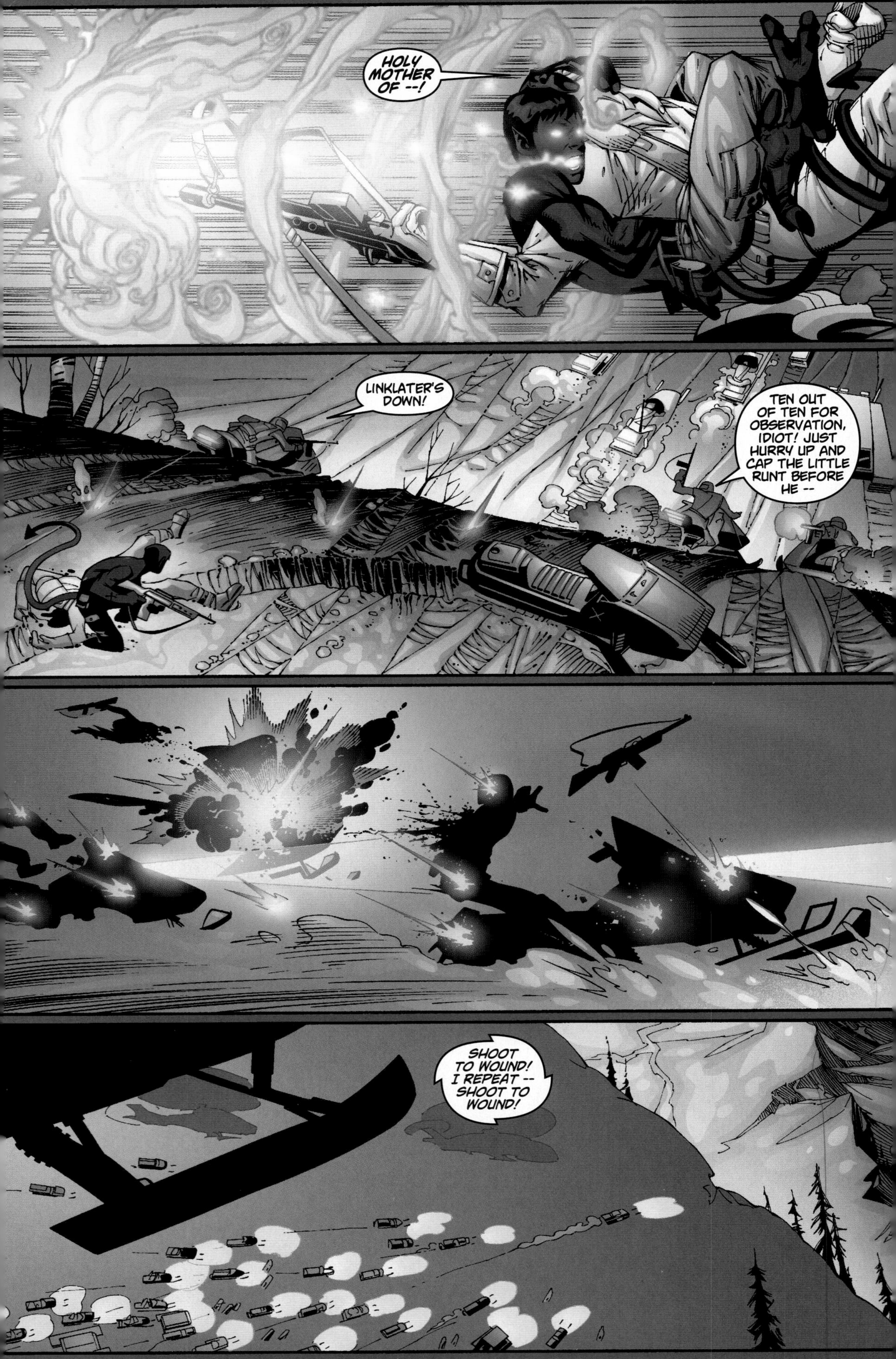
HOLY MOTHER OF --!
LINKLATER'S DOWN!
TEN OUT OF TEN FOR OBSERVATION, IDIOT! JUST HURRY UP AND CAP THE LITTLE RUNT BEFORE HE --
SHOOT TO WOUND! I REPEAT -- SHOOT TO WOUND!

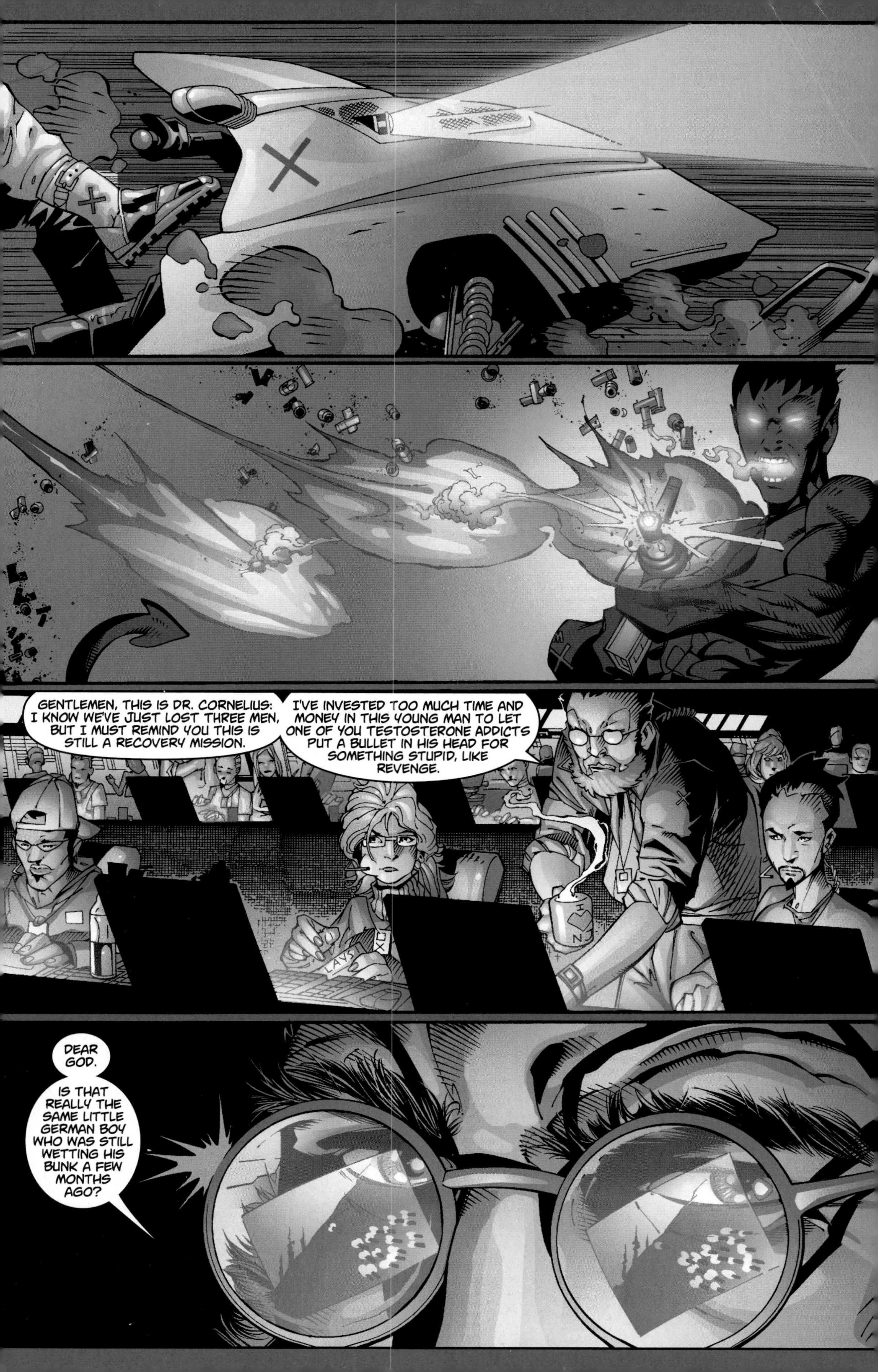
GENTLEMEN, THIS IS DR. CORNELIUS: I KNOW WE'VE JUST LOST THREE MEN, BUT I MUST REMIND YOU THIS IS STILL A RECOVERY MISSION.
I'VE INVESTED TOO MUCH TIME AND MONEY IN THIS YOUNG MAN TO LET ONE OF YOU TESTOSTERONE ADDICTS PUT A BULLET IN HIS HEAD FOR SOMETHING STUPID, LIKE REVENGE.
LAYS
DEAR GOD.
IS THAT REALLY THE SAME LITTLE GERMAN BOY WHO WAS STILL WETTING HIS BUNK A FEW MONTHS AGO?

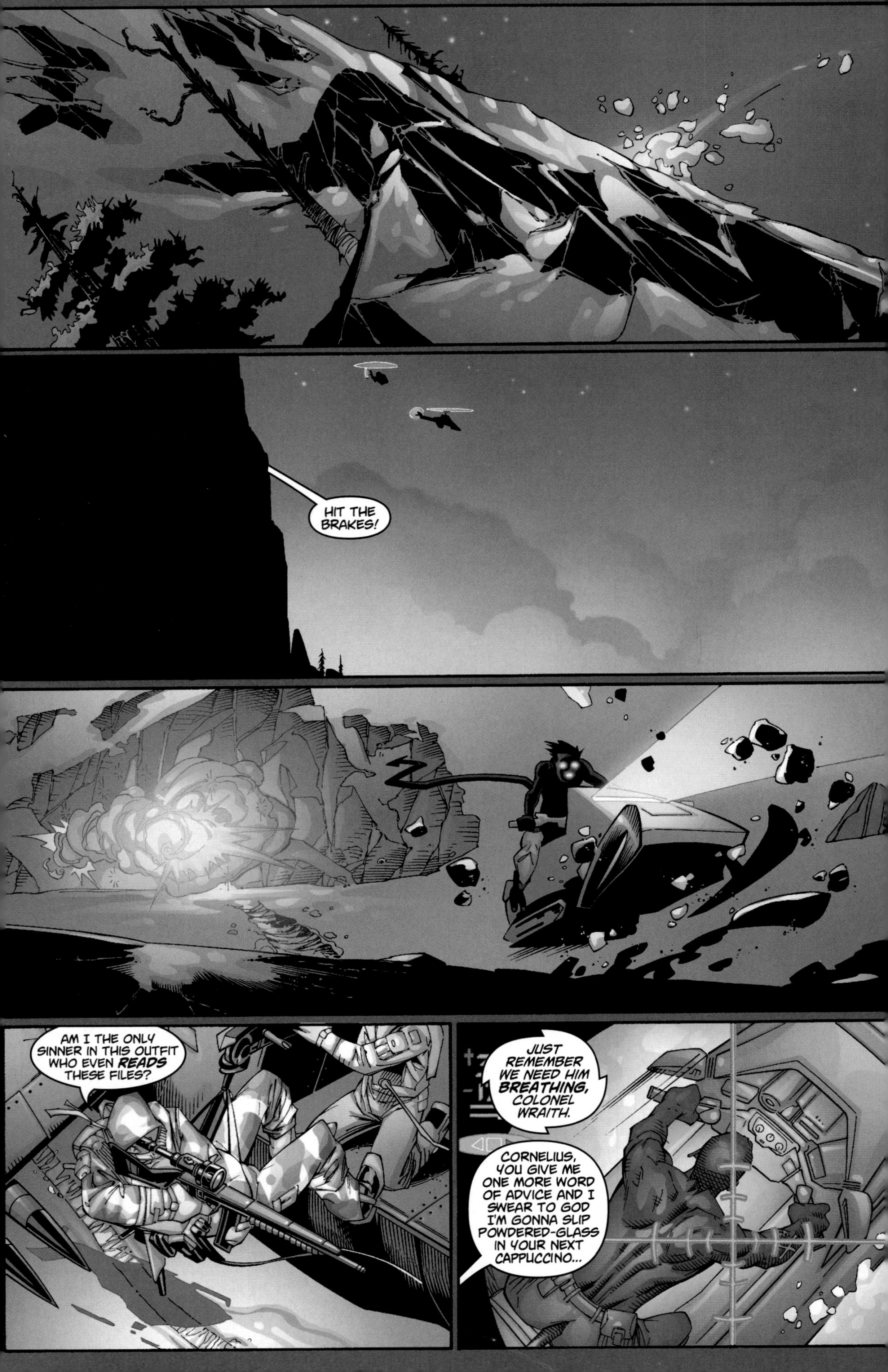
HIT THE BRAKES!
AM I THE ONLY SINNER IN THIS OUTFIT WHO EVEN READS THESE FILES?
JUST REMEMBER WE NEED HIM BREATHING, COLONEL WRAITH.
CORNELIUS, YOU GIVE ME ONE MORE WORD OF ADVICE AND I SWEAR TO GOD I'M GONNA SLIP POWDERED-GLASS IN YOUR NEXT CAPPUCCINO...

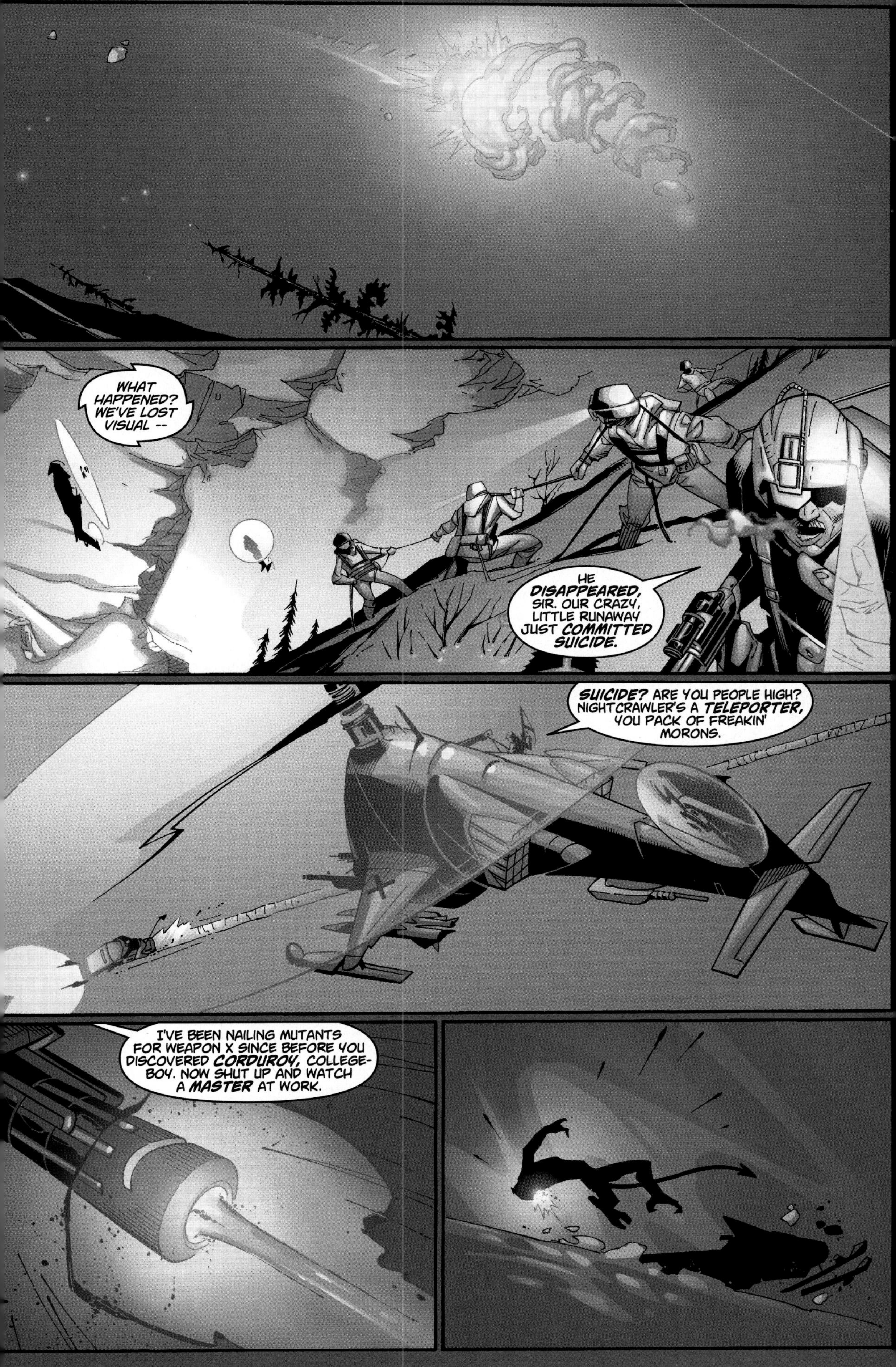
WHAT HAPPENED? WE'VE LOST VISUAL --
HE DISAPPEARED, SIR. OUR CRAZY, LITTLE RUNAWAY JUST COMMITTED SUICIDE.
SUICIDE? ARE YOU PEOPLE HIGH? NIGHTCRAWLER'S A TELEPORTER, YOU PACK OF FREAKIN' MORONS.
I'VE BEEN NAILING MUTANTS FOR WEAPON X SINCE BEFORE YOU DISCOVERED CORDUROY, COLLEGE-BOY. NOW SHUT UP AND WATCH A MASTER AT WORK.

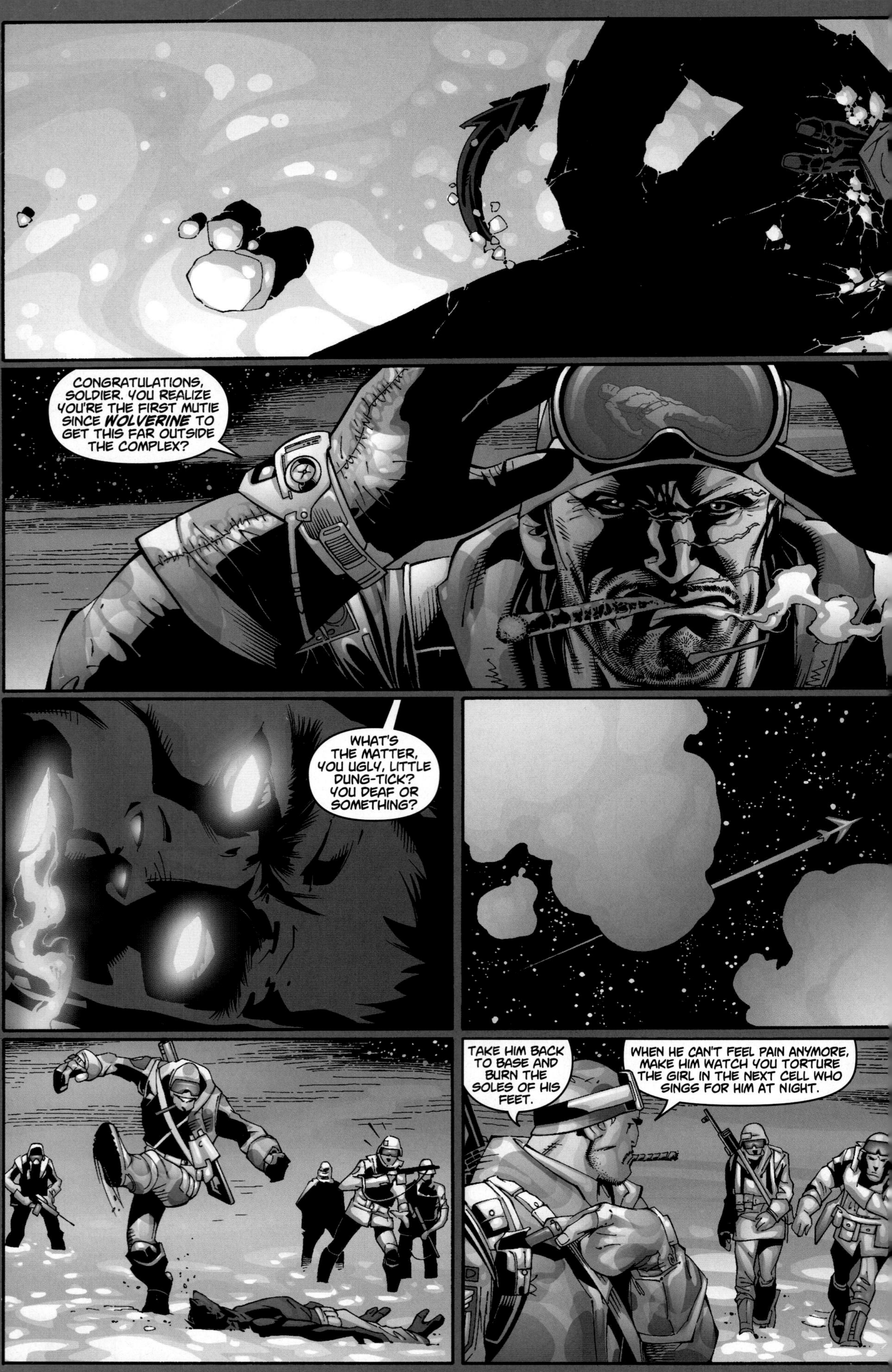
CONGRATULATIONS, SOLDIER. YOU REALIZE YOU'RE THE FIRST MUTIE SINCE WOLVERINE TO GET THIS FAR OUTSIDE THE COMPLEX?
WHAT'S THE MATTER, YOU UGLY, LITTLE DUNG-TICK? YOU DEAF OR SOMETHING?
TAKE HIM BACK TO BASE AND BURN THE SOLES OF HIS FEET.
WHEN HE CAN'T FEEL PAIN ANYMORE, MAKE HIM WATCH YOU TORTURE THE GIRL IN THE NEXT CELL WHO SINGS FOR HIM AT NIGHT.

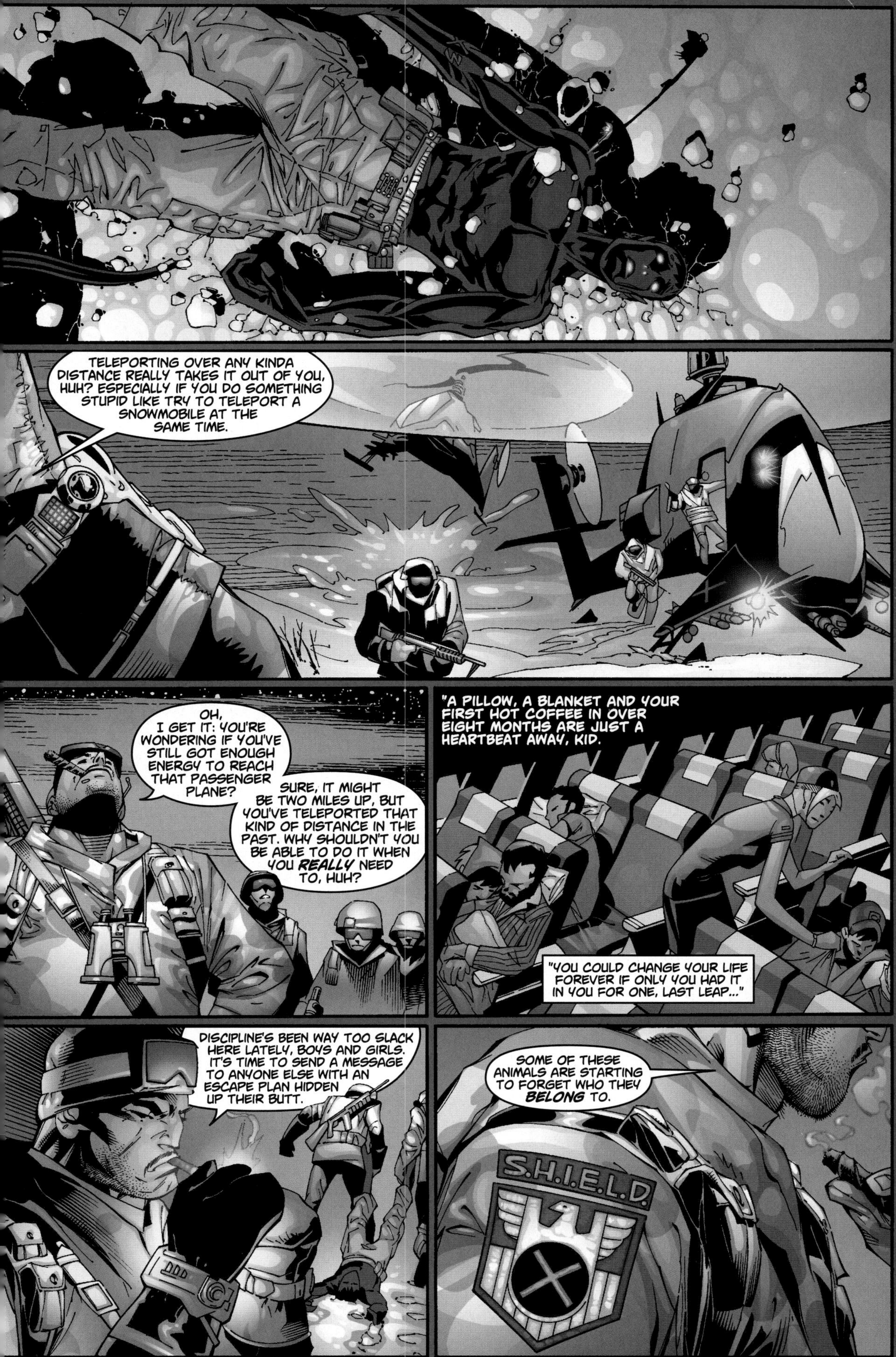
TELEPORTING OVER ANY KINDA DISTANCE REALLY TAKES IT OUT OF YOU, HUH? ESPECIALLY IF YOU DO SOMETHING STUPID LIKE TRY TO TELEPORT A SNOWMOBILE AT THE SAME TIME.
OH, I GET IT: YOU'RE WONDERING IF YOU'VE STILL GOT ENOUGH ENERGY TO REACH THAT PASSENGER PLANE?
SURE, IT MIGHT BE TWO MILES UP, BUT YOU'VE TELEPORTED THAT KIND OF DISTANCE IN THE PAST. WHY SHOULDN'T YOU BE ABLE TO DO IT WHEN YOU *REALLY* NEED TO, HUH?
"A PILLOW, A BLANKET AND YOUR FIRST HOT COFFEE IN OVER EIGHT MONTHS ARE JUST A HEARTBEAT AWAY, KID.
"YOU COULD CHANGE YOUR LIFE FOREVER IF ONLY YOU HAD IT IN YOU FOR ONE, LAST LEAP..."
DISCIPLINE'S BEEN WAY TOO SLACK HERE LATELY, BOYS AND GIRLS. IT'S TIME TO SEND A MESSAGE TO ANYONE ELSE WITH AN ESCAPE PLAN HIDDEN UP THEIR BUTT.
SOME OF THESE ANIMALS ARE STARTING TO FORGET WHO THEY *BELONG* TO.
S.H.I.E.L.D.

RETURN TO WEAPON X

A STAN LEE PRESENTATION

PART ONE OF SIX

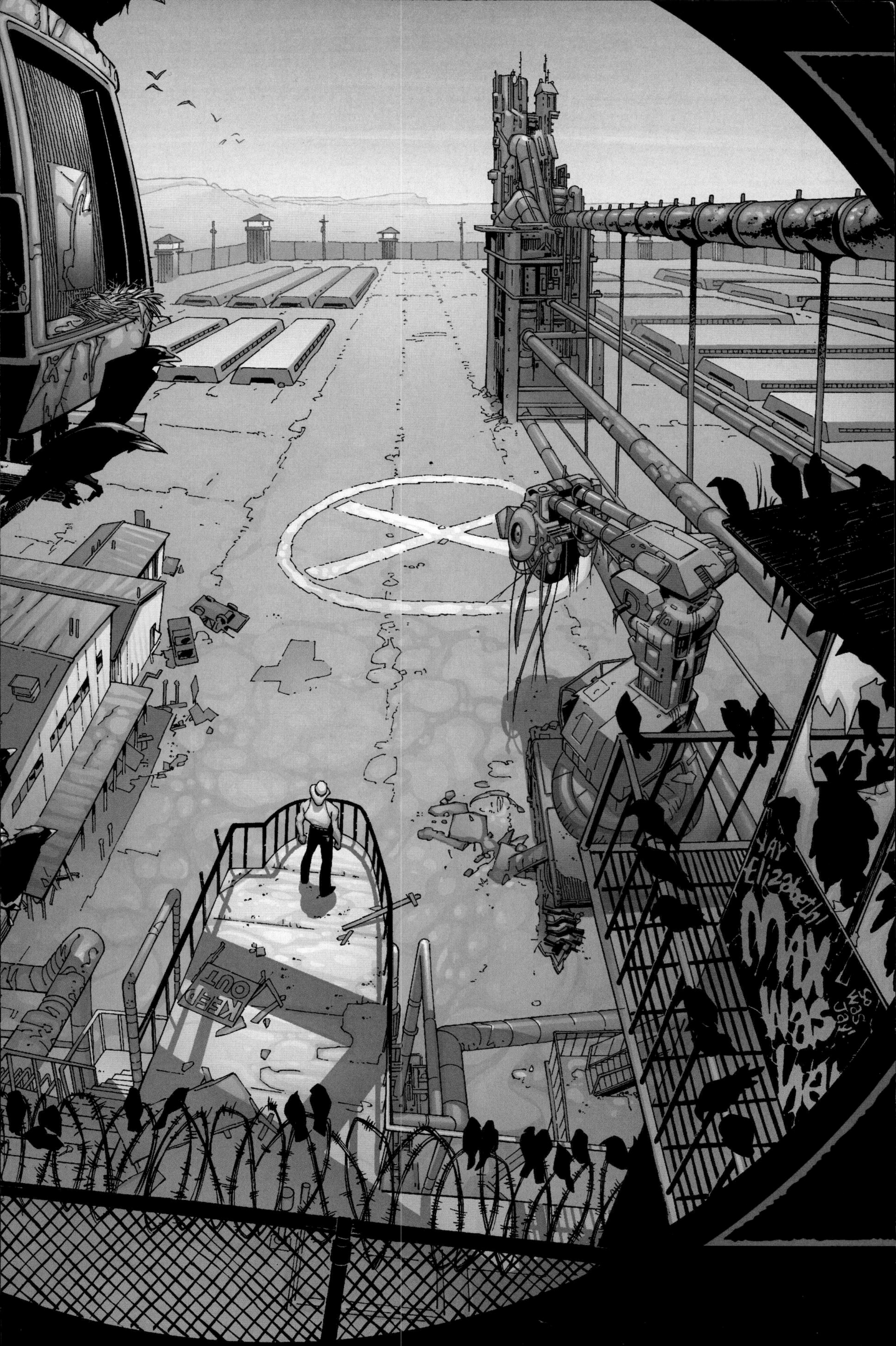
KEEP OUT
YAY Elizabeth!
Max was
So was Jay!

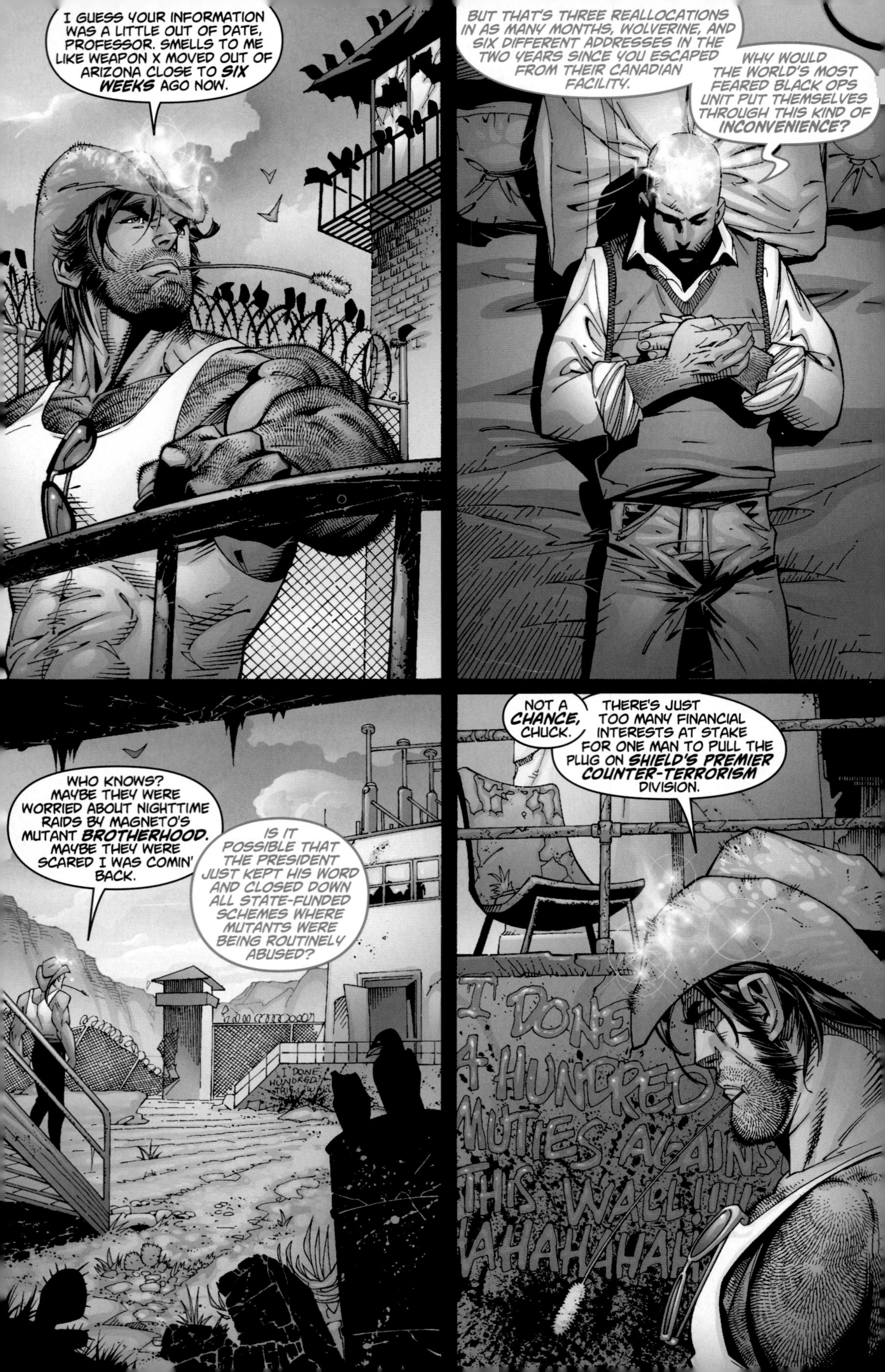
I GUESS YOUR INFORMATION WAS A LITTLE OUT OF DATE, PROFESSOR. SMELLS TO ME LIKE WEAPON X MOVED OUT OF ARIZONA CLOSE TO SIX WEEKS AGO NOW.
BUT THAT'S THREE REALLOCATIONS IN AS MANY MONTHS, WOLVERINE, AND SIX DIFFERENT ADDRESSES IN THE TWO YEARS SINCE YOU ESCAPED FROM THEIR CANADIAN FACILITY.
WHY WOULD THE WORLD'S MOST FEARED BLACK OPS UNIT PUT THEMSELVES THROUGH THIS KIND OF INCONVENIENCE?
WHO KNOWS? MAYBE THEY WERE WORRIED ABOUT NIGHTTIME RAIDS BY MAGNETO'S MUTANT BROTHERHOOD. MAYBE THEY WERE SCARED I WAS COMIN' BACK.
IS IT POSSIBLE THAT THE PRESIDENT JUST KEPT HIS WORD AND CLOSED DOWN ALL STATE-FUNDED SCHEMES WHERE MUTANTS WERE BEING ROUTINELY ABUSED?
NOT A CHANCE, CHUCK.
THERE'S JUST TOO MANY FINANCIAL INTERESTS AT STAKE FOR ONE MAN TO PULL THE PLUG ON SHIELD'S PREMIER COUNTER-TERRORISM DIVISION.
I DONE
4 HUNDRED
MUTIES AGAINS
THIS WALL!!!

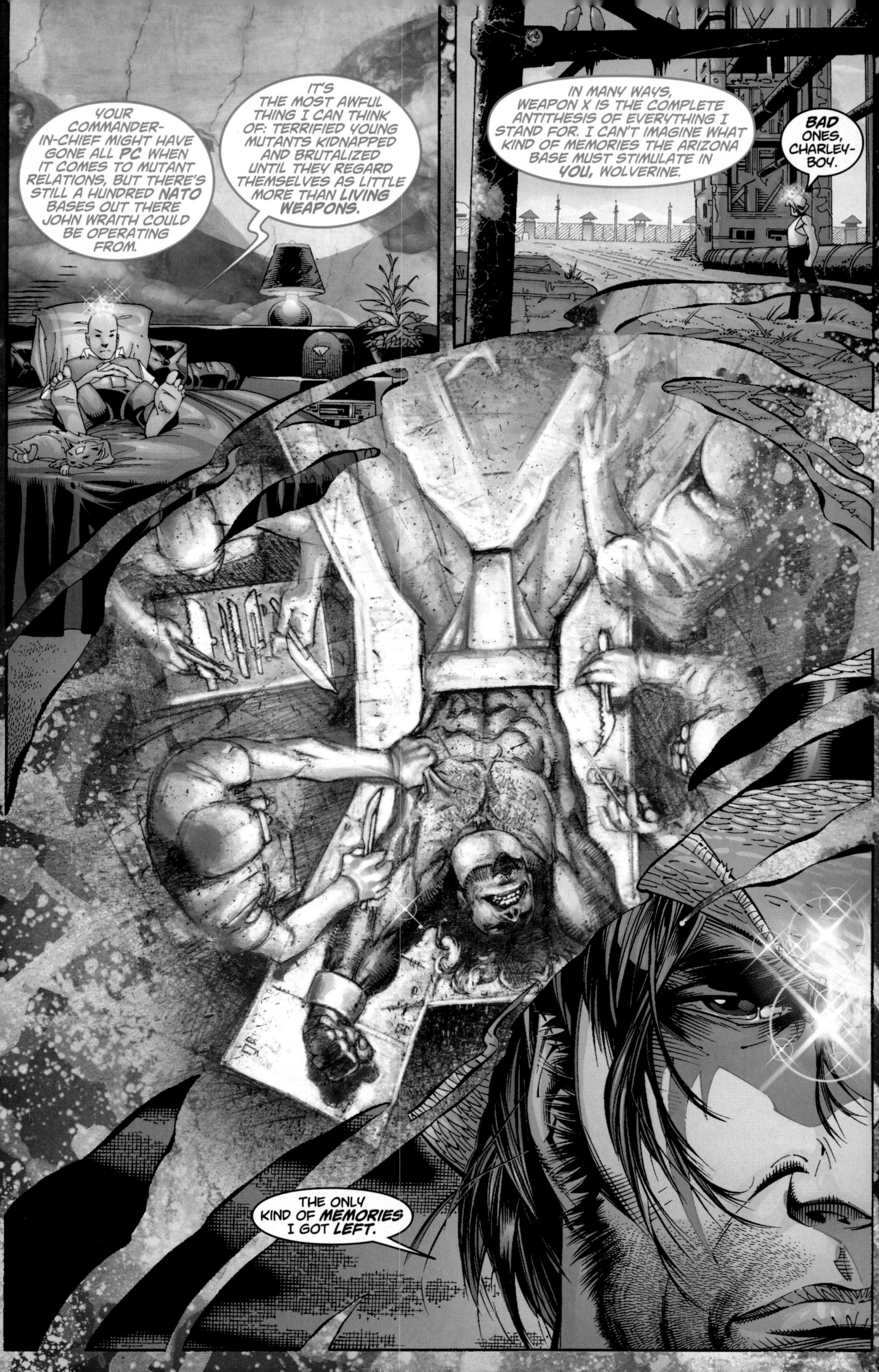
YOUR COMMANDER-IN-CHIEF MIGHT HAVE GONE ALL PC WHEN IT COMES TO MUTANT RELATIONS, BUT THERE'S STILL A HUNDRED NATO BASES OUT THERE JOHN WRAITH COULD BE OPERATING FROM.
IT'S THE MOST AWFUL THING I CAN THINK OF: TERRIFIED YOUNG MUTANTS KIDNAPPED AND BRUTALIZED UNTIL THEY REGARD THEMSELVES AS LITTLE MORE THAN LIVING WEAPONS.
IN MANY WAYS, WEAPON X IS THE COMPLETE ANTITHESIS OF EVERYTHING I STAND FOR. I CAN'T IMAGINE WHAT KIND OF MEMORIES THE ARIZONA BASE MUST STIMULATE IN YOU, WOLVERINE.
BAD ONES, CHARLEY-BOY.
THE ONLY KIND OF MEMORIES I GOT LEFT.

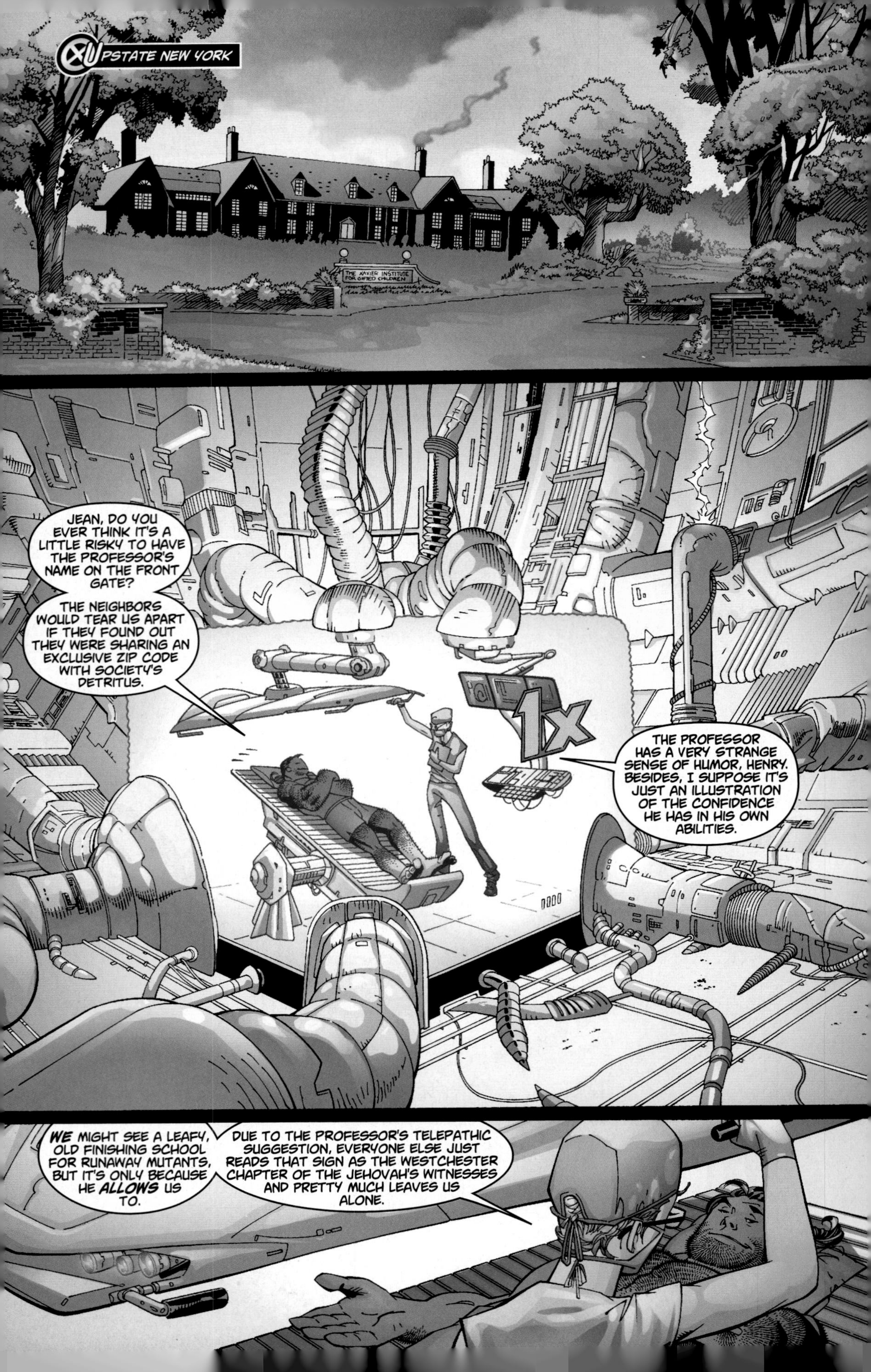
UPSTATE NEW YORK
THE XAVIER INSTITUTE FOR GIFTED CHILDREN
JEAN, DO YOU EVER THINK IT'S A LITTLE RISKY TO HAVE THE PROFESSOR'S NAME ON THE FRONT GATE?
THE NEIGHBORS WOULD TEAR US APART IF THEY FOUND OUT THEY WERE SHARING AN EXCLUSIVE ZIP CODE WITH SOCIETY'S DETRITUS.
1X
THE PROFESSOR HAS A VERY STRANGE SENSE OF HUMOR, HENRY. BESIDES, I SUPPOSE IT'S JUST AN ILLUSTRATION OF THE CONFIDENCE HE HAS IN HIS OWN ABILITIES.
WE MIGHT SEE A LEAFY, OLD FINISHING SCHOOL FOR RUNAWAY MUTANTS, BUT IT'S ONLY BECAUSE HE ALLOWS US TO.
DUE TO THE PROFESSOR'S TELEPATHIC SUGGESTION, EVERYONE ELSE JUST READS THAT SIGN AS THE WESTCHESTER CHAPTER OF THE JEHOVAH'S WITNESSES AND PRETTY MUCH LEAVES US ALONE.

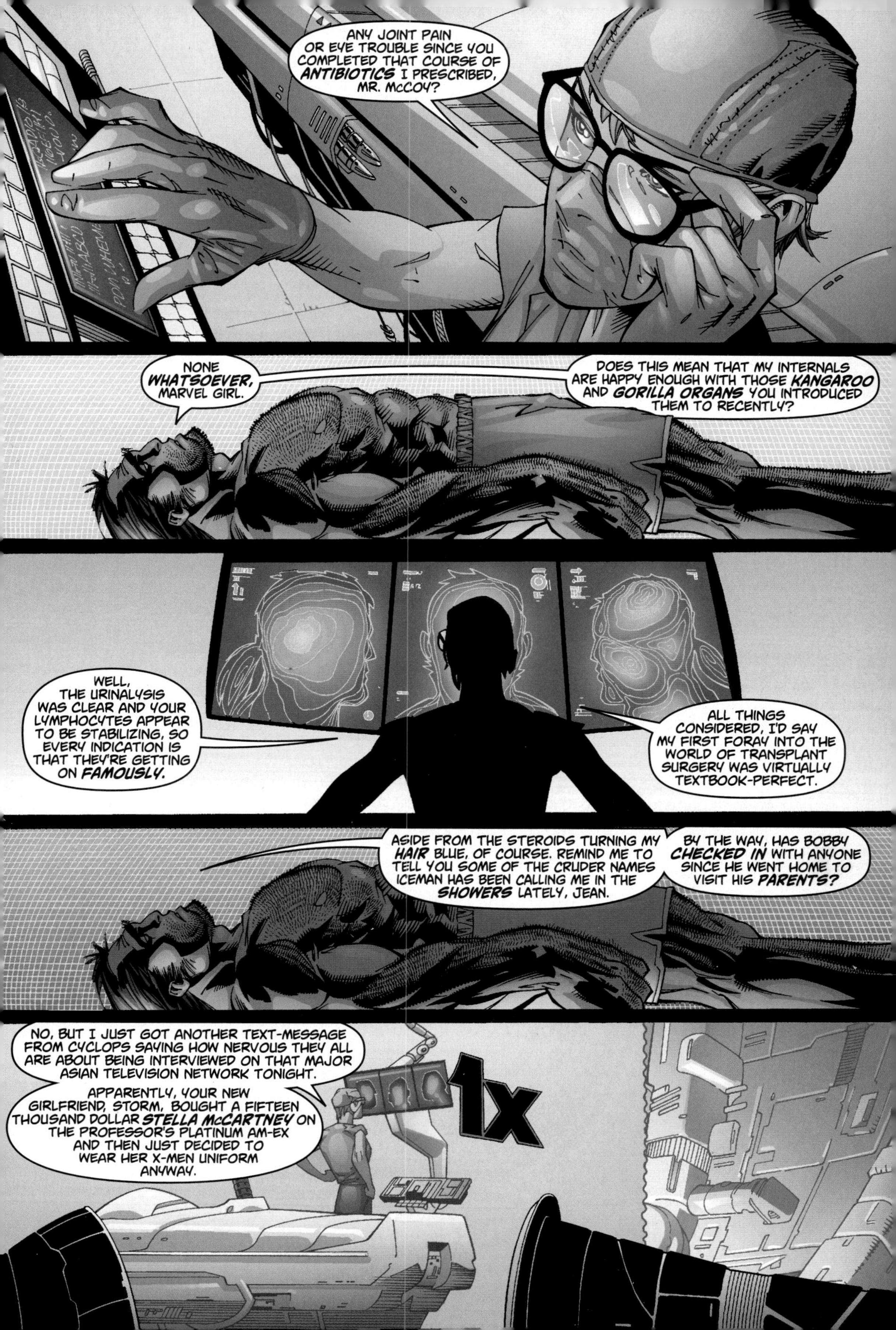
ANY JOINT PAIN OR EYE TROUBLE SINCE YOU COMPLETED THAT COURSE OF ANTIBIOTICS I PRESCRIBED, MR. McCOY?
NONE WHATSOEVER, MARVEL GIRL.
DOES THIS MEAN THAT MY INTERNALS ARE HAPPY ENOUGH WITH THOSE KANGAROO AND GORILLA ORGANS YOU INTRODUCED THEM TO RECENTLY?
WELL, THE URINALYSIS WAS CLEAR AND YOUR LYMPHOCYTES APPEAR TO BE STABILIZING, SO EVERY INDICATION IS THAT THEY'RE GETTING ON FAMOUSLY.
ALL THINGS CONSIDERED, I'D SAY MY FIRST FORAY INTO THE WORLD OF TRANSPLANT SURGERY WAS VIRTUALLY TEXTBOOK-PERFECT.
ASIDE FROM THE STEROIDS TURNING MY HAIR BLUE, OF COURSE. REMIND ME TO TELL YOU SOME OF THE CRUDER NAMES ICEMAN HAS BEEN CALLING ME IN THE SHOWERS LATELY, JEAN.
BY THE WAY, HAS BOBBY CHECKED IN WITH ANYONE SINCE HE WENT HOME TO VISIT HIS PARENTS?
NO, BUT I JUST GOT ANOTHER TEXT-MESSAGE FROM CYCLOPS SAYING HOW NERVOUS THEY ALL ARE ABOUT BEING INTERVIEWED ON THAT MAJOR ASIAN TELEVISION NETWORK TONIGHT.
APPARENTLY, YOUR NEW GIRLFRIEND, STORM, BOUGHT A FIFTEEN THOUSAND DOLLAR STELLA McCARTNEY ON THE PROFESSOR'S PLATINUM AM-EX AND THEN JUST DECIDED TO WEAR HER X-MEN UNIFORM ANYWAY.
1X

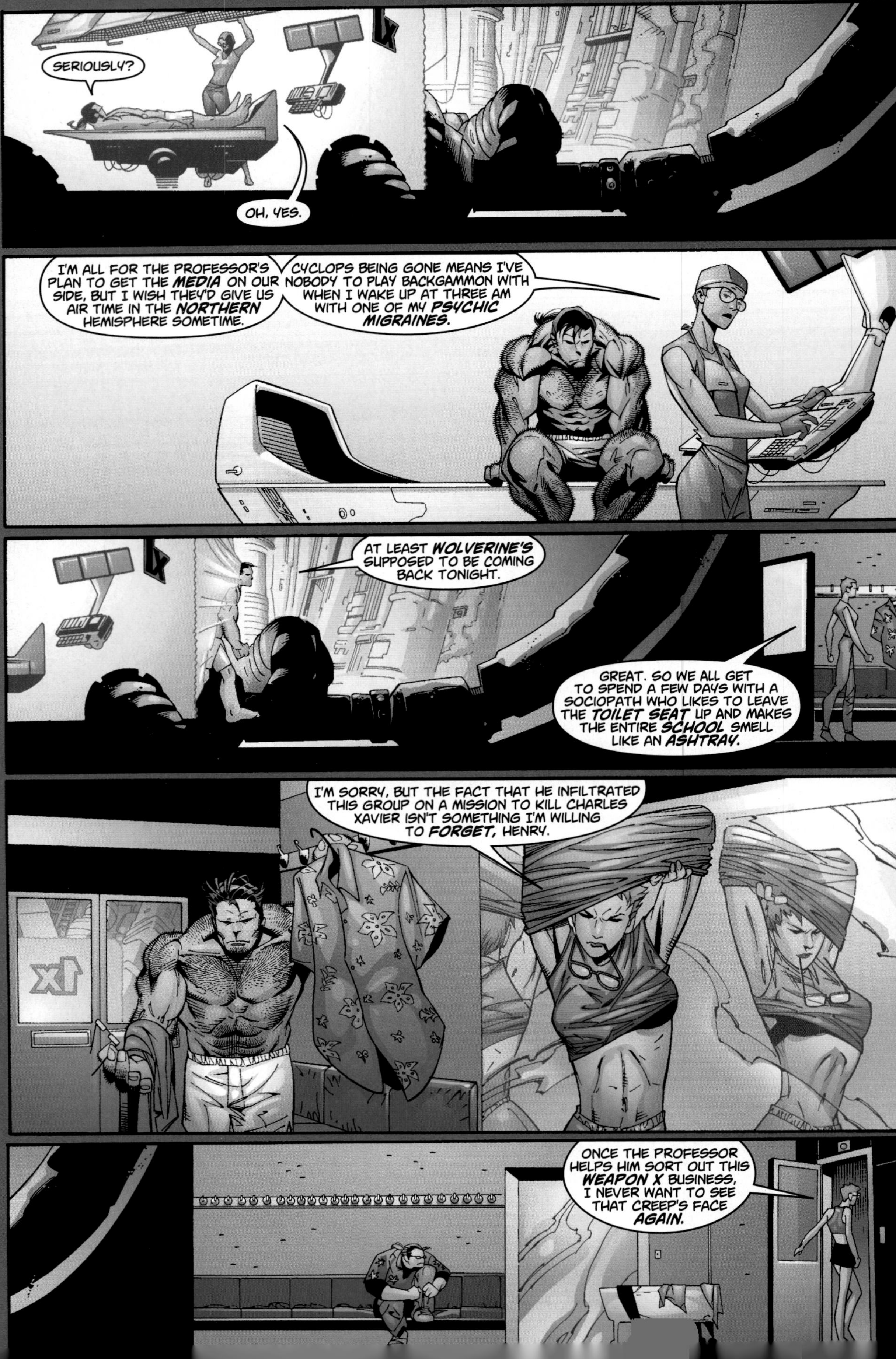
SERIOUSLY?
OH, YES.
I'M ALL FOR THE PROFESSOR'S PLAN TO GET THE MEDIA ON OUR SIDE, BUT I WISH THEY'D GIVE US AIR TIME IN THE NORTHERN HEMISPHERE SOMETIME.
CYCLOPS BEING GONE MEANS I'VE NOBODY TO PLAY BACKGAMMON WITH WHEN I WAKE UP AT THREE AM WITH ONE OF MY PSYCHIC MIGRAINES.
AT LEAST WOLVERINE'S SUPPOSED TO BE COMING BACK TONIGHT.
GREAT. SO WE ALL GET TO SPEND A FEW DAYS WITH A SOCIOPATH WHO LIKES TO LEAVE THE TOILET SEAT UP AND MAKES THE ENTIRE SCHOOL SMELL LIKE AN ASHTRAY.
I'M SORRY, BUT THE FACT THAT HE INFILTRATED THIS GROUP ON A MISSION TO KILL CHARLES XAVIER ISN'T SOMETHING I'M WILLING TO FORGET, HENRY.
ONCE THE PROFESSOR HELPS HIM SORT OUT THIS WEAPON X BUSINESS, I NEVER WANT TO SEE THAT CREEP'S FACE AGAIN.

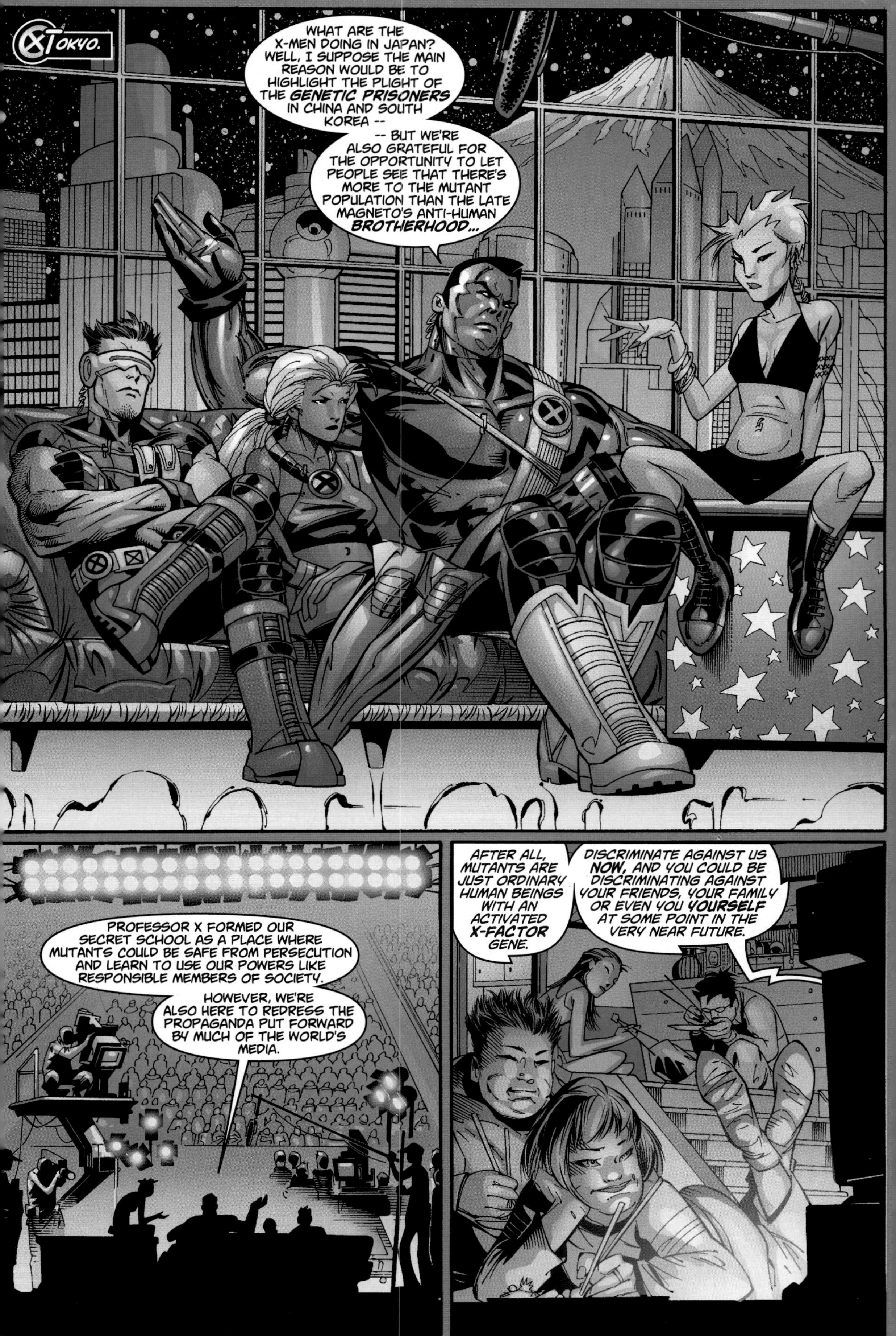
TOKYO.
WHAT ARE THE X-MEN DOING IN JAPAN? WELL, I SUPPOSE THE MAIN REASON WOULD BE TO HIGHLIGHT THE PLIGHT OF THE GENETIC PRISONERS IN CHINA AND SOUTH KOREA --
-- BUT WE'RE ALSO GRATEFUL FOR THE OPPORTUNITY TO LET PEOPLE SEE THAT THERE'S MORE TO THE MUTANT POPULATION THAN THE LATE MAGNETO'S ANTI-HUMAN BROTHERHOOD...
PROFESSOR X FORMED OUR SECRET SCHOOL AS A PLACE WHERE MUTANTS COULD BE SAFE FROM PERSECUTION AND LEARN TO USE OUR POWERS LIKE RESPONSIBLE MEMBERS OF SOCIETY.
HOWEVER, WE'RE ALSO HERE TO REDRESS THE PROPAGANDA PUT FORWARD BY MUCH OF THE WORLD'S MEDIA.
AFTER ALL, MUTANTS ARE JUST ORDINARY HUMAN BEINGS WITH AN ACTIVATED X-FACTOR GENE.
DISCRIMINATE AGAINST US NOW, AND YOU COULD BE DISCRIMINATING AGAINST YOUR FRIENDS, YOUR FAMILY OR EVEN YOU YOURSELF AT SOME POINT IN THE VERY NEAR FUTURE.

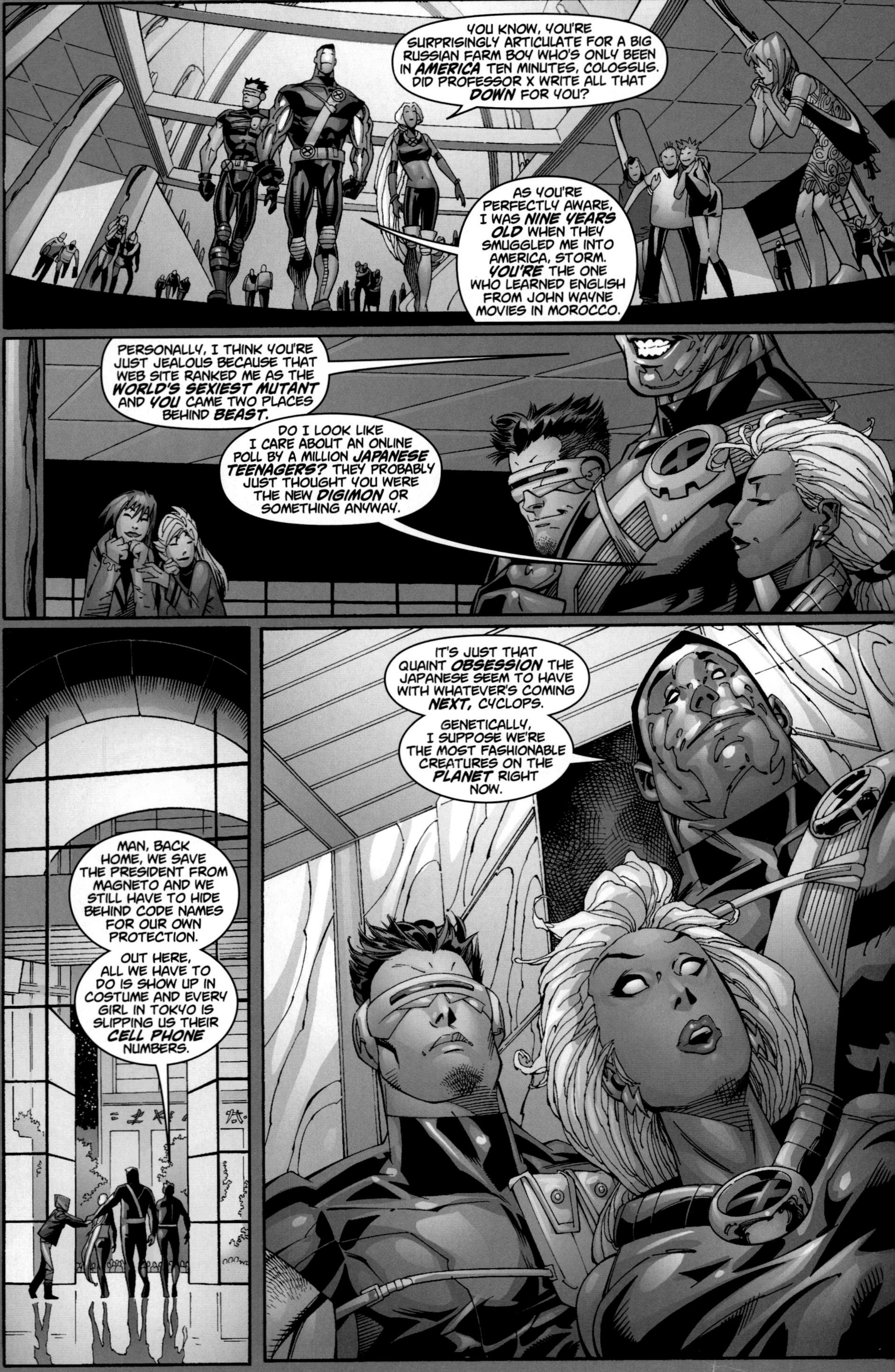
YOU KNOW, YOU'RE SURPRISINGLY ARTICULATE FOR A BIG RUSSIAN FARM BOY WHO'S ONLY BEEN IN AMERICA TEN MINUTES, COLOSSUS. DID PROFESSOR X WRITE ALL THAT DOWN FOR YOU?
AS YOU'RE PERFECTLY AWARE, I WAS NINE YEARS OLD WHEN THEY SMUGGLED ME INTO AMERICA, STORM. YOU'RE THE ONE WHO LEARNED ENGLISH FROM JOHN WAYNE MOVIES IN MOROCCO.
PERSONALLY, I THINK YOU'RE JUST JEALOUS BECAUSE THAT WEB SITE RANKED ME AS THE WORLD'S SEXIEST MUTANT AND YOU CAME TWO PLACES BEHIND BEAST.
DO I LOOK LIKE I CARE ABOUT AN ONLINE POLL BY A MILLION JAPANESE TEENAGERS? THEY PROBABLY JUST THOUGHT YOU WERE THE NEW DIGIMON OR SOMETHING ANYWAY.
MAN, BACK HOME, WE SAVE THE PRESIDENT FROM MAGNETO AND WE STILL HAVE TO HIDE BEHIND CODE NAMES FOR OUR OWN PROTECTION.
OUT HERE, ALL WE HAVE TO DO IS SHOW UP IN COSTUME AND EVERY GIRL IN TOKYO IS SLIPPING US THEIR CELL PHONE NUMBERS.
IT'S JUST THAT QUAINT OBSESSION THE JAPANESE SEEM TO HAVE WITH WHATEVER'S COMING NEXT, CYCLOPS.
GENETICALLY, I SUPPOSE WE'RE THE MOST FASHIONABLE CREATURES ON THE PLANET RIGHT NOW.

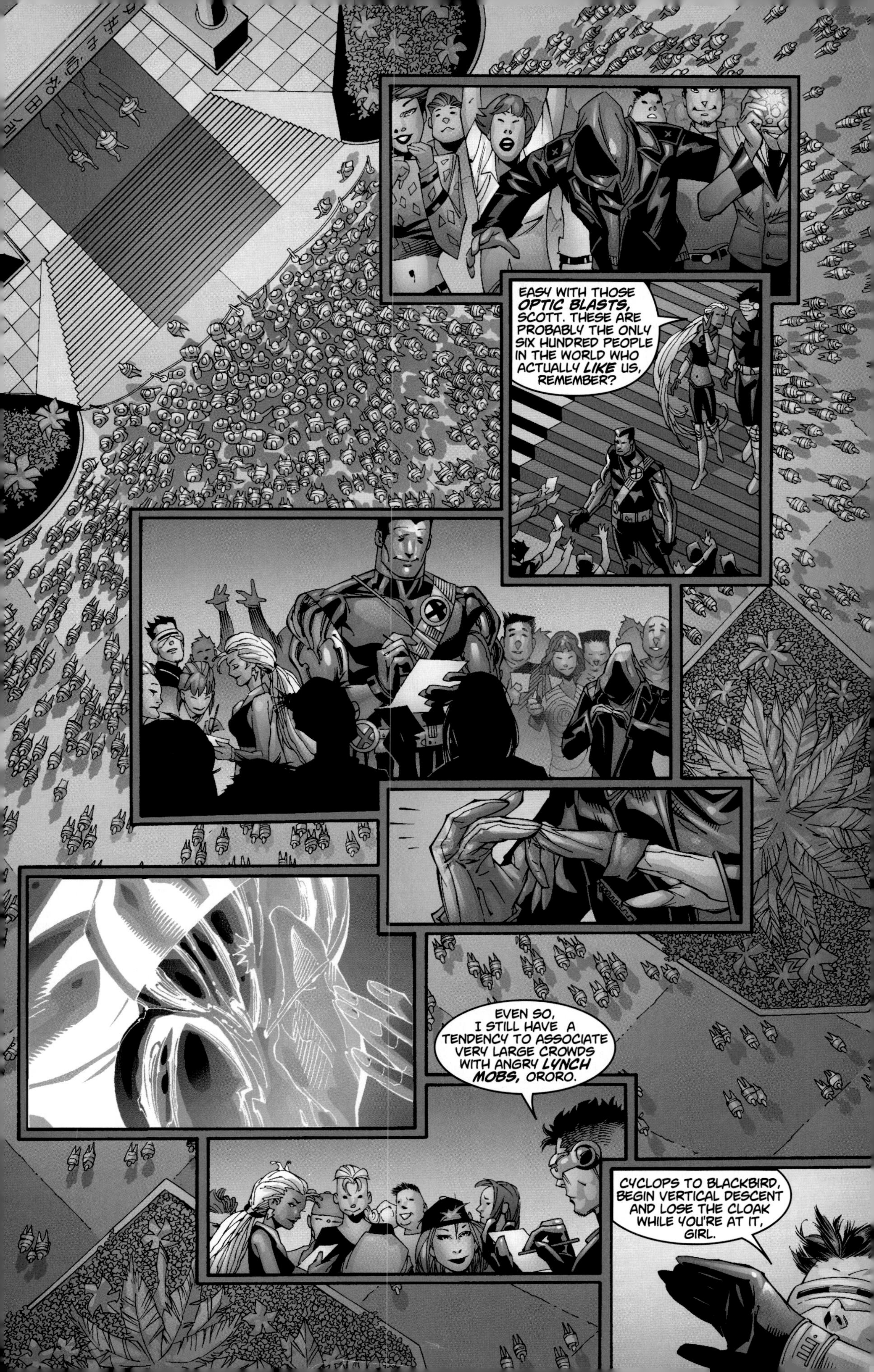
EASY WITH THOSE OPTIC BLASTS, SCOTT. THESE ARE PROBABLY THE ONLY SIX HUNDRED PEOPLE IN THE WORLD WHO ACTUALLY LIKE US, REMEMBER?
EVEN SO, I STILL HAVE A TENDENCY TO ASSOCIATE VERY LARGE CROWDS WITH ANGRY LYNCH MOBS, ORORO.
CYCLOPS TO BLACKBIRD, BEGIN VERTICAL DESCENT AND LOSE THE CLOAK WHILE YOU'RE AT IT, GIRL.

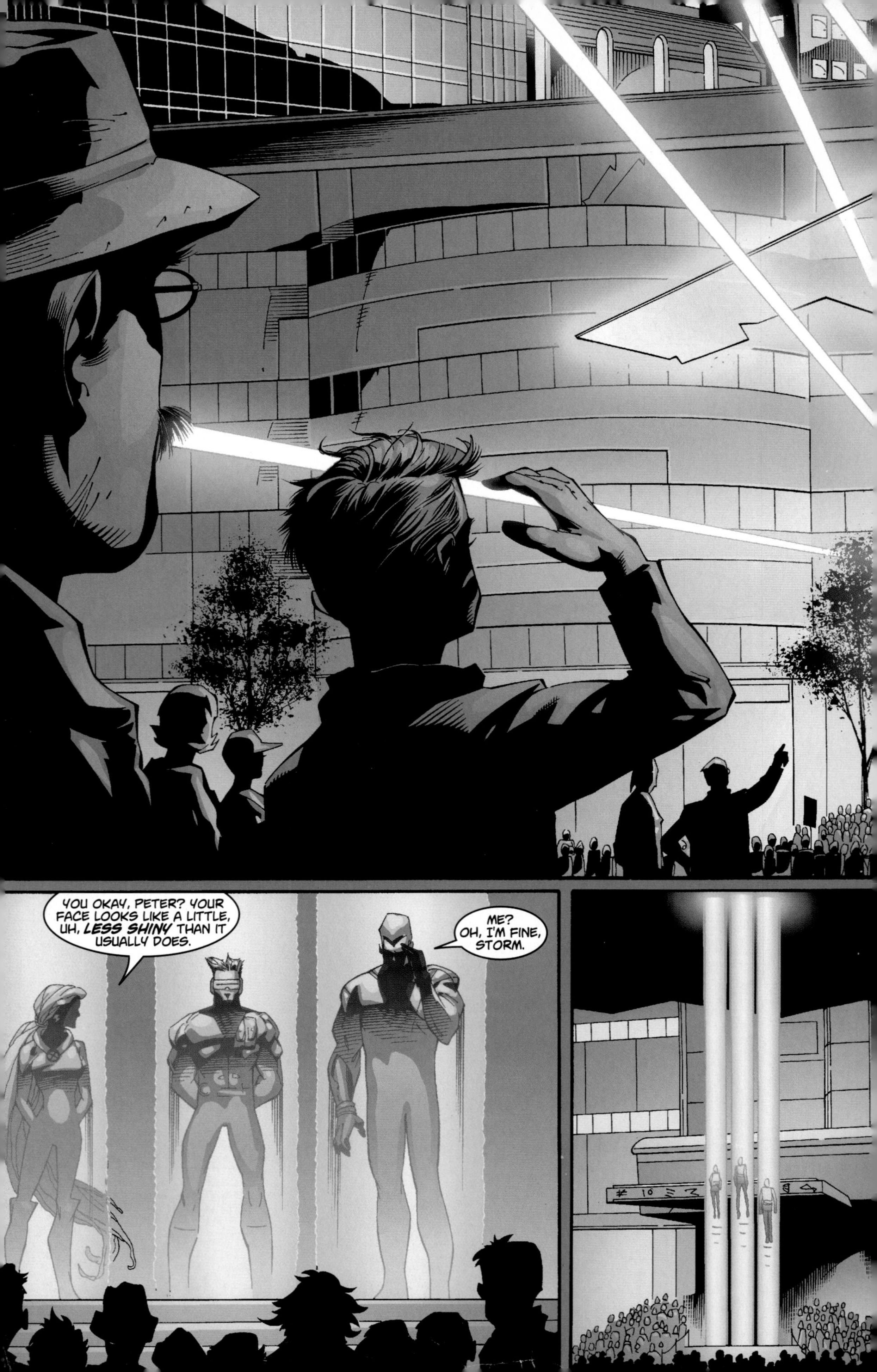

YOU OKAY, PETER? YOUR FACE LOOKS LIKE A LITTLE, UH, LESS SHINY THAN IT USUALLY DOES.
ME? OH, I'M FINE, STORM.

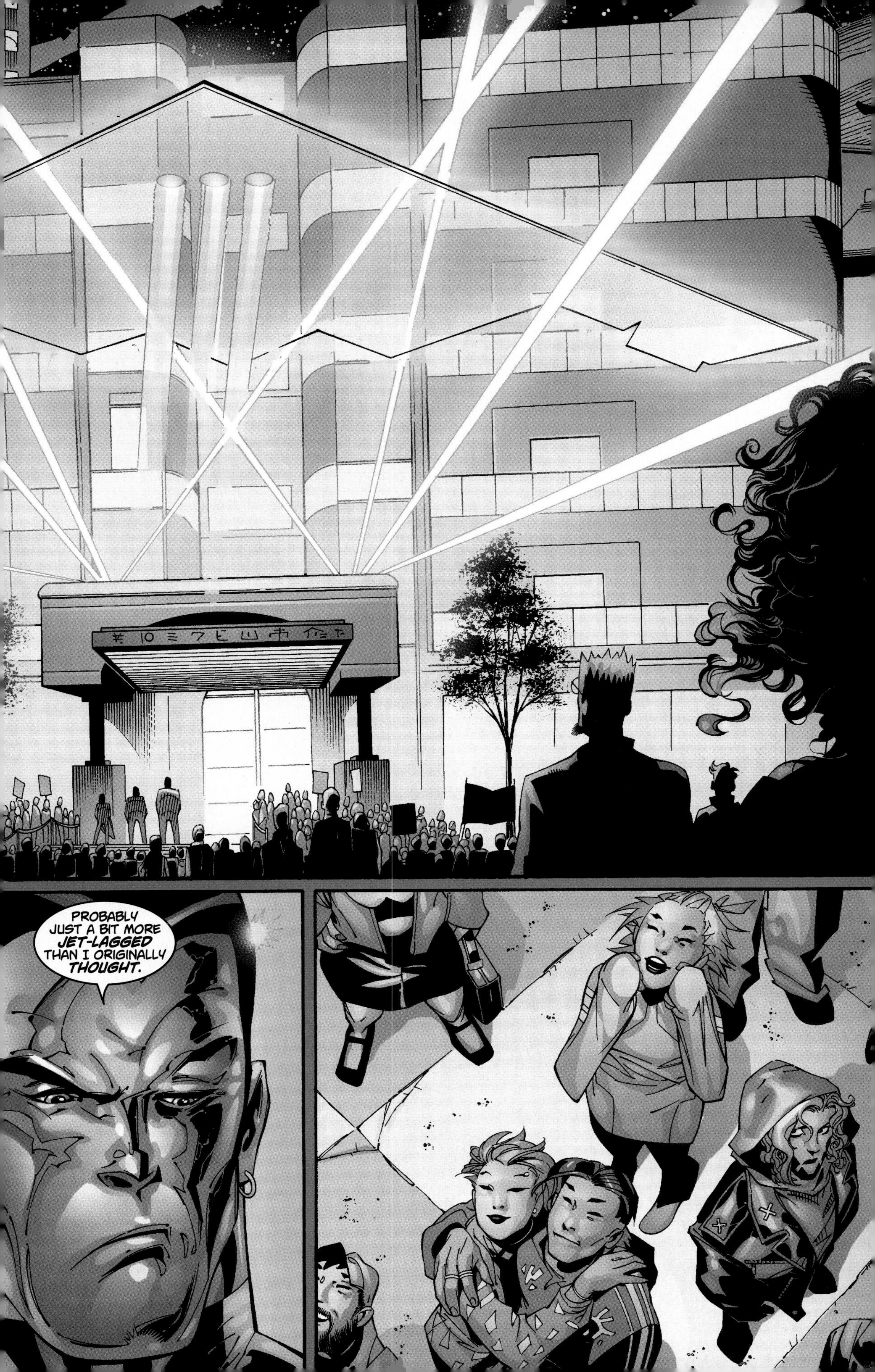
PROBABLY JUST A BIT MORE JET-LAGGED THAN I ORIGINALLY THOUGHT.

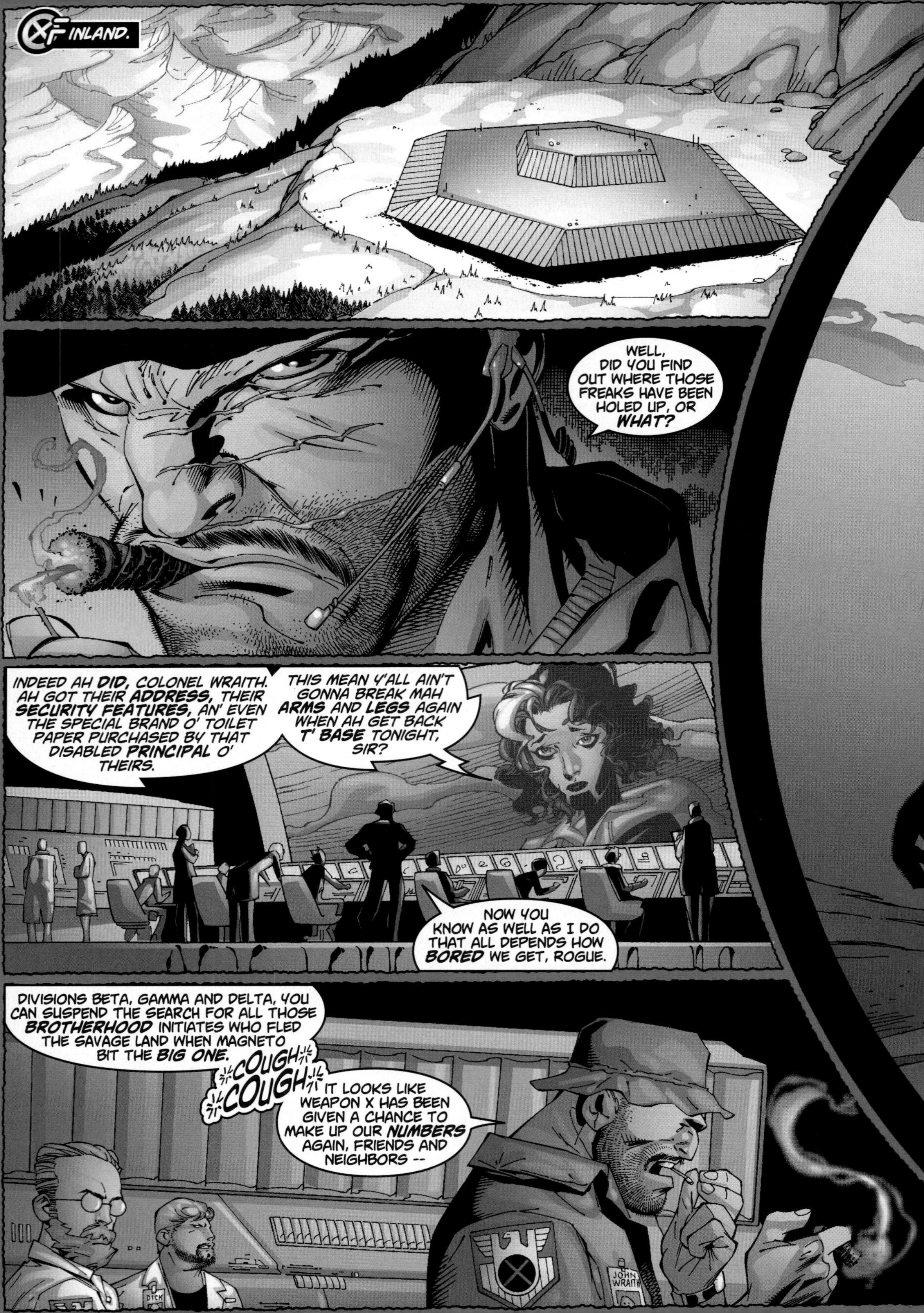
FINLAND.
WELL, DID YOU FIND OUT WHERE THOSE FREAKS HAVE BEEN HOLED UP, OR WHAT?
INDEED AH DID, COLONEL WRAITH. AH GOT THEIR ADDRESS, THEIR SECURITY FEATURES, AN' EVEN THE SPECIAL BRAND O' TOILET PAPER PURCHASED BY THAT DISABLED PRINCIPAL O' THEIRS.
THIS MEAN Y'ALL AIN'T GONNA BREAK MAH ARMS AND LEGS AGAIN WHEN AH GET BACK T' BASE TONIGHT, SIR?
NOW YOU KNOW AS WELL AS I DO THAT ALL DEPENDS HOW BORED WE GET, ROGUE.
DIVISIONS BETA, GAMMA AND DELTA, YOU CAN SUSPEND THE SEARCH FOR ALL THOSE BROTHERHOOD INITIATES WHO FLED THE SAVAGE LAND WHEN MAGNETO BIT THE BIG ONE.
COUGH COUGH
IT LOOKS LIKE WEAPON X HAS BEEN GIVEN A CHANCE TO MAKE UP OUR NUMBERS AGAIN, FRIENDS AND NEIGHBORS --
JOHN WRAITH
DICK

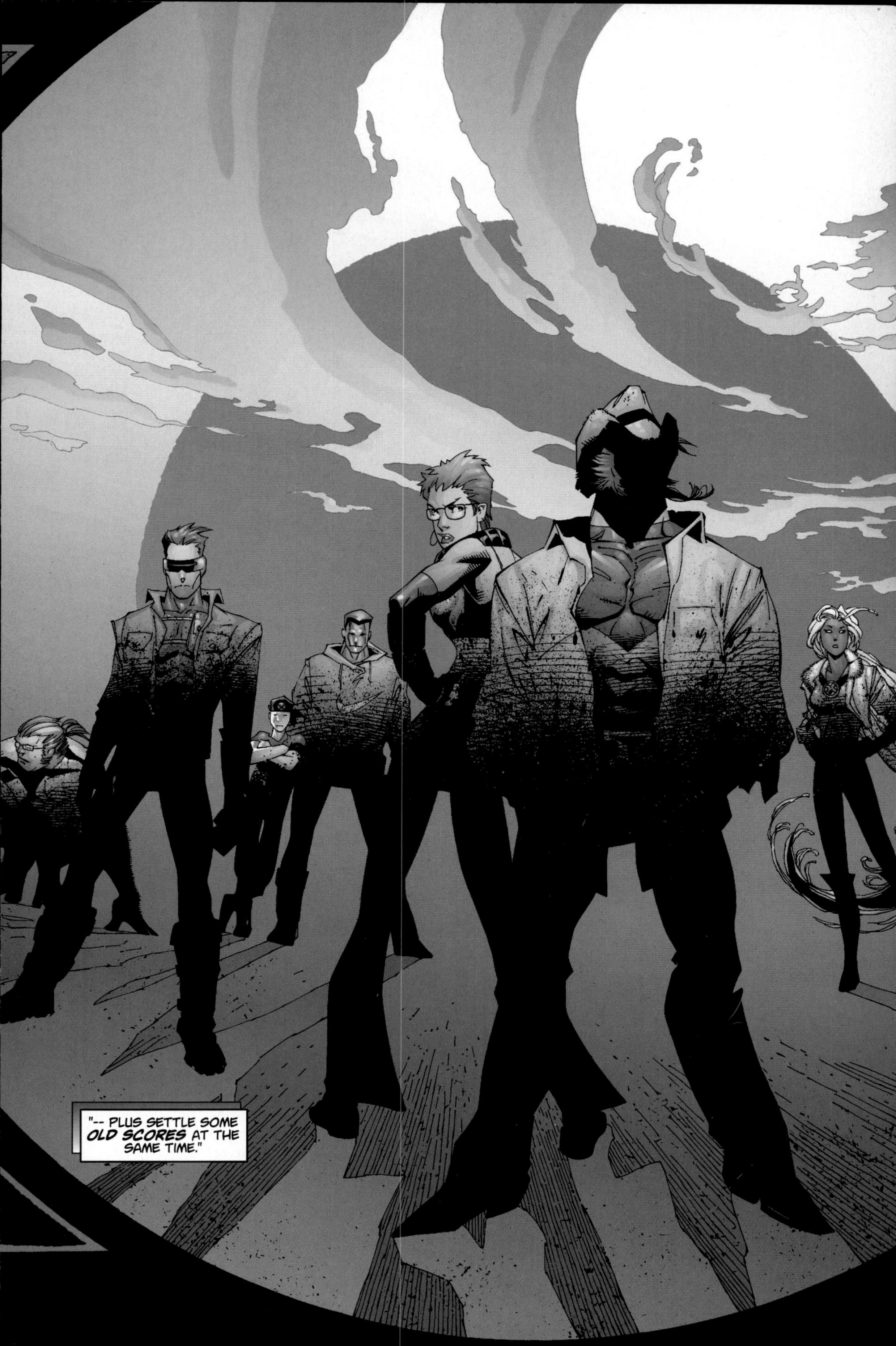
"-- PLUS SETTLE SOME OLD SCORES AT THE SAME TIME."

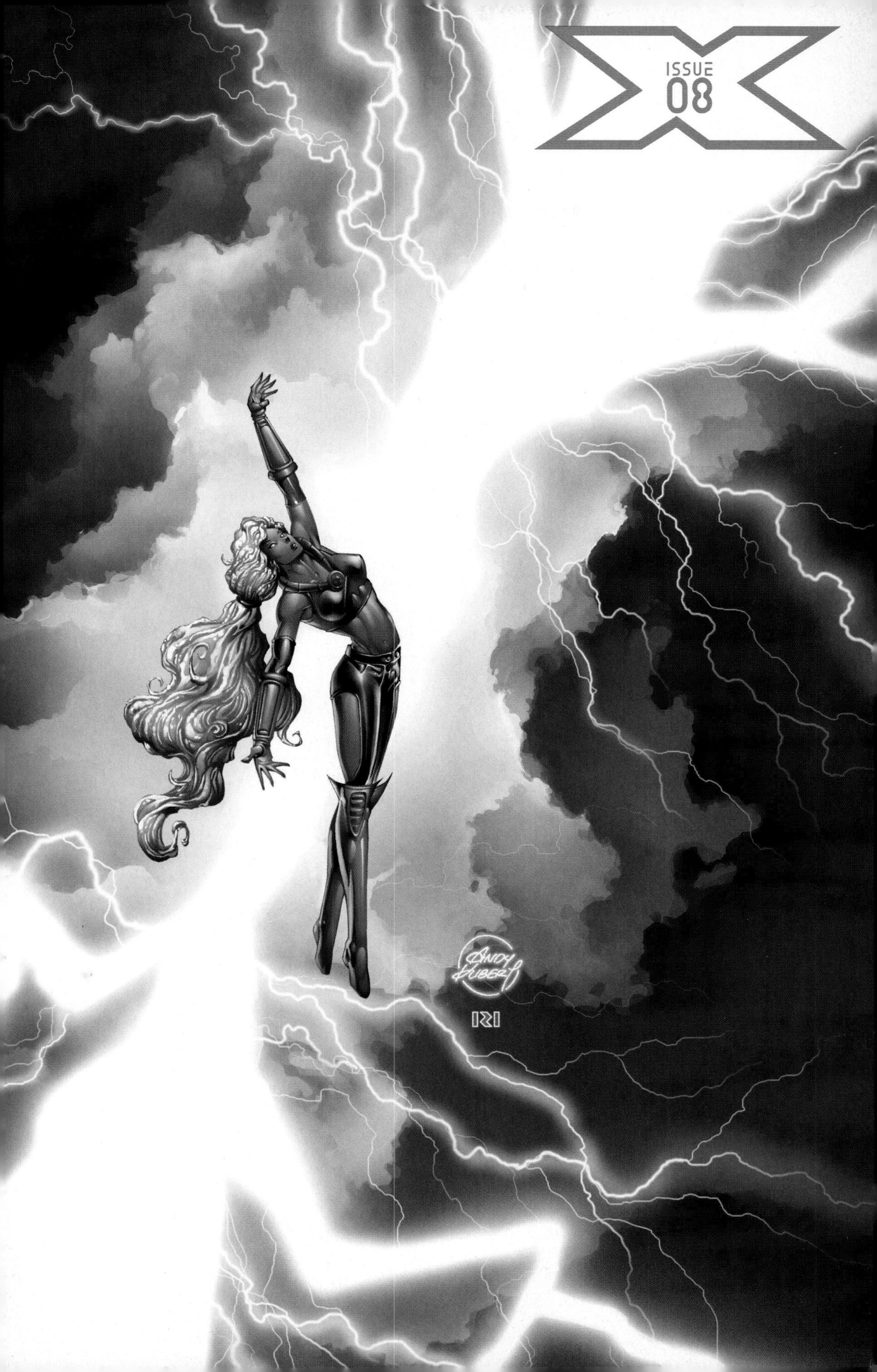
ISSUE
08
ANDY KUBERT

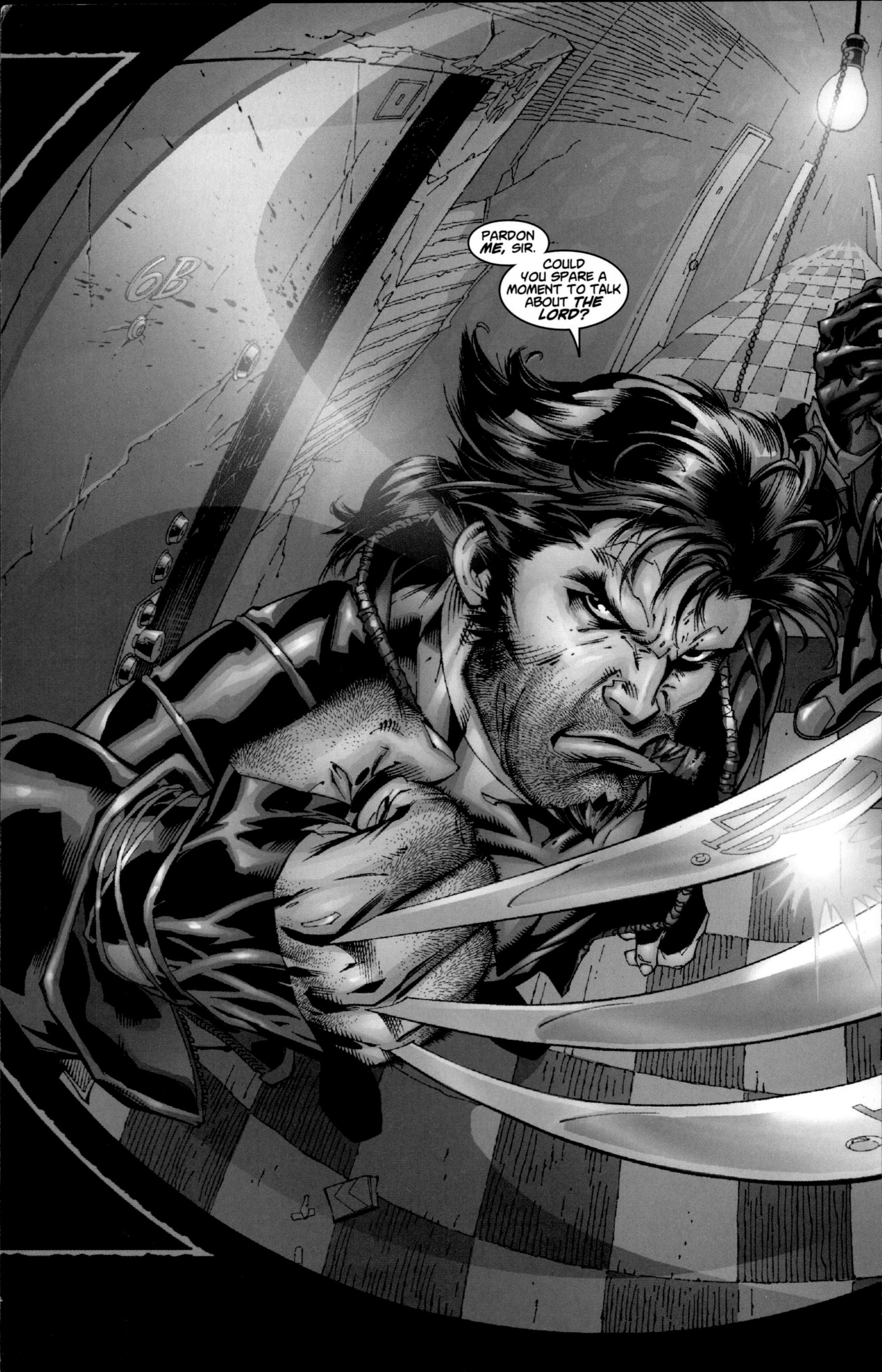
PARDON ME, SIR.
COULD YOU SPARE A MOMENT TO TALK ABOUT THE LORD?

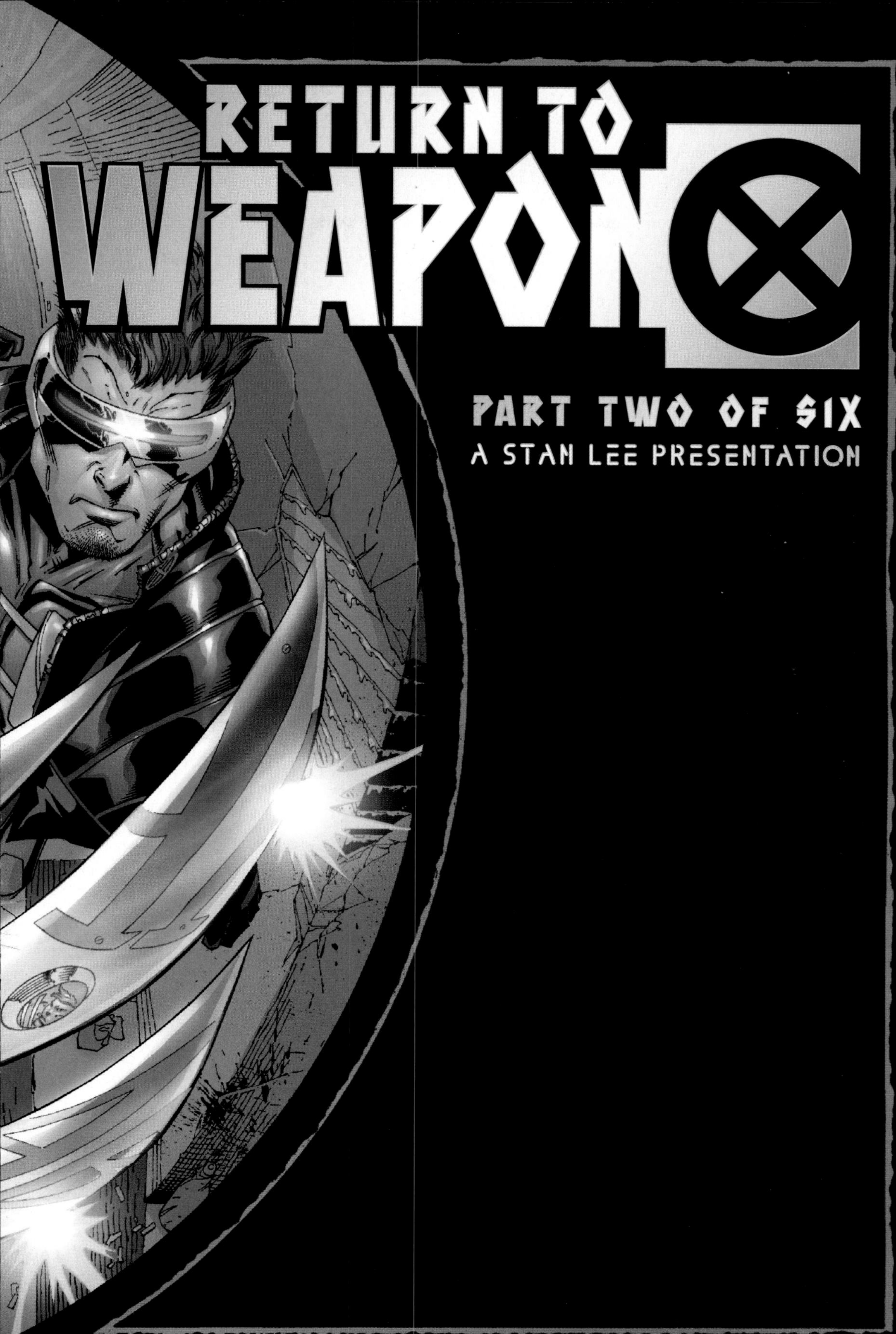
RETURN TO
WEAPON X
PART TWO OF SIX
A STAN LEE PRESENTATION

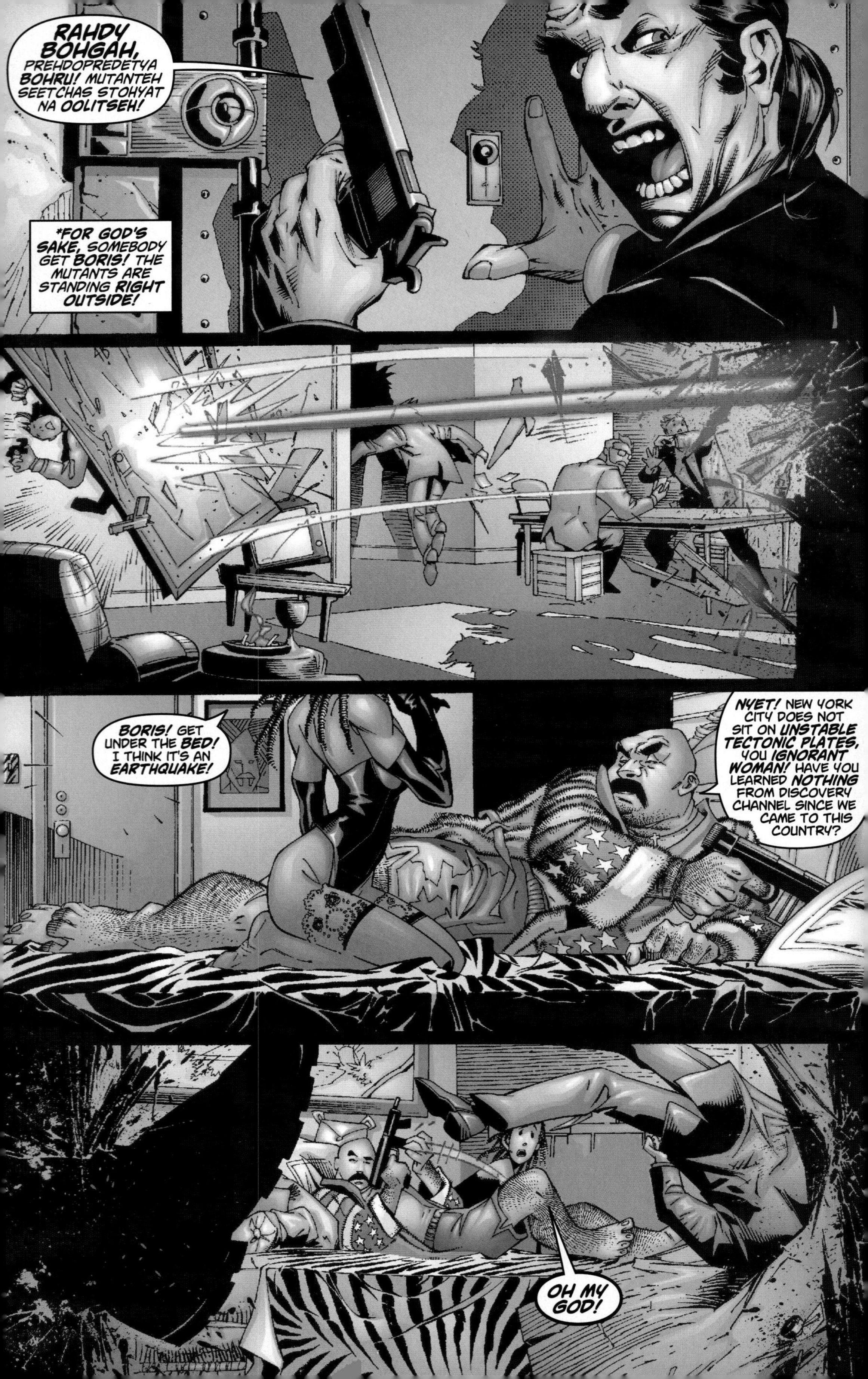
RAHDY BOHGAH, PREHDOPREDETYA BOHRU! MUTANTEH SEETCHAS STOHYAT NA OOLITSEH!
*FOR GOD'S SAKE, SOMEBODY GET BORIS! THE MUTANTS ARE STANDING RIGHT OUTSIDE!
BORIS! GET UNDER THE BED! I THINK IT'S AN EARTHQUAKE!
NYET! NEW YORK CITY DOES NOT SIT ON UNSTABLE TECTONIC PLATES, YOU IGNORANT WOMAN! HAVE YOU LEARNED NOTHING FROM DISCOVERY CHANNEL SINCE WE CAME TO THIS COUNTRY?
OH MY GOD!

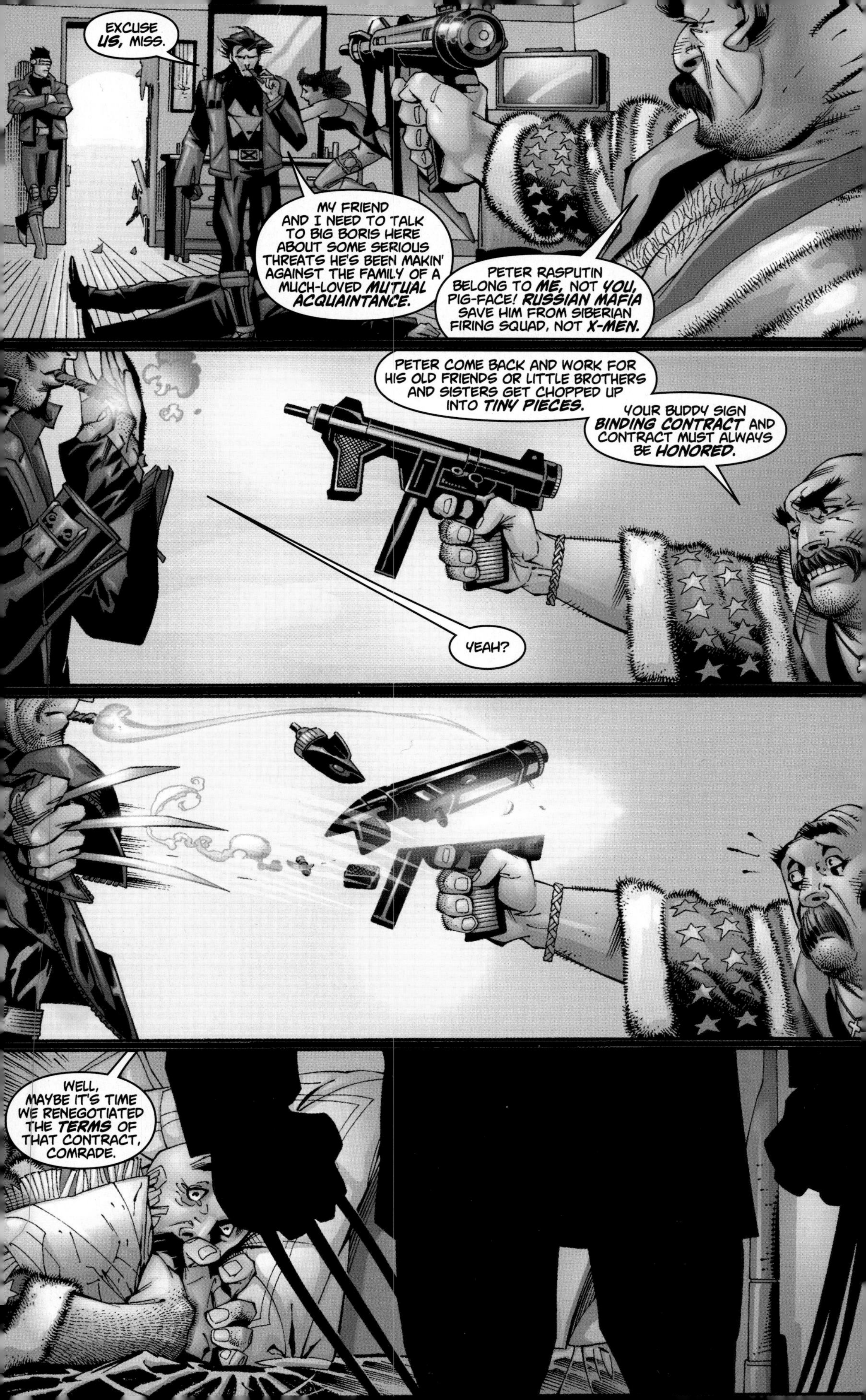
EXCUSE US, MISS.
MY FRIEND AND I NEED TO TALK TO BIG BORIS HERE ABOUT SOME SERIOUS THREATS HE'S BEEN MAKIN' AGAINST THE FAMILY OF A MUCH-LOVED MUTUAL ACQUAINTANCE.
PETER RASPUTIN BELONG TO ME, NOT YOU, PIG-FACE! RUSSIAN MAFIA SAVE HIM FROM SIBERIAN FIRING SQUAD, NOT X-MEN.
PETER COME BACK AND WORK FOR HIS OLD FRIENDS OR LITTLE BROTHERS AND SISTERS GET CHOPPED UP INTO TINY PIECES.
YOUR BUDDY SIGN BINDING CONTRACT AND CONTRACT MUST ALWAYS BE HONORED.
YEAH?
WELL, MAYBE IT'S TIME WE RENEGOTIATED THE TERMS OF THAT CONTRACT, COMRADE.

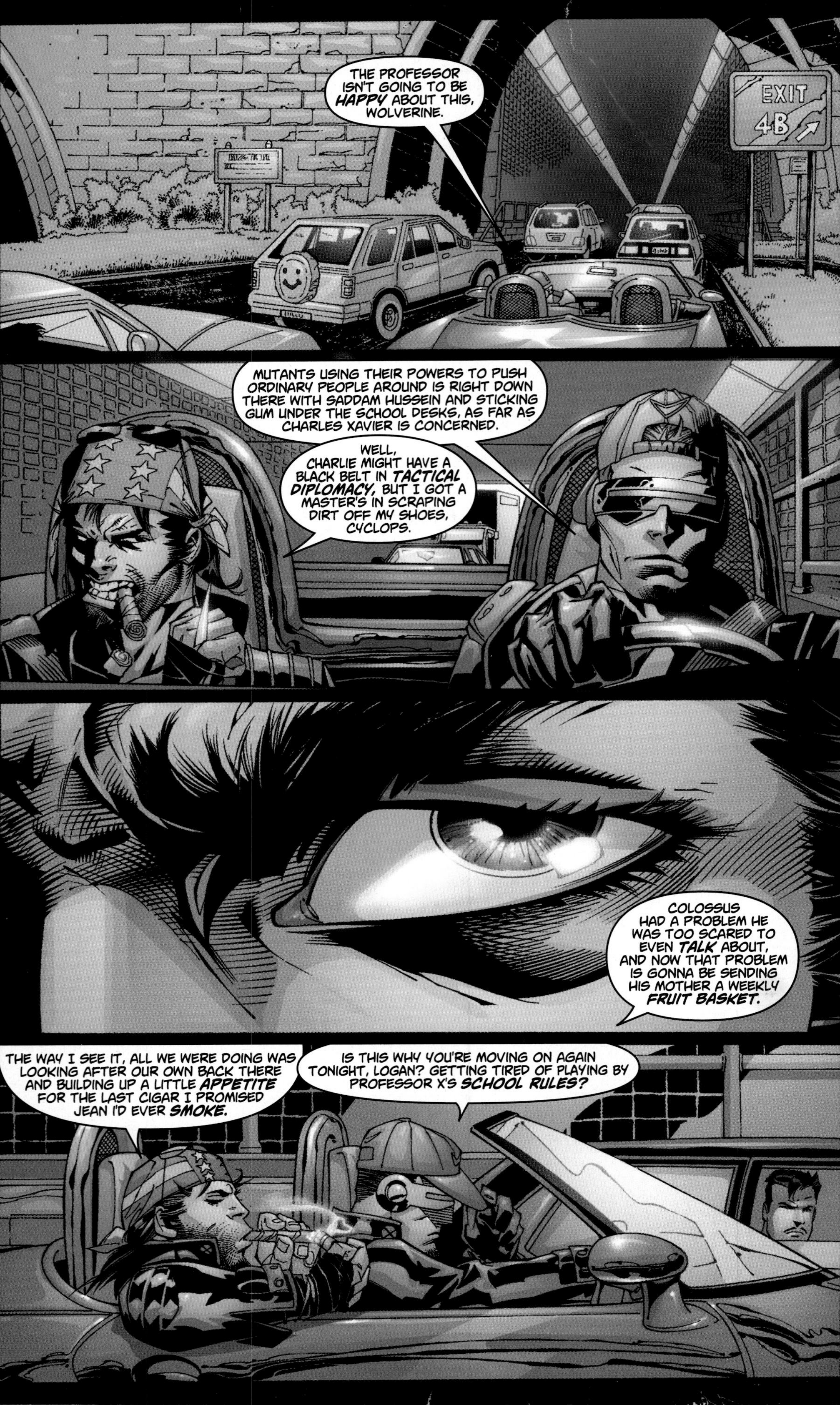
THE PROFESSOR ISN'T GOING TO BE HAPPY ABOUT THIS, WOLVERINE.
EXIT 4B
MUTANTS USING THEIR POWERS TO PUSH ORDINARY PEOPLE AROUND IS RIGHT DOWN THERE WITH SADDAM HUSSEIN AND STICKING GUM UNDER THE SCHOOL DESKS, AS FAR AS CHARLES XAVIER IS CONCERNED.
WELL, CHARLIE MIGHT HAVE A BLACK BELT IN TACTICAL DIPLOMACY, BUT I GOT A MASTER'S IN SCRAPING DIRT OFF MY SHOES, CYCLOPS.
COLOSSUS HAD A PROBLEM HE WAS TOO SCARED TO EVEN TALK ABOUT, AND NOW THAT PROBLEM IS GONNA BE SENDING HIS MOTHER A WEEKLY FRUIT BASKET.
THE WAY I SEE IT, ALL WE WERE DOING WAS LOOKING AFTER OUR OWN BACK THERE AND BUILDING UP A LITTLE APPETITE FOR THE LAST CIGAR I PROMISED JEAN I'D EVER SMOKE.
IS THIS WHY YOU'RE MOVING ON AGAIN TONIGHT, LOGAN? GETTING TIRED OF PLAYING BY PROFESSOR X'S SCHOOL RULES?

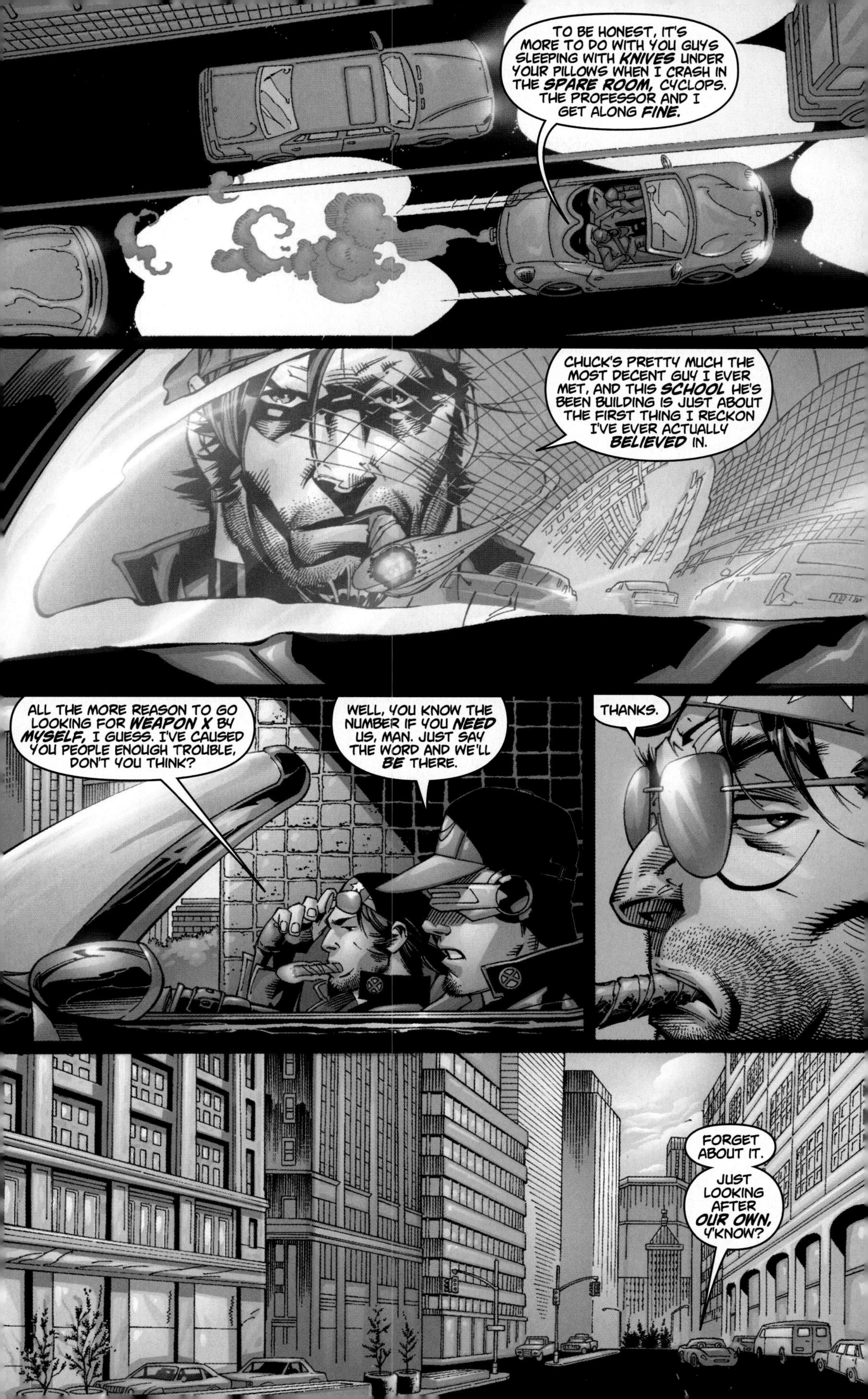
TO BE HONEST, IT'S MORE TO DO WITH YOU GUYS SLEEPING WITH **KNIVES** UNDER YOUR PILLOWS WHEN I CRASH IN THE **SPARE ROOM,** CYCLOPS. THE PROFESSOR AND I GET ALONG **FINE.**
CHUCK'S PRETTY MUCH THE MOST DECENT GUY I EVER MET, AND THIS **SCHOOL** HE'S BEEN BUILDING IS JUST ABOUT THE FIRST THING I RECKON I'VE EVER ACTUALLY **BELIEVED** IN.
ALL THE MORE REASON TO GO LOOKING FOR **WEAPON X** BY **MYSELF,** I GUESS. I'VE CAUSED YOU PEOPLE ENOUGH TROUBLE, DON'T YOU THINK?
WELL, YOU KNOW THE NUMBER IF YOU **NEED** US, MAN. JUST SAY THE WORD AND WE'LL **BE** THERE.
THANKS.
FORGET ABOUT IT.
JUST LOOKING AFTER **OUR OWN,** Y'KNOW?

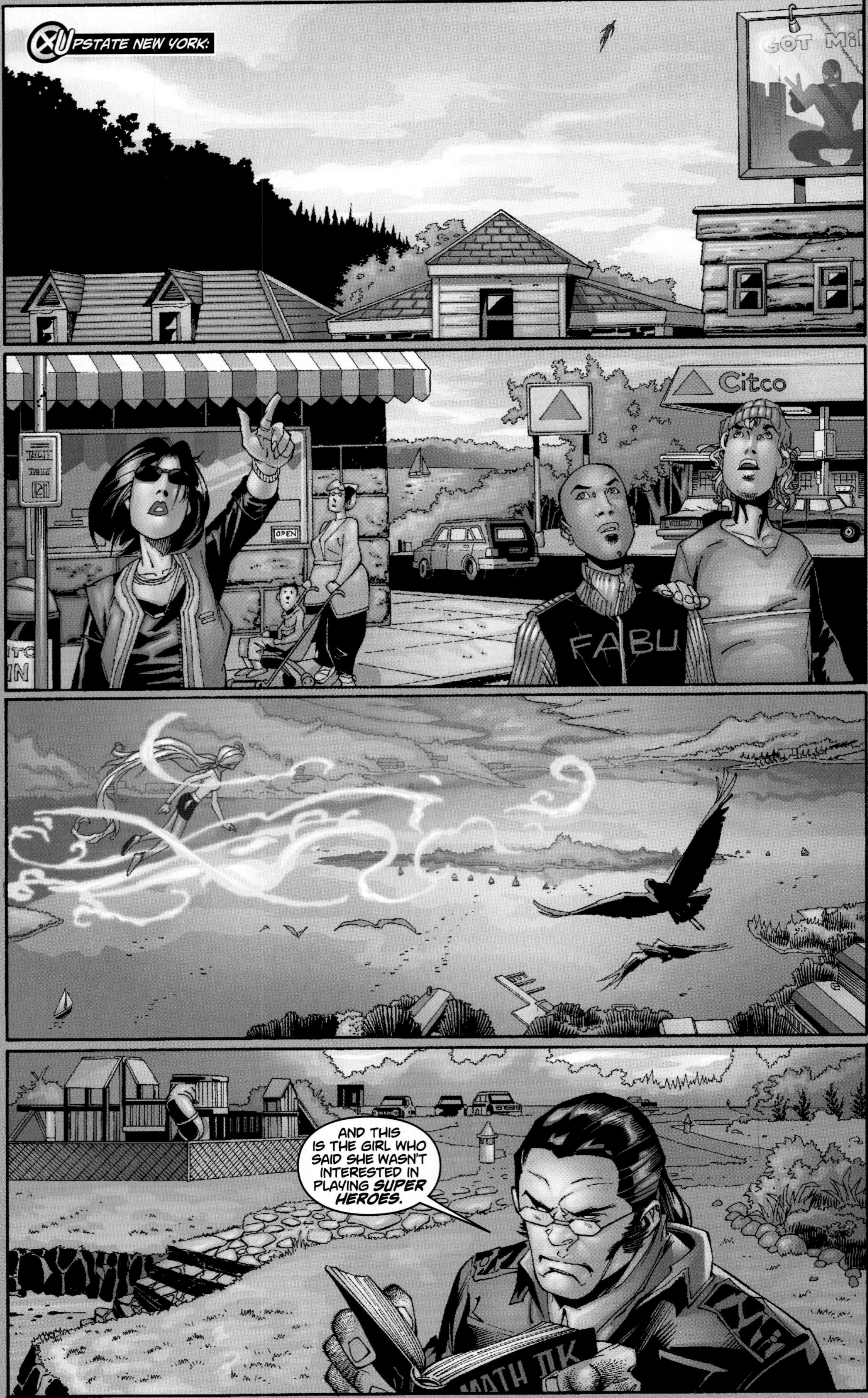
UPSTATE NEW YORK:
GOT MI
Citco
OPEN
FABU
AND THIS IS THE GIRL WHO SAID SHE WASN'T INTERESTED IN PLAYING SUPER HEROES.
MATH IIK

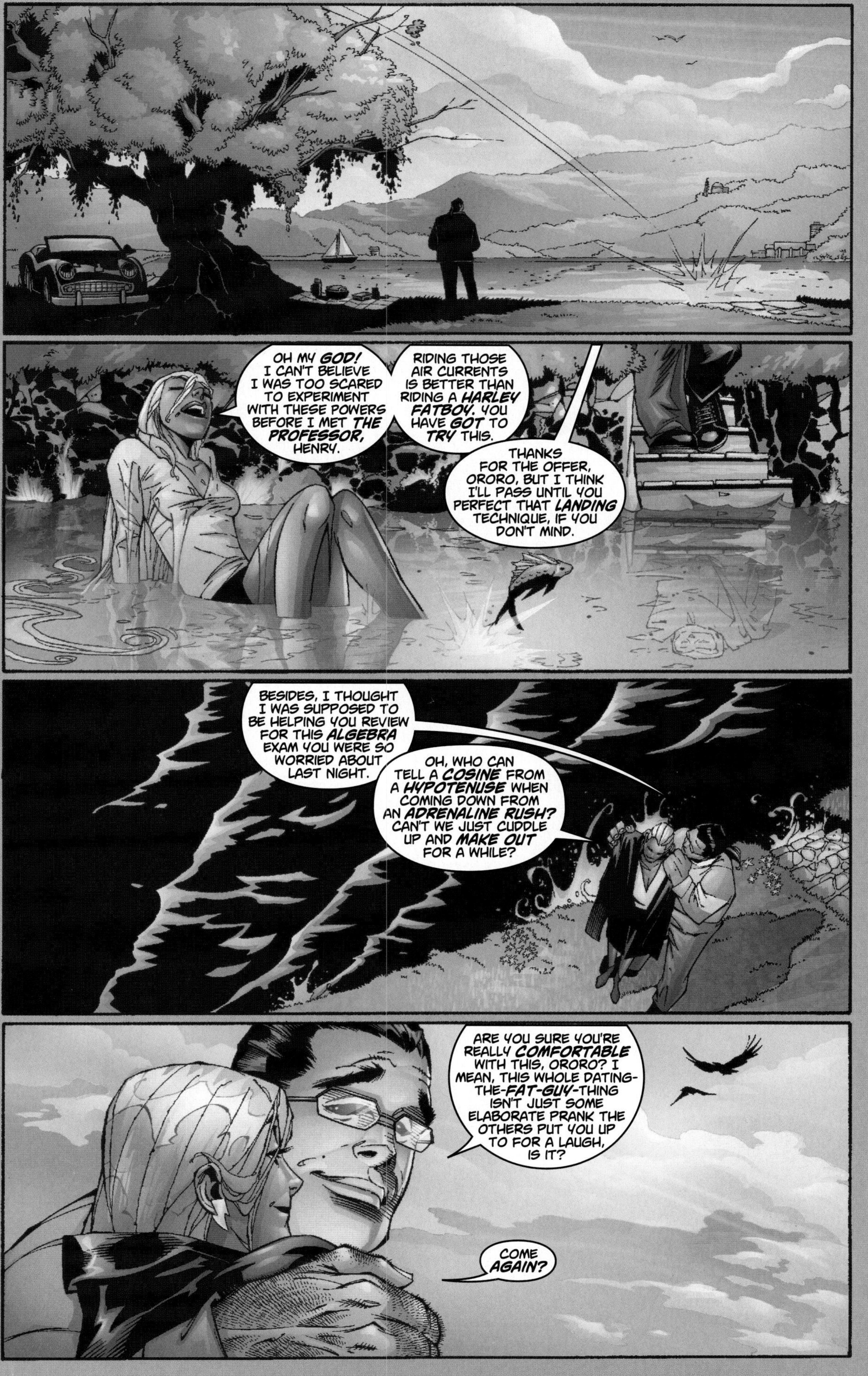

OH MY GOD! I CAN'T BELIEVE I WAS TOO SCARED TO EXPERIMENT WITH THESE POWERS BEFORE I MET THE PROFESSOR, HENRY.
RIDING THOSE AIR CURRENTS IS BETTER THAN RIDING A HARLEY FATBOY. YOU HAVE GOT TO TRY THIS.
THANKS FOR THE OFFER, ORORO, BUT I THINK I'LL PASS UNTIL YOU PERFECT THAT LANDING TECHNIQUE, IF YOU DON'T MIND.
BESIDES, I THOUGHT I WAS SUPPOSED TO BE HELPING YOU REVIEW FOR THIS ALGEBRA EXAM YOU WERE SO WORRIED ABOUT LAST NIGHT.
OH, WHO CAN TELL A COSINE FROM A HYPOTENUSE WHEN COMING DOWN FROM AN ADRENALINE RUSH? CAN'T WE JUST CUDDLE UP AND MAKE OUT FOR A WHILE?
ARE YOU SURE YOU'RE REALLY COMFORTABLE WITH THIS, ORORO? I MEAN, THIS WHOLE DATING-THE-FAT-GUY-THING ISN'T JUST SOME ELABORATE PRANK THE OTHERS PUT YOU UP TO FOR A LAUGH, IS IT?
COME AGAIN?

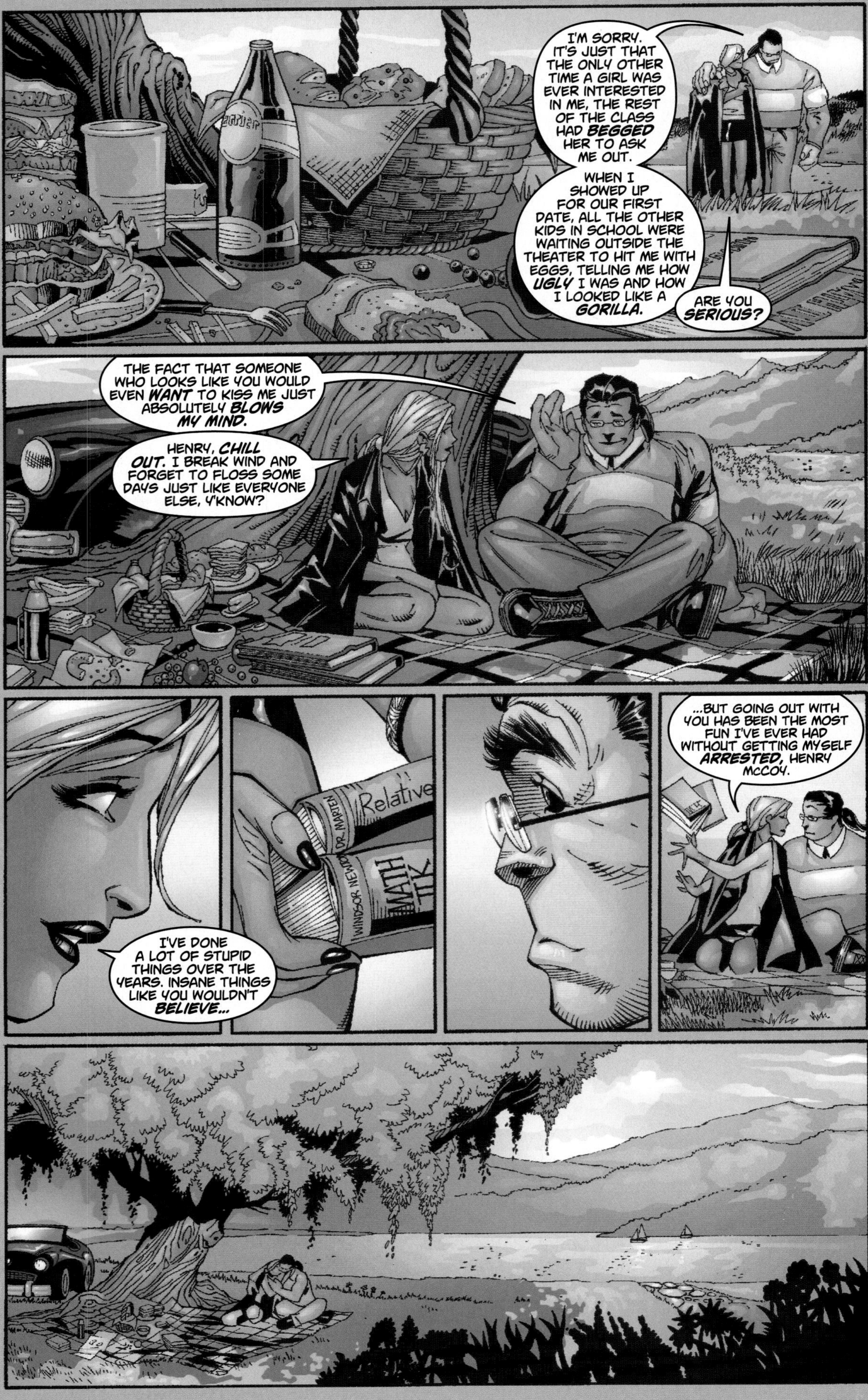
I'M SORRY. IT'S JUST THAT THE ONLY OTHER TIME A GIRL WAS EVER INTERESTED IN ME, THE REST OF THE CLASS HAD BEGGED HER TO ASK ME OUT.
WHEN I SHOWED UP FOR OUR FIRST DATE, ALL THE OTHER KIDS IN SCHOOL WERE WAITING OUTSIDE THE THEATER TO HIT ME WITH EGGS, TELLING ME HOW UGLY I WAS AND HOW I LOOKED LIKE A GORILLA.
ARE YOU SERIOUS?
THE FACT THAT SOMEONE WHO LOOKS LIKE YOU WOULD EVEN WANT TO KISS ME JUST ABSOLUTELY BLOWS MY MIND.
HENRY, CHILL OUT. I BREAK WIND AND FORGET TO FLOSS SOME DAYS JUST LIKE EVERYONE ELSE, Y'KNOW?
Relative
DR. MARTEN
WINDSOR NEWTON
MATH TIK
I'VE DONE A LOT OF STUPID THINGS OVER THE YEARS. INSANE THINGS LIKE YOU WOULDN'T BELIEVE...
...BUT GOING OUT WITH YOU HAS BEEN THE MOST FUN I'VE EVER HAD WITHOUT GETTING MYSELF ARRESTED, HENRY McCOY.

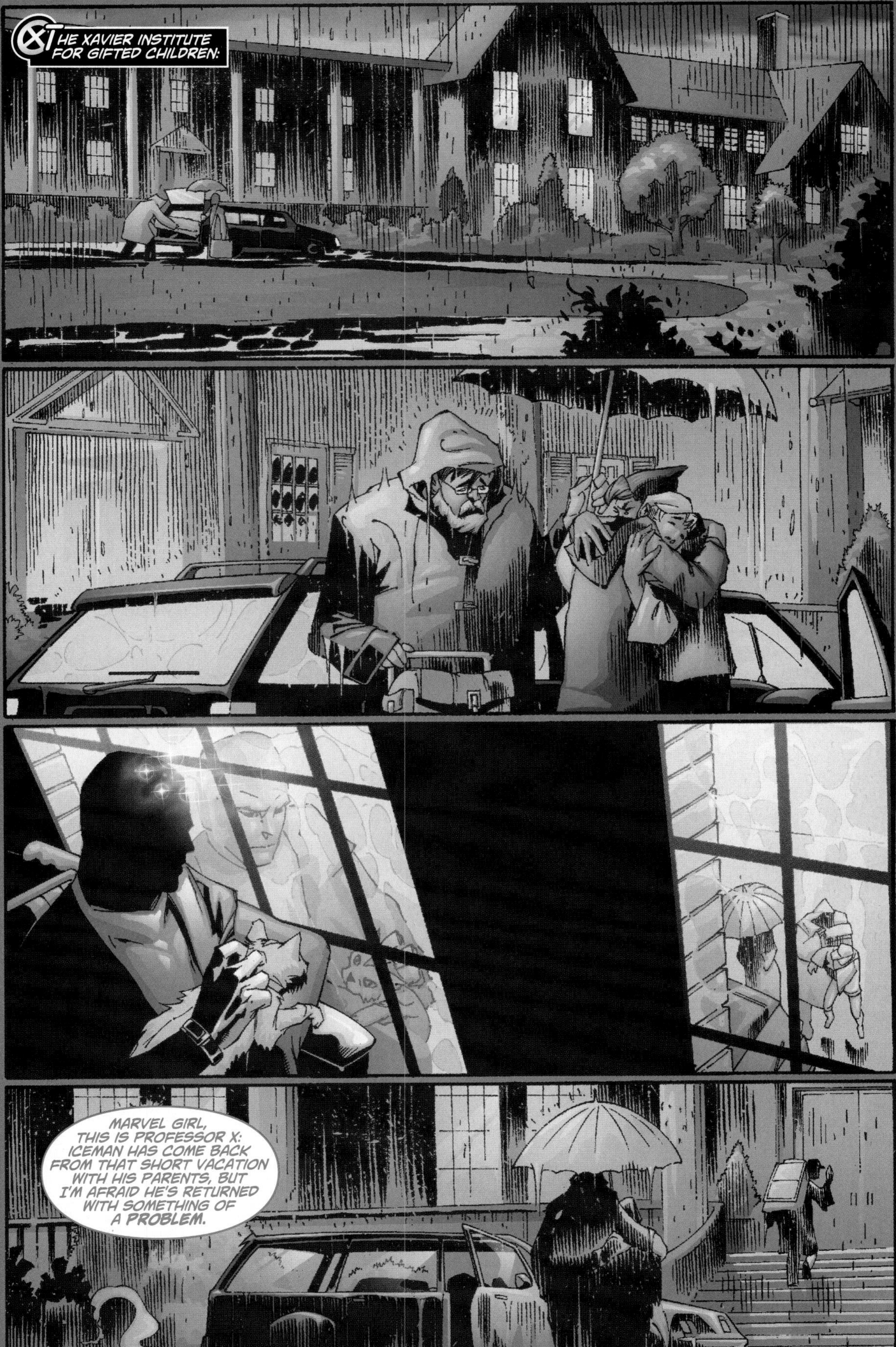
THE XAVIER INSTITUTE FOR GIFTED CHILDREN:
MARVEL GIRL, THIS IS PROFESSOR X: ICEMAN HAS COME BACK FROM THAT SHORT VACATION WITH HIS PARENTS, BUT I'M AFRAID HE'S RETURNED WITH SOMETHING OF A PROBLEM.

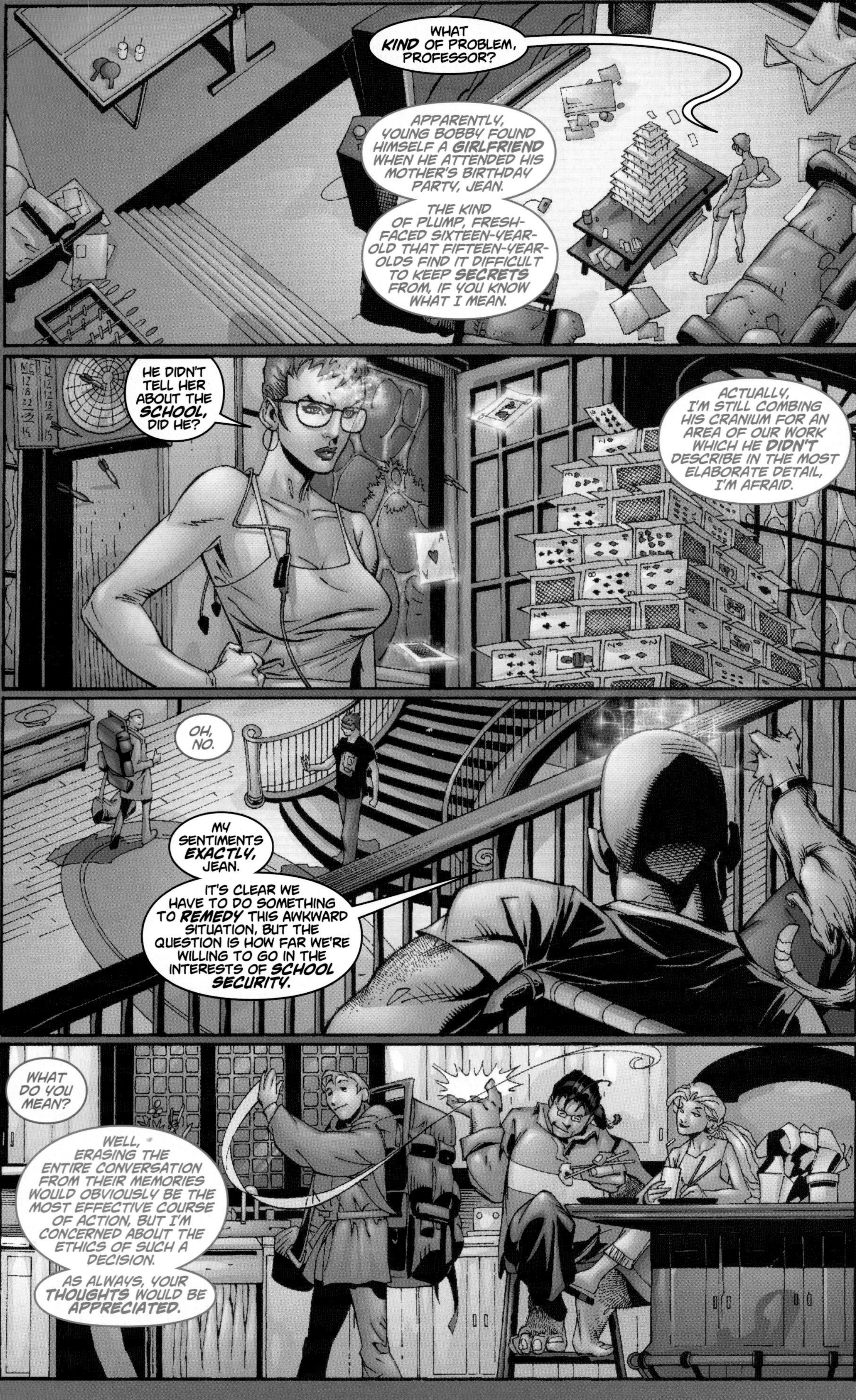

WHAT KIND OF PROBLEM, PROFESSOR?
APPARENTLY, YOUNG BOBBY FOUND HIMSELF A GIRLFRIEND WHEN HE ATTENDED HIS MOTHER'S BIRTHDAY PARTY, JEAN.
THE KIND OF PLUMP, FRESH-FACED SIXTEEN-YEAR-OLD THAT FIFTEEN-YEAR-OLDS FIND IT DIFFICULT TO KEEP SECRETS FROM, IF YOU KNOW WHAT I MEAN.
HE DIDN'T TELL HER ABOUT THE SCHOOL, DID HE?
ACTUALLY, I'M STILL COMBING HIS CRANIUM FOR AN AREA OF OUR WORK WHICH HE DIDN'T DESCRIBE IN THE MOST ELABORATE DETAIL, I'M AFRAID.
OH, NO.
MY SENTIMENTS EXACTLY, JEAN.
IT'S CLEAR WE HAVE TO DO SOMETHING TO REMEDY THIS AWKWARD SITUATION, BUT THE QUESTION IS HOW FAR WE'RE WILLING TO GO IN THE INTERESTS OF SCHOOL SECURITY.
WHAT DO YOU MEAN?
WELL, ERASING THE ENTIRE CONVERSATION FROM THEIR MEMORIES WOULD OBVIOUSLY BE THE MOST EFFECTIVE COURSE OF ACTION, BUT I'M CONCERNED ABOUT THE ETHICS OF SUCH A DECISION.
AS ALWAYS, YOUR THOUGHTS WOULD BE APPRECIATED.

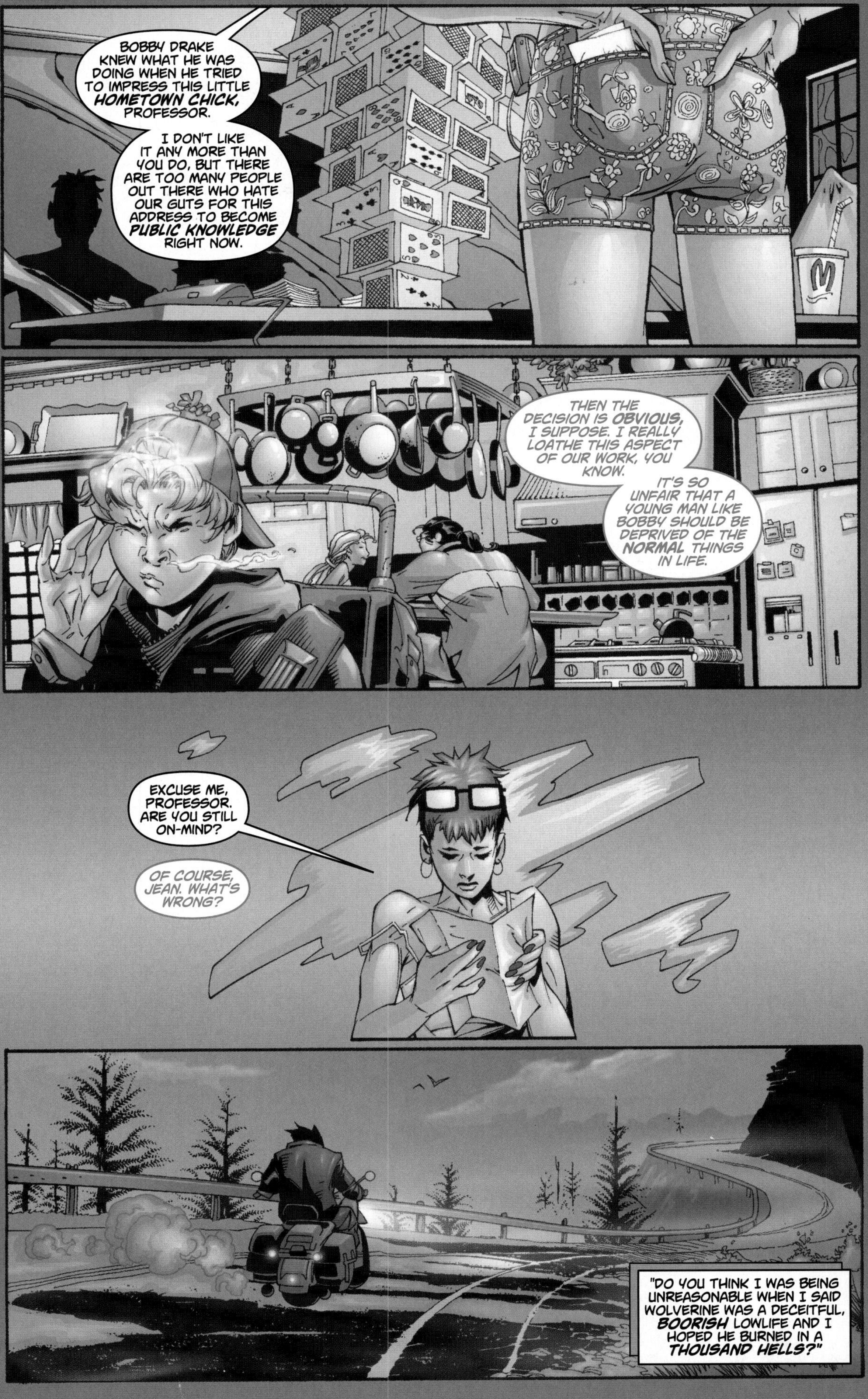
BOBBY DRAKE KNEW WHAT HE WAS DOING WHEN HE TRIED TO IMPRESS THIS LITTLE HOMETOWN CHICK, PROFESSOR.
I DON'T LIKE IT ANY MORE THAN YOU DO, BUT THERE ARE TOO MANY PEOPLE OUT THERE WHO HATE OUR GUTS FOR THIS ADDRESS TO BECOME PUBLIC KNOWLEDGE RIGHT NOW.
THEN THE DECISION IS OBVIOUS, I SUPPOSE. I REALLY LOATHE THIS ASPECT OF OUR WORK, YOU KNOW.
IT'S SO UNFAIR THAT A YOUNG MAN LIKE BOBBY SHOULD BE DEPRIVED OF THE NORMAL THINGS IN LIFE.
EXCUSE ME, PROFESSOR. ARE YOU STILL ON-MIND?
OF COURSE, JEAN. WHAT'S WRONG?
"DO YOU THINK I WAS BEING UNREASONABLE WHEN I SAID WOLVERINE WAS A DECEITFUL, BOORISH LOWLIFE AND I HOPED HE BURNED IN A THOUSAND HELLS?"

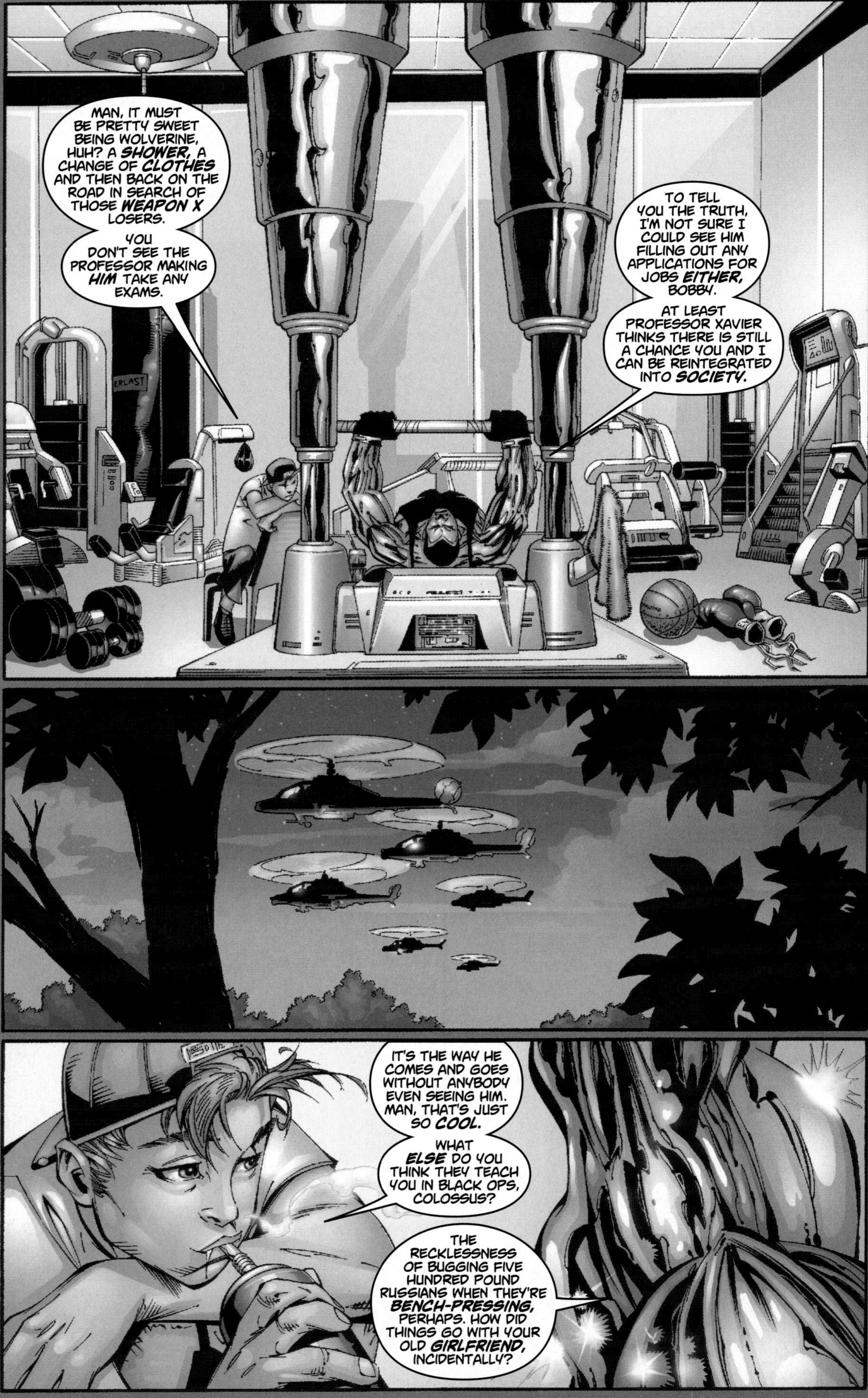
MAN, IT MUST BE PRETTY SWEET BEING WOLVERINE, HUH? A SHOWER, A CHANGE OF CLOTHES AND THEN BACK ON THE ROAD IN SEARCH OF THOSE WEAPON X LOSERS.
YOU DON'T SEE THE PROFESSOR MAKING HIM TAKE ANY EXAMS.
TO TELL YOU THE TRUTH, I'M NOT SURE I COULD SEE HIM FILLING OUT ANY APPLICATIONS FOR JOBS EITHER, BOBBY.
AT LEAST PROFESSOR XAVIER THINKS THERE IS STILL A CHANCE YOU AND I CAN BE REINTEGRATED INTO SOCIETY.
IT'S THE WAY HE COMES AND GOES WITHOUT ANYBODY EVEN SEEING HIM. MAN, THAT'S JUST SO COOL.
WHAT ELSE DO YOU THINK THEY TEACH YOU IN BLACK OPS, COLOSSUS?
THE RECKLESSNESS OF BUGGING FIVE HUNDRED POUND RUSSIANS WHEN THEY'RE BENCH-PRESSING, PERHAPS. HOW DID THINGS GO WITH YOUR OLD GIRLFRIEND, INCIDENTALLY?

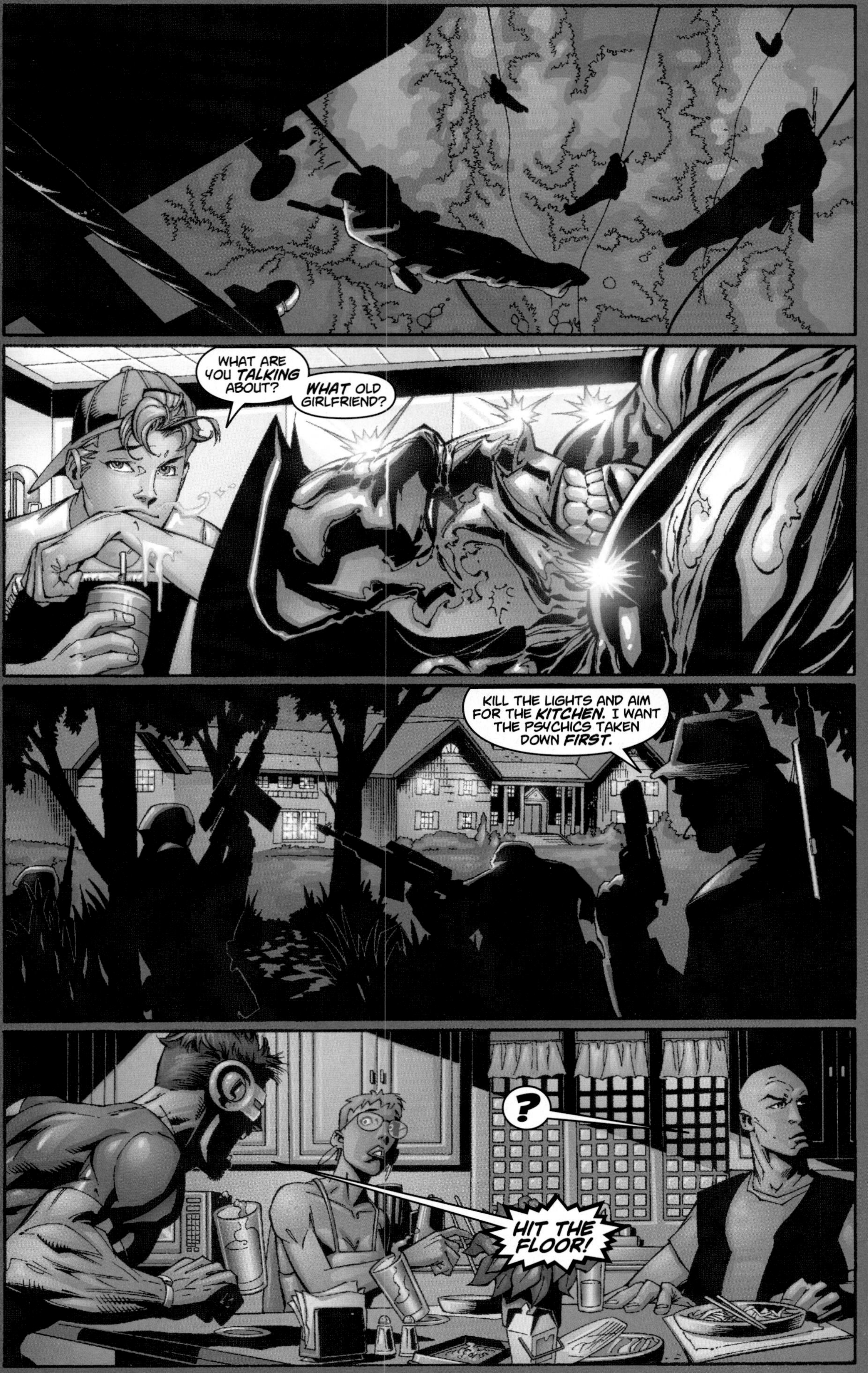
WHAT ARE YOU TALKING ABOUT?
WHAT OLD GIRLFRIEND?
KILL THE LIGHTS AND AIM FOR THE KITCHEN. I WANT THE PSYCHICS TAKEN DOWN FIRST.
?
HIT THE FLOOR!

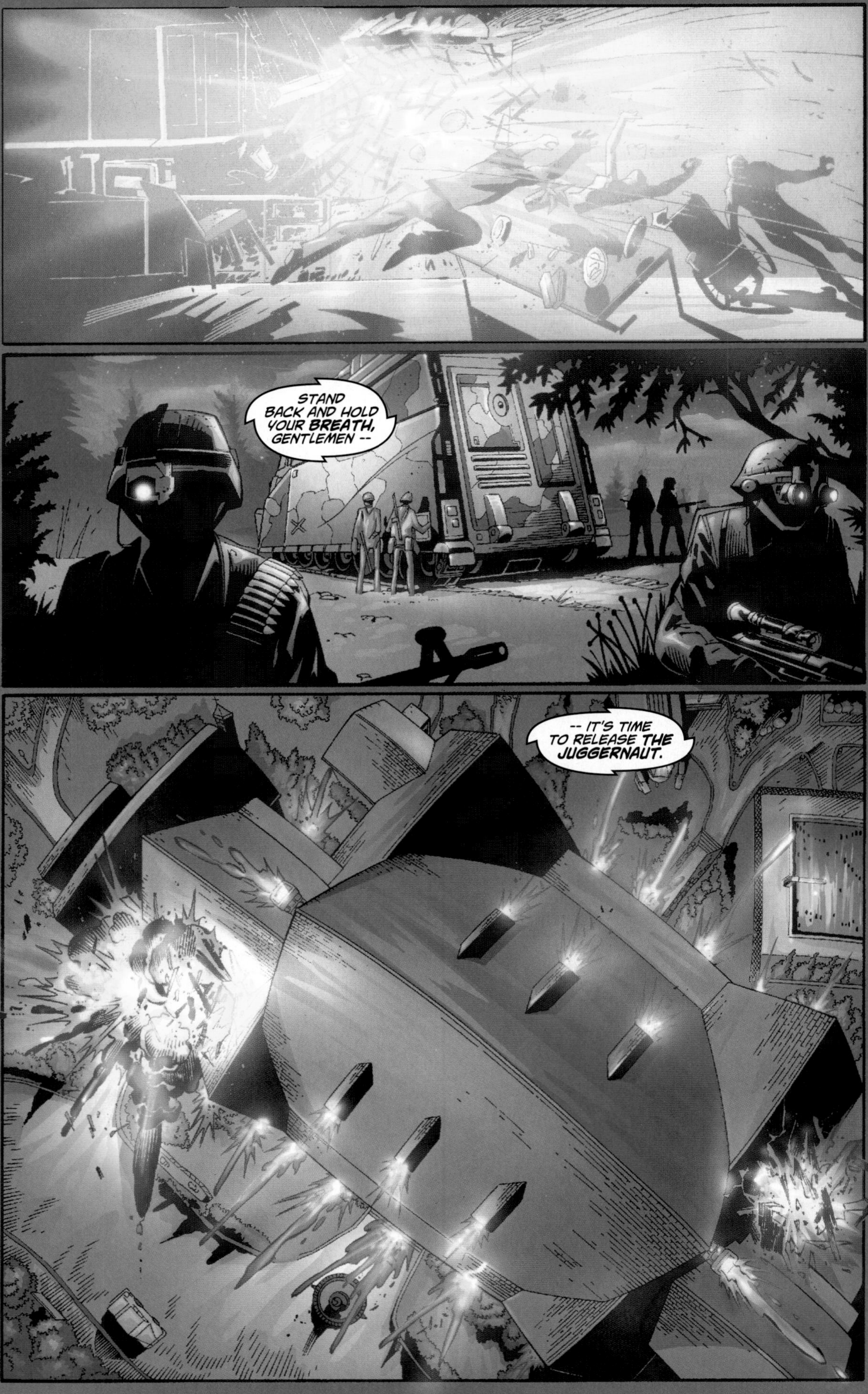
STAND BACK AND HOLD YOUR BREATH, GENTLEMEN --
-- IT'S TIME TO RELEASE THE JUGGERNAUT.

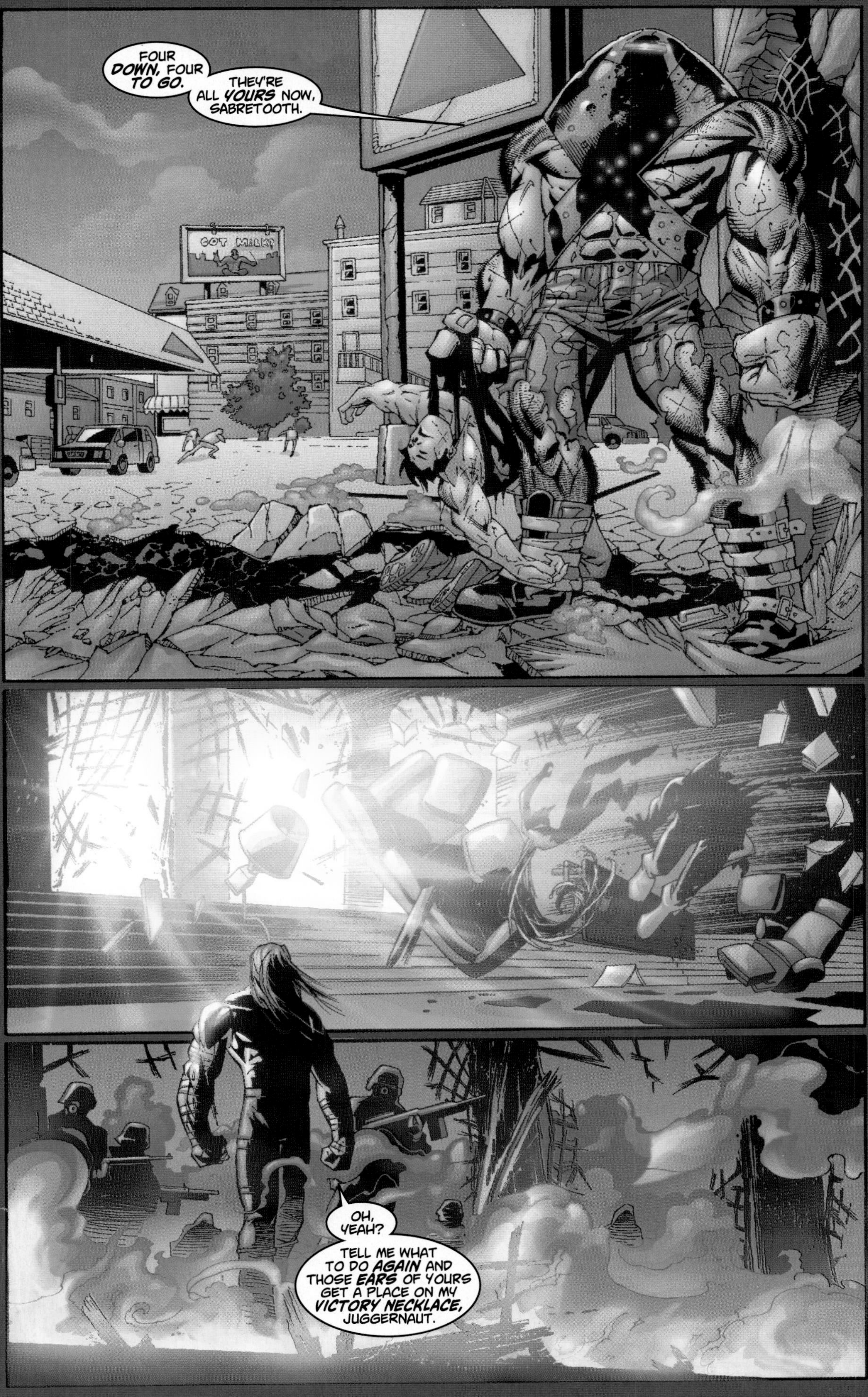
FOUR DOWN, FOUR TO GO.
THEY'RE ALL YOURS NOW, SABRETOOTH.
GOT MILK?
OH, YEAH?
TELL ME WHAT TO DO AGAIN AND THOSE EARS OF YOURS GET A PLACE ON MY VICTORY NECKLACE, JUGGERNAUT.

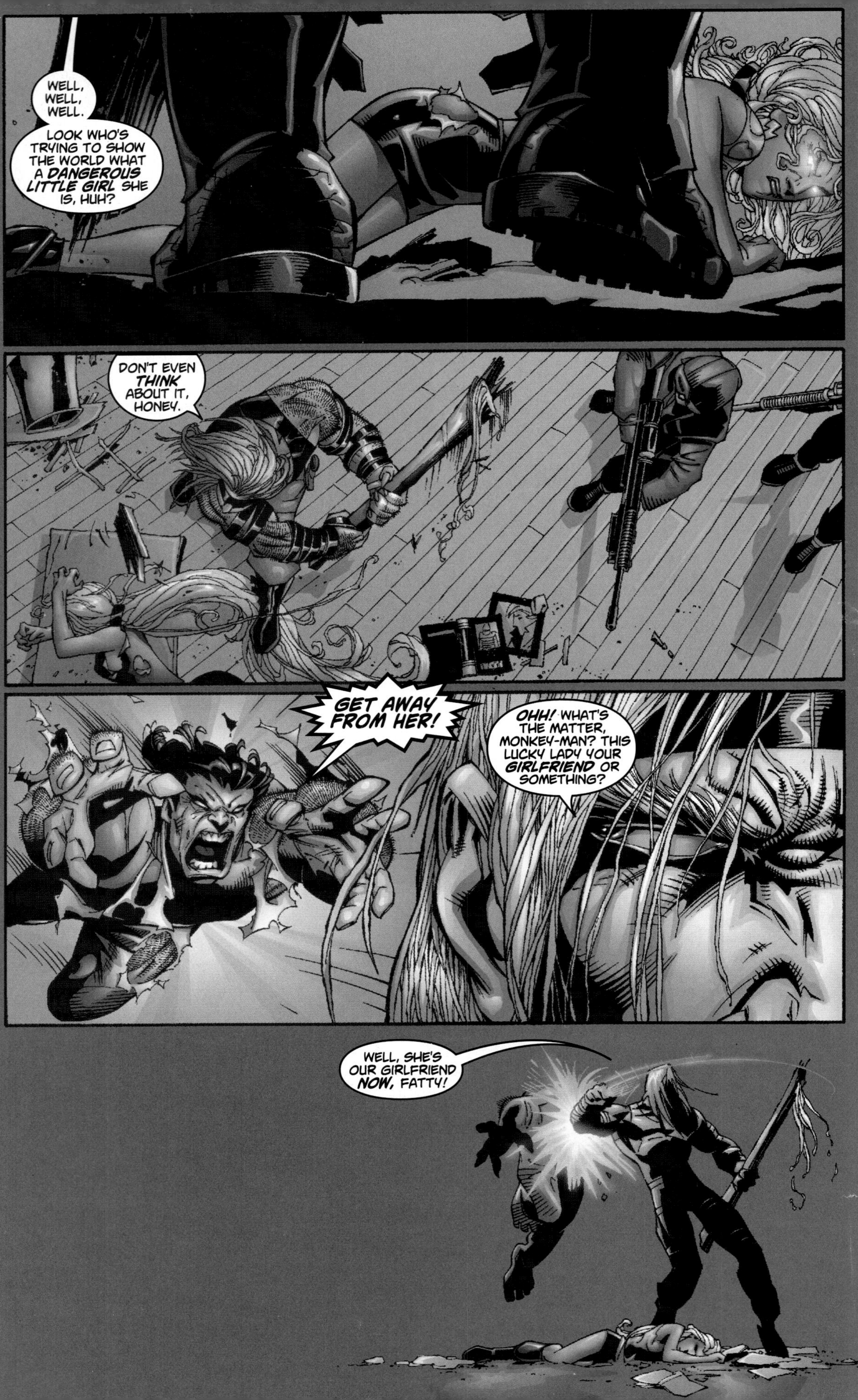

WELL, WELL, WELL.
LOOK WHO'S TRYING TO SHOW THE WORLD WHAT A **DANGEROUS LITTLE GIRL** SHE IS, HUH?
DON'T EVEN **THINK** ABOUT IT, HONEY.
GET AWAY FROM HER!
OHH! WHAT'S THE MATTER, MONKEY-MAN? THIS LUCKY LADY YOUR **GIRLFRIEND** OR SOMETHING?
WELL, SHE'S OUR GIRLFRIEND **NOW,** FATTY!

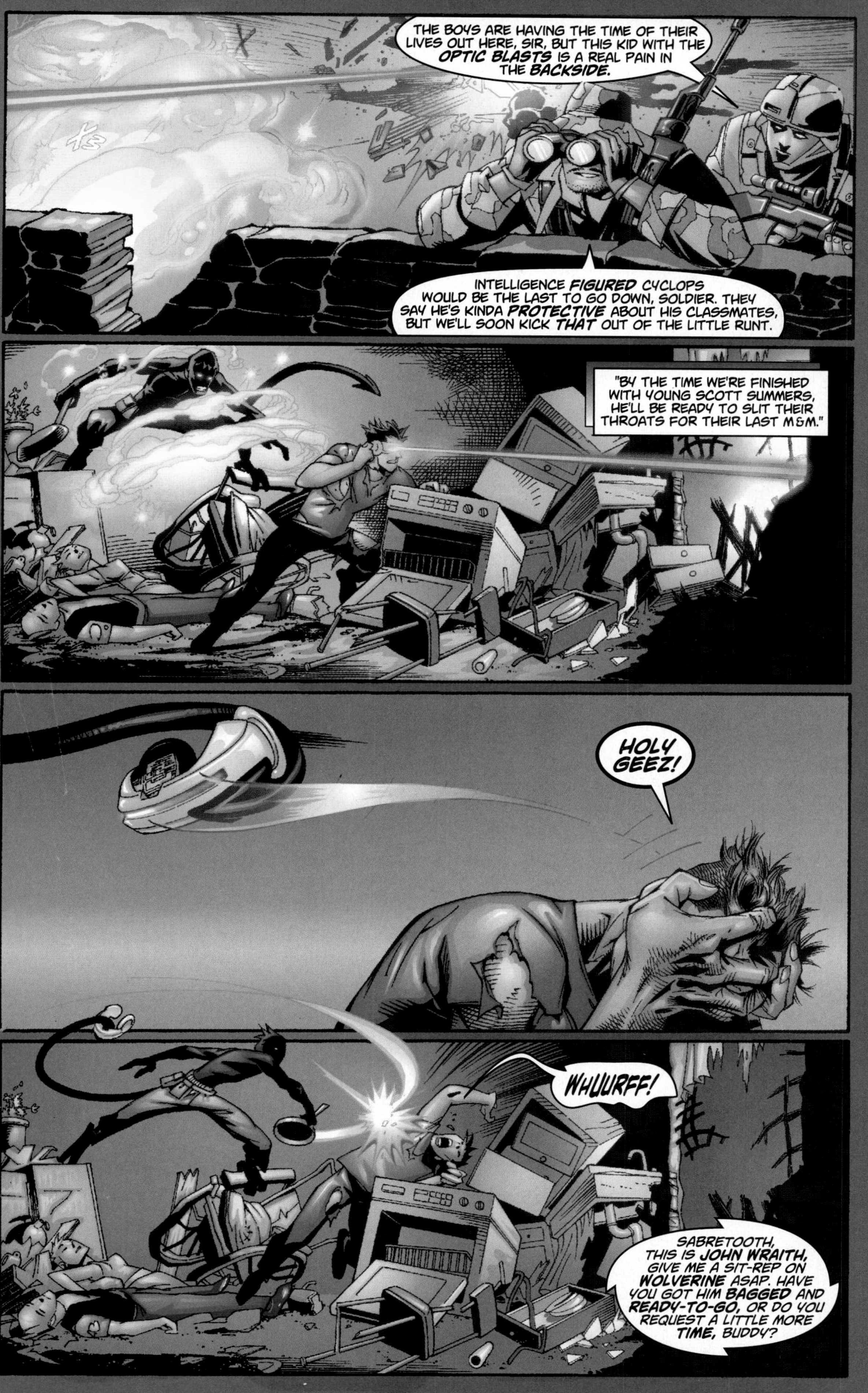
THE BOYS ARE HAVING THE TIME OF THEIR LIVES OUT HERE, SIR, BUT THIS KID WITH THE OPTIC BLASTS IS A REAL PAIN IN THE BACKSIDE.
INTELLIGENCE FIGURED CYCLOPS WOULD BE THE LAST TO GO DOWN, SOLDIER. THEY SAY HE'S KINDA PROTECTIVE ABOUT HIS CLASSMATES, BUT WE'LL SOON KICK THAT OUT OF THE LITTLE RUNT.
"BY THE TIME WE'RE FINISHED WITH YOUNG SCOTT SUMMERS, HE'LL BE READY TO SLIT THEIR THROATS FOR THEIR LAST M&M."
HOLY GEEZ!
WHUURFF!
SABRETOOTH, THIS IS JOHN WRAITH, GIVE ME A SIT-REP ON WOLVERINE ASAP. HAVE YOU GOT HIM BAGGED AND READY-TO-GO, OR DO YOU REQUEST A LITTLE MORE TIME, BUDDY?

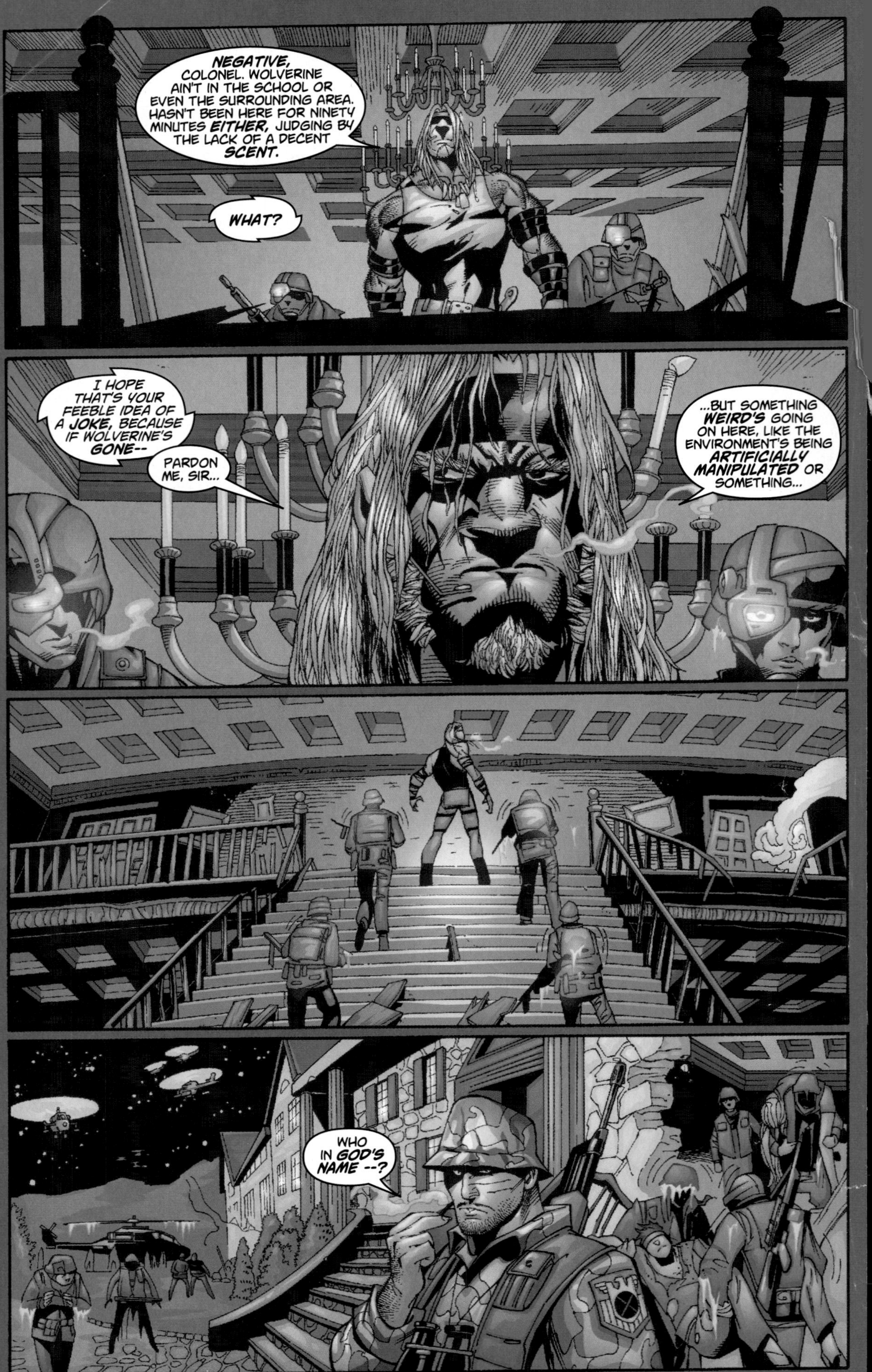
NEGATIVE, COLONEL. WOLVERINE AIN'T IN THE SCHOOL OR EVEN THE SURROUNDING AREA. HASN'T BEEN HERE FOR NINETY MINUTES EITHER, JUDGING BY THE LACK OF A DECENT SCENT.
WHAT?
I HOPE THAT'S YOUR FEEBLE IDEA OF A JOKE, BECAUSE IF WOLVERINE'S GONE--
PARDON ME, SIR...
...BUT SOMETHING WEIRD'S GOING ON HERE, LIKE THE ENVIRONMENT'S BEING ARTIFICIALLY MANIPULATED OR SOMETHING...
WHO IN GOD'S NAME --?

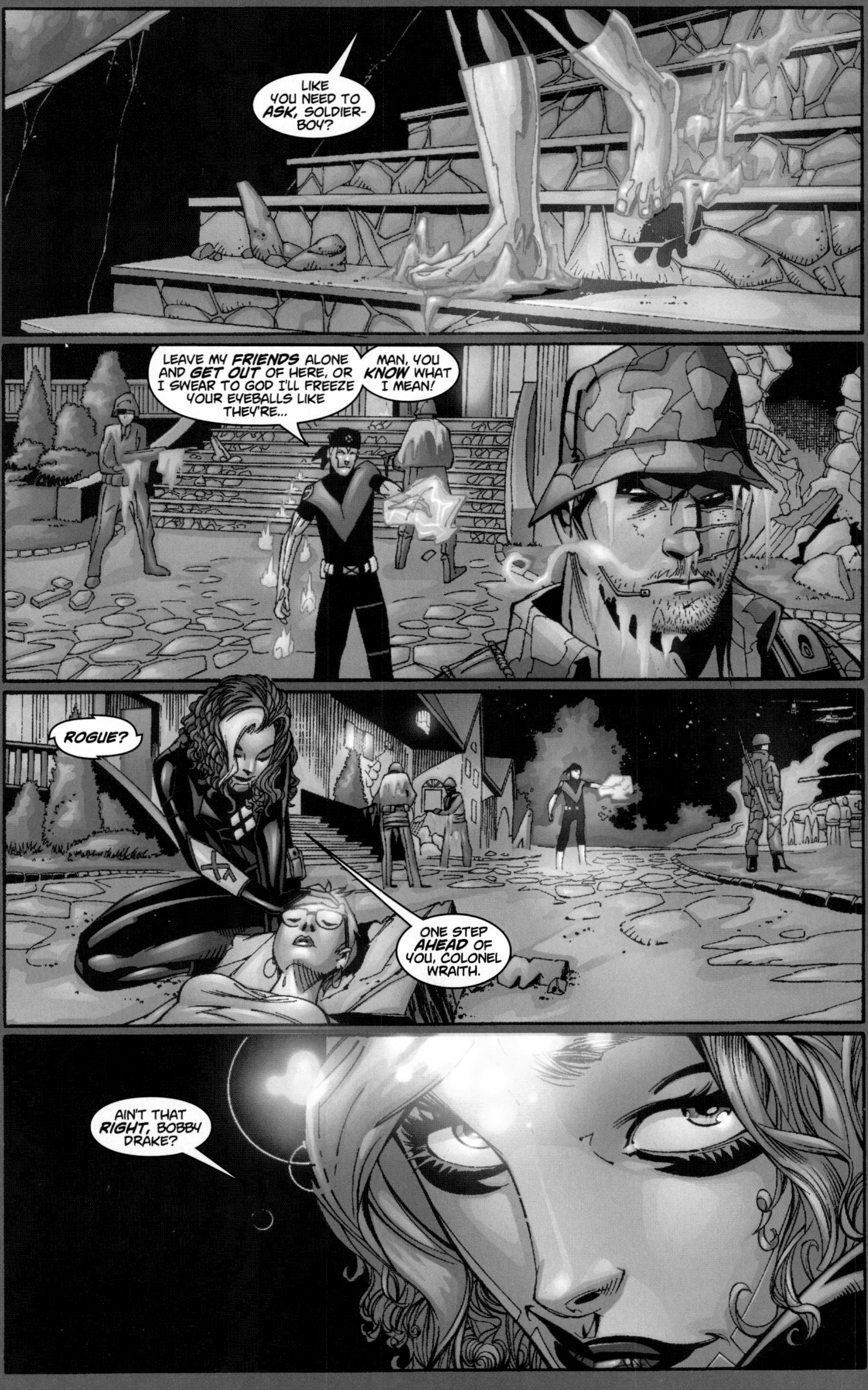
LIKE YOU NEED TO ASK, SOLDIER-BOY?
LEAVE MY FRIENDS ALONE AND GET OUT OF HERE, OR I SWEAR TO GOD I'LL FREEZE YOUR EYEBALLS LIKE THEY'RE...
MAN, YOU KNOW WHAT I MEAN!
ROGUE?
ONE STEP AHEAD OF YOU, COLONEL WRAITH.
AIN'T THAT RIGHT, BOBBY DRAKE?

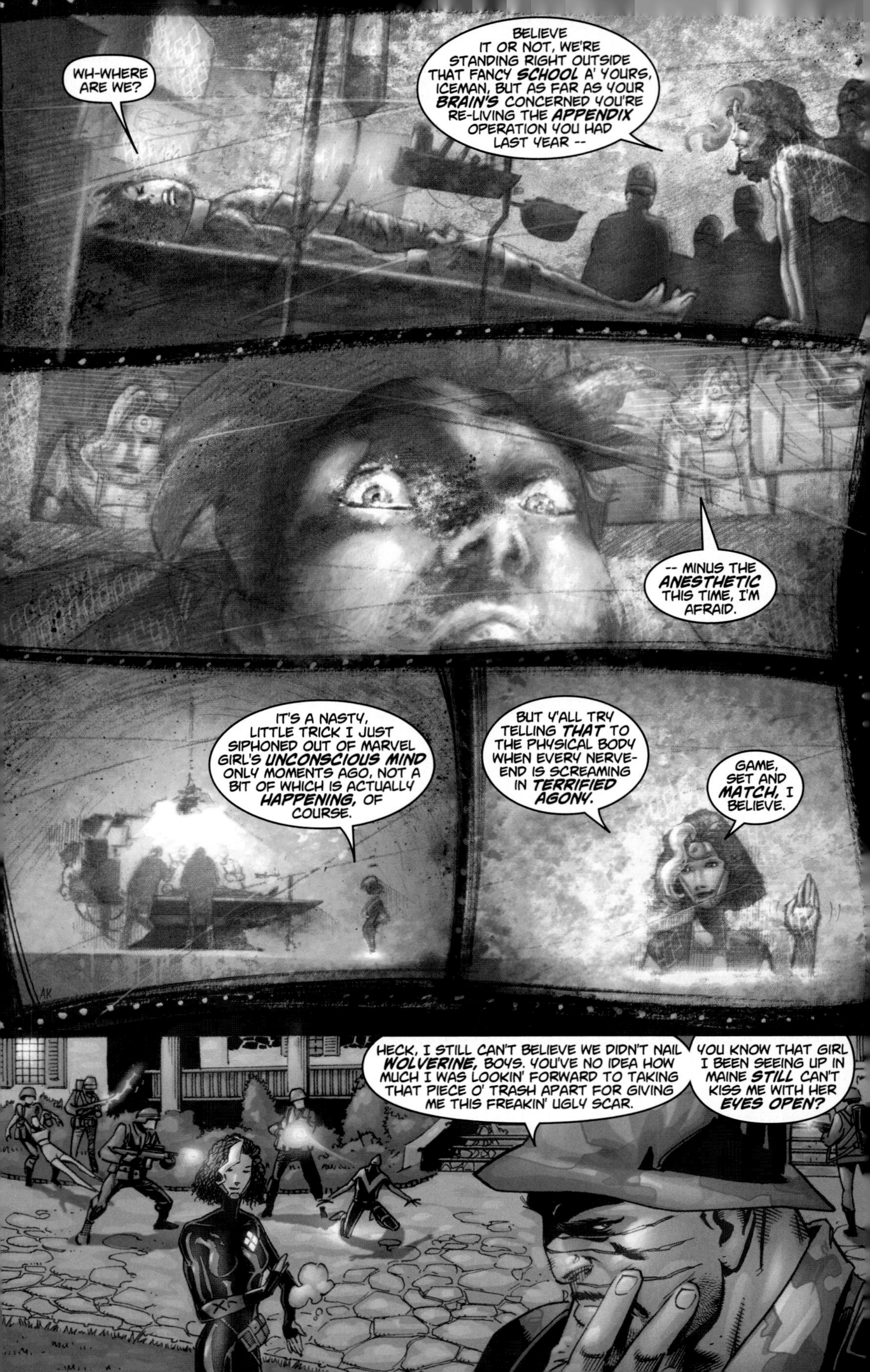
WH-WHERE ARE WE?
BELIEVE IT OR NOT, WE'RE STANDING RIGHT OUTSIDE THAT FANCY SCHOOL A' YOURS, ICEMAN, BUT AS FAR AS YOUR BRAIN'S CONCERNED YOU'RE RE-LIVING THE APPENDIX OPERATION YOU HAD LAST YEAR --
-- MINUS THE ANESTHETIC THIS TIME, I'M AFRAID.
IT'S A NASTY, LITTLE TRICK I JUST SIPHONED OUT OF MARVEL GIRL'S UNCONSCIOUS MIND ONLY MOMENTS AGO, NOT A BIT OF WHICH IS ACTUALLY HAPPENING, OF COURSE.
BUT Y'ALL TRY TELLING THAT TO THE PHYSICAL BODY WHEN EVERY NERVE-END IS SCREAMING IN TERRIFIED AGONY.
GAME, SET AND MATCH, I BELIEVE.
HECK, I STILL CAN'T BELIEVE WE DIDN'T NAIL WOLVERINE, BOYS. YOU'VE NO IDEA HOW MUCH I WAS LOOKIN' FORWARD TO TAKING THAT PIECE O' TRASH APART FOR GIVING ME THIS FREAKIN' UGLY SCAR.
YOU KNOW THAT GIRL I BEEN SEEING UP IN MAINE STILL CAN'T KISS ME WITH HER EYES OPEN?

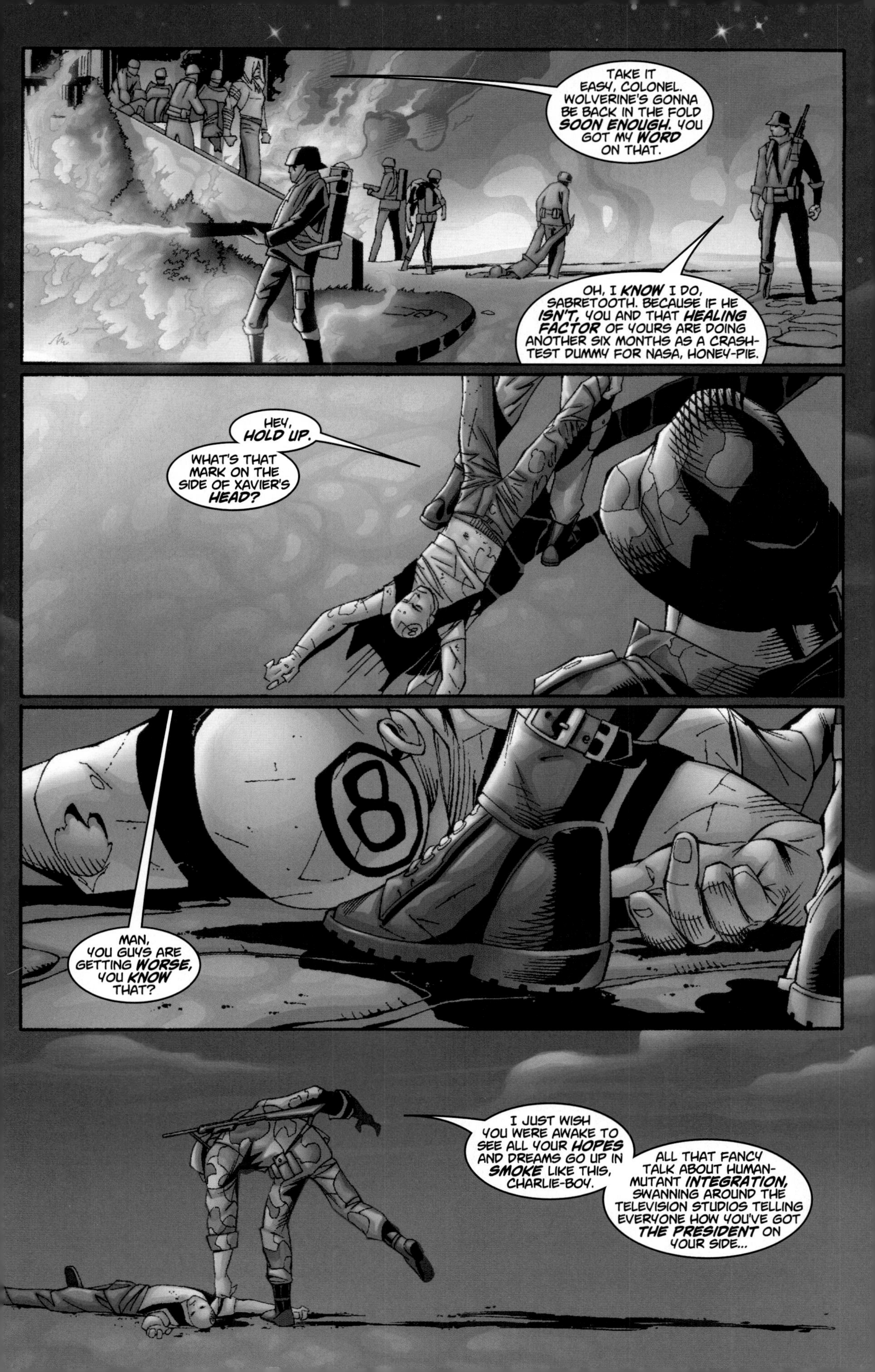
TAKE IT EASY, COLONEL. WOLVERINE'S GONNA BE BACK IN THE FOLD SOON ENOUGH. YOU GOT MY WORD ON THAT.
OH, I KNOW I DO, SABRETOOTH. BECAUSE IF HE ISN'T, YOU AND THAT HEALING FACTOR OF YOURS ARE DOING ANOTHER SIX MONTHS AS A CRASH-TEST DUMMY FOR NASA, HONEY-PIE.
HEY, HOLD UP.
WHAT'S THAT MARK ON THE SIDE OF XAVIER'S HEAD?
MAN, YOU GUYS ARE GETTING WORSE, YOU KNOW THAT?
I JUST WISH YOU WERE AWAKE TO SEE ALL YOUR HOPES AND DREAMS GO UP IN SMOKE LIKE THIS, CHARLIE-BOY.
ALL THAT FANCY TALK ABOUT HUMAN-MUTANT INTEGRATION, SWANNING AROUND THE TELEVISION STUDIOS TELLING EVERYONE HOW YOU'VE GOT THE PRESIDENT ON YOUR SIDE...

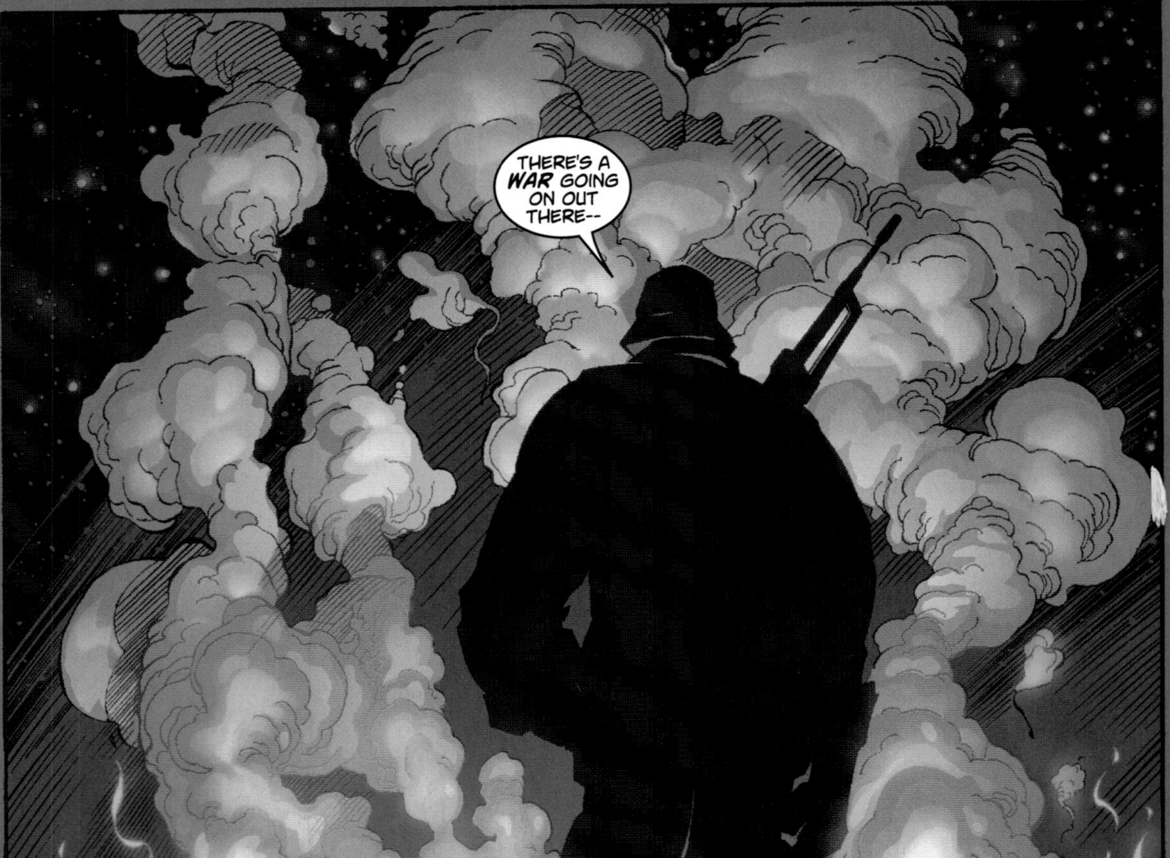
THERE'S A WAR GOING ON OUT THERE--

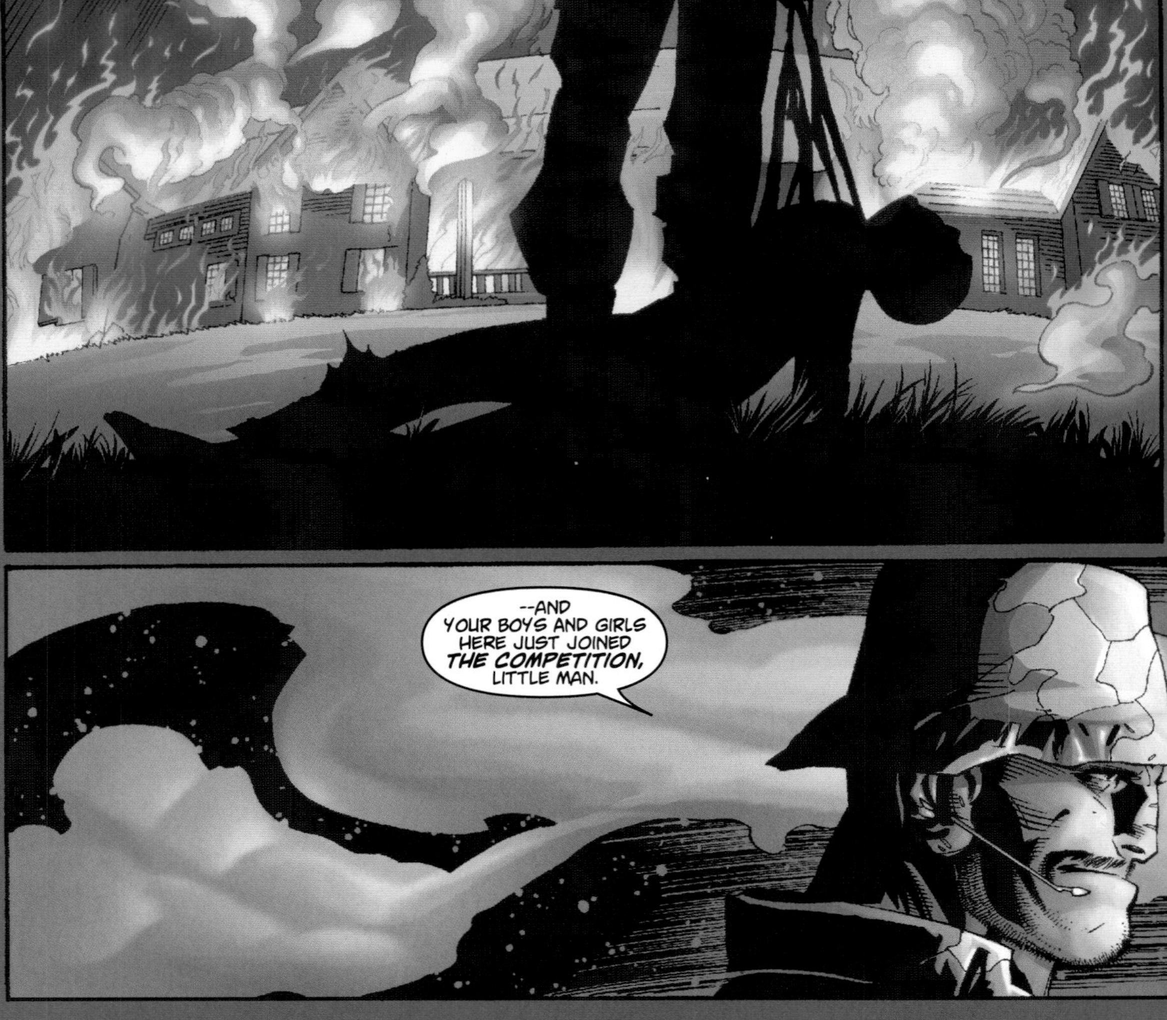
--AND YOUR BOYS AND GIRLS HERE JUST JOINED THE COMPETITION, LITTLE MAN.

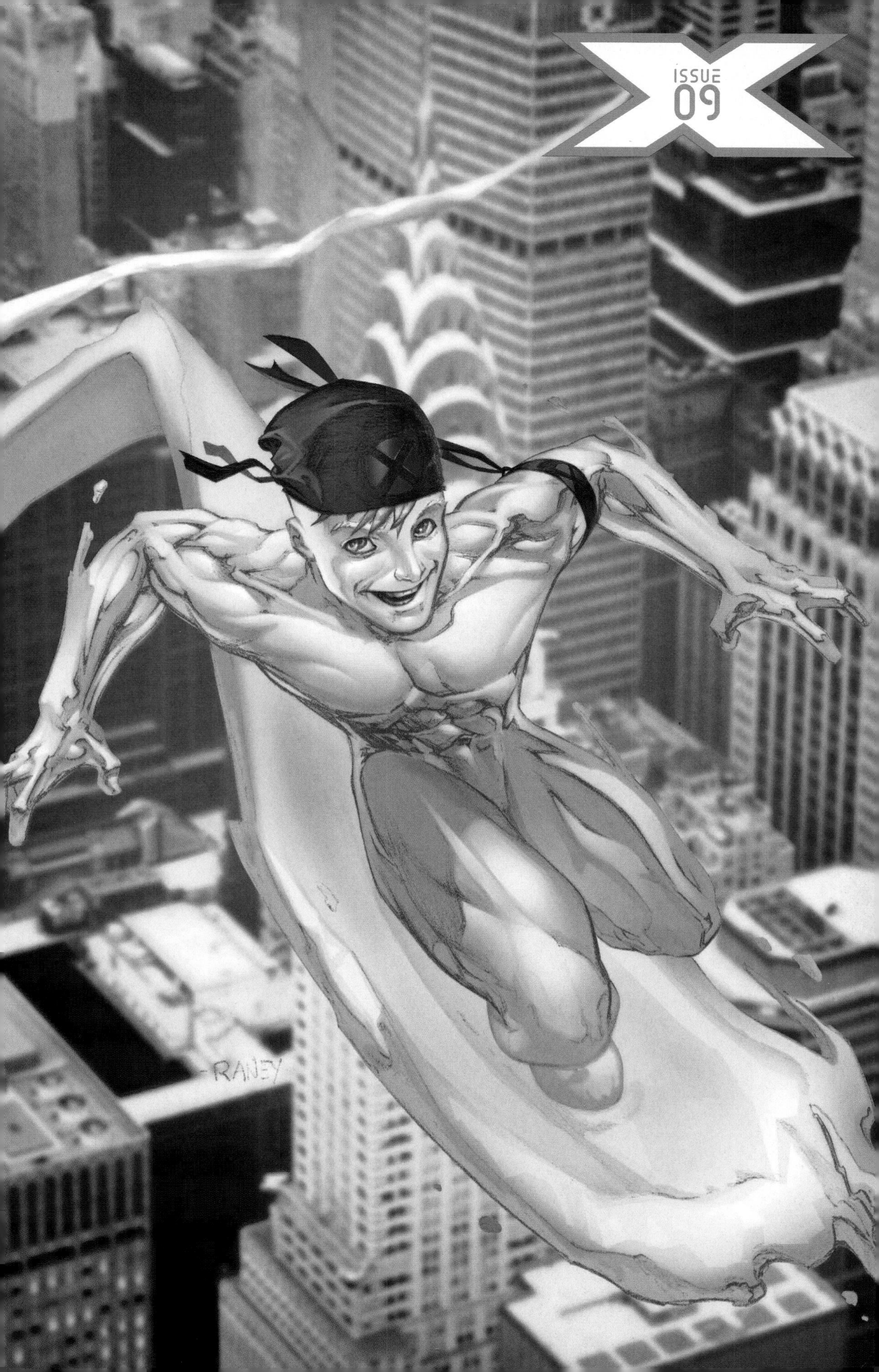
ISSUE
09
RANEY

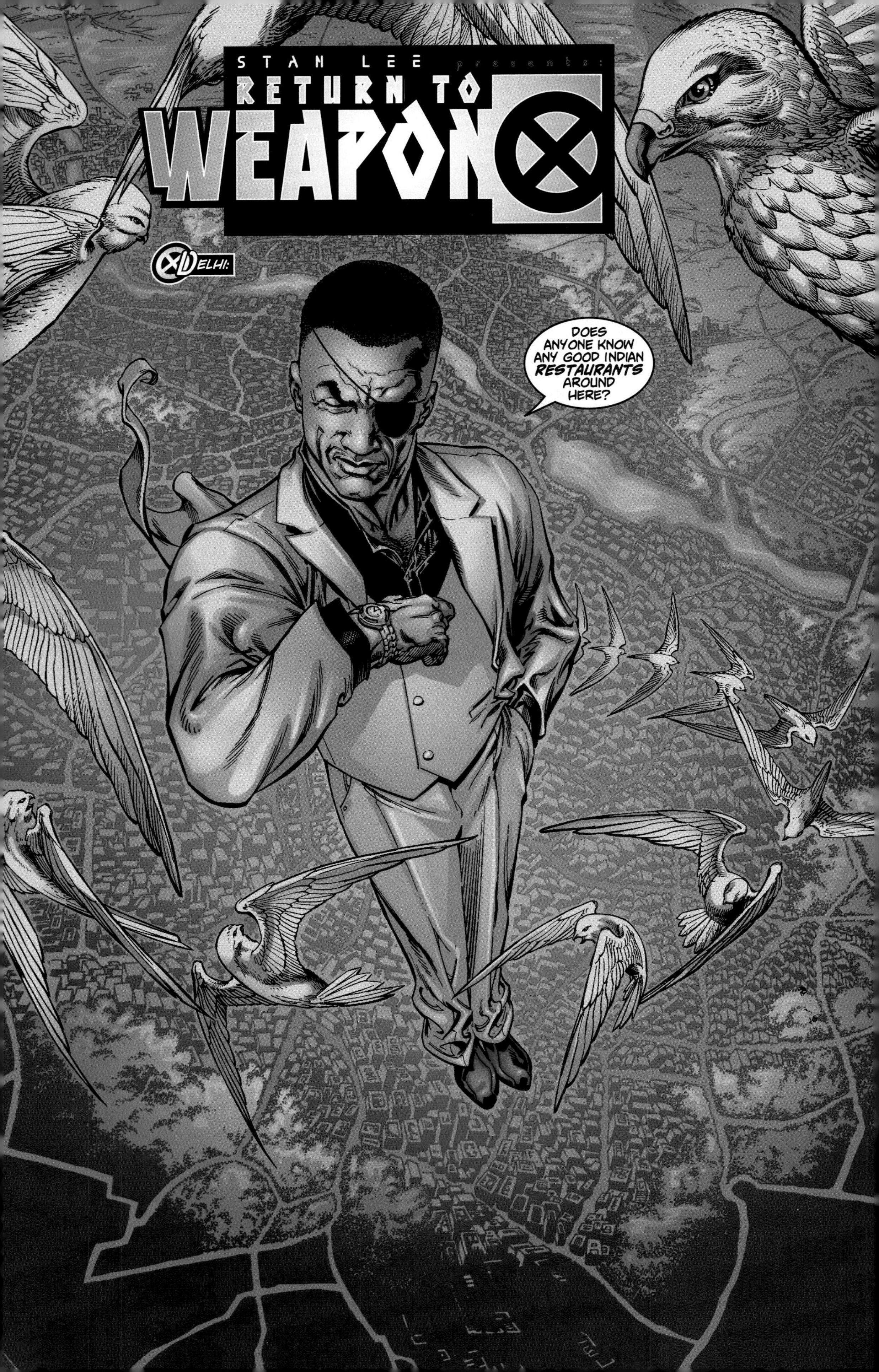
STAN LEE presents:
RETURN TO WEAPON X
DELHI:
DOES ANYONE KNOW ANY GOOD INDIAN RESTAURANTS AROUND HERE?

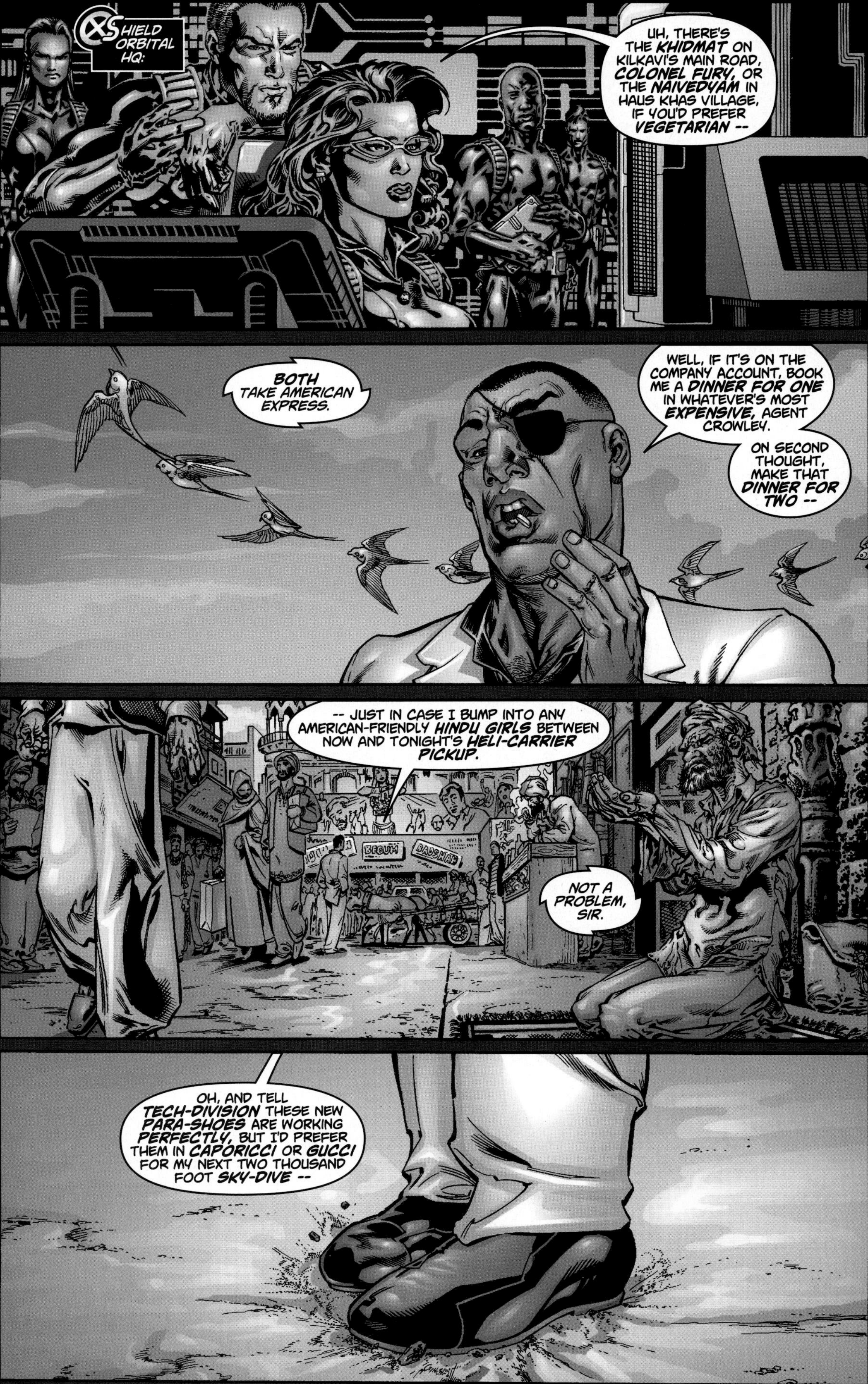
SHIELD ORBITAL HQ:
UH, THERE'S THE KHIDMAT ON KILKAVI'S MAIN ROAD, COLONEL FURY, OR THE NAIVEDYAM IN HAUS KHAS VILLAGE, IF YOU'D PREFER VEGETARIAN --
BOTH TAKE AMERICAN EXPRESS.
WELL, IF IT'S ON THE COMPANY ACCOUNT, BOOK ME A DINNER FOR ONE IN WHATEVER'S MOST EXPENSIVE, AGENT CROWLEY.
ON SECOND THOUGHT, MAKE THAT DINNER FOR TWO --
-- JUST IN CASE I BUMP INTO ANY AMERICAN-FRIENDLY HINDU GIRLS BETWEEN NOW AND TONIGHT'S HELI-CARRIER PICKUP.
BEGUM
BADSHAH
NOT A PROBLEM, SIR.
OH, AND TELL TECH-DIVISION THESE NEW PARA-SHOES ARE WORKING PERFECTLY, BUT I'D PREFER THEM IN CAPORICCI OR GUCCI FOR MY NEXT TWO THOUSAND FOOT SKY-DIVE --

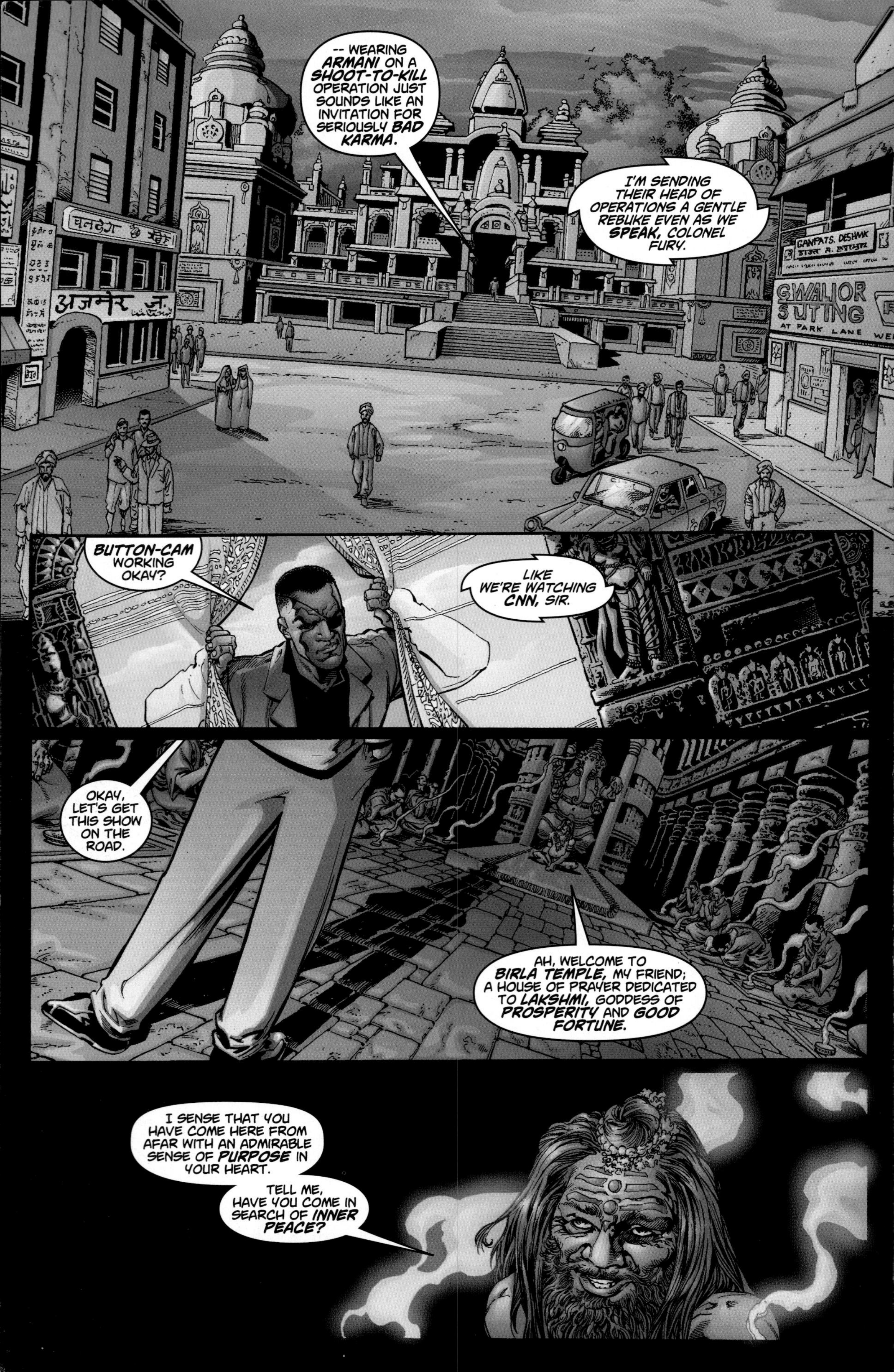
-- WEARING ARMANI ON A SHOOT-TO-KILL OPERATION JUST SOUNDS LIKE AN INVITATION FOR SERIOUSLY BAD KARMA.
I'M SENDING THEIR HEAD OF OPERATIONS A GENTLE REBUKE EVEN AS WE SPEAK, COLONEL FURY.
BUTTON-CAM WORKING OKAY?
LIKE WE'RE WATCHING CNN, SIR.
OKAY, LET'S GET THIS SHOW ON THE ROAD.
AH, WELCOME TO BIRLA TEMPLE, MY FRIEND; A HOUSE OF PRAYER DEDICATED TO LAKSHMI, GODDESS OF PROSPERITY AND GOOD FORTUNE.
I SENSE THAT YOU HAVE COME HERE FROM AFAR WITH AN ADMIRABLE SENSE OF PURPOSE IN YOUR HEART.
TELL ME, HAVE YOU COME IN SEARCH OF INNER PEACE?

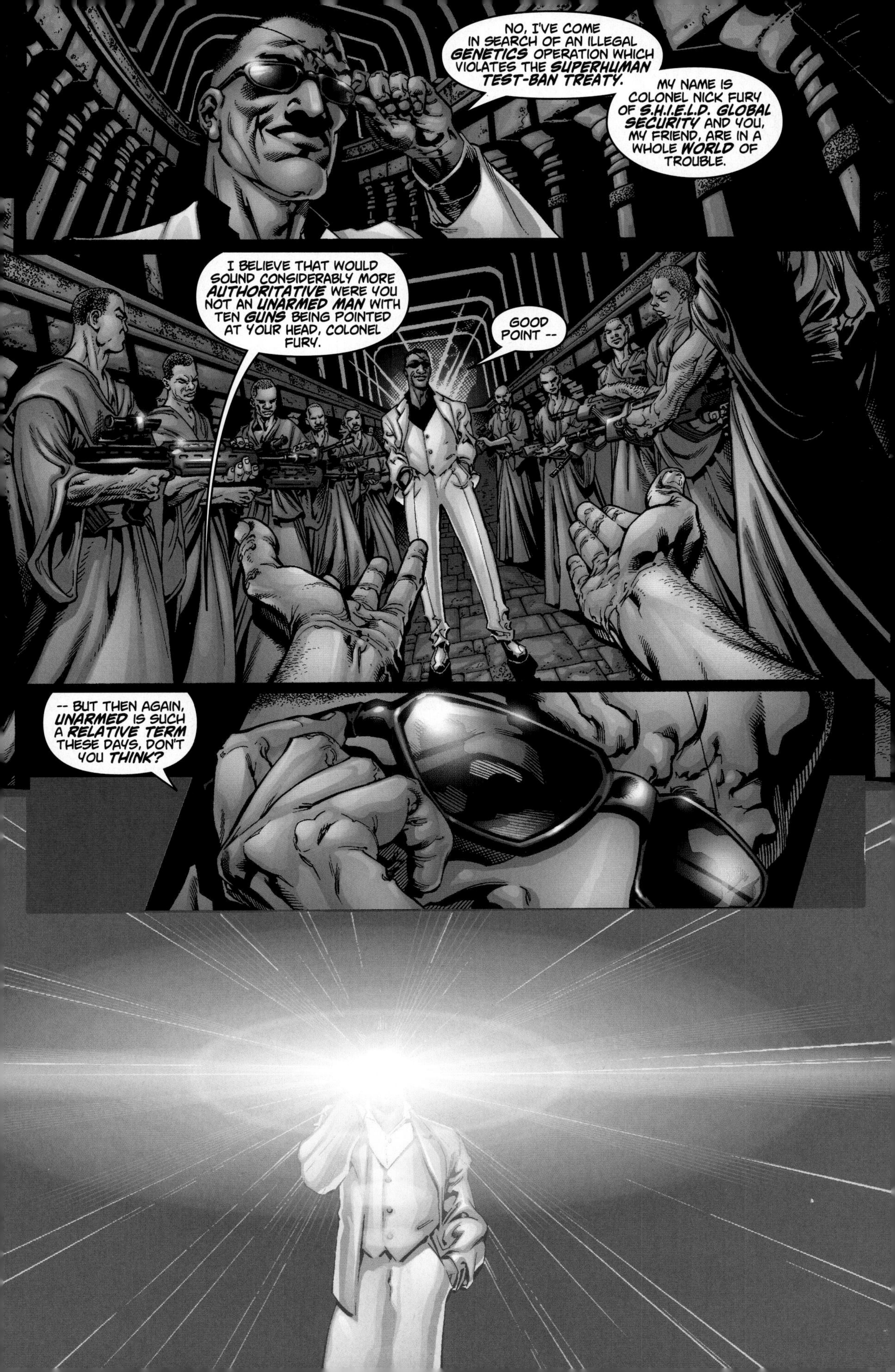
NO, I'VE COME IN SEARCH OF AN ILLEGAL GENETICS OPERATION WHICH VIOLATES THE SUPERHUMAN TEST-BAN TREATY.
MY NAME IS COLONEL NICK FURY OF S.H.I.E.L.D. GLOBAL SECURITY AND YOU, MY FRIEND, ARE IN A WHOLE WORLD OF TROUBLE.
I BELIEVE THAT WOULD SOUND CONSIDERABLY MORE AUTHORITATIVE WERE YOU NOT AN UNARMED MAN WITH TEN GUNS BEING POINTED AT YOUR HEAD, COLONEL FURY.
GOOD POINT --
-- BUT THEN AGAIN, UNARMED IS SUCH A RELATIVE TERM THESE DAYS, DON'T YOU THINK?

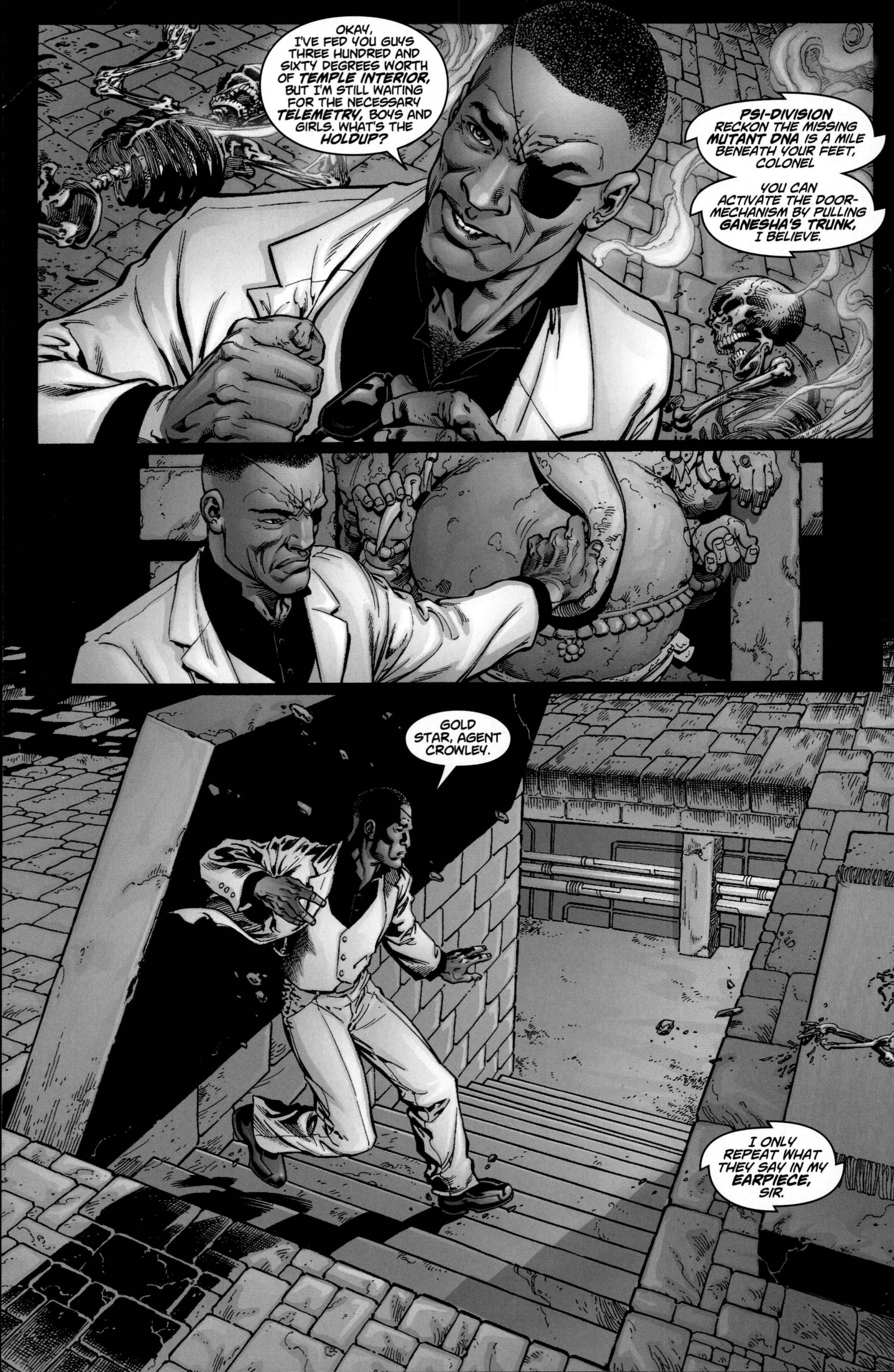
OKAY, I'VE FED YOU GUYS THREE HUNDRED AND SIXTY DEGREES WORTH OF TEMPLE INTERIOR, BUT I'M STILL WAITING FOR THE NECESSARY TELEMETRY, BOYS AND GIRLS. WHAT'S THE HOLDUP?
PSI-DIVISION RECKON THE MISSING MUTANT DNA IS A MILE BENEATH YOUR FEET, COLONEL
YOU CAN ACTIVATE THE DOOR-MECHANISM BY PULLING GANESHA'S TRUNK, I BELIEVE.
GOLD STAR, AGENT CROWLEY.
I ONLY REPEAT WHAT THEY SAY IN MY EARPIECE, SIR.

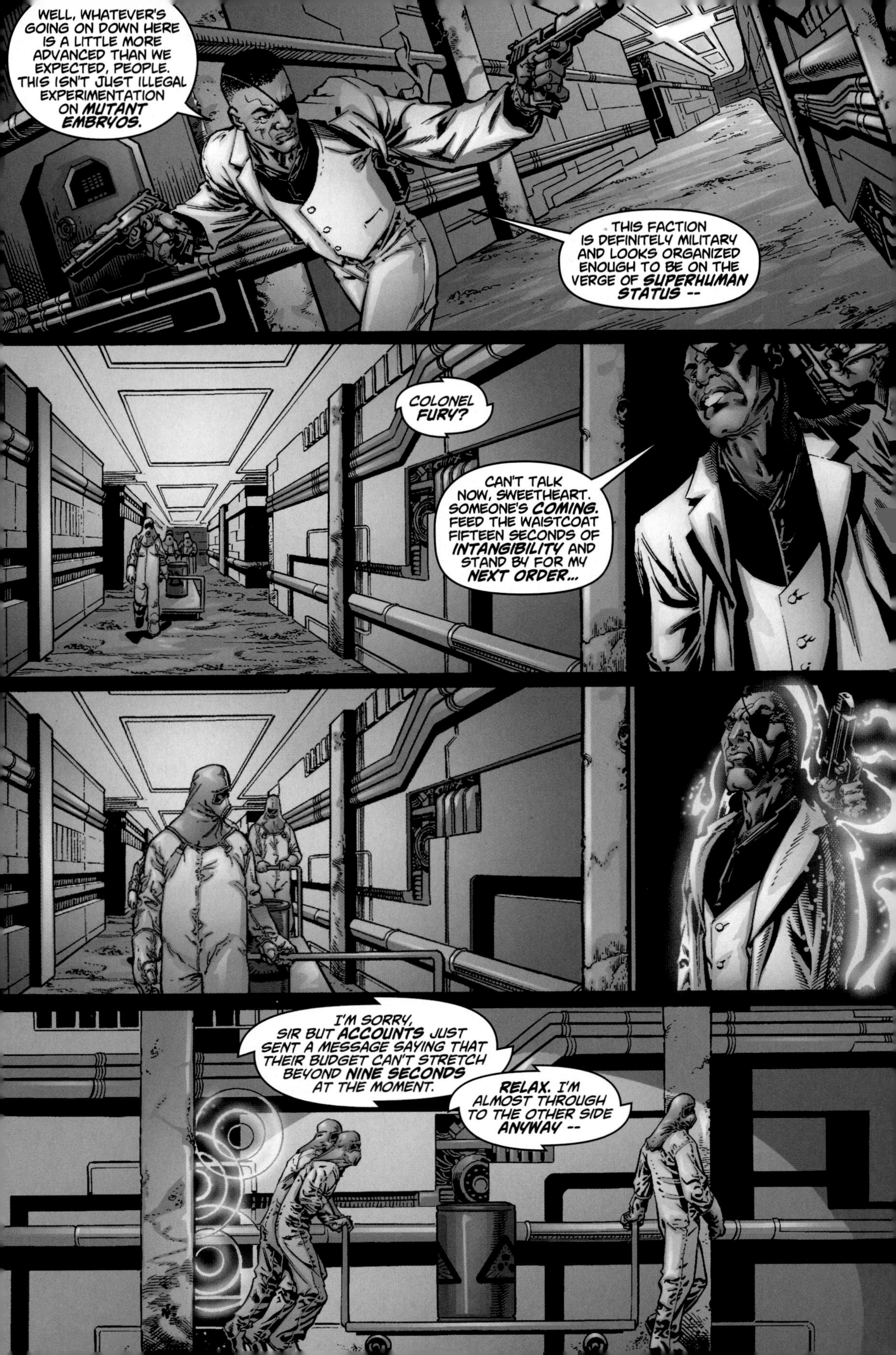
WELL, WHATEVER'S GOING ON DOWN HERE IS A LITTLE MORE ADVANCED THAN WE EXPECTED, PEOPLE. THIS ISN'T JUST ILLEGAL EXPERIMENTATION ON MUTANT EMBRYOS.
THIS FACTION IS DEFINITELY MILITARY AND LOOKS ORGANIZED ENOUGH TO BE ON THE VERGE OF SUPERHUMAN STATUS --
COLONEL FURY?
CAN'T TALK NOW, SWEETHEART. SOMEONE'S COMING. FEED THE WAISTCOAT FIFTEEN SECONDS OF INTANGIBILITY AND STAND BY FOR MY NEXT ORDER...
I'M SORRY, SIR BUT ACCOUNTS JUST SENT A MESSAGE SAYING THAT THEIR BUDGET CAN'T STRETCH BEYOND NINE SECONDS AT THE MOMENT.
RELAX. I'M ALMOST THROUGH TO THE OTHER SIDE ANYWAY --

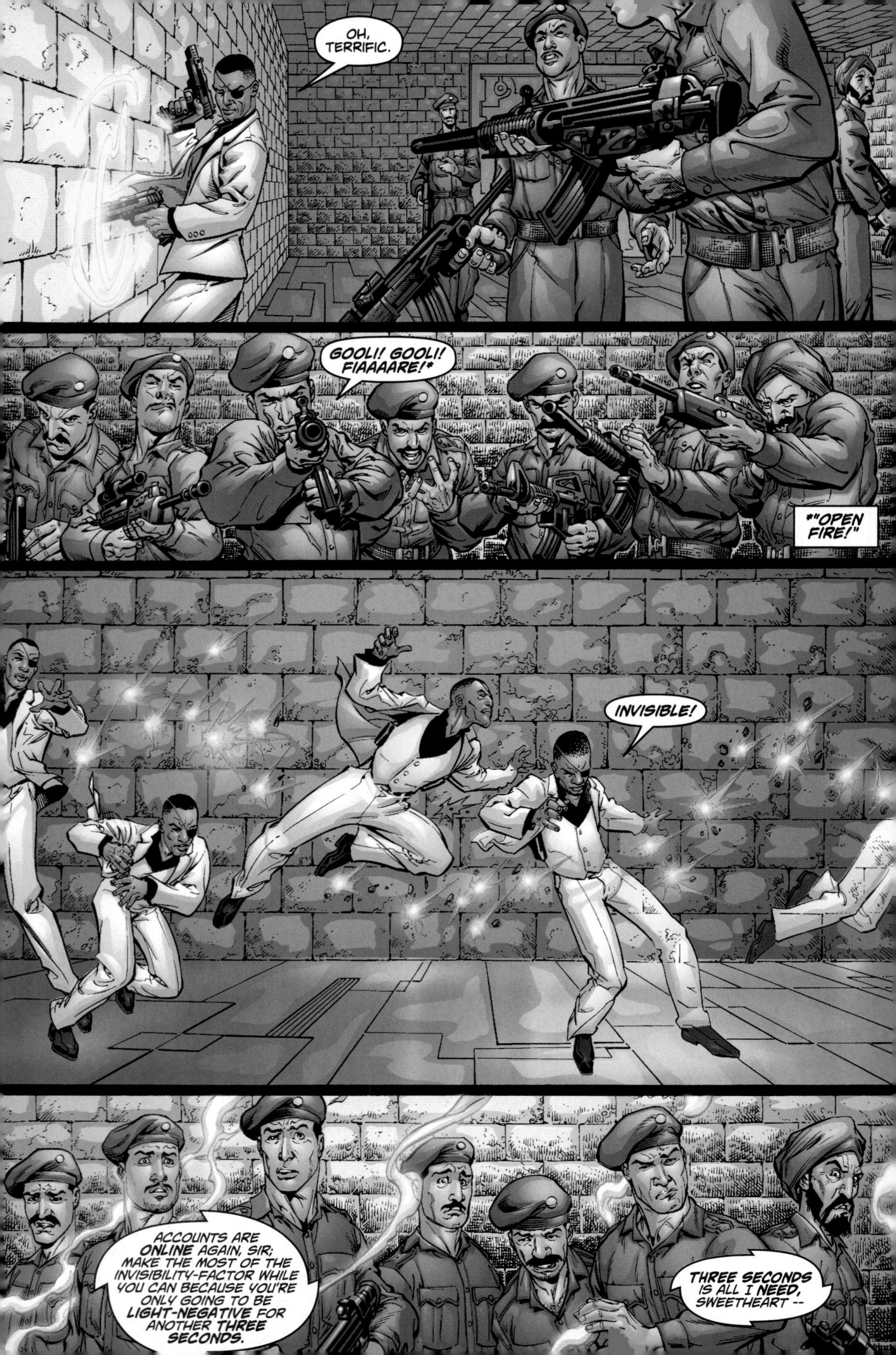
OH, TERRIFIC.
GOOLI! GOOLI! FIAAAARE!*
*"OPEN FIRE!"
INVISIBLE!
ACCOUNTS ARE ONLINE AGAIN, SIR; MAKE THE MOST OF THE INVISIBILITY-FACTOR WHILE YOU CAN BECAUSE YOU'RE ONLY GOING TO BE LIGHT-NEGATIVE FOR ANOTHER THREE SECONDS.
THREE SECONDS IS ALL I NEED, SWEETHEART --

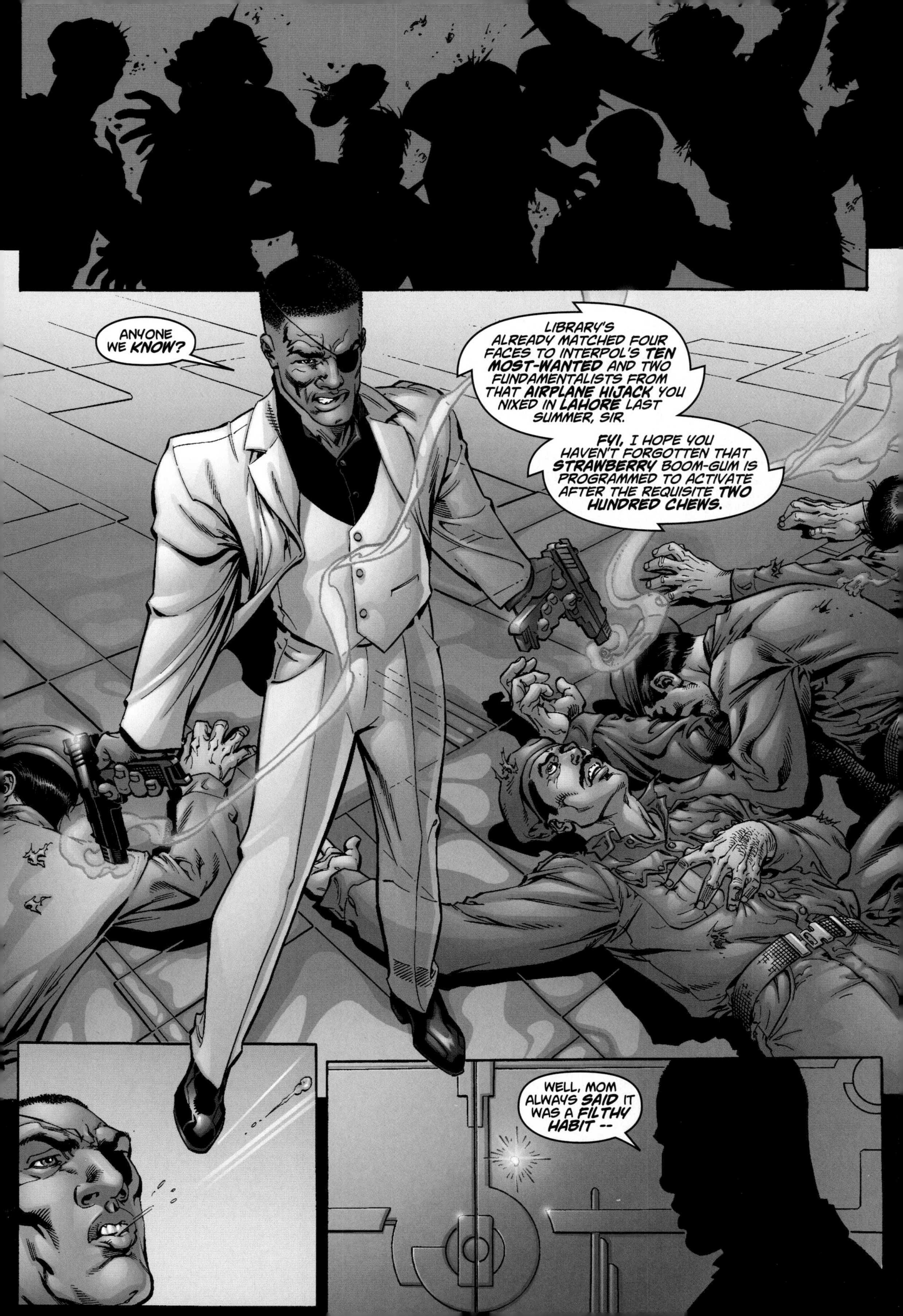
ANYONE WE KNOW?
LIBRARY'S ALREADY MATCHED FOUR FACES TO INTERPOL'S TEN MOST-WANTED AND TWO FUNDAMENTALISTS FROM THAT AIRPLANE HIJACK YOU NIXED IN LAHORE LAST SUMMER, SIR.
FYI, I HOPE YOU HAVEN'T FORGOTTEN THAT STRAWBERRY BOOM-GUM IS PROGRAMMED TO ACTIVATE AFTER THE REQUISITE TWO HUNDRED CHEWS.
WELL, MOM ALWAYS SAID IT WAS A FILTHY HABIT --

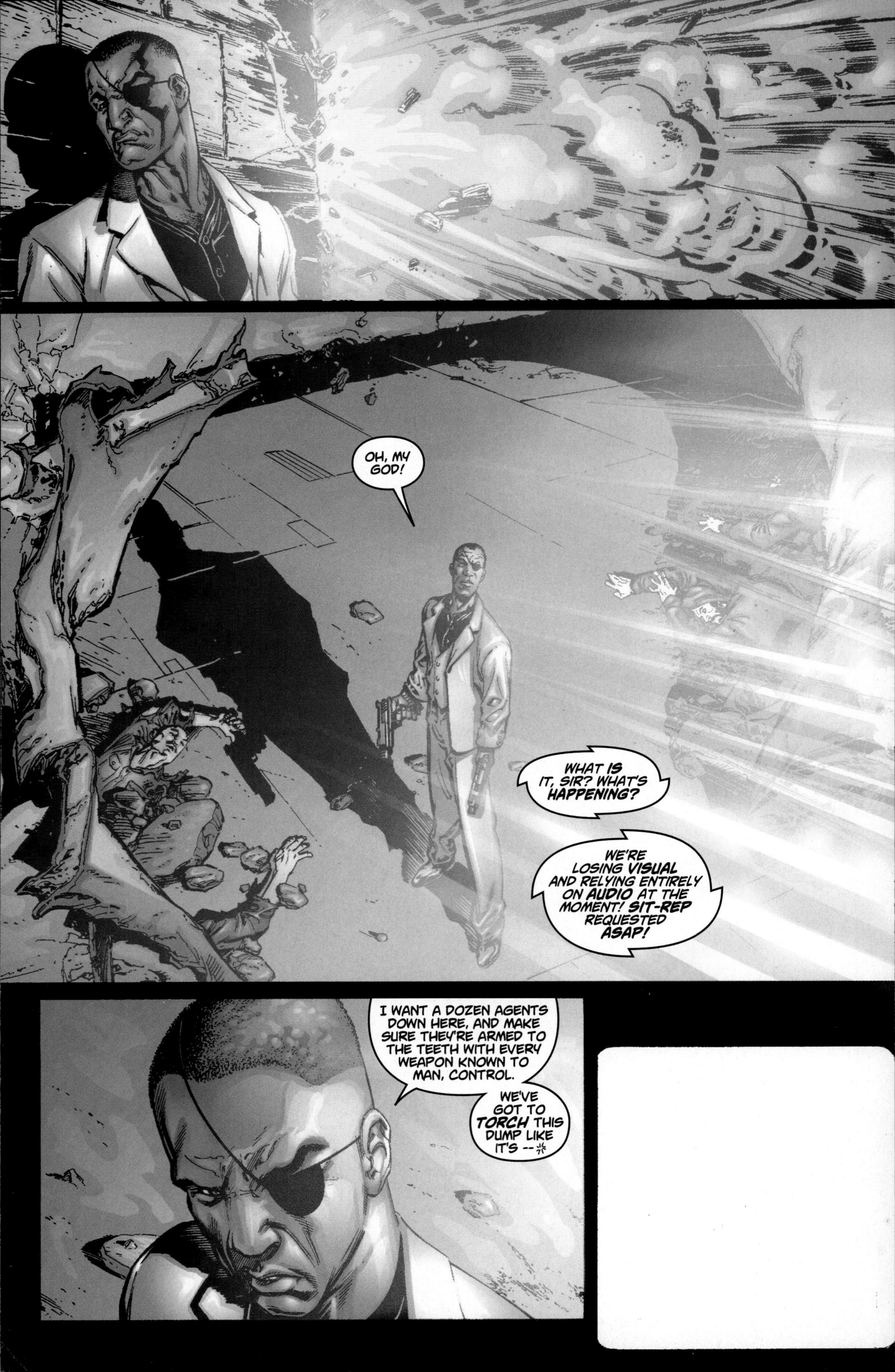
OH, MY GOD!
WHAT IS IT, SIR? WHAT'S HAPPENING?
WE'RE LOSING VISUAL AND RELYING ENTIRELY ON AUDIO AT THE MOMENT! SIT-REP REQUESTED ASAP!
I WANT A DOZEN AGENTS DOWN HERE, AND MAKE SURE THEY'RE ARMED TO THE TEETH WITH EVERY WEAPON KNOWN TO MAN, CONTROL.
WE'VE GOT TO TORCH THIS DUMP LIKE IT'S --

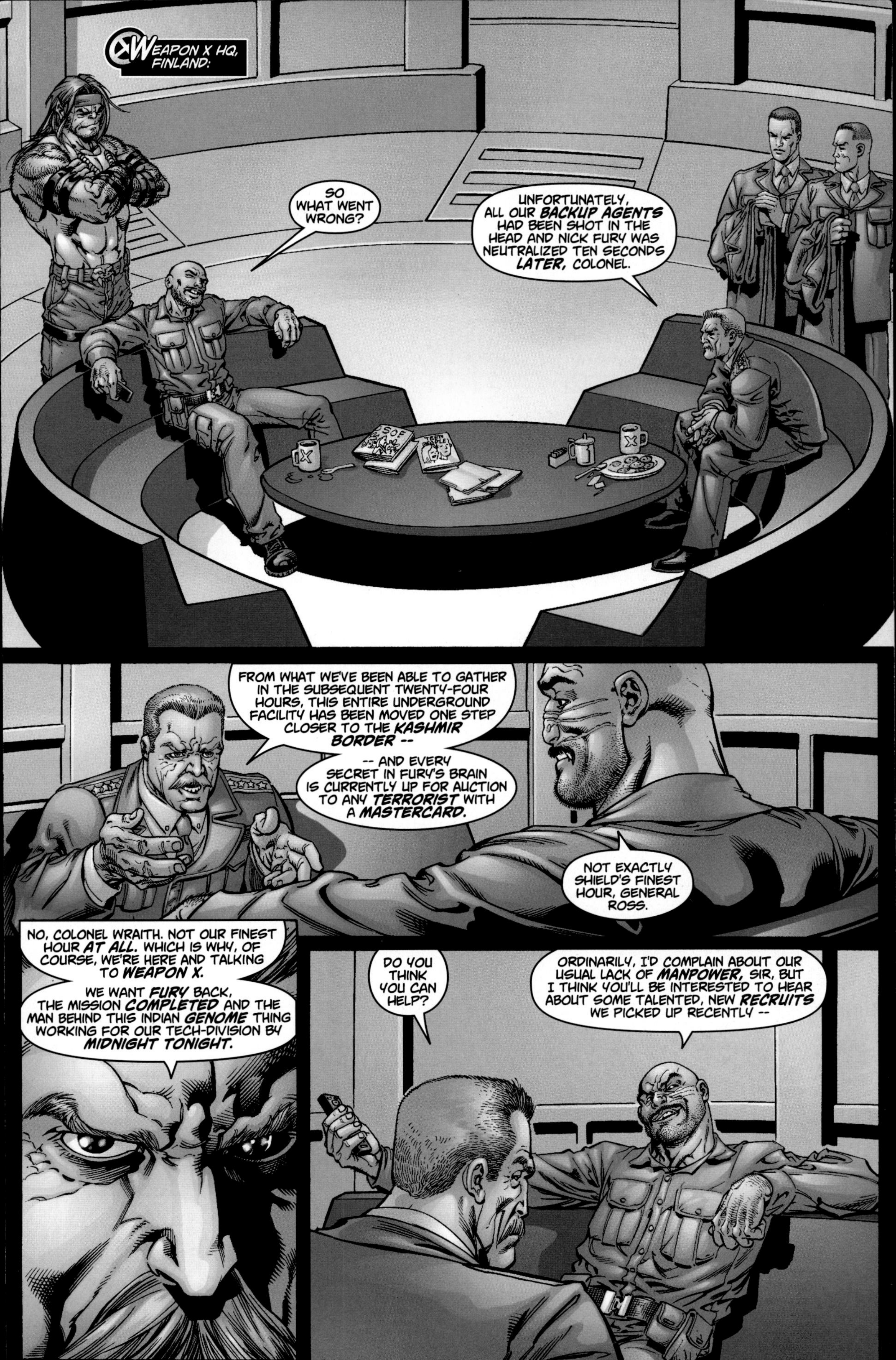
WEAPON X HQ, FINLAND:
SO WHAT WENT WRONG?
UNFORTUNATELY, ALL OUR BACKUP AGENTS HAD BEEN SHOT IN THE HEAD AND NICK FURY WAS NEUTRALIZED TEN SECONDS LATER, COLONEL.
FROM WHAT WE'VE BEEN ABLE TO GATHER IN THE SUBSEQUENT TWENTY-FOUR HOURS, THIS ENTIRE UNDERGROUND FACILITY HAS BEEN MOVED ONE STEP CLOSER TO THE KASHMIR BORDER --
-- AND EVERY SECRET IN FURY'S BRAIN IS CURRENTLY UP FOR AUCTION TO ANY TERRORIST WITH A MASTERCARD.
NOT EXACTLY SHIELD'S FINEST HOUR, GENERAL ROSS.
NO, COLONEL WRAITH. NOT OUR FINEST HOUR AT ALL. WHICH IS WHY, OF COURSE, WE'RE HERE AND TALKING TO WEAPON X.
WE WANT FURY BACK, THE MISSION COMPLETED AND THE MAN BEHIND THIS INDIAN GENOME THING WORKING FOR OUR TECH-DIVISION BY MIDNIGHT TONIGHT.
DO YOU THINK YOU CAN HELP?
ORDINARILY, I'D COMPLAIN ABOUT OUR USUAL LACK OF MANPOWER, SIR, BUT I THINK YOU'LL BE INTERESTED TO HEAR ABOUT SOME TALENTED, NEW RECRUITS WE PICKED UP RECENTLY --

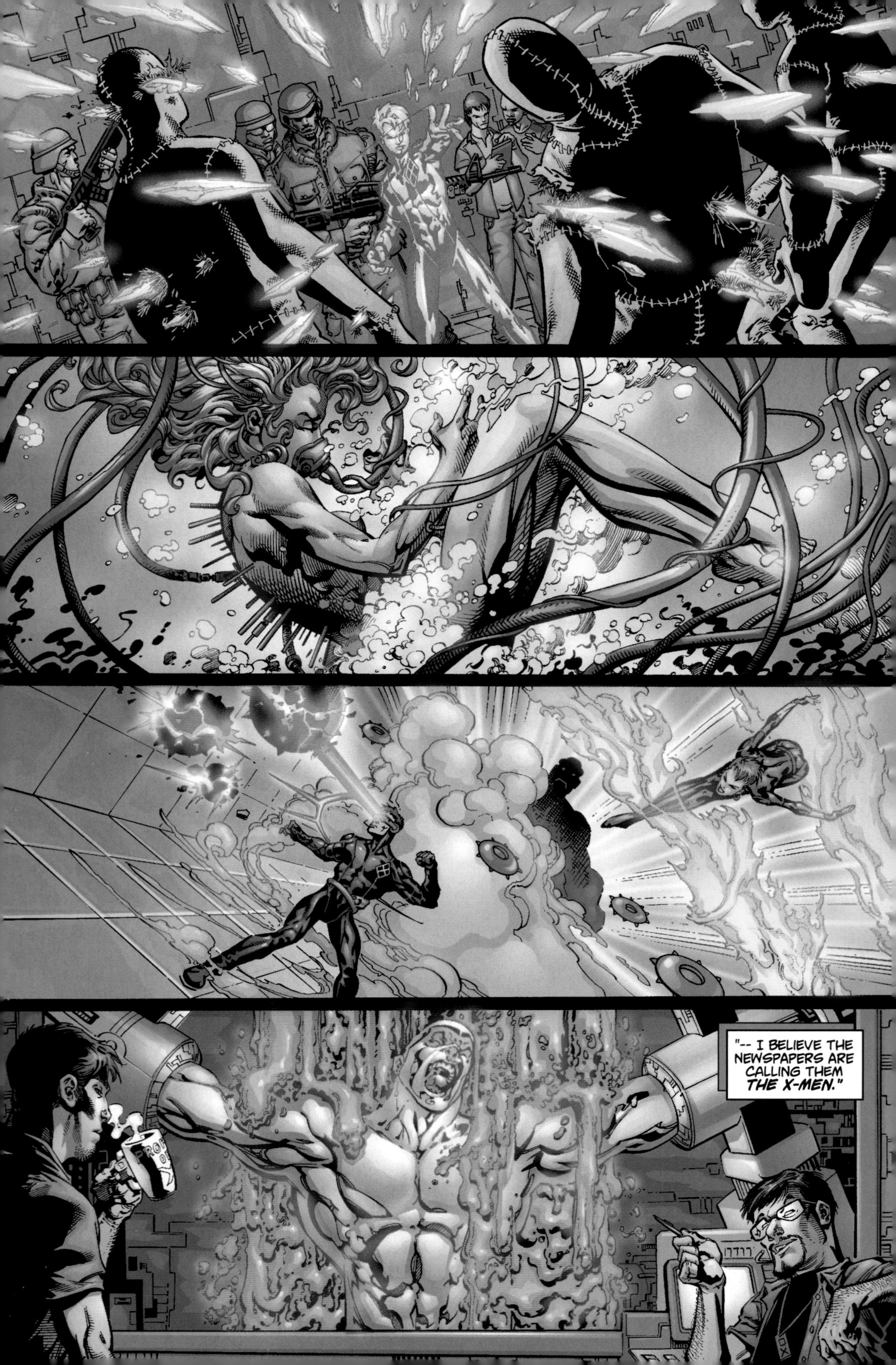
"-- I BELIEVE THE NEWSPAPERS ARE CALLING THEM THE X-MEN."

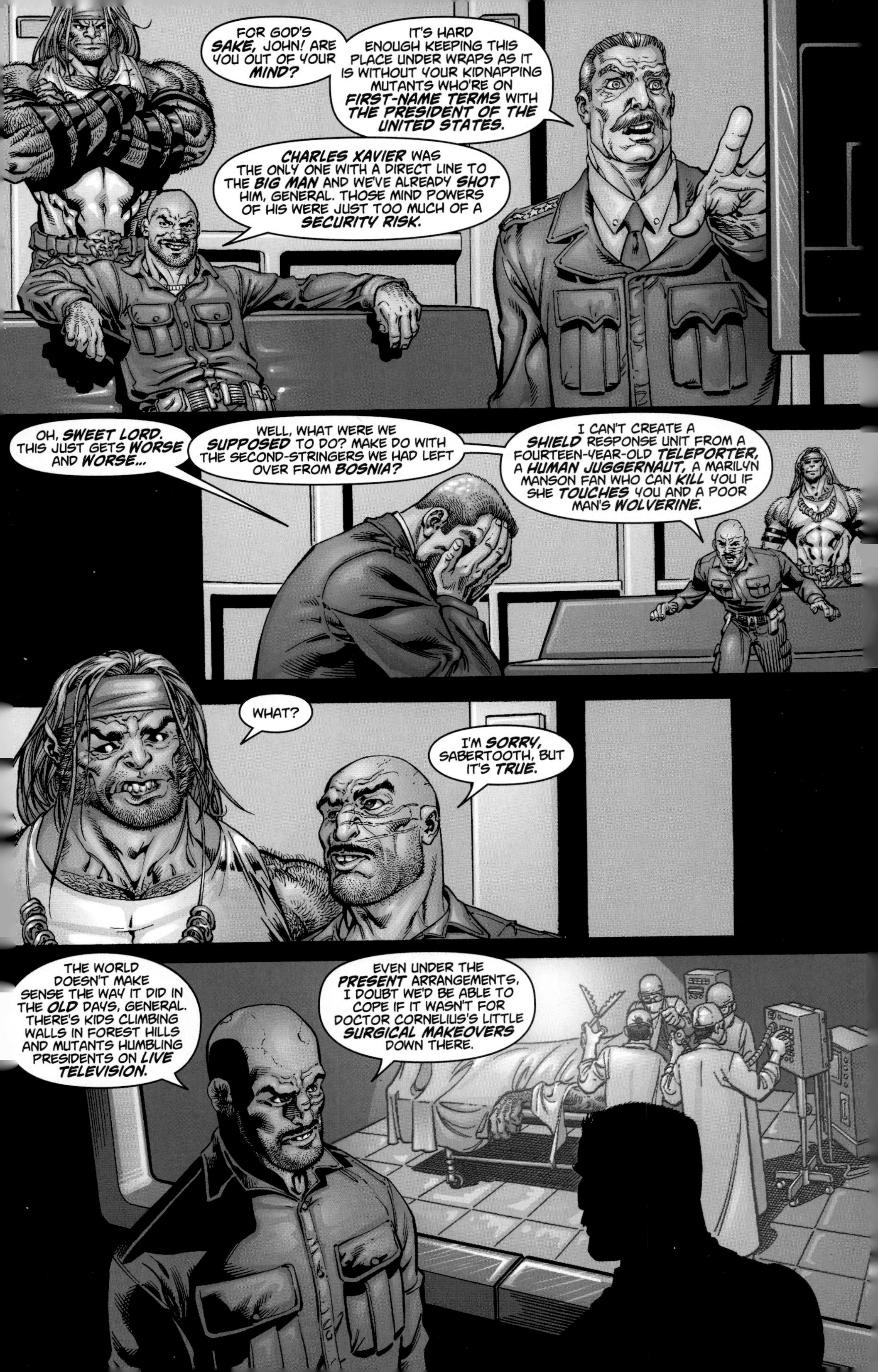
FOR GOD'S SAKE, JOHN! ARE YOU OUT OF YOUR MIND?
IT'S HARD ENOUGH KEEPING THIS PLACE UNDER WRAPS AS IT IS WITHOUT YOUR KIDNAPPING MUTANTS WHO'RE ON FIRST-NAME TERMS WITH THE PRESIDENT OF THE UNITED STATES.
CHARLES XAVIER WAS THE ONLY ONE WITH A DIRECT LINE TO THE BIG MAN AND WE'VE ALREADY SHOT HIM, GENERAL. THOSE MIND POWERS OF HIS WERE JUST TOO MUCH OF A SECURITY RISK.
OH, SWEET LORD. THIS JUST GETS WORSE AND WORSE...
WELL, WHAT WERE WE SUPPOSED TO DO? MAKE DO WITH THE SECOND-STRINGERS WE HAD LEFT OVER FROM BOSNIA?
I CAN'T CREATE A SHIELD RESPONSE UNIT FROM A FOURTEEN-YEAR-OLD TELEPORTER, A HUMAN JUGGERNAUT, A MARILYN MANSON FAN WHO CAN KILL YOU IF SHE TOUCHES YOU AND A POOR MAN'S WOLVERINE.
WHAT?
I'M SORRY, SABERTOOTH, BUT IT'S TRUE.
THE WORLD DOESN'T MAKE SENSE THE WAY IT DID IN THE OLD DAYS, GENERAL. THERE'S KIDS CLIMBING WALLS IN FOREST HILLS AND MUTANTS HUMBLING PRESIDENTS ON LIVE TELEVISION.
EVEN UNDER THE PRESENT ARRANGEMENTS, I DOUBT WE'D BE ABLE TO COPE IF IT WASN'T FOR DOCTOR CORNELIUS'S LITTLE SURGICAL MAKEOVERS DOWN THERE.

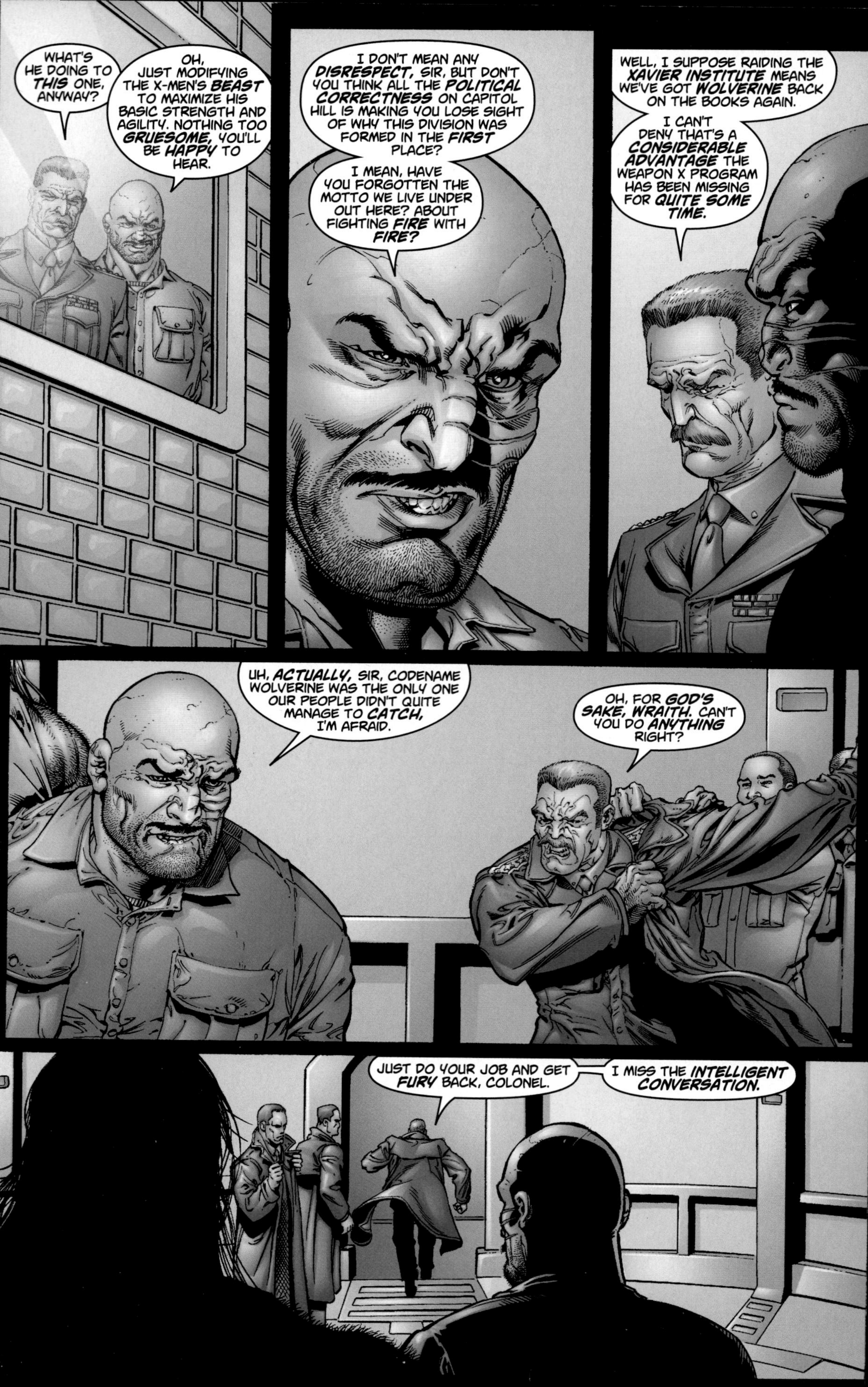
WHAT'S HE DOING TO THIS ONE, ANYWAY?
OH, JUST MODIFYING THE X-MEN'S BEAST TO MAXIMIZE HIS BASIC STRENGTH AND AGILITY. NOTHING TOO GRUESOME, YOU'LL BE HAPPY TO HEAR.
I DON'T MEAN ANY DISRESPECT, SIR, BUT DON'T YOU THINK ALL THE POLITICAL CORRECTNESS ON CAPITOL HILL IS MAKING YOU LOSE SIGHT OF WHY THIS DIVISION WAS FORMED IN THE FIRST PLACE?
I MEAN, HAVE YOU FORGOTTEN THE MOTTO WE LIVE UNDER OUT HERE? ABOUT FIGHTING FIRE WITH FIRE?
WELL, I SUPPOSE RAIDING THE XAVIER INSTITUTE MEANS WE'VE GOT WOLVERINE BACK ON THE BOOKS AGAIN.
I CAN'T DENY THAT'S A CONSIDERABLE ADVANTAGE THE WEAPON X PROGRAM HAS BEEN MISSING FOR QUITE SOME TIME.
UH, ACTUALLY, SIR, CODENAME WOLVERINE WAS THE ONLY ONE OUR PEOPLE DIDN'T QUITE MANAGE TO CATCH, I'M AFRAID.
OH, FOR GOD'S SAKE, WRAITH. CAN'T YOU DO ANYTHING RIGHT?
JUST DO YOUR JOB AND GET FURY BACK, COLONEL.
I MISS THE INTELLIGENT CONVERSATION.

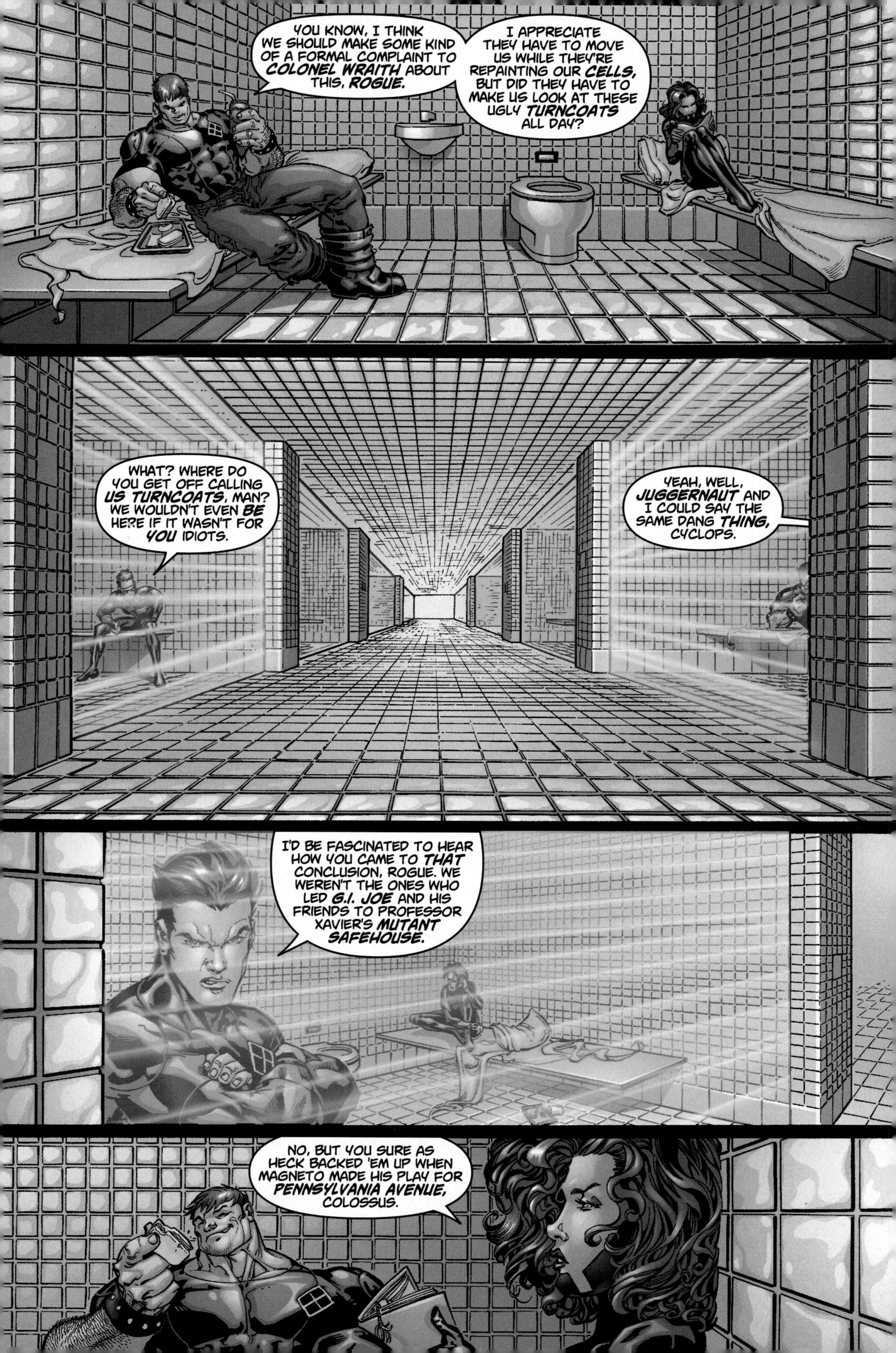
YOU KNOW, I THINK WE SHOULD MAKE SOME KIND OF A FORMAL COMPLAINT TO COLONEL WRAITH ABOUT THIS, ROGUE.
I APPRECIATE THEY HAVE TO MOVE US WHILE THEY'RE REPAINTING OUR CELLS, BUT DID THEY HAVE TO MAKE US LOOK AT THESE UGLY TURNCOATS ALL DAY?
WHAT? WHERE DO YOU GET OFF CALLING US TURNCOATS, MAN? WE WOULDN'T EVEN BE HERE IF IT WASN'T FOR YOU IDIOTS.
YEAH, WELL, JUGGERNAUT AND I COULD SAY THE SAME DANG THING, CYCLOPS.
I'D BE FASCINATED TO HEAR HOW YOU CAME TO THAT CONCLUSION, ROGUE. WE WEREN'T THE ONES WHO LED G.I. JOE AND HIS FRIENDS TO PROFESSOR XAVIER'S MUTANT SAFEHOUSE.
NO, BUT YOU SURE AS HECK BACKED 'EM UP WHEN MAGNETO MADE HIS PLAY FOR PENNSYLVANIA AVENUE, COLOSSUS.

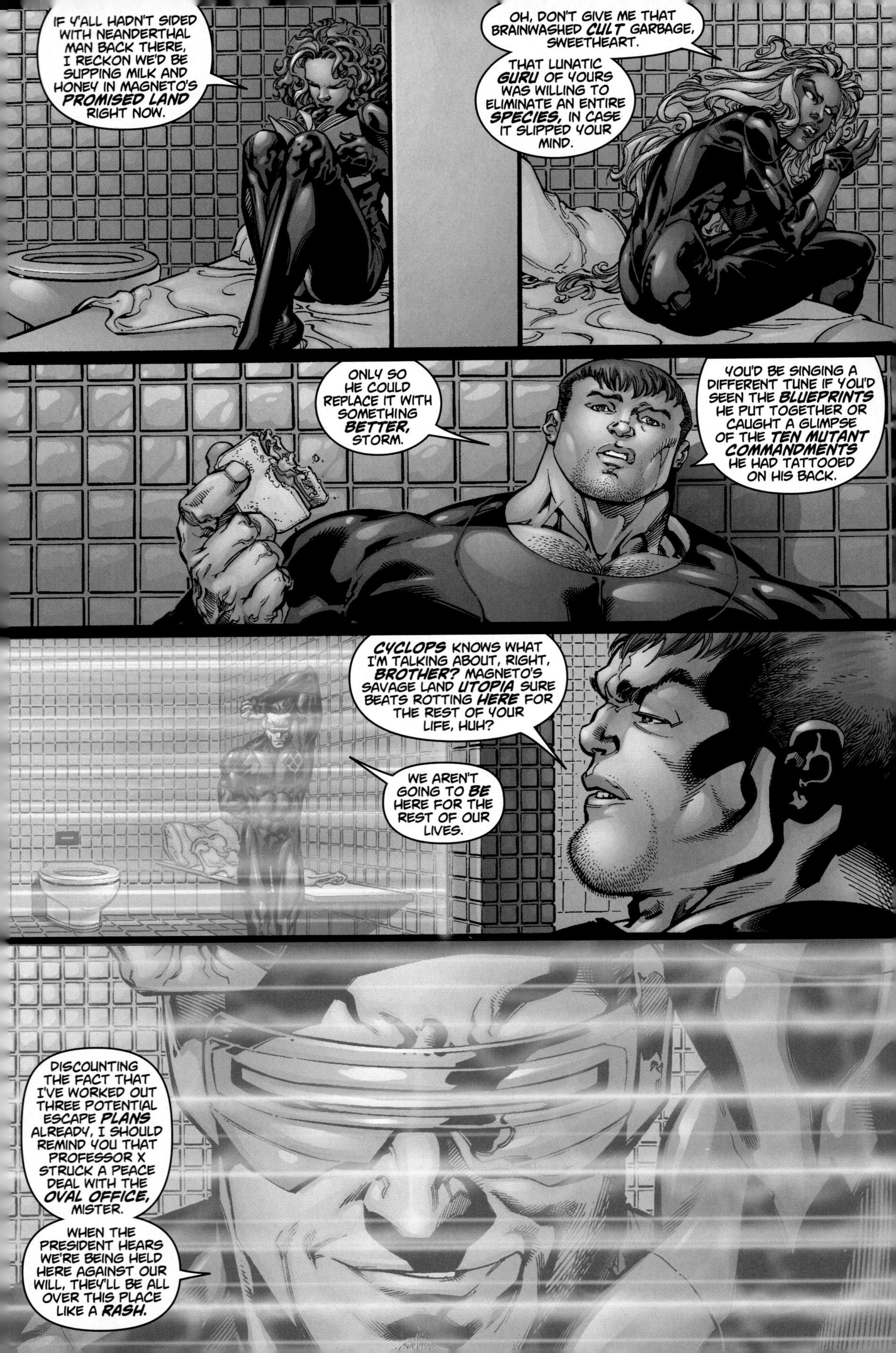
IF Y'ALL HADN'T SIDED WITH NEANDERTHAL MAN BACK THERE, I RECKON WE'D BE SUPPING MILK AND HONEY IN MAGNETO'S PROMISED LAND RIGHT NOW.
OH, DON'T GIVE ME THAT BRAINWASHED CULT GARBAGE, SWEETHEART.
THAT LUNATIC GURU OF YOURS WAS WILLING TO ELIMINATE AN ENTIRE SPECIES, IN CASE IT SLIPPED YOUR MIND.
ONLY SO HE COULD REPLACE IT WITH SOMETHING BETTER, STORM.
YOU'D BE SINGING A DIFFERENT TUNE IF YOU'D SEEN THE BLUEPRINTS HE PUT TOGETHER OR CAUGHT A GLIMPSE OF THE TEN MUTANT COMMANDMENTS HE HAD TATTOOED ON HIS BACK.
CYCLOPS KNOWS WHAT I'M TALKING ABOUT, RIGHT, BROTHER? MAGNETO'S SAVAGE LAND UTOPIA SURE BEATS ROTTING HERE FOR THE REST OF YOUR LIFE, HUH?
WE AREN'T GOING TO BE HERE FOR THE REST OF OUR LIVES.
DISCOUNTING THE FACT THAT I'VE WORKED OUT THREE POTENTIAL ESCAPE PLANS ALREADY, I SHOULD REMIND YOU THAT PROFESSOR X STRUCK A PEACE DEAL WITH THE OVAL OFFICE, MISTER.
WHEN THE PRESIDENT HEARS WE'RE BEING HELD HERE AGAINST OUR WILL, THEY'LL BE ALL OVER THIS PLACE LIKE A RASH.

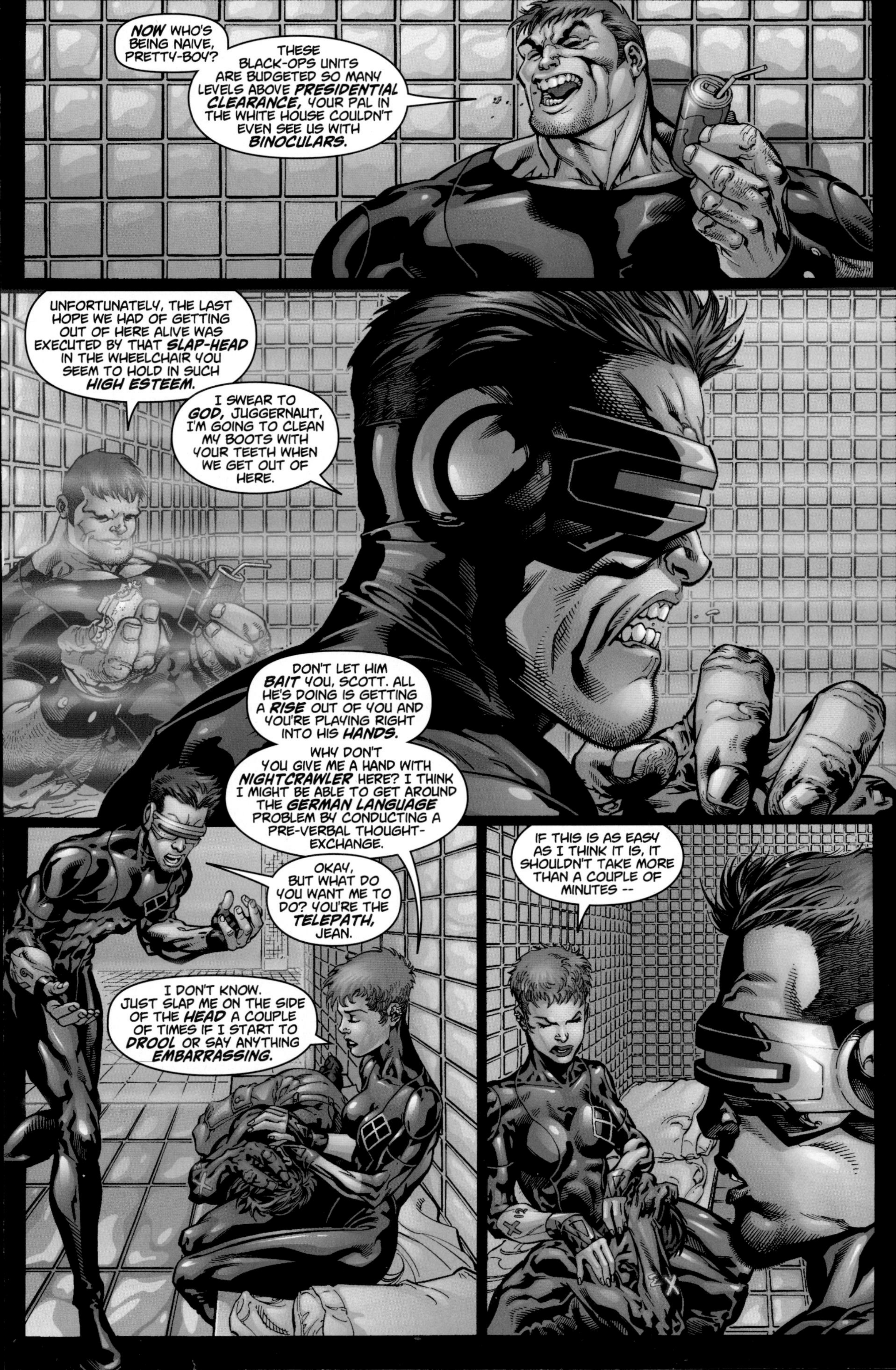

NOW WHO'S BEING NAIVE, PRETTY-BOY?
THESE BLACK-OPS UNITS ARE BUDGETED SO MANY LEVELS ABOVE PRESIDENTIAL CLEARANCE, YOUR PAL IN THE WHITE HOUSE COULDN'T EVEN SEE US WITH BINOCULARS.
UNFORTUNATELY, THE LAST HOPE WE HAD OF GETTING OUT OF HERE ALIVE WAS EXECUTED BY THAT SLAP-HEAD IN THE WHEELCHAIR YOU SEEM TO HOLD IN SUCH HIGH ESTEEM.
I SWEAR TO GOD, JUGGERNAUT, I'M GOING TO CLEAN MY BOOTS WITH YOUR TEETH WHEN WE GET OUT OF HERE.
DON'T LET HIM BAIT YOU, SCOTT. ALL HE'S DOING IS GETTING A RISE OUT OF YOU AND YOU'RE PLAYING RIGHT INTO HIS HANDS.
WHY DON'T YOU GIVE ME A HAND WITH NIGHTCRAWLER HERE? I THINK I MIGHT BE ABLE TO GET AROUND THE GERMAN LANGUAGE PROBLEM BY CONDUCTING A PRE-VERBAL THOUGHT-EXCHANGE.
OKAY, BUT WHAT DO YOU WANT ME TO DO? YOU'RE THE TELEPATH, JEAN.
I DON'T KNOW. JUST SLAP ME ON THE SIDE OF THE HEAD A COUPLE OF TIMES IF I START TO DROOL OR SAY ANYTHING EMBARRASSING.
IF THIS IS AS EASY AS I THINK IT IS, IT SHOULDN'T TAKE MORE THAN A COUPLE OF MINUTES --

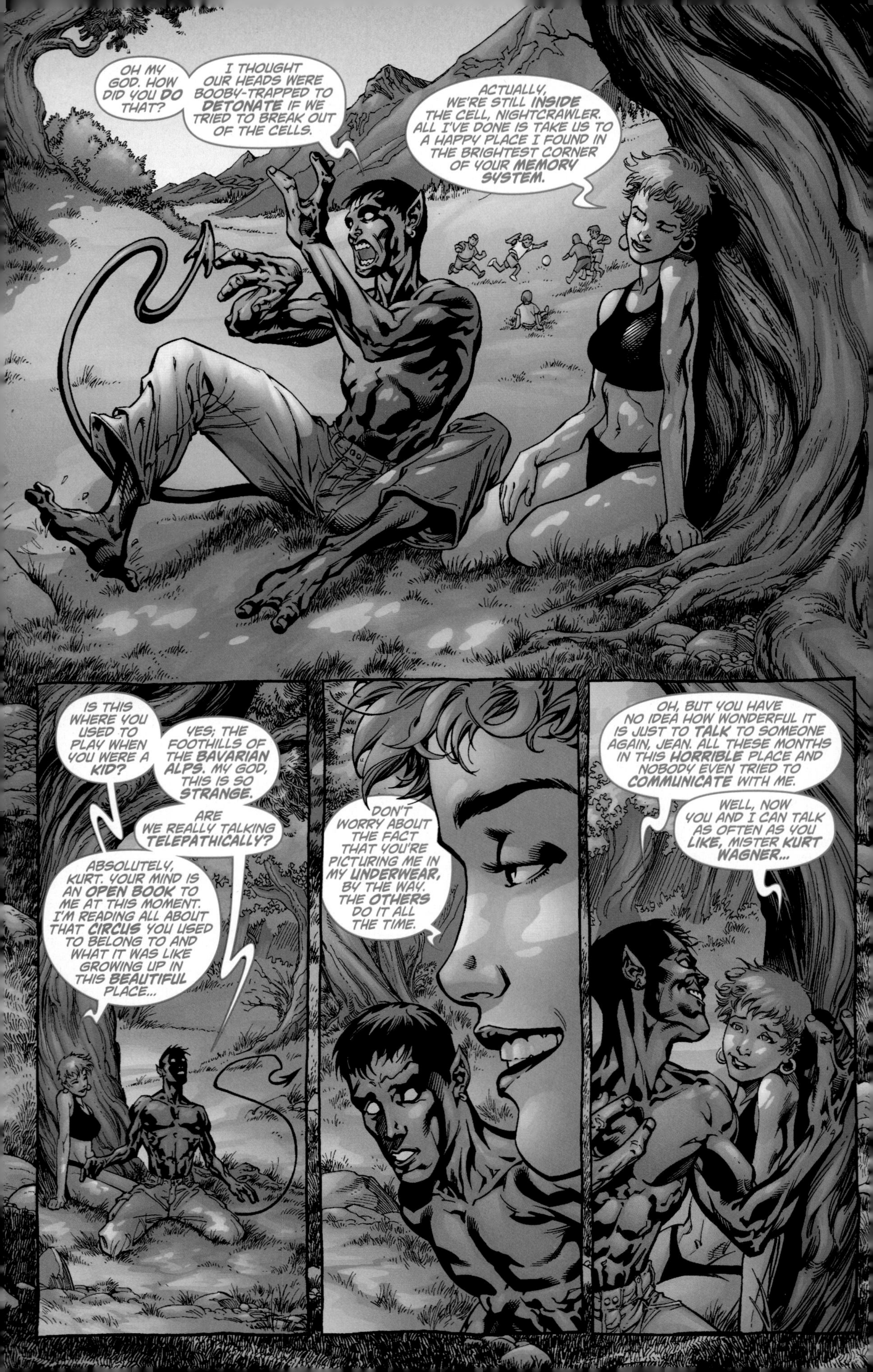
OH MY GOD. HOW DID YOU DO THAT?
I THOUGHT OUR HEADS WERE BOOBY-TRAPPED TO DETONATE IF WE TRIED TO BREAK OUT OF THE CELLS.
ACTUALLY, WE'RE STILL INSIDE THE CELL, NIGHTCRAWLER. ALL I'VE DONE IS TAKE US TO A HAPPY PLACE I FOUND IN THE BRIGHTEST CORNER OF YOUR MEMORY SYSTEM.
IS THIS WHERE YOU USED TO PLAY WHEN YOU WERE A KID?
YES; THE FOOTHILLS OF THE BAVARIAN ALPS. MY GOD, THIS IS SO STRANGE.
ARE WE REALLY TALKING TELEPATHICALLY?
ABSOLUTELY, KURT. YOUR MIND IS AN OPEN BOOK TO ME AT THIS MOMENT. I'M READING ALL ABOUT THAT CIRCUS YOU USED TO BELONG TO AND WHAT IT WAS LIKE GROWING UP IN THIS BEAUTIFUL PLACE...
DON'T WORRY ABOUT THE FACT THAT YOU'RE PICTURING ME IN MY UNDERWEAR, BY THE WAY. THE OTHERS DO IT ALL THE TIME.
OH, BUT YOU HAVE NO IDEA HOW WONDERFUL IT IS JUST TO TALK TO SOMEONE AGAIN, JEAN. ALL THESE MONTHS IN THIS HORRIBLE PLACE AND NOBODY EVEN TRIED TO COMMUNICATE WITH ME.
WELL, NOW YOU AND I CAN TALK AS OFTEN AS YOU LIKE, MISTER KURT WAGNER...

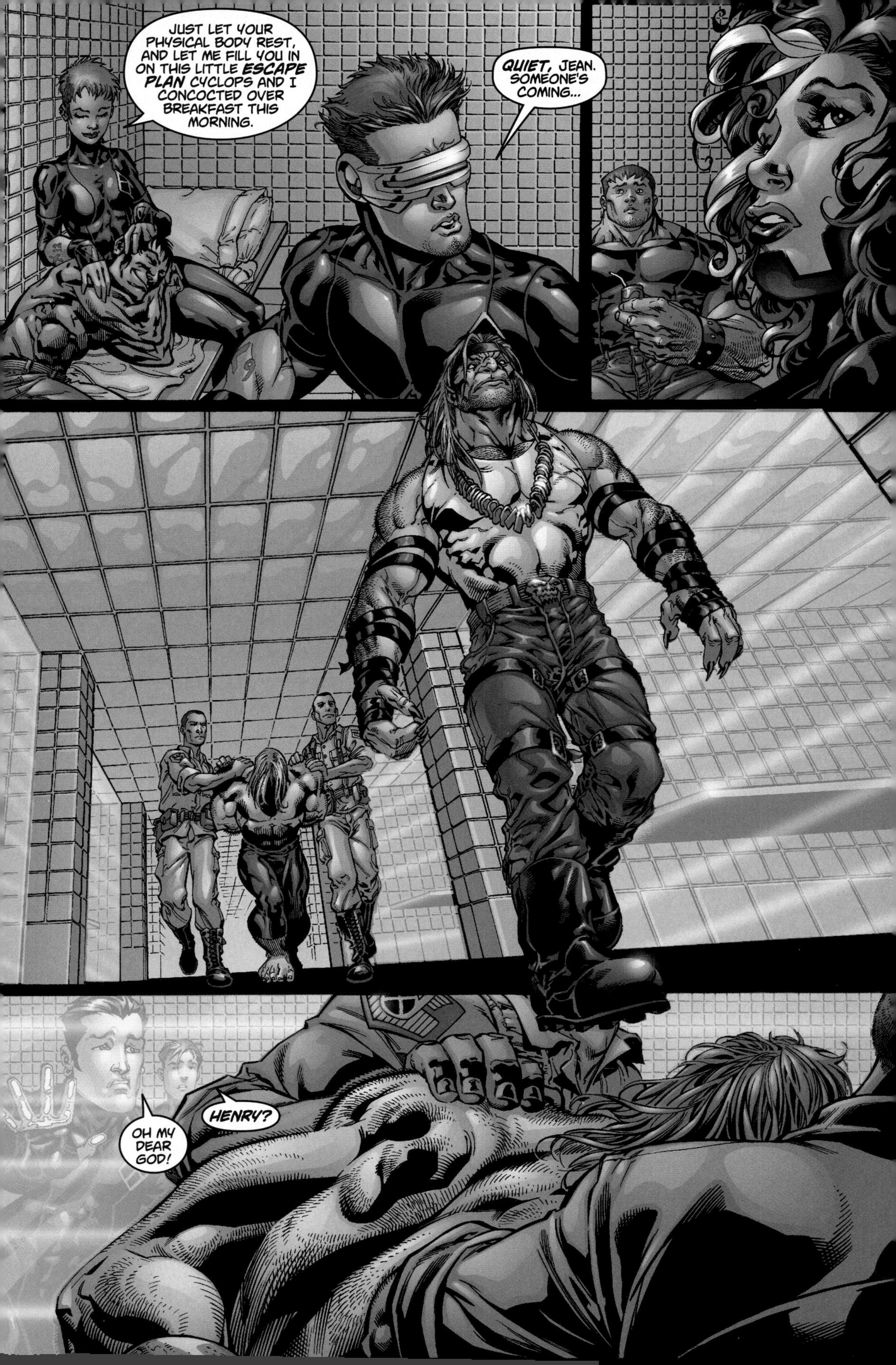
JUST LET YOUR PHYSICAL BODY REST, AND LET ME FILL YOU IN ON THIS LITTLE ESCAPE PLAN CYCLOPS AND I CONCOCTED OVER BREAKFAST THIS MORNING.
QUIET, JEAN. SOMEONE'S COMING...
HENRY?
OH MY DEAR GOD!

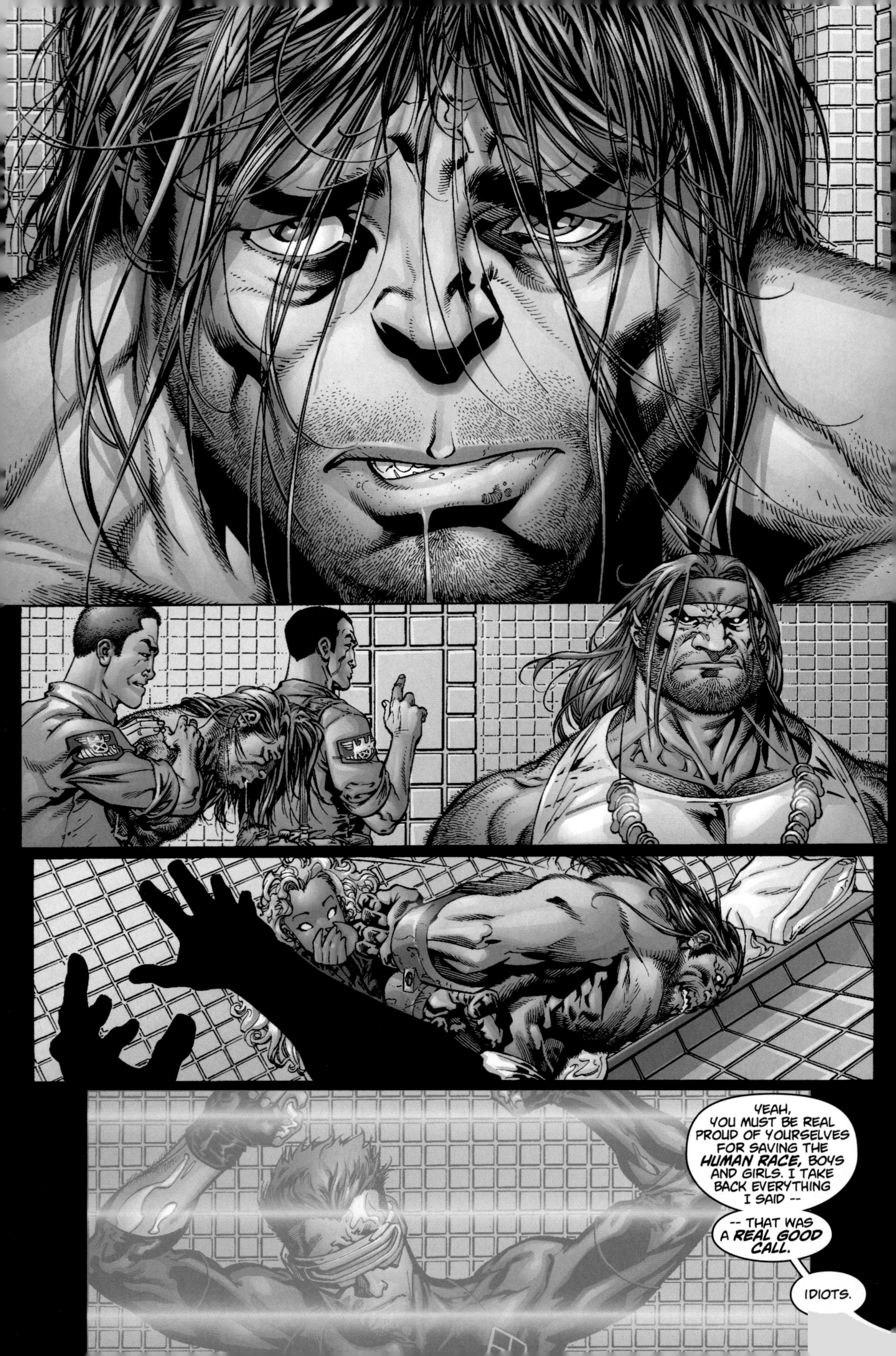
YEAH, YOU MUST BE REAL PROUD OF YOURSELVES FOR SAVING THE HUMAN RACE, BOYS AND GIRLS. I TAKE BACK EVERYTHING I SAID --
-- THAT WAS A REAL GOOD CALL.
IDIOTS.

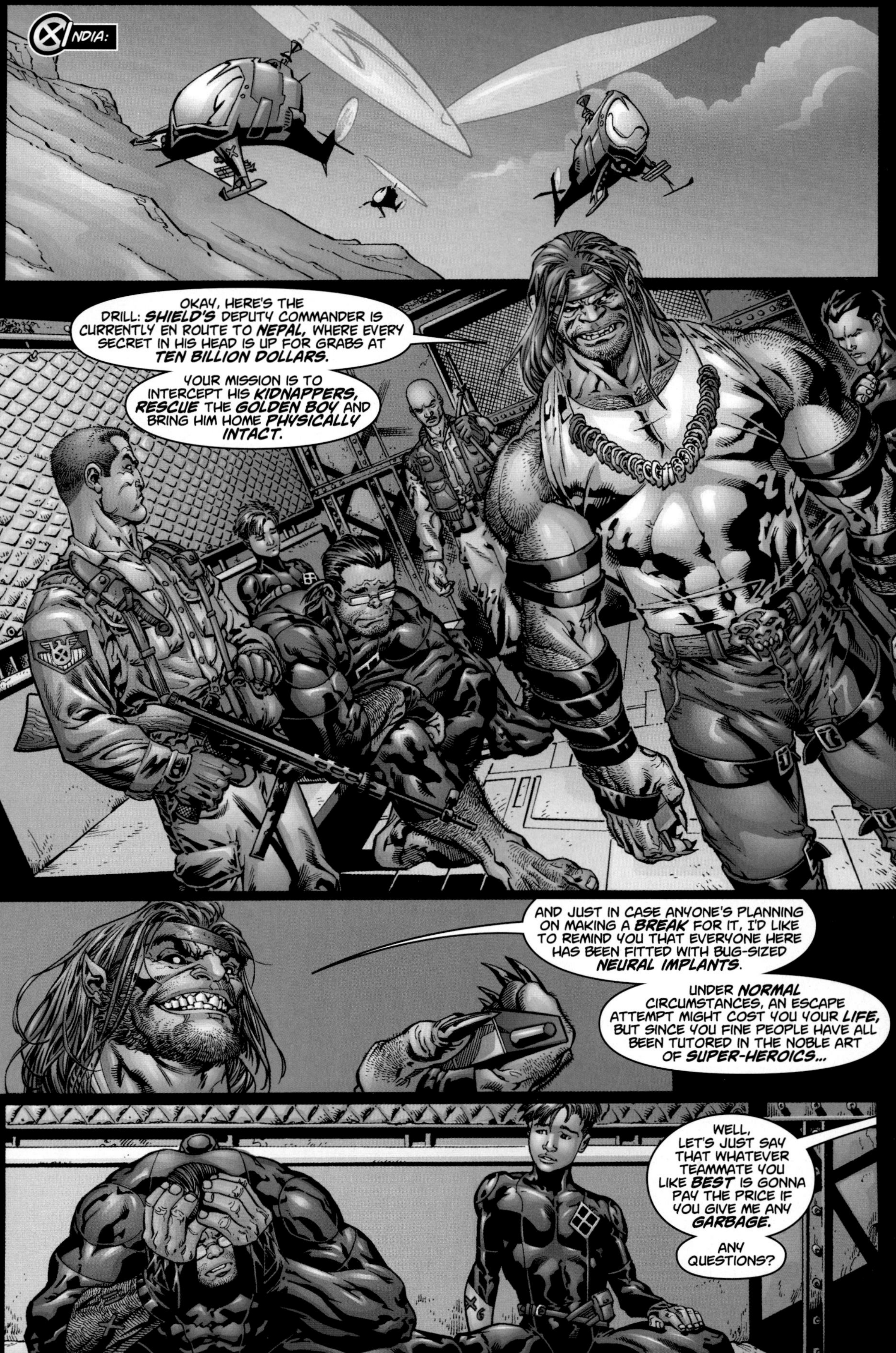
INDIA:
OKAY, HERE'S THE DRILL: SHIELD'S DEPUTY COMMANDER IS CURRENTLY EN ROUTE TO NEPAL, WHERE EVERY SECRET IN HIS HEAD IS UP FOR GRABS AT TEN BILLION DOLLARS.
YOUR MISSION IS TO INTERCEPT HIS KIDNAPPERS, RESCUE THE GOLDEN BOY AND BRING HIM HOME PHYSICALLY INTACT.
AND JUST IN CASE ANYONE'S PLANNING ON MAKING A BREAK FOR IT, I'D LIKE TO REMIND YOU THAT EVERYONE HERE HAS BEEN FITTED WITH BUG-SIZED NEURAL IMPLANTS.
UNDER NORMAL CIRCUMSTANCES, AN ESCAPE ATTEMPT MIGHT COST YOU YOUR LIFE, BUT SINCE YOU FINE PEOPLE HAVE ALL BEEN TUTORED IN THE NOBLE ART OF SUPER-HEROICS...
WELL, LET'S JUST SAY THAT WHATEVER TEAMMATE YOU LIKE BEST IS GONNA PAY THE PRICE IF YOU GIVE ME ANY GARBAGE.
ANY QUESTIONS?

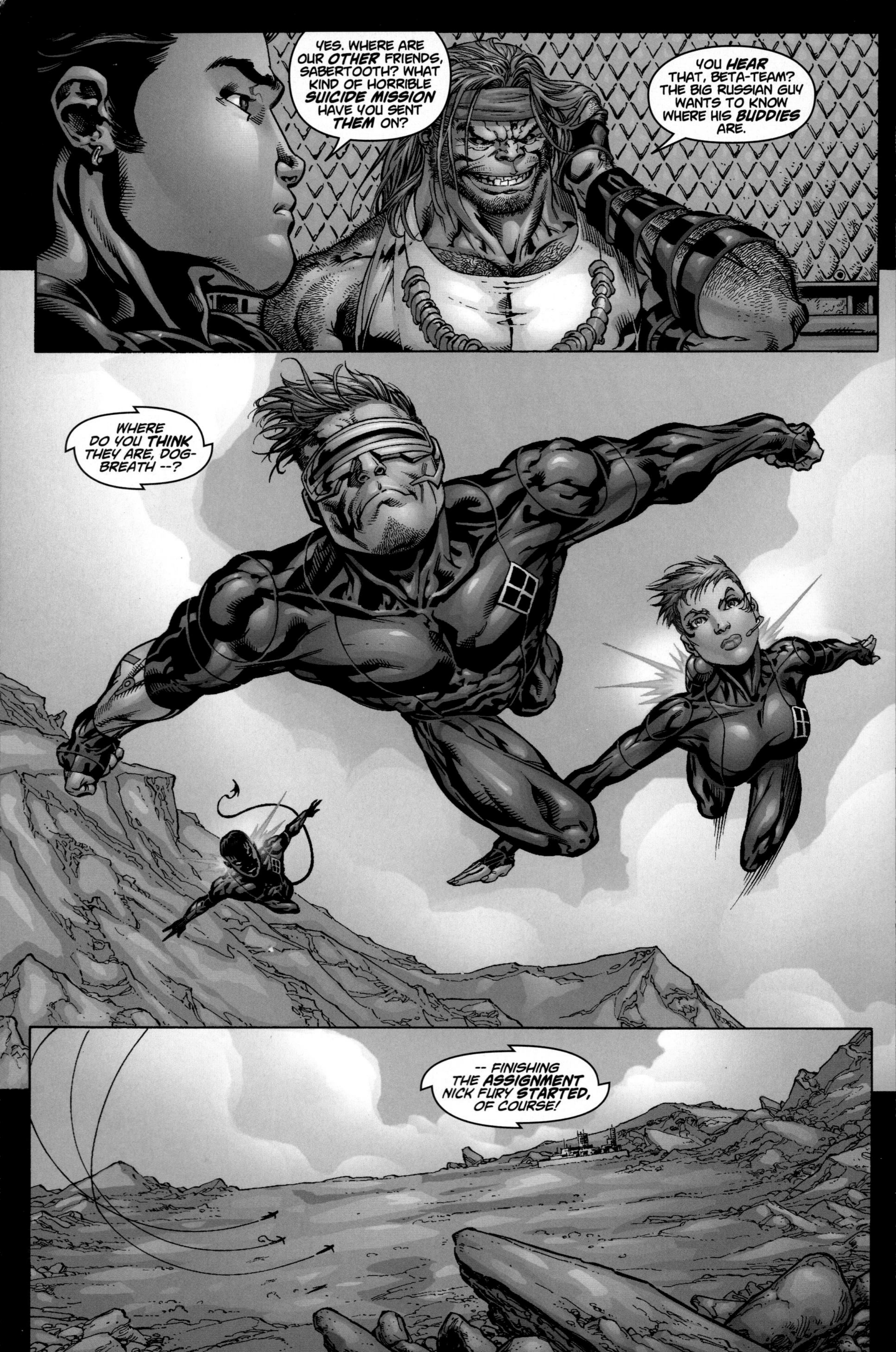
YES. WHERE ARE OUR OTHER FRIENDS, SABERTOOTH? WHAT KIND OF HORRIBLE SUICIDE MISSION HAVE YOU SENT THEM ON?
YOU HEAR THAT, BETA-TEAM? THE BIG RUSSIAN GUY WANTS TO KNOW WHERE HIS BUDDIES ARE.
WHERE DO YOU THINK THEY ARE, DOG-BREATH --?
-- FINISHING THE ASSIGNMENT NICK FURY STARTED, OF COURSE!

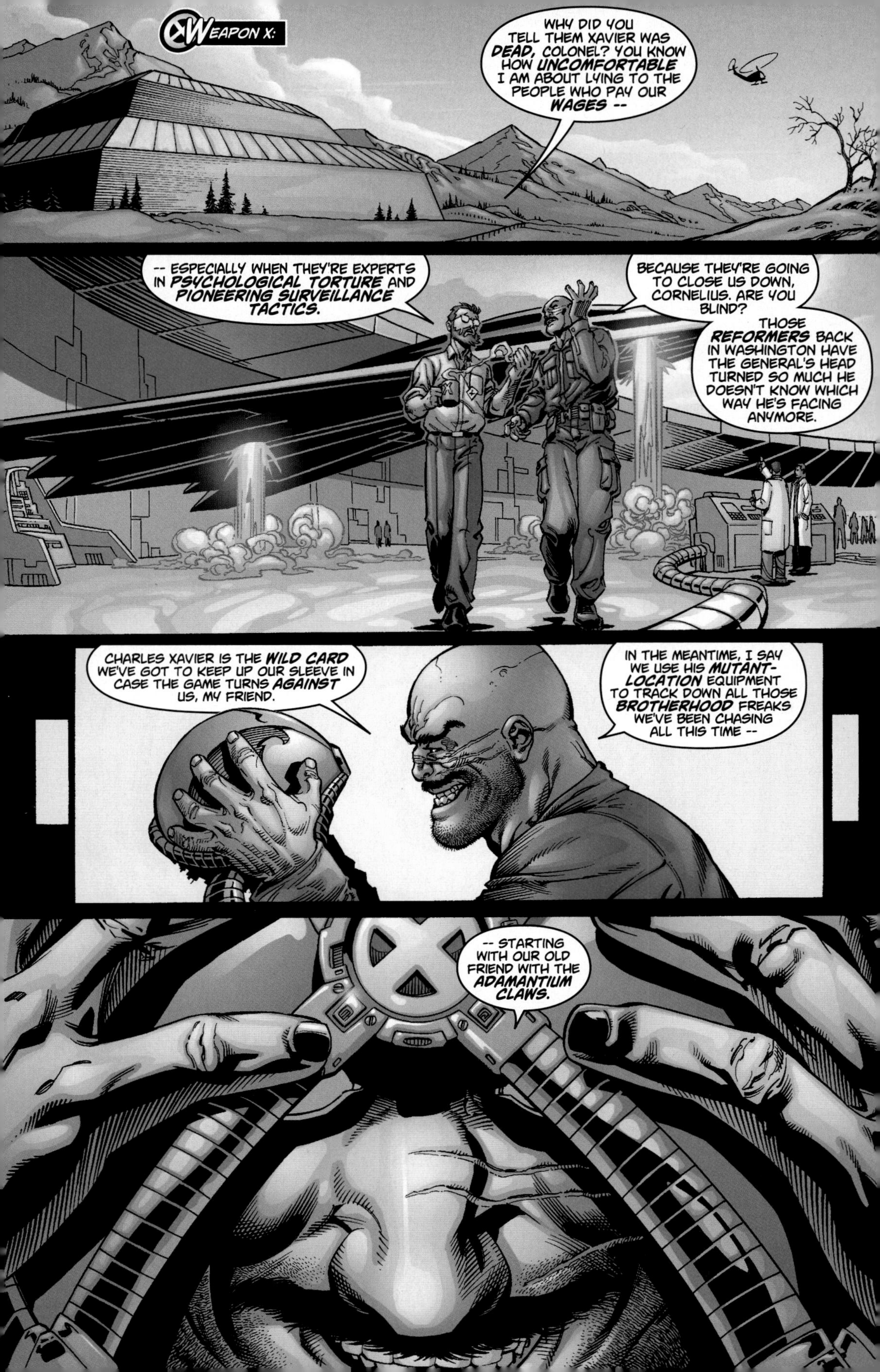
WEAPON X:
WHY DID YOU TELL THEM XAVIER WAS DEAD, COLONEL? YOU KNOW HOW UNCOMFORTABLE I AM ABOUT LYING TO THE PEOPLE WHO PAY OUR WAGES --
-- ESPECIALLY WHEN THEY'RE EXPERTS IN PSYCHOLOGICAL TORTURE AND PIONEERING SURVEILLANCE TACTICS.
BECAUSE THEY'RE GOING TO CLOSE US DOWN, CORNELIUS. ARE YOU BLIND?
THOSE REFORMERS BACK IN WASHINGTON HAVE THE GENERAL'S HEAD TURNED SO MUCH HE DOESN'T KNOW WHICH WAY HE'S FACING ANYMORE.
CHARLES XAVIER IS THE WILD CARD WE'VE GOT TO KEEP UP OUR SLEEVE IN CASE THE GAME TURNS AGAINST US, MY FRIEND.
IN THE MEANTIME, I SAY WE USE HIS MUTANT-LOCATION EQUIPMENT TO TRACK DOWN ALL THOSE BROTHERHOOD FREAKS WE'VE BEEN CHASING ALL THIS TIME --
-- STARTING WITH OUR OLD FRIEND WITH THE ADAMANTIUM CLAWS.

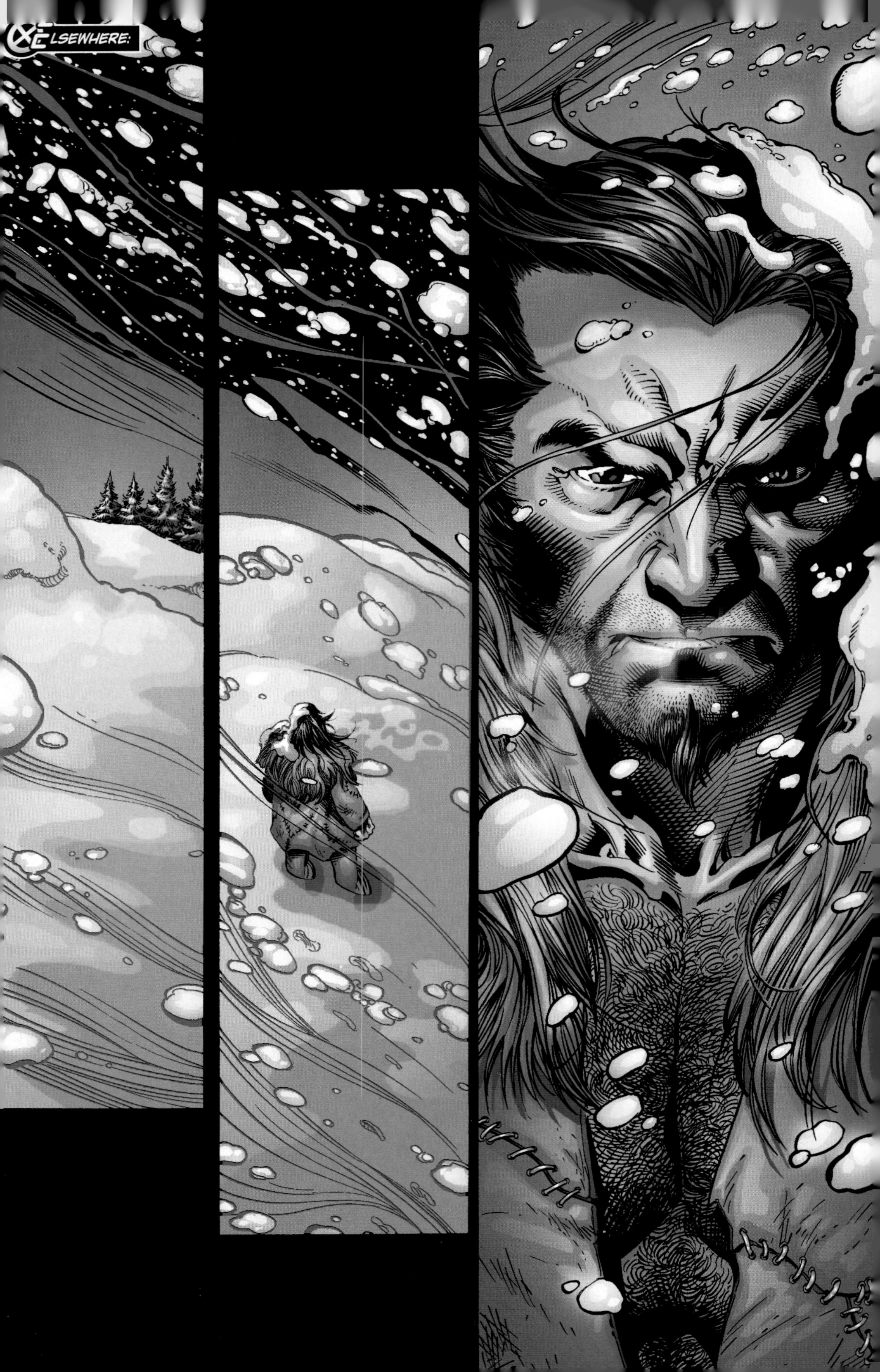
ELSEWHERE:

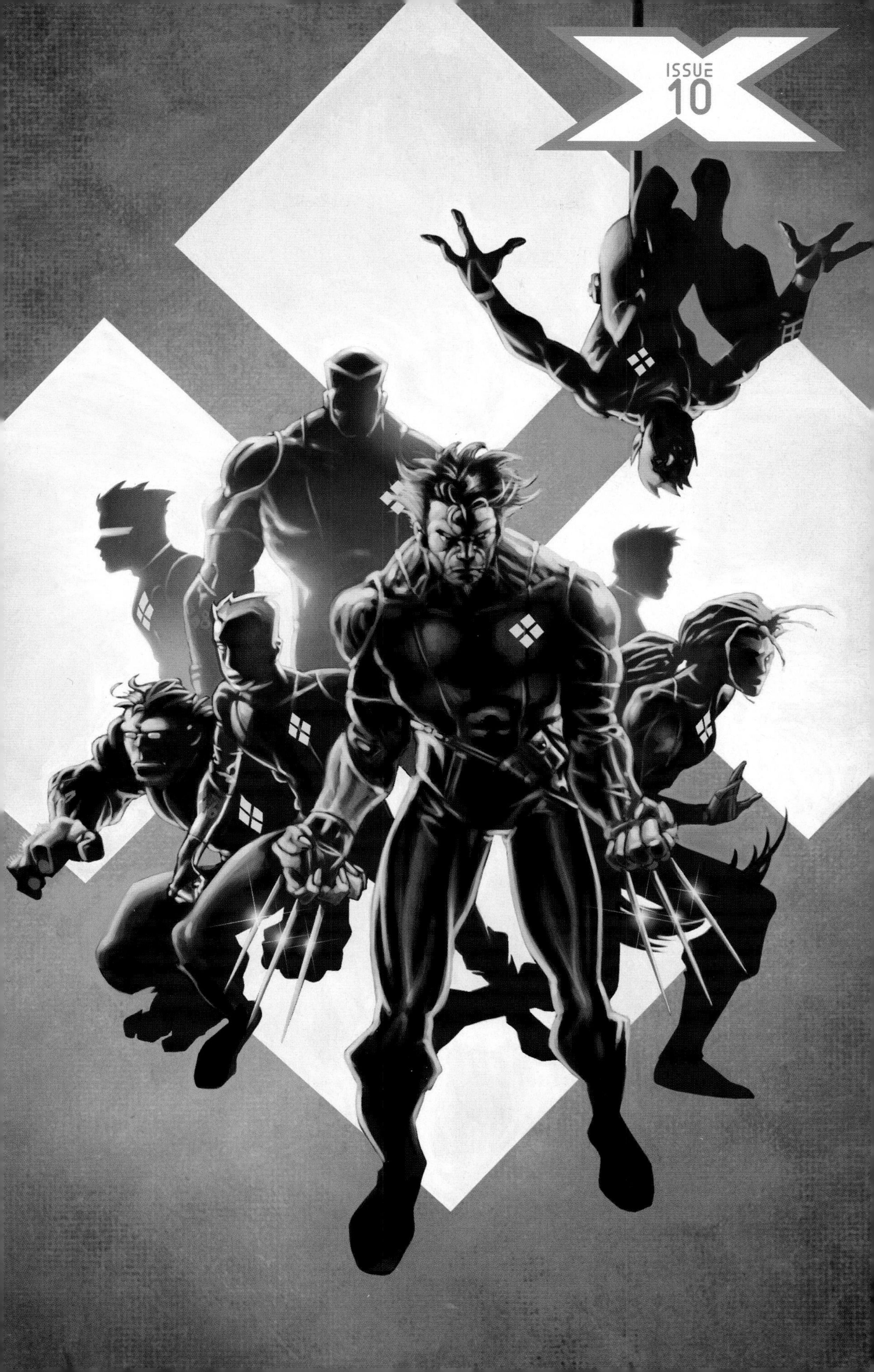
ISSUE
10

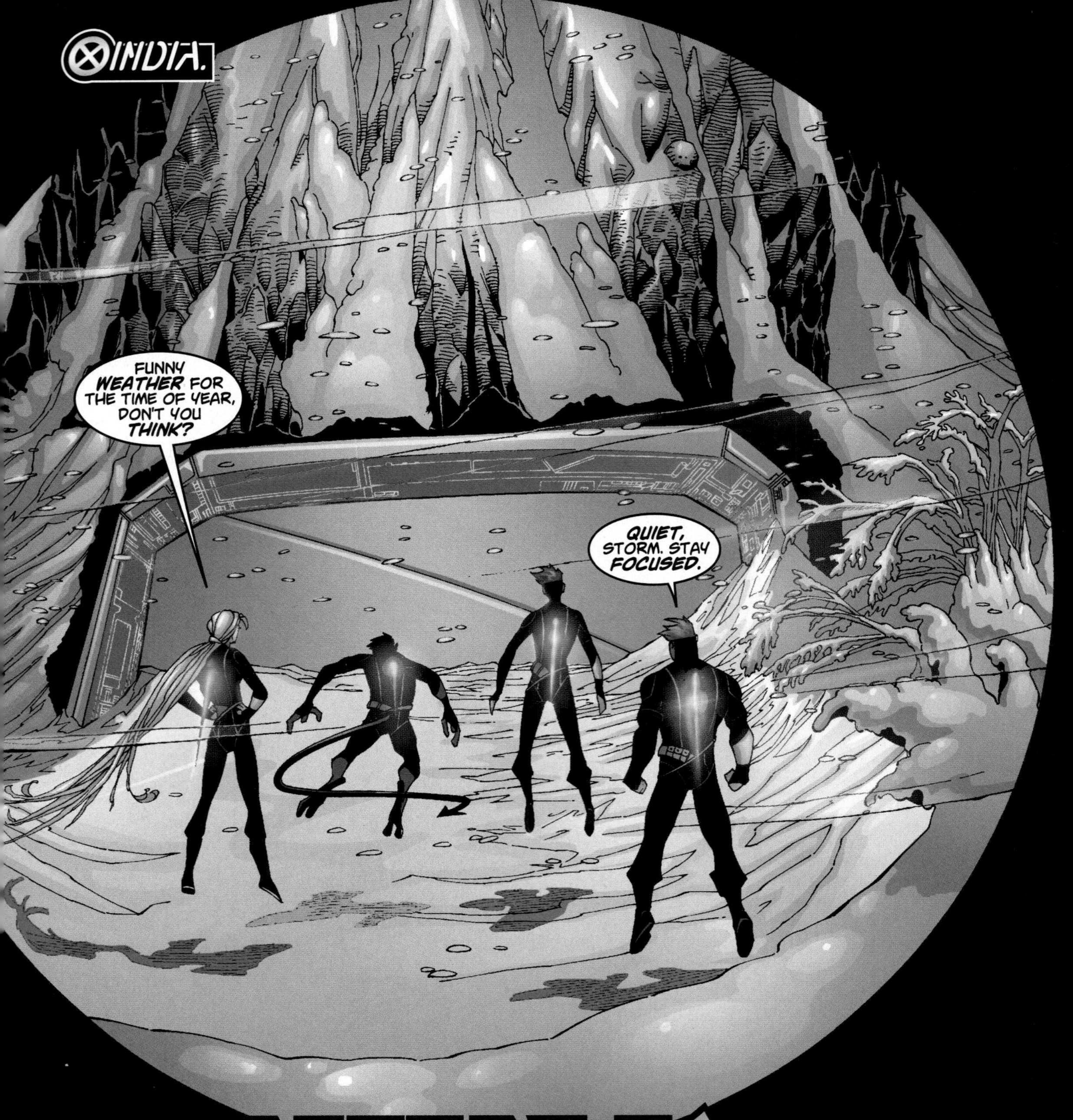
INDIA.
FUNNY WEATHER FOR THE TIME OF YEAR, DON'T YOU THINK?
QUIET, STORM. STAY FOCUSED.

RETURN TO WEAPON X

PART FOUR OF SIX

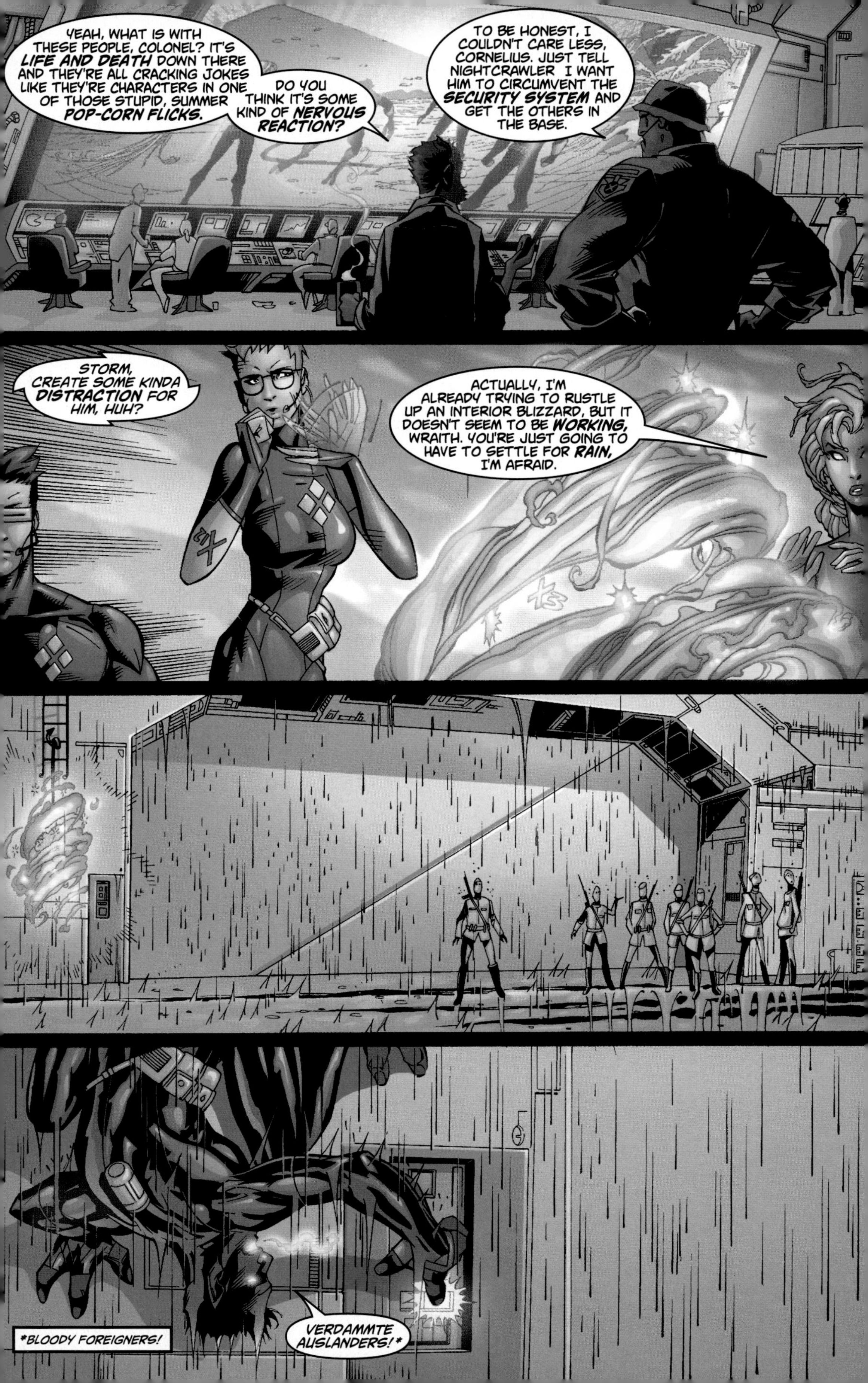
YEAH, WHAT IS WITH THESE PEOPLE, COLONEL? IT'S LIFE AND DEATH DOWN THERE AND THEY'RE ALL CRACKING JOKES LIKE THEY'RE CHARACTERS IN ONE OF THOSE STUPID, SUMMER POP-CORN FLICKS.
DO YOU THINK IT'S SOME KIND OF NERVOUS REACTION?
TO BE HONEST, I COULDN'T CARE LESS, CORNELIUS. JUST TELL NIGHTCRAWLER I WANT HIM TO CIRCUMVENT THE SECURITY SYSTEM AND GET THE OTHERS IN THE BASE.
STORM, CREATE SOME KINDA DISTRACTION FOR HIM, HUH?
ACTUALLY, I'M ALREADY TRYING TO RUSTLE UP AN INTERIOR BLIZZARD, BUT IT DOESN'T SEEM TO BE WORKING, WRAITH. YOU'RE JUST GOING TO HAVE TO SETTLE FOR RAIN, I'M AFRAID.
VERDAMMTE AUSLANDERS!*
*BLOODY FOREIGNERS!

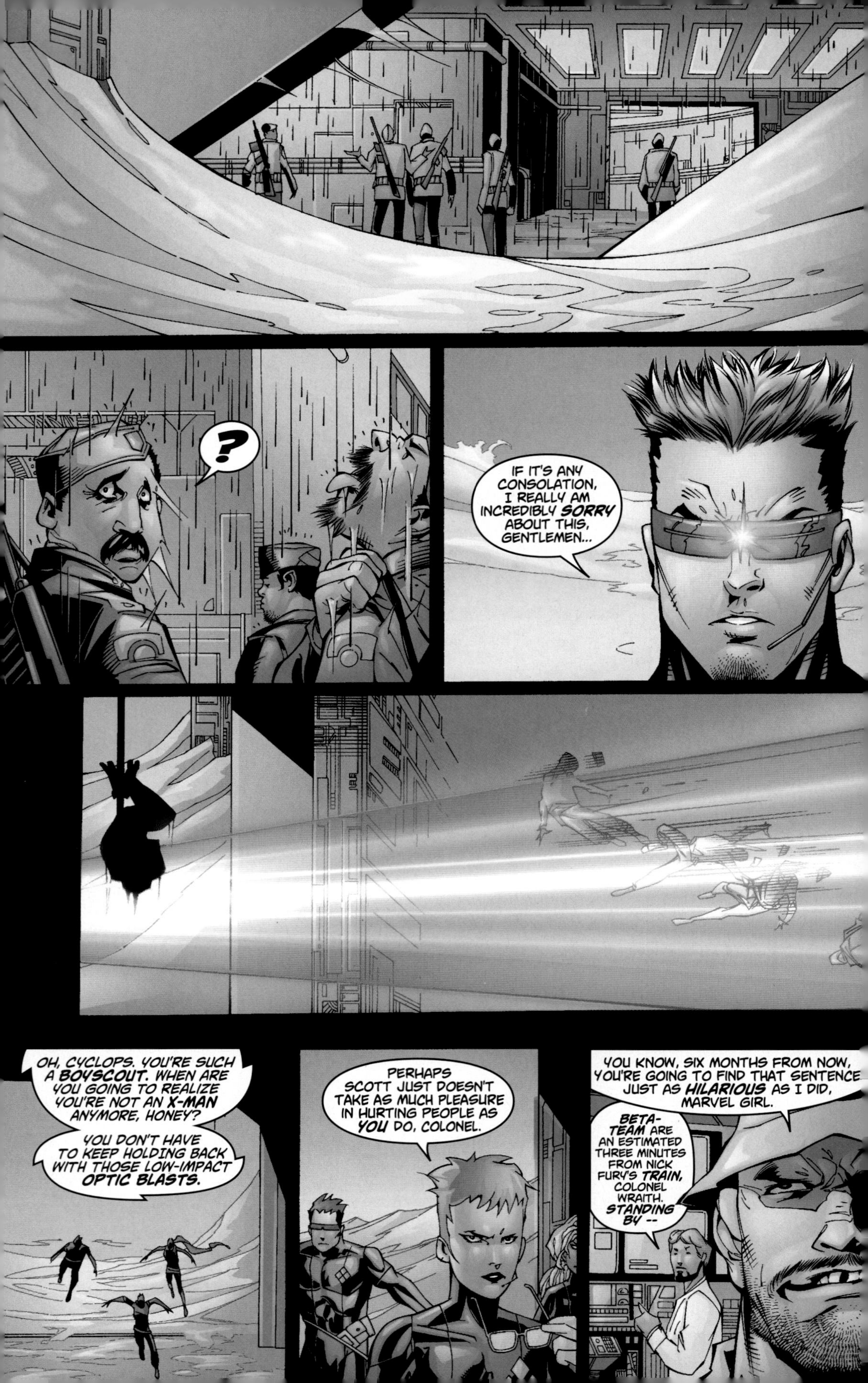
?
IF IT'S ANY CONSOLATION, I REALLY AM INCREDIBLY SORRY ABOUT THIS, GENTLEMEN...
OH, CYCLOPS. YOU'RE SUCH A BOYSCOUT. WHEN ARE YOU GOING TO REALIZE YOU'RE NOT AN X-MAN ANYMORE, HONEY?
YOU DON'T HAVE TO KEEP HOLDING BACK WITH THOSE LOW-IMPACT OPTIC BLASTS.
PERHAPS SCOTT JUST DOESN'T TAKE AS MUCH PLEASURE IN HURTING PEOPLE AS YOU DO, COLONEL.
YOU KNOW, SIX MONTHS FROM NOW, YOU'RE GOING TO FIND THAT SENTENCE JUST AS HILARIOUS AS I DID, MARVEL GIRL.
BETA-TEAM ARE AN ESTIMATED THREE MINUTES FROM NICK FURY'S TRAIN, COLONEL WRAITH. STANDING BY --

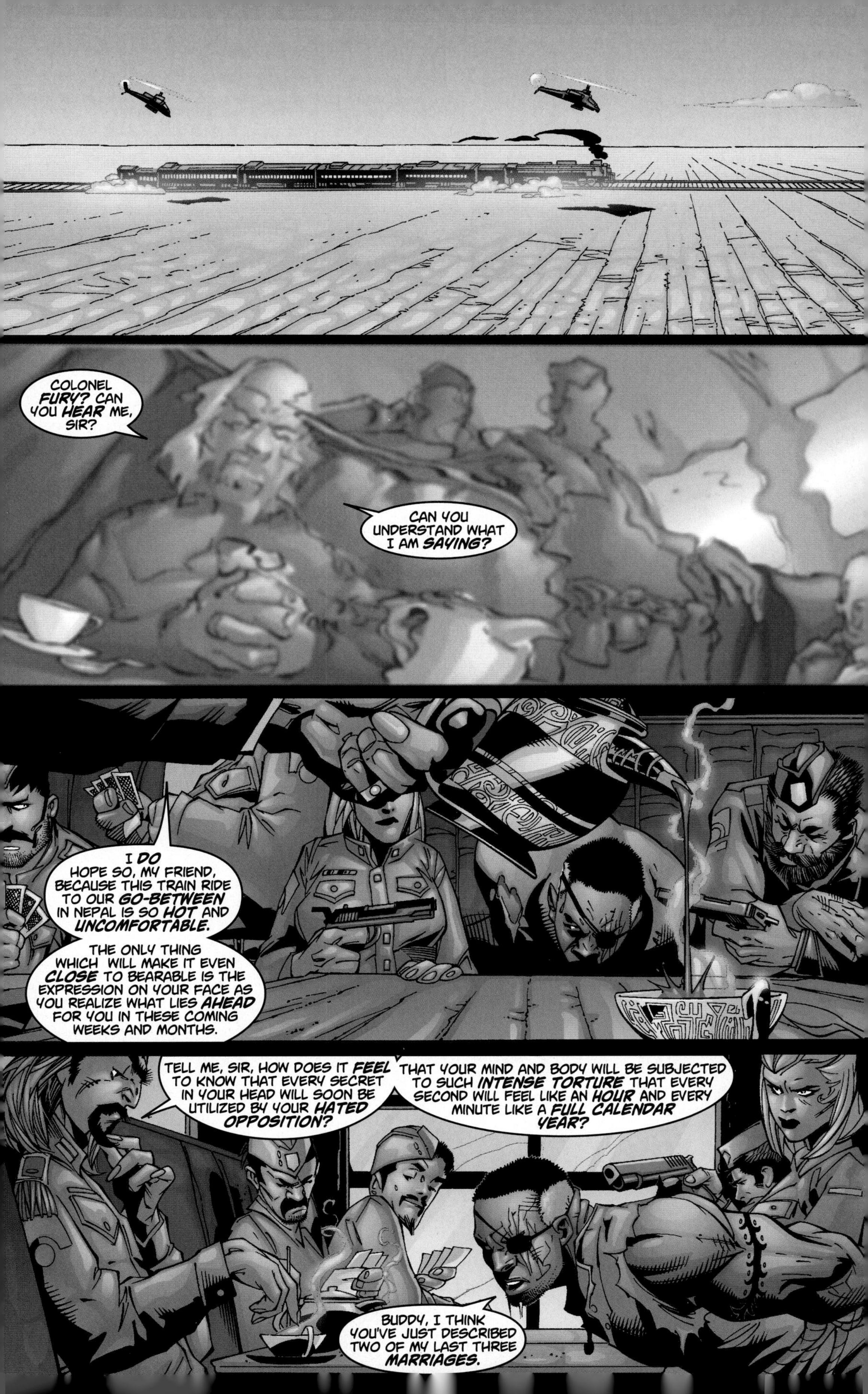
COLONEL FURY? CAN YOU HEAR ME, SIR?
CAN YOU UNDERSTAND WHAT I AM SAYING?
I DO HOPE SO, MY FRIEND, BECAUSE THIS TRAIN RIDE TO OUR GO-BETWEEN IN NEPAL IS SO HOT AND UNCOMFORTABLE.
THE ONLY THING WHICH WILL MAKE IT EVEN CLOSE TO BEARABLE IS THE EXPRESSION ON YOUR FACE AS YOU REALIZE WHAT LIES AHEAD FOR YOU IN THESE COMING WEEKS AND MONTHS.
TELL ME, SIR, HOW DOES IT FEEL TO KNOW THAT EVERY SECRET IN YOUR HEAD WILL SOON BE UTILIZED BY YOUR HATED OPPOSITION?
THAT YOUR MIND AND BODY WILL BE SUBJECTED TO SUCH INTENSE TORTURE THAT EVERY SECOND WILL FEEL LIKE AN HOUR AND EVERY MINUTE LIKE A FULL CALENDAR YEAR?
BUDDY, I THINK YOU'VE JUST DESCRIBED TWO OF MY LAST THREE MARRIAGES.

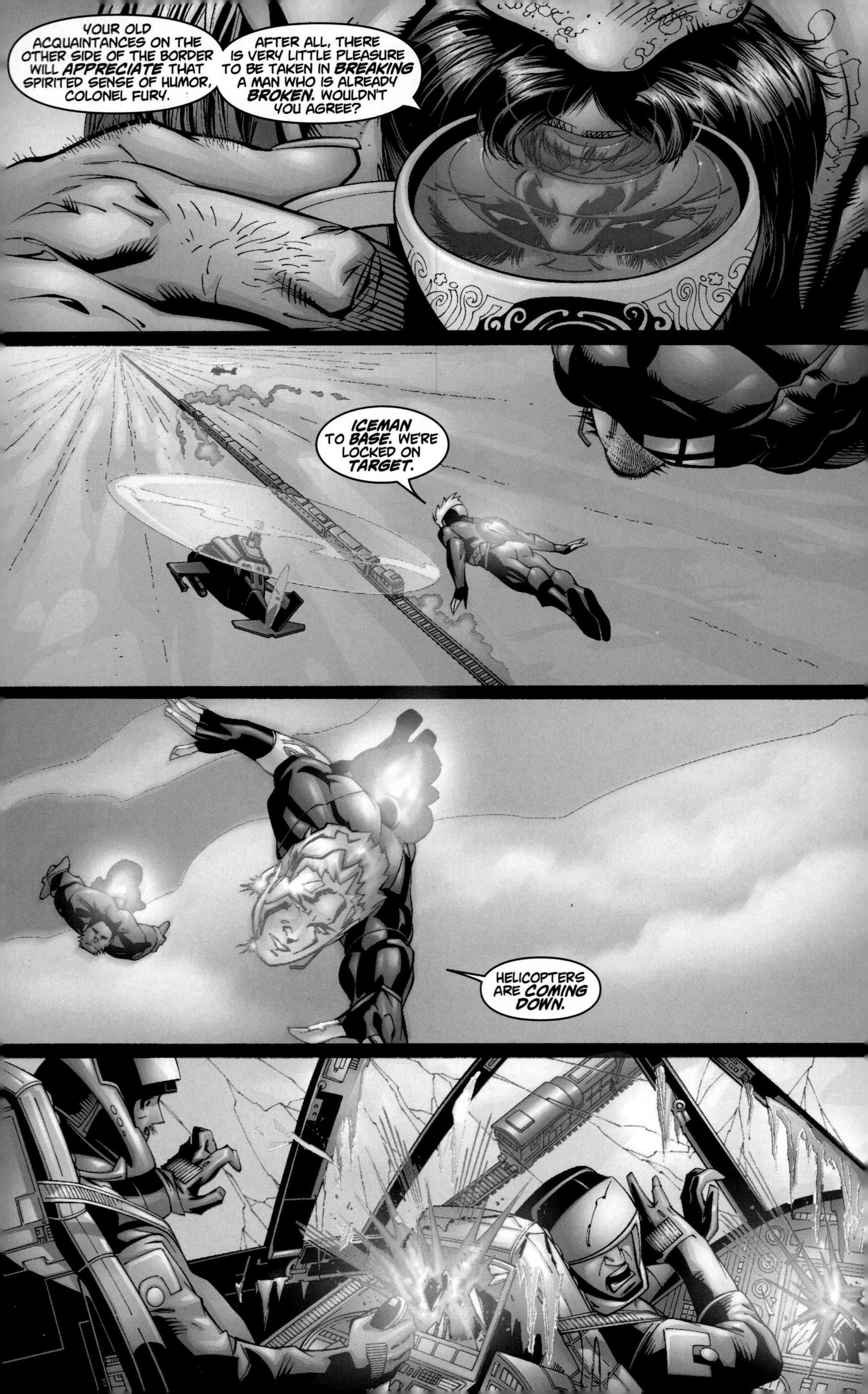
YOUR OLD ACQUAINTANCES ON THE OTHER SIDE OF THE BORDER WILL APPRECIATE THAT SPIRITED SENSE OF HUMOR, COLONEL FURY.
AFTER ALL, THERE IS VERY LITTLE PLEASURE TO BE TAKEN IN BREAKING A MAN WHO IS ALREADY BROKEN. WOULDN'T YOU AGREE?
ICEMAN TO BASE. WE'RE LOCKED ON TARGET.
HELICOPTERS ARE COMING DOWN.

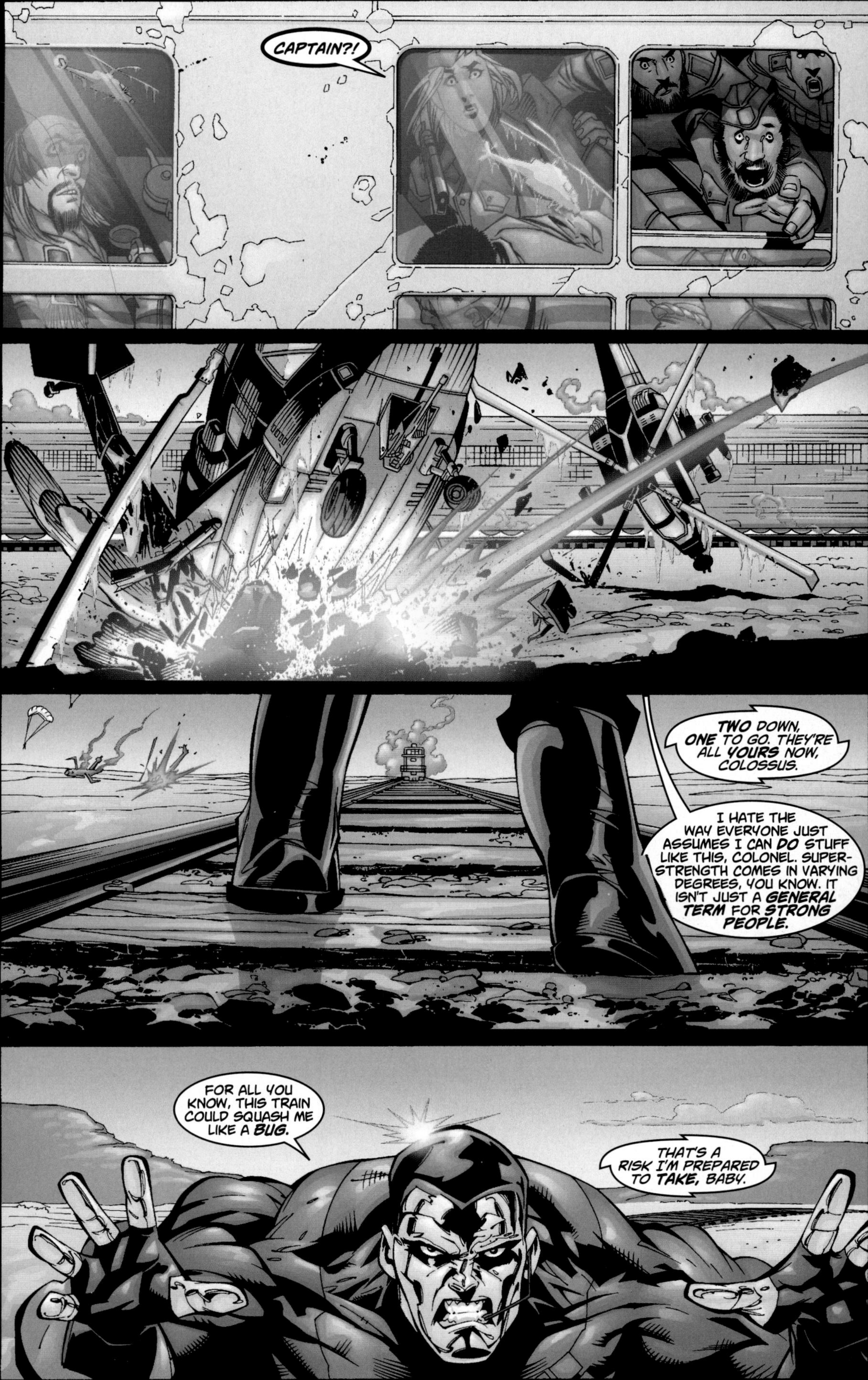
CAPTAIN?!
TWO DOWN, ONE TO GO. THEY'RE ALL YOURS NOW, COLOSSUS.
I HATE THE WAY EVERYONE JUST ASSUMES I CAN DO STUFF LIKE THIS, COLONEL. SUPER-STRENGTH COMES IN VARYING DEGREES, YOU KNOW. IT ISN'T JUST A GENERAL TERM FOR STRONG PEOPLE.
FOR ALL YOU KNOW, THIS TRAIN COULD SQUASH ME LIKE A BUG.
THAT'S A RISK I'M PREPARED TO TAKE, BABY.

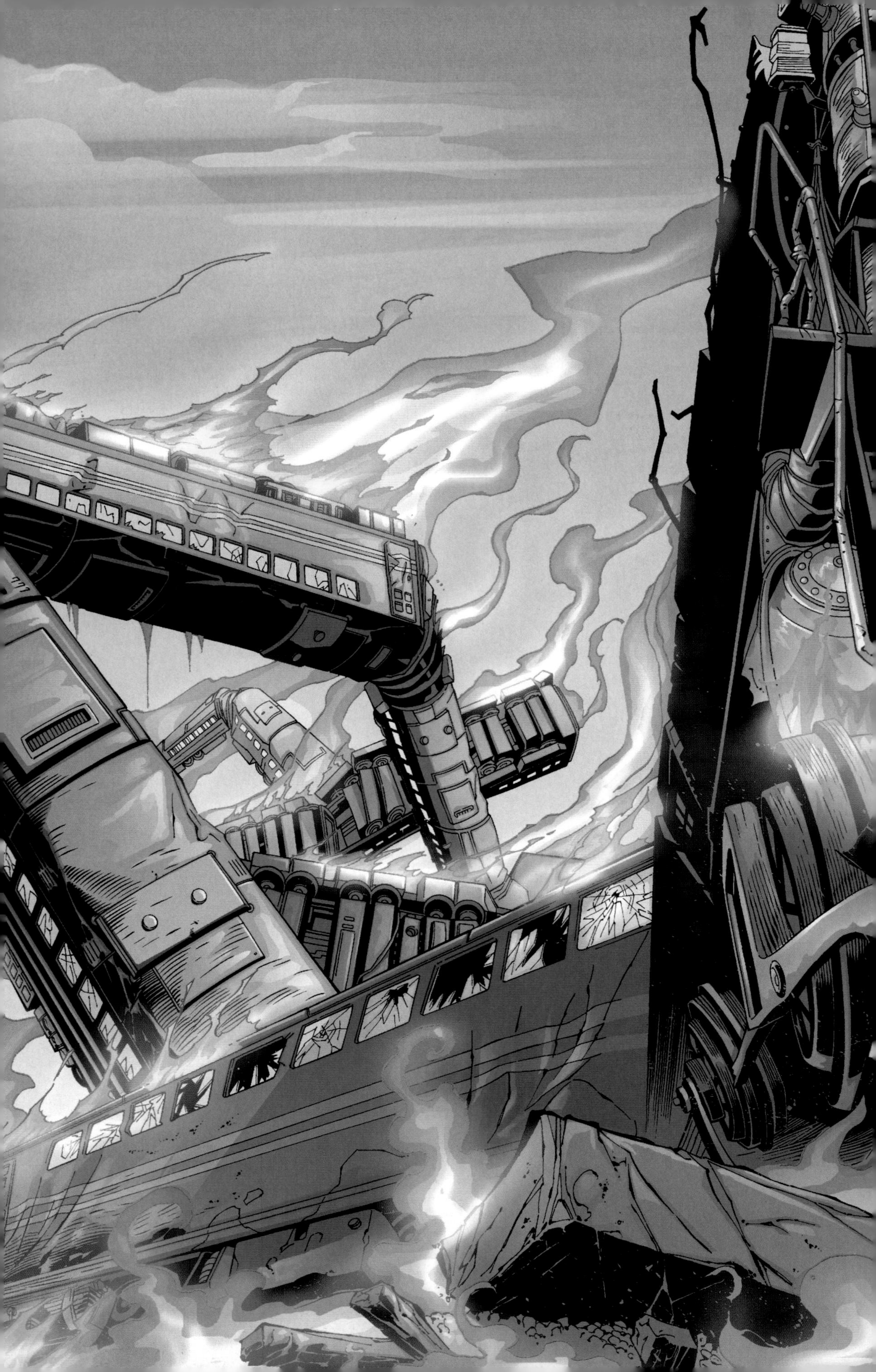

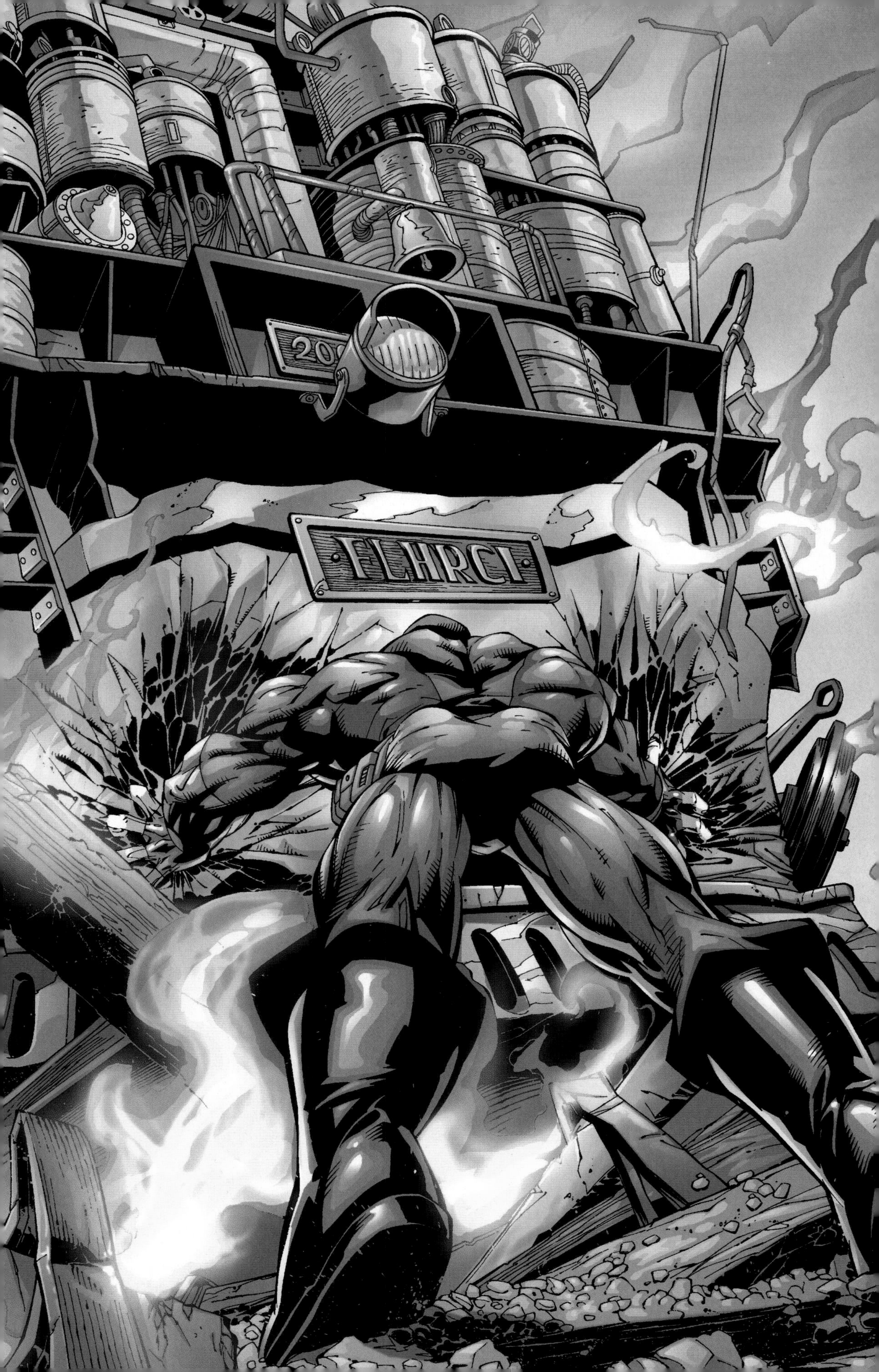
FLHRCI

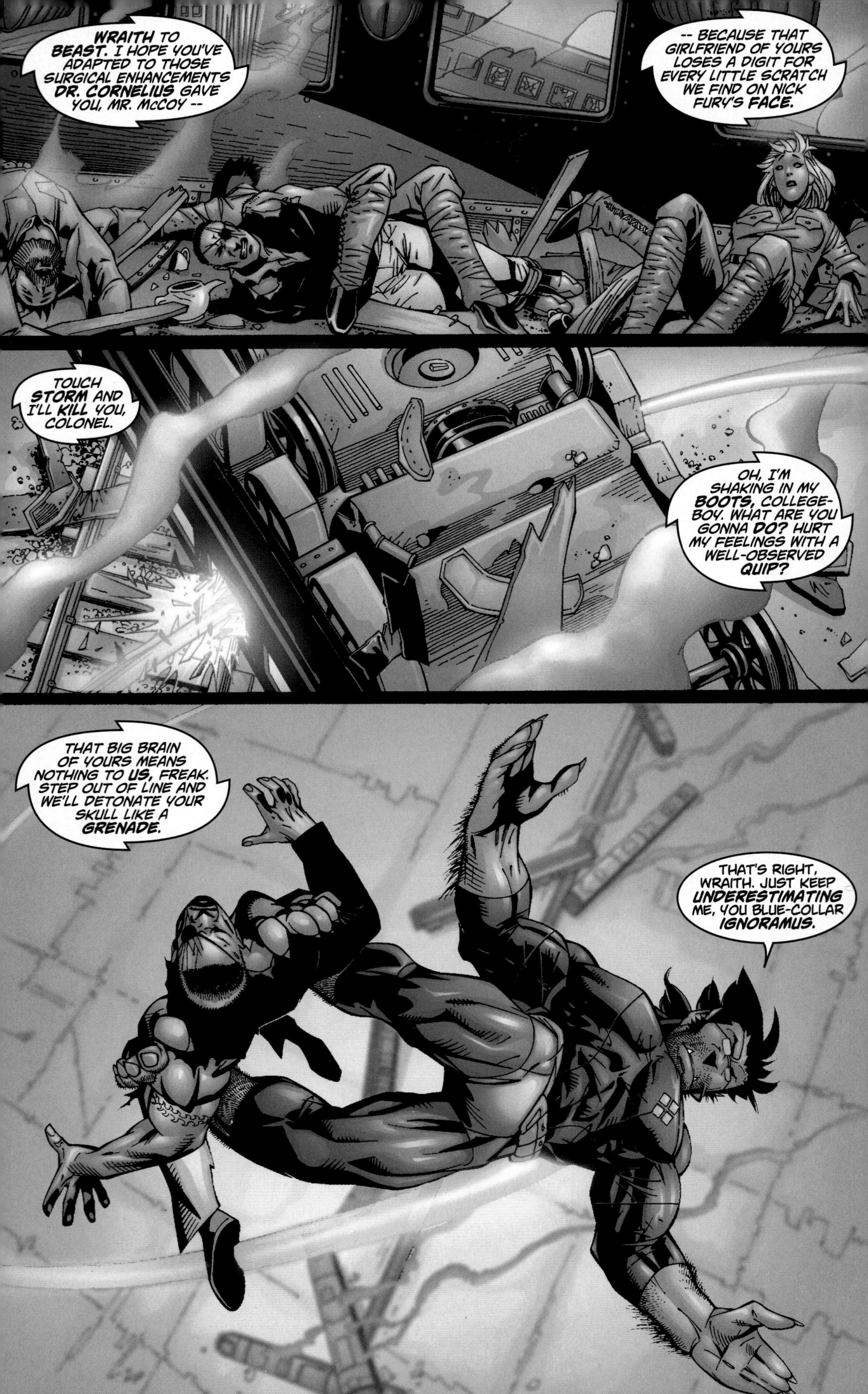
WRAITH TO BEAST. I HOPE YOU'VE ADAPTED TO THOSE SURGICAL ENHANCEMENTS DR. CORNELIUS GAVE YOU, MR. McCOY --
-- BECAUSE THAT GIRLFRIEND OF YOURS LOSES A DIGIT FOR EVERY LITTLE SCRATCH WE FIND ON NICK FURY'S FACE.
TOUCH STORM AND I'LL KILL YOU, COLONEL.
OH, I'M SHAKING IN MY BOOTS, COLLEGE-BOY. WHAT ARE YOU GONNA DO? HURT MY FEELINGS WITH A WELL-OBSERVED QUIP?
THAT BIG BRAIN OF YOURS MEANS NOTHING TO US, FREAK. STEP OUT OF LINE AND WE'LL DETONATE YOUR SKULL LIKE A GRENADE.
THAT'S RIGHT, WRAITH. JUST KEEP UNDERESTIMATING ME, YOU BLUE-COLLAR IGNORAMUS.

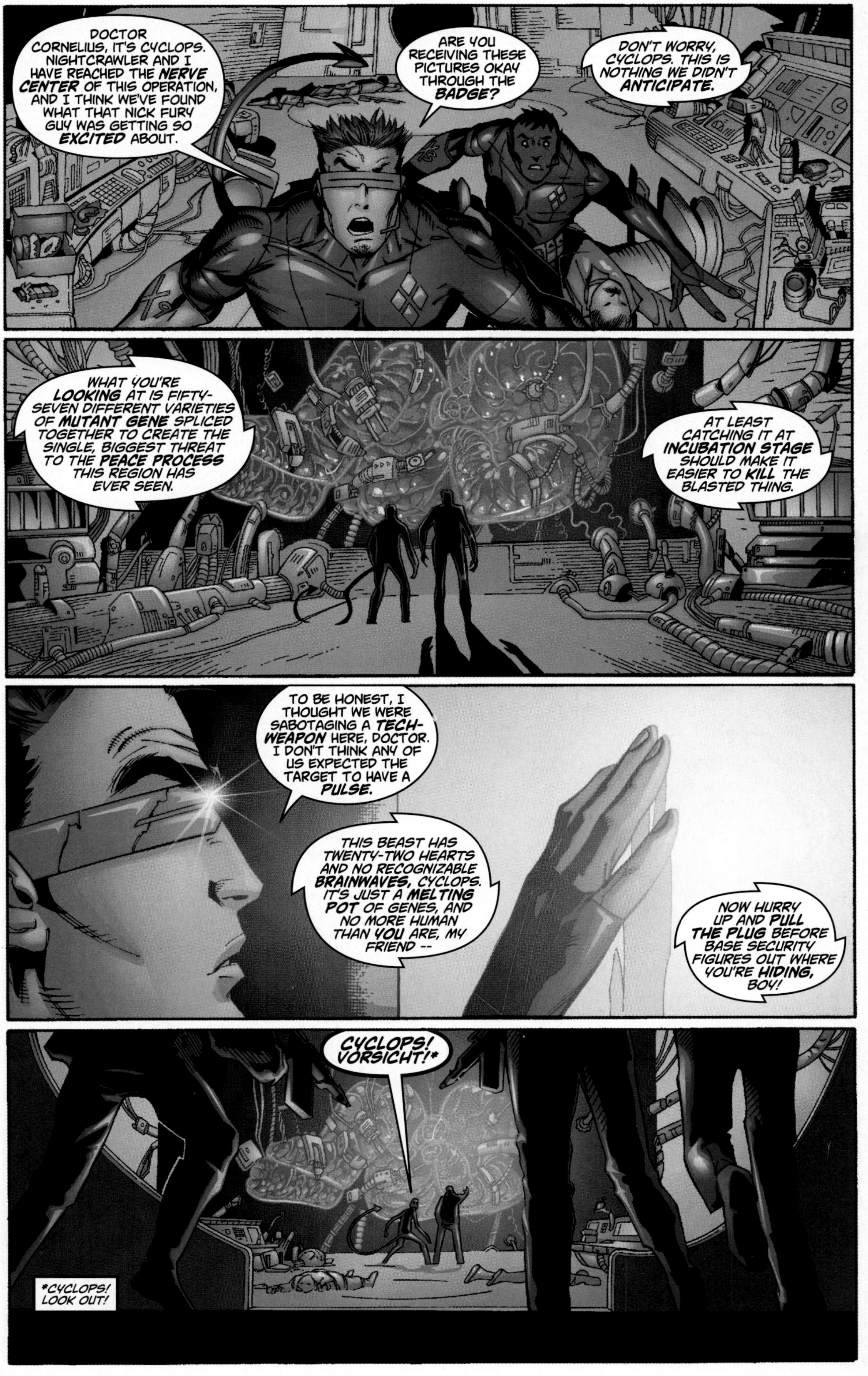
DOCTOR CORNELIUS, IT'S CYCLOPS. NIGHTCRAWLER AND I HAVE REACHED THE NERVE CENTER OF THIS OPERATION, AND I THINK WE'VE FOUND WHAT THAT NICK FURY GUY WAS GETTING SO EXCITED ABOUT.
ARE YOU RECEIVING THESE PICTURES OKAY THROUGH THE BADGE?
DON'T WORRY, CYCLOPS. THIS IS NOTHING WE DIDN'T ANTICIPATE.
WHAT YOU'RE LOOKING AT IS FIFTY-SEVEN DIFFERENT VARIETIES OF MUTANT GENE SPLICED TOGETHER TO CREATE THE SINGLE, BIGGEST THREAT TO THE PEACE PROCESS THIS REGION HAS EVER SEEN.
AT LEAST CATCHING IT AT INCUBATION STAGE SHOULD MAKE IT EASIER TO KILL THE BLASTED THING.
TO BE HONEST, I THOUGHT WE WERE SABOTAGING A TECH-WEAPON HERE, DOCTOR. I DON'T THINK ANY OF US EXPECTED THE TARGET TO HAVE A PULSE.
THIS BEAST HAS TWENTY-TWO HEARTS AND NO RECOGNIZABLE BRAINWAVES, CYCLOPS. IT'S JUST A MELTING POT OF GENES, AND NO MORE HUMAN THAN YOU ARE, MY FRIEND --
NOW HURRY UP AND PULL THE PLUG BEFORE BASE SECURITY FIGURES OUT WHERE YOU'RE HIDING, BOY!
CYCLOPS! VORSICHT!*
*CYCLOPS! LOOK OUT!

WHAT?
OH MY GOD!
WHAT ARE YOU WAITING FOR, NIGHTCRAWLER? GET US OUT OF HERE, MAN!
DRUEK AUF DEN ASLOESER! DRUEK ES!*
*HIT THE DETONATOR, YOU IDIOT! HIT IT!

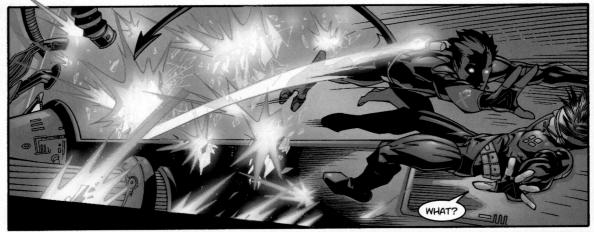

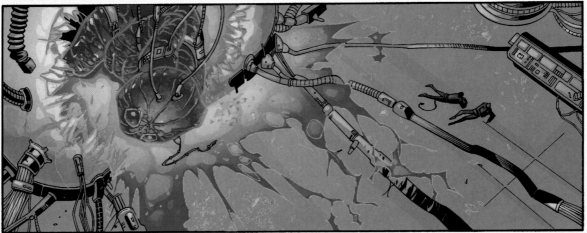

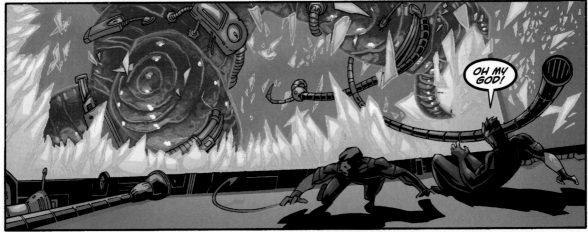

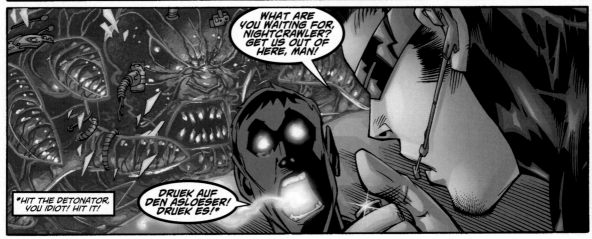

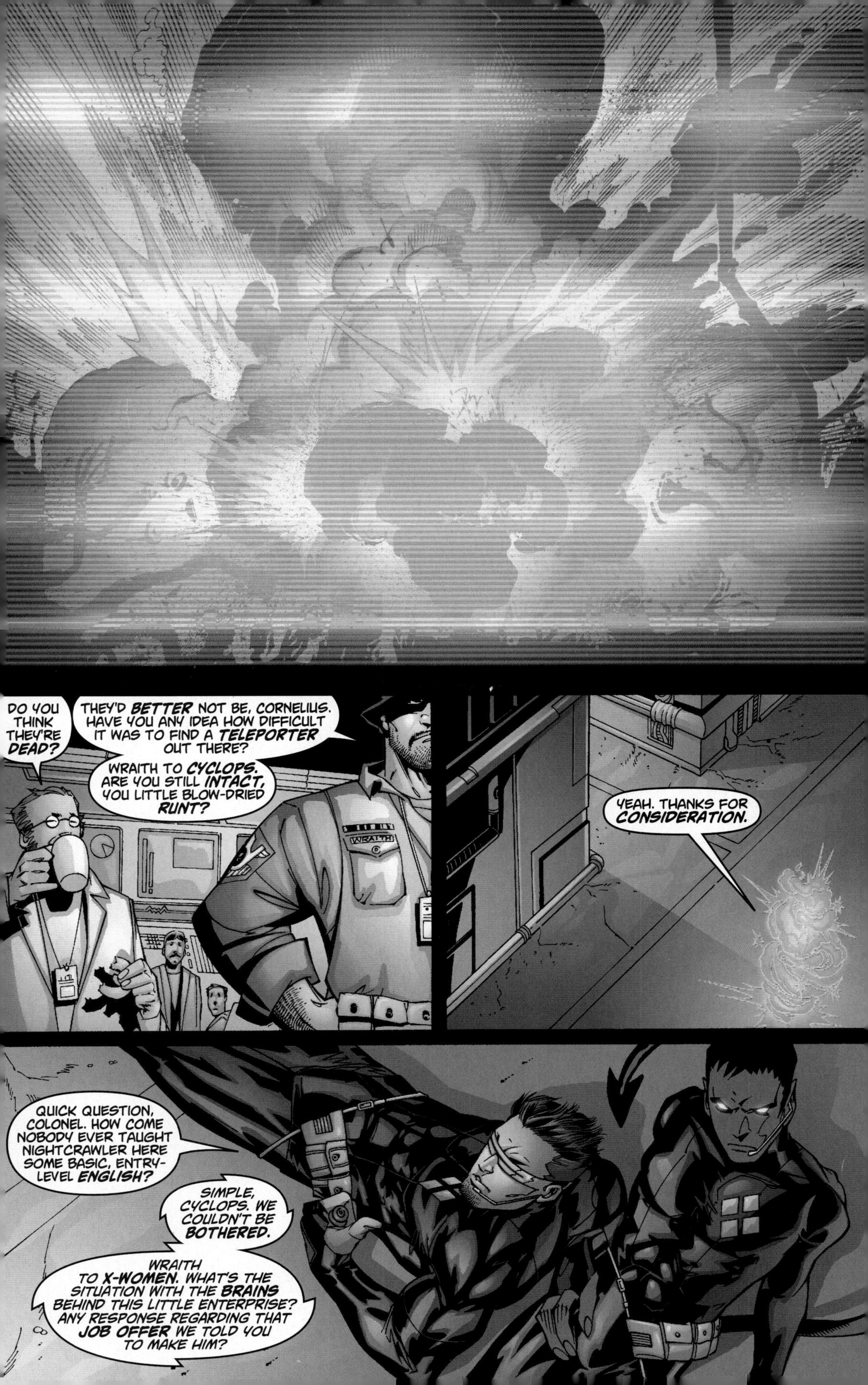
DO YOU THINK THEY'RE DEAD?
THEY'D BETTER NOT BE, CORNELIUS. HAVE YOU ANY IDEA HOW DIFFICULT IT WAS TO FIND A TELEPORTER OUT THERE?
WRAITH TO CYCLOPS. ARE YOU STILL INTACT, YOU LITTLE BLOW-DRIED RUNT?
WRAITH
YEAH. THANKS FOR CONSIDERATION.
QUICK QUESTION, COLONEL. HOW COME NOBODY EVER TAUGHT NIGHTCRAWLER HERE SOME BASIC, ENTRY-LEVEL ENGLISH?
SIMPLE, CYCLOPS. WE COULDN'T BE BOTHERED.
WRAITH TO X-WOMEN. WHAT'S THE SITUATION WITH THE BRAINS BEHIND THIS LITTLE ENTERPRISE? ANY RESPONSE REGARDING THAT JOB OFFER WE TOLD YOU TO MAKE HIM?

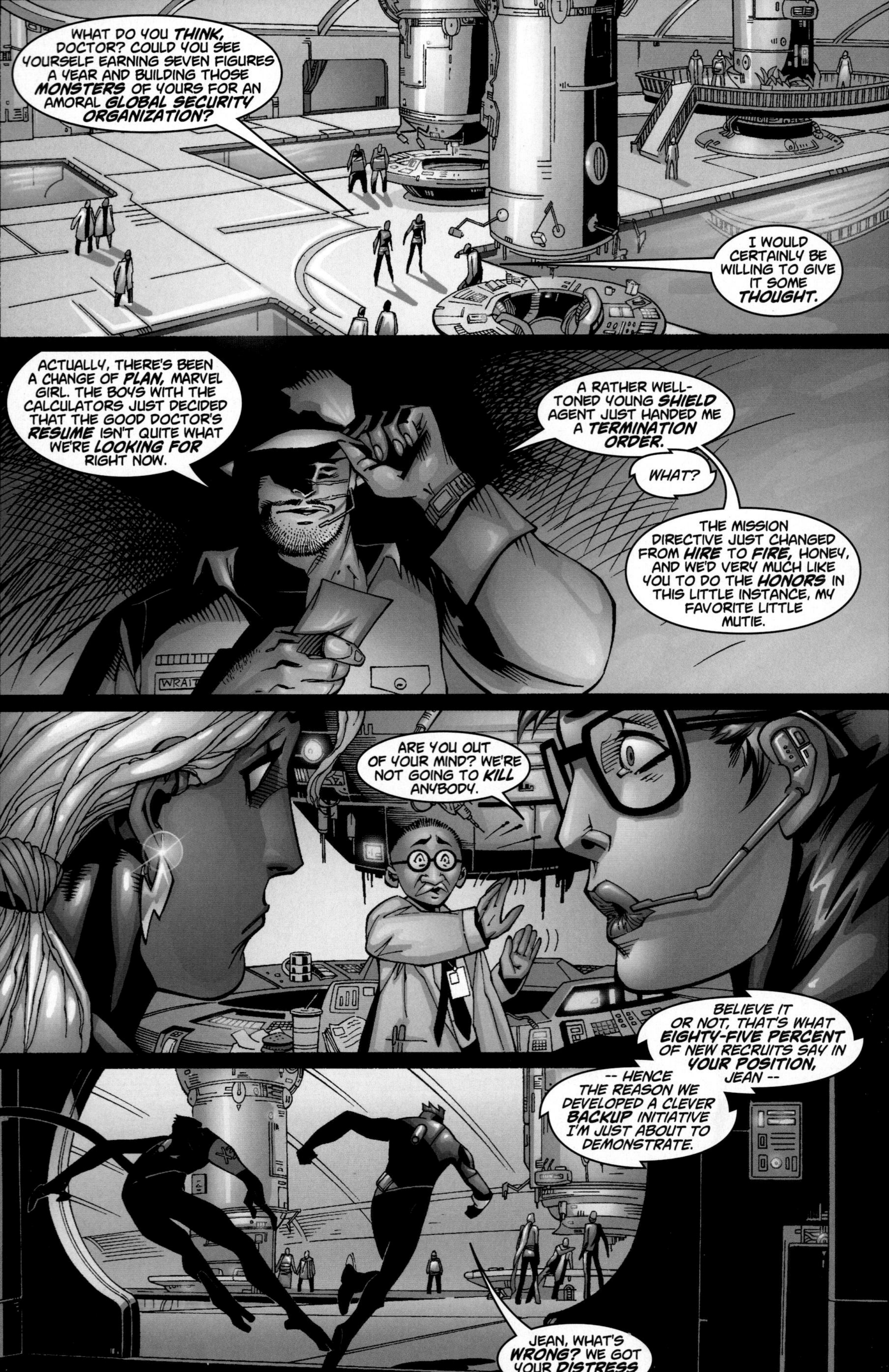
WHAT DO YOU THINK, DOCTOR? COULD YOU SEE YOURSELF EARNING SEVEN FIGURES A YEAR AND BUILDING THOSE MONSTERS OF YOURS FOR AN AMORAL GLOBAL SECURITY ORGANIZATION?
I WOULD CERTAINLY BE WILLING TO GIVE IT SOME THOUGHT.
ACTUALLY, THERE'S BEEN A CHANGE OF PLAN, MARVEL GIRL. THE BOYS WITH THE CALCULATORS JUST DECIDED THAT THE GOOD DOCTOR'S RESUME ISN'T QUITE WHAT WE'RE LOOKING FOR RIGHT NOW.
A RATHER WELL-TONED YOUNG SHIELD AGENT JUST HANDED ME A TERMINATION ORDER.
WHAT?
THE MISSION DIRECTIVE JUST CHANGED FROM HIRE TO FIRE, HONEY, AND WE'D VERY MUCH LIKE YOU TO DO THE HONORS IN THIS LITTLE INSTANCE, MY FAVORITE LITTLE MUTIE.
WRAIT
ARE YOU OUT OF YOUR MIND? WE'RE NOT GOING TO KILL ANYBODY.
BELIEVE IT OR NOT, THAT'S WHAT EIGHTY-FIVE PERCENT OF NEW RECRUITS SAY IN YOUR POSITION, JEAN --
-- HENCE THE REASON WE DEVELOPED A CLEVER BACKUP INITIATIVE I'M JUST ABOUT TO DEMONSTRATE.
JEAN, WHAT'S WRONG? WE GOT YOUR DISTRESS

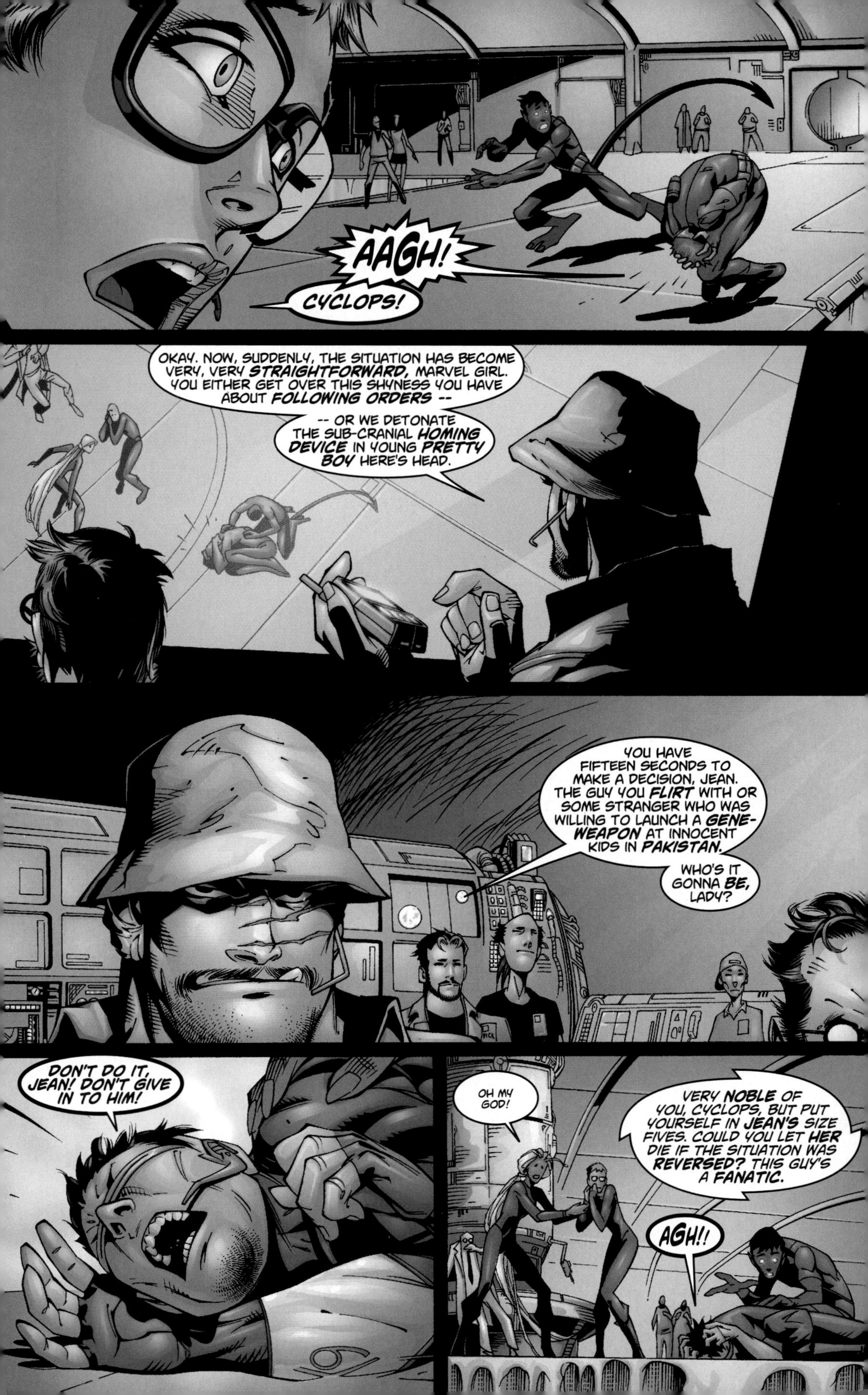
AAGH!
CYCLOPS!
OKAY. NOW, SUDDENLY, THE SITUATION HAS BECOME VERY, VERY STRAIGHTFORWARD, MARVEL GIRL. YOU EITHER GET OVER THIS SHYNESS YOU HAVE ABOUT FOLLOWING ORDERS --
-- OR WE DETONATE THE SUB-CRANIAL HOMING DEVICE IN YOUNG PRETTY BOY HERE'S HEAD.
YOU HAVE FIFTEEN SECONDS TO MAKE A DECISION, JEAN. THE GUY YOU FLIRT WITH OR SOME STRANGER WHO WAS WILLING TO LAUNCH A GENE-WEAPON AT INNOCENT KIDS IN PAKISTAN.
WHO'S IT GONNA BE, LADY?
DON'T DO IT, JEAN! DON'T GIVE IN TO HIM!
OH MY GOD!
VERY NOBLE OF YOU, CYCLOPS, BUT PUT YOURSELF IN JEAN'S SIZE FIVES. COULD YOU LET HER DIE IF THE SITUATION WAS REVERSED? THIS GUY'S A FANATIC.
AGH!!

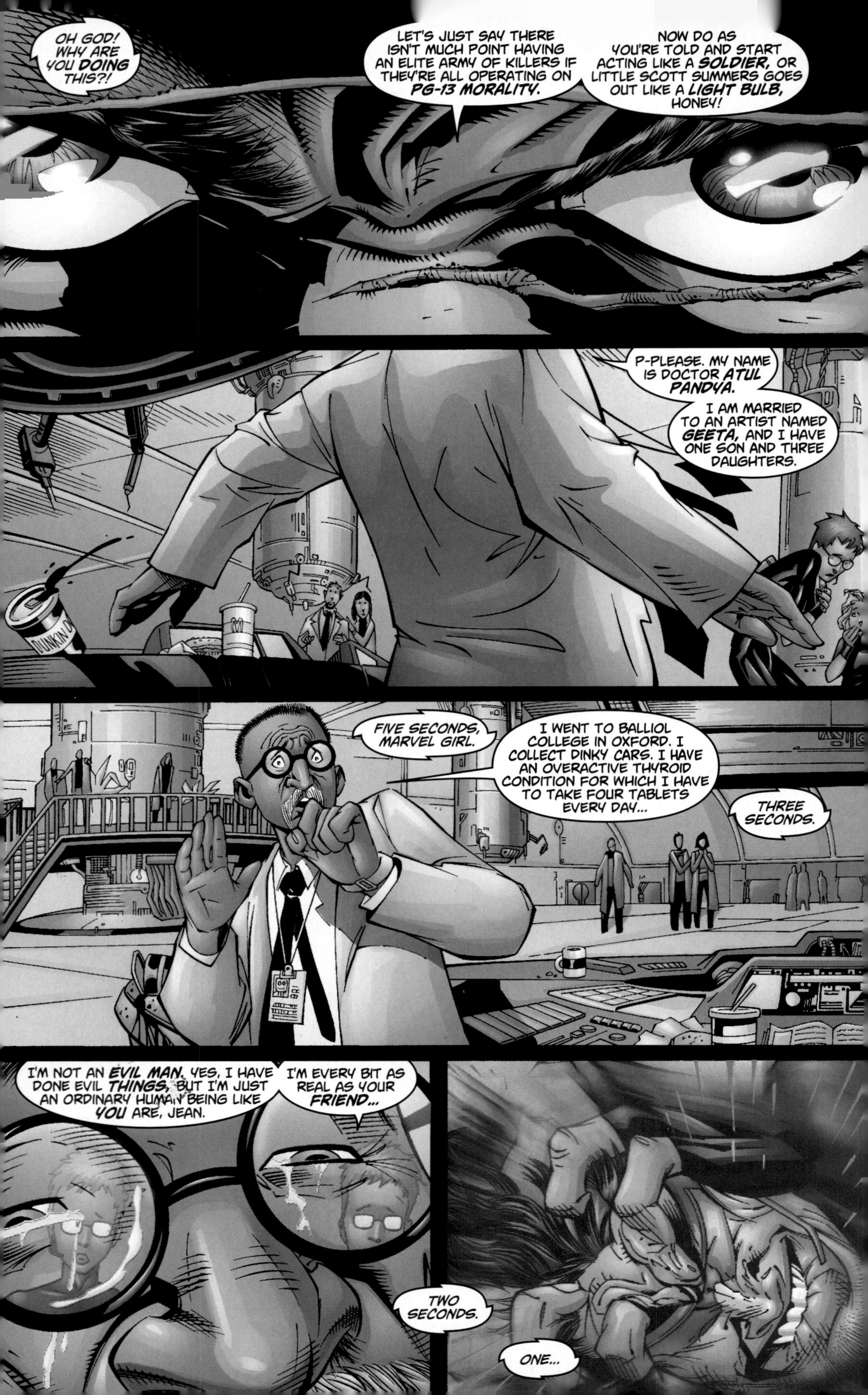

OH GOD! WHY ARE YOU DOING THIS?!
LET'S JUST SAY THERE ISN'T MUCH POINT HAVING AN ELITE ARMY OF KILLERS IF THEY'RE ALL OPERATING ON PG-13 MORALITY.
NOW DO AS YOU'RE TOLD AND START ACTING LIKE A SOLDIER, OR LITTLE SCOTT SUMMERS GOES OUT LIKE A LIGHT BULB, HONEY!
P-PLEASE. MY NAME IS DOCTOR ATUL PANDYA.
I AM MARRIED TO AN ARTIST NAMED GEETA, AND I HAVE ONE SON AND THREE DAUGHTERS.
FIVE SECONDS, MARVEL GIRL.
I WENT TO BALLIOL COLLEGE IN OXFORD. I COLLECT DINKY CARS. I HAVE AN OVERACTIVE THYROID CONDITION FOR WHICH I HAVE TO TAKE FOUR TABLETS EVERY DAY...
THREE SECONDS.
I'M NOT AN EVIL MAN. YES, I HAVE DONE EVIL THINGS, BUT I'M JUST AN ORDINARY HUMAN BEING LIKE YOU ARE, JEAN.
I'M EVERY BIT AS REAL AS YOUR FRIEND...
TWO SECONDS.
ONE...

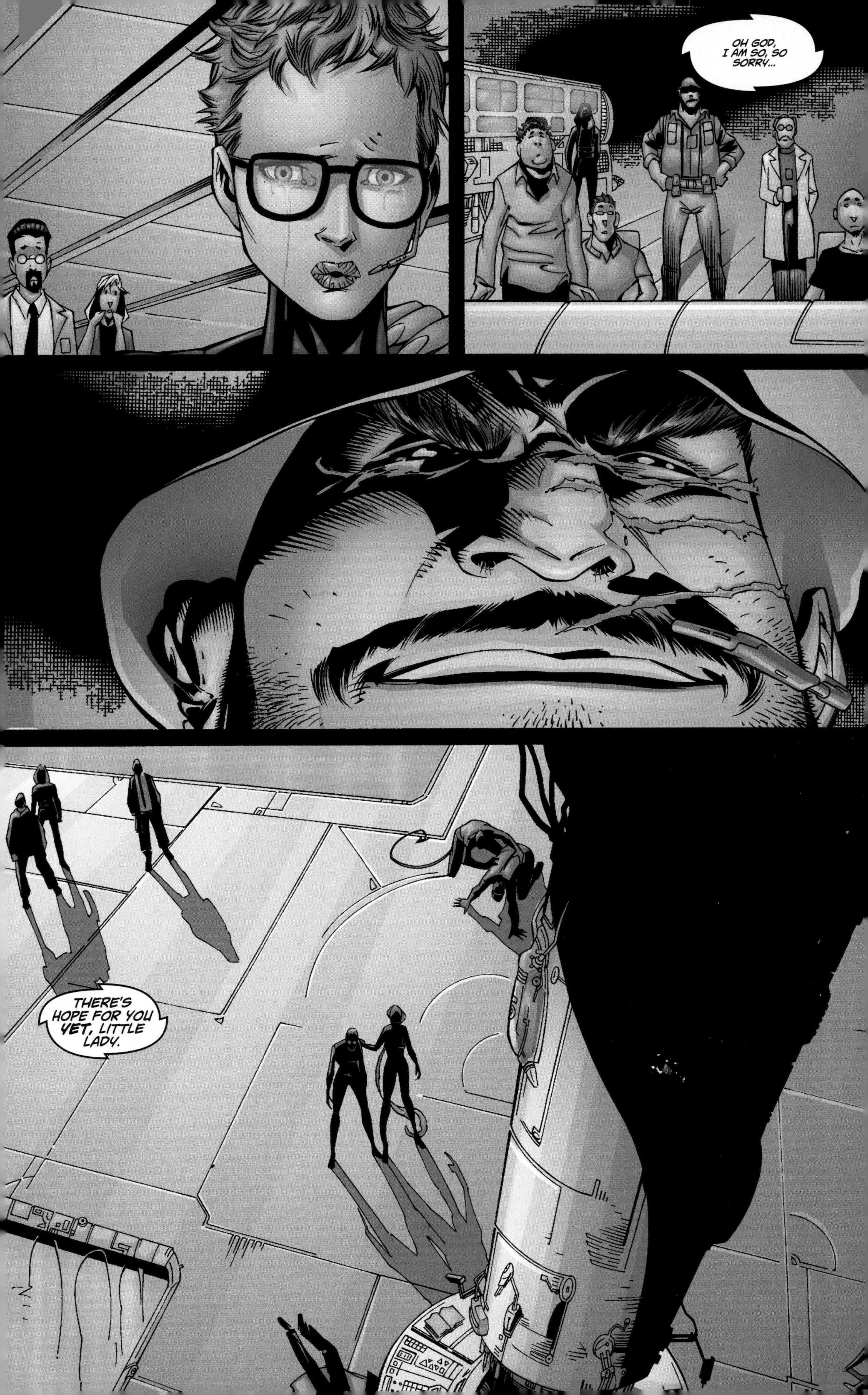
OH GOD, I AM SO, SO SORRY...
THERE'S HOPE FOR YOU YET, LITTLE LADY.

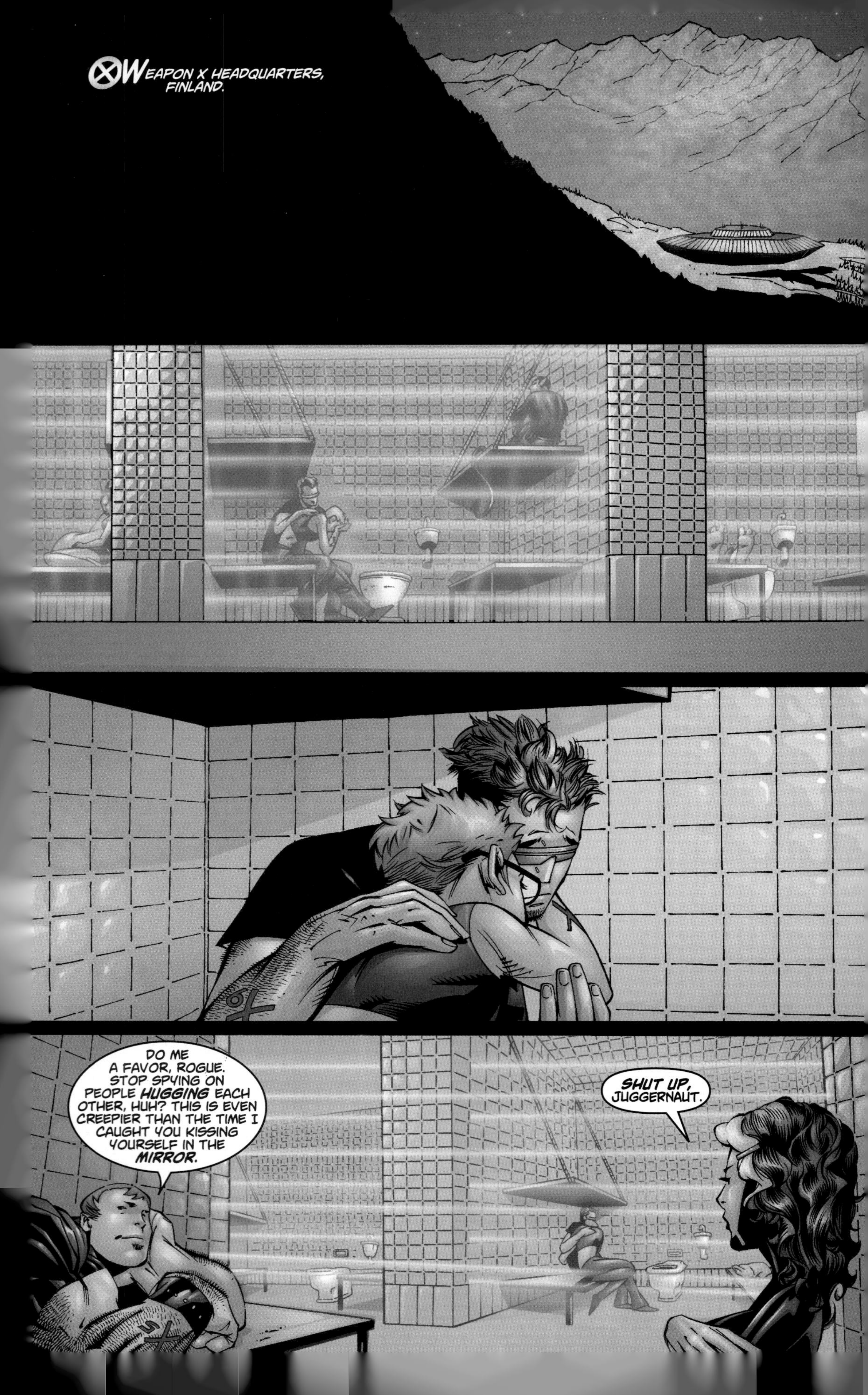
WEAPON X HEADQUARTERS, FINLAND.
DO ME A FAVOR, ROGUE. STOP SPYING ON PEOPLE HUGGING EACH OTHER, HUH? THIS IS EVEN CREEPIER THAN THE TIME I CAUGHT YOU KISSING YOURSELF IN THE MIRROR.
SHUT UP, JUGGERNAUT.

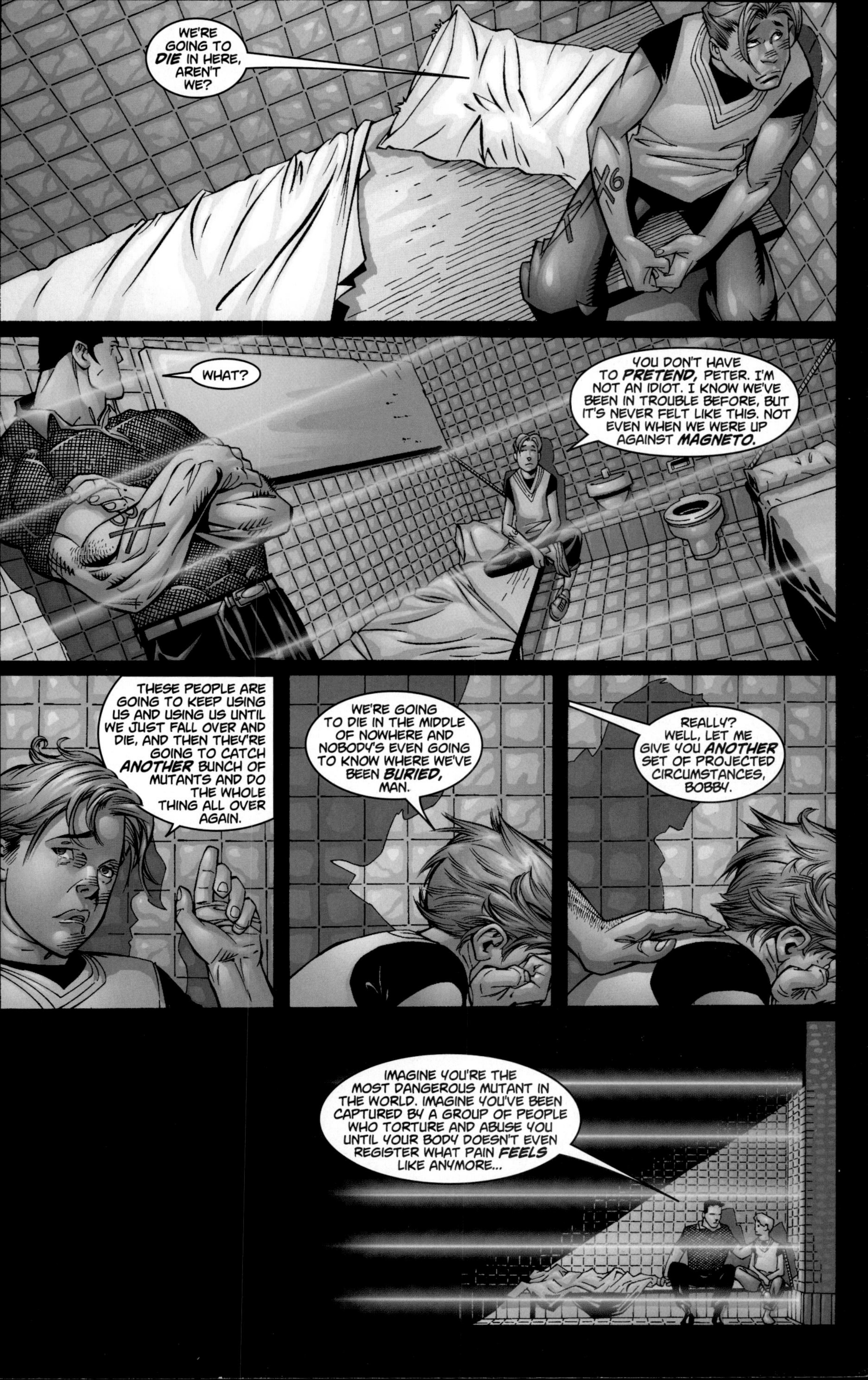
WE'RE GOING TO DIE IN HERE, AREN'T WE?
WHAT?
YOU DON'T HAVE TO PRETEND, PETER. I'M NOT AN IDIOT. I KNOW WE'VE BEEN IN TROUBLE BEFORE, BUT IT'S NEVER FELT LIKE THIS. NOT EVEN WHEN WE WERE UP AGAINST MAGNETO.
THESE PEOPLE ARE GOING TO KEEP USING US AND USING US UNTIL WE JUST FALL OVER AND DIE, AND THEN THEY'RE GOING TO CATCH ANOTHER BUNCH OF MUTANTS AND DO THE WHOLE THING ALL OVER AGAIN.
WE'RE GOING TO DIE IN THE MIDDLE OF NOWHERE AND NOBODY'S EVEN GOING TO KNOW WHERE WE'VE BEEN BURIED, MAN.
REALLY? WELL, LET ME GIVE YOU ANOTHER SET OF PROJECTED CIRCUMSTANCES, BOBBY.
IMAGINE YOU'RE THE MOST DANGEROUS MUTANT IN THE WORLD. IMAGINE YOU'VE BEEN CAPTURED BY A GROUP OF PEOPLE WHO TORTURE AND ABUSE YOU UNTIL YOUR BODY DOESN'T EVEN REGISTER WHAT PAIN FEELS LIKE ANYMORE...

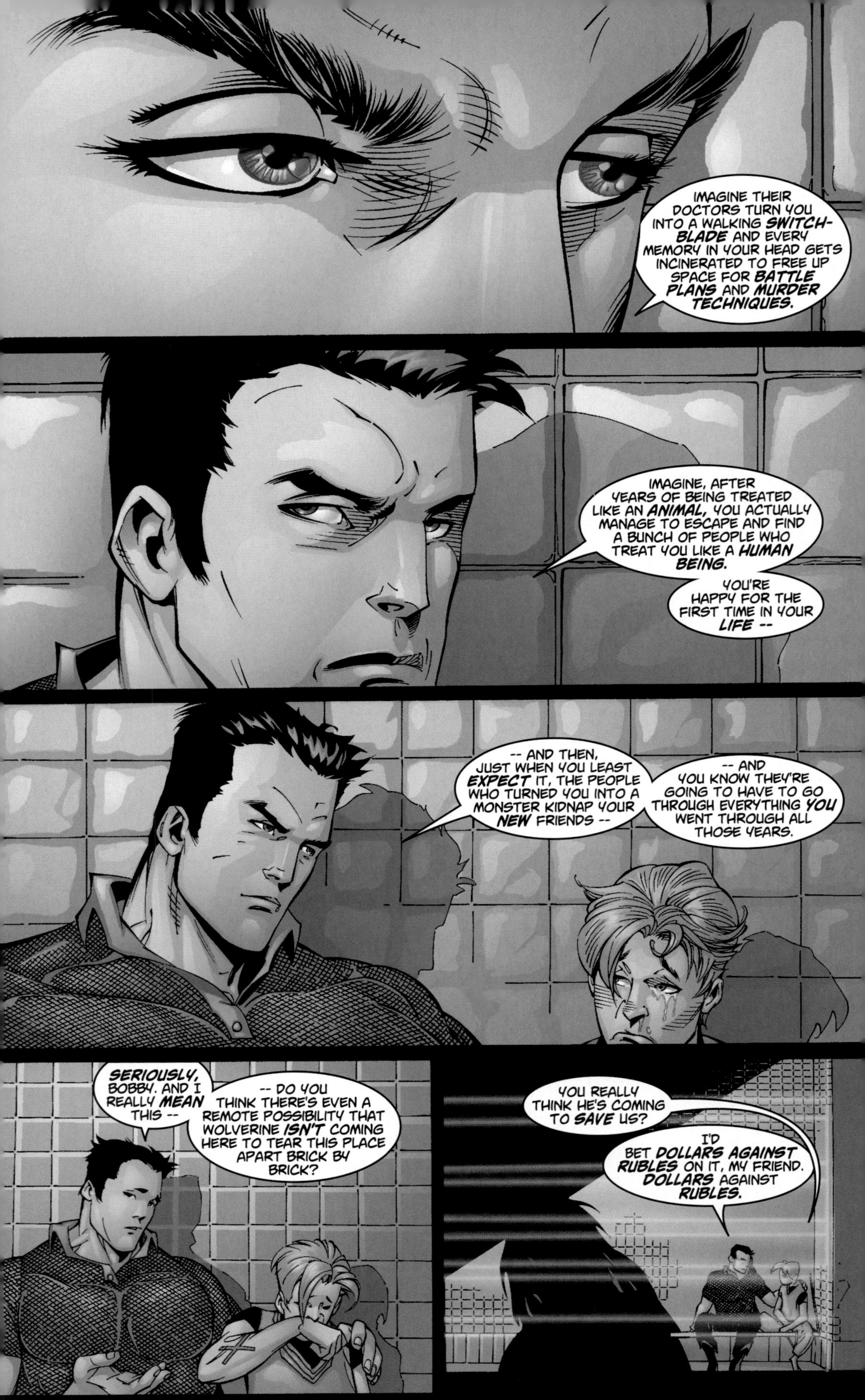
IMAGINE THEIR DOCTORS TURN YOU INTO A WALKING SWITCH-BLADE AND EVERY MEMORY IN YOUR HEAD GETS INCINERATED TO FREE UP SPACE FOR BATTLE PLANS AND MURDER TECHNIQUES.
IMAGINE, AFTER YEARS OF BEING TREATED LIKE AN ANIMAL, YOU ACTUALLY MANAGE TO ESCAPE AND FIND A BUNCH OF PEOPLE WHO TREAT YOU LIKE A HUMAN BEING.
YOU'RE HAPPY FOR THE FIRST TIME IN YOUR LIFE --
-- AND THEN, JUST WHEN YOU LEAST EXPECT IT, THE PEOPLE WHO TURNED YOU INTO A MONSTER KIDNAP YOUR NEW FRIENDS --
-- AND YOU KNOW THEY'RE GOING TO HAVE TO GO THROUGH EVERYTHING YOU WENT THROUGH ALL THOSE YEARS.
SERIOUSLY, BOBBY. AND I REALLY MEAN THIS --
-- DO YOU THINK THERE'S EVEN A REMOTE POSSIBILITY THAT WOLVERINE ISN'T COMING HERE TO TEAR THIS PLACE APART BRICK BY BRICK?
YOU REALLY THINK HE'S COMING TO SAVE US?
I'D BET DOLLARS AGAINST RUBLES ON IT, MY FRIEND. DOLLARS AGAINST RUBLES.

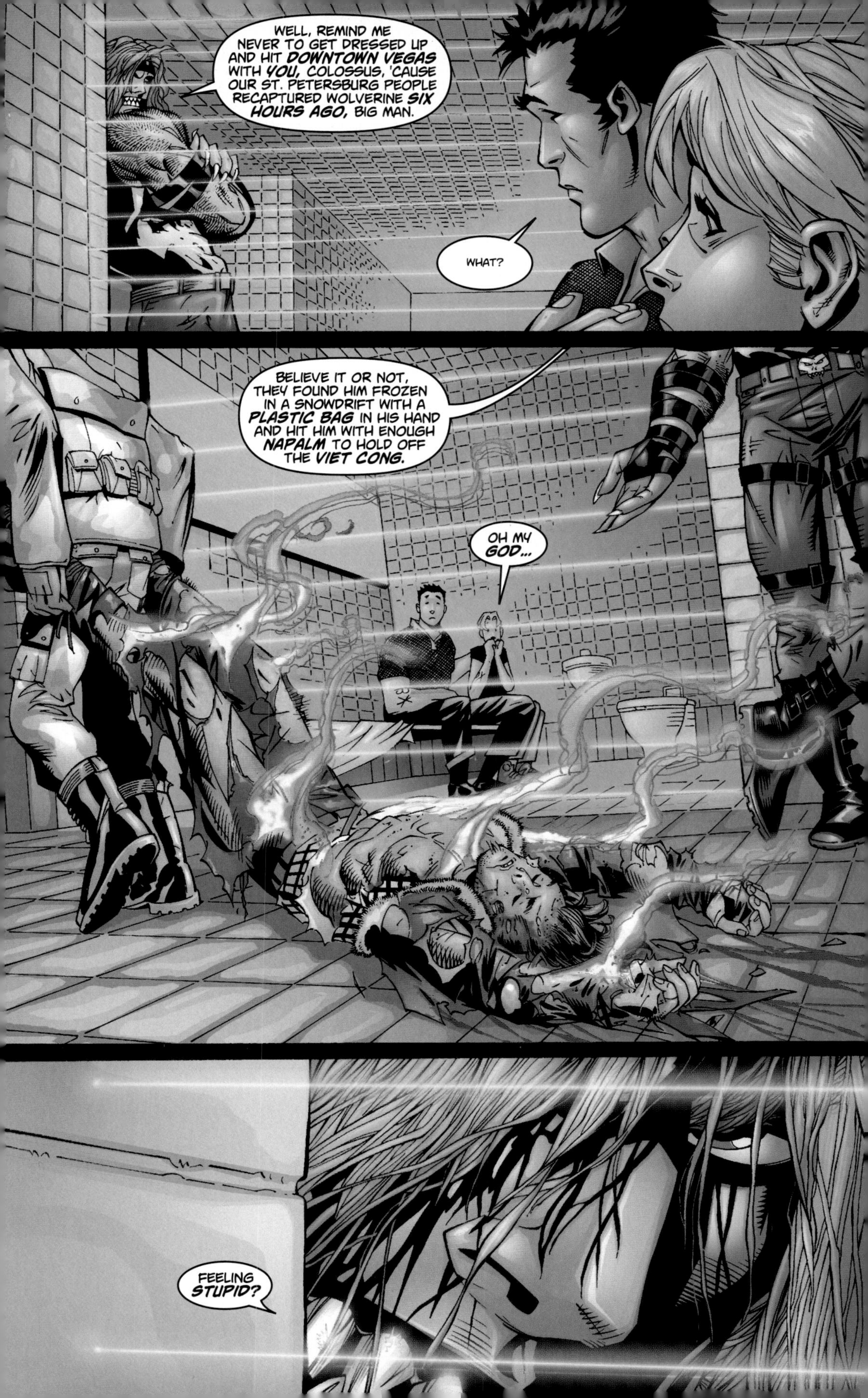
WELL, REMIND ME NEVER TO GET DRESSED UP AND HIT DOWNTOWN VEGAS WITH YOU, COLOSSUS, 'CAUSE OUR ST. PETERSBURG PEOPLE RECAPTURED WOLVERINE SIX HOURS AGO, BIG MAN.
WHAT?
BELIEVE IT OR NOT, THEY FOUND HIM FROZEN IN A SNOWDRIFT WITH A PLASTIC BAG IN HIS HAND AND HIT HIM WITH ENOUGH NAPALM TO HOLD OFF THE VIET CONG.
OH MY GOD...
FEELING STUPID?

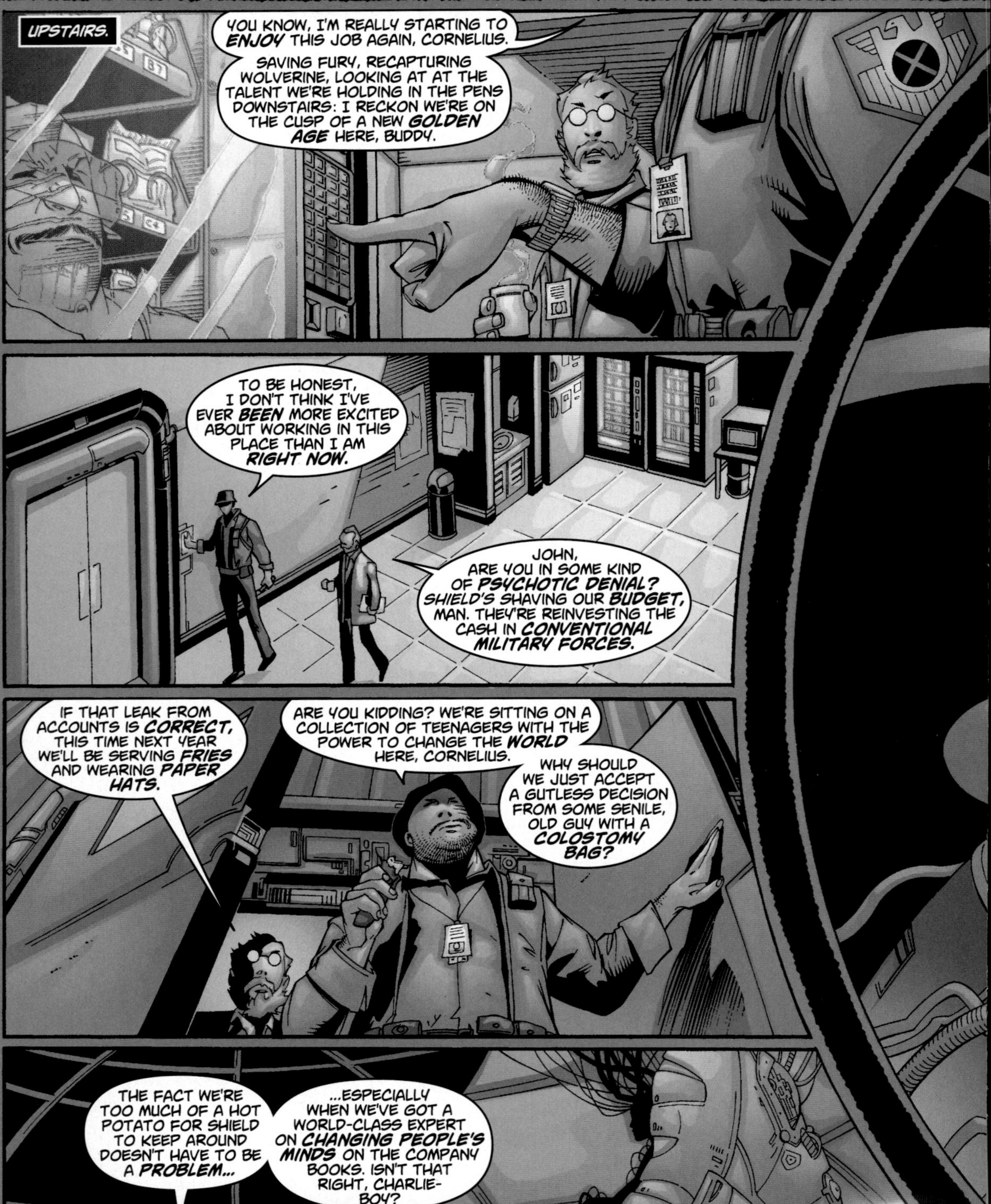
UPSTAIRS.
YOU KNOW, I'M REALLY STARTING TO ENJOY THIS JOB AGAIN, CORNELIUS.
SAVING FURY, RECAPTURING WOLVERINE, LOOKING AT AT THE TALENT WE'RE HOLDING IN THE PENS DOWNSTAIRS: I RECKON WE'RE ON THE CUSP OF A NEW GOLDEN AGE HERE, BUDDY.
TO BE HONEST, I DON'T THINK I'VE EVER BEEN MORE EXCITED ABOUT WORKING IN THIS PLACE THAN I AM RIGHT NOW.
JOHN, ARE YOU IN SOME KIND OF PSYCHOTIC DENIAL? SHIELD'S SHAVING OUR BUDGET, MAN. THEY'RE REINVESTING THE CASH IN CONVENTIONAL MILITARY FORCES.
IF THAT LEAK FROM ACCOUNTS IS CORRECT, THIS TIME NEXT YEAR WE'LL BE SERVING FRIES AND WEARING PAPER HATS.
ARE YOU KIDDING? WE'RE SITTING ON A COLLECTION OF TEENAGERS WITH THE POWER TO CHANGE THE WORLD HERE, CORNELIUS.
WHY SHOULD WE JUST ACCEPT A GUTLESS DECISION FROM SOME SENILE, OLD GUY WITH A COLOSTOMY BAG?
THE FACT WE'RE TOO MUCH OF A HOT POTATO FOR SHIELD TO KEEP AROUND DOESN'T HAVE TO BE A PROBLEM...
...ESPECIALLY WHEN WE'VE GOT A WORLD-CLASS EXPERT ON CHANGING PEOPLE'S MINDS ON THE COMPANY BOOKS. ISN'T THAT RIGHT, CHARLIE-BOY?

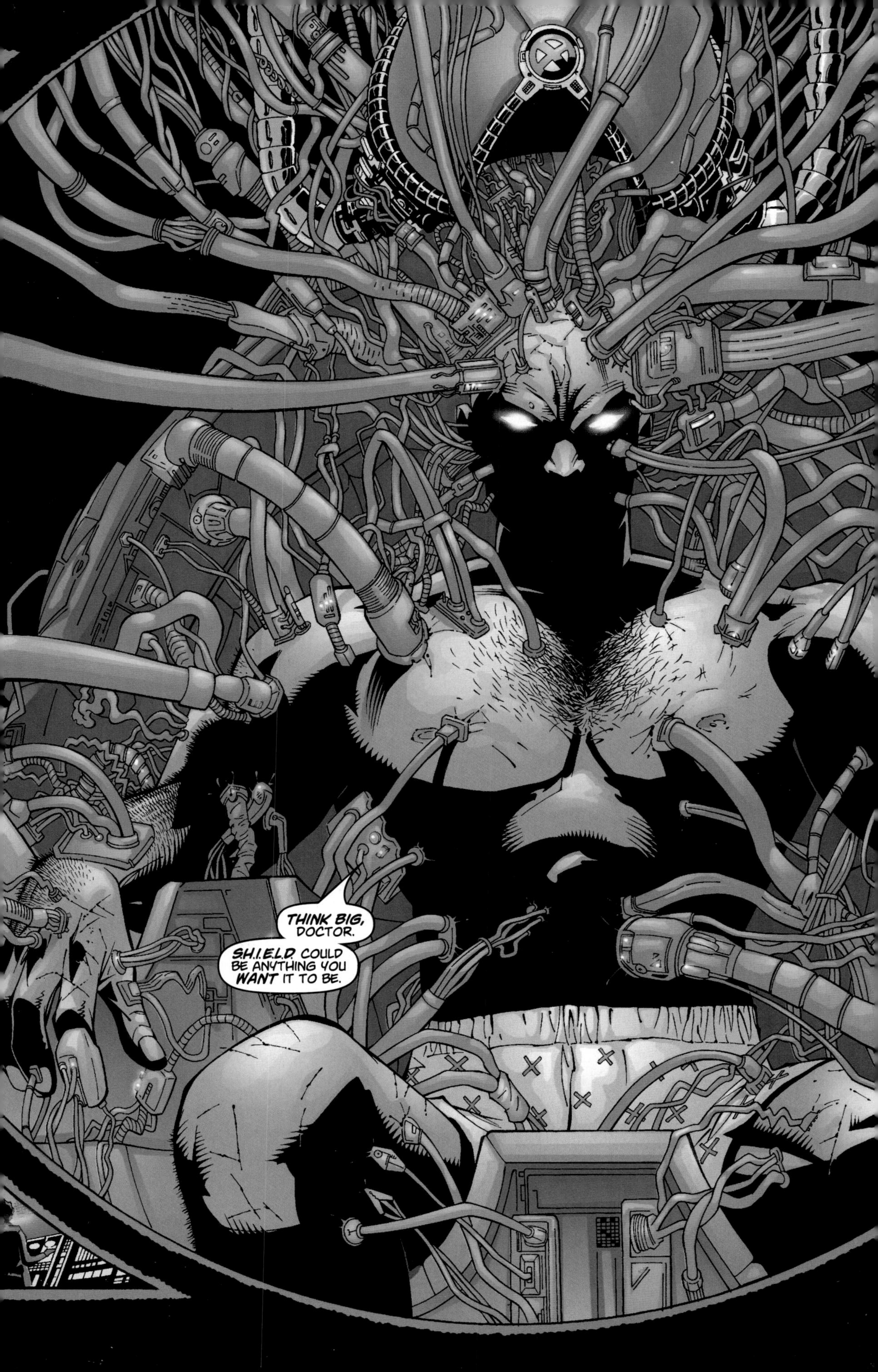
THINK BIG, DOCTOR.
S.H.I.E.L.D. COULD BE ANYTHING YOU WANT IT TO BE.

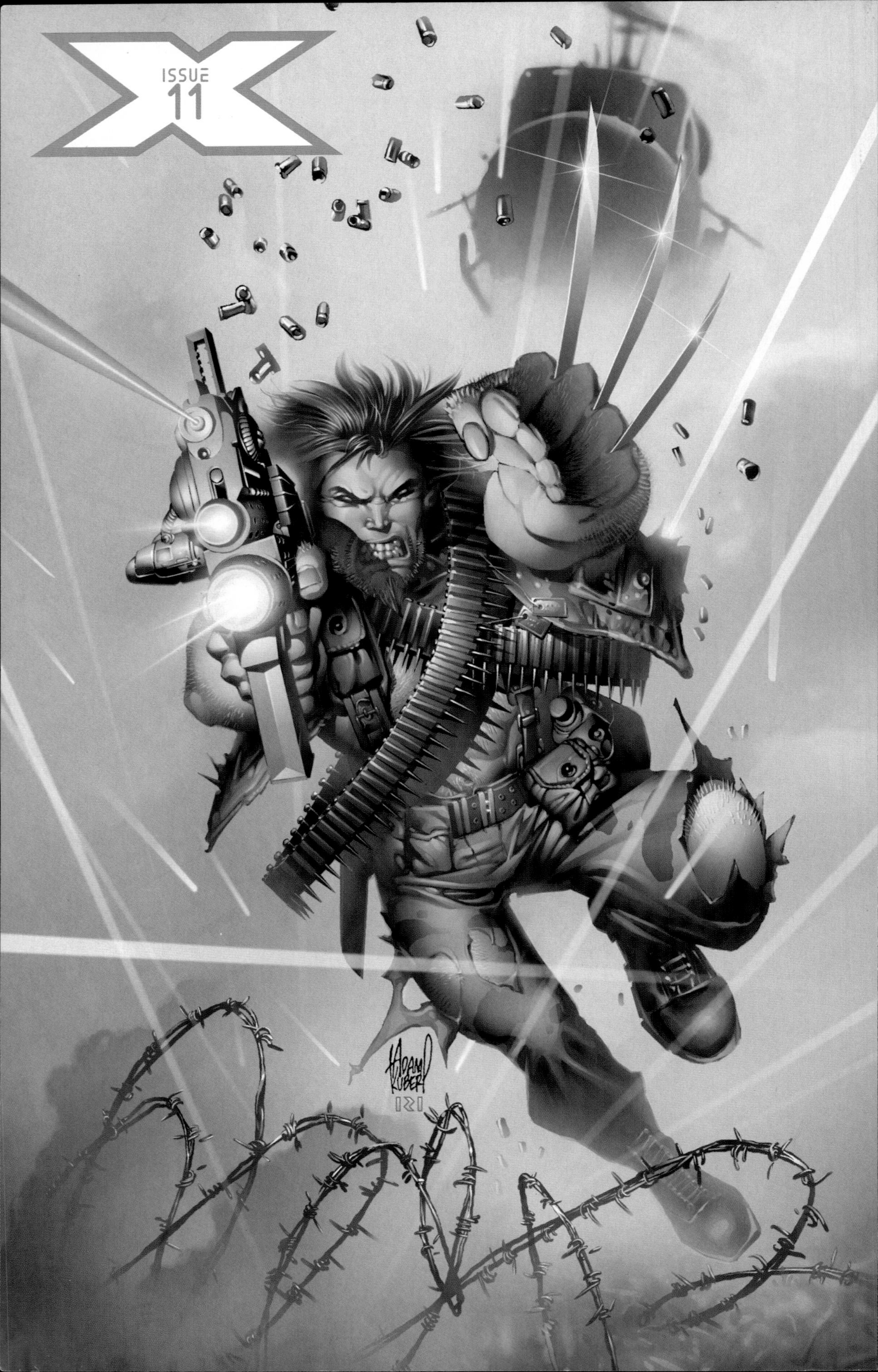
ISSUE
11

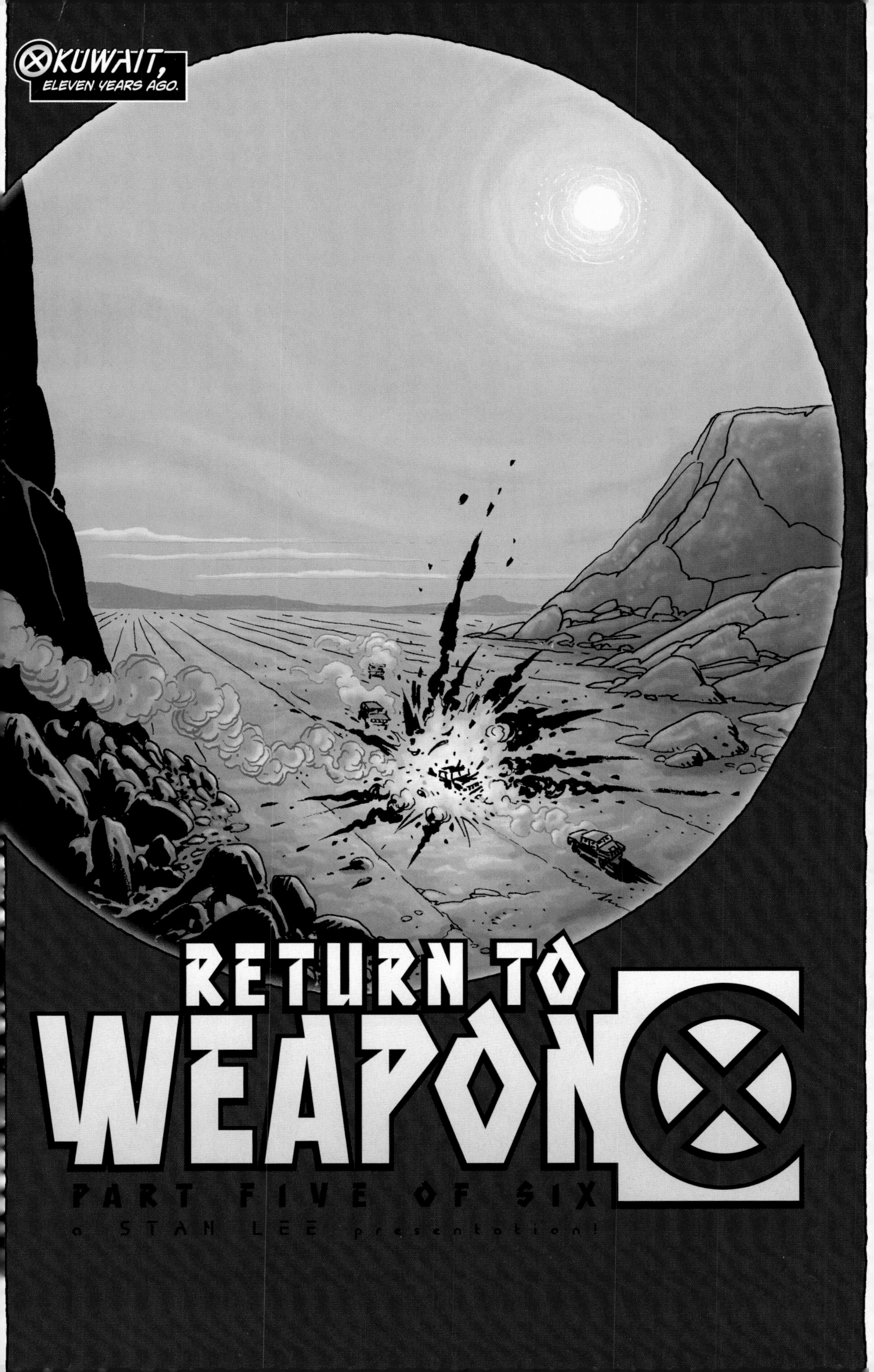
KUWAIT,
ELEVEN YEARS AGO.
RETURN TO
WEAPON X
PART FIVE OF SIX
a STAN LEE presentation!

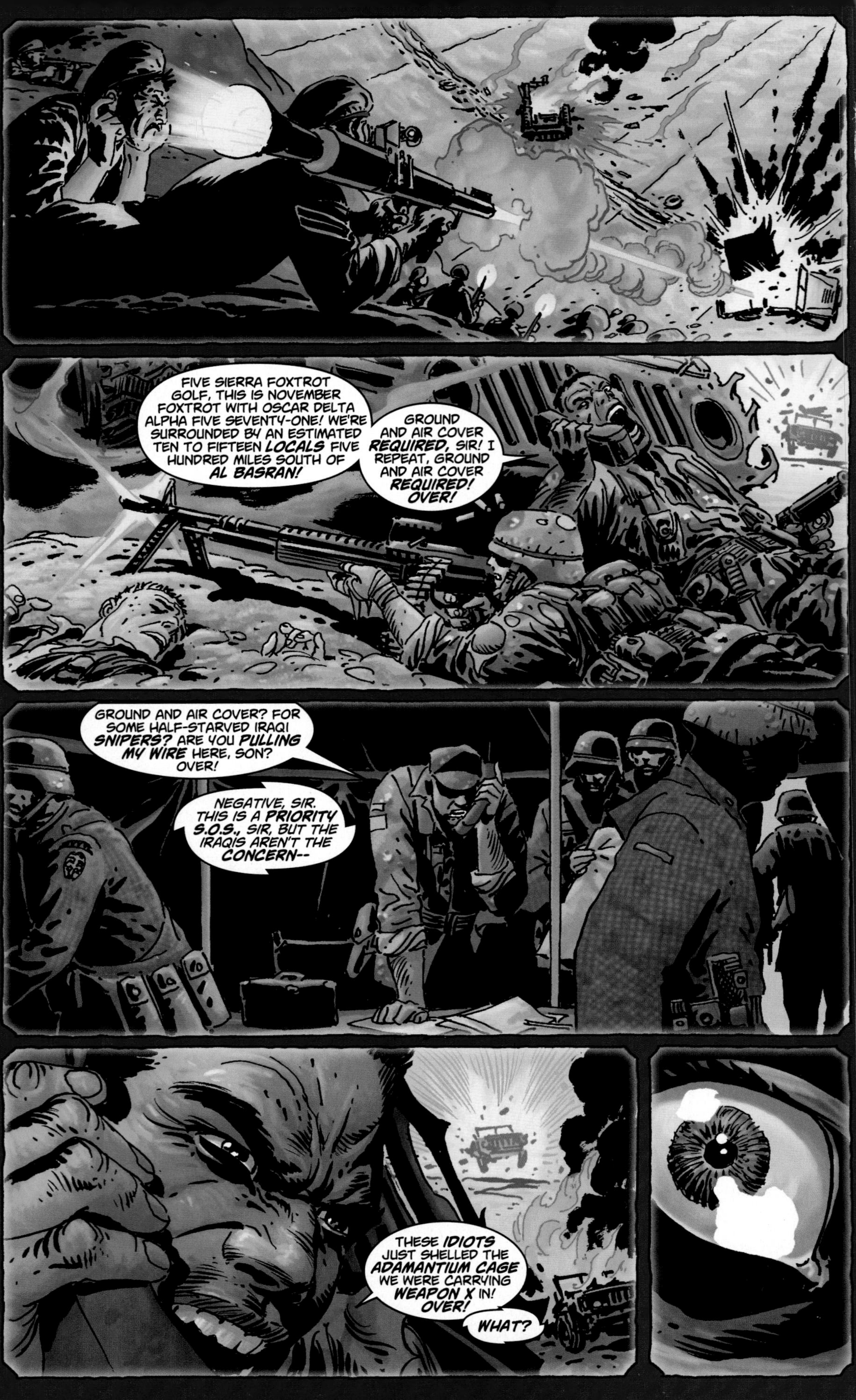
FIVE SIERRA FOXTROT GOLF, THIS IS NOVEMBER FOXTROT WITH OSCAR DELTA ALPHA FIVE SEVENTY-ONE! WE'RE SURROUNDED BY AN ESTIMATED TEN TO FIFTEEN LOCALS FIVE HUNDRED MILES SOUTH OF AL BASRAN!
GROUND AND AIR COVER REQUIRED, SIR! I REPEAT, GROUND AND AIR COVER REQUIRED! OVER!
GROUND AND AIR COVER? FOR SOME HALF-STARVED IRAQI SNIPERS? ARE YOU PULLING MY WIRE HERE, SON? OVER!
NEGATIVE, SIR. THIS IS A PRIORITY S.O.S., SIR, BUT THE IRAQIS AREN'T THE CONCERN--
THESE IDIOTS JUST SHELLED THE ADAMANTIUM CAGE WE WERE CARRYING WEAPON X IN! OVER!
WHAT?

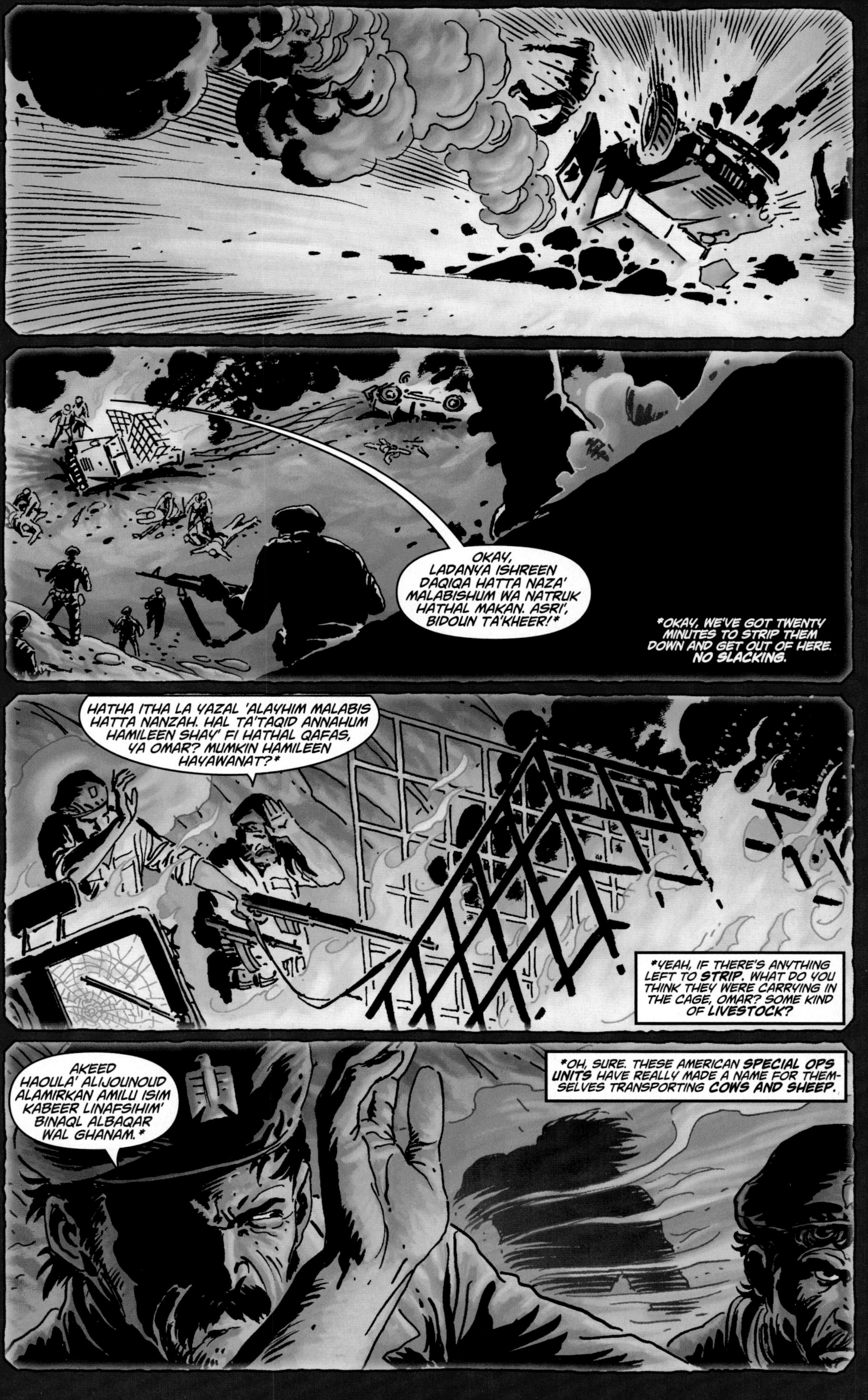
OKAY, LADANYA ISHREEN DAQIQA HATTA NAZA' MALABISHUM WA NATRUK HATHAL MAKAN. ASRI', BIDOUN TA'KHEER!*
*OKAY, WE'VE GOT TWENTY MINUTES TO STRIP THEM DOWN AND GET OUT OF HERE. NO SLACKING.
HATHA ITHA LA YAZAL 'ALAYHIM MALABIS HATTA NANZAH. HAL TA'TAQID ANNAHUM HAMILEEN SHAY' FI HATHAL QAFAS, YA OMAR? MUMKIN HAMILEEN HAYAWANAT?*
*YEAH, IF THERE'S ANYTHING LEFT TO STRIP. WHAT DO YOU THINK THEY WERE CARRYING IN THE CAGE, OMAR? SOME KIND OF LIVESTOCK?
AKEED HAOULA' ALIJOUNOUD ALAMIRKAN AMILU ISIM KABEER LINAFSIHIM' BINAQL ALBAQAR WAL GHANAM.*
*OH, SURE. THESE AMERICAN SPECIAL OPS UNITS HAVE REALLY MADE A NAME FOR THEMSELVES TRANSPORTING COWS AND SHEEP.

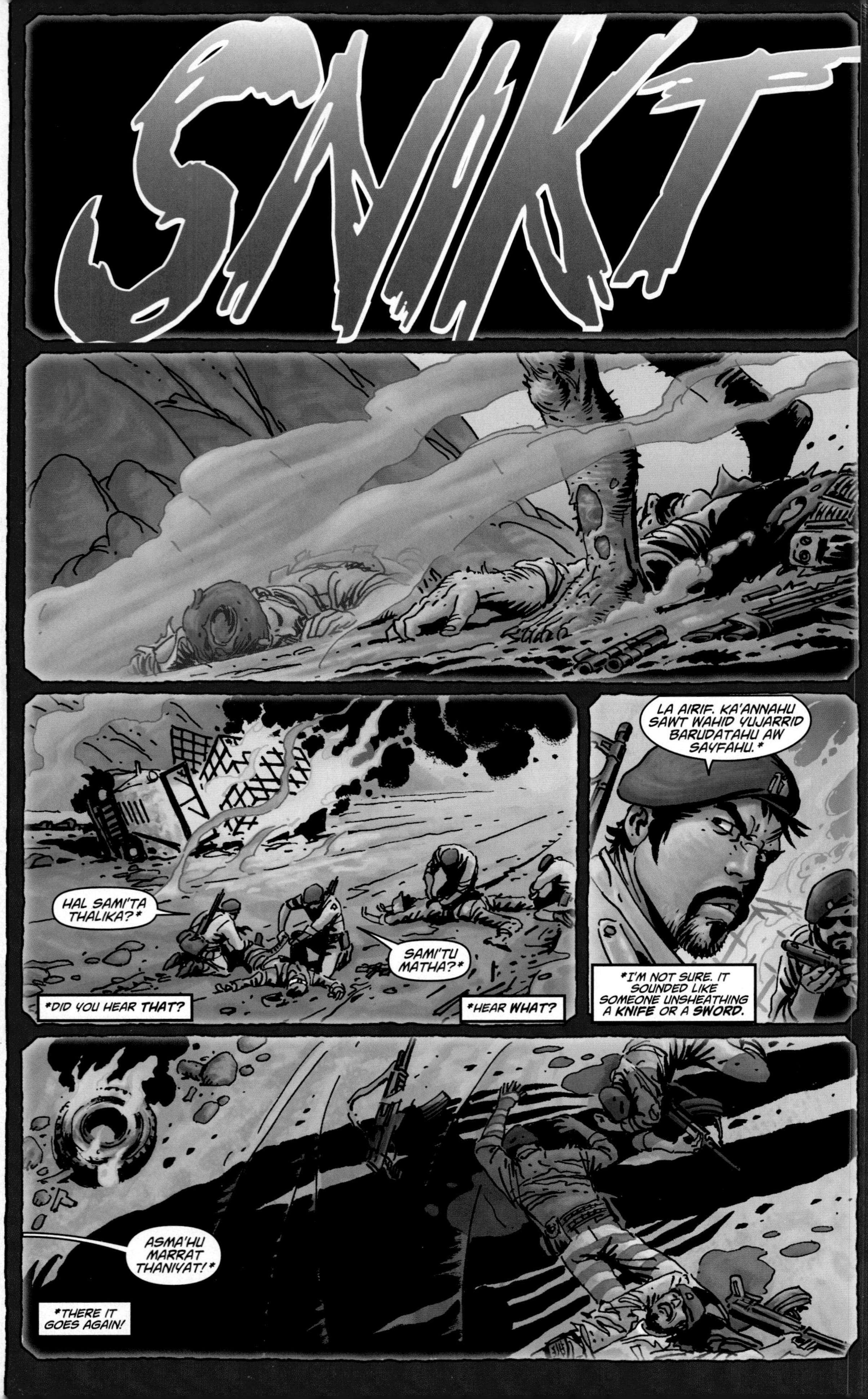
SNIKT
HAL SAMI'TA THALIKA?*
*DID YOU HEAR THAT?
SAMI'TU MATHA?*
*HEAR WHAT?
LA AIRIF. KA'ANNAHU SAWT WAHID YUJARRID BARUDATAHU AW SAYFAHU.*
*I'M NOT SURE. IT SOUNDED LIKE SOMEONE UNSHEATHING A KNIFE OR A SWORD.
ASMA'HU MARRAT THANIYAT!*
*THERE IT GOES AGAIN!

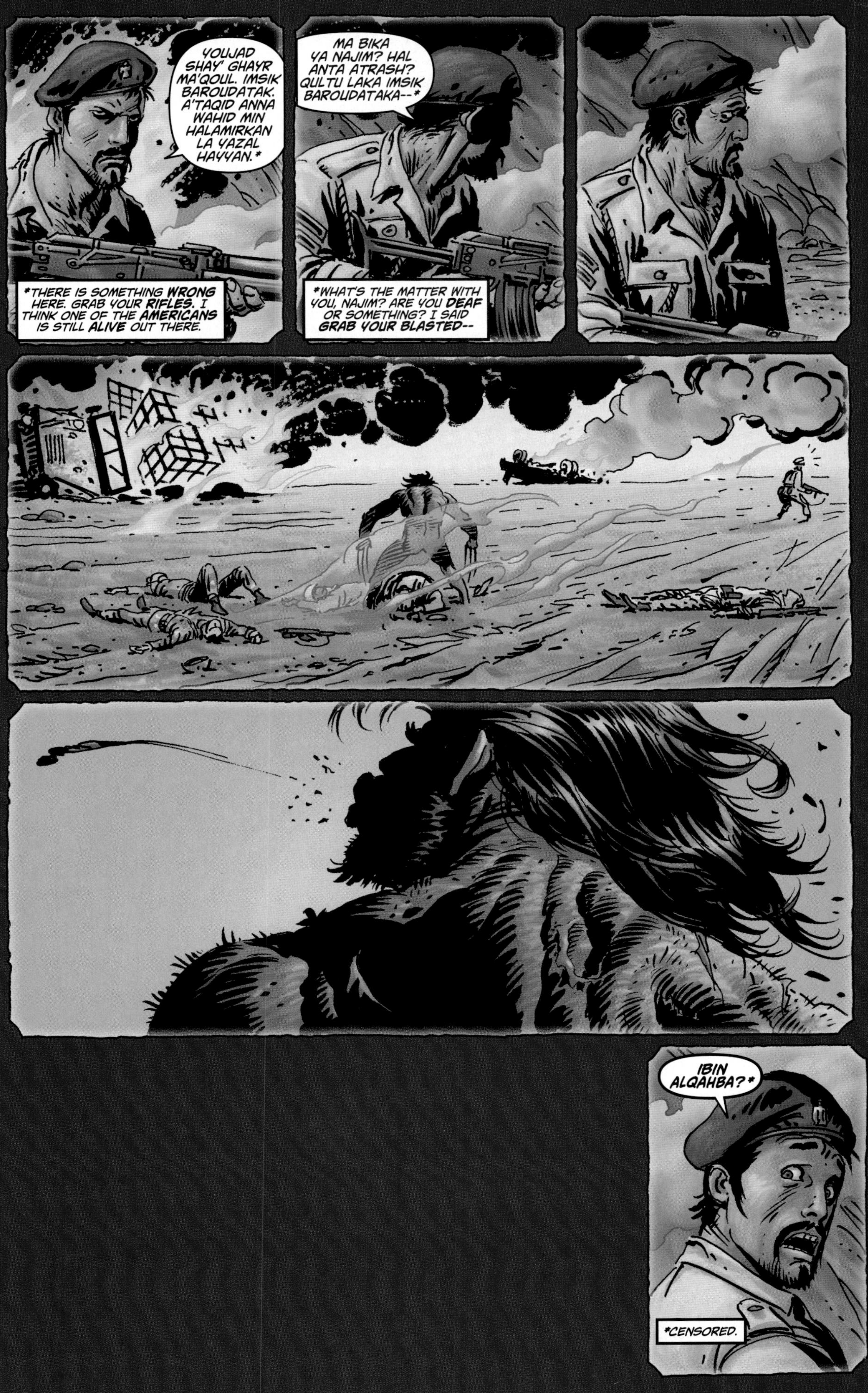
YOUJAD SHAY' GHAYR MA'QOUL. IMSIK BAROUDATAK. A'TAQID ANNA WAHID MIN HALAMIRKAN LA YAZAL HAYYAN.*
*THERE IS SOMETHING WRONG HERE. GRAB YOUR RIFLES. I THINK ONE OF THE AMERICANS IS STILL ALIVE OUT THERE.
MA BIKA YA NAJIM? HAL ANTA ATRASH? QULTU LAKA IMSIK BAROUDATAKA--*
*WHAT'S THE MATTER WITH YOU, NAJIM? ARE YOU DEAF OR SOMETHING? I SAID GRAB YOUR BLASTED--
IBIN ALQAHBA?*
*CENSORED.

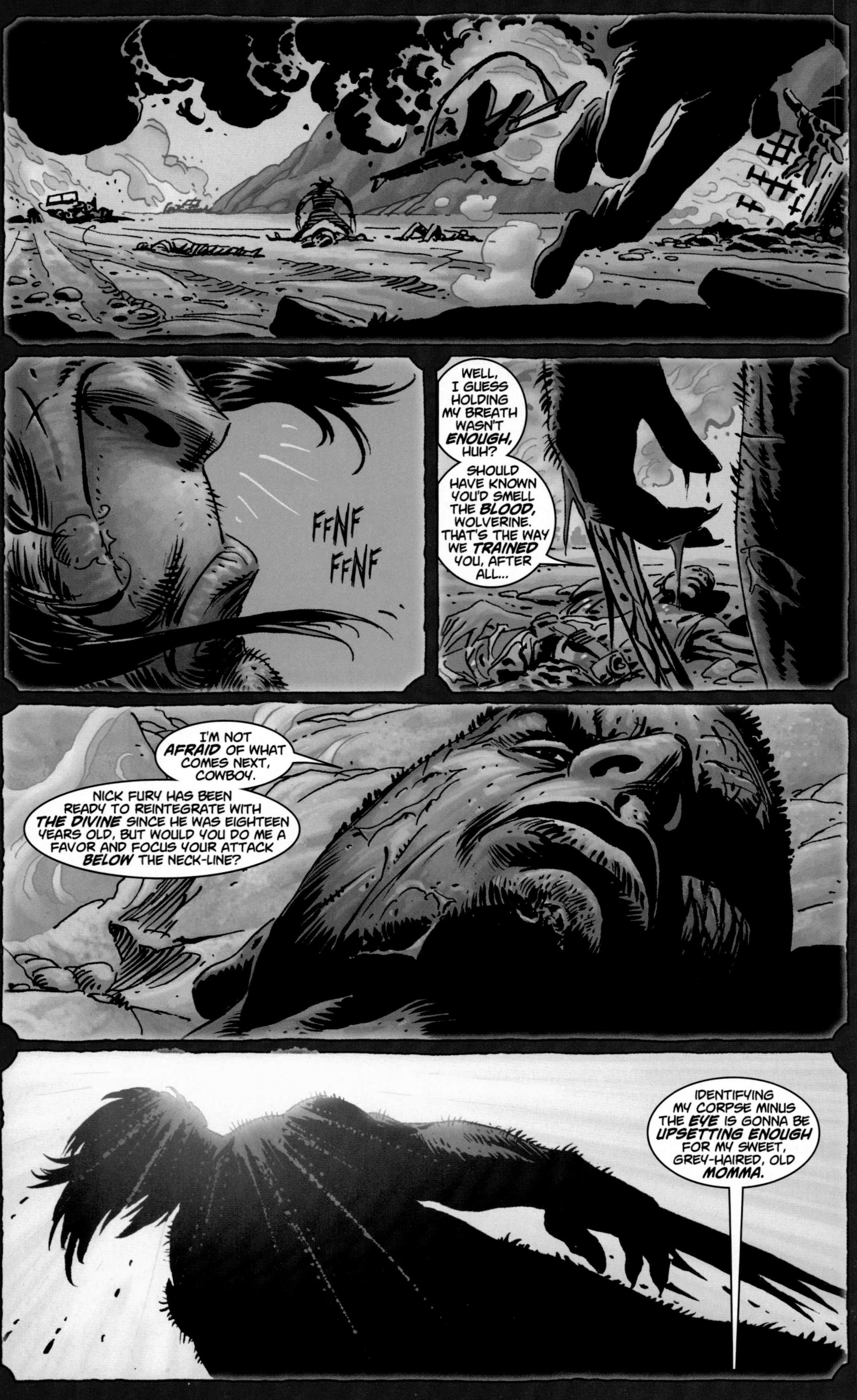
FFNF
FFNF
WELL, I GUESS HOLDING MY BREATH WASN'T ENOUGH, HUH?
SHOULD HAVE KNOWN YOU'D SMELL THE BLOOD, WOLVERINE. THAT'S THE WAY WE TRAINED YOU, AFTER ALL...
I'M NOT AFRAID OF WHAT COMES NEXT, COWBOY.
NICK FURY HAS BEEN READY TO REINTEGRATE WITH THE DIVINE SINCE HE WAS EIGHTEEN YEARS OLD, BUT WOULD YOU DO ME A FAVOR AND FOCUS YOUR ATTACK BELOW THE NECK-LINE?
IDENTIFYING MY CORPSE MINUS THE EYE IS GONNA BE UPSETTING ENOUGH FOR MY SWEET, GREY-HAIRED, OLD MOMMA.

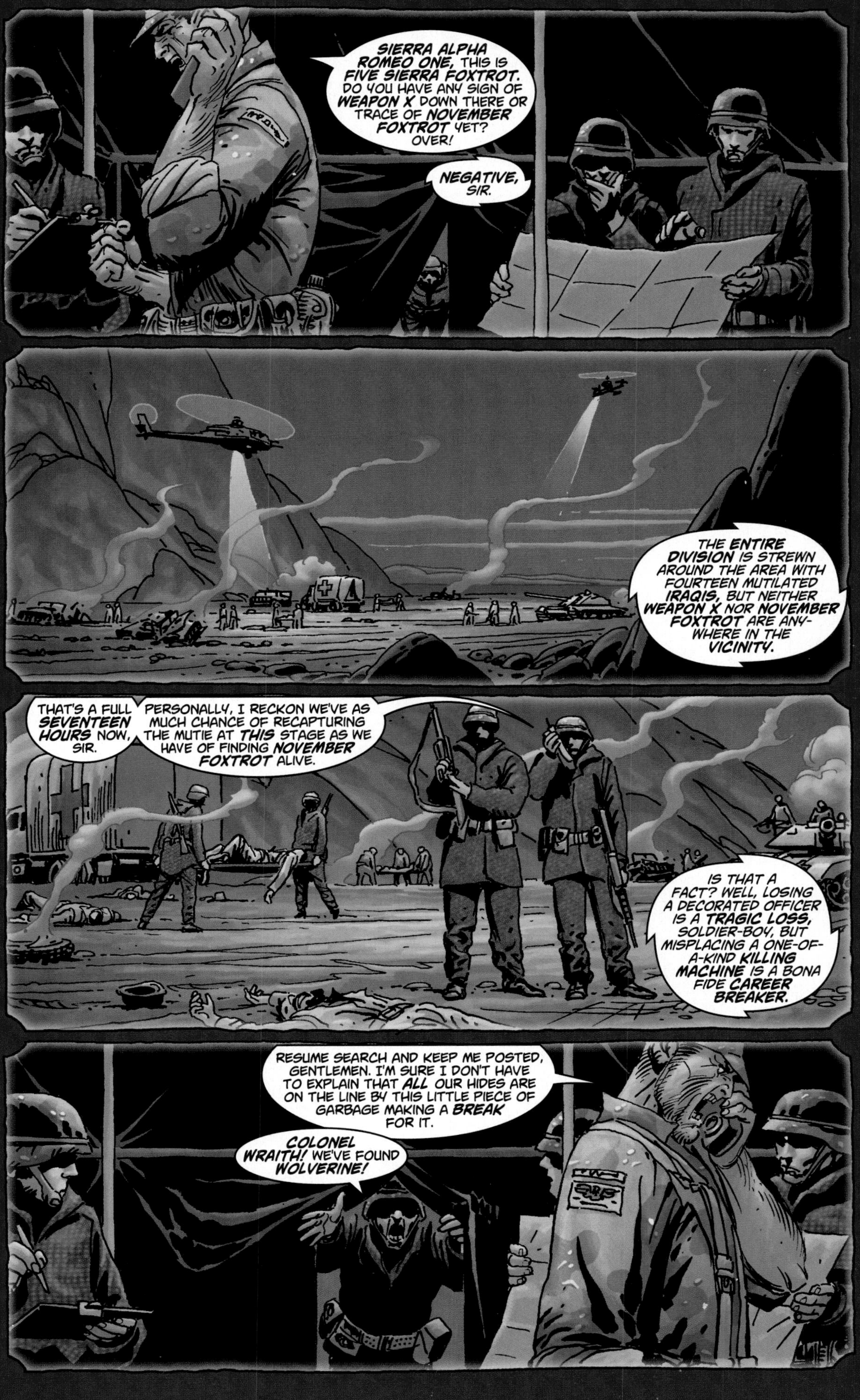
SIERRA ALPHA ROMEO ONE, THIS IS FIVE SIERRA FOXTROT. DO YOU HAVE ANY SIGN OF WEAPON X DOWN THERE OR TRACE OF NOVEMBER FOXTROT YET? OVER!
NEGATIVE, SIR.
THE ENTIRE DIVISION IS STREWN AROUND THE AREA WITH FOURTEEN MUTILATED IRAQIS, BUT NEITHER WEAPON X NOR NOVEMBER FOXTROT ARE ANYWHERE IN THE VICINITY.
THAT'S A FULL SEVENTEEN HOURS NOW, SIR.
PERSONALLY, I RECKON WE'VE AS MUCH CHANCE OF RECAPTURING THE MUTIE AT THIS STAGE AS WE HAVE OF FINDING NOVEMBER FOXTROT ALIVE.
IS THAT A FACT? WELL, LOSING A DECORATED OFFICER IS A TRAGIC LOSS, SOLDIER-BOY, BUT MISPLACING A ONE-OF-A-KIND KILLING MACHINE IS A BONA FIDE CAREER BREAKER.
RESUME SEARCH AND KEEP ME POSTED, GENTLEMEN. I'M SURE I DON'T HAVE TO EXPLAIN THAT ALL OUR HIDES ARE ON THE LINE BY THIS LITTLE PIECE OF GARBAGE MAKING A BREAK FOR IT.
COLONEL WRAITH! WE'VE FOUND WOLVERINE!

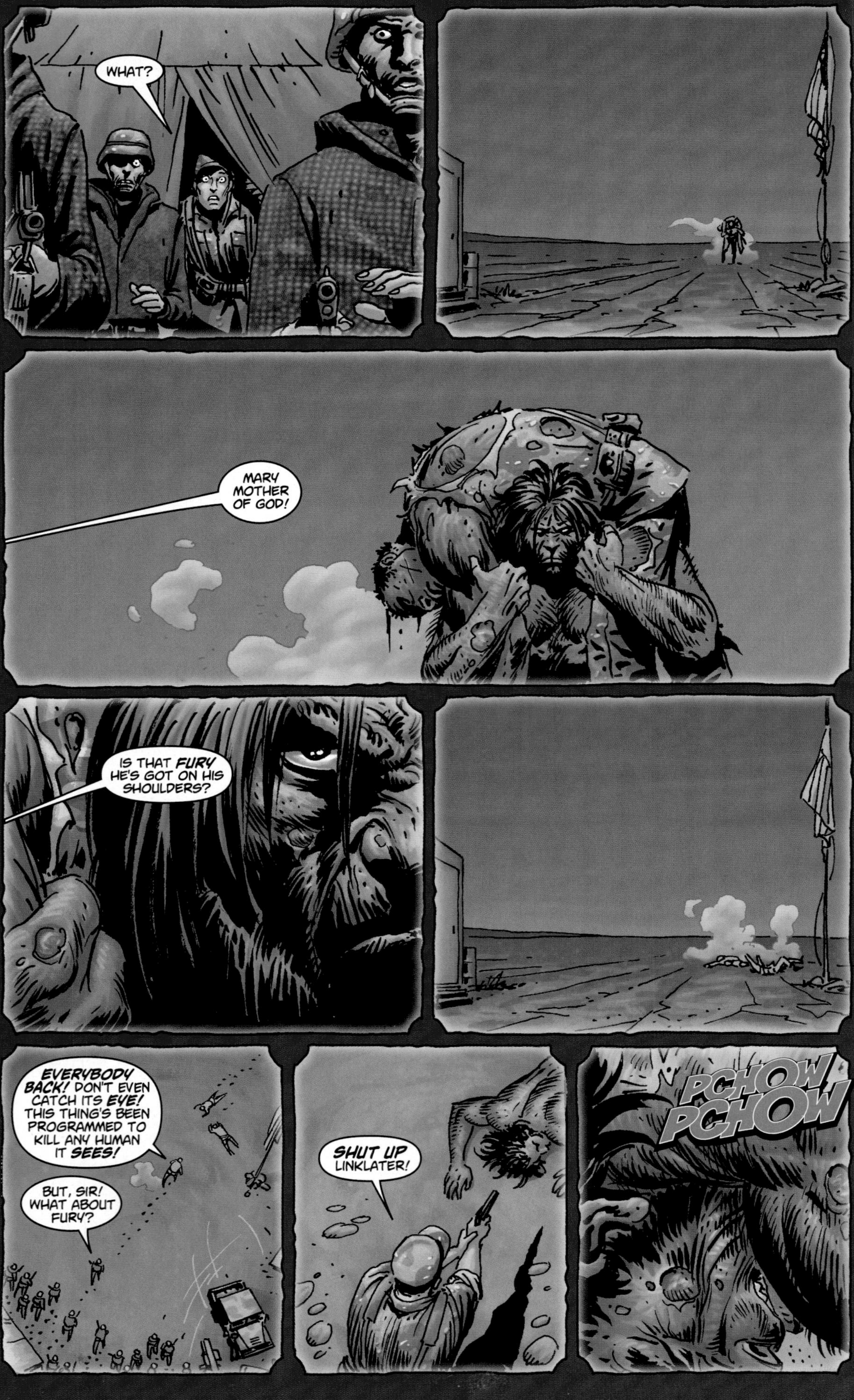
WHAT?
MARY MOTHER OF GOD!
IS THAT FURY HE'S GOT ON HIS SHOULDERS?
EVERYBODY BACK! DON'T EVEN CATCH ITS EYE! THIS THING'S BEEN PROGRAMMED TO KILL ANY HUMAN IT SEES!
BUT, SIR! WHAT ABOUT FURY?
SHUT UP LINKLATER!
PCHOW PCHOW

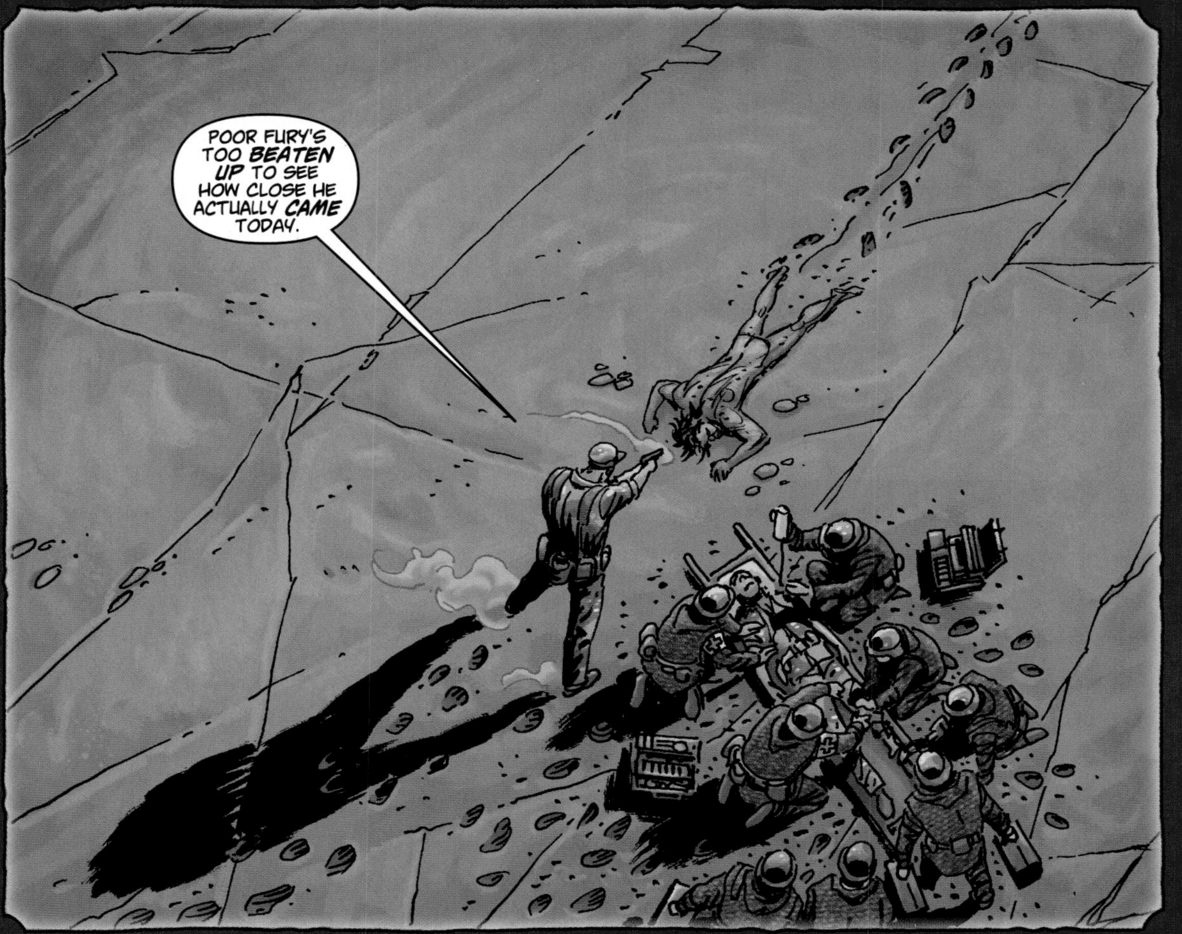
POOR FURY'S TOO BEATEN UP TO SEE HOW CLOSE HE ACTUALLY CAME TODAY.

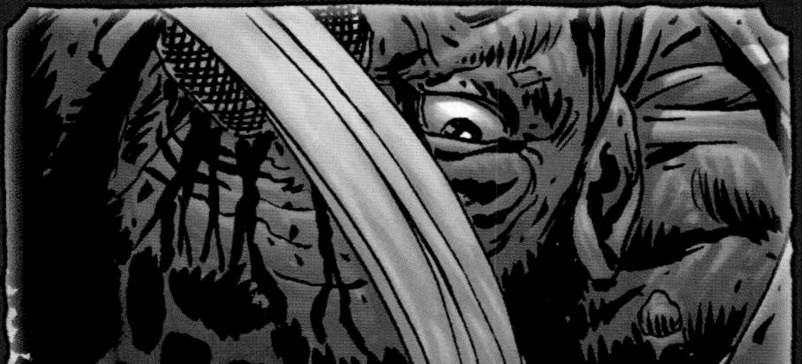

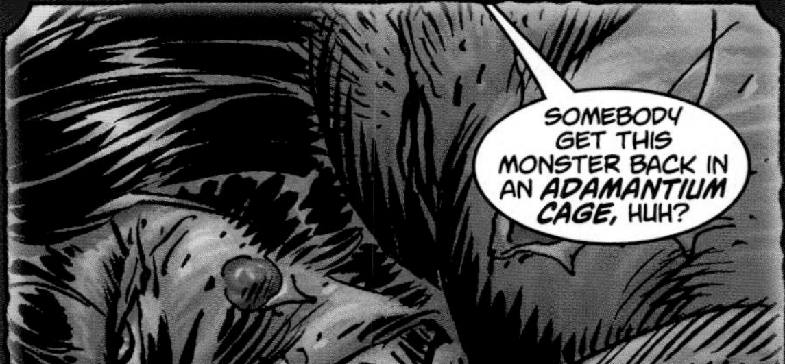
SOMEBODY GET THIS MONSTER BACK IN AN ADAMANTIUM CAGE, HUH?

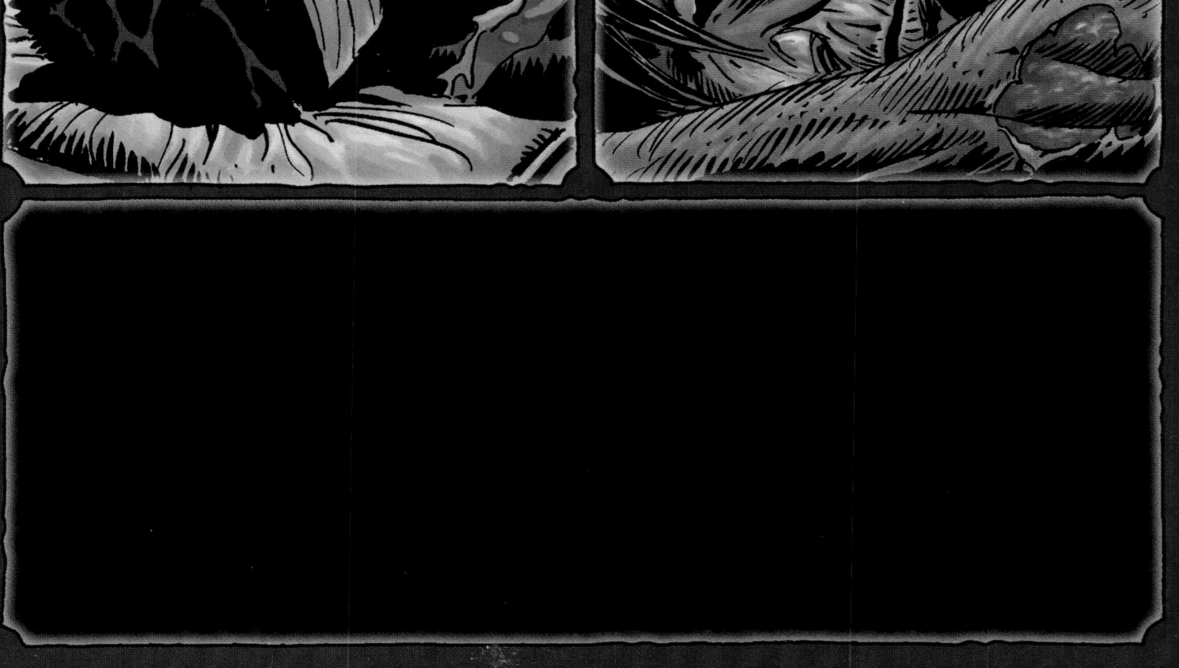

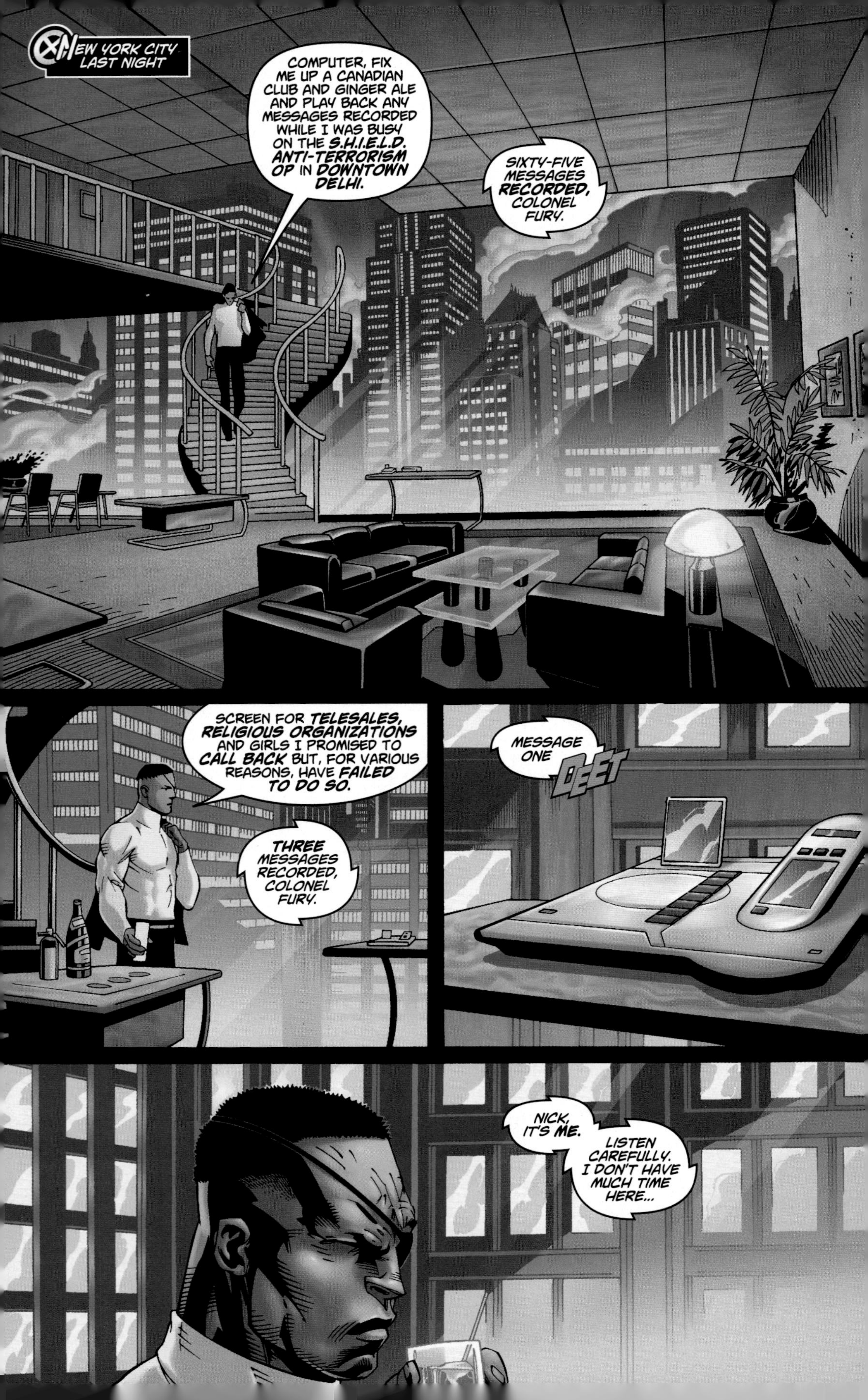
NEW YORK CITY LAST NIGHT
COMPUTER, FIX ME UP A CANADIAN CLUB AND GINGER ALE AND PLAY BACK ANY MESSAGES RECORDED WHILE I WAS BUSY ON THE S.H.I.E.L.D. ANTI-TERRORISM OP IN DOWNTOWN DELHI.
SIXTY-FIVE MESSAGES RECORDED, COLONEL FURY.
SCREEN FOR TELESALES, RELIGIOUS ORGANIZATIONS AND GIRLS I PROMISED TO CALL BACK BUT, FOR VARIOUS REASONS, HAVE FAILED TO DO SO.
THREE MESSAGES RECORDED, COLONEL FURY.
MESSAGE ONE
DEET
NICK, IT'S ME.
LISTEN CAREFULLY. I DON'T HAVE MUCH TIME HERE...

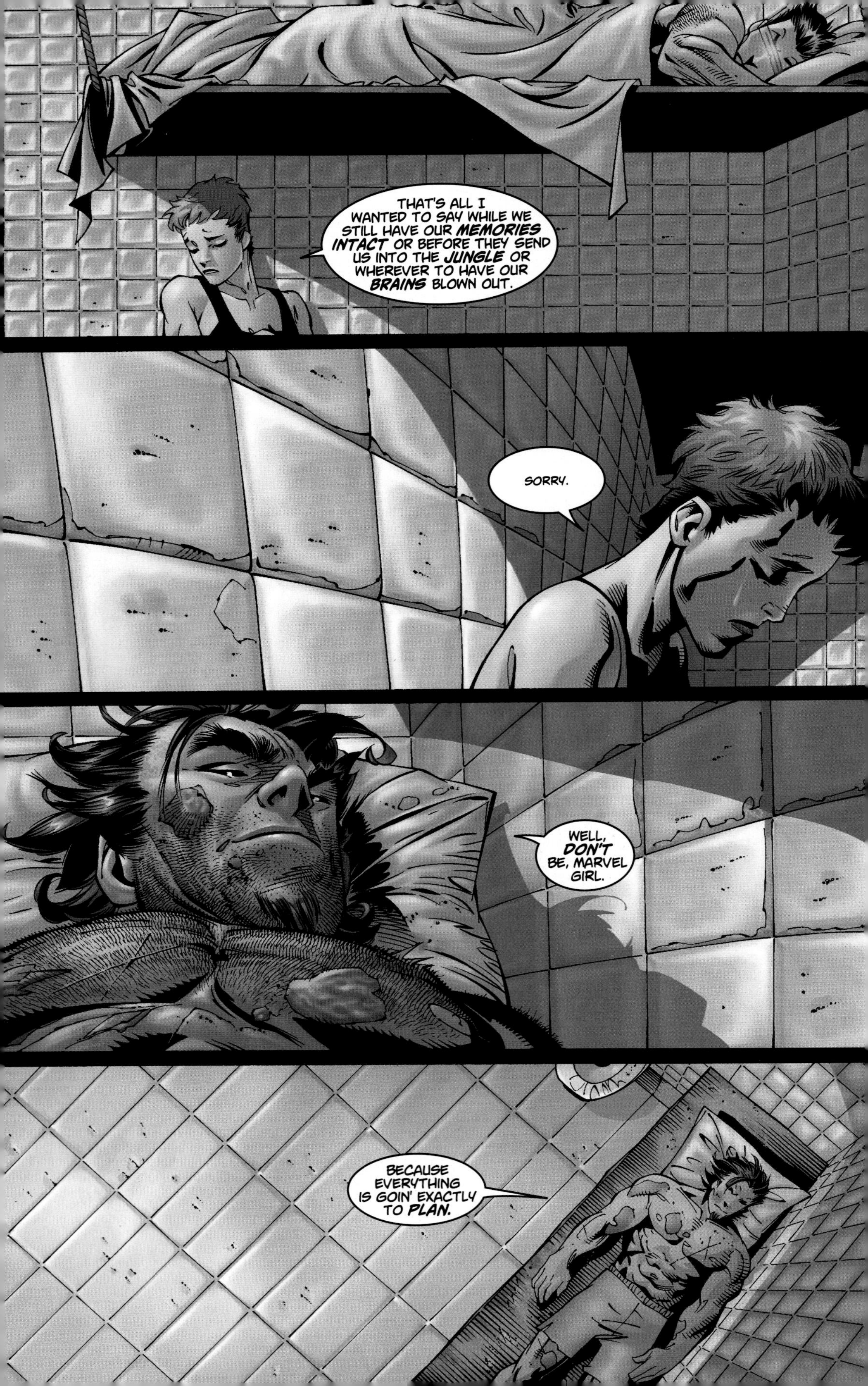
THAT'S ALL I WANTED TO SAY WHILE WE STILL HAVE OUR MEMORIES INTACT OR BEFORE THEY SEND US INTO THE JUNGLE OR WHEREVER TO HAVE OUR BRAINS BLOWN OUT.
SORRY.
WELL, DON'T BE, MARVEL GIRL.
BECAUSE EVERYTHING IS GOIN' EXACTLY TO PLAN.

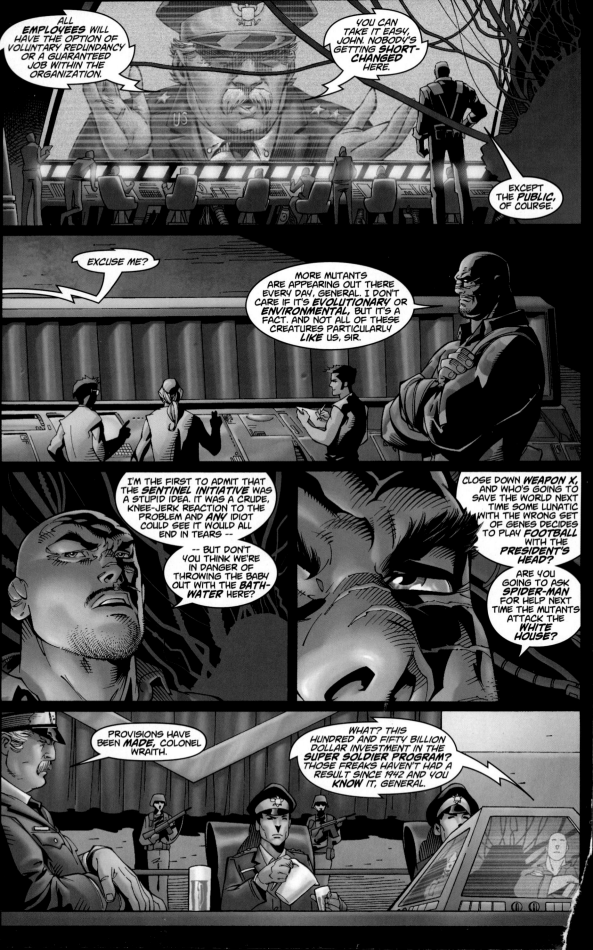

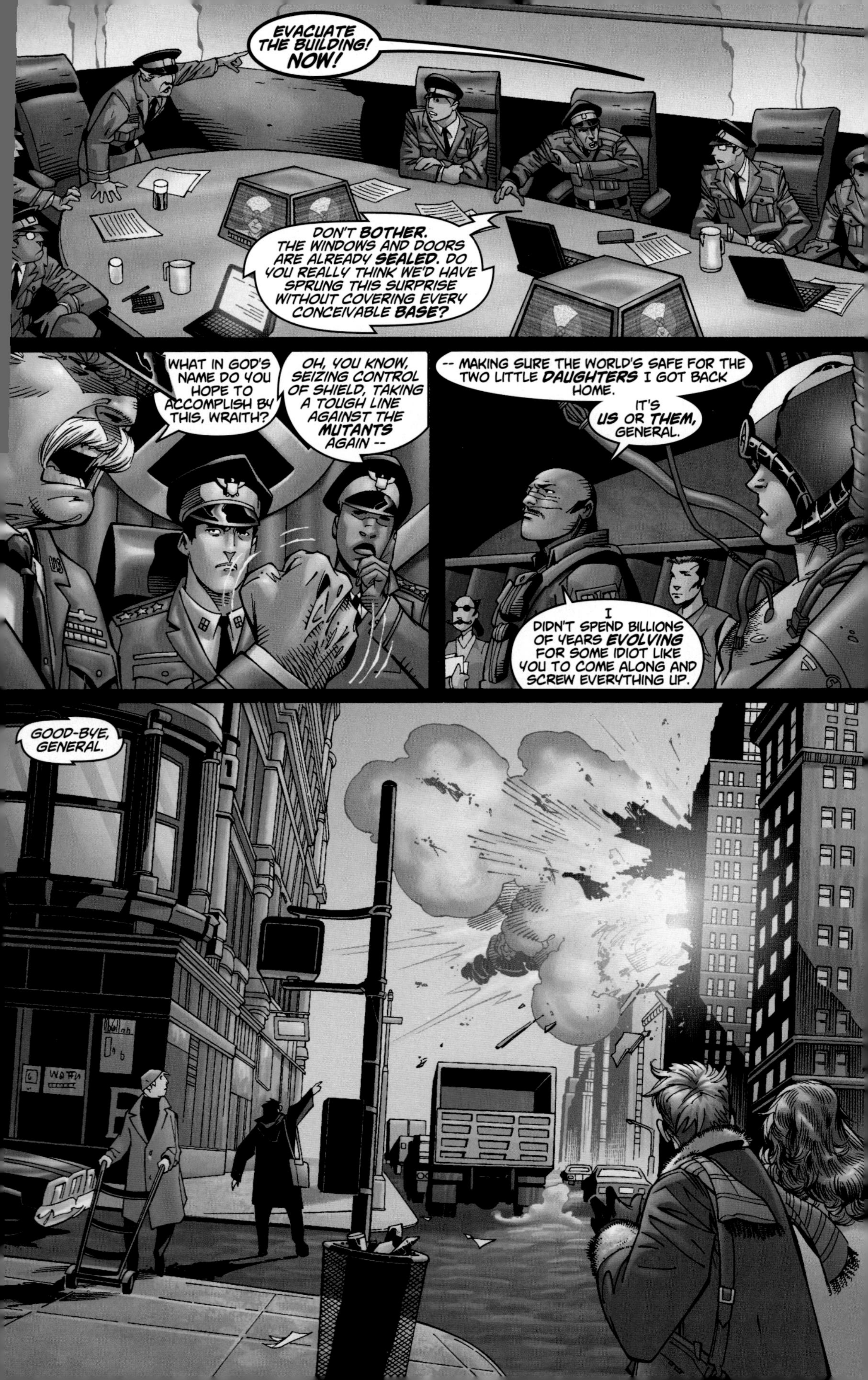
EVACUATE THE BUILDING! NOW!
DON'T BOTHER. THE WINDOWS AND DOORS ARE ALREADY SEALED. DO YOU REALLY THINK WE'D HAVE SPRUNG THIS SURPRISE WITHOUT COVERING EVERY CONCEIVABLE BASE?
WHAT IN GOD'S NAME DO YOU HOPE TO ACCOMPLISH BY THIS, WRAITH?
OH, YOU KNOW, SEIZING CONTROL OF SHIELD, TAKING A TOUGH LINE AGAINST THE MUTANTS AGAIN --
-- MAKING SURE THE WORLD'S SAFE FOR THE TWO LITTLE DAUGHTERS I GOT BACK HOME.
IT'S US OR THEM, GENERAL.
I DIDN'T SPEND BILLIONS OF YEARS EVOLVING FOR SOME IDIOT LIKE YOU TO COME ALONG AND SCREW EVERYTHING UP.
GOOD-BYE, GENERAL.

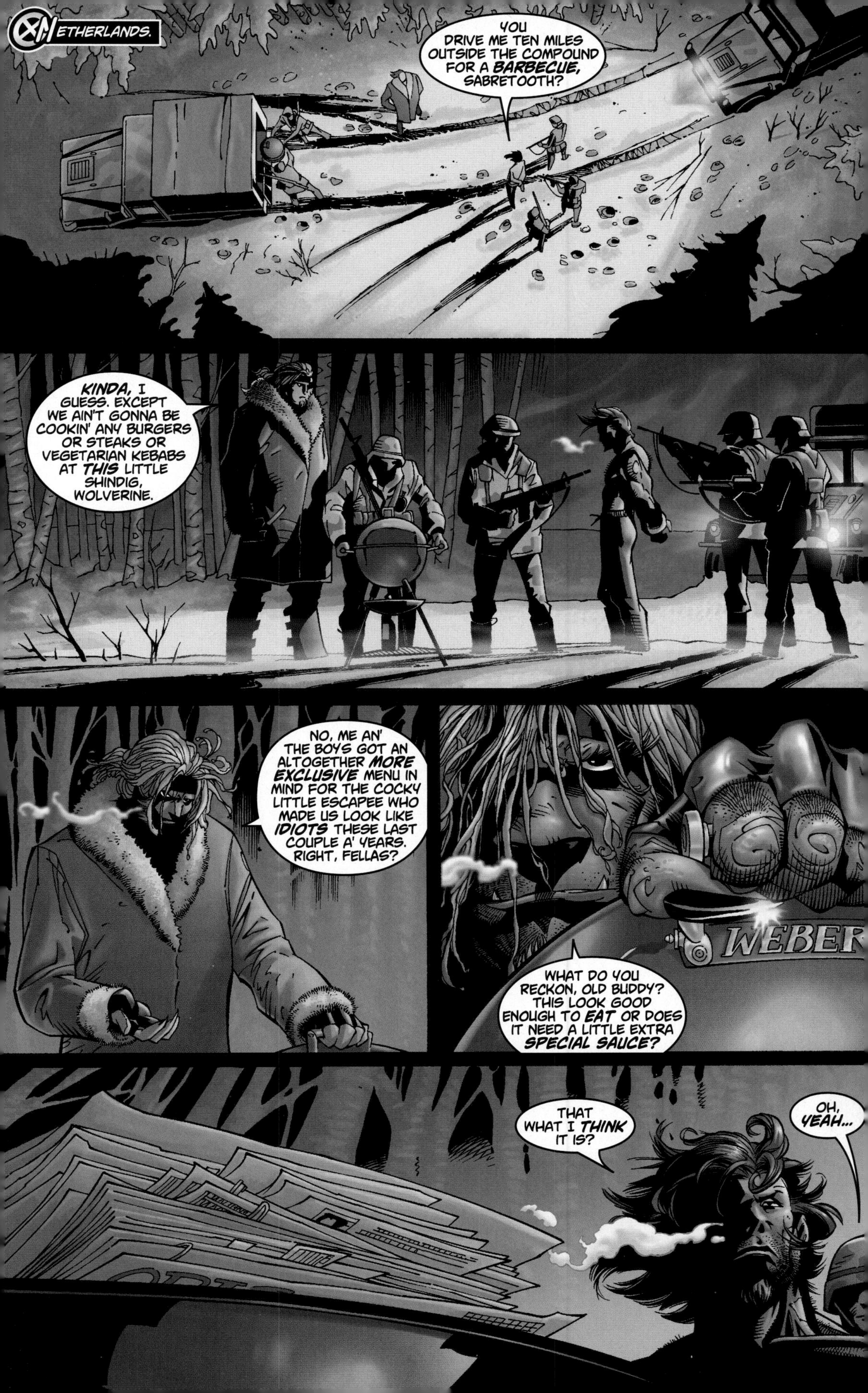
NETHERLANDS.
YOU DRIVE ME TEN MILES OUTSIDE THE COMPOUND FOR A BARBECUE, SABRETOOTH?
KINDA, I GUESS. EXCEPT WE AIN'T GONNA BE COOKIN' ANY BURGERS OR STEAKS OR VEGETARIAN KEBABS AT THIS LITTLE SHINDIG, WOLVERINE.
NO, ME AN' THE BOYS GOT AN ALTOGETHER MORE EXCLUSIVE MENU IN MIND FOR THE COCKY LITTLE ESCAPEE WHO MADE US LOOK LIKE IDIOTS THESE LAST COUPLE A' YEARS. RIGHT, FELLAS?
WEBER
WHAT DO YOU RECKON, OLD BUDDY? THIS LOOK GOOD ENOUGH TO EAT OR DOES IT NEED A LITTLE EXTRA SPECIAL SAUCE?
THAT WHAT I THINK IT IS?
OH, YEAH...

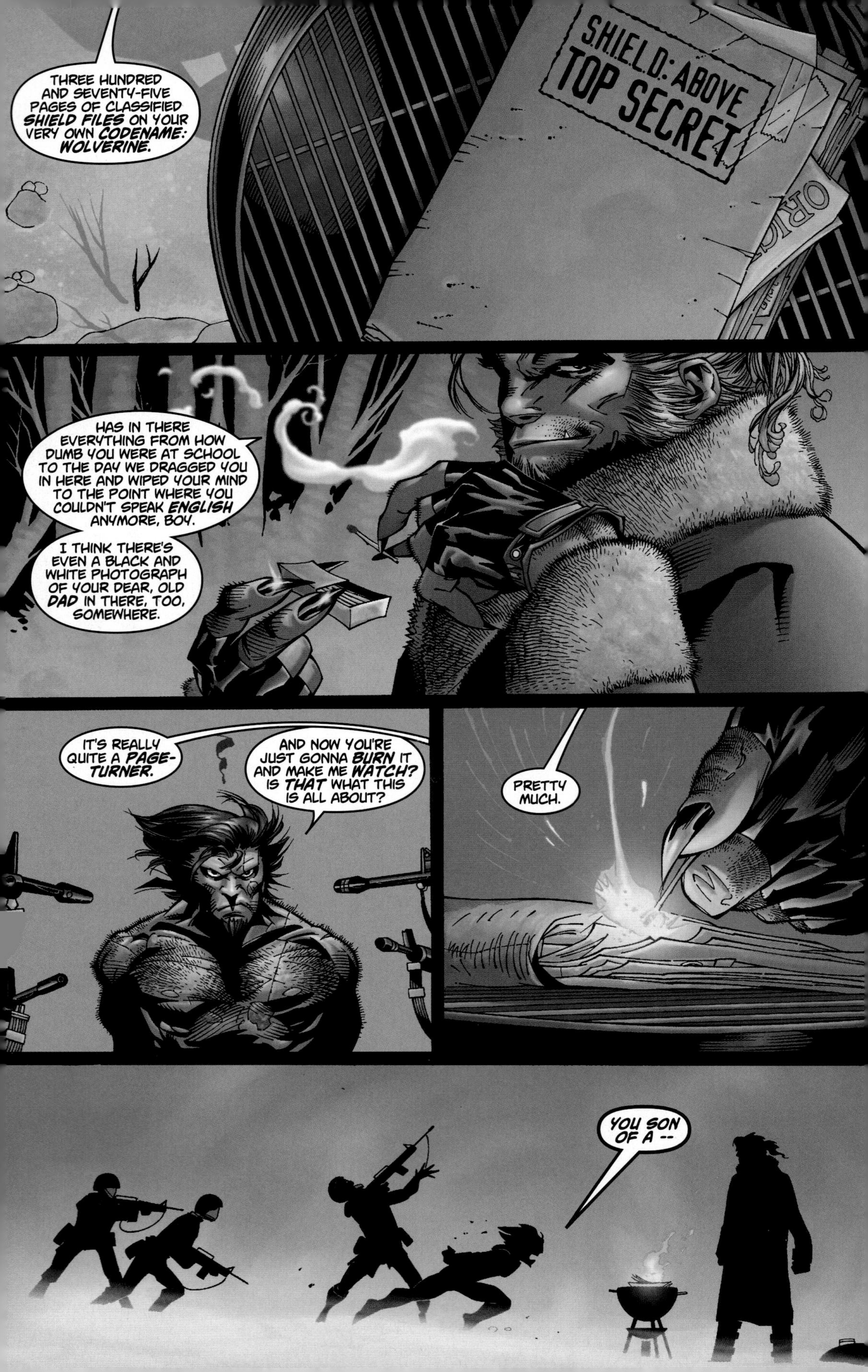

THREE HUNDRED AND SEVENTY-FIVE PAGES OF CLASSIFIED SHIELD FILES ON YOUR VERY OWN CODENAME: WOLVERINE.
S.H.I.E.L.D: ABOVE TOP SECRET
HAS IN THERE EVERYTHING FROM HOW DUMB YOU WERE AT SCHOOL TO THE DAY WE DRAGGED YOU IN HERE AND WIPED YOUR MIND TO THE POINT WHERE YOU COULDN'T SPEAK ENGLISH ANYMORE, BOY.
I THINK THERE'S EVEN A BLACK AND WHITE PHOTOGRAPH OF YOUR DEAR, OLD DAD IN THERE, TOO, SOMEWHERE.
IT'S REALLY QUITE A PAGE-TURNER.
AND NOW YOU'RE JUST GONNA BURN IT AND MAKE ME WATCH? IS THAT WHAT THIS IS ALL ABOUT?
PRETTY MUCH.
YOU SON OF A --

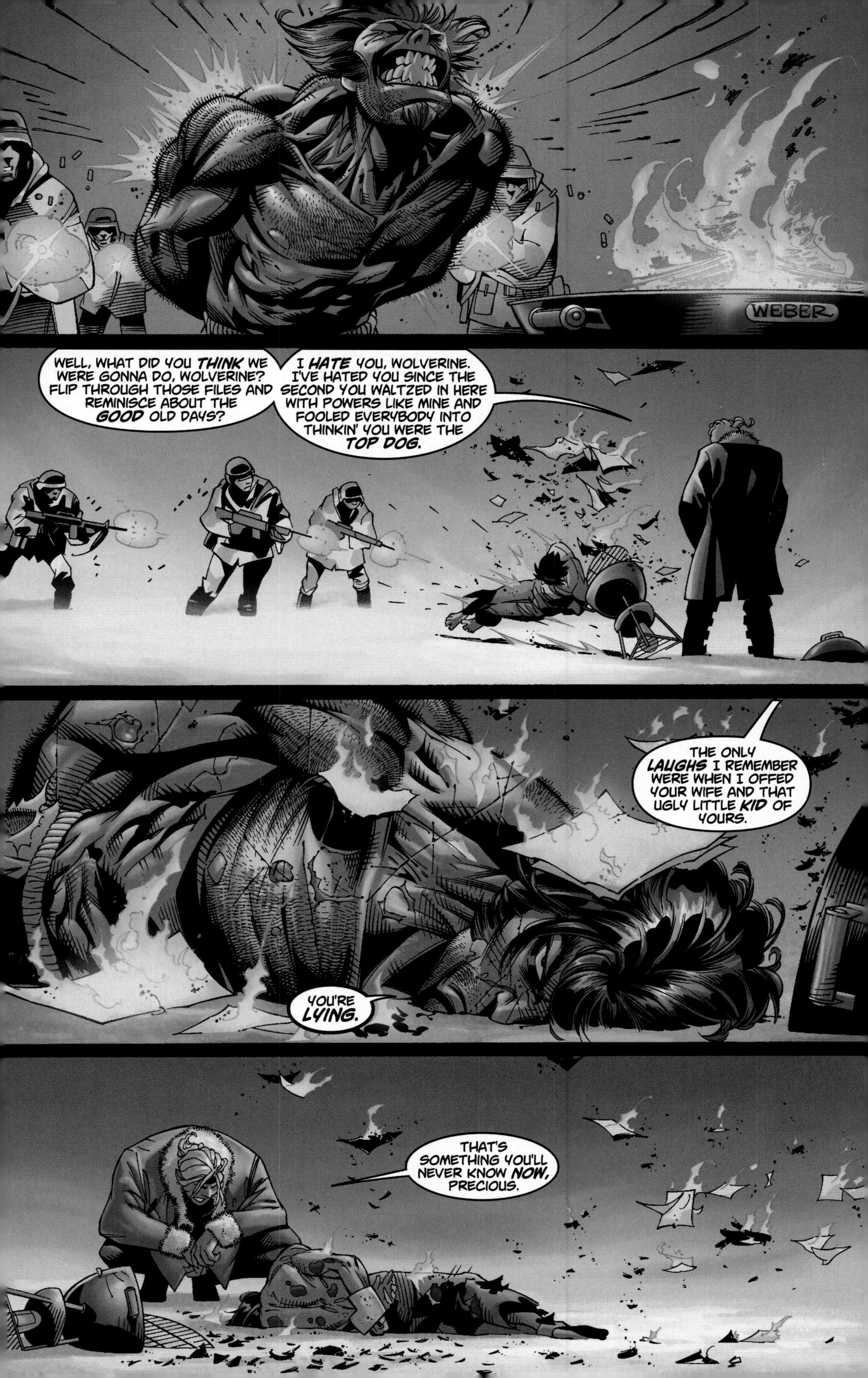
WEBER
WELL, WHAT DID YOU THINK WE WERE GONNA DO, WOLVERINE? FLIP THROUGH THOSE FILES AND REMINISCE ABOUT THE GOOD OLD DAYS?
I HATE YOU, WOLVERINE. I'VE HATED YOU SINCE THE SECOND YOU WALTZED IN HERE WITH POWERS LIKE MINE AND FOOLED EVERYBODY INTO THINKIN' YOU WERE THE TOP DOG.
THE ONLY LAUGHS I REMEMBER WERE WHEN I OFFED YOUR WIFE AND THAT UGLY LITTLE KID OF YOURS.
YOU'RE LYING.
THAT'S SOMETHING YOU'LL NEVER KNOW NOW, PRECIOUS.

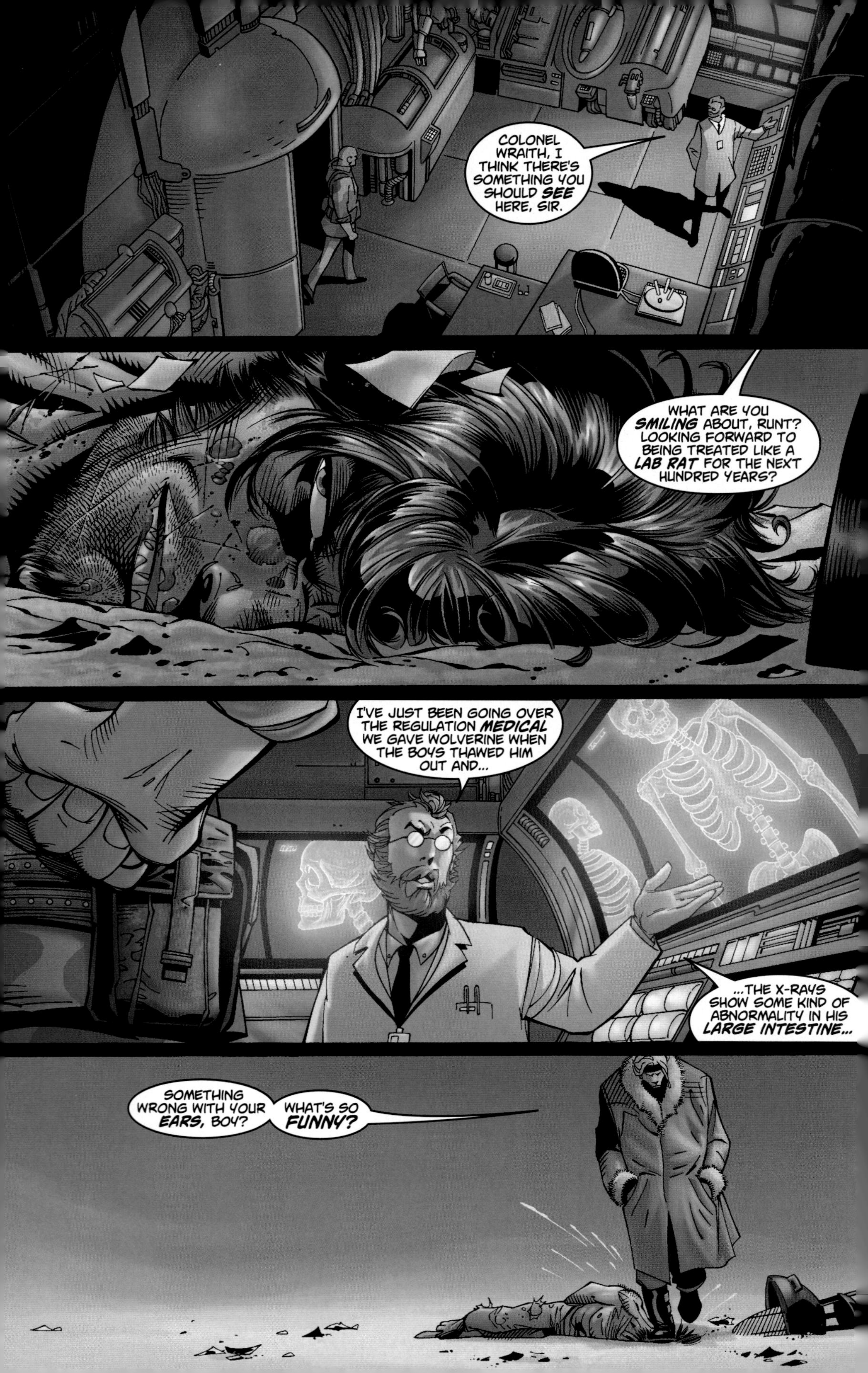
COLONEL WRAITH, I THINK THERE'S SOMETHING YOU SHOULD SEE HERE, SIR.
WHAT ARE YOU SMILING ABOUT, RUNT? LOOKING FORWARD TO BEING TREATED LIKE A LAB RAT FOR THE NEXT HUNDRED YEARS?
I'VE JUST BEEN GOING OVER THE REGULATION MEDICAL WE GAVE WOLVERINE WHEN THE BOYS THAWED HIM OUT AND...
...THE X-RAYS SHOW SOME KIND OF ABNORMALITY IN HIS LARGE INTESTINE...
SOMETHING WRONG WITH YOUR EARS, BOY?
WHAT'S SO FUNNY?

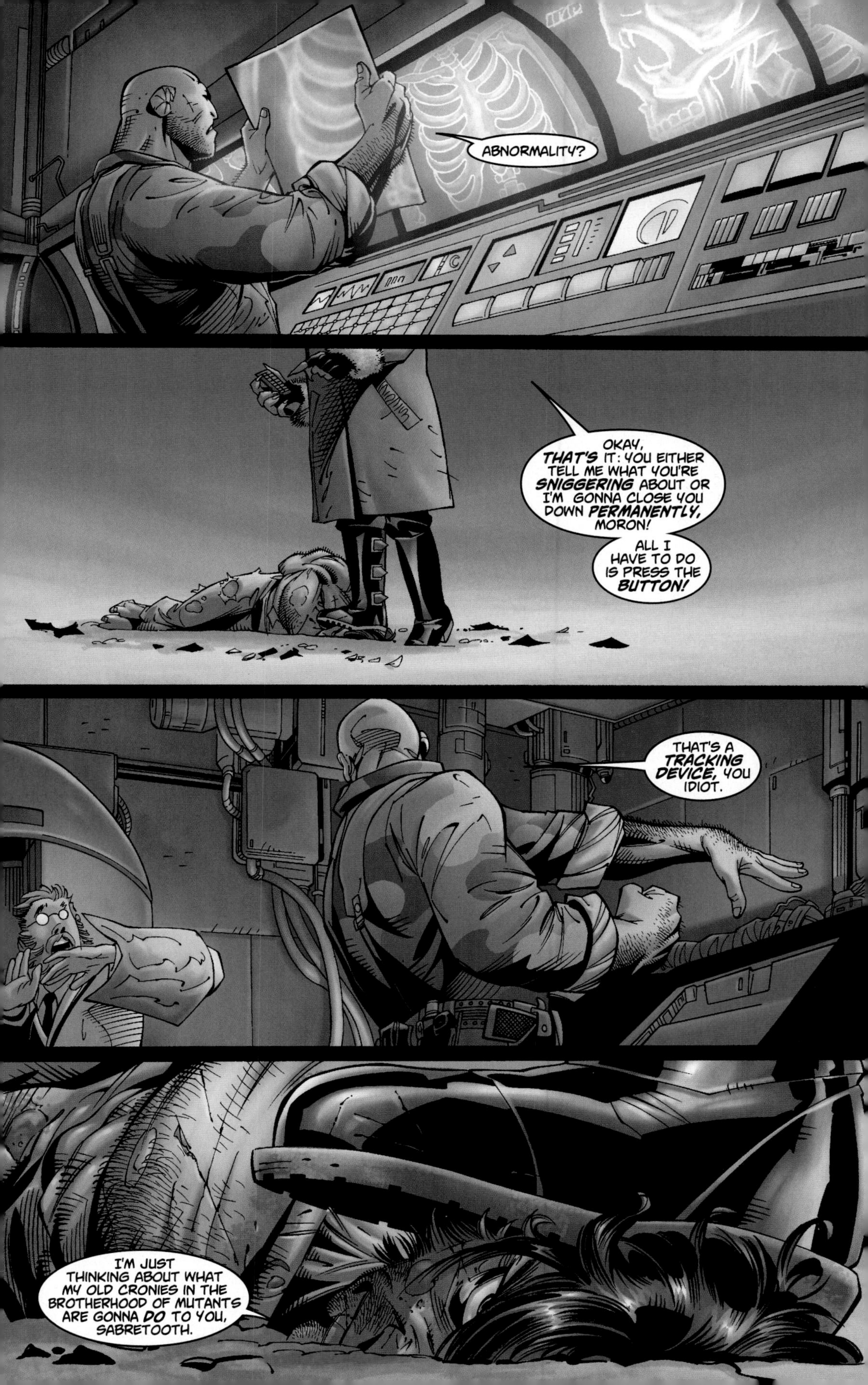
ABNORMALITY?
OKAY, THAT'S IT: YOU EITHER TELL ME WHAT YOU'RE SNIGGERING ABOUT OR I'M GONNA CLOSE YOU DOWN PERMANENTLY, MORON!
ALL I HAVE TO DO IS PRESS THE BUTTON!
THAT'S A TRACKING DEVICE, YOU IDIOT.
I'M JUST THINKING ABOUT WHAT MY OLD CRONIES IN THE BROTHERHOOD OF MUTANTS ARE GONNA DO TO YOU, SABRETOOTH.

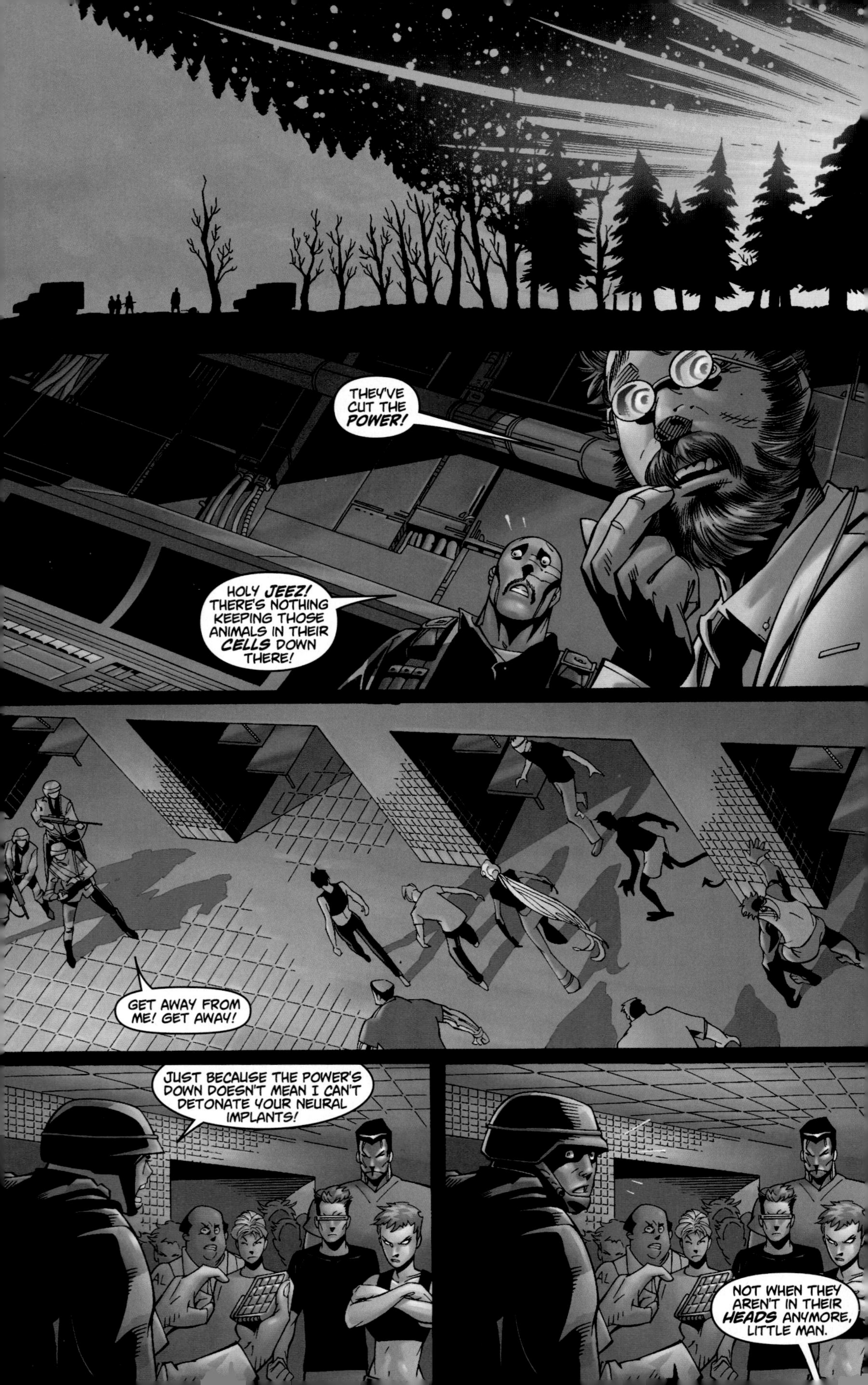
THEY'VE CUT THE POWER!
HOLY JEEZ! THERE'S NOTHING KEEPING THOSE ANIMALS IN THEIR CELLS DOWN THERE!
GET AWAY FROM ME! GET AWAY!
JUST BECAUSE THE POWER'S DOWN DOESN'T MEAN I CAN'T DETONATE YOUR NEURAL IMPLANTS!
NOT WHEN THEY AREN'T IN THEIR HEADS ANYMORE, LITTLE MAN.

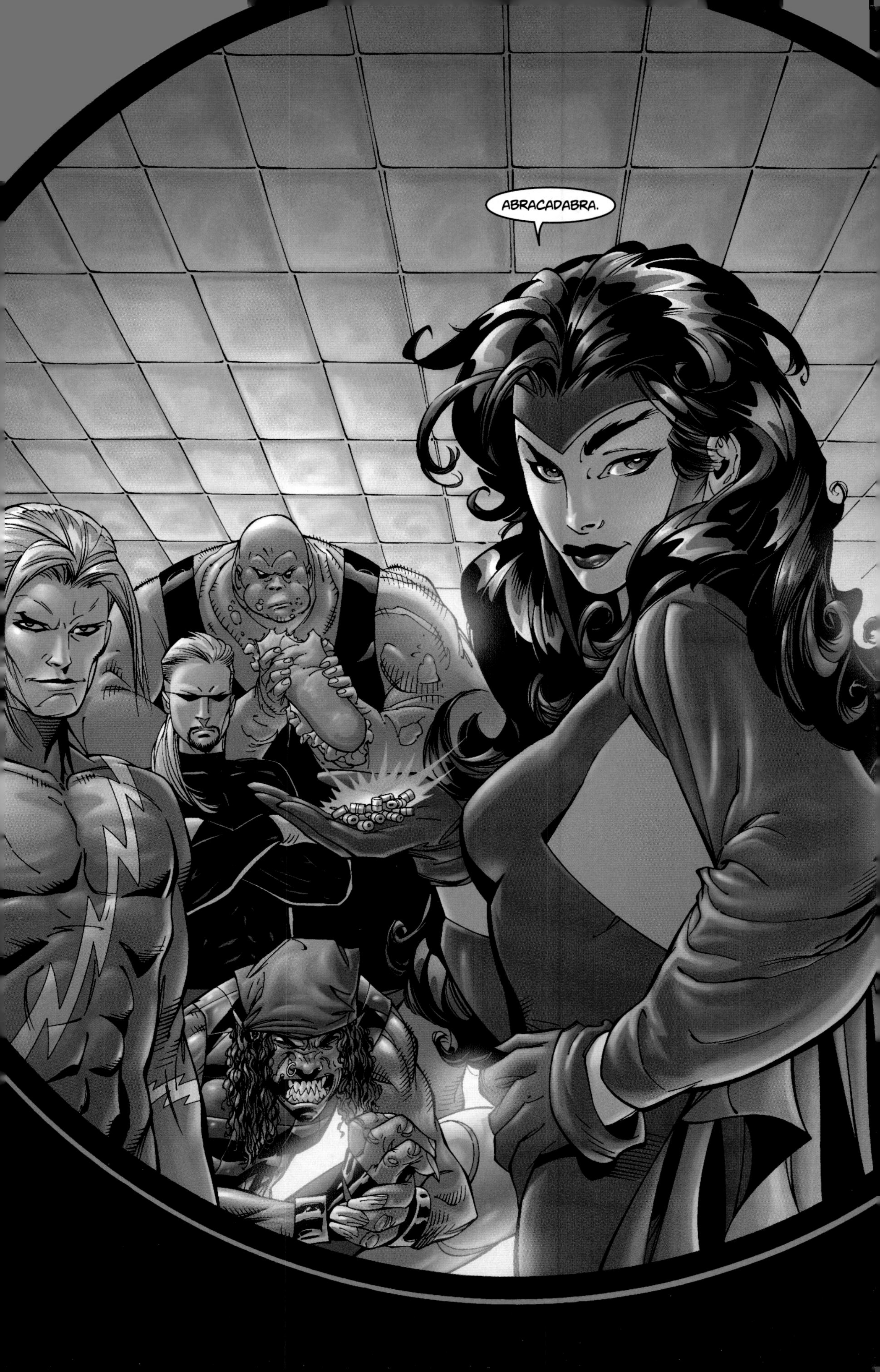
ABRACADABRA.

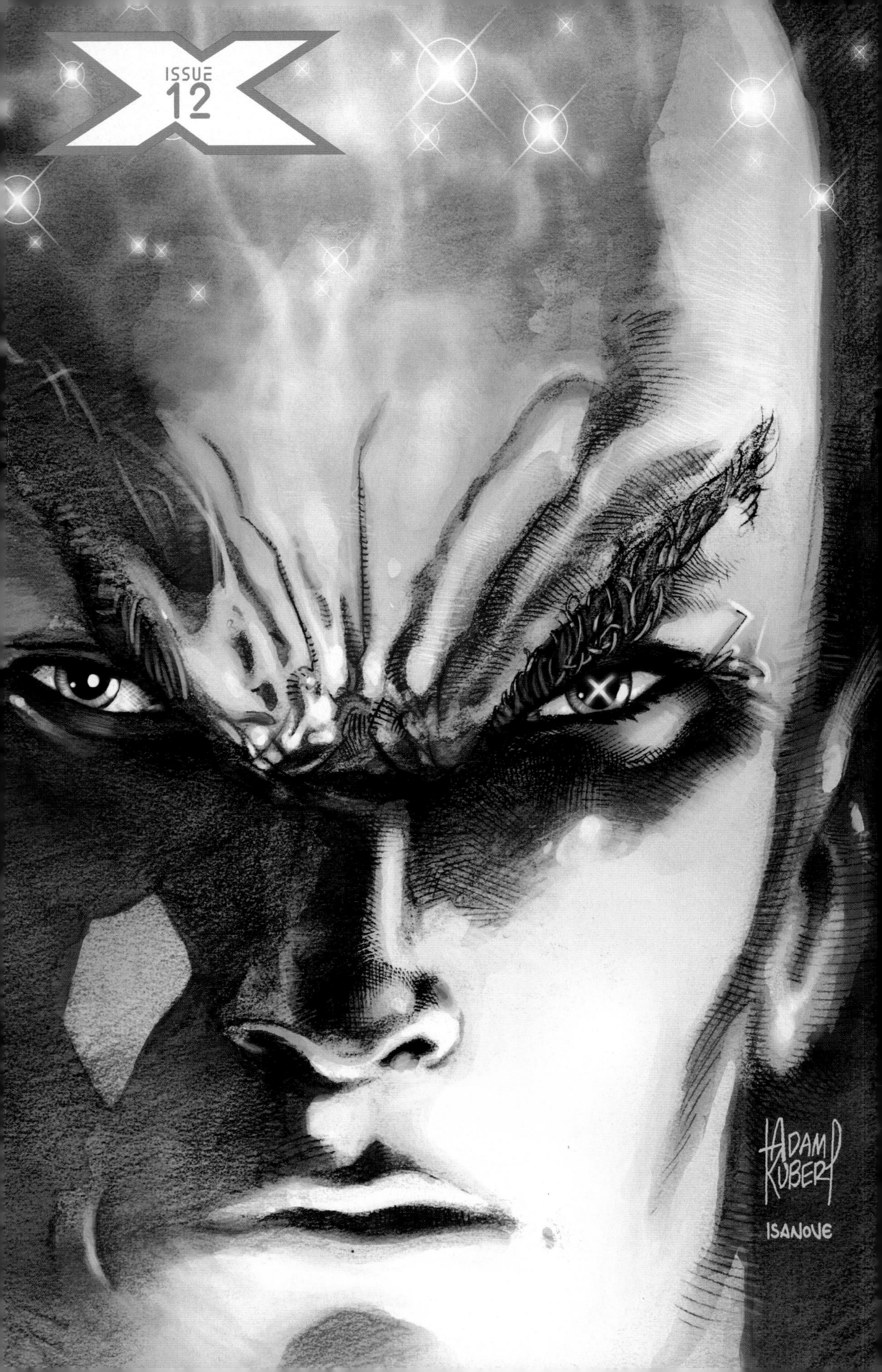
ISSUE
12
ADAM KUBERT
ISANOVE

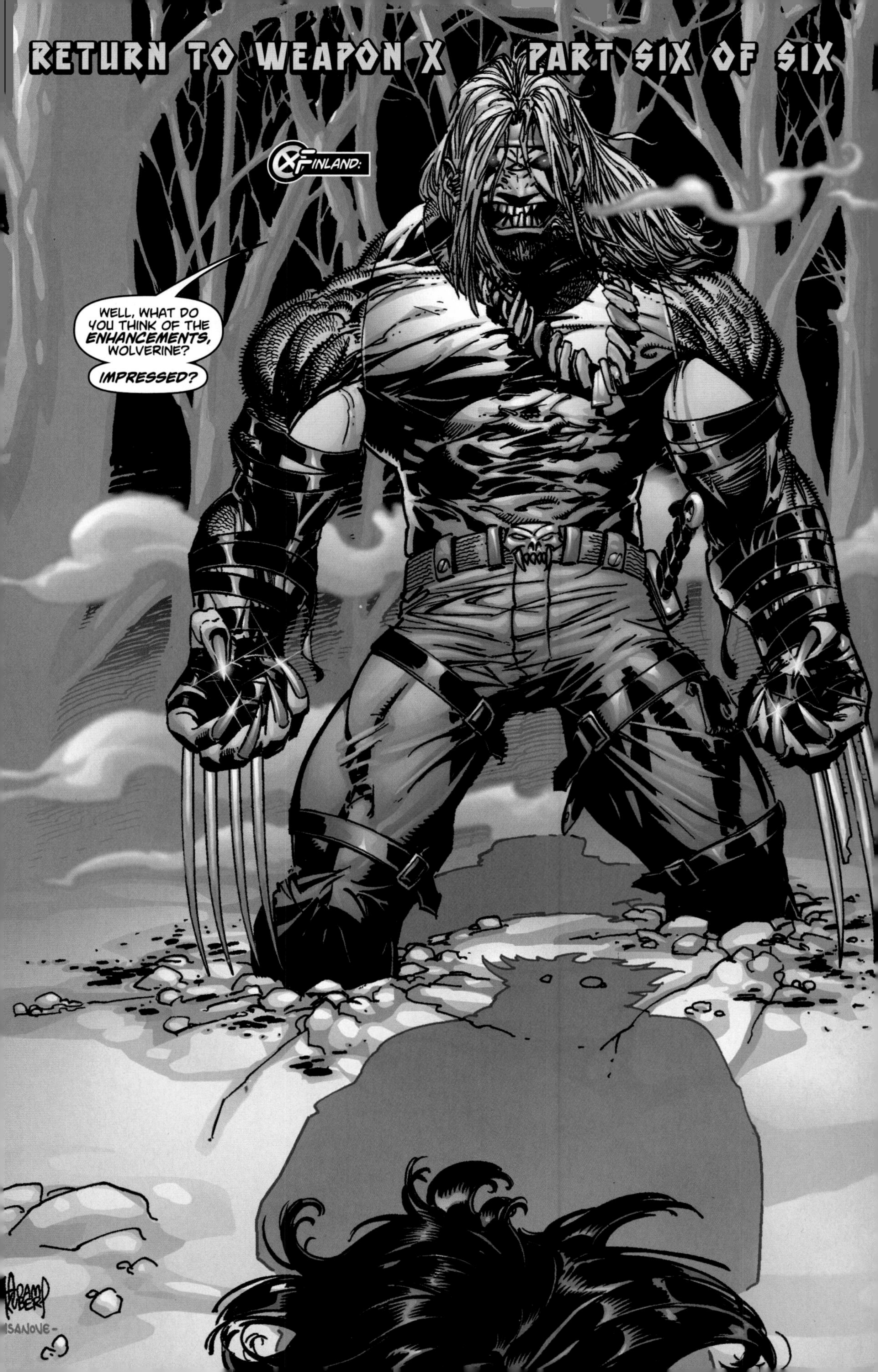
RETURN TO WEAPON X PART SIX OF SIX
FINLAND:
WELL, WHAT DO YOU THINK OF THE ENHANCEMENTS, WOLVERINE?
IMPRESSED?
ADAM KUBERT
ISANOVE

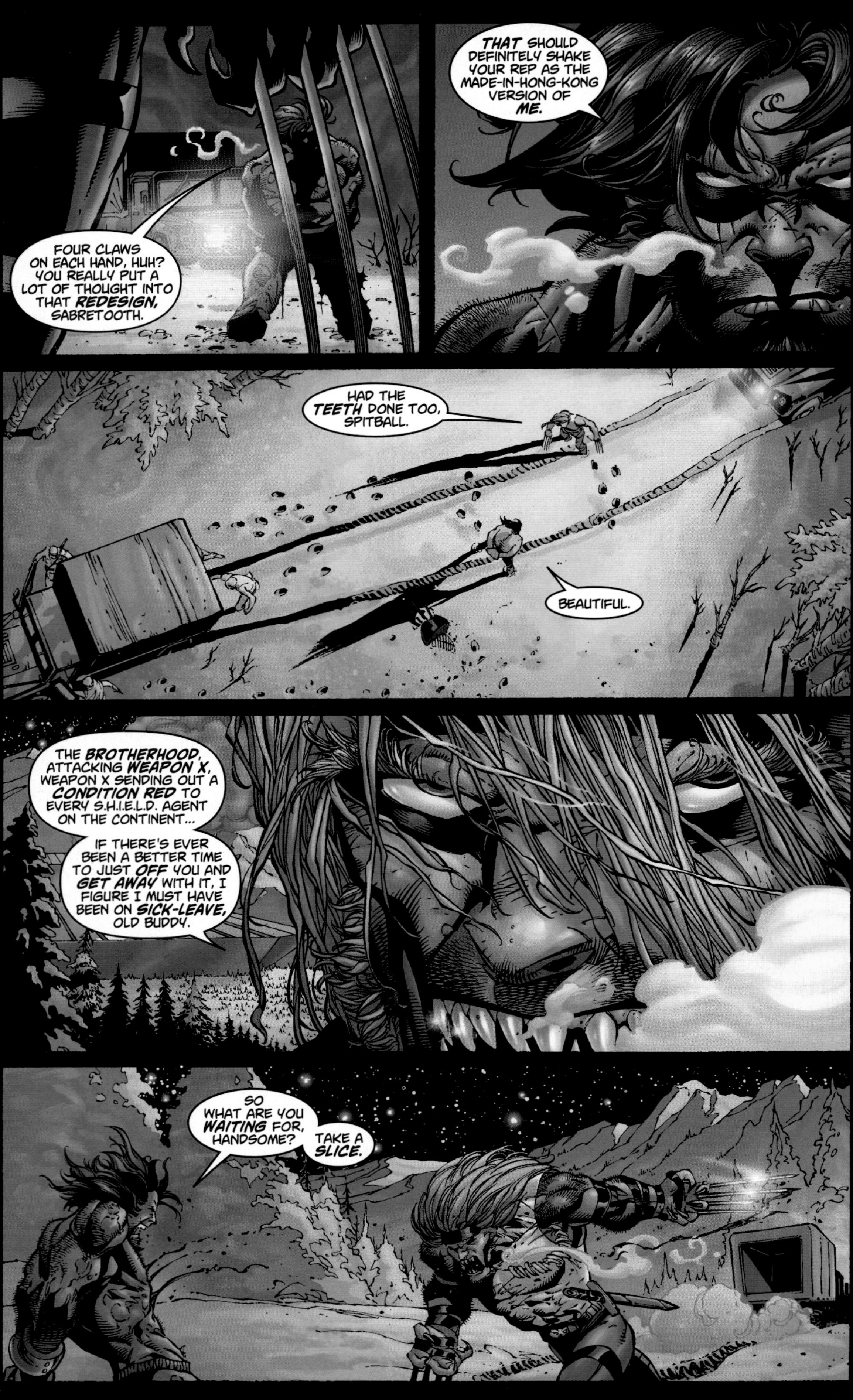
FOUR CLAWS ON EACH HAND, HUH? YOU REALLY PUT A LOT OF THOUGHT INTO THAT REDESIGN, SABRETOOTH.
THAT SHOULD DEFINITELY SHAKE YOUR REP AS THE MADE-IN-HONG-KONG VERSION OF ME.
HAD THE TEETH DONE TOO, SPITBALL.
BEAUTIFUL.
THE BROTHERHOOD, ATTACKING WEAPON X, WEAPON X SENDING OUT A CONDITION RED TO EVERY S.H.I.E.L.D. AGENT ON THE CONTINENT...
IF THERE'S EVER BEEN A BETTER TIME TO JUST OFF YOU AND GET AWAY WITH IT, I FIGURE I MUST HAVE BEEN ON SICK-LEAVE, OLD BUDDY.
SO WHAT ARE YOU WAITING FOR, HANDSOME?
TAKE A SLICE.

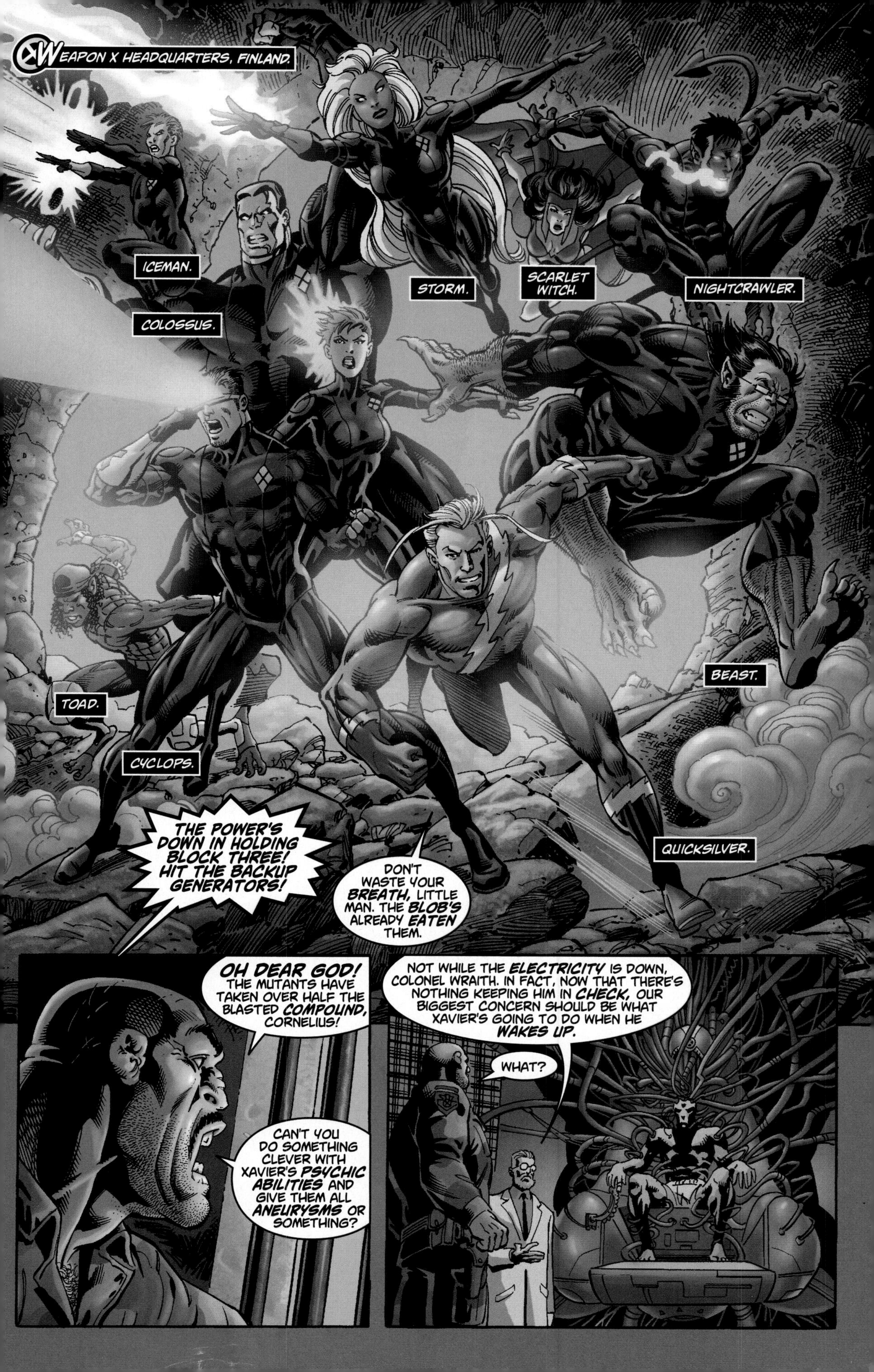
WEAPON X HEADQUARTERS, FINLAND.
ICEMAN.
COLOSSUS.
STORM.
SCARLET WITCH.
NIGHTCRAWLER.
BEAST.
TOAD.
CYCLOPS.
QUICKSILVER.
THE POWER'S DOWN IN HOLDING BLOCK THREE! HIT THE BACKUP GENERATORS!
DON'T WASTE YOUR BREATH, LITTLE MAN. THE BLOB'S ALREADY EATEN THEM.
OH DEAR GOD! THE MUTANTS HAVE TAKEN OVER HALF THE BLASTED COMPOUND, CORNELIUS!
CAN'T YOU DO SOMETHING CLEVER WITH XAVIER'S PSYCHIC ABILITIES AND GIVE THEM ALL ANEURYSMS OR SOMETHING?
NOT WHILE THE ELECTRICITY IS DOWN, COLONEL WRAITH. IN FACT, NOW THAT THERE'S NOTHING KEEPING HIM IN CHECK, OUR BIGGEST CONCERN SHOULD BE WHAT XAVIER'S GOING TO DO WHEN HE WAKES UP.
WHAT?

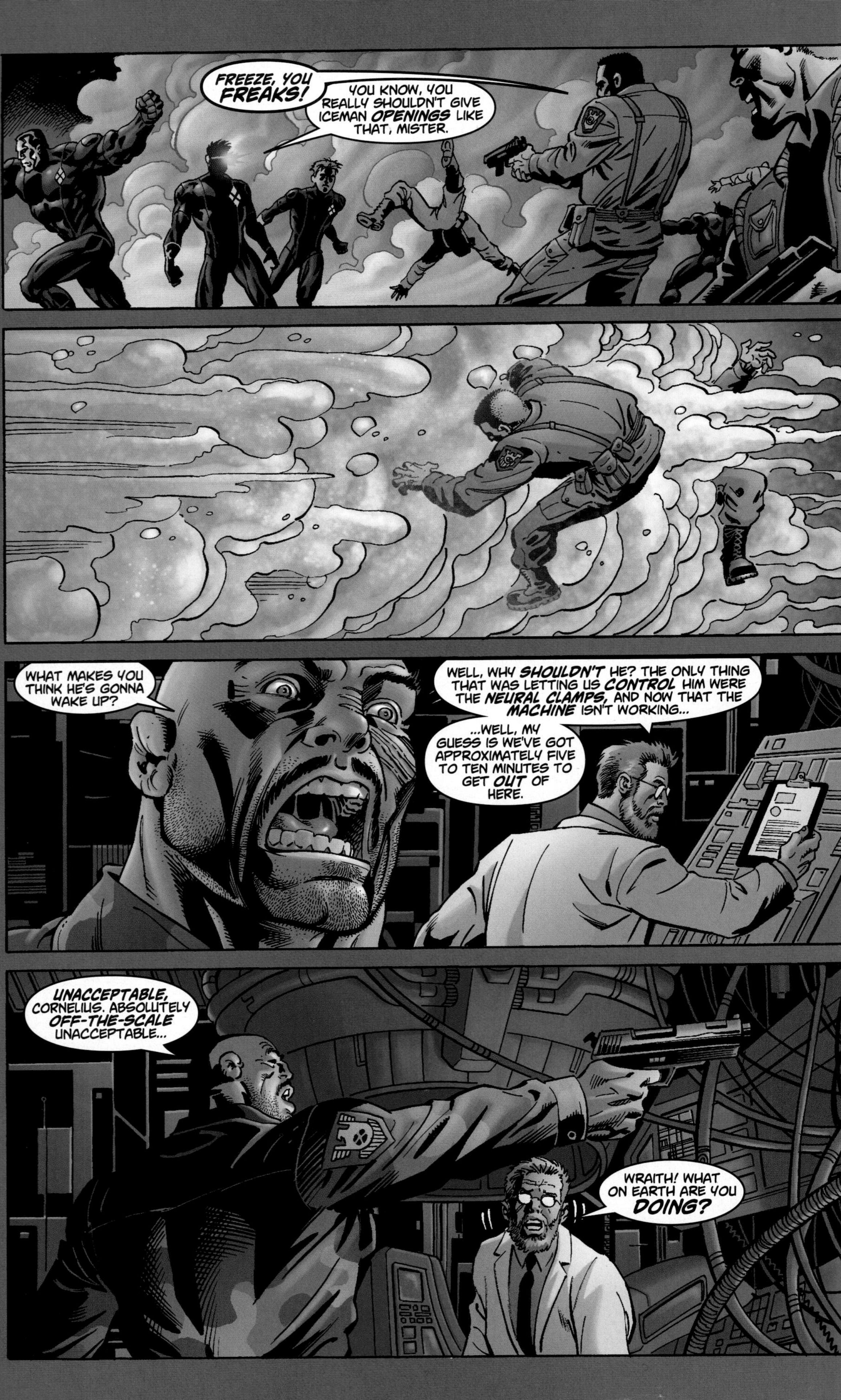
FREEZE, YOU FREAKS!
YOU KNOW, YOU REALLY SHOULDN'T GIVE ICEMAN OPENINGS LIKE THAT, MISTER.
WHAT MAKES YOU THINK HE'S GONNA WAKE UP?
WELL, WHY SHOULDN'T HE? THE ONLY THING THAT WAS LETTING US CONTROL HIM WERE THE NEURAL CLAMPS, AND NOW THAT THE MACHINE ISN'T WORKING...
...WELL, MY GUESS IS WE'VE GOT APPROXIMATELY FIVE TO TEN MINUTES TO GET OUT OF HERE.
UNACCEPTABLE, CORNELIUS. ABSOLUTELY OFF-THE-SCALE UNACCEPTABLE...
WRAITH! WHAT ON EARTH ARE YOU DOING?

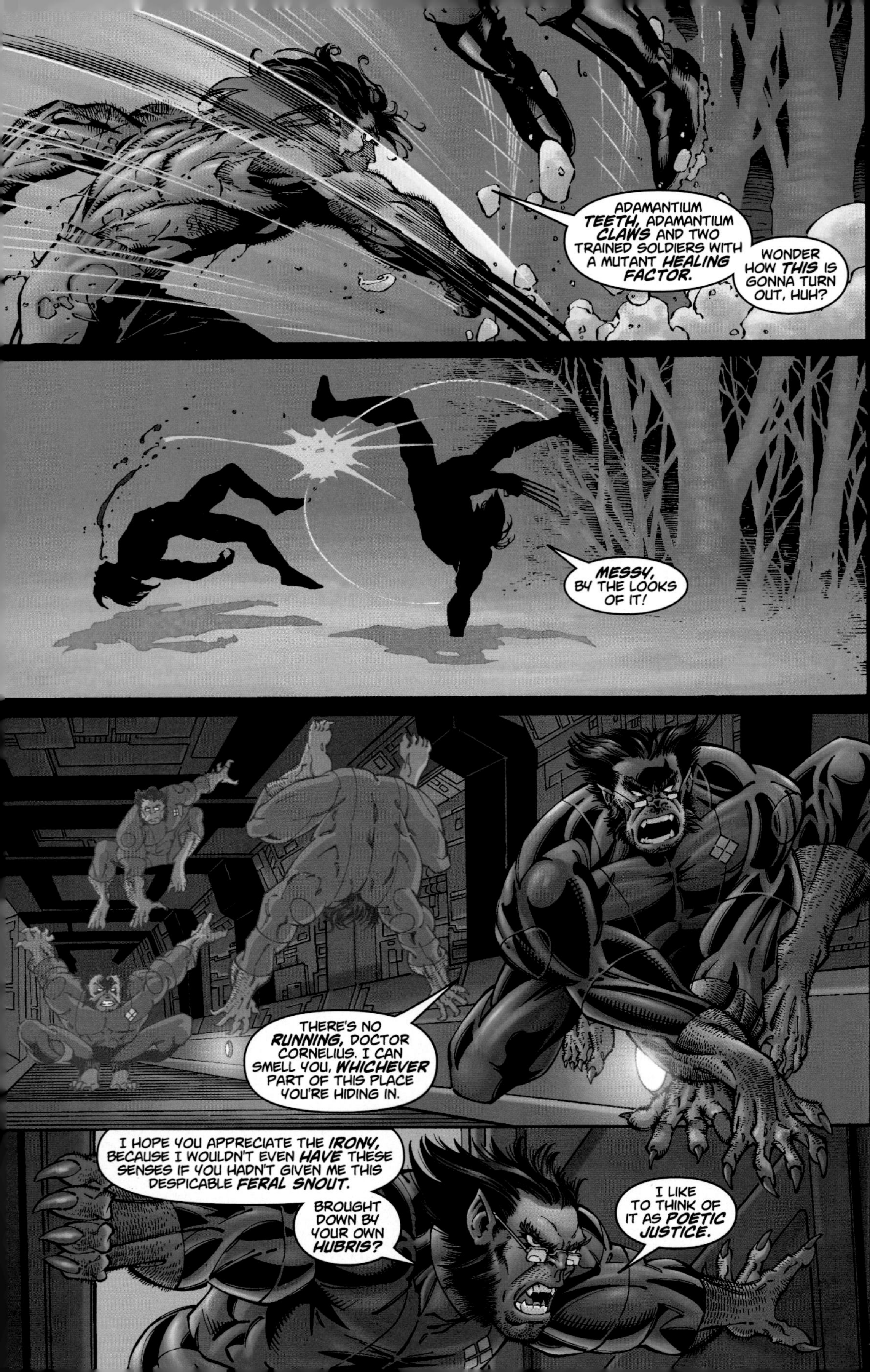

ADAMANTIUM TEETH, ADAMANTIUM CLAWS AND TWO TRAINED SOLDIERS WITH A MUTANT HEALING FACTOR.
WONDER HOW THIS IS GONNA TURN OUT, HUH?
MESSY, BY THE LOOKS OF IT!
THERE'S NO RUNNING, DOCTOR CORNELIUS. I CAN SMELL YOU, WHICHEVER PART OF THIS PLACE YOU'RE HIDING IN.
I HOPE YOU APPRECIATE THE IRONY, BECAUSE I WOULDN'T EVEN HAVE THESE SENSES IF YOU HADN'T GIVEN ME THIS DESPICABLE FERAL SNOUT.
BROUGHT DOWN BY YOUR OWN HUBRIS?
I LIKE TO THINK OF IT AS POETIC JUSTICE.

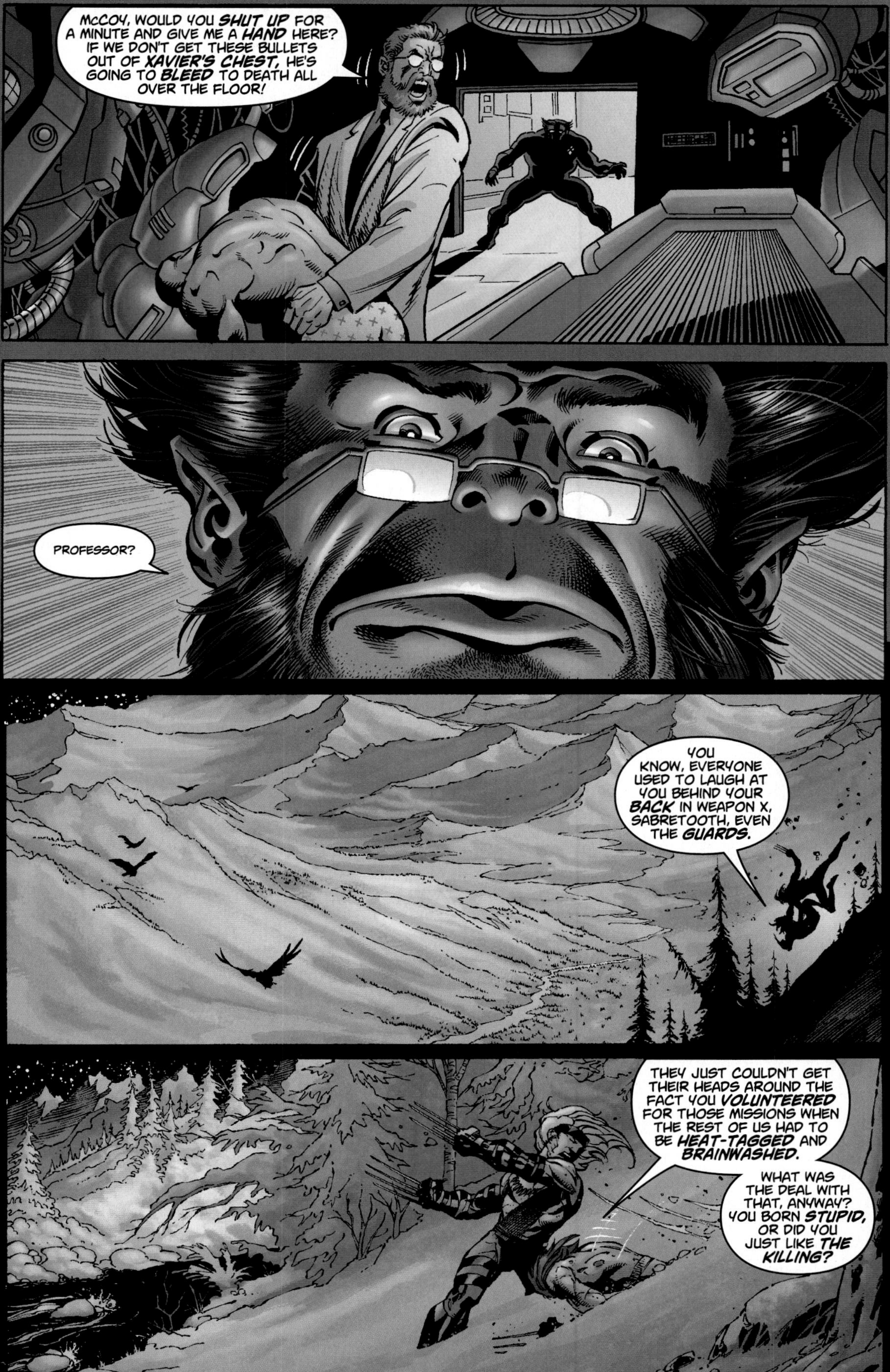
McCOY, WOULD YOU SHUT UP FOR A MINUTE AND GIVE ME A HAND HERE? IF WE DON'T GET THESE BULLETS OUT OF XAVIER'S CHEST, HE'S GOING TO BLEED TO DEATH ALL OVER THE FLOOR!
PROFESSOR?
YOU KNOW, EVERYONE USED TO LAUGH AT YOU BEHIND YOUR BACK IN WEAPON X, SABRETOOTH, EVEN THE GUARDS.
THEY JUST COULDN'T GET THEIR HEADS AROUND THE FACT YOU VOLUNTEERED FOR THOSE MISSIONS WHEN THE REST OF US HAD TO BE HEAT-TAGGED AND BRAINWASHED.
WHAT WAS THE DEAL WITH THAT, ANYWAY? YOU BORN STUPID, OR DID YOU JUST LIKE THE KILLING?

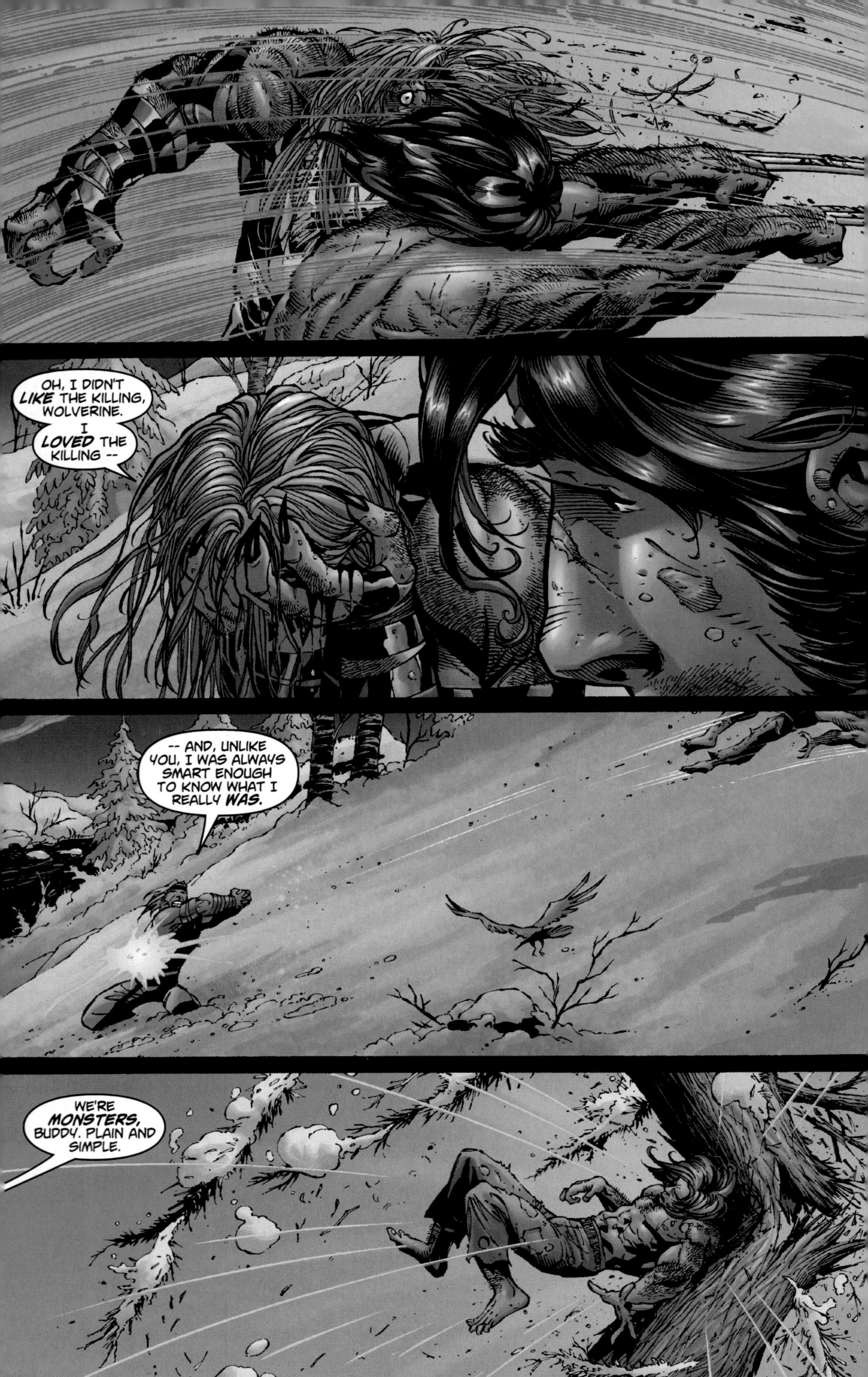
OH, I DIDN'T LIKE THE KILLING, WOLVERINE.
I LOVED THE KILLING --
-- AND, UNLIKE YOU, I WAS ALWAYS SMART ENOUGH TO KNOW WHAT I REALLY WAS.
WE'RE MONSTERS, BUDDY. PLAIN AND SIMPLE.

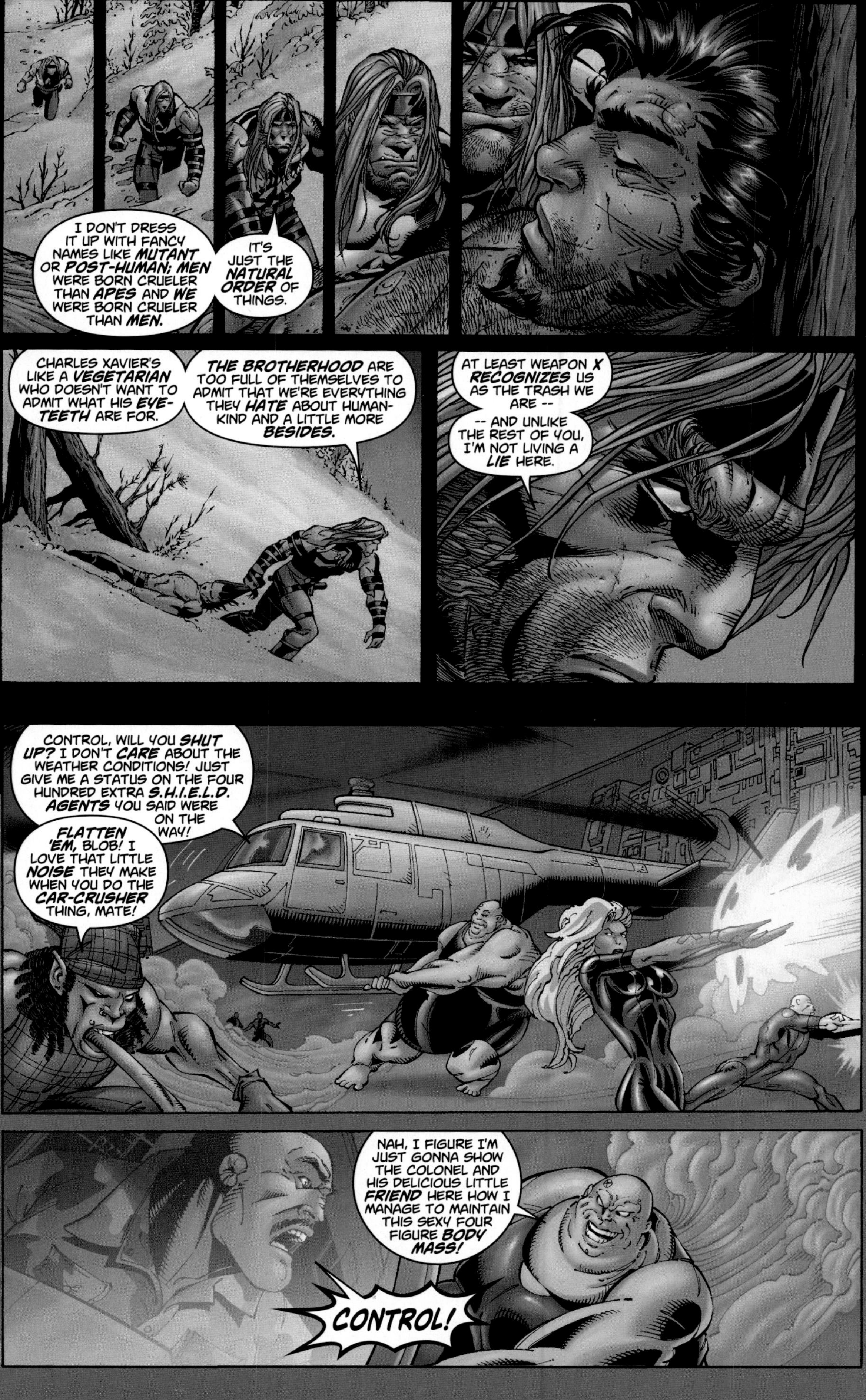
I DON'T DRESS IT UP WITH FANCY NAMES LIKE MUTANT OR POST-HUMAN; MEN WERE BORN CRUELER THAN APES AND WE WERE BORN CRUELER THAN MEN.
IT'S JUST THE NATURAL ORDER OF THINGS.
CHARLES XAVIER'S LIKE A VEGETARIAN WHO DOESN'T WANT TO ADMIT WHAT HIS EYE-TEETH ARE FOR.
THE BROTHERHOOD ARE TOO FULL OF THEMSELVES TO ADMIT THAT WE'RE EVERYTHING THEY HATE ABOUT HUMAN-KIND AND A LITTLE MORE BESIDES.
AT LEAST WEAPON X RECOGNIZES US AS THE TRASH WE ARE --
-- AND UNLIKE THE REST OF YOU, I'M NOT LIVING A LIE HERE.
CONTROL, WILL YOU SHUT UP? I DON'T CARE ABOUT THE WEATHER CONDITIONS! JUST GIVE ME A STATUS ON THE FOUR HUNDRED EXTRA S.H.I.E.L.D. AGENTS YOU SAID WERE ON THE WAY!
FLATTEN 'EM, BLOB! I LOVE THAT LITTLE NOISE THEY MAKE WHEN YOU DO THE CAR-CRUSHER THING, MATE!
NAH, I FIGURE I'M JUST GONNA SHOW THE COLONEL AND HIS DELICIOUS LITTLE FRIEND HERE HOW I MANAGE TO MAINTAIN THIS SEXY FOUR FIGURE BODY MASS!
CONTROL!

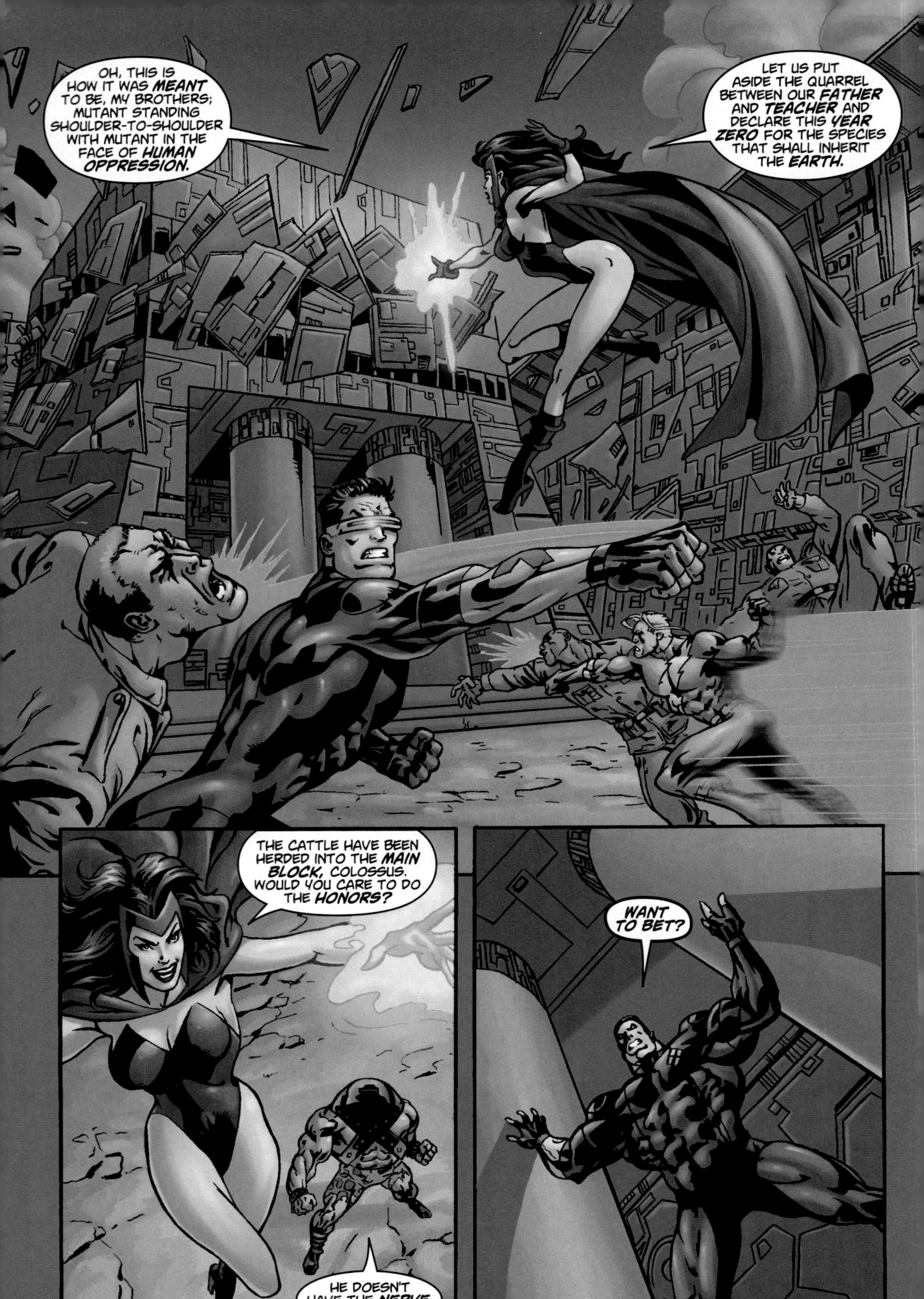
OH, THIS IS HOW IT WAS MEANT TO BE, MY BROTHERS; MUTANT STANDING SHOULDER-TO-SHOULDER WITH MUTANT IN THE FACE OF HUMAN OPPRESSION.
LET US PUT ASIDE THE QUARREL BETWEEN OUR FATHER AND TEACHER AND DECLARE THIS YEAR ZERO FOR THE SPECIES THAT SHALL INHERIT THE EARTH.
THE CATTLE HAVE BEEN HERDED INTO THE MAIN BLOCK, COLOSSUS. WOULD YOU CARE TO DO THE HONORS?
HE DOESN'T HAVE THE NERVE, WANDA.
WANT TO BET?

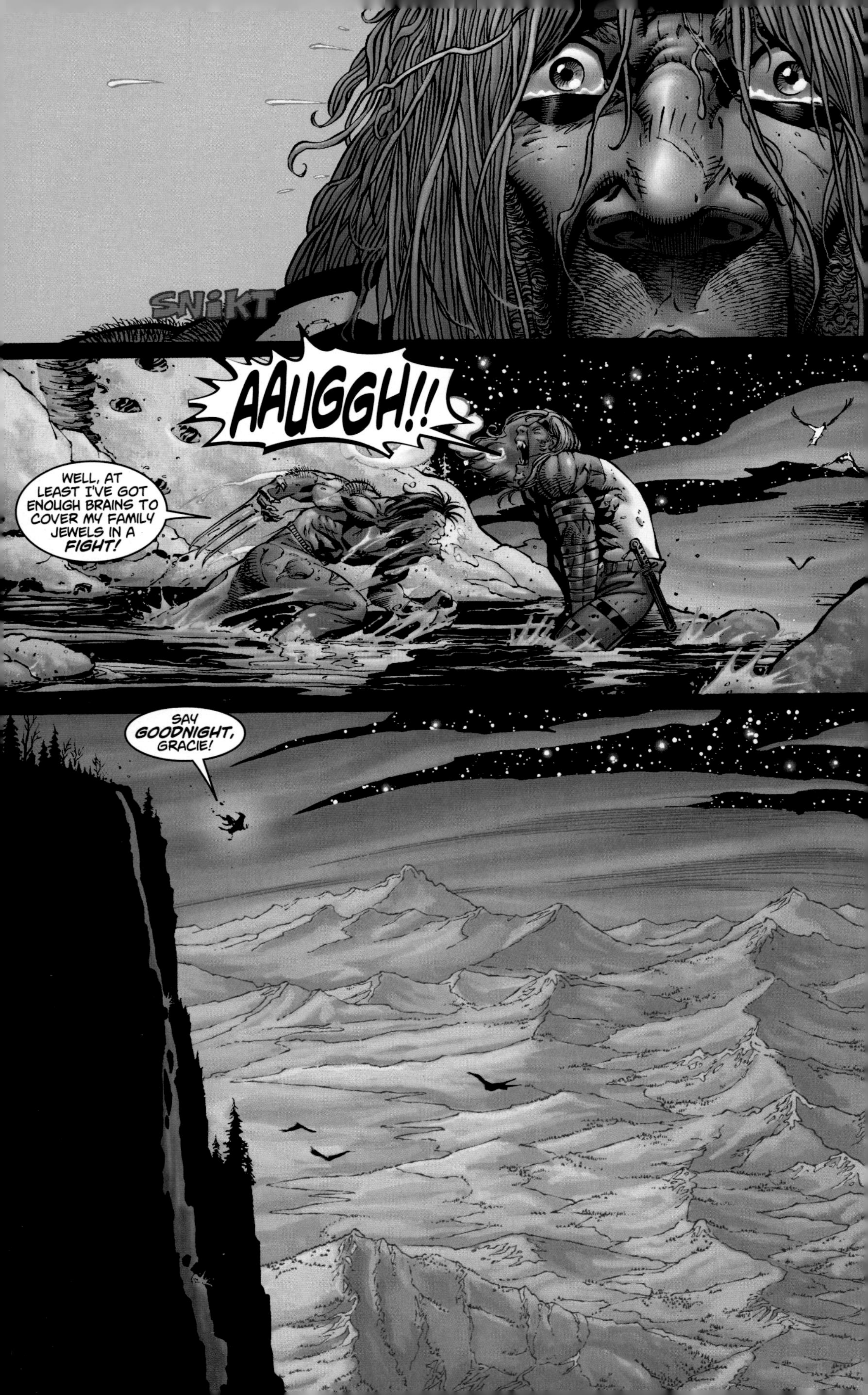
SNIKT
AAUGGH!!
WELL, AT LEAST I'VE GOT ENOUGH BRAINS TO COVER MY FAMILY JEWELS IN A FIGHT!
SAY GOODNIGHT, GRACIE!

WHAT ARE YOU *WAITING* FOR, COLOSSUS? THESE PEOPLE DIDN'T HESITATE WHILE THEY WERE TORTURING *YOU* AND YOUR *MUTANT BROTHERS.*

FINISH THE JOB BEFORE THAT *S.H.I.E.L.D* TEAM ARRIVES, YOU IDIOT.

I'M NOT *HESITATING* HERE, QUICKSILVER, MY *ARMS* JUST AREN'T LISTENING TO MY *BRAIN* FOR SOME REASON.

THAT'S BECAUSE I'M *DISRUPTING THE SIGNAL,* PETER.

WHAT?

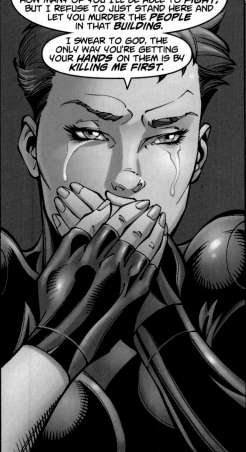

I DON'T KNOW HOW LONG I CAN *HOLD* IT OR HOW MANY OF YOU I'LL BE ABLE TO *FIGHT,* BUT I REFUSE TO JUST STAND HERE AND LET YOU MURDER THE *PEOPLE* IN THAT *BUILDING.*

I SWEAR TO GOD, THE ONLY WAY YOU'RE GETTING YOUR *HANDS* ON THEM IS BY *KILLING ME FIRST.*

PLEASE, YOU KNOW I'M RIGHT. DON'T MAKE ME FIGHT YOU JUST BECAUSE YOU'RE ANGRY AT A BUNCH OF MOTHER-FIXATED, EMOTIONALLY-DETACHED *ABUSERS* IN THERE.

GIRL, SOMEBODY NEEDS TO *SHUT* YOU --

OW!

THAT ACTUALLY *HURT*, YOU LITTLE SLEAZE.

SHE'S *RIGHT*, ROGUE. NOBODY'S KILLING *ANYONE*.

I DON'T KNOW ABOUT THE REST OF YOU, BUT I'M WITH JEAN.

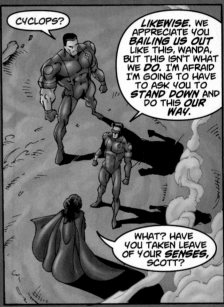

CYCLOPS?

LIKEWISE. WE APPRECIATE YOU *BAILING US OUT* LIKE THIS, WANDA, BUT THIS ISN'T WHAT WE *DO*. I'M AFRAID I'M GOING TO HAVE TO ASK YOU TO *STAND DOWN* AND DO THIS *OUR WAY.*

WHAT? HAVE YOU TAKEN LEAVE OF YOUR *SENSES,* SCOTT?

YEAH, WHY SHOULD WE JUST LET THIS GO BECAUSE YOU'RE TOO SCARED TO DISAGREE WITH *LITTLE MISS EMPATHIC* HERE? HAVE YOU FORGOTTEN WHAT THESE MONSTERS DID TO *HENRY*, CYCLOPS?

NO, BUT WHAT'S YOUR SOLUTION, STORM?

MURDERING FIVE HUNDRED *S.H.I.E.L.D.* TROOPS AND *OFFICE STAFF* ISN'T GOING TO MAKE HIM LOOK HUMAN AGAIN, *EITHER.*

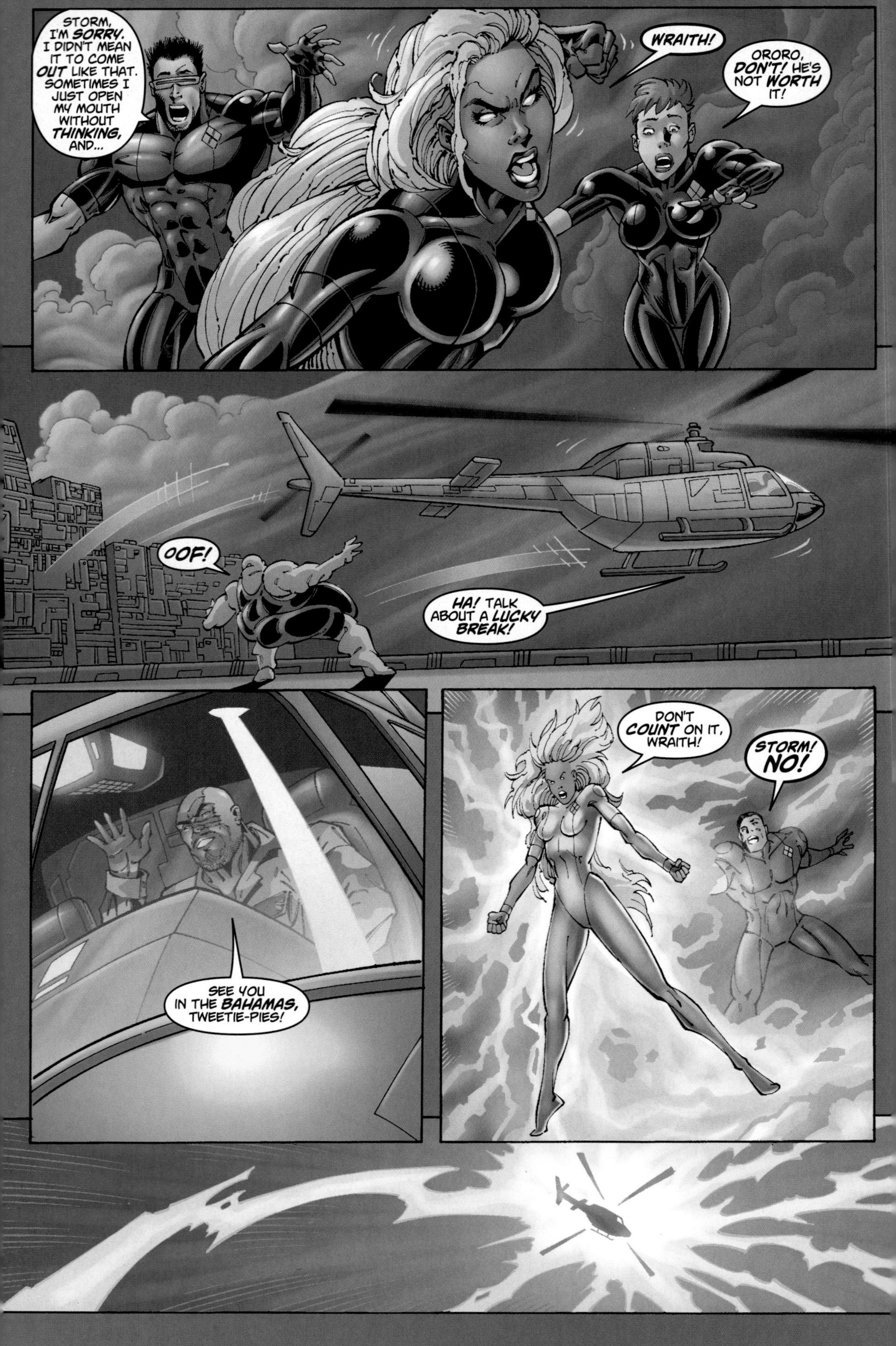

STORM, I'M SORRY. I DIDN'T MEAN IT TO COME OUT LIKE THAT. SOMETIMES I JUST OPEN MY MOUTH WITHOUT THINKING, AND...
WRAITH!
ORORO, DON'T! HE'S NOT WORTH IT!
OOF!
HA! TALK ABOUT A LUCKY BREAK!
SEE YOU IN THE BAHAMAS, TWEETIE-PIES!
DON'T COUNT ON IT, WRAITH!
STORM! NO!

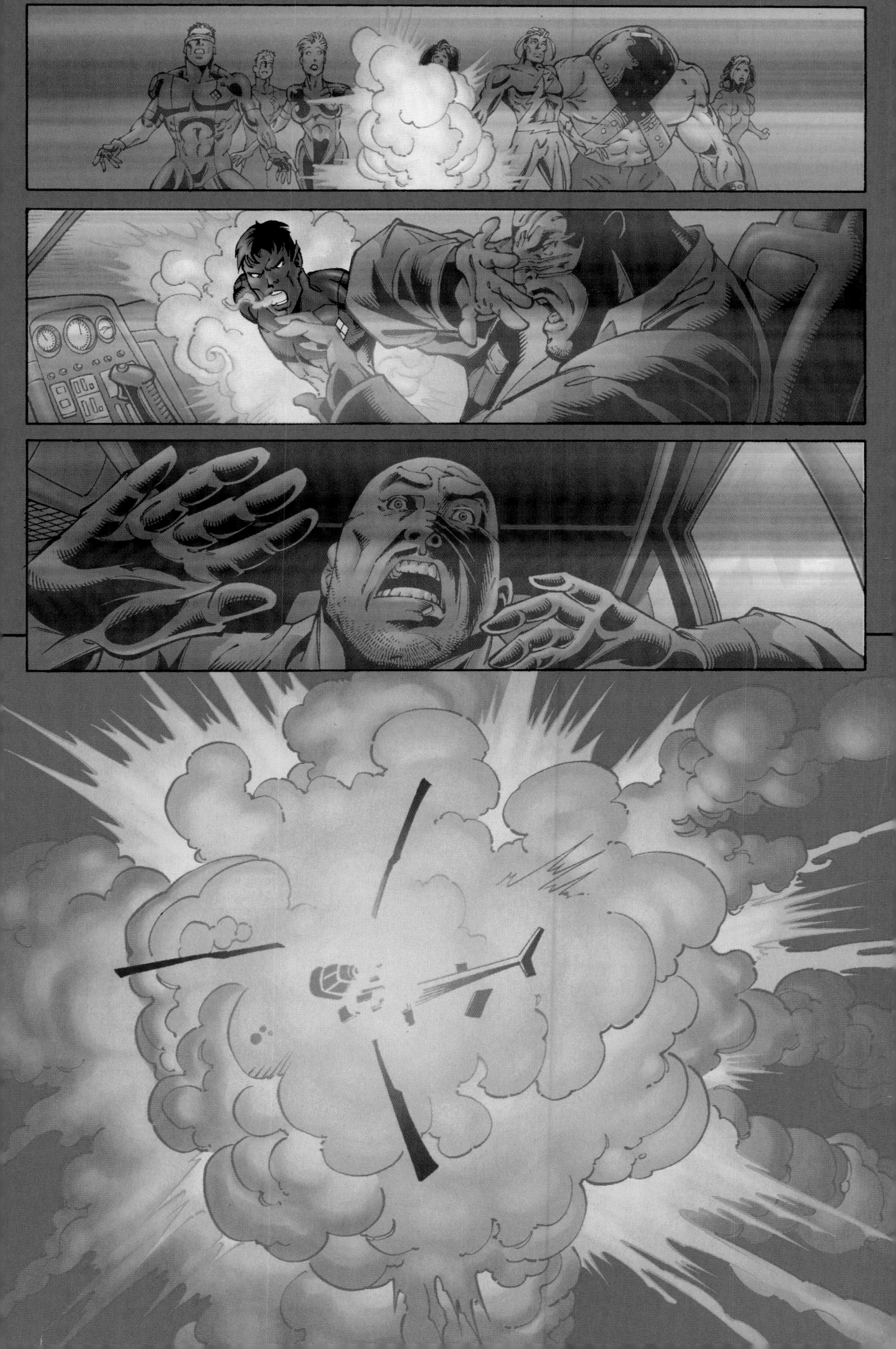

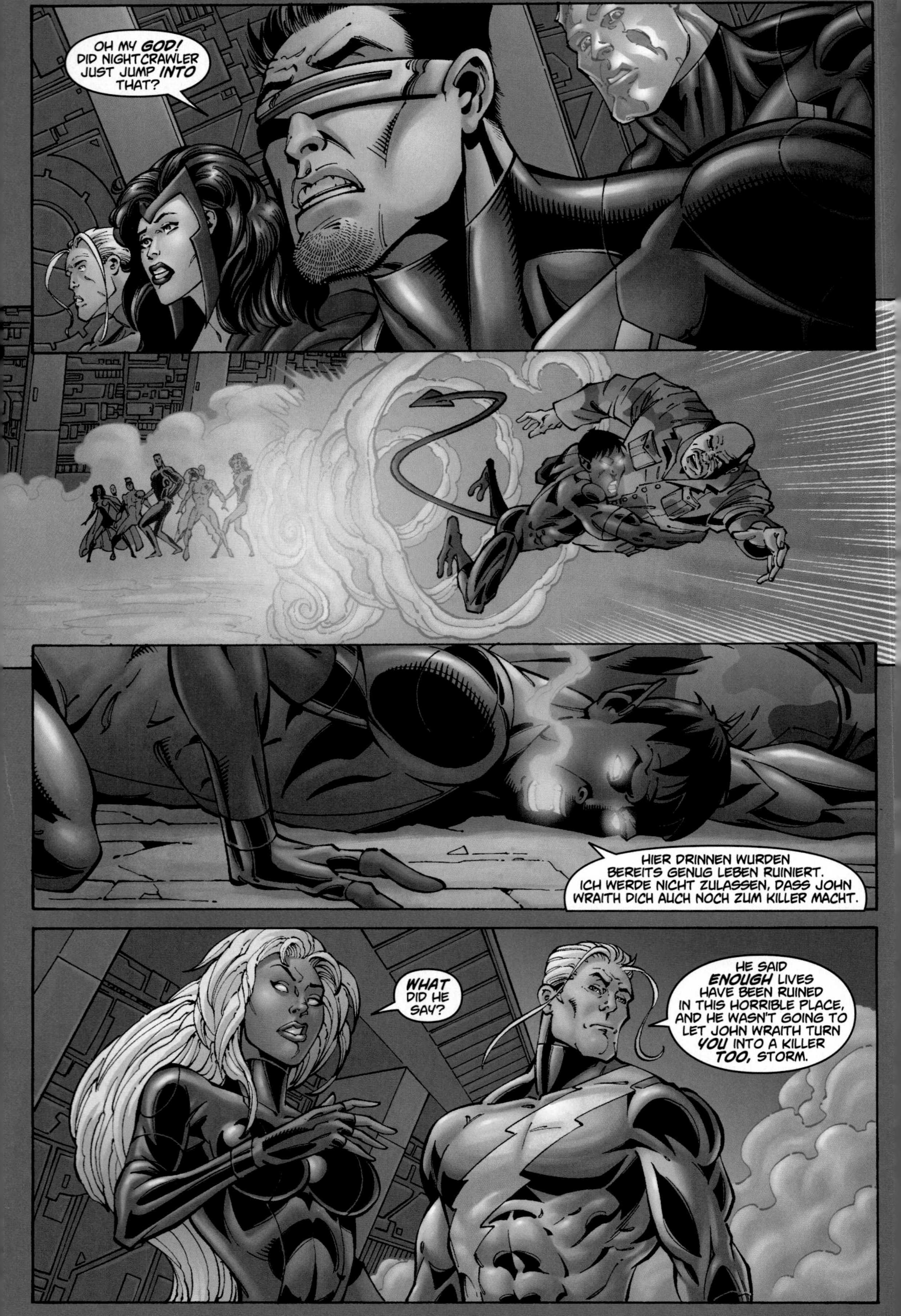
OH MY GOD! DID NIGHTCRAWLER JUST JUMP INTO THAT?
HIER DRINNEN WURDEN BEREITS GENUG LEBEN RUINIERT. ICH WERDE NICHT ZULASSEN, DASS JOHN WRAITH DICH AUCH NOCH ZUM KILLER MACHT.
WHAT DID HE SAY?
HE SAID ENOUGH LIVES HAVE BEEN RUINED IN THIS HORRIBLE PLACE, AND HE WASN'T GOING TO LET JOHN WRAITH TURN YOU INTO A KILLER TOO, STORM.

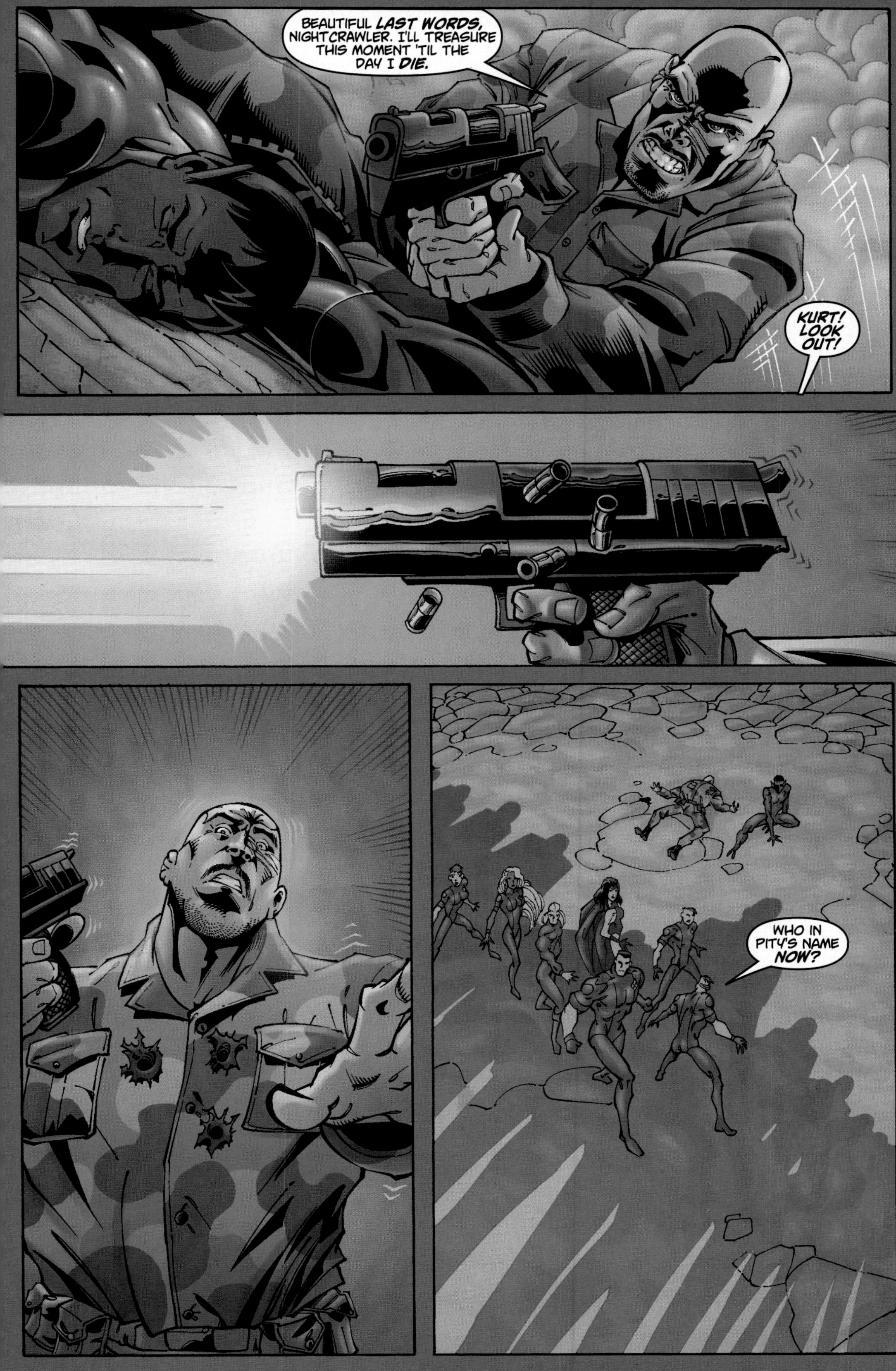
BEAUTIFUL LAST WORDS, NIGHTCRAWLER. I'LL TREASURE THIS MOMENT 'TIL THE DAY I DIE.
KURT! LOOK OUT!
WHO IN PITY'S NAME NOW?

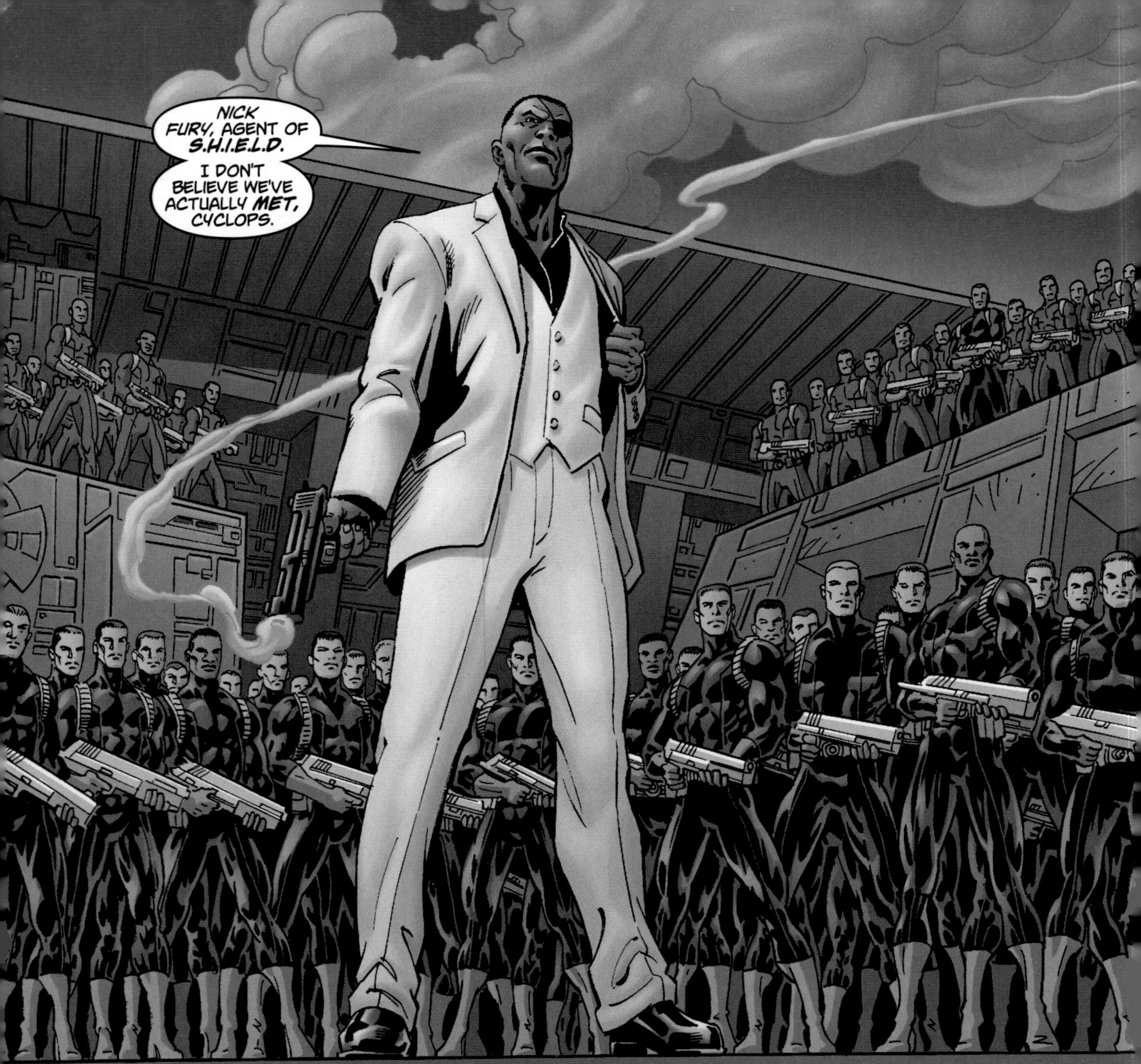
NICK FURY, AGENT OF S.H.I.E.L.D.
I DON'T BELIEVE WE'VE ACTUALLY MET, CYCLOPS.

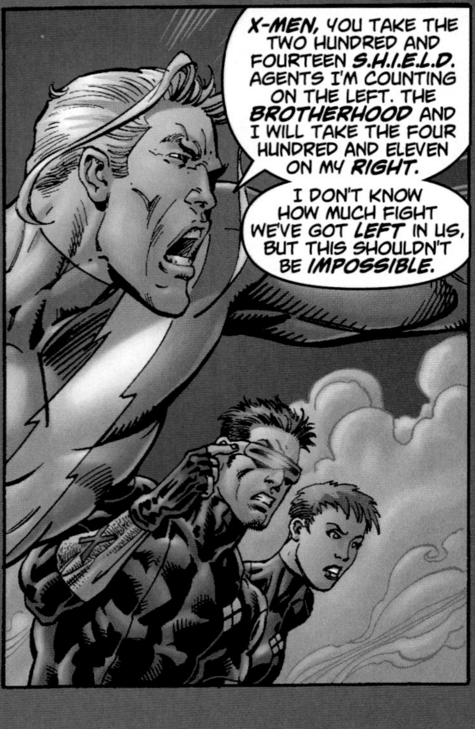
X-MEN, YOU TAKE THE TWO HUNDRED AND FOURTEEN S.H.I.E.L.D. AGENTS I'M COUNTING ON THE LEFT. THE BROTHERHOOD AND I WILL TAKE THE FOUR HUNDRED AND ELEVEN ON MY RIGHT.
I DON'T KNOW HOW MUCH FIGHT WE'VE GOT LEFT IN US, BUT THIS SHOULDN'T BE IMPOSSIBLE.

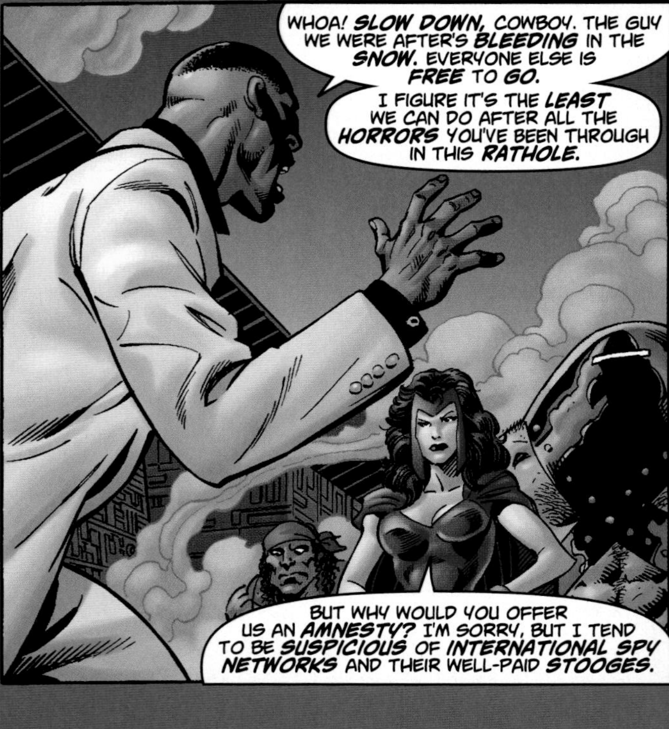
WHOA! SLOW DOWN, COWBOY. THE GUY WE WERE AFTER'S BLEEDING IN THE SNOW. EVERYONE ELSE IS FREE TO GO.
I FIGURE IT'S THE LEAST WE CAN DO AFTER ALL THE HORRORS YOU'VE BEEN THROUGH IN THIS RATHOLE.
BUT WHY WOULD YOU OFFER US AN AMNESTY? I'M SORRY, BUT I TEND TO BE SUSPICIOUS OF INTERNATIONAL SPY NETWORKS AND THEIR WELL-PAID STOOGES.

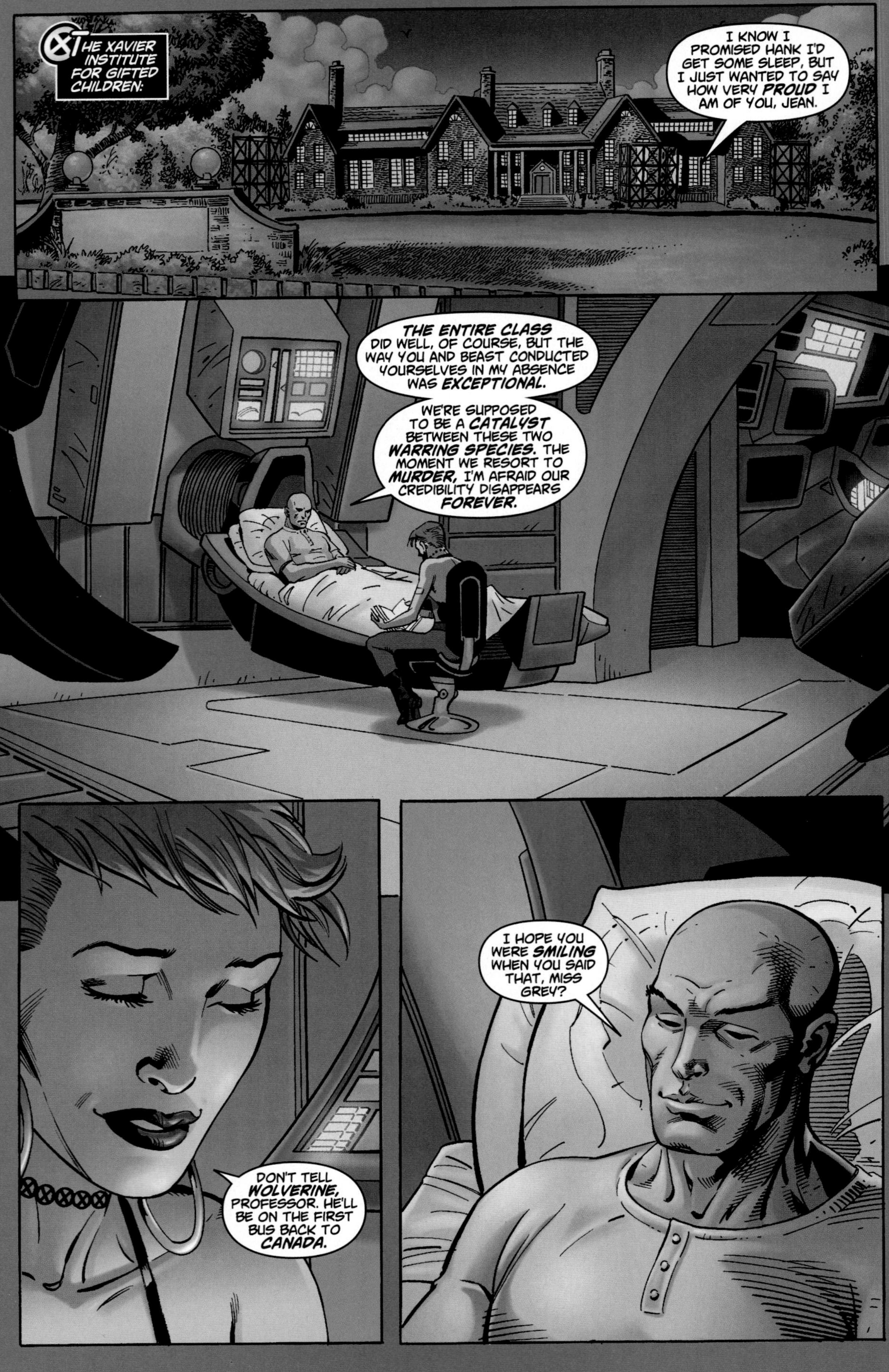
THE XAVIER INSTITUTE FOR GIFTED CHILDREN:
I KNOW I PROMISED HANK I'D GET SOME SLEEP, BUT I JUST WANTED TO SAY HOW VERY PROUD I AM OF YOU, JEAN.
THE ENTIRE CLASS DID WELL, OF COURSE, BUT THE WAY YOU AND BEAST CONDUCTED YOURSELVES IN MY ABSENCE WAS EXCEPTIONAL.
WE'RE SUPPOSED TO BE A CATALYST BETWEEN THESE TWO WARRING SPECIES. THE MOMENT WE RESORT TO MURDER, I'M AFRAID OUR CREDIBILITY DISAPPEARS FOREVER.
DON'T TELL WOLVERINE, PROFESSOR. HE'LL BE ON THE FIRST BUS BACK TO CANADA.
I HOPE YOU WERE SMILING WHEN YOU SAID THAT, MISS GREY?

Although he later turned down the gig, Brian Michael Bendis initially pitched to write *Ultimate X-Men* during the project's early stages. Presented here is his script for what could have been a very different take on *Ultimate X-Men #1*.

X-MEN
GROUND ZERO
PROJECT SCRIPT
ISSUE ONE
BY BRIAN MICHAEL BENDIS

PAGE 1-

PANEL 1-

1- An almost totally black panel. Forty or fifty little digital blue dots spring up out of the black.

It looks as if the dots could be infrared readings, but they have a different halo to them...a different ambiance.

Voices are heard. They are placed almost on top of each other: a street hustle is in progress and the patter is fast and furious.

REMY
What's it going to be, mon ami? I'm dying a slow death.

VOICE
I don't know. I just don't-

ROGUE
I would do it.

VOICE
You would do it?

ROGUE
Totally would do it.

VOICE
Then go ahead and do it. Here-

ROGUE
Do I even look like I got a pot to-?

GAMBIT
Old age! Dying! Me!

2- A high and wide shot of New York City. Looking down on the teeming metropolis from the tops of its tallest buildings all the way down to the teeming hustle and bustle below.

ROGUE
If I had a finsky- I would. But I don't. I'm living vicariously.

VOICE
I don't know.

REMY
You don't know what?

VOICE
What's the bet again?
And if I bet twenty, I win what?

REMY
Forty, aye?

VOICE
Twenty gets me forty?
REMY
Is there an echo?

ROGUE
Wish I had the coinage. I so know how to do this.

REMY
Big talk, little girl. It's a simple question, boyo, what's it going to be? In or out.

VOICE
Um...
Believe it or not, I do have a life.

VOICE (CONT'D)
I'm thinking.

Page 2-3

DOUBLE PAGE SPREAD

1- Wide. A street scene- Washington Square Park. Day.

It's a rocking good time under the arch of the square, hackie sackers, pop potatoes and skate boarders hang around and chitchat.

A colorful gang of teens from all walks of rebellious life play out whatever soap opera they are involved in.

Street performers, horse carriages. Caricature artists, jewelry makers selling their wares.

Skateboarders are sliding across stairs and banisters trying to impress girls who aren't even paying attention.

In the background, Remy. GAMBIT, 17, a devilish looking Leonardo look-a-like, with a hint of his French lineage. He is wearing a long coat with tank top underneath. He looks like he is always up to something.

He is running a **THREE CARD MONTY GAME** to the delight and confusion of his gathered crowd.
He is mixing the cards. His crowd is mixed with tourists and older people charmed by the street con.

Also in the middle crowd is **ROGUE, A YOUNG-LOOKING 16**, with shocking pink hair. Like a teen Gwen Stefani from No Doubt, she is **REMY**'s plant in the crowd.

They are pretending not to know each other, she is egging on...

The doughy guy MARK in front of REMY, the proverbial sucker born every minute. He is the target of the hustle.

REMY
Call it the way you see it, yes?

Simple for you. Watch my hands. Pick the ace.

You pick the ace you win the bank.

MARK
So I gotta pick the ace?

2- Tight on REMY. Our first good look at him. He looks up at Rogue. He is giving her the signal.

REMY
That's all you gotta do.

3- Rogue standing next to the mark. Rogue looks back at Remy with a smirk. She knows what to do. The mark is transfixed on the cards.

MARK
I don't know. I heard there was a trick to this or something...

4- Rogue slips off her pink leather glove.

REMY
A trick? News to me.

5- Tight on her hand just barely touching the back of the mark's arm.

There is **A BLUE SPARK BETWEEN HER FINGERTIPS** and the hair on the back of his arm. The mark doesn't notice.

MARK
I think I'm going to get outta here. I saw a guy take a guy's shoes once playing this.

6- REMY looks to Rogue.

REMY
Took a guy's shoes?

7- Rogue holds up a two sign with her fingers.

8- Profile of group. **REMY** looks back to the mark.

REMY (CONT'D)
Two hundred gets you five.

MARK
Five?

REMY
Bet goes up the bank goes up.

MARK
Five, huh?

REMY
If you got it.

9- The mark thinks, he seems a bit woozy now, from Rogue's touch.

10- His **POV** of the cards. A tad blurry.

11- Rogue looks at him. She knows he is going to go for it.

12- The mark digs into his pocket

Gambit sketch by J.H. Williams III

MARK

OK- uh- OK. Big shot, let's see you do it.

PAGE 4-

1- REMY shuffles the cards. The mark throws down his money. A couple of the younger members of the gathered crowd, obvious locals, egg on REMY.

YOUNG PUNK

Yo REMY boy, do the thing.

YOUNG PUNK 2

Come on, give them a treat...

2- Rogue rolls her eyes. The mark looks at the kids not knowing what this means.

MARK

What?

3- REMY smiles and holds his hands over the cards.

REMY

Alright, alright...

Pick it, my friend.

4- The mark nervously picks the middle card.
MARK
There. Yeah there- the middle one.

5- REMY. a devil's smile, his hands still over the cards.

REMY

The middle one?

MARK

Yes.

REMY

Not the left one?

MARK

No.

6- The left card EXPLODES like a piece of purple magnesium. A flash of light and a poof. Like a magic trick.

SPX: PIFF

PAGE 5-

1- The crowd JUMPS out of their skin. The locals smile.

They love the trick

WOMAN

Aahh!

MARK

Oh sh-!!

2- REMY his hands still over the cards. They don't move.

REMY

Not the right one?

MARK

N-no.

3- The right card EXPLODES the same way.

SPX: PIFF!

4- The crowd has gone from shock to delight. The middle age woman is clapping her hands from the thrill.

REMY

Then this one?

MARK

Yes.

REMY

Flip it then...

Page 6-

1- The nervous mark looks at REMY.

2- The mark flips the card himself.

3- It's a 5 OF SPADES.

4- Bigger panel. The mark deflates and the crowd erupts in applause. Rogue just smirks

5- REMY scoops up his money.

MARK

Damn it! Damn it! But- I- I saw it.

WOMAN

How did you do that?

REMY

It's the Orleans, baby. Magic's in the air. I'm your big bad voodoo daddy.

6- A slight bird's eye. A looming shadow towers over REMY resetting his game.

MONEY B
What did I tell you about hustlin' in the pavilion
till you pay me my bank, you little-?!

7- Same angle, but tighter. REMY looks up.

Page 7-

1- From REMY's and Rogue's P.O.V. Two huge
Rastafarian street hoods/ drug dealer types. They are
pissed. The huge Ice Cube look-a-like dude talking is
MONEY B!

MONEY B (CONT'D)
What did I tell you? I told you I was taking you
in next time, right boy?

2- BIG TALL PANEL. In a blink, REMY grabs everything and
FLIPS OVER BACKWARDS over a large shrub.
Rogue leaps the shrub as well.

3- REMY and Rogue run down street at top speed. His
long jacket blows behind him. They are dodging the New
York City street crowds gracefully.

4- The Rastafarian street hoods chase.

5- REMY and Rogue turn into an alley

6- REMY grabs a fire escape ladder...

7- and grabs Rogue's hand with the other hand.

8- ...and with the grace of a gymnast heaves himself and
her up to the second story window.

Page 8-

1- REMY and Rogue run across a rooftop. They are both
laughing and running. New York City in the background.

It is as much a victory lap as a getaway.

ROGUE
Two hundred!! Hot diggity diggity dog!

REMY
Girl, today we are super-sizing those Happy
Meals.

ROGUE
Thank god REMY, I am a starvin' piece of
chicken!

2- Bird's eye looking down on the two teens running
across the rooftop.

3- Same shot, but it is a A CEREBRO PROJECT

PANEL. Like the first panel of the book, this is a series
of panels throughout the book that will represent how
CEREBRO reads mutant energy in the New York area.

CEREBRO panels are A BLUE HUED DIGITAL
READING ALMOST LIKE A HIGH TECH
INFRA RED HEAT READER BUT DIFFERENT.
Something we haven't seen before in a comic book.

The figures of REMY and Rogue are glowing with energy.
Rogue is glowing a little brighter.
4- Same, but tighter. It is a frozen computer image of last
panel. Type is on the side and white boxes are around the
two figures.

The type reads as follows.

Located:

REMY De la St. Croix. Class level three. Last
sighted 5-5-99 status: same.

Located:

Rogue, class level four. Last sighted 5-5-99
status: same.

Page 9-

1- A leaf falls off a tree. A single green leaf. We hear the
voice of Ororo. She is reading street poetry.

ORORO
BLACK CHAMPAGNE GASOLINE
PUDDLES
NIGHTCLUBS DRIPPING WITH
NEON SIGNS
STREETLIGHTS BLAZING WHITE
ON BLACK.
BUT THAT ISN'T WHERE MY HEAD
IS AT.

2- The leaf falls toward the earth. Think the feather in
Forrest Gump.

ORORO (CONT'D)
CAR HORNS BLARING
CUT GLASS TOWERS INTO NIGHT
BLACK NIGHT BLACK SILK BLACK
RAIN. BUT MY BLACK SKIN IS
NOTHING WITHOUT THE SUN.

3- The leaf falls in front of ORORO.

Ororo is sixteen, African American, earthy beauty. If not
for her crunchy granola fashion she would look like royalty.
(Think a young Lauren Hill meets Tracy Chapman.)

Ororo reads from her worn journal. She has a beatific smile. Ororo the artist is a happy and confident girl. Ororo is outside in a city park.

ORORO (CONT'D)
GLITTER SEQUINS OVER SKYLINE
HEELS CLICKING DOWN THE
STREET
DESERTED DESOLATE.

4- The floating leaf catches Ororo's eye. She is a little entranced by it.

ORORO (CONT'D)

BLACK STREET
BLACK NIGHT BLACK SKIN
I PAY IT NO MIND AT ALL
SILENT

5- Same. Ororo continues her poem, but she puts out her hand under the floating leaf.

Is Ororo keeping the leaf afloat with her powers? She stares at the leaf like it is the center of her universe.

ORORO (CONT'D)
SILVER ORCHID IN A BLACK,
BLACK STREET

6- The leaf defies gravity and floats back up to the sky.

STORM-ORORO: I THOUGHT IT MORE INTERESTING TO GET RID OF THE CAPE. IT SEEMS TO GIVE HER MORE ATTITUDE WITHOUT IT. SHE HAS A MORE VOLUPTUOUS BODY COMPARED TO JEAN GREY. NOTE THE TRIBAL TATTOOS.

Storm sketch by J.H. Williams III

ORORO (CONT'D)

BLACKOUT

7- Wide shot of an outdoor Bleeker Street cafe. Ororo has just performed her poem for a smattering of her peers and a couple of walkbys.

A smattering of applause to her beautiful poem. She accepts it gracefully.

LYNDSAY
YAY!

ORORO
Thank you, guys.

Thanks.

Page 10-

1- Over Ororo's shoulder, from the small crowd, Lyndsay, Ororo's best friend (think Brandi), leaps up from the crowd in approval and support of her friend's performance.

Most of the rest of the crowd is talking amongst themselves.

Maybe a skateboarding guy is staring at Ororo in the background. Awestruck by her beauty.

LYNDSAY
Ororo, that was amazing!! You did it!

ORORO
It was OK.

LYNDSAY
Girl! You are so the performer!

2- Same, but Lyndsay's face has dropped. She is looking at something over Ororo's shoulder. Something she is sad to see.

LYNDSAY (CONT'D)
That was really fun to-

3- Same angle, Ororo turns her head around to see what her friend Lyndsay is looking at so miserably.

LYNDSAY (CONT'D)
That dog-

4- Over both Lyndsay and Ororo's shoulder, they have both turned their bodies to face...

A handsome young BLACK MAN who is hanging all over a fly girl.

The couple are oblivious to the fact that they are being watched by the two young girls. There is a small smattering of people walking around the open park.

5- Tighter on the young couple slobbering on each other

6- Lyndsay and Ororo frowning at the sight. Ororo looks really hurt. This is obviously her boyfriend or a boy she liked.

The SKY BEHIND THEM IS TURNING DARKER with a twinge of orange from an electrical orange. The wind is picking up.

                    LYNDSAY (CONT'D)
        He's a dog, O.

Page 11-

1- Tight on Ororo. She is really mad and hurt. We can see that Ororo is no wallflower. She is emotional and tempestuous-

2- Mid shot of the two girls. Lyndsay yells out toward the couple. Ororo still stares ahead in quiet rage.
The WIND has really picked up. Leaves are blowing. The people in the park are starting to run. A STORM IS COMING.

Behind them the sky has turned into A DARK STORMY WEATHER COLOR. The fury of the earth is brewing.

                    LYNDSAY (CONT'D)
              YOU DOG!!!

3- The couple breaks their revelry. The girl looks to the sky noticing the crazy weather all of a sudden.

The boy looks right at Ororo.

4- big panel. Ororo looks right at him. A single tear falls down one of her angry eyes.

Way behind her A HUGE LIGHTNING BOLT TOUCHES DOWN. A lone raindrop hits her forehead.

SPX: KRAKABOOM!

PAGE 12-

1- High shot of the park but A CEREBRO PROJECT PANEL. Ororo's figure in the middle. The energy off her is huge, almost white.

It looks like a Doppler weather pattern. She is the eye of

the storm. It is a beautiful sight in a way.

2- Same. The image is frozen and digitized like the Rogue and REMY one before.

The white computer type on the side reads

LOCATED:

ORORO MUNROE. CLASS LEVEL SEVEN. LAST SIGHTED 6-8-99 STATUS: AGGRAVATED

3- The same computer screen image is in the middle of the panel. But the hint of a man looking at the screen curiously is in the foreground.

Whatever we can make of his bald features is totally silhouetted and backlit to the light of the screen.

Maybe hints of other screens popping out of the corners of the panel.

Page 13-

1- Wide shot of a beautiful gated mansion on a hill. A stunning piece of architecture.

On the gating in the foreground is a Gothic "W"

2- Tight on coat-sleeved hands slicing an apple.

3- The hands pick up the fancy food tray and start to walk with it. On the tray are two sliced apples, a big bottle of water and a napkin.

4- A white-coated servant type, his back now to us, is walking the tray to a backyard patio. The surroundings are serene, but there is something sad about them.

5- Tight on the butler, he is looking up curiously to the sky.

6- He puts an oddly shaped whistle to his mouth and blows it gentlemanly.

Page 14-

1- Wide shot of the patio.

In the foreground, we can see the figure of what seems like a HUGE BIRD approaching. It is backlit to the sun.

2- Same but the figure swoops down from the sky. The same arcing trajectory of a bird coming in for a landing. They all watch.

3- Big, big panel. But it isn't a bird.

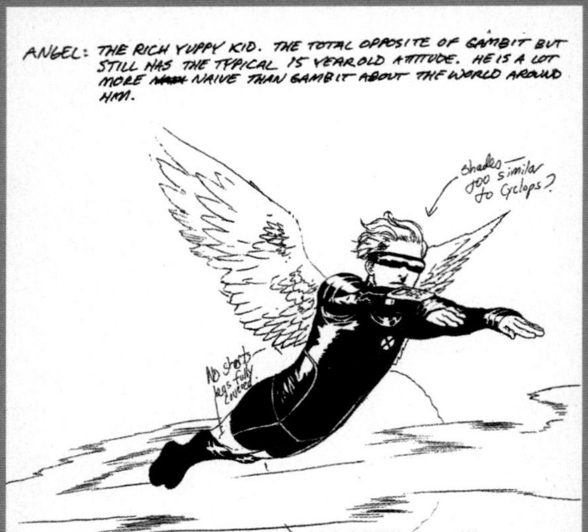
ANGEL: THE RICH YUPPY KID. THE TOTAL OPPOSITE OF GAMBIT BUT STILL HAS THE TYPICAL 15 YEAROLD ATTITUDE. HE IS A LOT MORE NAIVE THAN GAMBIT ABOUT THE WORLD AROUND HIM.
shades too similar to Cyclops?
No shorts- legs fully covered.

Angel sketch by J.H. Williams III

It is the beautiful WINGED FIGURE OF WARREN WORTHINGTON III...

A beautiful blond boy of 17. (think Kurt Cobain) He has a six foot WHITE WINGSPAN spread wide as he has stopped and hovers just above ground level in front of the meeting.

His face is humble, almost embarrassed. He doesn't look anyone in the eye. His left wing gleams off the sun..

He truly looks like AN ANGEL.

BUTLER

Master, your lunch is ready.

4- Warren sits on the roof of the mansion eating his food in an odd birdlike way. There is a quiet nobility about him.

5- A CEREBRO shot. Looking down from the sky on the top of the Worthington estate, a white bracket around him, a glow from his wings.

The white computer type on the side reads

Located:

Warren Worthington III. Class level three. Last sighted 8-18-99 status: same.

Page 15-

1- Same as last page, last panel but pull out to reveal the silhouette of the bald man watching the computer screen.

2- Same but wider. A bank of blue-hued computer screens surround the bald man sitting in the foreground. In each screen is a different situation, a different mutant teen being looked down from above.

3- Same, but wider. We now see the full scope of the room. The man sitting before the screens back still to us. He has quite a task in front of him and is fully prepared to do it.

A voice comes from off screen. It is VICTOR CREED'S.

VOICE

Doctor? Doctor Xavier? It's time.

Doctor?

4- Our first look at the face of CHARLES XAVIER. Bald, handsome. Early thirties. He is woken from his concentration by the voice behind him.

CREED

Doctor?!

XAVIER

Wha-? Oh- yes.

Yes, it's time. Thank you, Mr. Creed.

5- Standing in the doorway to Charles' office/ CEREBRO monitoring station is VICTOR CREED (think Henry Rollins). A big yet intelligent man.

Xavier is turned to see him.

CREED

Well, Charles, let's go.

They are not the type of men that are used to being kept waiting.

6- Full figure shot. Charles has spun HIS WHEELCHAIR around to face his supervisor. He has a file folder with papers in his lap. He is wearing a handsome suit.

7- Tight on Charles' face. The lighting is from below. His face is emotionless.

XAVIER

Mutant!

Page 16-17

Double page spread.

1- Long shot across both pages.

For the first time we see that Charles Xavier is bound to a wheelchair. He sits profile to us in the left side of the panel as he addresses a group of faceless and nameless government black-suited war room types.

In fact, they are all seated in a war room type setting. Dim lighting. Much of the room is drenched in shadow.

Not too dissimilar to the war room setting of Dr. Strangelove. Very top secret looking. Very covert. We should be able to tell just from the look of the room that nothing said in it is ever spoken of outside of this room.

Illumination comes from the maps of New York City on the otherwise black walls, a map very similar to the very first image we saw in this book. A **CEREBRO** shot pinpointing the mutant activity in the New York area.

Victor Creed, notebook held to his chest, stands at a podium not far from Xavier. He obviously has handed the spotlight over to Charles for this part of the briefing.

All listen intently to Xavier's emotionless briefing.

XAVIER (CONT'D)
Homo sapien. Homo mutatis. The next step of human evolution? Still a point of wide speculation.

But- they are individuals, people just like you and me, who find themselves with abilities beyond the norm.

Abilities that they have had since birth but in most cases don't blossom or manifest themselves until puberty.

They walk among us. Some not even aware of their power.

But the mutations to their base human biology is so diverse- as unique to the individual as their fingerprint-

that previously it has been near impossible to get a foothold of where these mutants are and what they are doing.

I am pleased to announce to the council that I have spent the last six months refining the **CEREBRO** satellite technology.

And I can tell you that CEREBRO is a success.

2- Tight on the CEREBRO map.

XAVIER (CONT'D)
In laymen's terms, **CEREBRO** is now able not only to locate mutant activity, but it is able to catalogue the specific genetic code, tag it, and keep tabs and records of it.

The **CEREBRO** satellite is in geo-

synchronistic orbit on the G3-1212 ban.

3- Tight on Ororo's picture

XAVIER (CONT'D)
Also, if abnormal amounts of activity are registered, CEREBRO acts as an alarm system, not too dissimilar to the effects of a Doppler weather tracking system.

4- Xavier talking. Reading his notes.

XAVIER (CONT'D)
So, not only are we now able to pinpoint mutant activity, we are able to analyze and record it.

My hope, gentlemen, is that we will be able to use this information wisely.

That we will learn from the lessons that history has taught us.

5- A shot of three of the shadowed VIP's Xavier is talking to. Maybe cigar smoke is coming from where one of their mouths would be.

VOICE
And what lesson is that, Dr. Xavier?

6- Xavier looking them in the eye. Not reading from his notes.

XAVIER
That- that it is easier and more humane to attempt to peacefully coexist than it is to-

7- Same as five. The men pause. This is obviously not a popular opinion.

8- Same as seven. One of the other men talks.

VOICE 2
And what if that other party has no intention of peaceful coexistence?

Page 18-

1- Xavier talks, Creed is looking at Xavier in disapproval, but Xavier is focused on his immediate audience and not paying Creed mind.

XAVIER
That's the thing, sir.

There is no other party- no other side in this.

It's a smattering of individuals. Many of them

young. They have no agenda. No movement.

I think that the-

2- The trio. Another one speaks.

VOICE

What about Magnus Lehnsherr? And that anti-human campaigning?

3- Tight profile of Xavier.

XAVIER

Sir, that has nothing to do with the CEREBRO project.
Our research will- should be used to help pinpoint those citizens who need our help to-

4- Same as two. The one on the right's hand gestures are erratic and combative.

VOICE

I don't- what are we talking about here?

I thought we were going to be briefed on what happened to the 18.1 billion dollars we approved for the-

5- Same as three tighter. Xavier is confused.

XAVIER

Eighteen- sir, I assure you that the budget for our-

6- Same as 3.

VOICE

No. No. Not your little light show.

The WEAPON X project! What happened to the-?

Page 19-

1- Xavier is confused by this information and is looking to Creed. Creed has his hand on Charles' shoulder.

XAVIER

I don't-

CREED

Charles, thank you for your time.

Everyone has a copy of your leave-behind and we await your next report.

XAVIER

But-

2- From Charles' POV. An eerie lit Creed looking down on Charles.

CREED

Thank you, Charles, the rest of the briefing is level nine clearance.

Thank you.

3- Charles pauses. Looks to the shadow men.

4- The shadow men sit quiet waiting for him to leave.

5- Charles leaves rolling through the door to the hallway outside. He is almost totally backlit to the hallway lighting.

Page 20-

1- Tight on Charles' eye. It is intense. a roll of sweat is rolling down his brow

2- Same shot. His mouth grimacing. His jaw clenched.

XAVIER

NNNFFF.....

3- Tight on his biceps. It is taut. In motion. A vein popping out. Bigger than you would have first imagined.
4- Tight on his hand. Gripping a balance beam for all it's worth.
5- Mid shot of Xavier in a tank top pushing his whole body up with both arms on balance beams.

XAVIER (CONT'D)

RRRFFF!

He is pulling his body out of the water of a indoor Olympic-sized swimming pool. Using the balance beams to do pull ups out of the water. It is hydrotherapy for paraplegics.

He looks as if he is on his fiftieth pull-up in a row. Xavier is in incredible physical shape. A strong intense man.

6- Tight on his eye again. This is a man of intense determination.

MCCOY

(off panel)
Charles, are you ignoring me or just...?

7- Wide shot of the pool area. They are the only ones there.

Standing right in front of Charles at the far end of the pool is SENATOR James McCoy, late 50's, presidential (think Martin Sheen.).

is suit is expensive, his hair is immaculate. His skin is
ale, almost green. His suave demeanor is only surface.

MCCOY (CONT'D)
First you don't return my calls and now here I
am standing in front of you- and I can't get your
attention.

XAVIER
No- No- I-

Nothing like that, Senator, I was- I was
concentrating...

MCCOY
Come on out of there. Let's talk.

Page 21-

- Still in the pool area. Charles sits in his wheelchair a
owel around his neck. The senator is looking around the
ool area suspiciously.

MCCOY (CONT'D)
Charles, I've called you twice in the last week.

XAVIER
Yes.

MCCOY
"Yes?" That's what you have to say.

I thought you were going to say: "I'm a busy
man, McCoy."

2- McCoy smiles, but it is a sad smile.

MCCOY (CONT'D)
And then I was going to say: "No, Charles, I'm
the busy man."

3- Xavier serious. Not one for small talk or this reunion.

XAVIER
What brings you up here to New York City,
Senator? I would think-

4- Tighter two shot of the two. There is a history between
hem.

MCCOY
Polite of you not to pick at my head to find out,
Charles.

XAVIER
I try not to do that anymore. You know that.

MCCOY
I would.

5- McCoy looks around.

MCCOY (CONT'D
This is a nice little niche you carvec
here, huh?

6- Charles doesn't respond. Just
quizzically.

7- Same as five.

MCCOY (CONT'D
A far cry from the bedlam we were
in back in the day, huh?

8- Charles doesn't respond.

9- McCoy looks back at Charles.

MCCOY (CONT'D
Sort of the point though, right?

Page 22-

1- McCoy gestures toward the locker r
turns toward the door to see why. A bo
doorway humbly.

MCCOY (CONT'D
I wanted you to meet someone, Ch

Come here, Henry.

3- Wide. ENTER Hank MCCOY. 17

His clothes are that of a rich kid tryir
messy. His hands are in his pockets
handsome.

He seems nervous to meet Xavier bu
show it.

MCCOY (CONT'D
Henry, I want you to meet a very
mine.

This is the man I told you about.

This is Professor Charles Xavier.

With an X.

4- Charles stretches out his hand to s
XAVIER
Henry-

5- Hank looks at Charles' hand.

his father, concerned.

ssion.

        MCCOY
. Charles is a good friend.

Charles' hand to shake it. HENRY'S
GE! Twice the size of Charles' hand and

is normal teenage size. But this HAND

shoulder looking down, Charles looks at

' shoulder, Henry never makes eye

        XAVIER
you, Henry.

        HANK

        XAVIER

assed by his kid.

        MCCOY

ough a Hank/ Henry thing.

arles is warm. Good with kids.

        XAVIER
ent through a Charlie/ Charles

gives Charles a little smile for the first
Hank a small smile back.

AVIER (CONT'D)
ther when he was your age.

Charles intently.

he we see words on the screen
balloon or tail to them. Just
ke, but readable words. These
CHIC TALK.

s psychic conversations, we will

---

have psychic and real conversations going o
at once, and this technique will be a cool wa
to do that.

        HANK PSYCHIC
My father says you can read people's thoughts.
Is that true?

7- Charles looks at him. This hurts to do.

        XAVIER PSYCHIC
No.

8- Hank smiles wildly. He likes Charles.

        HANK PSYCHIC
Oh my god! That is so cool.

9- Wide of room.

McCoy is looking down. Hank rolls his eyes. Charles seem
to be in a little pain from that display.

        MCCOY
Henry, can Charles and I speak privately?

        HANK
What am I supposed to do?

        MCCOY
Go for a walk.

        XAVIER
It was good to meet you, then - Hank.

10- Hank at the door. Tips his imaginary hat.

        HANK
Thank you, Charles.

Page 24-

1- Wide of room. Charles waits for McCoy to speak
McCoy's tone is very serious.

        MCCOY
It happened to him about a year ago.

        XAVIER
Just the hands...

        MCCOY
His hands and feet.

He's- y'know- he's pretty athletic now.

Sometimes spectacularly so.

2- Henry is standing in the hallway, right by the door, he is eavesdropping. His teenage face confused by what he is hearing.

MCCOY (CONT'D)
And his intelligence levels are- pfftt- off the charts.

XAVIER
Sounds pretty promising, all things considered.

Seems like a nice boy.

3- Same. Henry winces at his secret revealed.

MCCOY
He's a mutant, Charles.

4- Charles and James talk.

XAVIER
Maybe he's just a smart kid with-

MCCOY
I had him tested.

He's a class four mutant.

6- Over Henry's shoulder.
He peeks into the room. Wide shot of room. McCoy paces in the foreground. Charles is patient. Neither facing Henry's direction.

MCCOY (CONT'D)
So I guess you can appreciate the delicate situation this whole thing puts me in-

Considering my position in life.

Considering the political climate.

XAVIER
(sarcastic)
And what climate is that?

MCCOY
Charles.

7- Same. Xavier turns his chair toward McCoy. McCoy turns to his friend. Henry slinks so he can't be seen.

XAVIER
I don't think I understand what this meeting is about.

MCCOY
Yes, you do.

1- James turns to Charles. Serious.

MCCOY (CONT'D)
The boy needs attention, Charles.

Training.

XAVIER
Of course he does.

MCCOY
Yes.

XAVIER
Oh. I-I don't think I can help you, Jim. That's not really my-

2- Charles listens intently and is defiant to the offer.

MCCOY
The way I see it, you're the only one that can.

XAVIER
I can barely control my own abilities anymore. You know that. Ever since-

I am hardly the one to teach another-

3- McCoy, serious and gesticulating his point.

MCCOY
That's why you're perfect.

Who better than someone who can teach by example?

If not you- who?

4- Wide of Charles.

XAVIER
Jim, listen.

I appreciate your position. Really.

5- Same, but tighter. Charles really believes what he is saying.

XAVIER (CONT'D)
But I have my research and the project-

And I think I am doing a lot more good for more people than I would just tutoring a-

6- McCoy, serious as a heart attack.

MCCOY
Charles, what exactly do you think you are doing here?

You and your project?

7- Same as five.

8- Same as six, but tighter.

MCCOY (CONT'D)
Get dressed.

This isn't the place for this.

Page 26-

1- Wide shot of Central Park.

It's a nice green sunny weekday as opposed to the blue and grey gloom of the project safehouse that Xavier works in.
Kids are playing on a tree as mom looks on. A mime/clown is performing for no one in particular. Lovebirds walk by.

Sitting at an inconspicuous park bench is Senator James McCoy. He is now wearing sunglasses and reading a paper for cover.

Sitting next to him in his chair but facing the opposite direction is Xavier. They are having a talk.

Think the scene in JFK where Donald Sutherland is telling Xavier all his secret information. It just looks like two guys talking, but in actuality, incredibly important matters are being discussed.

Hank is there too but he is just pacing around out of earshot waiting for his dad. He is staring at his shoes and daydreaming.

MCCOY (CONT'D)
There are things going on now- things brewing on the horizon-

Things that would make your skin crawl if you knew about them, Charles.

But you don't- because that is the way they wanted it.

XAVIER
They?

2- Two shot of the two men facing opposite direction.

MCCOY
And I am truly sorry that this is how I am coming to you- to tell you this.

But, see, it's different for me now.

I don't want my son to pay for my mistakes.

XAVIER
What are we talking about?

MCCOY
What do you think your research is going for?

3- Xavier doesn't answer. He waits for the answer.

4- A different two shot of the two of them not facing each other as they talk.

MCCOY (CONT'D)
CEREBRO isn't a research project, Charles. It's a cover.

XAVIER
A cover?

MCCOY
A cover for a paramilitary covert operation called WEAPON X.

XAVIER
What are you-?

MCCOY
It's a front. The information you are gathering- have you heard the term Weapon X before?

XAVIER
Only recently.

5- McCoy talks and looks at his paper.

MCCOY
They can't wait for the mutant scare to build on its own... like Communism did. So they are trying to manufacture it all by themselves.

From the makers of the Iran Contra campaign and Watergate, we bring you the latest in government abuse of power.

But let me tell you, from what I know, it's a sloppy mishmash of mutant paranoia, Charles-

The research you are gathering is being funneled into this Weapon X project right under your nose.